Public International Law

Public International Law: A Multi-Perspective Approach is a comprehensive yet critical introduction to the diverse field of public international law.

Bringing together a unique range of perspectives from around the world and from different theoretical approaches, this textbook introduces both the overarching questions and doctrines of public international law, as well as the specialised sub-fields. These include emerging fields such as international law in cyberspace, international migration law, and the international climate regime. The book includes numerous case examples, references to debates and controversies in the literature, and focus sections addressing topics in more depth.

Featuring an array of pedagogical features, including learning objectives, suggested further reading and resources, and QR codes to interactive exercises, this book is ideal for students studying this field for the first time and also offers something new for students who would like to deepen their knowledge via a diverse and engaging range of perspectives.

Sué González Hauck is a postdoctoral scholar at the German Center for Integration and Migration Studies (DeZIM), Berlin and at the Helmut-Schmidt University, Hamburg.

Raffaela Kunz is a postdoctoral scholar and lecturer at the University of Zurich.

Max Milas is a PhD student at the University of Münster.

'Public international law scholarship has since the days of its "founding fathers" been dominated by single authored sums. The biases inherent in such a model have become all too obvious, which is why *Public International Law: A Multi-Perspective Approach* is just the collection we needed. International law will only be reconfigured in decades to come if the extent to which it has meant very different things for different people is recognized in textbooks themselves. We owe the diversity of our students this very diversity of perspectives'.

Frédéric Mégret, *Full Professor, Co-director of the Centre for Human Rights and Legal Pluralism, Hans & Tamar Oppenheimer Chair in Public International Law, McGill University*

'Put together with both care and flair, featuring terrific voices both seasoned and new, covering both key concepts and contemporary concerns, taking us from history to future, deep sea to outer space, cores to peripheries, and open access to boot, this is a delightful cocktail of a textbook. I look forward to many happy hours with it'.

Surabhi Ranganathan, *Professor of International Law and Director of Postgraduate Education, University of Cambridge*

Public International Law

A MULTI-PERSPECTIVE APPROACH

EDITED BY SUÉ GONZÁLEZ HAUCK, RAFFAELA KUNZ, AND MAX MILAS

Routledge
Taylor & Francis Group

LONDON AND NEW YORK

Designed cover image: oobqoo/Getty Images ©

First published 2024
by Routledge
4 Park Square, Milton Park, Abingdon, Oxon OX14 4RN

and by Routledge
605 Third Avenue, New York, NY 10158

Routledge is an imprint of the Taylor & Francis Group, an informa business

This publication was funded by the German Federal Ministry for Family Affairs, Senior Citizens, Women and Youth.

British Library Cataloguing-in-Publication Data
A catalogue record for this book is available from the British Library

Library of Congress Cataloging-in-Publication Data
Names: Hauck, Sué González, editor. | Kunz, Raffaela, editor. | Milas, Max, editor.
Title: Public international law : a multi-perspective approach / edited by Sué González Hauck, Raffaela Kunz, and Max Milas.
Description: Abingdon, Oxon [UK] ; New York, NY : Routledge, 2024. | Includes bibliographical references and index.
Identifiers: LCCN 2023048214 | ISBN 9781032587479 (hardback) | ISBN 9781032587448 (paperback) | ISBN 9781003451327 (ebook)
Subjects: LCSH: International law.
Classification: LCC KZ3410 .P83 2024 | DDC 341—dc23/eng/20231013
LC record available at https://lccn.loc.gov/2023048214

ISBN: 978-1-032-58747-9 (hbk)
ISBN: 978-1-032-58744-8 (pbk)
ISBN: 978-1-003-45132-7 (ebk)

DOI: 10.4324/9781003451327

Typeset in Avenir, Bell and Bembo
by Apex CoVantage, LLC

https://openrewi.org/en/projects/project-public-international-law/

CONTENTS

Part II
General International Law

CONTRIBUTORS

Shubhangi Agarwalla, Yale University, New Haven, USA

Thamil Venthan Ananthavinayagan, Department of Justice, Dublin, Ireland

Walter Arévalo-Ramírez, Universidad del Rosario, Bogotá, Colombia

Kanad Bagchi, University of Amsterdam, Amsterdam, The Netherlands

Grażyna Baranowska, Hertie School/Polish Academy of Sciences, Berlin, Germany/Warsaw, Poland

Bernardo Mageste Castelar Campos, Università degli Studi di Milano-Bicocca (UNIMIB), Milan, Italy

He Chi, Tongji University, Shanghai, China

Vishakha Choudhary, World Trade Organization, Geneva, Switzerland

Annalisa Ciampi, University of Verona, Verona, Italy

Alex P. Dela Cruz, University of Melbourne, Melbourne, Australia

Anne Dienelt, University of Hamburg, Hamburg, Germany

Craig Eggett, Maastricht University, Maastricht, The Netherlands

Viljam Engström, Åbo Akademi University, Turku/Åbo, Finland

Başak Etkin, Université Paris 2 Panthéon-Assas, Paris, France

Taxiarchis Fiskatoris, University of the Western Cape/University of Marburg, Bellville, South Africa/Marburg, Germany

Sué González Hauck, Deutsches Zentrum für Integrations- und Migrationsforschung/Helmut-Schmidt University, Berlin/Hamburg, Germany

Alex Green, University of York, York, UK

Anna Hankings-Evans, Greenberg Traurig LLP, Berlin, Germany

Pia Hüsch, University of Glasgow, Glasgow, Scotland

Patrick Lukusa Kadima, University of the Witwatersrand, Johannesburg, South Africa

Verena Kahl, University of Hamburg, Hamburg, Germany

Deepa Kansra, Jawaharlal Nehru University, New Delhi, India

Raffaela Kunz, University of Zurich, Zurich, Switzerland

Lucas Carlos Lima, Universidade Federal de Minas Gerais, Minas Gerais, Brasil

Marnie Lloydd, Te Herenga Waka–Victoria University of Wellington, Wellington, New Zealand

Miriam Bak McKenna, Roskilde University, Roskilde, Denmark

Max Milas, University of Münster, Münster, Germany

Tamsin Phillipa Paige, Deakin University, Melbourne, Australia

Anne Peters, Max Planck Institute for Comparative Public Law and International Law/Universities of Heidelberg, FU Berlin and Basel, Heidelberg, Germany

Abbas Poorhashemi, Canadian Institute for International Law Expertise, Toronto, Canada

Daniel Ricardo Quiroga-Villamarín, Geneva Graduate Institute, Geneva, Switzerland

Adamantia Rachovitsa, University of Groningen, Groningen, The Netherlands

Andrés Rousset-Siri, National University of Cuyo, Mendoza, Argentina

Juliana Santos de Carvalho, Geneva Graduate Institute, Geneva, Switzerland

Silvia Steininger, Hertie School, Berlin, Germany

Victor Stoica, University of Bucharest, Bucharest, Romania

Marko Svicevic, Palacký University/University of Johannesburg, Olomouc, Czech Republic

Jens T. Theilen, Helmut Schmidt University, Hamburg, Germany

Imdad Ullah, National University of Sciences and Technology, Islamabad, Pakistan

Raghavi Viswanath, European University Institute, Florence, Italy

Thalia Viveros-Uehara, Tilburg University, Tilburg, The Netherlands

Beatrice A. Walton, Debevoise & Plimpton, New York, USA

PREFACE/FOREWORD

The teaching of international law is governed by exclusions. Although international law – like no other field of law – is shaped by global, universal aspirations, its teaching is provincial financially, personally, geographically, and epistemologically. With this perspective in mind, we decided to initiate this textbook on public international law in spring 2021. It has been created within the fabric of OpenRewi. Initially, OpenRewi, which stands for open *rechtswissenschaft* (German: 'legal scholarship' or 'legal science'), was founded in Germany and focused on publishing German textbooks and casebooks. The idea behind the initiative is to use the possibilities the internet offers to contribute to reducing some of the existing exclusions: today it is possible to publish digitally and make content available at no cost to everyone around the globe with an internet connection. Accordingly, all teaching materials created by OpenRewi are published as Open Educational Resources (OER). This allows students and teachers to freely access, use, modify, and share these resources independent of institutional affiliation, region, and economic status.

However, a perhaps even greater need for OER exists in the field of international law, with huge global disparities existing in terms of access to high quality teaching materials. It is not farfetched to say that the potential offered by the internet to make knowledge widely accessible has not been realised in international law. If textbooks are available digitally, they remain behind a paywall. Indeed, to the best of our knowledge, not a single international law textbook exists which is freely accessible and reusable in line with Open Access terms.

Amid a global pandemic and after numerous all-too-familiar video conferences, we thus decided to fill this gap. Timidly and uncertainly, we published a call for authors. This call aimed at overcoming legal and technical barriers to create the first-ever collaboratively written and openly accessible textbook in international law.

It quickly turned out that our worries were unfounded. Over 100 authors, among them both established scholars and younger researchers, responded with their ideas. It became obvious that the idea of an open textbook hit a nerve, and that many shared our feeling that teaching materials in international law need to become more accessible. However, it was evident to us that Open Access has to mean more than facilitating access. What need to be 'opened' are also processes of knowledge production and scholarship themselves.

The approach we thus opted for in elaborating this textbook is reflected in its title: we deliberately chose a *multi-perspectivist* approach. With this, we mean that the textbook aims to represent a diversity of perspectives in at least three ways: intellectual approaches, gender, and regional representation. We were partially successful in this respect. Never before have so many critical scholars contributed to a textbook on public international law. Never before have authors of an international law textbook lived on all inhabited continents. Never before have more women and non-binary people than men contributed to an international law textbook as authors. However, we must also concede and disclose that we did, to some extent, reproduce existing power structures and hierarchies when selecting authors. We have shared our call for authors on platforms that are primarily read by people from the Global North. We selected authors based on proposals that seemed familiar to us in terms of language and thinking. Only one author based at an institution on the African continent and one Chinese author contributed to our textbook. The textbook is published in English and therefore requires a certain language proficiency, which presupposes economic and cultural capital that is unequally distributed globally. Furthermore, selections also cause rejections, and so we would like to express gratitude to all unsuccessful applicants once again.

Multi-perspectivism for us also meant designing the writing process in ways that allowed for inclusivity. After we had selected the authors, further video conferences followed in which we discussed the structure, content, and approach of the textbook as a collective. The result of these discussions was the table of contents and didactic concept of this textbook described in more detail below. Based on this, all authors could choose their desired chapters. Like other OpenRewi projects, we used the Wikimedia Foundation's open platform Wikibooks to create our textbook. The platform enables the free creation and publication of digital books. Each chapter of our book has been allocated its own page on Wikibooks. This allows readers, authors, and editors to track, comment, and correct all developments of a chapter.

The goal of this multi-perspectivist approach to producing a textbook consists in not only reproducing conventional knowledge about international law but also allowing students to question it. Multi-perspectivism, therefore, also means departing from the standard of the textbook genre. The genre of the textbook has been one of the main tools through which a particular perspective – the perspective of a white, European man – has been allowed to portray itself as objective and thus usurp the place of the universal. Three main features of the book's composition are supposed to work to break up this standard narrative: First, even though there is a distinct part covering history, theory, and methodology, the chapters in this part are only supposed to deliver the relevant background knowledge to be able to understand the historical and theoretical underpinnings of each chapter. Most chapters contain extensive historical and theoretical contextualisations themselves instead of just reproducing the standard textbook narrative. Second, chapters on different approaches and methodologies are relatively detailed and focused on critical approaches. While it may be confusing for students to some degree to be introduced in relative detail (compared to other textbooks) to, for example, Feminist, Marxist, and Third World Approaches to International Law, and with interdisciplinarity, without first being introduced to the core concepts that usually stand at the beginning of a textbook, this confusion is not accidental but calculated. The idea is that students will encounter ways of looking critically at the standard way of conceiving international law before they encounter this standard narrative – not the other way around, as is most often the case. Third, and maybe most obviously, the book is not pretending to offer a single perspective that could be framed as universal. The authors who have contributed to the book come from diverse backgrounds and have received their professional formation in different ways. While we have, of course, strived for a degree of cohesiveness that allows students to work with this book as a coherent whole rather than as a set of loosely connected individual chapters, we have not imposed a single perspective or approach on our diverse authors. Their individual voice and perspective are palpable, and students will be able to appreciate each of these perspectives as what it is – a perspective that they can take as a reliable source for the knowledge and the skills they need in order to be able to craft an international legal argument but still one perspective that they are invited to question.

However, some limitations remain. Writing a textbook as a collective composed of a majority of female and non-binary scholars and of many scholars located in or having a diasporic or ancestral connection to the Global South does not eliminate all the problems of exclusion and hierarchisation inherent in writing a textbook. Writing a textbook that counts as an instance of the genre involves reproducing, at least to some degree, the standard textbook narrative associated with mainstream international law. Reproducing this standard narrative is not only a matter of complying with the conventions of the genre, but it also has connections to questions of how to contribute to a profession of international law that is more accessible. Access to the profession is mediated through examinations that students have to pass. These examinations, in most non-elite places of higher education, will ask students to reproduce the standard textbook narrative in some form. Therefore, where this textbook adheres to this narrative it does so not in spite of but because of the fact that this is the narrative that has established itself as dominant – not through intellectual persuasion but through imperialism and hegemonic moves. Part of the dominant narrative this textbook knowingly reproduces is the distinction between the different parts of the textbook, split into a first part covering 'History, Theory, and Methods', a second part devoted to 'General International Law', and a third part introducing students to 'Specialised Fields' of international law. Nothing beyond the conventions of the field provides an explanation for why, for example, international human rights law counts as a specialised field whereas the law of immunities or diplomatic relations pertains to 'general international law'. The same can be said for many aspects reflected in the composition and content of the book. We hope, however, that the multi-perspectivist approach can allow students to not only familiarise themselves with the standard textbook narrative but to see its contingency from the beginning and therefore embark on their international law journey with their critical minds sharpened.

From the beginning, we wanted to publish the textbook in a printed version as well, with an established publisher, in order to raise its visibility, and to offer its readership a further seal of quality in addition to the open peer review process. After some informational contact with well-known publishers since the beginning of 2023, we were incredibly grateful when Routledge got back to us with enthusiasm. From that point on, it was clear to us that we wanted to publish the textbook with Routledge. We are sincerely grateful to Emily Kindleysides and Chloe Herbert at Routledge for their professional, kind, and efficient support. We received financial support from the German Centre for Integration and Migration Studies (DeZIM) with funds from the German Ministry of Family Affairs, Senior Citizens, Women and Youth. This financial support has made it possible for us to keep this publication Open Access. We therefore remain deeply grateful to DeZIM, particularly to Dr. Noa Ha, Volker Knoll-Hoyer, Dr. Cihan Sinanoglu, and Benjamin Schwarze. Eva Vogel has been immensely helpful, supporting us in finishing the manuscript and providing feedback from a student's perspective.

§ § §

PART I
HISTORY, THEORY, AND METHODS

1

CHAPTER 1
HISTORY OF
INTERNATIONAL LAW

SUÉ GONZÁLEZ HAUCK

BOX 1.1 Required Knowledge and Learning Objectives

Required knowledge: None

Learning objectives: Understanding the historical references in other chapters of the book; common references to international law's historical origins and development.

BOX 1.2 Interactive Exercises

Access *interactive exercises for this chapter*[1] by positioning your smartphone camera at the dot-filled box, also known as a QR code.

Figure 1.1 QR code referring to interactive exercises.

A. INTRODUCTION

Scholarly disciplines are constituted through how they tell their history. It is impossible to understand public international law without understanding its history. This does not imply revealing the true essence of international law by pinpointing a fixed origin or unveiling the correct way to interpret specific legal doctrines through their origins.[2] Nevertheless, histories of international law do teach about the creation of rules,

---

1 https://openrewi.org/en-projects-project-public-international-law-history-of-international-law/
2 Anne Orford, *International Law and the Politics of History* (CUP 2021).

DOI: 10.4324/9781003451327-2

institutions, concepts, and doctrines, shedding light on how the law perpetuates past injustices into the present.[3] Importantly, learning about international law's contribution to domination, exploitation, and injustice entails learning how the world can be changed for the better.

B. OF ORIGINS AND FOUNDING MYTHS

I. CHOOSING A STARTING POINT

Histories necessarily require a starting point. Distinct approaches to international legal history are, in part, characterised by differing methods of selecting and portraying this starting point. While some accounts trace international law's origins to the rules governing inter-polity relations in ancient India, Mesopotamia, Syria, Egypt, Greece, and Rome,[4] the most prevalent starting point consists of the combination of Hugo Grotius' work *De jure belli ac pacis* (Latin: 'Of the Law on War and Peace') in 1625 and the Peace of Westphalia in 1648. This common point of departure typically aligns with a conception of history as an endeavour that portrays 'how things actually were' in the past.[5] Not all approaches to history, however, assume 'the existence of immobile forms that precede the external world of accident and succession'.[6] An alternative perspective on origins seeks starting points not as temporal markers for the foundation of something, but as the circumstances that best explain its emergence, formation, and heritage.[7] Another approach to history rejects such origin stories altogether, arguing that past events, ideas, and people must be examined only for their role in their own time.[8] However, lawyers are typically 'trained in the art of making meaning move across time'.[9]

Choosing a starting point for the history of international law presupposes knowing, at least roughly, what international law is. The dominant understanding of international law portrays it as the legal framework governing relationships between sovereign States.[10] From this point of view, the starting point in the history of international law must depict how States and sovereignty emerged and when sovereign States started to have relationships governed by law. If international law is, more broadly, understood as law of global encounter,[11] one may infer that the interactions shaping the laws currently

---

3 Cf. Alasia Nuti, *Injustice and the Reproduction of History: Structural Inequalities, Gender and Redress* (CUP 2019).

4 Hiralal Chatterjee, *International Law and Inter-State Relations in Ancient India* (Mukhopadhyay 1958); David J Bederman, *International Law in Antiquity* (CUP 2004).

5 Leopold von Ranke, *Geschichten der romanischen und germanischen Völker von 1494 bis 1514* (Duncker & Humblot 1885) 8.

6 Michel Foucault, 'Nietzsche, Genealogy, History' in Michel Foucault and Donald F Bouchard (eds), *Language, Counter-Memory, Practice* (Donald F Bouchard and Sherry Simon trans., Cornell University Press 1977) 142.

7 Ibid 145.

8 Mark Bevir, 'The Contextual Approach' in George Klosko (ed), *The Oxford Handbook of the History of Political Philosophy* (OUP 2011) 11.

9 Anne Orford, 'On International Legal Method' (2013) 1 LRIL 166, 172.

10 On States, see Green, § 7.1, in this textbook.

11 Sundhya Pahuja, 'Laws of Encounter: A Jurisdictional Account of International Law' (2013) 1 LRIL 63.

governing global encounters did not primarily and exclusively arise from interactions between States but between Empires, the inhabitants of the land these Empires sought to conquer, and the companies they sponsored to carry out these conquests.

II. INTERNATIONAL LAW'S FOUNDING MYTHS AND THE PROBLEM WITH HISTORIES OF GREAT MEN

International law is famously riddled with institutional anxiety: 'Does it even exist?', 'Does it *matter*?', 'Is it *really* law?',[12] and, 'Are we, international lawyers, the good guys' or, as the popular meme goes, 'Are we the baddies?'[13] International law has affirmed its existence by providing a 'birth certificate' (the Peace Treaties of Münster and Osnabrück or 'Peace of Westphalia') and a 'father' (mainly Hugo Grotius).[14] Together, the Peace of Westphalia and Grotius' work *De iure belli ac pacis libri tres* (Latin: 'Three books on the law of war and peace') established State sovereignty as the source of international law's binding force, thus establishing international law as *real* law. Additionally, grounding international law's existence in peace treaties and casting Hugo Grotius as a secular, peace-loving humanitarian has allowed international lawyers to see themselves as invested in a project serving humanity in the pursuit of peace, order, and justice. In contrast, Third World Approaches to International Law[15] (TWAIL) scholars have drawn attention to international law's sustained and central role in legitimising and maintaining the colonial project. These critical histories of international law draw a different line of continuity from the writings of Hugo Grotius and Francisco de Vitoria to the establishment of international law as a formalised discipline in the 19th century and to international law in its present form.

As the newly founded Dutch Republic was looking to assert itself against Portugal and Spain, the Dutch East India Company (VOC) asked Grotius to write a defence of the Company's privateering campaign in waters under Portuguese control.[16] Grotius completed the resulting manuscript, *De Indis*, in 1607–1608 and published part of it in 1609 under the title *Mare Liberum* (Latin: 'The Free See'). In his subsequent work, *De jure belli ac pacis*, Grotius provided a comprehensive treatise on international law combining natural law perspectives – grounding legal validity in sources beyond law, such as God or reason – with positivist concepts, deriving legal validity from rules and the sovereign's will and consent.[17] The comprehensive systematicity and fusion of

---

12 See Quiroga-Villamarín, § 2.3; and Etkin and Green, § 3.1, in this textbook.

13 https://imgflip.com/i/5uzgnv

14 See Randall Lesaffer, 'The Grotian Tradition Revisited: Change and Continuity in the History of International Law' (2002) 73 BYBIL 103, 104, with further references.

15 See González Hauck, § 3.2, in this textbook.

16 Martine Julia van Ittersum, 'Hugo Grotius: The Making of a Founding Father of International Law' in Anne Orford and Florian Hoffmann (eds), *The Oxford Handbook of the Theory of International Law* (OUP 2016) 82, 84.

17 David J Bederman, 'Reception of the Classical Tradition in International Law: Grotius' De Jure Belli ac Pacis' (1996) 10 Emory International Law Review 1, 2; Stefan Kadelbach, 'Hugo Grotius: On the Conquest of Utopia by Systematic Reasoning' in Stefan Kadelbach and others (eds), *System, Order, and International Law* (OUP 2017) 134.

naturalist and positivist legal concepts in *De jure belli ac pacis* led to Grotius being dubbed the 'father of international law'.[18]

As scholars of international law and international relations sought to reinvigorate the project of a peaceful international order created and maintained by international law after the Second World War (WWII), they did so by reclaiming Grotius and sketching a 'Grotian tradition' of international law and international relations. In a 'Grotian' international community, the power of the sovereign State is supposed to be restricted by the rationality of the law.[19] Recent work focusing on the connection between Grotius' work and colonialism not only calls into question the flattering self-image of international law as a peace-seeking humanitarian discipline. It also challenges the assumption that the origins of modern international law can be found exclusively in Europe. Placing Grotius in the context of his role as legal advisor to the VOC shows that the questions he addressed in his work did not originate on the European continent but, outside Europe, through the colonial encounter.[20]

Hugo Grotius' strongest competitor for the role of 'father of international law' is Francisco de Vitoria. Vitoria was the first scholar to adapt the Roman concept of *ius gentium* (Latin: 'Law of Peoples') to what we recognise now as an international context,[21] namely the colonial encounter between the Spanish Empire and indigenous peoples in what is now known as South America and the Caribbean.[22] The question of whether Vitoria was using *ius gentium* to condemn or at least reign in colonial violence or whether he was justifying and thereby enabling it is a hotly debated question. It is debated so fiercely because it is equated with the question of whether international law has been, from the beginning, humanitarian or imperialist in nature.[23]

Other figures on whom international legal scholars have relied as 'fathers' include Francisco Suárez (1548–1617), Alberico Gentili (1552–1603), Emer de Vattel (1714–1767), and Jeremy Bentham (1748–1832), who coined the term 'public international law'. As international law as a discipline is increasingly trying to increase

---

18 Martine Julia van Ittersum, 'Hugo Grotius: The Making of a Founding Father of International Law' in Anne Orford and Florian Hoffmann (eds), *The Oxford Handbook of the Theory of International Law* (OUP 2016) 82, 88–89.

19 Hedley Bull, *The Anarchical Society* (Macmillan 1977) 23–25; Barry Buzan, 'The English School' (2001) 27 Review of International Studies 471, 476; Richard Little, 'The English School's Contribution to the Study of International Relations' (2000) 6 European Journal of International Relations 395, 396; Hersch Lauterpacht, 'The Grotian Tradition in International Law' (1946) 23 British Yearbook of International Law 1; Stefan Kadelbach, 'Hugo Grotius: On the Conquest of Utopia by Systematic Reasoning' in Stefan Kadelbach, Thomas Kleinlein, and David Roth-Isigkeit (eds), *System, Order, and International Law* (OUP 2017) 134, 155.

20 José-Manuel Barreto, '*Cerberus*: Rethinking Grotius and the Westphalian System' in Martti Koskenniemi and others (eds), *International Law and Empire: Historical Explorations* (OUP 2017) 149, 154.

21 James Brown Scott, *The Spanish Origins of International Law: Francisco de Vitoria and His Law of Nations* (Clarendon Press 1934) 3.

22 Antony Anghie, *Imperialism, Sovereignty, and the Making of International Law* (CUP 2005) 13–14.

23 Paolo Amorosa, *Rewriting the History of the Law of Nations: How James Brown Scott Made Francisco de Vitoria the Founder of International Law* (OUP 2019) 1.

female representation not only in international institutions but also in the history of international (legal) thought,[24] Christine de Pizan has emerged as the strongest contender for the title of 'mother of international law'.[25] Her claim to the title rests on the fact that she wrote a book on the laws of war and that she did so long before Grotius and even before Vitoria, Gentili, and Suárez.[26] However, for feminist and critical histories to fulfil their objectives of challenging conventional narratives and fostering change in our perception of the past, present, and future, it is essential to prioritise amplifying the voices and visibility of historically marginalised people as well as underscoring the collective components of scholarly pursuits, rather than simply substituting traditional accounts of great men with those of great women.

C. TURNING POINTS IN HISTORIES OF INTERNATIONAL LAW

I. PORTUGUESE AND SPANISH COLONIAL CONQUEST AND THE TREATY OF TORDESILLAS

As aforementioned, one way of telling the history of international law is as a history of colonial encounter. The first period of European colonialism featured a rivalry between Portugal and Spain. The Portuguese, over the course of the 15th century, sailed the Atlantic coast of Africa, reached the Indian Ocean, and, in 1452, obtained a series of papal grants allowing them to conquer the lands they encountered and to enslave their inhabitants.[27] The 'Catholic Monarchs' Isabella I of Castile and Ferdinand II of Aragon, in turn, funded Christopher Columbus' expedition aimed at discovering a westward route to the Indies through the Atlantic. Instead of India, Columbus landed on a small island in the Bahamas.[28] The 'discovery' of this island and other islands in the Caribbean during Columbus' initial voyage led the Catholic Monarchs to seek Pope Alexander VI's endorsement of their claim to the 'New World'. After ongoing colonial rivalries between the Spanish and Portuguese monarchs and respective papal bulls and treaties,[29] the Catholic Monarchs and João II, King of Portugal, divided up their spheres of influence in the Atlantic by agreeing on a demarcation line in the Treaty of Tordesillas, signed on 7 June 1494.[30] The Treaty of Tordesillas marks an important turning point

---

24 Immi Tallgren, *Portraits of Women in International Law: New Names and Forgotten Faces?* (OUP 2023); See Santos de Carvalho and Kahl, § 7.5, in this textbook.

25 Maria Teresa Guerra Medici, 'The Mother of International Law: Christine de Pisan' (1999) 19(1) Parliaments, Estates and Representation 15–22.

26 Franck Latty, 'Founding "Fathers" of International Law' (*EJIL: Talk!*, 15 January 2019) <www.ejiltalk.org/founding-fathers-of-international-law-recognizing-christine-de-pizan/> accessed 25 August 2023.

27 Wilhelm Grewe, *The Epochs of International Law* (M Byers, trans., de Gruyter 2000) 230 et seq.

28 See David S Berry, 'The Caribbean' in Bardo Fassbender and Anne Peters (eds), *The Oxford Handbook of the History of International Law* (OUP 2012) 578.

29 For an overview, see Thomas Duve, 'Treaty of Tordesillas' (*Max Planck Encyclopedia of Public International Law*) <https://opil.ouplaw.com/display/10.1093/law:epil/9780199231690/law-9780199231690-e2088> accessed 5 August 2023, paras 4–10.

30 Ibid.

in the history of international law, not only because the spheres of influence outlined in this treaty established the division between Hispanic and Portuguese parts of the Americas – the latter constituting today's State of Brazil – but also because it marks a step away from relying on purely papal authority and grounding legal claims in inter-State agreements instead.[31] In this sense, the Treaty of Tordesillas is a plausible starting point for histories of international law both as the law of inter-State relationships and as the law of colonial encounter.

II. SOVEREIGNTY, SECULARISM, AND THE MYTH OF 'WESTPHALIA'

The late 16th century and, more importantly, the 17th century were pivotal in shaping sovereignty as the dominant paradigm for governing political interactions in Europe. Jean Bodin's publication of *Six Livres de la République* (French: 'Six Books of the Republic' or 'Six Books on the Commonwealth') in 1576,[32] which encapsulated the now canonical definition of sovereignty as absolute and perpetual power, accountable to no higher earthly authority,[33] initially remained largely aspirational.[34] However, during the 17th century, sovereign States gradually acquired the capacity to assert control over their territories, shifting authority from interpersonal dynamics to a territorial framework.[35]

Simultaneously, chartered companies like the VOC, established in 1602, wielded sovereignty over territories and parts of the sea where they pursued trading monopolies. In areas where they lacked the necessary monopolistic control, these companies advocated for free travel and trade.[36] As seen above, among the influential figures who advocated for freedom of the seas and free trade in the interest of the VOC was Hugo Grotius.[37] Alongside Grotius, another component in many narratives of international law's origins is the Peace of Westphalia in 1648. The peace agreements in Münster and

---

31 Ibid, paras 15–21.

32 Jean Bodin, *On Sovereignty: Four Chapters from 'The Six Books of the Commonwealth'* (Julian H Franklin, trans., CUP 1992)

33 Sophie Nicholls, 'Sovereignty and Government in Jean Bodin's *Six Livres de la République (1576)*' (2019) 80 Journal of the History of Ideas 47, 49, 63; Daniel Lee, *The Right of Sovereignty: Jean Bodin on the Sovereign State and the Law of Nations* (OUP 2021).

34 William F Church, *Constitutional Thought in Sixteenth-Century France: A Study in the Evolution of Ideas* (Harvard University Press 1941).

35 Hendrik Spruyt, *The Sovereign State and Its Competitors* (Princeton University Press 1994).

36 For more information on chartered companies and their impact on international law and international relations, see González Hauck, § 7.7, in this textbook; Sudipta Sen, *Empire of Free Trade: The East India Company and the Making of the Colonial Marketplace* (University of Pennsylvania Press 1997); HV Bowen, *The Business of Empire: The East India Company and Imperial Britain, 1756–1833* (CUP 2006); Emily Erikson, *Between Monopoly and Free Trade: The English East India Company, 1600–1757* (Princeton University Press 2014); Rupali Mishra, *A Business of State: Commerce, Politics, and the Birth of the East India Company* (Harvard University Press 2018); Andrew Phillips and JC Sharman, *Outsourcing Empire: How Company-States made the Modern World* (Princeton University Press 2020).

37 Martine van Ittersum, *Profit and Principle: Natural Rights Theories and the Rise of Dutch Power in the East Indies, 1595–1615* (Brill 2006).

Osnabrück collectively constitute the Peace of Westphalia, concluding the Thirty Years' War in Europe. The Peace of Westphalia was the focal point of a longer development resulting in the establishment of a system of sovereign States centred around territoriality.[38]

'Westphalia' is frequently used to describe an international system characterised by unfettered State sovereignty and little to no rules governing how States are to exercise their sovereignty – especially within their territories.[39] This myth of 'Westphalia' tells a story in which the peace settlements of Münster and Osnabrück established a system of sovereign States that persists today.[40] However, attributing the establishment of modern international law based on State sovereignty to the Peace of Westphalia is, at best, a simplification.[41] Particularly, the cornerstone of the 'Westphalian System', territorial sovereignty, was not explicitly referenced in the treaties. The peace treaties did presuppose the sovereignty of the Swedish and French kings in the sense that they were not subordinate to the authority of the Emperor or the Pope. However, this conception of sovereignty differed from the characteristics of the 19th-century conception.[42] The latter, commonly associated with the 'Westphalian System', included the sovereign authority to dictate the law. In contrast, the sovereignty referenced in the peace treaties of Münster and Osnabrück was grounded in natural law ideas and the ideal of solidarity among monarchs.[43] Rather than introducing a system of abstract territorial sovereignty, the Peace of Westphalia maintained a period of personal power relations within a complex patchwork of imperial and princely sovereignties until the early 19th century and the final breakdown of the Holy Roman Empire.[44]

The simplifications of historical processes and the habitual reference to 'classical' international law or 'classical' notions of sovereignty as 'Westphalian' have consequences for present-day arguments about international law. The myth of 'Westphalia' establishes a hierarchy where arguments derived from sovereignty seem to align with the system, and arguments encroaching on this sovereignty are framed as exceptions. Moreover, it portrays this normative hierarchy as 'natural'. By presenting these conditions as natural, the myth of 'Westphalia' and its associations obscure the functioning of international law as a language of power.[45]

---

38 Bardo Fassbender, 'Westphalia, Peace of (1648)' (*The Max Planck Encyclopedia of Public International Law*, February 2011) <https://opil.ouplaw.com/display/10.1093/law:epil/9780199231690/law-9780199231690-e739?prd=EPIL> accessed 25 August 2023.

39 Leo Gross, 'The Peace of Westphalia, 1648–1948' (1948) 42 AJIL 20.

40 Ibid; Gerard J Mangone, *A Short History of International Organization* (McGraw-Hill 1954) 100.

41 Andreas Osiander, 'Sovereignty, International Relations, and the Westphalian Myth' (2001) 55 IO 251, 260–262.

42 Cf. Saskia Sassen, *Territory, Authority, Rights: From Medieval to Global Assemblages* (Princeton University Press 2008).

43 Fassbender (n 38) para 21.

44 Maïa Pal, *Jurisdictional Accumulation. An Early Modern History of Law, Empires, and Capital* (CUP 2021) 35.

45 Tamsin Phillipa Paige, *Petulant and Contrary: Approaches by the Permanent Five Members of the UN Security Council to the Concept of 'Threat to the Peace' Under Article 39 of the UN Charter* (Brill Nijhoff 2019) 29.

III. REVOLUTIONS IN THE UNITED STATES OF AMERICA, FRANCE, AND HAITI

Histories of international law encompass more than just inter-State relations or imperial domination. Individual and collective self-determination and resistance form another vital thematic strand. Among the first turning points in this context are the revolutions in the United States of America, France, and Haiti.

The US Declaration of Independence of 1776 proclaimed it to be 'self-evident' 'that all men are created equal' and 'endowed by their Creator with certain unalienable rights'. It states further that governments are instituted to safeguard these rights, deriving their legitimacy from the consent of the governed and that, when a government undermines these principles, the people possess the right to alter or replace it. The Declaration of Independence thus marked an important turning point in the development of human rights and of self-determination as a legal norm.[46] However, the rights contained in the Declaration of Independence only applied to white male settlers and not to the indigenous population whose land the settlers had appropriated, not to Black people who remained enslaved – even by some of the signatories of the Declaration of Independence themselves – and not to women, who remained excluded from the right to vote and subject to the authority of their fathers or husbands.[47]

Similar contradictions characterised the French Revolution. Article 1 of the 1789 Declaration of the Rights of Man and of the Citizen asserted that 'men are born and remain free and equal in rights'. Article 2 affirmed that '[t]he aim of all political association is the preservation of the natural and imprescriptible rights of man', including 'liberty, property, security, and resistance to oppression'. Despite the universalist rhetoric, the declaration did not alter the status of women, Black people enslaved in French colonies, other colonial subjects, and Jews, most of whom were denied citizenship.[48] Olympe de Gouges, who pronounced the Declaration of the Rights of Woman and of the Female Citizen in 1791, was tried and convicted for treason and executed by the revolutionary government for this act.[49]

Also in 1791, enslaved Black people in what was then called Saint-Domingue initiated a coordinated attack against the slaveholders and French colonial authorities.[50] The

---

46 Jörg Fisch, 'Peoples and Nations' in Fassbender and Peters (n 28) 27, 34.

47 Robert J Allison, *The American Revolution: A Concise History* (OUP 2011).

48 Shanti Singham, 'Betwixt Cattle and Men: Jews, Blacks and Women, and the Declaration of the Rights of Man' in Dale Van Kley (ed), *The French Idea of Freedom: The Old Regime and the Declaration of Rights of 1789* (Stanford University Press 1994) 114.

49 Annamaria Loche, 'Gouges, Olympe de' in Gianfrancesco Zanetti, Mortimer Sellers, and Stephan Kirste (eds), *Handbook of the History of the Philosophy of Law and Social Philosophy* (Springer 2023) 253.

50 CLR James, *The Black Jacobins: Toussaint L'Ouverture and the San Domingo Revolution* (Vintage 1989); Carolyn E Fick, *The Making of Haiti: Saint Domingue Revolution from Below* (University of Tennessee Press 1990); Laurent Dubois, *A Colony of Citizens: Revolution & Slave Emancipation in the French Caribbean, 1787–1804* (Omohundro Institute and UNC Press 2004).

revolutionaries forced the legal abolition of slavery and defeated French, British, and Spanish forces. In 1804, the former slaves proclaimed the Republic of Haiti's independence, paying homage to the island's original Taíno name, Ayiti. The Haitian Declaration of Independence and the following 1805 Constitution inverted the labelling of 'civilised' versus 'barbarians', which the European colonisers had used all over the world to legitimise their acts of conquest, appropriation, murder, and enslavement.[51] The Haitian Revolution was 'a true world-historical moment in ways that are increasingly acknowledged today' and 'the most radical . . . assertion of the right to have rights in human history'.[52]

IV. THE CONGRESS OF VIENNA AND THE CONCERT OF EUROPE

Following the turbulence of the French Revolution, Napoleon's ascent, and the ensuing Napoleonic wars, the Congress of Vienna convened in 1814 with the objective of re-establishing order in Europe.[53] The envisioned restoration of order aimed at establishing a balance of power among European States, primarily those that emerged victorious from joint conflicts against Napoleon. These triumphant powers encompassed Britain, Russia, Austria, and Prussia. Between November 1814 and June 1815, representatives from over 200 European political entities gathered in Vienna to configure a new European political and legal order. In what became a model for future multilateral conferences, the Congress of Vienna, in addition to the many bilateral treaties that were signed there, adopted the Final Act of Vienna of 9 June 1815.[54] Not only did the order instituted by the Congress of Vienna establish an order based on the idea of balance of power, it also embraced the so-called Great Power principle.[55] During the congress, even though more than 200 polities participated, most decisions were made either in the Committees of Five (comprising Britain, Russia, Austria, Prussia, and France) or the Committees of Eight (which, in addition, also included Spain, Sweden, and Portugal).[56] Immediately after and in close connection with the Congress of Vienna, the Second Peace of Paris of 20 November 1815 instituted a system in which the Great Powers would convene regularly and discuss how best to maintain peace and order in Europe, while reserving the right to maintain this peace even through military intervention.[57] This system, which bears obvious

---

51 Liliana Obregón Tarazona, 'The Civilized and the Uncivilized' in Fassbender and Peters (n 28) 917, 923.

52 Laurent Dubois, 'Why Haiti Should Be at the Center of the Age of Revolution' (*Aeon Essays,* 7 November 2016) <https://aeon.co/essays/why-haiti-should-be-at-the-centre-of-the-age-of-revolution> accessed 1 July 2023. On the right to have rights, see Hannah Arendt, *The Origins of Totalitarianism* (Harcourt Brace Jovanovich 1973); Leila Faghfouri Azar, 'Hannah Arendt: The Right to Have Rights' (*Critical Legal Thinking,* 12 July 2019) <https://criticallegalthinking.com/2019/07/12/hannah-arendt-right-to-have-rights/> accessed 1 July 2023.

53 Gerry Simpson, *Great Powers and Outlaw States: Unequal Sovereigns in the International Legal Order* (CUP 2004) 91.

54 Anne Peters and Simone Peter, 'International Organizations: Between Technocracy and Democracy' in Fassbender and Peters (n 28) 170, 171–172.

55 Simpson (n 53) 94 et seq.

56 Randall Lesaffer, 'The Congress of Vienna' (*Oxford Historical Treaties*) <https://opil.ouplaw.com/page/477> accessed 25 August 2023.

57 Heinz Duchhardt, 'From the Peace of Westphalia to the Congress of Vienna' in Fassbender and Peters (n 28) 628, 651.

resemblance to present-day formats like the Permanent Members of the United Nations Security Council (UNSC) or the G7, was called the 'Concert of Europe', and it structured European politics and diplomacy until the unification of Germany in 1871.[58]

V. THE EMERGENCE OF INTERNATIONAL ORGANISATIONS

The Concert of Europe operated on what scholars commonly refer to as the 'law of coexistence', a concept coined by Wolfgang Friedmann.[59] Beginnings of what Friedmann, in contrast, calls the 'law of co-operation' can also be observed in the first half of the 19th century.[60] The first international organisations,[61] so-called river commissions like the Central Commission for the Navigation of the Rhine (1815) and the European Danube Commission (1856), as well as 'technical unions' including the International Telegraph Union (1865), the Universal Postal Union (1874), and the International Association of Railway Congresses (1884), expressed a common interest in effective and efficient transnational transport and communication and acknowledged the need of cooperation to ensure this. This form of cooperation responded to the changes brought about by the Industrial Revolution and the emergence and expansion of capitalism.[62] In Friedmann's account, these commissions and unions were technical in the sense that they did not touch on the question of internal politics, and yet they can be seen as first instances of an international law of co-operation, which he sees as marked by a more 'vertically' oriented interest in common welfare, as opposed to the purely 'horizontal' law of coexistence focusing on inter-State relationships.[63] The fact that these commissions and unions were not quite as unpolitical as they seemed, however, can be observed in their operation at the European peripheries and in European colonies.[64] The commissions regarding the Danube and the Rhine were not the only river commissions. Similar commissions were set up regarding the Nile and Congo Rivers and the Suez Canal. These river commissions – much like other seemingly technical organisations including the international sanitary councils in Istanbul, Alexandria, and Teheran, can be seen as vehicles of a 'civilising mission' aimed at imposing European conceptions of order and government while gaining access to resources.[65]

VI. THE FORMALISATION OF COLONIAL EMPIRES IN ASIA AND AFRICA

The second half of the 19th century, often termed the 'Age of Empire',[66] saw colonising States administer Asian and African colonies directly, contrasting with prior indirect

---

58 Simpson (n 53) 92.

59 Wolfgang Friedmann, *The Changing Structure of International Law* (Columbia University Press 1967) 367.

60 Ibid.

61 See Baranowska, Engström, and Paige, § 7.3, in this textbook.

62 Craig N Murphy, *International Organization and Industrial Change: Global Governance Since 1850* (Wiley 1994).

63 Ibid.

64 Guy Fiti Sinclair, 'Teaching Statehood' in Jan Klabbers (ed), *The Cambridge Companion to International Organizations Law* (Columbia University Press 2022) 212.

65 Ibid.

66 Eric Hobsbawm, *The Age of Empire: 1875–1914* (Vintage 1989).

control through chartered companies and other agents.[67] In 1858, the British Crown took over the British East India Company's possessions and armed forces, and proclaimed that it would enter and maintain all treaties and engagements made between the East India Company and 'the native princes of India'.[68] The defining turning point within this age of formalised empire is, however, the Berlin Conference of 1884–1885. At this conference, European powers, the US, and the Ottoman Empire convened under the guise of managing 'free trade' in Africa.[69] The resultant General Act of Berlin formalised African subordination and partition. Contemporary African State borders still largely reflect the colonial boundaries drawn in 1885.[70] Other lastingly influential aspects of the General Act of Berlin included an explicit reference to 'spheres of influence' as grounds for international obligations, and the establishment of the principle of 'effective occupation' as grounds for acquiring rights over colonial lands.[71] This led, among other things, to the first genocide of the 20th century, the genocide of imperial Germany against the Herero and Nama.[72] Another gruesome result of the Berlin Conference was the creation of the so-called 'Congo Free State', over which the Belgian King Leopold II exercised rights of property and sovereignty and in which he introduced unimaginably cruel practices to maximise rubber extraction.[73] Colonial officers in the Congo Free State killed and mutilated people for failing to meet rubber collection quotas. More than 10 million people died due to these and other colonial practices.

VII. THE FIRST WORLD WAR AND ITS AFTERMATHS

The First World War (WWI), waged between 1914 and 1918, pitted the Central Powers (Germany, Austria, the Ottoman Empire, and Bulgaria) against the Allies or Entente powers (France, the UK, Russia, the US, Italy, and Japan). Although its origins were European, the war's global scope emerged due to combat on and over European colonies.

After the Central Powers' defeat, WWI led to significant shifts in international organisation and colonial arrangement. Woodrow Wilson, then the US president, articulated Fourteen Points in a congressional speech to guide post-war reconstruction.[74] These principles included open diplomacy, freedom of navigation, free trade, arms reduction, and colonial reorganisation, as well as some points

---

67 Upendra Baxi, 'India-Europe' in Fassbender and Peters (n 28) 744, 755.

68 Ibid.

69 Matthew Craven, 'Between Law and History: The Berlin Conference of 1884–1885 and the Logic of Free Trade' (2015) 3 LRIL 31.

70 Cf. AI Asiwaju, *Artificial Boundaries* (Lagos University Press 1984).

71 Taslim Olawale Elias, *Africa and the Development of International Law* (Richard Akinjide, ed, Martinus Nijhoff 1988) 16.

72 Zoé Samudzi, 'Paradox of Recognition: Genocide and Colonialism' (2021) 31 Postmodern Culture 1.

73 Martin Ewans, *European Atrocity, African Catastrophe: Leopold II, the Congo Free State and Its Aftermath* (Routledge 2015).

74 Woodrow Wilson, 'Wilson's Address to Congress, Stating the War Aims and Peace Terms of the United States (Delivered in Joint Session, 8 January 1918)' in A Shaw (ed), *State Papers and Addresses by Woodrow Wilson* (George H Doran 1918) 464.

regarding the creation of new States like Turkey and Poland and the readjustment of borders on the European continent. Of utmost significance was the 14th point, envisaging '[a] general association of nations . . . under specific covenants for the purpose of affording mutual guarantees of political independence and territorial integrity to great and small States alike'. Subsequently, the League of Nations (LoN or League) was founded at the Paris Peace Conference, which ended WWI. The Covenant of the League of Nations was included in the Treaty of Versailles. In the preamble, the Covenant set out the goal of the League, namely 'to promote international co-operation and to achieve international peace and security'. To this end, articles 8 to 17 set out provisions regarding disarmament and arms control, collective security, protection of minorities, and peaceful dispute settlement. The major organs instituted by the Covenant were, according to article 2, the Secretariat, the Assembly, which represented all member States, and the Council, comprising major powers as permanent members and additional non-permanent members.[75] The Council went on to create the Permanent Court of International Justice, the precursor of the International Court of Justice.[76]

Colonial reorganisation materialised within the LoN through the Mandate System,[77] transferring former German and Ottoman colonies to other colonial powers. Article 22 of the Covenant referred to the people living in these territories as 'peoples not yet able to stand by themselves under the strenuous conditions of the modern world' and stated that 'the well-being and development of such peoples should form a sacred trust of civilisation'. This was a typical reflection of the 'standard of civilisation' and of the 'white man's burden'.[78] The 'standard of civilisation', rooted in racism and colonial paternalism, implies that certain cultures and societies were considered less advanced or developed, necessitating the guidance and control of more 'civilised' nations. The concept of the 'white man's burden', in an attempt to legitimise colonial domination, encapsulated the belief that Western powers had a moral duty to educate and uplift these supposedly less advanced societies. Article 22 also introduced a three-tiered system according to which the administration of the mandates was supposed to reflect 'the stage of the development of the people, the geographical situation of the territory, its economic conditions and other similar circumstances'. This system formally introduced and entrenched a clearly racist hierarchy not only between Europeans and 'others', but also among negatively racialised people. Just as most of the institutional makeup of the LoN was later reintroduced – with some aspects of it reformed – with the foundation of the United Nations, the Mandate System carried on in a slightly changed manner within the Trusteeship system instituted by the UN.[79] TWAIL scholars have also argued that understanding the Mandate System is crucial

---

75 Peter Krüger, 'From the Paris Peace Treaties to the End of the Second World War' in Fassbender and Peters (n 28) 679, 684 et seq.

76 See Choudhary, § 12, in this textbook.

77 Susan Pedersen, *The Guardians: The League of Nations and the Question of Empire* (OUP 2015).

78 Ntina Tzouvala, *Capitalism as Civilisation: A History of International Law* (CUP 2020) 96 et seq.

79 Ralph Wilde, *International Territorial Administration: How Trusteeship and the Civilizing Mission Never Went Away* (OUP 2008).

to understanding present-day institutions like the World Bank and the International Monetary Fund[80] as well as contemporary conceptions of peripheral or Third World sovereignty more broadly.[81]

VIII. THE SECOND WORLD WAR AND ITS AFTERMATH

The LoN was not able to achieve its goal of preserving peace or at least of preventing another war of the dimensions of the First World War. Shortly after Hitler came to power in Germany in 1933, Nazi Germany left the LoN.[82] Japan left the League in 1933 after it had invaded Manchuria in 1931, and Fascist Italy left in 1937 after having occupied Ethiopia in 1936.[83] In 1939, Nazi Germany started WWII by invading Poland.[84] The atrocities of the war itself were accompanied by the industrialised genocide against Jewish people (Holocaust or *Shoa*, Hebrew: 'great catastrophe') and against Sinti and Romani people (*Porajmos*, Romani: 'the devouring'), eugenicist policies involving the systematic murder, forced sterilisation, and imprisonment of people with disabilities, homosexual, trans, and intersex people, persecution and also forced sterilisation of Black people, and colonial *Großraum* (German: 'greater area') policies regarding Eastern Europe, which lead to mass deportation, starvation, forced labour, and extermination of Polish, Ukrainian, Czech, Russian, and other Slavic people.[85] Six million Jewish people and 24 million people across the Soviet Union died. Only a few of the people facing persecution, deportation, and death could find refuge in other countries. The US enforced a particularly restrictive refugee policy claiming that Jewish refugees constituted a threat to order and security.[86] The cruelty of this restrictive refugee policy is exemplified by the case of the M.S. *St. Louis*, a ship with 937 passengers, who were almost all Jewish. The ship was sent back from the port of Miami, Florida, to Hamburg, Germany. Upon arrival, the passengers were immediately deported to concentration camps, where over a quarter of them died.[87] After the war, the Refugee Convention was adopted in 1951 to prevent such cruel policies and acts in the future.[88] One of its cornerstones is the principle of non-refoulement, which prohibits States from returning refugees to a country where they face serious threats.[89]

---

80 Anghie (n 22) 115 et seq. See Bagchi, § 23.3, in this textbook.

81 Usha Natarajan, 'Creating and Recreating Iraq: Legacies of the Mandate System in Contemporary Understandings of Third World Sovereignty' (2011) 24 LJIL 799.

82 Krüger (n 75) 693.

83 Ibid.

84 Ibid 694.

85 Mathias Schmöckel, *Die Großraumtheorie: Ein Beitrag zur Geschichte der Völkerrechtswissenschaft im Dritten Reich, insbesondere der Kriegszeit* (Duncker & Humblot 1994); Bardo Fassbender, 'Stories of War and Peace: On Writing the History of International Law in the "Third Reich" and After' (2002) 13 EJIL 479.

86 Norman L Zucker and Naomi Flink Zucker, *The Guarded Gate: The Reality of American Refugee Policy* (Harcourt Brace Jovanovich 1987).

87 Allison Lawlor, *'The Saddest Ship Afloat': The Tragedy of the MS St. Louis* (Nimbus 2016).

88 Convention Relating to the Status of Refugees (adopted 18 July 1951, entered into force 22 April 1954) 189 UNTS 137; On international migration law, see Kadima, § 18, in this textbook.

89 Penelope Mathew, 'Non-Refoulement' in Cathryn Costello, Michelle Foster, and Jane McAdam (eds), *The Oxford Handbook of International Refugee Law* (OUP 2021).

The development of international human rights law[90] in the form of, inter alia, the Universal Declaration of Human Rights,[91] the Genocide Convention,[92] the Convention on the Elimination of Racial Discrimination,[93] and the two Human Rights Covenants[94] was also motivated by the goal of not letting the atrocities committed during WWII happen again.[95]

In the Atlantic Charter,[96] a declaration signed in 1941 by US President Franklin D. Roosevelt and British Prime Minister Winston Churchill, the two heads of State laid out the cornerstones of what the post-war international order should look like.[97] The principles affirmed in this declaration included self-determination, free trade and free access to resources, economic cooperation, improved labour standards, social security, and the abandonment of the use of force. The Atlantic Charter laid out the foundations for the creation of the United Nations, which was created in 1945 at the San Francisco Conference, in which 50 States participated.[98] The purposes of this new international organisation with a universalist mandate, as laid out in the preamble and in article 1 UN Charter,[99] are to maintain international peace and security, to develop friendly relations based on equal rights and self-determination of peoples, to achieve international cooperation in economic, social, cultural and humanitarian matters, and to promote and encourage respect for human rights. Unlike the LoN, the UN was not designed to ensure these goals through detailed legal procedures but through Great Power cooperation, as expressed most strikingly in the key role given to the five Permanent Members of the UN Security Council (UNSC; the UK, China, France, the Soviet Union, and the US).[100]

IX. FORMAL DECOLONISATION

After most of the Americas had gained independence from the colonial metropoles in the 19th century and after some LoN mandates like Egypt, Lebanon, Syria, and Iraq

---

90 See Ciampi, § 21, in this textbook.

91 Universal Declaration of Human Rights (adopted 10 December 1948) UNGA Res 217 A(III).

92 Convention on the Prevention and Punishment of the Crime of Genocide (adopted 9 December 1948, entered into force 12 January 1951) 78 UNTS 277.

93 International Convention on the Elimination of All Forms of Racial Discrimination (adopted 7 March 1966, entered into force 4 January 1969) 660 UNTS 195.

94 International Covenant on Civil and Political Rights (adopted 16 December 1966, entered into force 23 March 1976) 999 UNTS 171; International Covenant on Economic, Social and Cultural Rights (adopted 16 December 1966, entered into force 3 January 1976) 993 UNTS 3.

95 Alejandro Baer and Natan Sznaider, *Memory and Forgetting in the Post-Holocaust Era: The Ethics of Never Again* (Routledge 2017).

96 Declaration of Principles (signed and entered into force 14 August 1941) 204 LNTS 381.

97 Krüger (n 75) 695.

98 Ibid 696.

99 Charter of the United Nations (concluded 26 June 1945, entered into force 24 October 1945) 1 UNTS XVI.

100 Martti Koskenniemi, 'History of International Law, Since World War II' in Rüdiger Wolfrum (ed), Max Planck Encyclopedia of International Law (2011) <https://opil.ouplaw.com/display/10.1093/law:epil/9780199231690/law-9780199231690-e714> accessed 7 August 2011, para 6; See Baranowska, Engström, and Paige, § 7.3, in this textbook.

had become independent in the first half of the 20th century, it was after the conclusion of WWII that a tidal wave of decolonisation swept across the globe. The struggle for independence during this time was explicitly and tightly linked to the struggle over public international law.[101]

In 1947 the partition of British India into independent India and Pakistan marked the beginning of this post-WWII decolonisation era.[102] Meanwhile, the ideals of Pan-Africanism began to gather momentum, championed by figures like the Jamaican journalist Marcus Garvey and taken up by Kwame Nkrumah, who would become Ghana's first president, and Patrice Lumumba, the first prime minister of the Republic of the Congo, who was later murdered at the orders of Belgian officers, among others.[103] The year 1960 saw not only a multitude of African countries gaining their independence but also the adoption of the Declaration on the Granting of Independence to Colonial Countries and Peoples by the UNGA, stating that foreign rule was a violation of human rights, reiterating the right to self-determination, and calling for an immediate end of all forms of colonial rule.[104] This declaration was a major achievement for the newly independent States that had become members of the UN, transforming the UNGA into a platform for anti-colonial resistance.[105]

Amid the ideological divide of the Cold War (see C.X.), leaders like Sukarno of Indonesia, Jawaharlal Nehru of India, Josip Broz Tito of Yugoslavia, and Gamal Abdel Nasser of Egypt convened the Non-Aligned Movement. This coalition of nations, seeking to avoid alignment with the superpowers and rejecting imperialistic ambitions, found its roots in the 1955 Bandung Conference[106] and was formally established in 1961 in Belgrade.

Economic justice played a vital role in post-colonial aspirations. The creation of the United Nations Conference on Trade and Development (UNCTAD) in 1964 aimed to challenge the current international economic system and promote a New International Economic Order (NIEO).[107] The principles of the NIEO encompassed the freedom of newly independent nations to regulate multinational corporations, nationalise foreign property, form commodity associations (like OPEC), and establish equitable prices for raw materials. Furthermore, it emphasised technology transfer and development

---

101 Sundhya Pahuja, *Decolonising International Law: Development, Economic Growth and the Politics of Universality* (CUP 2011); Jochen von Bernstorff and Philipp Dann (eds), *The Battle for International Law: South-North Perspectives on the Decolonization Era* (OUP 2019).

102 Ian Talbot, *A History of Modern South Asia: Politics, States, Diasporas* (Yale University Press 2016) 131 et seq; Priyasha Saksena, 'Building the Nation: Sovereignty and International Law in the Decolonisation of South Asia' (2020) JHIL 1.

103 Adom Getachew, *Worldmaking After Empire: The Rise and Fall of Self-Determination* (Princeton University Press 2019) 6 et seq.

104 UNGA Res 1514 (XV) (1960), GAOR 15th Session Supp 16, 66.

105 Getachew (n 103) 73 et seq.

106 Luis Eslava, Michael Fakhri, and Vasuki Nesiah (eds), *Bandung, Global History, and International Law: Critical Pasts and Pending Futures* (CUP 2017).

107 Antony Anghie, 'Legal Aspects of the New International Economic Order' (2015) 6 Humanity 145.

assistance devoid of conditionalities. Other international instruments related to the NIEO include the Declaration on Permanent Sovereignty over Natural Resources[108] and the Charter of Economic Rights and Duties of States.[109]

X. THE COLD WAR

WWII's conclusion in 1945 marked the beginning of the Cold War,[110] a time of confrontation between the Western capitalist bloc led by the US and the Eastern communist bloc led by the Soviet Union (USSR). This period, characterised by ideological and geopolitical rivalry between these superpowers, lasted until the USSR's collapse in 1991. The Cold War was a 'hot' war in many parts of the world, as the US and the Soviet Union intervened militarily in the regions they deemed to belong to their 'spheres of influence' and engaged in proxy wars. These interventions and proxy wars were so widespread that prominent international legal scholars argued over whether the relatively new prohibition of the use of force enshrined in article 2(4) UN Charter had already died.[111] Among the proxy wars were the Korean War and the Vietnam War, as well as the wars in Afghanistan and Angola.

Japan had previously annexed Korea, and after Japan's defeat in WWII the US and the USSR divided Korea into two zones of occupation, which later became two sovereign States, communist North Korea and capitalist South Korea. In 1950, North Korean military forces crossed the border, giving rise to a violent conflict. As the USSR was temporarily protesting the UNSC's failure to let the recently established People's Republic of China take China's UNSC seat, the UNSC passed several resolutions condemning North Korea's action and authorising military force in support of South Korea.[112] After the USSR realised that its intended boycott had not reached its goal of paralysing the UN, it took up its seat again and vetoed further resolutions on the conflict.[113] Subsequently, the UNGA passed a resolution titled 'Uniting for Peace', in which it claimed authority to issue resolutions on matters of the maintenance of international peace and security in cases where the UNSC failed to do so.[114] It was, in fact, the UNGA under this Uniting for Peace Resolution that authorised the first UN peacekeeping force, the United Nations Emergency Force, in the Suez War.[115] In this case, it was the French and British vetoes that had paralysed the UNSC.[116]

---

108 UNGA Res 1803 (1962) GAOR 17th Session Supp 17, 15.
109 UNGA Res 3281 (1974) GAOR 29th Session Supp 31, 50.
110 See Matthew Craven and others (eds), *International Law and the Cold War* (CUP 2020).
111 Thomas Franck, 'Who Killed Article 2(4)? Or: Changing Norms Governing the Use of Force by States' (1970) 64 AJIL 809; Louis Henkin, 'Reports of the Death of Article 2(4) Are Greatly Exaggerated' (1971) 65 AJIL 544.
112 Nico Krisch, 'The Security Council and the Great Powers' in Vaughan Lowe and others (eds), *The United Nations Security Council and War* (OUP 2008) 133, 149.
113 Dominik Zaum, 'The Security Council, the General Assembly, and War: The Uniting for Peace Resolution' in Vaughan Lowe and others (n 112) 154, 156–157.
114 UNGA Res 377 (1950) GAOR 5th Session Supp 20, 10.
115 UNGA Res 1000 (1956) GAOR 1st Emergency Special Session Supp 1, 2.
116 Zaum (n 113) 154.

The Vietnam War began in 1955 as a similar proxy war between communist North Vietnam, backed by China and the USSR, and capitalist South Vietnam, backed by the US and its allies. The main fight was between the South Vietnam military with heavy US support on one side and communist Viet Cong guerrilla troops on the other side. While some international legal historians claim that the Vietnam War was 'conducted without any serious discussion of its lawfulness',[117] there were at least some prominent debates in this regard.[118] More pertinent, however, was the question of how to account for *how* this war was carried out. US war crimes in Vietnam were the subject of the first international people's tribunal, the so-called Russell Tribunal, which served as a model for later civil society investigations into human rights abuses.[119]

From 1979 to 1989, Afghanistan was another battleground for superpower rivalry. The communist government in Afghanistan was facing resistance from mujahideen fighters, which led the Soviet Union to intervene on behalf of the Afghan government. The US, in turn, provided the mujahideen with arms, training, and funding.[120] The withdrawal of Soviet forces in 1989 not only signalled the erosion of Soviet power and influence, but it also set the stage for protracted instability and wars in Afghanistan and the whole region.[121] The Taliban, which later assumed power over Afghanistan, were one faction of the mujahideen, who had been supported by the US.

Both Soviet and US foreign policy during the Cold War were defined by doctrines reflecting their perspectives on intervention and control in what they considered their spheres of influence.[122] The Soviet Brezhnev Doctrine, proclaimed in 1968, asserted the Soviet Union's right to intervene militarily in any socialist country and was used to justify interventions in Hungary (1956) and Czechoslovakia (1968).[123] The US doctrines were rooted in the 1823 Monroe Doctrine, according to which European interference in the affairs of the Western Hemisphere would be considered a threat to US interests and which the US had since then used as a rationale for interventions and influence in Latin America and the Caribbean. The Truman Doctrine from 1947 took this idea of a US sphere of influence further so that it developed global reach. The Johnson Doctrine from 1965 combined the Monroe and the Truman Doctrines and was used to justify US military interventions in the Dominican Republic in 1965;

---

117 Koskenniemi (n 100) para 28.

118 John Norton Moore, *Law and the Indo-China War* (Princeton University Press 1972) 358 et seq; Richard Falk, 'International Law and the United States Role in the Viet Nam War' (1966) 75 Yale Law Journal 1122.

119 John Duffett (ed), *Against the Crime of Silence: Proceedings of the Russell International War Crimes Tribunal* (Bertrand Russell Peace Foundation 1968).

120 Shri Prakash, 'US Involvement in Afghanistan: Implications for the Future' (2003) 10 Journal of Peace Studies 1, 6.

121 Rafael Reuveny and Aseem Prakash, 'The Afghanistan War and the Breakdown of the Soviet Union' (1999) 25 Review of International Studies 693.

122 Thomas D Grant, 'Doctrines (Monroe, Hallstein, Brezhnev, Stimson)' (Max Planck Encyclopedia of Public International Law, March 2014) <https://opil.ouplaw.com/display/10.1093/law:epil/9780199231690/law-9780199231690-e697?rskey=e8aNEz&result=11&prd=MPIL> accessed 24 August 2023.

123 Leon Romaniecki, 'Sources of the Brezhnev Doctrine of Limited Sovereignty and Intervention' (1970) 5 Israel Law Review 527.

the support of the anti-communist 'Contras' in Nicaragua, which led to the landmark *Nicaragua* ICJ judgment;[124] and the US intervention in Grenada in 1983.[125]

Given that both the Soviet Union and the US possessed nuclear weapons, the threat of nuclear destruction loomed over the whole period of the Cold War. International organisations and international diplomacy, therefore, focused on disarmament and non-proliferation of nuclear weapons. Three landmark ICJ cases, the *Nuclear Weapons Advisory Opinion*,[126] the *Nuclear Tests* case,[127] and the *Marshall Islands* case,[128] deal with questions relating to nuclear weapons and international law.

XI. IMPORTANT DEVELOPMENTS IN THE 21ST CENTURY

The end of the Cold War with the collapse of the USSR sparked a sense of optimism amid everyone committed to liberal internationalism and even famously prompted Francis Fukuyama to declare 'the end of history'.[129] Post-Soviet transitions and increased international cooperation fostered hopes for a more peaceful world in what many call the 'golden nineties'. The NATO intervention in Kosovo in 1999, carried out without UNSC authorisation, shattered this optimism.[130]

The international climate changed completely with the attacks on the World Trade Center in New York City on 11 September 2001 carried out by the terrorist network al-Qaeda, operating out of Afghanistan. A few days after the attacks, US President George W Bush declared the so-called War on Terror and, later that year, invaded Afghanistan. The UNSC adopted Resolution 1368[131] on 12 September 2001 condemning the attacks and declaring them to be a threat to international peace and security. Resolution 1373, adopted later in the same month,[132] went a lot further and became one of the central elements of international law arguments related to the 'War on Terror'.[133] Another war related to the War on Terror was the US invasion of Iraq in 2003. A broad consensus

---

124 *Military and Paramilitary Activities in and Against Nicaragua (Nicaragua v United States of America)* (Merits) [1986] ICJ Rep 14.

125 Isaak I Dore, 'The US Invasion of Grenada: Resurrection of the Johnson Doctrine' (1984) Stanford Journal of International Law 173.

126 *Legality of the Threat or Use of Nuclear Weapons* (Advisory Opinion) [1996] ICJ Rep 226.

127 *Nuclear Tests (Australia v France) (Judgment)* [1974] ICJ Rep 253.

128 *Obligations Concerning Negotiations Relating to Cessation of the Nuclear Arms Race and to Nuclear Disarmament (Marshall Islands v United Kingdom)* (Preliminary Objections, Judgment) [2016] ICJ Rep 833.

129 Francis Fukuyama, *The End of History and the Last Man* (Free Press 1992).

130 Martti Koskenniemi, ' "The Lady Doth Protest Too Much" Kosovo, and the Turn to Ethics in International Law' (2002) 65 MLR 159.

131 UNSC Res 1368 (2001) 4370th meeting.

132 UNSC Res 1373 (2001) 4385th meeting

133 José E Alvarez, 'The UN's "War" on Terrorism' (2003) 31 International Journal of Legal Information 238; Ntina Tzouvala, 'The "Unwilling or Unable" Doctrine and the Political Economy of the War on Terror' (2023) 14 Humanity 19.

among most international lawyers was that this war was blatantly unlawful, and demonstrations across the world denounced this war using the language of international law, which also sparked debates among critical international lawyers on whether and how they should engage in such arguments.[134]

Moving into the 2010s, the Arab Spring emerged as a significant phenomenon reshaping the international legal landscape.[135] Originating in Tunisia, these anti-government protests and uprisings quickly spread to countries like Libya, Egypt, Yemen, Syria, and Bahrain. These events led to the deposition of the rulers in Tunisia, Libya, Egypt, and Yemen but were also met with increasingly violent responses by autocratic governments, with the civil war in Syria being the most extreme example.

Beyond these events, the 21st century has seen a myriad of developments unfold that continue to shape international law. Rapid technological advancements, including the proliferation of the internet, have led to new legal challenges in the realms of privacy, security, and sovereignty.[136] Climate change has fuelled debates surrounding environmental protection, responsibility, and the rights of future generations.[137] Additionally, the emergence of right-wing populist movements, shifting power dynamics, and evolving regional conflicts have demanded responses from the international community.

D. CONCLUSION

Histories of international law are marked by trajectories of both empire and resistance. From early instances of imperial conquest, international legal norms evolved to legitimise and regulate colonisation. The balance of power principle that emerged from the Congress of Vienna further exemplified how international law has been used by powerful States to assert dominance over weaker ones. The aftermath of the world wars epitomise the dual nature of international law. The League of Nations' Covenant entrenched imperial interests through the Mandate System, perpetuating hierarchical control over former colonies. Simultaneously, the principles of self-determination and sovereignty facilitated the rise of decolonisation movements. Multiple revolutionary movements across the globe and throughout the history of international law show, however, that international law can also be harnessed for liberation. Recognising this dual nature of international law is crucial to shaping a more just and equitable future, where international law serves as a catalyst for justice and the dismantling of systems of empire.

---

134 Robert Knox, 'Strategy and Tactics' (2010) 21 FYBIL 193; Usha Natarajan, 'A Third World Approach to Debating the Legality of the Iraq War' (2007) 9 IntCLRev 405.

135 Ayodeji K Perrin, 'Introduction to the Special Issue on the Arab Spring' (2013) 34 UPaJIntlL i.

136 See Hüsch, § 19, in this textbook.

137 See Viveros-Uehara, § 17, in this textbook.

BOX 1.3 Further Readings and Further Resources

Further Readings

- Matthew Craven, Malgosia Fitzmaurice, and Maria Vogiatzi (eds), *Time, History and International Law* (Brill 2007)

- Bardo Fassbender and Anne Peters (eds), *The Oxford Handbook of the History of International Law* (OUP 2012)

- Anne Orford, *International Law and the Politics of History* (CUP 2021)

Further Resources

- Thomas Skouteris, 'The Turn to History in International Law' (*Oxford Bibliographies*, June 2017) <www.oxfordbibliographies.com/display/document/obo-9780199796953/obo-9780199796953-0154.xml> accessed 26 August 2023

- 'The History of International Law [Timeline]' <https://blog.oup.com/2015/09/history-international-law-timeline/> accessed 26 August 2023

§ § §

2

CHAPTER 2
OVERARCHING QUESTIONS

SUÉ GONZÁLEZ HAUCK, MARNIE LLOYDD,
DANIEL RICARDO QUIROGA-VILLAMARÍN,
AND MIRIAM BAK MCKENNA

INTRODUCTION
SUÉ GONZÁLEZ HAUCK

BOX 2.1 Required Knowledge and Learning Objectives

Required knowledge: History of International Law

Learning objectives: Understanding why the overarching questions chosen to be treated as such in this textbook play a pivotal role across different approaches and subject areas.

BOX 2.2 Interactive Exercises

Access *interactive exercises for this chapter*[1] by positioning your smartphone camera at the dot-filled box, also known as a QR code.

Figure 2.1 QR code referring to interactive exercises.

A. INTRODUCTION

This book – in this sense a typical representative of the textbook genre – mostly treats questions pertaining to international law within separate 'boxes', labelled either

---

1   https://openrewi.org/en-projects-project-public-international-law-nature-and-purpose-of-international-law/

DOI: 10.4324/9781003451327-3

according to a specific approach, method, or subject area pertaining to 'general international law' or to 'specialised fields'. These boxes, of course, are not entirely self-contained. As the many cross-references between chapters throughout this book illustrate, different approaches to international law and different subject areas overlap significantly. This is true well beyond the overarching questions we have chosen to treat in this chapter. The overarching questions presented in this chapter, however, escape these boxes altogether. This short introductory section explains why the questions of international law and violence, consent, enforcement, and self-determination require being placed outside the brackets of other chapters devoted to specific approaches or subject areas and provides a glimpse into the following chapters dealing with these questions in more detail.

B. OVERARCHING QUESTIONS

The first question spanning multiple subject areas, which is crucial for any treatment of international law, is the question of international law and violence. International law as a discipline often portrays itself as working towards the good of humanity as a whole – particularly when it comes to eliminating violence.[2] Many students become interested in international law precisely because they think international law is a tool that serves to make the world a better place. The section on international law and violence,[3] without trying to disillusion students who may approach international law with this disposition, complicates this narrative. It offers a detailed account of how international law does seek to prevent violence but also of how international law accepts and regulates certain forms of violence. It further introduces avenues for critical reflection about the complex relationship between violence and international law.

The second question with an overarching character, which warrants separate treatment, is the question pertaining to consent in the international legal order.[4] Consent is traditionally considered to be the basis of international law as a whole, the ultimate source of validity of every international legal rule.[5] The chapter devoted to consent presents this classical narrative and introduces some of the theoretical problems that arise when trying to conceptualise consent as the expression of the 'free will' of States, explores connections between consent and anarchy, delves into different types of consent in international law, and highlights the relationship between consent and colonialism.

Intricately linked to the idea of international law as a consent-based legal order is the third overarching question, namely the question of enforcement.[6] In the absence

---

2   See e.g. Antônio Augusto Cançado Trindade, *International Law for Humankind: Towards a New Jus Gentium* (3rd edn, Brill 2020); Anne Peters, 'Humanity as the A and Ω of Sovereignty' (2009) 20 EJIL 513.

3   See Lloydd, § 2.1, in this textbook.

4   See González Hauck, § 2.2, in this textbook.

5   *Legality of the Threat or Use of Nuclear Weapons* (Advisory Opinion) [1996] ICJ Rep 226 [21].

6   See Quiroga-Villamarín, § 2.3, in this textbook.

of a centralised government, international law lacks the enforcement mechanisms of many other legal systems. From this stems a question that has been haunting internal law for centuries: is international law really law? International legal theorists have devoted significant intellectual energy to finding convincing answers to this question. The section on enforcement highlights how European legal scholars have tried to provide answers through a concern for the systematicity and interconnectedness of international legal rules while scholars from the US have focused on a more informal conception of 'process'. It thus introduces the most influential accounts of why international law is deemed to count as law, without losing sight of what is left outside of this framing.

Finally, the fourth overarching question concerns self-determination.[7] The previous chapter on the history of international law has portrayed international law not only as an instrument of colonial and imperialist domination but also as a tool for resistance. The main avenue through which resistance has been pursued within international law is through self-determination. The chapter on self-determination locates this notion within wider theoretical debates about recognition, statehood, political communities, and sovereignty in international legal theory and practice. It draws on the key international instruments and rulings that define its legal scope and application and discusses its inherent conceptual and legal tensions. Among the different contexts in which self-determination has played a key role, the section highlights self-determination against colonial domination, against alien subjugation, domination, or exploitation, as well as internal or democratic self-determination, remedial self-determination, and indigenous and minority self-determination.

C. CONCLUSION

The following sections on international law and violence, on consent, enforcement, and self-determination, concern questions that shape international law across subject areas. They pertain to the central characteristics of international law as a legal order. As students embarking on a journey of learning about international law, you can reassess your previously held assumptions about international law and keep whatever further reflections the following sections will inspire in mind as you unpack the individual 'boxes' in the rest of this book.

§ § §

---

7   See Bak McKenna, § 2.4, in this textbook.

§ 2.1 INTERNATIONAL LAW AND VIOLENCE

MARNIE LLOYDD

BOX 2.1.1 Required Knowledge and Learning Objectives

Required knowledge: None

Learning objectives: Acknowledging that international law seeks to prevent violence but also accepts and regulates certain forms of violence; introducing avenues for critical reflection about the complex relationship between violence and international law.

A. INTRODUCTION

A key aim of the international legal system is to protect future generations from the 'scourge of war'.[8] International law therefore requires States to settle their international disputes by peaceful means and outlaws aggression between them.[9] Other rules place significant restraints on how wars may be fought; for example, not allowing civilians or hospitals to be targeted, to reduce war's humanitarian consequences. Many students become interested in international law precisely because it is seen as an aspirational vehicle for 'making the world a better place'.

Much has been achieved in suppressing the right to make war and restricting the means and methods of warfare.[10] Still, aspirations for a peaceful and just world have not (yet) been achieved. Partly, armed violence occurs in violation of international legal norms – the illegal invasion of a sovereign State, a terrorist attack on a market square, attacks against a particular ethnic group. However, armed violence is also undertaken in compliance with international law. Specifically, self-defence and collective security measures adopted by the UN Security Council (UNSC) are accepted within the system as a way to counter insecurity. Thus, there are important exceptions to the general norm against using force.[11] International law is not pacifist and its functioning as intended involves violence. Reflecting this, the preamble of the UN Charter sets out that 'armed force shall not be used, save in the common interest'.

---

8 *Charter of the United Nations,* 1945, 1 UNTS XVI (UN Charter) preamble.
9 UN Charter, arts 2(3), 2(4). See also art 1(1). See also UNGA Res 3314 (XXIX) (14 December 1974), Annex: Definition of Aggression; Rome Statute of the International Criminal Court 2187 UNTS 3 (opened for signature 17 July 1998, entered into force 1 July 2002) (ICC Statute) art 8*bis*.
10 See, for instance, Marc Weller, 'Use of Force' in Jacob Katz Cogan, Ian Hurd, and Ian Johnstone (eds), *Oxford Handbook of International Organisations* (OUP 2016) 625.
11 See Svicevic, § 13, in this textbook.

It may seem paradoxical that peace and security are sought through war and violence. Because violence can be oppressive but also potentially emancipatory, '[p]lacing limits around violence remains . . . one of the hardest challenges of the human condition'.[12] So, who gets to decide what is in the 'common interest' and how armed violence might be used 'in the right way and for the right reasons'?[13] In their application of international law, different thinkers, actors, and traditions will have different readings of a situation and different legal, political, and moral judgements and arguments as to the values and interests to be prioritised. These priorities can change over time and context. The relevant norms and exceptions, and their application, are neither neutral or inevitable nor technical and universally agreed, but highly political and contested.[14]

B. WHAT IS MEANT BY 'VIOLENCE'?

Exploring the relationship(s) between international law and violence is a potentially wide-ranging endeavour since there is no reason the term 'violence', and even more so 'harm', must be limited to armed force and its direct physical and psychological consequences. For example, the humanitarian consequences of armed conflict can also include knock-on effects such as displacement and the breakdown of essential infrastructure and services leading to increased sickness and death.[15] Importantly, violence could also be thought of as structural, a less visible part of many people's everyday experiences of discrimination leading to injustice, exploitation or exclusion, economic or political inequalities, or activities that degrade the environment.[16] Moreover, such issues can contribute to conflict and outbreaks of violence.

Nevertheless, this chapter focuses on organised physical violence during armed conflict and discusses international law related to the use of force and the UN Charter (i.e. rules on starting or joining hostilities) and regulating those hostilities once they are underway (known as the law of armed conflict or international humanitarian law [IHL]).[17]

Within that narrower focus, the term 'violence' is not defined in international law but does appear in certain international instruments, most commonly related to acts

---

12 Hugo Slim, *Killing Civilians: Method, Madness and Morality in War* (Hurst 2007) 295.

13 See discussion in Helen Dexter, 'Peace and Violence' in Paul D Williams and Matt McDonald, *Security Studies: An Introduction* (Vol 1, 3rd edn, Routledge 2018) 209.

14 Anne Orford, *International Authority and the Responsibility to Protect* (CUP 2011) 212; MS Wallace, *Security without Weapons: Rethinking Violence, Nonviolent Action, and Civilian Protection* (Routledge 2017) 12–13; Noelle Crossley, 'Is R2P Still Controversial? Continuity and Change in the Debate on 'Humanitarian Intervention' (2018) 31(5) Cambridge Review of International Affairs 415, 428.

15 ICRC, *War in Cities: Preventing and Addressing the Humanitarian Consequences for Civilians* (ICRC 2023) 55.

16 Johan Galtung, 'Violence, Peace and Peace Research' (1969) 6(3) Journal of Peace Research 167. See also Hilary Charlesworth's discussion of 'international law of everyday life' compared to responding always to crises: 'International Law: A Discipline of Crisis' (2002) 65(3) Modern Law Review 377, 391–392. Note also the risk of violence as a concept becoming so broad as to become unworkable discussed in Dexter (n 13) 211. For a Marxist understanding of violence, see Bagchi, § 3.4.C., in this textbook.

17 See Dienelt and Ullah, § 14, in this textbook.

committed against individuals, including violence against women or children, and sexual and gender-based violence.[18] Otherwise, acts of violence are often described through offences such as murder, extermination, torture, enforced disappearance, and bodily or mental harm, or through terms that have been defined or have developed specific meanings, such as 'attack', 'armed attack', and 'aggression'.[19] Other language is broader, such as 'the scourge of war', 'use of force', 'armed force', and 'threat to international peace and security', referred to in the United Nations Charter.[20]

If 'violence' is hard to define, 'war', 'peace', and 'security' can be even more difficult. 'Peace' sometimes refers to the absence of war, and sometimes to a more expansive idea including also the achievement of social justice.[21] 'Security' often refers to State security but, like 'peace', has more recently also been thought of within the broader idea of 'human security'.[22] Reflecting this, the UN Charter preamble expresses concern not only with international peace and security but human rights and social justice.

C. DISCUSSION: A COMPLEX AND CONTESTED RELATIONSHIP BETWEEN VIOLENCE AND INTERNATIONAL LAW

I. THE EXAMPLE OF THE MILITARY INTERVENTION IN LIBYA 2011

In February 2011, anti-government demonstrations started in the north-eastern city of Benghazi before spreading to other parts of Libya. Libya's leader, Colonel Muammar al-Qadhafi, responded with military force against dissenters. Helped by some defections from the military, anti-government forces managed to take control of certain areas of

---

18 See e.g. Convention (I) for the Amelioration of the Condition of the Wounded and Sick in Armed Forces in the Field 75 UNTS 31 (opened for signature 12 August 1949, entered into force 21 October 1950) arts 3, 12, 18; Convention (II) for the Amelioration of the Condition of Wounded, Sick and Shipwrecked Members of Armed Forces at Sea 75 UNTS 85 (opened for signature 12 August 1949, entered into force 21 October 1950) art 12; Convention (III) relative to the Treatment of Prisoners of War 75 UNTS 135 (opened for signature 12 August 1949, entered into force 21 October 1950) arts 13, 93; Convention (IV) relative to the Protection of Civilian Persons in Time of War 75 UNTS 287 (opened for signature 12 August 1949, entered into force 21 October 1950) art 27; Protocol Additional to the Geneva Conventions of 12 August 1949, and relating to the Protection of Victims of International Armed Conflicts 1125 UNTS 3 (opened for signature 8 June 1977, entered into force 7 December 1978) (AP I) arts 17, 51, 75; Protocol Additional to the Geneva Conventions of 12 August 1949, and relating to the Protection of Victims of Non-International Armed Conflicts 1125 UNTS 609 (opened for signature 8 June 1977, entered into force 7 December 1978) arts 1(2), 4(2)(a) and 13(2); ICC Statute arts 7(1)(g), 8(2)(d), 8(2)(f), 36(8)(b), 42(9), 54(1)(b); Convention on the Rights of the Child (adopted 20 November 1989, entered into force 2 September 1990) 1577 UNTS 3 art 19(1).

19 See AP I art 49; UN Charter art 51; UNGA Res 3314 (XXIX) (14 December 1974), Annex: Definition of Aggression.

20 UN Charter preamble, arts 2(4), 42.

21 Referred to as 'negative' and 'positive' peace: Galtung (n 16). For a good summary, see Dexter (n 13).

22 Fen Osler Hampson, 'Human Security' in Paul D Williams and Matt McDonald (eds), *Security Studies: An Introduction* (2nd edn, Routledge 2014).

eastern Libya. The situation escalated into an armed conflict between opposition forces and forces loyal to the al-Qadhafi regime.[23]

The UNSC quickly demanded an end to the violence, referred the situation to the International Criminal Court, and imposed an arms embargo and other sanctions on members of the Libyan regime.[24]

With the hostilities approaching the opposition stronghold, Benghazi, which the regime had reportedly threatened to attack with 'no mercy',[25] the UN Secretary-General expressed concern about the endangering of civilians should an assault on Benghazi occur.[26] Adopting Resolution 1973 on 17 March 2011, the UNSC reaffirmed its 'strong commitment to the sovereignty, independence, territorial integrity and national unity' of Libya. It also imposed a no-fly zone and authorised States 'to take all necessary measures . . . to protect civilians and civilian populated areas under threat of attack' in Libya.[27] 'All necessary measures' is a phrase used by the UNSC to include military force.

NATO member States rapidly initiated military operations on 19 March 2011. In addition to actions to protect civilians from the advancing Libyan government forces and to enforce the no-fly zone, those air operations subsequently directly supported the opposition forces. Intervention operations continued until October 2011, by which time al-Qadhafi had been killed, and a majority of States recognised the opposition National Transitional Council as Libya's new interim government.

The years following the intervention proved difficult with deteriorating security and reignition of civil war between different Libyan factions in 2014, as well as a growing ISIS presence.[28] Following a 2020 ceasefire agreement, political instability, human rights abuses, and other violations have continued.[29]

---

23 For a timeline, see 'Timeline of the Libyan Crisis/War (2011)' in Dag Henriksen and Ann Karin Larssen (eds), *Political Rationale and International Consequences of the War in Libya* (OUP 2016).

24 UNSC Res 1970 (26 February 2011).

25 M Golovina and P Worsnip, 'UN Okays Military Action on Libya; Gaddafi Warns' (*Reuters*, 18 March 2011) <www.reuters.com/article/libya/wrapup-2-un-okays-military-action-on-libya-gaddafi-warns-idUSLDE72H00K20110318> accessed 20 June 2023.

26 'Assault on Benghazi Would Endanger Masses of Libyan Civilians, Ban Warns' (*UN News*, 16 March 2011) <https://news.un.org/en/story/2011/03/369182> accessed 20 June 2023.

27 UNSC Res 1973 (17 March 2011) preamble, [4], [6].

28 K Knipp, 'Ten Years After NATO Intervention, Libya Remains Unstable' (*DeutscheWelle*, 18 March 2021) <www.dw.com/en/libya-still-plagued-by-conflict-10-years-after-nato-intervention/a-56921306> accessed 20 June 2023; AL Jacobz, 'Libya 10 Years After the NATO Intervention: U.N. Report Explains Challenges' (*Arab Gulf States Institute in Washington*, 24 March 2021) <https://agsiw.org/libya-10-years-after-the-nato-intervention-u-n-report-explains-challenges/> accessed 20 June 2023; Soufan Center, 'IntelBrief: Ten Years After NATO's Intervention in Libya, a Transitional Government Takes Control' (*Soufan Center*, 26 March 2021) <https://thesoufancenter.org/intelbrief-2021-march-26/> accessed 20 June 2023.

29 International Crisis Group, 'U.N. Plan to Reunite Libya: Four Obstacles' (*International Crisis Group*, 4 May 2023) <www.crisisgroup.org/middle-east-north-africa/north-africa/libya/un-plan-reunite-libya-four-obstacles> accessed 20 June 2023; Report of the Independent Fact-Finding Mission on Libya, A/HRC/52/83 (3 March 2023).

II. CONTESTED NATURE OF ACHIEVING PEACE OR PROTECTION OF CIVILIANS THROUGH MILITARY FORCE

Does the Libya 2011 example provoke any particular gut reaction from you?

Some commentators applauded that the UNSC had been able to react promptly to a humanitarian crisis, and that States were willing to take action.[30] This reflects how the promotion of fundamental freedoms and human rights, and the growing notion that mass atrocities within a State could threaten international peace and security, have strengthened the moral authority of arguments justifying armed responses to such threats as being in the common interest.[31] This more expansionist view has, in turn, impacted on what might be described as a more restrictive and universal holding to norms respecting sovereignty and non-intervention. Indeed, Resolution 1973 was the first time that the UNSC had recognised and put into action the so-called responsibility to protect (R2P), which authorised military force as an exception to the general prohibition on the use of force between States for the purpose of protecting individuals at risk where the State in question was not meeting that responsibility.[32] Accepting it might be an imperfect and rather 'blunt instrument' but perhaps the best we have in a bad situation,[33] and/or that learning from previous experiences might help ensure future operations do more good than harm,[34] many accept such interventions as the lesser evil because they are conducted in the hope of averting even greater suffering.[35] Regarding Libya, for example, reports indicated that NATO bombing killed 72 civilians but averted a potentially far larger massacre in Benghazi.[36]

Other commentators have expressed concern about the implementation and/or consequences of the intervention. Amongst criticisms is that the NATO

---

30 See e.g. Thomas G Weiss, 'Libya, R2P, and the United Nations' in Dag Henriksen and Ann Karin Larssen (eds), *Political Rationale and International Consequences of the War in Libya* (OUP 2016) 228; Sally Khalifa Isaac, 'NATO's Intervention in Libya: Assessment and Implications' (2012) IEMed Mediterranean Yearbook 121–123.

31 Anne Orford, 'Moral Internationalism and the Responsibility to Protect' (2013) 24 EJIL 83, 98. See also Pierre Thielbörger, 'The Status and Future of International Law after the Libya Intervention' (2012) 4(1) Goettingen Journal of International Law 11; Jessica Whyte, 'The "Dangerous Concept of the Just War": Decolonization, Wars of National Liberation, and the Additional Protocols to the Geneva Conventions' (2018) 9(3) Humanity 313, 330–331; Sigmund Simonsen, 'The Intervention in Libya in a Legal Perspective: R2P and International Law' in Dag Henriksen and Ann Karin Larssen (eds), *Political Rationale and International Consequences of the War in Libya* (OUP 2016) 245, 249–251; Russell Buchan and Nicholas Tsagourias, *Regulating the Use of Force in International Law: Stability and Change* (Edward Elgar 2021) 213.

32 *2005 World Summit Outcome*, GA Res 60/1, UN Doc A/RES/60/1 (24 October 2005, adopted 16 September 2005) [138]–[139].

33 Alex J Bellamy, 'Libya and the Responsibility to Protect: The Exception and the Norm' (2011) Ethics & International Affairs 1, 7.

34 See Taylor B Seybolt, *Humanitarian Military Intervention: The Conditions for Success and Failure* (OUP 2008).

35 See e.g. Michael Ignatieff, *The Lesser Evil: Political Ethics in an Age of Terror* (Princeton University Press 2005); but contrast also Eyal Weizman, *The Least of All Possible Evils: A Short History of Humanitarian Violence* (Verso 2017) 6.

36 Wallace (n 14) 1 citing Human Rights Watch 2012. But see also discussion in Alan J Kuperman, 'A Model Humanitarian Intervention?: Reassessing NATO's Libya Campaign' (2013) 38(1) International Security 105, 121–123.

intervention exceeded the UNSC's authorisation in Resolution 1973 by actively
supporting regime change, arguably turning the lawful intervention into an
unlawful one.[37] This might be compared with the earlier situation in Kosovo
where NATO controversially undertook an air campaign against Yugoslavia in
1999 without UNSC authorisation, with the operation subsequently being labelled
as 'illegal' since it was unauthorised but 'legitimate' under the circumstances.[38]
Relatedly, while not opposed to R2P, some commentators have examined whether
in the particular case of Libya, required legal and ethical thresholds to justify
intervention such as last resort, sufficiently serious situation, or purpose, were
met.[39] The instability and civil war in the years following the Libya intervention,
as well as an argument that NATO operations gave cover to violations committed
by anti-regime forces, also led to critiques about ill judgement, the intervention
worsening the situation, or, at least, that the international community inadequately
supported Libya post-conflict.[40] Those same reasons contributed to arguments that
the 'disaster' of Libya made it unlikely that similar humanitarian actions would be
adopted in the future.[41]

Arguments about 'mission creep' were also made by those voicing a broader
wariness of military operations undertaken for humanitarian and protective
purposes. There is concern, including for many developing States, about seemingly
expanding powers of such 'muscular humanitarianism'[42] and the risks of exploitation
by militarily powerful States.[43] Commentators have noted the discretion and

---

37 Patrick CR Terry, 'The Libya Intervention (2011): Neither Lawful, Nor Successful' (2015) 48(2) Comparative
    and International Law Journal of Southern Africa 162; Geir Ulfstein and Hege Føsund Christiansen, 'The
    Legality of the NATO Bombing in Libya' (2013) 62(1) ICLQ 159; Benedetta Berti, 'Forcible Intervention
    in Libya: Revamping the "Politics of Human Protection"?' (2014) 26(1) Global Change, Peace & Security
    21, 37. In contrast, arguing the operations did not exceed the mandate, Chris De Cock, 'Operation Unified
    Protector and the Protection of Civilians in Libya' in MN Schmitt and L Arimatsu (eds), Yearbook of International
    Humanitarian Law (Vol 14, TMC Asser Press 2011) 213; 'Libya Letter by Obama, Cameron and Sarkozy: Full
    Text' (BBC News, 15 April 2011) <www.bbc.com/news/world-africa-13090646> accessed 20 June 2023.

38 Independent International Commission on Kosovo, 'The Kosovo Report' (Oxford, 23 October 2000) 4
    <http://www.kosovocommission.org> accessed 20 June 2023.

39 See e.g. James Pattison, 'The Ethics of Humanitarian Intervention in Libya' (2011) 25(3) Ethics & International
    Affairs 271; Simonsen (n 31) 254–259; Berti (n 37).

40 Wallace (n 14) 1; Kuperman (n 36) 125–133. See also generally, Alex J Bellamy, 'The Responsibility to Protect'
    in Paul D Williams and Matt McDonald (eds), Security Studies: An Introduction (2nd edn, Routledge 2014) 422,
    432–433.

41 Terry (n 37) 181; Ulfstein and Christiansen (n 37) 169–171. For other discussion regarding Libya and Syria, see
    Simonsen (n 31) 262–265; Spencer Zifcak, 'The Responsibility to Protect After Libya and Syria' (2012) 13(1)
    MJIL 59.

42 Anne Orford, 'Muscular Humanitarianism: Reading the Narratives of New Interventionism' (1999) 10
    EJIL 679.

43 Iain Scobbie, 'War' in Jean d'Aspremont and Sahib Singh (eds), Concepts for International Law (Edward Elgar
    2019) 900, 912: '[secure] some States' freedom of action [while eroding] the prohibition of the use of force in
    the territory of another State' (citations omitted). See also Thilo Marauhn, 'How Many Deaths Can Article
    2(4) UN Charter Die?' in Lothar Brock and Hendrik Simon (eds), The Justification of War and International Order
    (OUP 2021) 449; Rajan Menon, The Conceit of Humanitarian Intervention (OUP 2016); Terry (n 37).

selectivity in responses to situations considered crises.[44] For some, claims that norms justifying military action are universal ring rather hollow given the 'lopsided global arrangements in which some forms of suffering are recognized while a great many more are not'.[45] This has led to accusations of Western leadership using international law 'to target its enemies while protecting its friends'.[46] As David Kennedy has expressed, one

> must imagine that claims to make war in the name of right will rarely sound sincere or seem persuasive to those who believe the truth lies elsewhere – who oppose the war, are disgusted by the tactic, or simply expect themselves to be maimed or killed.[47]

Relatedly, critical scholarship has pointed out how race, gender, and class continue to be implicated in the legal justifications made for intervention, replicating historical experiences of domination of the so-called Global South in the application of international law, including to curb emancipatory struggles.[48] While not always ruling out the need for military action in exceptional circumstances involving intentional attacks against civilians, some call for prudence and an overwhelming consensus of the international community before the resort to force.[49]

---

44 See e.g. Pattison (n 39) 276; Martti Koskenniemi, ' "The Lady Doth Protest Too Much" Kosovo, and the Turn to Ethics in International Law' (2002) 65(2) MLR 159, 172–173; Christine M Chinkin, 'A "Good" or "Bad" War?' (1999) 93(4) AJIL 841, 847. Regarding the deaths of some people being more 'grievable', and worth saving or defending, than others, see Judith Butler, *Precarious Life: The Powers of Mourning and Violence* (Verso 2004); Judith Butler, *Frames of War: When Is Life Grievable?* (Verso 2009). On the role of international law in these hierarchies, Thomas Gregory, 'Potential Lives, Impossible Deaths' (2012) 14(3) International Feminist Journal of Politics 327. But see also a contrasting discussion of selectivity/inconsistency in Alex J Bellamy, 'The Responsibility to Protect Turns Ten' (2015) 29(2) Ethics & International Affairs 161, 171–175.

45 Darryl Li, ' "Afghan Arabs", Real and Imagined' (2011) 260 Middle East Report 2, 7.

46 Anne Orford, 'What Kind of Law Is This? Libya and International Law' (*London Review of Books*, 29 March 2011) <https://www.lrb.co.uk/blog/2011/march/what-kind-of-law-is-this> accessed 6 December 2023.

47 David Kennedy, 'Lawfare and Warfare' in James Crawford and Martti Koskenniemi (eds), *The Cambridge Companion to International Law* (CUP 2012) 177.

48 See e.g. Katherine Fallah and Ntina Tzouvala 'Deploying Race, Employing Force: "African Mercenaries" and the 2011 NATO Intervention in Libya' (2021) 67(6) UCLA Law Review 1580; Anne-Charlotte Martineau, 'Concerning Violence: A Post-Colonial Reading of the Debate on the Use of Force' (2016) 29 LJIL 95; Parvathi Menon, 'We're (Not) Talkin' Bout a Revolution: Anti-Colonial Struggles and Their (Un)justifications (*Völkerrechtsblog*, 1 June 2021) <https://voelkerrechtsblog.org/were-not-talkin-bout-a-revolution-anti-colonial-struggles-and-their-unjustifications/> accessed 20 June 2023. See also regarding IHL and the right to wage war, Claire Vergerio, *War, States and International Order* (CUP 2022) 259–261. See also Ananthavinayagan and Theilen, § 21.8, in this textbook.

49 See e.g. BS Chimni, 'Justification and Critique: Humanitarianism and Imperialism Over Time' in Lothar Brock and Hendrik Simon (eds), *The Justification of War and International Order* (OUP 2021) 471, 485 and 487; Kuperman (n 36) 136. See also Koskenniemi (n 44) 174, discussing that if there is no longer room for neutral formalism because of a turn to ethics in legal argumentation, and while ethics is also politics, it might provide space at least for a good or better politics if it could involve a 'culture of restraint, a commitment to listening to others' (emphasis omitted).

Finally, approaches based in pacifism or non-violence have long accompanied the development of international law and are seeing renewed interest.[50] For some, what is important is that the means used to counter ills such as insecurity or terrorism are 'consistent with the changes we wish to bring about'.[51] On a practical level, some researchers argue that violent methods have been overused and have largely failed (e.g. to counter terror) while non-violent strategies have proven more successful.[52] Even those supporting R2P have reinforced the importance of preventing violence in preference to military responses once a crisis breaks out.[53]

Once in those crises, the dilemma often appears as one between action and inaction, where 'doing something' tends to be understood as a military response. Reflecting this, pacifist or non-violent philosophies have been labelled as overly idealistic and morally challenging, that remaining neutral or non-active implicates the acceptance of violence and might reinforce the dominant order.[54] Yet, nonviolent approaches do not equate with doing nothing and might still persuade or even be coercive.[55] Similarly, there is a vast range of different ways military operations to protect civilians could be undertaken.[56] Limiting the options to either intervening militarily or standing idly by arguably blinkers us to other possible responses, as well as to a situation's historical and political context; for example, understanding better how the earlier involvement of other States and international institutions might have contributed to the situation at hand.[57] Some thus believe pacifist and non-violent

---

50 Wallace (n 14); Richard Jackson, 'The Challenges of Pacifism and Nonviolence in the Twenty-First Century' (2023) 1 Journal of Pacifism and Nonviolence 28, 30; Alexandre Christoyannopoulos, 'Pacifism and Nonviolence: Discerning the Contours of an Emerging Multidisciplinary Research Agenda' (2023) 1 Journal of Pacifism and Nonviolence 1; Helen Dexter, 'Pacifism and the Problem of Protecting Others' (2019) 56 International Politics 243; Jeremy Moses, 'Anarchy, Pacifism and Realism: Building a Path to a Non-Violent International Law' (2018) 6(2) Critical Studies on Security 221.

51 S Lindahl, 'A CTS Model of Counterterrorism' (2017) 10(3) Critical Studies on Terrorism 523, 528–29. See also Wallace (n 14) 13, 25–27, arguing that the problem of disagreement about the ends requires us to derive legitimacy from the means we employ; Hannah Arendt, *On Violence* (Harcourt Brace Jovanovich 1970) 4: 'the end is in danger of being overwhelmed by the means which it justifies and which are needed to reach it'.

52 See e.g. Richard Jackson 'CTS, Counterterrorism and Non-Violence' (2017) 10(2) Critical Studies on Terrorism 357; MJ Stephan and E Chenoweth, 'Why Civil Resistance Works: The Strategic Logic of Nonviolent Conflict' (2008) 33(1) International Security 7–44; Wallace (n 14) ch 2.

53 Bellamy (n 33) 427–429, 434–435.

54 Christoyannopoulos (n 50) 11; J Ashley Foster, 'Writing Was Her Fighting: Three Guineas as a Pacifist Response to Total War' in Kathryn Stelmach Artuso (ed), *Critical Insights: Virginia Woolf and 20th Century Women Writers* (Salem Press 2014) 59; Richard Jackson, 'Pacifism: The Anatomy of a Subjugated Knowledge' (2018) 6(2) Critical Studies on Security 160, 167.

55 Jackson (n 54) 166; Wallace (n 14).

56 Jennifer Welsh, 'Civilian Protection in Libya: Putting Coercion and Controversy Back into RtoP' (2011) 25(3) Ethics & International Affairs 255, 261.

57 Gina Heathcote, *The Law on the Use of Force: A Feminist Analysis* (Taylor & Francis 2011) 4, 29; Anne Orford, *Reading Humanitarian Intervention: Human Rights and the Use of Force in International Law* (CUP 2003) 15; Sundhya Pahuja, '"Don't Just Do Something, Stand There!" Humanitarian Intervention and the Drowning Stranger' (2005) 5 Human Rights & Human Welfare 51, 52–53.

approaches can open up spaces for alternative discussions, destabilising assumptions about militarism, and might have potential for being more global and inclusive than the current international system.[58]

III. CONTESTED NATURE OF CIVILIAN CASUALTIES DURING THE PROTECTION OF CIVILIANS

In Libya in 2011, civilians in several areas became very unsafe because of the fighting and many were killed or injured. This harm was reportedly caused by all parties.[59]

Once an armed conflict starts, IHL places limits on the means and methods of waging war to protect those not participating (e.g. civilians) and no longer participating (e.g. wounded or captured combatants). Reflecting the non-pacifist nature of the international legal system, IHL does not prohibit violence outright, even violence affecting civilians. Rather, trade-offs formulated within IHL accept that wars will happen but place restraints on warring parties, balancing humanitarian protections with military necessity.[60] Concretely, although IHL prohibits direct and indiscriminate attacks against civilians, it accepts certain incidental harm, known colloquially as 'collateral damage' (during proportionate attacks on military objectives undertaken with sufficient precautions to avoid civilian harm).[61] Imagine, for example, an air strike targeting enemy forces which also kills a nearby civilian. This means that a civilian casualty in Libya in 2011 might or might not be a result of a violation of IHL depending on the circumstances. IHL is far less protective than the rules otherwise regulating force, such as during law enforcement operations by the police.[62]

IHL advocates argue in support of the vital restraints IHL places on warring parties and point out how beneficial increased compliance would be in protecting people during war; moreover, that IHL also does much good that goes unnoticed.[63]

Other commentators appear less enamoured with IHL. On the abstract level, one might accept some harm to bystanders as unavoidable and part of the 'lesser evil'. Yet,

---

58 Jackson (n 54) 169; Neta C Crawford, 'The Critical Challenge of Pacifism and Nonviolent Resistance Then and Now' (2023) 1 Journal of Pacifism and Nonviolence 140; Karen C Sokol, 'East Meets West in Civil Disobedience Theory and Beyond' in Giuliana Ziccardi Capaldo (ed), *The Global Community Yearbook of International Law and Jurisprudence 2015* (OUP 2016) 125; Wallace (n 14) 253–254 regarding paying attention to the enemy other's moral frameworks.

59 Report of the International Commission of Inquiry on Libya, A/HRC/19/68, 8 March 2012, [87]–[89].

60 See e.g. ICRC, 'The Principles of Humanity and Necessity' (March 2023) <www.icrc.org/sites/default/files/wysiwyg/war-and-law/02_humanity_and_necessity-0.pdf> accessed 20 June 2023. See also Uday Singh Mehta, 'Gandhi and the Common Logic of War and Peace' (2010) 30(1) Raritan 134, 147 on IHL providing moral constraint but accepting the logic braiding together war, peace, and politics.

61 See Dienelt and Ullah, § 14, in this textbook.

62 See ICRC, *Violence and the Use of Force* (ICRC July 2011).

63 Helen Durham, 'Atrocities in Conflict Mean We Need the Geneva Conventions More Than Ever' (*The Guardian*, 5 April 2016) <www.theguardian.com/global-development/2016/apr/05/atrocities-in-conflict-mean-we-need-the-geneva-conventions-more-than-ever> accessed 20 June 2023.

many people would be unwilling to accept this if they were directly affected, and in practice, not all populations are subject to the same risks. Moreover, in the moment, it presumably matters little to a family whether the bombs they are fleeing were launched compliantly or not; and, in practice, investigations into such civilian harm allegations often struggle to pronounce definitively whether an attack was proportionate or not, or even to determine who is a civilian.[64] IHL's acceptance that civilians can be lawfully (albeit incidentally) killed, even during operations intended to protect them, can therefore create an underlying uneasiness.

As such, some commentators consider IHL to have been formulated to privilege military necessity over humanitarian considerations.[65] Experience also shows that conflict parties have at times argued, especially related to counterterrorism, that existing rules were insufficient or inapplicable to the response needed for an exceptional threat.[66] This is seen to risk a gradual loosening of the rules,[67] particularly where an operation is for a 'good cause' and the underlying 'fault' for the violence is perceived to lie with the 'terrorists' or other 'bad guys'.[68] Despite a stated purpose of protecting civilians, the aim might actually be to defeat the enemy, with increased risks for civilians.[69]

Stepping further back, when IHL was first codified in the 19th century, some hoped that rules restraining the means and methods of warfare could progressively lead to greater restrictions and ultimately the elimination of war. Others feared that such rules would operate to shift focus to the legal technicalities, postponing calls in peace activism for the abolition of war.[70] More recent UN 'Women, Peace, and Security' initiatives, which endorsed greater institutional participation of women in peace-building and were perhaps hoped by women's networks to progressively transform militarism, have arguably resulted in a similar muffling of important feminist peace activism and critiques

---

64 Christiane Wilke, 'Civilians, Combatants, and Histories of International Law' (*Critical Legal Thinking*, 28 July 2014) <https://criticallegalthinking.com/2014/07/28/civilians-combatants-histories-international-law/> accessed 20 June 2023.

65 Chris AF Jochnick and Roger Normand, 'The Legitimation of Violence: A Critical History of the Laws of War' (1994) 35(1) HILJ 49, 65, 68; Amanda Alexander, 'A Short History of International Humanitarian Law' (2015) 26(1) EJIL 109, 113.

66 Michael Glennon, 'Forging a Third Way to Fight; "Bush Doctrine" for Combating Terrorism Straddles Divide Between Crime and War' (*Legal Times*, 24 September 2001) 68, discussed in Frédéric Mégret, '"War"? Legal Semantics and the Move to Violence' (2002) 13(2) EJIL 361, 386.

67 Amanda Alexander, 'The Ethics of Violence: Recent Literature on the Creation of the Contemporary Regime of Law and War' (2021) Journal of Genocide Research 1, 13.

68 See e.g. ICRC (n 15) 45–47.

69 Ibid 47.

70 André Durand, 'Gustave Moynier and the Peace Societies' (1996) IRRC 314; Samuel Moyn, 'From Antiwar to Antitorture Politics' in Sarat and others (eds), *Law and War* (Stanford University Press 2014) 154; Samuel Moyn, *Humane: How the United States Abandoned Peace and Reinvented War* (Farrar, Strauss and Giroux 2021); David Kennedy, *Of Law and War* (Princeton University Press 2006); Marnie Lloydd, '"A Few Not Too Troublesome Restrictions": Humanitarianism, Solidarity, Anti-Militarism, Peace' (*Critical Legal Thinking*, 22 November 2022) <https://criticallegalthinking.com/2022/11/22/a-few-not-too-troublesome-restrictions-humanitarianism-solidarity-anti-militarism-peace/> accessed 20 June 2023; Dianne Otto, 'Rethinking "Peace" in International Law and Politics from a Queer Feminist Perspective' (2020) 126 Feminist Review 19, 27–30.

of militarism.[71] Relatedly, some argue that the denunciation of certain forms of violence as particularly problematic, such as the prosecution of war crimes, creates a boundary which normalises other forms of violence.[72]

To conclude, while the formulation of IHL fits within the logic of the current international legal system, and the humanitarian consequences of armed conflict would undoubtedly be less disastrous if warring parties complied more faithfully with IHL, more critical arguments that IHL might ultimately facilitate and legitimate rather than successfully restrain violence also hold some weight.[73] Eyal Weizman describes how some violence occurs with the 'terrible force of the law' rather than in violation of it.[74]

IV. INTERNATIONAL LAW *OR* VIOLENCE, INTERNATIONAL LAW *AND* VIOLENCE, INTERNATIONAL LAW *AS* VIOLENCE?

The preceding discussion suggests that it becomes overly simplistic to say that law and war are of two different worlds – that in war, law falls silent or that the presence of violence alerts us to law's failings.[75] More accurately, while different instances of violence may indeed be of a different nature or purpose, we can recognise the complex relationship(s) between international law and violence. They are not of two different worlds rubbing up against each other but are already 'an old couple'.[76]

In practice, international law and violence are certainly interconnected since legal argumentation has become a key part of warfighting, often referred to as 'lawfare'.[77] Concerning legal theory, scholars argue that if we could reach that utopia where peace and security were maintained, the law would lose its driving force; that violence helps establish or construct the law by giving it meaning and social relevance.[78] Part of the social relevance of violence to the law relates to an assumption that we cannot (yet) have both security and non-violence. Security and violence are understood as a natural and never-ending dilemma that needs to be reconciled by finding an appropriate balance,

---

71 Dianne Otto, 'Women, Peace, and Security: A Critical Analysis of the Security Council's Vision' in Fionnuala Ní Aoláin and others (eds), *The Oxford Handbook of Gender and Conflict* (OUP 2018); Sheri Gibbings, 'Governing Women, Governing Security: Governmentality, Gender Mainstreaming and Women's Activism at the UN' (LLM Thesis, York University, Toronto 2004), 67–68.

72 Alexander (n 67) 2; Heathcote (n 57) 22.

73 See also Kennedy (n 47) 181.

74 Eyal Weizman, 'Legislative Attack' (2010) 27(6) *Theory, Culture & Society* 11, 12.

75 Kennedy (n 47) 158. See also Austin Sarat and Thomas Kearns, *Law's Violence* (University of Michigan Press 1995) 2.

76 Vanja Hamzić, 'International Law as Violence: Competing Absences of the Other' in Dianne Otto (ed), *Queering International Law: Possibilities, Alliances, Complication, Risks* (Taylor & Francis 2017) 77.

77 See e.g. Kennedy (n 47); Lawrence Douglas and others 'Law and War: An Introduction' in Sarat and others (eds), *Law and War* (Stanford University Press 2014) 3–4.

78 Hamzić (n 76) 77; Ntina Tzouvala, 'Eye in the Sky: Drones, the (Human) Ticking-Time Bomb Scenario and Law's Inhumanity' (*Critical Legal Thinking*, 19 April 2016) <https://criticallegalthinking.com/2016/04/19/eye-sky-drones-human-ticking-time-bomb-scenario-laws-inhumanity/> accessed 20 June 2023.

such that certain forms of violence remain a necessary evil.[79] Law works to define the boundaries/balance of what is perceived to be needed. Austin Sarat's statement about law more generally seems to apply also to international law: law 'is always violent but never only violent; always oriented towards justice but never fully just'.[80]

D. CONCLUSION

Key instruments of international law, such as the UN Charter or the Geneva Conventions 1949, are commonly seen as significant milestones marking progressive achievement towards the 'abandonment of the use of force' and full disarmament.[81] As such, the basic design of collective security might be seen as the only 'stable workhorse' available, its imperfect functioning being primarily due to a lack of genuine willingness of States,[82] as well as to the realist view that certain actors need to be allowed to retain their arms in order to enforce the disarmament and defend themselves or others.[83]

Other thinkers appear less willing to sit in the 'not yet' of peace and justice, and view international law as having a more contested, even conspiratory, role in violence. Consider, for example, Dianne Otto's question about 'how law helps to reproduce the inevitability of the deadly, anthropocentric, imperial, neoliberal military-industrial-complex' and 'whether there remain any remnants of opportunity in law' with which one might yet work if one wanted to imagine alternative notions of peace.[84] In that dire description, current international law no longer appears as an aspirational vehicle for making the world a better place. Rather, the logic, practice, and demonstrated interests of the entire system are being critiqued and challenged.

The point is not only how challenging these questions are, but rather the resulting plurality of views on violence and international law. Different thinkers and actors will have different readings of a situation of violence, and different legal, political, and moral judgements and arguments in their application of international law. International legal argument might appear neutral or universal – for example, when an actor or institution claims to be acting objectively in the interests of humanity or for the common good – but the arguments being relied upon will be based on certain underlying assumptions about the world, about international law, and about particular authorities being able to make those determinations.[85] The values being prioritised are not necessarily held in common, and can also change over time and in different political contexts, or in hindsight. Describing international law as a conversation, David Kennedy says

---

79 See also Mehta (n 60).
80 Austin Sarat, 'Situating Law Between the Realities of Violence and the Claims of Justice: An Introduction' in Austin Sarat (ed), *Violence, and the Possibility of Justice* (Princeton University Press 2001) 13.
81 Atlantic Charter between the United States and the United Kingdom 1941, final provision.
82 Weller (n 10) 642–643.
83 Ibid 629.
84 Otto (n 70) 21.
85 Jan Klabbers, *International Law* (CUP 2013), 3–4; Orford (n 14) 193.

[i]nternational law reminds us to pay attention to opinion elsewhere in the world, to think about consistency over time, to remember that what we do today may come back to haunt us . . . international law only rarely offers a definitive judgment on who is right.[86]

Regarding not only armed violence but most issues of interest to international law, international lawyers should, then, look closely and empathetically at the particular context, but also consciously and continually step back to reflect critically about the bigger picture.[87] Rather than only working out what, in one's opinion, the law says, it becomes important to pay attention to narratives being used about any instance of violence, by whom, to serve what purpose, and with what political consequence. Moreover, who gets to decide? Critical reflection can also include considerations of 'when, how, and at the behest of whom those rules have emerged and developed'.[88]

This final section, therefore, proposes questions which may help foster exploration of students' individual legal, political, and moral positions around the complex and enduring relationships between violence and international law.

- What language is being used in political or public dialogue to describe the violence or the parties involved? By whom? For what purpose?
- What values are being expressed by a particular actor's position? Is it being described as objective, universal, or in the common interest?
- If the one who can define or decide what is legitimate and what is not is the one with true power,[89] who is deciding in the situation at hand?
- Do the acts of violence reproduce any power dynamics that made those acts possible in the first place? In your view, '[i]s violence necessary at times, and if so, does it, or can it, put an end to further violence' in the context at hand?[90]
- In what ways has compliance with the law protected people from harm? Or put them at risk of harm?
- In which situations could a non-violent option have been chosen, or in what situations were non-violent responses rejected or made impossible? What future paths do those decisions possibly close off? What might have been the imaginable results of other possible paths not taken or actively rejected?
- Is 'war talk' used to frame a crisis, threat, or problem (e.g. war on drugs, fight against climate change)? To what effect?[91]

---

86 David Kennedy, *The Dark Side of Virtue: Reassessing International Humanitarianism* (Princeton University Press 2004), 273.

87 Anne Orford, 'The Politics of Collective Security' (1996) 17(2) MJIL 373, 407–409.

88 Helen M Kinsella and Giovanni Mantilla, 'Contestation Before Compliance: History, Politics, and Power in International Humanitarian Law' (2020) 64(3) ISQ 649, 653.

89 Richard Devetak, 'Post-Structuralism' in Burchill and others (eds), *Theories of International Relations* (5th edn, Bloomsbury 2013) 194 citing Derrida.

90 See discussion in Aisha Karim and Bruce B Lawrence, *On Violence: A Reader* (Duke University Press 2007) 78 citing Fanon.

91 Eliana Cusato, 'Beyond War Narratives: Laying Bare the Structural Violence of the Pandemic' in Makane Moïse Mbengue and Jean D'Aspremont (eds), *Crisis Narratives in International Law* (Brill 2022) 109.

BOX 2.1.2 Further Readings and Further Resources

Further Readings

- A Alexander, 'The Ethics of Violence: Recent Literature on the Creation of the Contemporary Regime of Law and War' (2021) Journal of Genocide Research 1

- H Dexter, 'Peace and Violence' in Paul D Williams and Matt McDonald (eds), *Security Studies: An Introduction* (3rd edn, Routledge 2018)

- D Kennedy, 'Lawfare and Warfare' in James Crawford and Martti Koskenniemi (eds), *The Cambridge Companion to International Law* (CUP 2012)

- M Koskenniemi, ' "The Lady Doth Protest Too Much" Kosovo, and the Turn to Ethics in International Law' (2002) 65(2) MLR 159

- A Martineau, 'Concerning Violence: A Post-Colonial Reading of the Debate on the Use of Force' (2016) 29 LJIL 95

Further Resources

- Gavin Hood, 'Eye in the Sky' (Entertainment One 2015) (Film)

- Olivier Sarbil, *Mosul* (PBS/Frontline 2017) (Documentary Series)

- Brad Evans and others, *Portraits of Violence: An Illustrated History of Radical Thinking* (New Internationalist 2017)

---

§ § §

§ 2.2 CONSENT

SUÉ GONZÁLEZ HAUCK

BOX 2.2.1 Required Knowledge and Learning Objectives

Required knowledge: History of International Law; Overarching Questions

Learning objectives: Understanding key components of the notion of consent and assessing the central role it plays in the international legal system.

A. INTRODUCTION

Perhaps no other notion is as central to understanding international law as the notion of consent. It is the bedrock of classical doctrinal accounts of international law. This chapter familiarises students with the notion of consent, introducing the classical notion as expressed by the Permanent Court of International Justice. It hints at some of the difficulties that come with the classical conception of consent in international law, discusses the connection between consent and anarchy, introduces different types of consent that are prevalent in international law, explores the relationship between consent and colonialism, and, finally, sketches some of the limits on State consent in the international legal system.

B. THE CENTRALITY OF CONSENT IN INTERNATIONAL LAW

The degree to which consent is taken to structure the international legal system depends on whether and to what degree one subscribes to voluntarist theories of validity of international legal rules. The famous *Lotus* case is the often-cited point of anchoring for such voluntarist conceptions of international law. The relevant passage from the *Lotus* dictum reads:

> International law governs relations between independent States. The rules of law binding upon States therefore emanate from their own free will as expressed in conventions or by usages generally accepted as expressing principles of law and established in order to regulate the relations between these co-existing independent communities or with a view to the achievement of common aims. Restrictions upon the independence of States cannot therefore be presumed.[92]

Consent is thus supposed to be the expression of the 'free will' of a sovereign State and the source of obligations under international law. The principle of consent is reflected in

---

92 *Lotus (France v Turkey)* PCIJ Rep Series A No 10, 18.

the way international law is formed. This is most obvious in the cases of treaties, which are, in principle, only binding on a State if this State has expressed its consent to be bound by the respective treaty (cf. articles 11–17 VCLT).[93] Consent is also an essential part of international dispute resolution. Under article 36 of the Statute of the International Court of Justice (ICJ),[94] States can accept the ICJ's jurisdiction either by signing the ICJ Statute or by making a special declaration recognising the ICJ's jurisdiction in a particular case. This means that a State can only be brought before the ICJ if it has consented to the ICJ's jurisdiction either generally or specifically in a particular case.

Two main issues arise regarding the voluntarist conception of the role of consent in international rule-making. First, given that States are legal entities who cannot form and express a 'free will' in the same way an individual person can, the question of whether and how one can attribute a free will to a State and which expressions of such an attributed will count as expressions of State consent remains one of the enigmas at the heart of international law.[95] Second, the prevailing formalised conception of consent, which flows from the idea of sovereign equality among States, does not consider material inequalities. A formally 'free' expression of consent may reveal to be the result of coercion once one considers the material circumstances. Not all forms of coercion have the effect of rendering an expression of consent void under international law – especially not economic coercion.[96]

It is commonplace among international lawyers to juxtapose an extreme version of a voluntarist conception of international law, in which consent and only consent is supposed to be the source of obligations under international law, and a conception of international law based on community values. According to Martti Koskenniemi, this contrast between consent and justice is one of the many ways in which international legal arguments permanently oscillate between 'concreteness' and 'normativity'.[97]

C. CONSENT, CONSENSUS, AND ANARCHY

The importance of consent in international law stems from the fact that there is no centralised international government. The absence of government or hierarchical rule in the sense of a centralised authority able to make and enforce laws can be defined as anarchy.[98] In the absence of formal hierarchical rule and thus under

---

93 Vienna Convention on the Law of Treaties (adopted 23 May 1969, entered into force 27 January 1980) 1155 UNTS 331.

94 Statute of the International Court of Justice (adopted 26 June 1945, entered into force 24 October 1945) 1 UNTS XVI.

95 Cf. Jochen von Bernstorff, *The Public International Law Theory of Hans Kelsen: Believing in International Law* (CUP 2010) 26–37; 61–69.

96 Cf. Mohamed S Helal, 'On Coercion in International Law' (2019) 52 NYU JILP 1.

97 Martti Koskenniemi, *From Apology to Utopia: The Structure of International Legal Argument* (Reissue with a new Epilogue, CUP 2006) 65.

98 Hedley Bull, *The Anarchical Society* (3rd edn, Palgrave Macmillan 2002) 44; Kenneth Waltz, *Theory of International Politics* (McGraw-Hill 1979) 88, 102; Helen Milner, 'The Assumption of Anarchy in International Relations Theory: A Critique' (1991) 17 Review of International Studies 67, 70–74.

conditions of formal equality, the subjects of international law (i.e. mainly States) can only be bound by a rule of international law if they have given their consent. This mirrors the ideal of consensual decision-making and unanimity, which communal anarchist theories embrace.[99] However, these theories were developed with smaller communities of individuals in mind, not with a global community of States. The difference between the community-oriented idea of anarchy and the prevailing international notion of anarchy is reflected in the difference between group-oriented notions of consensus and unanimity in contrast to individualist, voluntarist notions of consent.

D. TYPES OF CONSENT IN INTERNATIONAL LAW

Stephen Neff distinguishes three kinds of consent: 'outcome consent', 'rule consent', and 'regime consent'.[100] Outcome consent refers to a specific situation and it transforms the outcome of this situation. An act that would otherwise be unlawful is transformed into a lawful act because the State affected by this act has given its consent. Rule consent refers to the voluntary acceptance of a specific rule of international law. This kind of consent is at the basis of classical positivist and voluntarist conceptions of international law sources and of international law's validity. Regime consent refers not to a specific rule but, more generally, to be bound by the rules created within a specific system (e.g. an international organisation). In the terminology introduced by HLA Hart, rule consent can be characterised as consent to primary rules (i.e. rules involving substantive obligations), while regime consent refers to secondary rules (i.e. rules about rule-making).[101] Arguments involving a generalised kind of consent to the whole of international law have played a key role in the era of formal decolonisation (i.e. mainly in the 1960s and 1970s). The 'newly independent States' that were created as a result of this formal decolonisation argued that they had not consented to previously existing international legal rules and could therefore start with a clean slate. The counterargument, which prevailed, was based on a form of regime consent: international lawyers from the Global North argued that the newly independent States had given a generalised consent to the international legal system by attaining independence as States.[102] This argument, of course, seems rather cynical given the fact that the form of the State was the only form through which formerly colonised peoples were able to gain independence.[103]

---

99 See Andrew Fiala, 'Anarchism' (*The Stanford Encylopedia of Philosophy*, Winter 2021) <https://plato.stanford.edu/archives/win2021/entries/anarchism/> accessed 26 August 2023.

100 Stephen Neff, 'Consent' in Jean d'Aspremont and Sahib Singh (eds), *Concepts for International Law: Contributions to Disciplinary Thought* (Edward Elgar 2019) 128–129.

101 Ibid 130–131.

102 DP O'Connell, 'The Role of International Law' (1966) 95 Daedalus 627, 628.

103 Sundhya Pahuja, *Decolonising International Law: Development, Economic Growth and the Politics of Universality* (CUP 2011) 44 et seq; Cf. Sué González Hauck, 'It's the System, Stupid!: Systematicity as a Conceptual Weapon' (*Völkerrechtsblog*, 29 December 2020) <doi:10.17176/20210107-181817-0>.

E. CONSENT AND COLONIALISM

The role of generalised regime consent in the formal decolonisation era has not been the only connection between consent and colonialism in the development of international law. State consent obtained its status as the ultimate source of international legal obligations in the 19th century, as international law was established as a 'scientific' discipline and as legal positivists purportedly broke ties with the natural law tradition.[104] The 19th century was also the time during which European States formalised their colonial endeavours. Consent as a foundational principle of international law was supposed to flow from State sovereignty. Consequently – but not incidentally – there was no place in 19th-century positivist accounts of international law for consent of people and communities that were not organised in the form of European States.[105]

On the other hand, colonial powers used a formalised notion of consent to legitimise their claim to colonial domination. European States did not recognise indigenous polities in the Americas, Africa, and Australia as sovereign entities with the power to contribute to international law-making and with the protection that the principle of non-intervention and other corollaries of sovereignty provide. They did, however, recognise indigenous authorities and their capacity to enter into legally binding obligations when it came to formally ceding title to land. This practice entirely neglected the coercive circumstances that accompanied formal declarations of consent.[106] Contemporary international legal rules take into account indigenous people's rights by requiring their free, prior, and informed consent regarding policies and projects that directly affect them.[107]

F. LIMITS ON STATE CONSENT UNDER CONTEMPORARY POSITIVE INTERNATIONAL LAW

The most important limits on State consent under contemporary positive law flow from article 53 VCLT and article 103 of the UN Charter. Both of these norms establish a hierarchy of rules, limiting States' ability to enter into and uphold agreements that conflict either with *jus cogens* or with the UN Charter.[108] *Jus cogens*, or a peremptory norm of general international law, is, according to article 53 VCLT,

---

104 Amnon Lev, 'The Transformation of International Law in the 19th Century' in Alexander Orakhelashvili (ed), *Research Handbook on the Theory and History of International Law* (Edward Elgar 2011).

105 Antony Anghie, *Imperialism, Sovereignty and the Making of International Law* (CUP 2005) 34; James Anaya, *Indigenous Peoples in International Law* (OUP 2000) 19 et seq.

106 Mieke van der Linden, *The Acquisition of Africa (1870–1914): The Nature of International Law* (Brill Nijhoff 2017); Anaya (n 105) 17.

107 See Viswanath, § 7.2.D.IV., in this textbook.

108 Cf. Prosper Weil, 'Towards Relative Normativity in International Law?' (1983) 77 AJIL 413; Karen Knop, 'Introduction to the Symposium on Prosper Weil, "Towards Relative Normativity in International Law?"' (2020) 114 AJIL Unbound 67.

a norm accepted and recognized by the international community of States as a whole as a norm from which no derogation is permitted and which can be modified only by a subsequent norm of general international law having the same character.

This means that States cannot modify *jus cogens* through other treaties or through customary law. Examples of jus cogens include the prohibition of genocide, crimes against humanity, slavery, and torture, and the principle of non-refoulement. Article 103 of the United Nations Charter is another key aspect of limits to State consent in international law. This article provides that in the event of a conflict between the obligations of a State under the Charter and its obligations under another international agreement, the obligations under the Charter shall take precedence.

G. CONCLUSION

In the absence of a centralised international government and, therefore, what many scholars call 'anarchy' on the international plane, consent is the main source of validity of international legal rules. It can be expressed as 'outcome consent', 'rule consent', or 'regime consent'. However, the notion of consent is not as straightforward as it may seem. The fiction of attributing a 'will' to an abstract entity like a State comes with its difficulties, as does the fact that consent completely disregards material inequalities and thus forms of coercion that may hamper true consent. This is best illustrated in the way in which consent as a notion was selectively employed to legitimise colonial appropriation and domination. Contemporary international law tries to mitigate this, especially in the field of the rights of indigenous peoples, which includes the right to free, prior, and informed consent. Finally, the limits on State consent that arise from peremptory rules of international law and from the system established through the UN Charter show that consent, if it ever was, is no longer the sole pillar on which the house of international law rests.

BOX 2.2.2 Further Readings

Further Readings

- S Neff, 'Consent' in Jean d'Aspremont and Sahib Singh (eds), *Concepts for International Law: Contributions to Disciplinary Thought* (Edward Elgar 2019)

- P Weil, 'Towards Relative Normativity in International Law?' (1983) 77 AJIL 413

- K Knop, 'Introduction to the Symposium on Prosper Weil, "Towards Relative Normativity in International Law?"' (2020) 114 AJIL Unbound 67

---

§§§

§ 2.3 ENFORCEMENT

DANIEL RICARDO QUIROGA-VILLAMARÍN

BOX 2.3.1 Required Knowledge and Learning Objectives

Required knowledge: International Law and Violence

Learning objectives: Evaluating the reasons why certain legal scholars have considered international law to be 'incomplete'; examining how different schools of international legal thought have problematised this 'incompleteness' critique and reframed the problem of compliance – or lack thereof – of international law; understanding the divergence in North Atlantic international legal thought between a European concern for 'system' and a US focus on 'process' – without losing sight of what is left outside of this framing.

A. INTRODUCTION

Could international law be neither 'international' nor even 'law'? Such 'institutional anxieties' have long haunted our profession.[109] In this chapter, I provide an introduction to the second anxiety by reviewing different ways our discipline has engaged with questions related to the enforcement – or lack thereof – of international legal categories.[110]

B. FACING THE AUSTINIAN CHALLENGE

Since 1832, international law has been haunted by the English legal theorist John Austin.[111] In his influential lectures, titled 'The Providence of Jurisprudence Determined',[112] Austin claimed that 'international law' was but a contradiction in terms. As committed positivist theorist who distinguished between 'laws strictly so called' and 'morality' (as only the former fell within the purview of 'the science of jurisprudence'), Austin saw international law as an imprecise misnomer.[113] Perhaps one could talk of a science of 'positive international morality' – but were there such things as international 'positive laws'?[114] Given that Austin understood a law to be a general command

---

109 See González Hauck, § 1, in this textbook.

110 On the first anxiety, see Anthea Roberts, *Is International Law International?* (OUP 2017).

111 Antony Anghie, 'Towards a Postcolonial International Law' in Prabhakar Singh and Benoît Mayer (eds), *Critical International Law* (OUP 2014) 124–125.

112 John Austin, *The Province of Jurisprudence Determined* (John Murray 1832).

113 Ibid 132. See also Etkin and Green, § 3.1, in this textbook.

114 Ibid.

delivered by a sovereign authority,[115] he was sceptical that there could really be 'law' in the non-hierarchical structures of inter-polity relations. Without supranational enforcement, there can be no international law 'strictly so called'.

International lawyers have strived to face this 'Austinian challenge'.[116] Considering that Austin himself experienced 'self-distrust' throughout his intellectual career,[117] it is perhaps ironic that his writings ultimately transferred some of these 'institutional anxieties' to the international legal profession.[118] Some scholars have embraced its alleged 'incompleteness', often by defending the international legal order as a 'primitive' but functional system.[119] Others have resisted the analogy between domestic and international law.[120] In 1995, Franck claimed that international law had entered its 'post-ontological era', a time when '[i]ts lawyers need no longer defend [its] very existence'.[121] However, as he was quick to concede,[122] this early optimism – so typical of the post–Cold War North Atlantic faith in liberal legalism[123] – could do with some Austinian scepticism, as questions of non-compliance still haunt the discipline.[124] For better or worse, we have been unable to fully exorcise Austin's spectre. In what follows, I review how different schools of international legal thought have attempted, even if unsuccessfully, to do so.[125]

C. 'DIFFERENT WAYS OF THINKING' ABOUT COMPLIANCE[126]

Despite Austin's challenge, it seems that 'almost all nations observe almost all principles of international law and almost all of their obligations almost all of the time', as Henkin once speculated.[127] Over time, European and US traditions have tended to diverge in

---

115 Ibid 18.

116 Ignacio De La Rasilla Del Moral, 'The Shifting Origins of International Law' (2015) 28 LJIL 419, 425.

117 HLA Hart, 'Introduction' in *The Province of Jurisprudence Determined: and, The Uses of the Study of Jurisprudence* (Hackett 1998) viii.

118 See González Hauck, § 1, in this textbook.

119 Yoram Dinstein, 'International Law as a Primitive Legal System' (1986) 19 NYUJILP 1.

120 Ian Hurd, 'The International Rule of Law and the Domestic Analogy' (2015) 4 GlobCon 365.

121 Thomas Franck, *Fairness in International Law and Institutions* (OUP 1995) 6.

122 Thomas Franck, 'The Power of Legitimacy and the Legitimacy of Power: International Law in an Age of Power Disequilibrium' (2006) 100 AJIL 88, 91.

123 Daniel Ricardo Quiroga-Villamarín, 'From Speaking Truth to Power to Speaking Power's Truth: Transnational Judicial Activism in an Increasingly Illiberal World' in Lena Riemer and others (eds), *Cynical International Law? Abuse and Circumvention in Public International and European Law* (Springer 2020) 11–133.

124 Michael Bothe, 'Compliance in International Law' (*Oxford Bibliographies*, 2020) <https://oxfordbibliographies.com/view/document/obo-9780199796953/obo-9780199796953-0213.xml>

125 Benedict Kingsbury, 'The Concept of Compliance as a Function of Competing Conceptions of International Law' (1998) 19 MichJIntlL 345.

126 With apologies to Andrea Bianchi, *International Law Theories: An Inquiry into Different Ways of Thinking* (OUP 2016).

127 Louis Henkin, *How Nations Behave: Law and Foreign Policy* (Council on Foreign Relations 1968) 42.

how to make sense of this fact. I focus on these rather parochial schools not because of their analytical precision, but because they became dominant through force or persuasion in 'almost all' countries throughout the 20th century.[128] In a global textbook that aspires to reach an international audience I chose to focus on these traditions *not in spite of but because of* their imperial significance.

I. INTERNATIONAL LAW AS A *SYSTEM*: EUROPEAN APPROACHES

European traditions emphasised the *systematicity* of international law, arguing that norms did not operate on the basis of single regulations but were linked in a dense arrangement 'within a hierarchy, composing together a coherent logical order'.[129] Building on this 'Germanic' focus,[130] they defended international law – albeit with melancholy about the deficiencies of this international system compared to the 'mature' domestic State.[131] 'Like a Phoenix', different iterations of this argument have surfaced in 20th-century mainstream international legal thought,[132] with echoes found in later debates regarding fragmentation,[133] or Global Constitutionalism.[134]

An example of this can be found in the 'Grotian tradition'. While the 19th century has been read as one marked by the rise of 'positive' law,[135] natural law commitments have remained strong in the international legal profession well into the present day.[136] In his 1946 article defending (and perhaps 'inventing') this tradition,[137] Lauterpacht argues that a 'Grotian' approach placed 'the value of human will as an agency shaping the destiny of men [sic]' at the forefront of the goals of international law[138] and subjected 'the totality of international relations to the rule of law'.[139] A 'Grotian' rejoinder to Austin argues that one cannot understand how international law is enforced without paying attention to these higher values, for they explain why 'members of good societies agree to live in peace and expect mutual benefits' from mutual cooperation.[140] Recognising that law

---

128 Anghie, 'Towards a Postcolonial International Law' (n 111) 127.

129 Eyal Benvenisti, 'The Conception of International Law as a Legal System' (2008) 50 GYIL 393.

130 Martti Koskenniemi, 'Between Coordination and Constitution: International Law as a German Discipline' (2011) 15 Redescriptions 45.

131 Daniel Ricardo Quiroga-Villamarín, 'Black Flowers of Civilization: Violence, Colonial Institutions, and the Law in Coetzee's Waiting for the Barbarians' (2020) 2 The Graduate Press 37.

132 Bianchi (n 126) 39–43.

133 Martti Koskenniemi and Päivi Leino, 'Fragmentation of International Law? Postmodern Anxieties' (2002) 15 LJIL 553.

134 Anne Peters, 'The Merits of Global Constitutionalism' (2009) 16 Indiana Journal of Global Legal Studies 397; Bianchi (n 126) 44–71.

135 Stephen Neff, *Justice among Nations: A History of International Law* (Harvard University Press 2014) 215; Mónica García-Salmones-Rovira, *The Project of Positivism in International Law* (OUP 2013).

136 Stephen Hall, 'The Persistent Specter: Natural Law, International Order and the Limits of Legal Positivism' (2001) 12 EJIL 269.

137 Eric Hobsbawm, 'Introduction: Inventing Traditions' in Eric Hobsbawm and Terence Ranger (eds), *The Invention of Tradition* (CUP 2012) 1–14.

138 Hersch Lauterpacht, 'The Grotian Tradition of International Law' (1946) 23 BYBIL 1, 5.

139 Ibid 19.

140 Martti Koskenniemi, 'Imagining the Rule of Law: Rereading the Grotian "Tradition"' (2019) 30 EJIL 17.

and morality are separate spheres of knowledge, the Grotian argues that one cannot fully expunge the 'human sense of justice' from the (international) legal system.[141] This does not mean one should expect the international legal order to be upheld in every occasion. It can find itself questioned and challenged, but however long the arc of the moral universe might be, it ultimately bends towards justice.[142] Gaps in enforcement are but a signal of international law's incompleteness.

Other perspectives responded to Austin from within legal positivism. Given that the most famous positivist authors, Kelsen and Hart, are further discussed in this volume, I will only highlight the crucial role of 'primitiveness' in their approaches to enforcement.[143] Hart, a former student of Austin, noted in *The Concept of Law* that international law was marked by its 'absence of an international legislature, courts with compulsory jurisdiction, and centrally organized sanctions'[144] – earning him 'few friends' in our discipline.[145] Hart considered that international law's lack of 'secondary rules' (meta-norms governing the making or breaking of primary obligations, including those that create consequences for non-compliance), undermined international law's systematicity. Moreover, Hart noted that '[o]ne of the most persistent sources of perplexity about the obligatory character of international has been the difficulty felt in accepting or explaining the fact that a state which is sovereign may also be bound by . . . international law'.[146] European legal thought took Hart's seemingly unsolvable conundrum to 'square the circle' of compliance. In the famous *S.S. Wimbledon* case of 1923, the PCIJ concluded that the 'the right of entering into international engagements is an attribute of state sovereignty' – even if such agreement entails 'an abandonment' of sovereignty.[147]

Kelsen also lamented the 'primitiveness' of the international order.[148] In his 1953 Hague Academy lectures, he concluded that 'primitive juridical communities' are those in which sanctions are yet to be centralised[149] – a condition that, alas, also holds true for the 'international community'.[150] This didn't undermine international law's claim to be a system, but it entailed that it was one with 'decentralised' enforcement mechanisms, often requiring parties to seek justice through their own measures.[151] Like his Grotian contemporaries, Kelsen defended international law's incompleteness and eagerly

---

141 Janne Nijman, 'Grotius' 'Rule of Law' and the Human Sense of Justice: An Afterword to Martti Koskenniemi's Foreword' (2019) 30 EJIL 1105.

142 With apologies to Samuel Moyn, 'Dignity's Due' (*The Nation*, 16 October 2013) <www.thenation.com/article/archive/dignitys-due/> accessed 25 August 2023.

143 Etkin and Green, § 3.1, in this textbook.

144 HLA Hart, *The Concept of Law* (2nd edn, OUP 1994) 214.

145 David Lefkowitz, 'What Makes a Social Order Primitive? In Defense of Hart's Take on International Law' (2017) 23 Legal Theory 258.

146 Hart, *The Concept of Law* (n 144). 220.

147 PCIJ, *Case of the S.S. 'Wimbledon'* (17 August 1923) 25.

148 Jochen von Bernstorff, *The Public International Law Theory of Hans Kelsen: Believing in Universal Law* (CUP 2010) 90–93.

149 Hans Kelsen, *Théorie Du Droit International Public* (1994) 84 RdC 71.

150 Ibid 11.

151 Charles Leben, 'Hans Kelsen and the Advancement of International Law' (1998) 9 EJIL 287, 289–292.

anticipated its maturation through the establishment of permanent and supranational institutions – courts and tribunals chief among them. Both positivist and natural-law–inflected traditions in Europe saw the Austinian challenge as an incentive to work towards the 'completion' of the international legal system. In their view, international law – however 'primitive' – was never only 'a random collection' of norms but perhaps a system (flawed, but improvable and ultimately lovable) in its own terms.[152]

II. INTERNATIONAL LAW AS A *PROCESS*: US PERSPECTIVES

US legal thought took another path. Instead of focusing on international law's systematicity, this tradition foregrounded the *processes* of international law-making, enforcement, and non-compliance. Inspired by legal realist thought,[153] Unitedstateseans downplayed the importance of legal concepts, studying instead how actors used international legal remedies to enforce rights.[154] The best example of this movement can be found in two 1968 student casebooks: *International Legal Process* by Abram Chayes, Thomas Ehrlich, and Andreas Lowenfeld,[155] and *Transnational Legal Problems* by Detlev Vagts and Henry Steiner.[156] These two books show the decisive influence of a realist concern for process over substance that would be characteristic of this turn. In certain circles, this approach would still place certain 'human values' or 'legitimacy' at the forefront, especially in the so-called New Haven School[157] and in the later Manhattan School.[158] In any case, US engagement with the empirical methods of the social sciences – especially to measure compliance – did mark an important difference with European traditions.[159]

This concern for process has been influential, especially when it comes to enforcement. A surge of interventions have called for its renewal: from 'New International Legal Process'[160] to a 'new New Haven School'[161] or a 'New Realist Approach'.[162] A good

---

152 ILC, Conclusions of the work of the Study Group on the Fragmentation of International Law (2006) UN Doc A/61/10, para 251.

153 For an overview, see Justin Desautels-Stein, *The Jurisprudence of Style: A Structuralist History of American Pragmatism and Liberal Legal Thought* (CUP 2018); John Henry Schlegel, *American Legal Realism and Empirical Social Science* (University of North Carolina Press 2011); AL Escorihuela, 'Alf Ross: Towards a Realist Critique and Reconstruction of International Law' (2003) 14 EJIL 703.

154 Dinah Shelton, *Remedies in International Human Rights Law* (2nd edn, OUP 2006).

155 Abram Chayes, Thomas Ehrlich, and Andreas Lowenfeld, *International Legal Process: Materials for an Introductory Course* (Little, Brown 1968).

156 Detlev Vagts and Henry Steiner, *Transnational Legal Problems; Materials and Text* (Foundation Press 1968).

157 Michael Reisman, Siegfried Wiessner, and Andrew Willard, 'The New Haven School: A Brief Introduction' (2007) 32 YJIL 575; Bianchi, *International Law Theories* (n 126) 91–109.

158 Samuel Moyn, 'The International Law That Is America: Reflections on the Last Chapter of the Gentle Civilizer of Nations' (2013) 27 TempInt'l & CompLJ 399, 403–405.

159 Tom Ginsburg, Daniel Abebe, and Adam Chilton, 'The Social Science Approach to International Law' (2021) 22 Chicago JIL 1. See also Ryan Goodman and Derek Jinks, *Socializing States: Promoting Human Rights Through International Law* (OUP 2013); Steininger and Paige, § 4.2, in this textbook.

160 Mary Ellen O'Connell, 'New International Legal Process' (1999) 93 AJIL 334.

161 Harold Hongju Koh, 'Is There a 'New' New Haven School of International Law?' (2007) 106 YJIL 2599.

162 Gregory Shaffer, 'The New Legal Realist Approach to International Law' (2015) 28 LJIL 189.

example is the tide of interest in 'Transnational Law'[163] – a term first coined by Jessup in 1956 to theorise the interstices of public/private and domestic/international that has since taken 'many lives'.[164] This focus on 'problems and process' – to paraphrase the title of Rosalyn Higgins' famous monograph from 1994[165] – has now been widely accepted. In contemporary scholarship, the imprint of this US foregrounding of 'process' shines brightly in Global Administrative Law,[166] inquiries into 'informal' law-making,[167] and International Law and Economics.[168]

D. CONCLUSION

For better or worse, international legal thought is also haunted by dichotomies.[169] Most legal theories ground their approach in an intrinsic difference between categories like public/private, normativity/morality, domestic/international, and law-making/law-breaking – often with terrible consequences, as feminist legal critique has convincingly argued.[170] Sadly, this chapter is also organised around a series of binaries including US/European and system/process. I do not offer them as fixed categories but rather as tentative guideposts that might orientate a newcomer to the vast literature on enforcement in international law. At the same time, we cannot forget that other ways of seeing international law might be excluded from this framing – and that will be developed further in this volume, in relation to feminist and queer, postcolonial and decolonial, and Marxist voices.[171] The real challenge ahead for 21st-century international legal thought is to finally exorcise the ghosts of ages past – including the Austinian challenge's discoloured wraith.

Instead of focusing on the binary disobedience/compliance, these other voices have highlighted the 'world-making' function of international law,[172] for our discipline is not an external patina which is applied unevenly to the real, but rather a frame that

---

163 Philip Jessup, *Transnational Law* (Yale University Press 1956).

164 Peer Zumbansen (ed), *The Many Lives of Transnational Law: Critical Engagements with Jessup's Bold Proposal* (CUP 2020).

165 Rosalyn Higgins, *Problems and Process: International Law and How We Use It* (OUP 1994).

166 See Benedict Kingsbury, Nico Krisch, and Richard Stewart, 'The Emergence of Global Administrative Law' (2005) 68 LCP 15.

167 Joost Pauwelyn, Ramses Wessel, and Jan Wouters, 'When Structures Become Shackles: Stagnation and Dynamics in International Lawmaking' (2014) 25 EJIL 733. See also Kunz, Lima, and Castelar Campos, § 6.4, in this textbook.

168 Jack Goldsmith and Eric Posner, *The Limits of International Law* (OUP 2007). See also Steininger and Paige, § 4.2, in this textbook.

169 Jean d'Aspremont, *After Meaning: The Sovereignty of Forms in International Law* (Edward Elgar 2021) 8–9.

170 Hilary Charlesworth, Christine Chinkin, and Shelley Wright, 'Feminist Approaches to International Law' (1991) 85 AJIL 613, 625–634. See also Kahl and Paige, § 3.3, in this textbook.

171 See González Hauck, § 3.2; Kahl and Paige, § 3.3; and Bagchi, § 3.4, in this textbook.

172 Negar Mansouri, 'International Organizations and World Making Practices: Some Notes on Method' (2022) 19 IOLR 528, among others.

allows us to open the window and *see* a 'world of nation states' – where questions of compliance can be meaningfully posed and answered.[173] But it is never too late to start questioning our ways of seeing international (dis)order.[174]

BOX 2.3.2 Further Readings

Further Readings

- A Bianchi, *International Law Theories: An Inquiry Into Different Ways of Thinking* (OUP 2016)

- R Higgins, *Problems and Process: International Law and How We Use It* (OUP 2001)

- R Goodman and D Jinks, *Socializing States: Promoting Human Rights Through International Law* (OUP 2013)

- D Shelton, *Remedies in International Human Rights Law* (2nd edn, OUP 2006)

- A Thompson, 'Coercive Enforcement of International Law' in Jeffrey Dunoff and Mark Pollack (eds), *Interdisciplinary Perspectives on International Law and International Relations* (CUP 2012) 502

---

§ § §

---

173 David Kennedy, 'One, Two, Three, Many Legal Orders: Legal Pluralism and the Cosmopolitan Dream' (2006) 31 NYU Review of Law & Social Change 641, 650.

174 Negar Mansouri and Daniel Ricardo Quiroga-Villamarín (eds), *Ways of Seeing International Organisations: New Perspectives for International Institutional Law* (CUP forthcoming 2024).

§ 2.4 SELF-DETERMINATION

MIRIAM BAK MCKENNA

BOX 2.4.1 Required Knowledge and Learning Objectives

Required knowledge: History of International Law

Learning objectives: Understanding the history, philosophy, and practical implications of self-determination in international law.

A. INTRODUCTION

Self-determination is among the most politicised principles of the post–WWII international legal system. This section provides a brief overview of the history, conceptual underpinnings, and diverse meanings ascribed to self-determination in the international legal system, along with the tensions and controversies that have accompanied its circulation as a legal idea.

Incorporated as a principle in the UN Charter, and as a right in the ICCPR and ICESCR, self-determination has been elevated to the status of *erga omnes* (Latin: 'among all'),[175] or even *jus cogens* (peremptory norms of international law)[176] and has been recognised by the ICJ as constituting one of international law's 'essential principles'.[177] Yet, there exists little consensus on its precise definition or scope as a legal rule or principle.

While its linguistic sources can be traced to German Enlightenment figures and the international socialist movement, as a conceptual idea it holds deep resonance across cultures.[178] Self-determination was popularised in the inter-war period by figures such as Woodrow Wilson and Vladimir Lenin as a collectivist notion linked to ideologies of

---

175 See Judge Weeramantry, Dissenting Opinion, *Case Concerning East Timor (Portugal v. Australia)* [1995] ICJ Rep 142, 172–3; Judge Higgins, Separate Opinion, *Legal Consequences of the Construction of a Wall in the Occupied Palestinian Territory* (Advisory Opinion) [2004] ICJ Rep [379]; Judge Kooijmans, Separate Opinion, *Ibid* [404]; Judge Al Khasawneh, Separate Opinion, *Ibid* [13]; Judge Elaraby, Separate Opinion, *Ibid* [3.4]; Antonio Cassese, *Self-Determination of Peoples: A Legal Reappraisal* (CUP 1995) at 3, 1–34, 15–23, 17–78; Benedict Kingsbury, 'Restructuring Self-Determination: A Relational Approach' in P Aikio and M Scheinin (eds), *Operationalizing the Right of Indigenous Peoples to Self-determination* (Åbo Akademi University 2000) 19, 22.

176 In support see Judge Ammoun, Separate Opinion, *Barcelona Traction, Second Phase* (Merits) [1970] ICJ Rep 304; Casssese *Ibid* 140; Ian Brownlie, *Principles of Public International Law* (4th edn, Clarendon Press 1990) at 513. On *erga omnes* and *jus cogens* rules, see Eggett, Introduction to § 6, in this textbook.

177 *Case Concerning East Timor (Portugal v Australia)* (Judgment) [1995] ICJ Rep 4, 102 [29].

178 Eric D Weitz, 'Self-Determination: How a German Enlightenment Idea Became the Slogan of National Liberation and a Human Right' (2015) 120 The American Historical Review 462–496.

national unification and liberation. In the post-war period, anticolonial thinkers and activists mobilised self-determination as the legal basis for the emancipation of peoples from colonial rule. Even though the applicability and practical implications of self-determination outside of the colonial context has been subject to continuing debate, self-determination remains the catchcry of movements around the globe demanding greater autonomy in shaping their own future.

B. CONCEPTUAL AND LEGAL TENSION

In its broadest legal sense, self-determination denotes the right of all peoples 'to freely determine their political status and freely pursue their economic, social and cultural development' (ICCPR article 1(1)).[179] Due to, or perhaps in spite of, its relationship to freedom, there lies a paradoxical tension at its core: 'self-determination both *legitimates* and *challenges* sovereign authority'.[180]

The concept of sovereignty is perhaps the most widely articulated form of self-determination in international law, providing a sphere free from external threat and interference in which peoples may freely determine the ways in which they wish to govern themselves. The legitimacy of States is largely dependent upon their embodiment of self-determination, as they provide a setting in which groups and individuals give expression to their values, culture, and sense of themselves.[181] However, self-determination simultaneously provides a normative platform for people to alter how they are governed, thereby pitting the validity of current political arrangements against the validity of possible alternatives.[182]

The destabilising potential of self-determination has been balanced by the demand that any exercise of self-determination respect territorial integrity and the retention of present international and internal boundaries. The right of colonial peoples to freely choose their political status is therefore restrained by the application of the principle of *uti possidetis* (Latin: 'as [you] possess under law'), which requires the retention of existing colonial boundaries[183] despite the fact that these were drawn largely 'with little consideration for factors of geography, ethnicity, economic convenience or reasonable means of communication'.[184] *Uti possidetis* has also

---

179 See also UNGA Res 1514 (1960) GAOR 15th Session Supp 16; UNGA Res 2625 (1970) GAOR 25th Session Supp 28; the *Helsinki Final Act*, 14 ILM (1975); *Vienna Declaration and Programme of Action*, 32 ILM (1993).

180 Martti Koskenniemi, 'National Self-Determination Today: Problems of Legal Theory and Practice' (1994) 43 ICLQ 241, 245.

181 Andrew Hurrell, 'The Making and Unmaking of Boundaries in International Law' in A Buchanan and M Moore (eds), *States, Nations and Borders: The Ethics of Making Boundaries* (CUP 2003) 283.

182 Patrick Macklem, 'Distributing Sovereignty: Indian Nations and Equality of Peoples' (1992–1993) 45 Stanford Law Review 1311, 1346–1347.

183 *Frontier Dispute (Burkina Faso v Mali)* (Judgment) [1986] ICJ Rep 554.

184 *Territorial Dispute (Libyan Arab Jamahiriya v Chad)* (Separate Opinion of Judge Ajibola) [1994] ICJ Rep 6 [8].

been applied outside of the colonial context, for example during the breakup of Yugoslavia.[185] The international community has been reluctant to allow self-determination to ground or endorse claims of separation and secession. The result, as Karen Knop points out, is that 'some states in international law represent the exercise of self-determination by a people, others do not. Some peoples have their own State, others do not'.[186]

C. DEFINING PEOPLE

Self-determination is structured around the notion of the 'people' as the legitimate bearer of the right. As Sir Ivor Jennings archly noted, self-determination at first glance offers a reasonable proposition: let the people decide their own fate. The problem is that 'the people cannot decide until someone decides who are the people'.[187] The main difficulty is that there is rarely a perfect overlap between those who find themselves territorially bounded and those who identify themselves members of the 'self'. In the context of modern statehood, this is the 'Janus face of the modern nation'.[188] The tension between the conception of the self-determining State entity and other competing claims to 'selfhood' has been the primary source of conflict in the practical application of self-determination.

The two dominant interpretations to the term 'peoples' emerging from self-determination discourse largely correspond to that of *ethnos* (i.e. an imaginary community of descent or affiliation such as the nation) and *demos* (i.e. a politically defined community). The latter holds that a 'people' entitled to self-determination is the whole of a population within the generally accepted boundaries of an independent State or a territory of a classical colonial type. The difficulty, as James Anaya asserts, is in the underlying view that *only* such units of human aggregation – the *whole* of the people of a State or colonial territory – are beneficiaries of self-determination.[189] 'This approach', Anaya notes, 'renders the norm inapplicable to the vast number of contemporary claims of sub-state groups that represent many of the world's most pressing problems in the post-colonial age'.[190]

---

185 Allain Pellet, 'Note sur la Commission d'arbitrage de la Conférence européenne pour la paix en Yougoslavie' (1991) 37 Ann fr dr int 329 at 337; Allain Pellet, 'L'Activité de la Commission d'arbitrage de la Conférence européenne pour la paix en Yougoslavie' (1992) 38 Ann fr dr int 220; Allain Pellet, 'L'Activité de la Commission d'arbitrage de la Conférence internationale pour l'ancienne Yougoslavie' (1993) 39 Ann fr dr int 286.

186 Karen Knop, 'Statehood: Territory, People, Government' in James Crawford and Martti Koskenniemi (eds), *The Cambridge Companion to International Law* (CUP 2012) 107.

187 Sir Ivor Jennings, *The Approach to Self-Government* (CUP 1956) 55–56.

188 Jürgen Habermas, 'A Genealogical Analysis of the Cognitive Content of Morality' in *The Inclusion of the Other: Studies in Political Theory* (MIT Press 1998).

189 James Anaya, 'Self-Determination as a Collective Right Under Contemporary International Law' in Pekka Aikio and Martin Scheinin (eds), *Operationalizing the Right of Indigenous Peoples to Self-Determination* (Åbo Akademi University 2000) 10.

190 Ibid.

D. FORMS OF SELF-DETERMINATION

I. GENERAL NORM

Having been included in the Atlantic Charter, the joint declaration of allied post-war aims, and its demands for the restoration of sovereignty and self-government, self-determination was invoked as one of the founding principles of the UN Charter in articles 1 and 55, linked to developing 'friendly relations among nations' and promoting the 'equal rights . . . of peoples'.[191] While not implying a legal right per se, the reference to self-determination in the UN Charter is widely understood as bolstering the territorial and sovereign sanctity of the State against foreign incursions, as well as guaranteeing a people's 'choice of a political, economic, social and cultural system, and the formulation of foreign policy', as affirmed by the ICJ in its *Nicaragua* decision.[192] In its 2004 *Wall* opinion, concerning the construction by Israel of a wall in occupied Palestinian territory, the ICJ affirmed that self-determination had acquired the status of a legal right under international law, placing States under an obligation to 'refrain from any forcible action which deprives peoples . . . of their right to self-determination', as well as 'to promote the realization of [self-determination] and to respect it'.[193]

II. COLONIAL SELF-DETERMINATION

With many colonial powers reluctant to relinquish their colonial holdings, references to self-determination are conspicuously absent from the UN Charter chapters relating to both the non-self-governing territories and the trusteeships. In subsequent decades, however, anti-colonialists successfully transformed self-determination into a legal and normative platform for decolonisation. Drawing a direct line between colonialism and the violation of not only human rights and human dignity, but the broader aims of the international system contained in the UN Charter, anti-colonialists laid the foundations for a legal challenge to empire. Following its inclusion in the final statement of the Bandung Conference of Afro-Asian Countries in 1955, self-determination was successfully incorporated into the landmark Declaration on the Granting of Independence to Colonial Countries and Peoples (Resolution 1514 (XV)) in 1960 by the General Assembly.[194] Calling for an immediate end to all forms of colonial rule, the resolution granted colonial peoples a legal right to independence or to adopt any other status they freely chose. The ICJ later affirmed the colonial right to self-determination in its *Namibia*,[195]

---

191 Antonio Cassese, *Self-Determination of Peoples: A Legal Appraisal* (CUP 1995) 37.

192 *Case Concerning Military and Paramilitary Activities in and against Nicaragua* (Nicaragua v. United States of America) (Merits) [1986] ICJ Rep 14.

193 *Legal Consequences of the Construction of a Wall in the Occupied Palestinian Territory* (Advisory Opinion) [2004] ICJ Rep 136 [88].

194 UNGA Res 1514 (1960) GAOR 15th Session Supp 16.

195 *Legal Consequences for States of the Continued Presence of South Africa in Namibia (South West Africa) Notwithstanding Security Council Resolution 276 (1970) (Advisory Opinion)* [1971] ICJ Rep 16.

Western Sahara,[196] and *East Timor*[197] decisions. With no formal definition of colony, however, the right was restricted in practice to territories geographically separate and culturally and ethnically distinct from the administering power, excluding settler colonies and their indigenous peoples from the ambit of the right.[198]

III. ALIEN SUBJUGATION, DOMINATION, OR EXPLOITATION

Following the height of the decolonisation era, the right of self-determination was broadened to include cases in which a people is subject to 'alien subjugation, domination or exploitation'.[199] The situations in Afghanistan, Lebanon, Uganda, Cambodia, Grenada, Palestine, South Africa, Southern Rhodesia, and Central America dominated UN debates in which self-determination was raised in terms of foreign domination. Concerns over neo-colonial and Cold War intervention also saw self-determination cast as a corollary of non-interference, sovereign equality, and economic sovereignty. The 1965 Declaration on the Inadmissibility of Intervention in the Domestic Affairs of States[200] solidified a sovereignty-based notion of self-determination as a buffer against interference and 'foreign pressure', while economic self-determination featured prominently in demands for a New International Economic Order by States from the Global South in the 1970s. The right to economic self-determination was strengthened by the inclusion of the right to permanent sovereignty over natural resources in common article 1(2) of the ICCPR and ICESCR, which declared 'all peoples may, for their own ends, freely dispose of their natural wealth and resources without prejudice'. Within the text of the Friendly Relations Declaration from 1970, an authoritative restatement of the UN Charter principles, a clear line emerged that the promotion and implementation of self-determination and equal rights were among the most important measures to ensure universal peace.

IV. INTERNAL OR DEMOCRATIC SELF-DETERMINATION

While absent from the Universal Declaration of Human Rights (UDHR), the right to self-determination features prominently in several human rights instruments, most notably common article 1 of the ICCPR and ICESCR and the African Charter on Human and Peoples Rights. Political participation, democratic government, free and fair elections, and public accountability are increasingly referred to as falling within the rubric of 'internal' self-determination, which is said to create international standards regarding the form and function of a State's internal political order.[201] During the

---

196 *Western Sahara* (Advisory Opinion) [1975] ICJ Rep 12.

197 *Case Concerning East Timor (Portugal v Australia)* [1995] ICJ Rep 142.

198 UNGA Res 1541 (1960) GAOR 15th Session Supp 16.

199 See *Friendly Relations Declaration*, GA Res 2625 (1970) GAOR 25th Session Supp 28.

200 1965 Declaration on the Inadmissibility of Intervention in the Domestic Affairs of States.

201 For example, Resolution 1995/60 on 'ways and means of overcoming obstacles to the establishment of a democratic society and requirements for the maintenance of democracy', UN Commission on Human Rights ESCOR Supp 4, UN Doc. E/CN.4/1995/60 (1995), preamble.

immediate post–Cold War period, many States along with prominent jurists such as Thomas Franck and Antonio Cassese sought to link self-determination to a right of democratic governance.[202] Discussions over self-determination's link to 'legitimate' forms of internal political functioning and democratic governance are also enmeshed in debates over the resurgence in concepts such as trusteeship, protectorate, and international administration and the rise of post–conflict reconstruction missions.[203]

V. REMEDIAL SELF-DETERMINATION

In cases where States failed to uphold these protections, the possibility has been raised that a right of 'remedial' self-determination or secession could exist. This is based on a reading of the so-called safeguard clause contained in the Friendly Relations Declaration, which extends the right of territorial integrity to governments '*representing the whole people* belonging to the territory *without distinction* as to race, creed or colour'. Similar arguments of exceptionality in cases in which a group suffers systematic and gross violations of human rights have been raised in the Aaland Islands decisions, concerning a Swedish-speaking minority in Finland,[204] the Supreme Court of Canada in *Re Secession of Quebec*, responding to Quebec's request for secession,[205] and by some States in their submissions to the ICJ's Advisory Opinion regarding Kosovo's unilateral declaration of independence from Serbia in 2008.[206] However, while the recognition of Kosovo's independence by over 100 States raises the possibility that a new category of 'remedial secession' may exist, no right of secession has yet been recognised under international law.

VI. INDIGENOUS AND MINORITY SELF-DETERMINATION

Self-determination is also increasingly viewed as encapsulating a wide spectrum of rights for sub-State groups aimed at protecting their culture, identity, and self-governing capacity. Rights of ethnic and national minorities, while traditionally falling within human rights frameworks, were linked to the broad principle of self-determination. This was prominently seen in the aftermath of the breakups of the USSR and Yugoslavia, where the retention of existing boundaries necessitated an accommodation of cultural and ethnic claims by minorities.

---

202 See Thomas Franck, 'The Emerging Right to Democratic Governance' (1992) 86 AJIL 46.

203 See Ralph Wilde, *International Territorial Administration: How Trusteeship and the Civilizing Mission Never Went Away* (OUP 2008).

204 *Report of the International Commission of Jurists Entrusted by the Council of the League of Nations with the Task of Giving an Advisory Opinion Upon the Legal Aspects of the Aaland Islands Question*, League of Nations Official Journal, Special Supplement No 3 (October 1920); *The Aaland Islands Question: Report Submitted to the Council of the League of Nations by the Commission of Rapporteurs*, League of Nations Doc B7 [C] 21/68/106 (April 1921).

205 *Re Reference by the Governor in Council Concerning Certain Questions Relating to the Secession of Quebec from Canada*, [1998] 1 16 1 DLR (4) 385.

206 *Accordance with International Law of the Unilateral Declaration of Independence in Respect of Kosovo (Request for Advisory Opinion)* [2010] ICJ Rep 423.

Indigenous rights have become increasingly articulated within the framework of self-determination, as an important restorative step towards redressing stolen sovereignty by granting decision-making over their traditional lands and natural resources.[207] The International Labour Organization's Convention 169 of 1989 was crucial milestone in this regard, employing for the first time the term 'peoples' in referring to indigenous groups, and laying out the entitlements of self-governance in relation to matters connected with their lands, beliefs, and economic and cultural development.[208] Indigenous self-determination was bolstered in 2006 with the adoption of the UN Declaration on the Rights of Indigenous Peoples, which affirmed the right to self-determination,[209] linking it to self-government and autonomy 'in matters relating to their internal and local affairs, as well as ways and means for financing their autonomous functions'.[210]

Appeals to indigenous self-determination are thus taking place against the backdrop of broader debates surrounding the Statist paradigm of international law, with autonomy rights and devolutionary arrangements directed towards the goal of renegotiating sovereignty. Self-determination also continues to figure prominently in independence claims by numerous groups, including in Palestine, Catalonia, and Kurdistan, and by groups seeking greater control over issues affecting them. Self-determination is also increasingly being linked to redressing the ongoing legacy of colonialism,[211] seen most prominently in the successful challenge to the UK's occupation of the Chagos Islands by Mauritius in a 2019 ICJ Advisory Opinion.[212]

E. CONCLUSION

Self-determination may be one of the most unsettled norms in international law, yet it is also one of the most resonant. Despite its shifting legal content, normatively it provides the cornerstone for an international system which appeals to the equality and worth of the multitude of social, cultural and political identities which exist across the globe, providing a powerful platform for change. As Upendra Baxi surmises, self-determination 'insists that every human person has a right to a *voice* . . . the right to bear witness to violation, a right to immunity against *disarticulation* by concentrations of economic, social, and political formations . . . thus opening up sites of resistance'.[213]

---

207 See James Crawford (ed), *The Rights of Peoples* (Clarendon Press 1988); Benedict Kingsbury, 'Claims by Non-State Groups in International Law' (1992) 25(1) Cornell Int'l LJ 48; Patrick Thornberry, *International Law and the Rights of Minorities* (Clarendon Press 1991).

208 Article 7 of ILO Convention 169 concerning Indigenous and Tribal Peoples in Independent Countries (adopted on 27 June 1989). Prior to this, ILO Convention 107 from 1957 used the term 'populations'.

209 UNGA Res 61/295 (2007) GAOR 61st Session Supp 49, para 3.

210 Ibid article 4.

211 Marc Weller, *Escaping the Self-Determination Trap* (Martinus Nijhoff 2009) 19.

212 *Legal Consequences of the Separation of the Chagos Archipelago from Mauritius in 1965* (Advisory Opinion) [2019] ICJ Rep 95.

213 Upendra Baxi, *The Future of Human Rights* (OUP 2002) 36.

BOX 2.4.2 Further Readings and Further Resources

Further Readings

- A Cassese, *Self-Determination of Peoples: A Legal Reappraisal* (CUP 1995)

- K Knop, *Diversity and Self-Determination in International Law* (CUP 2002)

- MB McKenna, *Reckoning With Empire: Self-Determination in International Law* (Brill 2023)

- A Getachew, *Worldmaking After Empire: The Rise and Fall of Self-Determination* (Princeton University Press 2020)

- T Sparks, *Self-Determination in the International Legal System: Whose Claim, to What Right?* (Hart 2023)

Further Resources

- Olivier Magis, 'Another Paradise' (2019) (Film) <www.truestory.film/another-paradise> accessed 25 August 2023

- Maya Newell, 'In My Blood It Runs' (2019) (Film) <www.imdb.com/title/tt8192948/> accessed 25 August 2023

§ § §

3

CHAPTER 3
APPROACHES

SUÉ GONZÁLEZ HAUCK, VERENA KAHL, BAŞAK
ETKİN, ALEX GREEN, TAMSIN PHILLIPA PAIGE,
AND KANAD BAGCHI

INTRODUCTION
SUÉ GONZÁLEZ HAUCK AND VERENA KAHL

BOX 3.1 Required Knowledge and Learning Objectives

Required knowledge: None

Learning objectives: Understanding what is typically meant by an 'approach' to international law.

BOX 3.2 Interactive Exercises

Access *interactive exercises for this chapter*[1] by positioning your smartphone camera at the dot-filled box, also known as a QR code.

Figure 3.1 QR code referring to interactive exercises.

A. INTRODUCTION

This chapter introduces some of the most important approaches to international law, while the next chapter introduces methods in working within international law. The distinction between 'approaches' and 'methods' mirrors the distinction between

---

1   https://openrewi.org/en-projects-project-public-international-law-approaches-to-international-law/

DOI: 10.4324/9781003451327-4

methodology and method.[2] This introductory section, first, introduces this distinction and thereby tries to illustrate what 'approaches' to international law are. Second, it reflects on the traditional approach to international law and on its relationship with positivism. Third, it briefly introduces commonalities among and pluralities within critical approaches to international law.

B. WHAT IS AN APPROACH? METHODOLOGY AND METHOD

The different approaches presented in this chapter represent different methodologies, that is, different sets of ontological and epistemological premises, which shape any intellectual enterprise. Premises are the starting point of an argument. They are the statements that are taken for granted as the point of departure. Ontological premises, simply put, are premises on *what there is* in the world, that is, on whether there is an objective truth and/or fixed reality 'out there' and on which elements in the world determine such truths and realities. Epistemological premises are premises on what we can know and on how we can acquire and establish knowledge. No intellectual enterprise can be carried out consistently and rigorously without, at the outset, gaining clarity about ontological and epistemological premises. The terms 'method' and 'methodology' are often used interchangeably.[3] However, a useful distinction between the two consists in understanding methodology as a set of ontological and epistemological premises and therefore the point of departure, as explained above, and method as the roadmap guiding the individual steps to be taken from this point of departure. 'Method', then, refers to the concrete application of the conceptual apparatus of a specific approach.[4]

C. TRADITIONAL INTERNATIONAL LAW AND LEGAL POSITIVISM

Despite influential figures like Ian Brownlie having argued that theory is but fog that obscures the more interesting legal questions,[5] no inquiry into international law is possible without theory. It is necessary to at least be aware of the set of premises from which one is starting. The standard way of engaging with international law in the traditional approach, which Brownlie epitomises, consists in laying out 'what the law is' on a particular question by deriving the relevant

---

2   Cf. Rossana Deplano and Nicholas Tsagourias, 'Introduction' in idem (eds), *Research Methods in International Law: A Handbook* (Edward Elgar 2021) 1–5.

3   Sundhya Pahuja, 'Methodology: Writing About How We Do Research' in Rossana Deplano and Nicholas Tsagourias (eds), *Research Methods in International Law: A Handbook* (Edward Elgar 2021) 61.

4   Andrea Bianchi, *International Law Theories: An Inquiry into Different Ways of Thinking* (OUP 2017) viii.

5   Ian Brownlie, 'International Law at the Fiftieth Anniversary of the United Nations – General Course on Public International Law (1995) 255 RdC 9, 30.

rules from the sources of international law (mainly treaties, custom, and general principles, article 38(1) ICJ Statute[6]) and by interpreting and applying these rules in accordance with existing authoritative interpretations and applications. This approach can be labelled 'doctrinal', 'traditional',[7] 'orthodox',[8] or simply 'mainstream'.[9] Making a claim to knowledge about 'what the law is', however, necessarily involves adopting a position on what 'law' *is* and on how we can know it, which means departing from a specific set of ontological and epistemological premises. Therefore, it is impossible to state what the law is without, implicitly, adopting a specific theoretical approach in doing so. A position that claims to discard theory altogether will often just adopt an inconsistent theoretical position as the starting point of its argument.[10] This is often the case with the doctrinal, traditional, or orthodox approach. Another label which is often attached to this approach is 'positivist'.[11] Positivism, generally, is a label attached to the set of ontological and epistemological premises according to which there is a single, objective truth 'out there' and that it is possible for human beings to know this truth reliably. Legal positivism, as a philosophical position,[12] adopts these premises *only* for the established (i.e. 'positive') law, not for moral and other considerations, which are considered to be separate from law. Consequently, at least in 'hard cases', that is, when the law employs vague terms like 'proportionality' or when the law has to be applied to circumstances not clearly reflected in the law, law is no longer a matter of cognition but of (usually a court's) decision. Philosophical legal positivists therefore agree that, at least in these 'hard cases', there is no single right answer to legal questions. However, practitioners who claim to be only interested in positive law and doctrinal scholars whose commitment to legal positivism mainly consists in adopting the perspective of practitioners and providing guidance by systematising existing legal materials often operate under the assumption that answers about 'what the law is' have a single correct answer and that this answer can be found.[13] 'Positivism' in the sense of the traditional doctrinal approach is therefore often incompatible with philosophical legal positivism.

---

6 Statute of the International Court of Justice (adopted 26 June 1945, entered into force 18 April 1946) 33 UNTS 993.

7 Bianchi (n 4) 21.

8 Jörg Kammerhofer, 'International Legal Positivism' in Florian Hoffmann and Anne Orford (eds), *The Oxford Handbook of the Theory of International Law* (OUP 2016) 413.

9 Srinivas Burra, 'Teaching Critical International Law: Reflections from the Periphery' (*TWAILR Reflections*, 12 March 2023) <https://twailr.com/teaching-critical-international-law-reflections-from-the-periphery/> accessed 22 June 2023.

10 Sué González Hauck, 'The Outside Keeps Creeping In: On the Impossibility of Engaging in Purely Doctrinal Scholarship' (*Völkerrechtsblog*, 23 February 2021) <https://voelkerrechtsblog.org/de/the-outside-keeps-creeping-in-on-the-impossibility-of-engaging-in-purely-doctrinal-scholarship/> accessed 22 June 2023.

11 Bruno Simma and Andreas L Paulus, 'The Responsibility of Individuals for Human Rights Abuses in Internal Conflicts: A Positivist View' (1999) 93 AJIL 302.

12 See Etkin and Green, § 3.1, in this textbook.

13 Danae Azaria, '"Codification by Interpretation": The International Law Commission as an Interpreter of International Law' (2020) 31 EJIL 171–200, at 176.

D. CRITICAL INTERNATIONAL LAW

Critical approaches to international law emerged from the Critical Legal Studies (CLS) movement in the United States, which was heavily influenced by both postmodern philosophy and Legal Realism. From postmodern and (post)structuralist philosophy, Critical Legal Studies and critical approaches to international law derive the premises that there is no objective and single truth 'out there' and that knowledge creation is not about neutral and objective cognition of a pre-existing truth but rather about the 'conditions of possibility' for expressing certain claims and for having these claims recognised and count as knowledge.

A central methodological tool deployed by critical legal scholars is deconstruction, a mode of thought developed by Jacques Derrida.[14] Deconstruction in this sense can be understood as a never-ending process of questioning existing and accepted structures of dominance, which are perceived as objective, neutral, or natural.[15] As a result, it reveals the existence of other competing forms of interpretation, alternative views, which have been ignored, overshadowed, or suppressed, thereby opening the door to new possibilities and structures.[16] The concept of deconstruction therefore rejects the idea of an absolute truth or natural referent,[17] but rather searches for 'the tensions, the contradictions, the heterogeneity'.[18] In its ability to show pluralities and different options, deconstruction creates space for (ongoing) transformation and reconstruction. With this in mind, '[it] is only through this element of endless analysis, criticism and deconstruction that we can prevent existing structures of dominance from reasserting themselves'.[19]

The main characteristic that critical approaches have derived from the project of deconstructing international law consists in the claim that international law is radically indeterminate.[20] Radical indeterminacy, in this sense, means that any course of action can be defended or rejected in terms of international law,[21] and that the

---

14 For Derrida's idea of deconstruction see, inter alia, Jacques Derrida, *Of Grammatology* (Gayatri Chakravorty Spivak, trans., Johns Hopkins University Press 2016); Jacques Derrida, *Deconstruction in a Nutshell: A Conversation with Jacques Derrida* (John D Caputo ed, Fordham University Press 2020). For an analysis of deconstruction regarding law and justice see Jacques Derrida, 'Force of Law: The "Mystical Foundation of Authority"' in Drucilla Cornell and others (eds), *Deconstruction and the Possibility of Justice* (Routledge 1992) 3–677.

15 See Catherine Turner, 'Jacques Derrida: Deconstruction' (*Critical Legal Thinking*, 27 May 2016) <https://criticallegalthinking.com/2016/05/27/jacques-derrida-deconstruction/> accessed 26 August 2023.

16 Ibid.

17 Ibid.

18 Derrida, *Deconstruction in a Nutshell* (n 14) 9.

19 Turner (n 15).

20 For a more detailed introduction to Koskenniemi's argument on radical indeterminacy, see Jean-François Thibault, 'Martti Koskenniemi: Indeterminacy' (*Critical Legal Thinking*, 8 December 2017) <https://criticallegalthinking.com/2017/12/08/martti-koskenniemi-indeterminacy/> accessed 23 June 2023.

21 Martti Koskenniemi, *From Apology to Utopia: The Structure of International Legal Argument. Reissue with a New Epilogue* (CUP 2006) 591.

question of which position prevails is not a question of sound legal argument or correct legal method but of politics.[22] This critique of the distinction between law and politics is what critical approaches to international law share with Legal Realism. Martti Koskenniemi, who, together with David Kennedy,[23] has been the main figure in articulating, defending, and popularising this position, argues in his famous work *From Apology to Utopia* that 'international law is singularly useless as a means for justifying or criticizing international behaviour'.[24] The reason for international law's radical indeterminacy, in Koskenniemi's account, is its fundamentally and irresolvably contradictory nature, which causes international legal arguments to oscillate between the poles of concreteness and normativity, apology and utopia.[25] Concreteness means that the law's content has to be verified 'not against some political principle but by reference to the concrete behaviour, will and interest of the States'.[26] Simultaneously, the law has to be normative in the sense that it has to be 'opposable to State policy'.[27] The contradiction inherent in the need for both normativity and concreteness leads to constant oscillations between these positions. To seem coherent, individual arguments have to stress either normativity or concreteness. In doing so, however, they become vulnerable to valid criticism from the opposing perspective. 'The choice of solution is dependent on an ultimately arbitrary choice to stop the criticisms at one point instead of another'.[28] Koskenniemi highlights, however, that even though it is possible to justify any kind of practice in terms of international legal argument, in practice, it is not arbitrary at all which actions are justified and which ones are condemned. This is due to what Koskenniemi calls 'structural bias'.[29]

Even though they do not all adopt Koskenniemi's linguistic analysis of international law and differ from Koskenniemi in many other aspects, one way of characterising the other critical approaches to international law, which will be presented in the following sub-chapters, is that they offer focused accounts on specific 'structural biases' of international law. Feminist and queer theory approaches critique international law's bias favouring and centring cis men, while Third World Approaches focus on how international law is structured in a way that favours the Global North, thereby harming the Global South. Marxist approaches offer an entirely different view on international law's contradictory nature and oppressive structure. They do, however, share the view that international law produces and favours the status quo with all its exploitation and violence. Further premises will be laid out in the respective sections.

---

22 Martti Koskenniemi, 'The Politics of International Law' (1990) 1 EJIL 4–32.

23 See e.g. David Kennedy, *International Legal Structures* (Nomos 1987).

24 Martti Koskenniemi, *From Apology to Utopia: The Structure of International Legal Argument. Reissue with a New Epilogue* (CUP 2006) 67.

25 Ibid 58.

26 Ibid.

27 Ibid.

28 Ibid 67.

29 Ibid 605–606.

E. CONCLUSION

The approaches presented in this chapter offer different ways of thinking about international law. Any way of engaging with international law presupposes doing so using a specific lens or approach. This is true even and especially for the traditional doctrinal approach, even though this approach is rarely made explicit. The following sections present positivism, Third World Approaches to International Law, feminist and queer theory, and Marxist approaches to international law in more detail.

BOX 3.3 Further Readings

Further Readings

- A Bianchi, *International Law Theories: An Inquiry Into Different Ways of Thinking* (OUP 2016)

- A Orford and F Hoffmann (eds), *The Oxford Handbook of the Theory of International Law* (OUP 2016)

---

§ § §

§ 3.1 POSITIVISM

BAŞAK ETKİN AND ALEX GREEN

BOX 3.1.1 Required Knowledge and Learning Objectives

Required knowledge: History of International Law; Approaches

Learning objectives: Understanding analytical and normative legal positivism and their differences from international legal positivism; identifying the major critiques of positivism.

A. INTRODUCTION

One of the more influential theories in contemporary legal theory, positivism is often treated as a catch-all term within international legal scholarship. In order to identify its different uses, this section will first discuss 'analytical' positivism as it appears in general legal theory, and then 'normative' positivism, its most common version in international law. Then, we will focus on the critique of positivism by canvassing three reasons why one might adopt a non-positivist approach.

B. POSITIVISM AS METHOD AND IDEOLOGY

Legal positivism is a theory about law determination. Law determination concerns what it means for the content of the law to be 'fixed' or 'made what it is' (e.g. the threat or use of force within international relations is unlawful because art. 2.4 of the UN Charter forbids both). Legal positivism asserts that 'legal facts' (i.e. facts about the existence and content of the law as it currently exists) are determined by 'social facts' alone, and that all law is posited/positive. Social facts, in this sense, are value-neutral descriptions of social behaviour, such as the fact that people take their hats off when entering a church. Within the framework of positivism, the social facts relevant to the existence and content of law are those recognised as being relevant by the officials of a legal system (the 'social thesis'). Legal positivism first emerged as a reaction to 'natural law' theories in the 18th century. Its roots within Anglophone legal scholarship are in the works of Jeremy Bentham (1748–1832),[30] who sought to both criticise and discredit natural law theories. 'Analytical legal positivism' (the view that positivism is the correct theory of law on logical or conceptual grounds) is and has been one of the more

---

30 Jeremy Bentham, *Of Laws in General* (Unpublished Manuscript, HLA Hart ed) (Athlone Press 1970); Jeremy Bentham, *An Introduction to the Principles of Morals and Legislation* (first published 1789, JH Burns and HLA Hart eds) (OUP 1996).

influential modern legal theories as far as international law is concerned, to the extent
that some scholars will often misuse 'positivism' to describe all 'mainstream' doctrinal
approaches to international law.[31]

I. ANALYTICAL POSITIVISM

As their main point of convergence, all legal positivists agree upon the 'separability
thesis', which holds that law and morality are not necessarily linked. According to
positivists, it is the separation of law and morality that makes criticising the content
of law possible. However, to what degree law and morality are separated is a point of
contention between inclusive (soft) and exclusive (hard) positivists. Inclusive positivists
allow for moral elements to be included directly or indirectly in the rule of recognition:
the 'master rule' of any legal order, which provides that order with its criteria for
legal validity. Exclusive legal positivists, on the other hand, reject any moral elements
entering the rule of recognition. Both sides of the argument agree that when the rule of
recognition does not give a clear answer to the question 'What is the law?', courts must
either create new law or else simply state the answer to be undetermined.[32]

Within the anglosphere, analytical positivism was first popularised by John
Austin[33] (1790–1859), who developed the 'command theory', the notion that law
consists of 'orders backed by threats'. Here, 'orders' represent the command of a
sovereign whose will is habitually obeyed and disobedience to whom is sanctioned by
a 'threat'.

HLA Hart (1907–1992), an inclusive legal positivist and a prominent critic of
Austin, offered a comprehensive critique of the command theory in his influential
book *The Concept of Law*.[34] Hart's arguments demonstrated three main issues with
command theory: it cannot account for customary law,[35] not all laws command or
prohibit specific actions,[36] and it is impossible in virtually all jurisdictions to identify
sovereigns with unlimited law-making powers.[37] Hart proposed an alternative account
of law, characterising it as 'a union of primary and secondary rules'.[38] Primary rules
establish obligations and confer rights to guide human conduct (e.g. it is forbidden
to cross the street when the red light is on). In some communities described by Hart
as 'primitive', law consists solely of these primary rules, but primary rules alone do
not make a legal system, which also requires secondary rules. Secondary rules are

---

31 Andrea Bianchi, *International Law Theories: An Inquiry into Different Ways of Thinking* (OUP 2016) 22–43.

32 Especially when facing extra-legal notions such as 'proportional' or 'reasonable'.

33 John Austin, *The Province of Jurisprudence Determined* (First Published 1832) (CUP 1995); John Austin, *Lectures on Jurisprudence, or the Philosophy of Positive Law* (First Published 1879) (R Campbell ed, 4th edn, Thoemmes Press 2002).

34 HLA Hart, *The Concept of Law* (2nd edn, OUP 1994). See also HLA Hart, 'Positivism and the Separation of Law and Morals' (1958) 71 Harvard Law Review 593.

35 Ibid 44–49.

36 Ibid 27–44.

37 Ibid 66–71.

38 Ibid 79–99.

those that serve as organisational meta-rules, or that govern primary rules. According to Hart, these secondary rules address three main shortcomings: (1) the uncertainty around which rules are valid in this system, (2) the static character of the rules, and (3) the inefficiency of the rules. These problems are solved by, respectively, (1) the rule of recognition, providing the criteria of legal validity and answering the question 'What is the law?'; (2) rules of change, establishing the procedures for introducing new primary rules, modifying existing ones, and abolishing old ones, answering the question 'How does the law change?'; and (3) rules of adjudication, determining who has the authority to adjudicate and how they must do so, answering the question 'How to implement the law?' All secondary rules can be classified under one of these three categories.

Hart is often presented in opposition to his continental counterpart Hans Kelsen (1881–1973), an Austrian jurist, who is more influential in civil law systems. Kelsen was closer to Austin's look than Hart, as in his view laws were norms addressed to officials and not at subjects – that is, they are norms to be applied by courts and other legal authorities in particular circumstances.[39] Another point of divergence between Hart and Kelsen is legal validity. For Hart, legal validity depends ultimately upon social recognition but, for Kelsen, legal validity was an entirely normative ('ought', not 'is') question. He argued that legal rules are valid only when they are validated by 'higher' norms, following prescribed procedure. This stepped construction (*Stufenbau*) culminates in the *Grundnorm* (English: basic norm), as Kelsen presented in *Reine Rechtslehre* (English: Pure Theory of Law).[40] The *Grundnorm* is the presupposed legal proposition at the foundation of any legal system: a simple fiction to uphold validity.[41]

Another prominent figure in legal positivism is the Israeli legal philosopher Joseph Raz (1939–2022). In *The Authority of Law: Essays on Law and Morality*,[42] Raz developed both the social thesis and the sources thesis (the view that law is identified only by reference to its social sources), asserting that law's existence and content cannot rely on moral facts. As an exclusive positivist, Raz further explored the normative aspects of legal systems in his *Practical Reasons and Norms*[43] and made the case for legal rules offering a practical justification for obedience, while excluding other justifications.

Most recently, Scott Shapiro's book *Legality* offers an alternative approach to legal positivism.[44] Shapiro's 'planning theory' of law contends that legal systems are compulsory planning organisations, while his 'moral aim thesis' suggests that law provides content-independent normative guidance to bypass moral disagreements.

---

39 Hans Kelsen, *General Theory of Law and State* (A Wedberg, trans., Harvard University Press 1945) 8–64.

40 Hans Kelsen, *Pure Theory of Law* (M Knight, trans., 2nd edn, University of California Press 1967).

41 Ibid 193–221.

42 Joseph Raz, *The Authority of Law: Essays on Law and Morality* (2nd edn, OUP 2009).

43 Joseph Raz, *Practical Reasons and Norms* (2nd edn, OUP 1999).

44 Scott Shapiro, *Legality* (Belknap Press 2011).

II. INTERNATIONAL LEGAL POSITIVISM AND NORMATIVE POSITIVISM

Normative positivism, traditionally more prevalent in international legal scholarship than purely analytical positivism, defends the idea that positivism is not only true, but also valuable. Normative positivism in this sense should not be confused with analytically normative approaches, such as Kelsen's. Jeremy Waldron argues that true normative positivism, which emphasises the value of reasoning about law in particular ways, is more faithful to positivism's origins, as Bentham's intention was not to separate law and morality conceptually but to coordinate conflict resolution between law and personal judgments about morality.[45] Lassa Oppenheim (1858–1919) also defended this point of view, suggesting that positivism was the best suited concept to advance particular moral and political values, as demonstrated by his advocacy of 'international society'.[46] Also adopted by Prosper Weil, this has been a particularly influential approach in international law.[47]

Some obsolete versions of analytical positivism might seem incompatible with international law, such as Austin's command theory, which might cast doubt upon its general veracity, given the lack of a sovereign in the international arena.[48] Another potential issue surrounds Kelsen's account of legal validity, which, through its appeal to successively higher levels of normative validation, appears to favour 'monism' (the view that the different branches of international law, and all domestic legal systems, constitute a unified regime).[49] International law is a highly fragmented domain with numerous regional and international regimes, and it is often difficult to establish hierarchically superior norms in each situation. However, modern legal positivism has evolved quite significantly and has developed sophisticated answers to questions that arise within international law.

International legal positivism (i.e. positivism as understood and upheld by international lawyers), much like its analytical counterpart explained above, is far from being a monolith, and in some ways it diverges from legal positivism.[50] Most notably, international legal positivism is, partially because of the weight given to State will in international law, often confused with consensualism or voluntarism.[51] However,

---

45 Jeremy Waldron, 'Normative (or Ethical) Positivism' in J Coleman (ed), *Hart's Postscript: Essays on the Postscript to 'The Concept of Law'* (OUP 2001).

46 Lassa Oppenheim, 'The Science of International Law: Its Task and Method' (1908) 2 AJIL 313; Benedict Kingsbury, 'Legal Positivism as Normative Politics: International Society, Balance of Power and Lassa Oppenheim's Positive International Law' (2002) 13 EJIL 401.

47 Prosper Weil, 'Towards Relative Normativity in International Law?' (1983) 77 AJIL 413.

48 On enforcement, see Quiroga-Villamarín, § 2.3, in this textbook.

49 On international law and domestic law, see Kunz, § 5, in this textbook.

50 Başak Etkin, 'Legal Positivism' in Christina Binder and others (eds), *Elgar Encyclopedia of Human Rights* (Edward Elgar 2022) 412–417; Jean d'Aspremont, 'International Legal Positivism' in Mortimer Sellers and Stephan Kirste (eds), *Encyclopedia of the Philosophy of Law and Social Philosophy* (Springer 2017); Jörg Kammerhofer, 'International Legal Positivism' in Anne Orford and Florian Hoffmann (eds), *The Oxford Handbook of the Theory of International Law* (OUP 2016) 407–426.

51 On consent, see González Hauck, § 2.2, in this textbook.

treaties are the only consent-based source of international law, assuming a strict
understanding of consent. Therefore, the rule of recognition of international law
does not include consent, and the sources thesis applied to international law does not
paint a consensualist picture.[52] While neo-voluntarists survive, many contemporary
international legal positivists separate the objective international legal order and the
subjective will of States.[53]

International law's compatibility with positivism is also called into question regarding
jus cogens (peremptory norms of general international law). These peremptory norms
are 'accepted and recognised . . . as a norm from which no derogation is permitted',
according to the 1969 Vienna Convention on the Law of Treaties. This means that
the idea of *jus cogens* does not necessarily breach the separability thesis, even though
one can identify its moral undertone once a series of examples are given: prohibitions
of genocide, torture, and slavery. Some exclusive legal positivists believe that
acknowledging the existence of *jus cogens* undermines the separability thesis, but this
problem can be solved by saying that the moral belief or judgment shared by States is a
social fact, and that is what makes a norm *jus cogens*, not its inherent moral value.[54]

C. CRITIQUES OF POSITIVISM

Legal positivism, as we have seen, is the view that the content of international legal
norms is made what it is (i.e. determined or 'fixed') by social facts alone. These social
facts typically relate to the 'pedigree' of those norms: their historical roots in particular
social sources, such as treaty texts or expressions of *opinio juris* (short for *opinio juris sive
necessitates*; in English: 'an opinion of law or necessity'). The inverse view, held by 'non-
positivists', is that international legal norms are necessarily determined *not only* by social
facts *but also* by facts about political morality,[55] which include moral values, genuine
normative principles, and practical reasons that govern how individuals should 'live
together', organise themselves, and behave in national and international society.

Consider an uncontroversial claim such as 'the 1969 Vienna Convention on the Law
of Treaties expresses true propositions of international law'. For non-positivists, this
will only be true insofar as the law-determining function of the Convention is morally
valuable in some way. This reliance upon political morality is also entailed by the beliefs
of normative positivists, who argue that *for moral reasons* international legal norms
must be identified via social facts alone. To continue with the example, a normative
positivist and a committed non-positivist might agree that the Vienna Convention helps
to fix international law because treaties have a coordinating function, which benefits
the stability and predictability of international relations. For both scholars, in other

---

52 On sources, see Eggett, Introduction to § 6, in this textbook.
53 Jörg Kammerhofer and Jean d'Aspremont (eds), *International Legal Positivism in a Post-Modern World* (CUP 2014).
54 Asif Hameed, 'Unravelling the Mystery of Jus Cogens in International Law' (2014) 84 BYBIL 2.
55 Hasan Dindjer, 'The New Legal Anti-Positivism' (2020) 26(3) Legal Theory 181.

words, treaty texts help to fix the content of international legal norms because there are compelling reasons why those texts *should* have this effect.[56]

What, then, distinguishes *non*-positivists from *normative* positivists? Non-positivists, whilst agreeing that facts about political morality partly determine the content of the law, *disagree* that moral reasoning should be excluded from the identification of legal norms.[57] Normative positivists, as noted above, argue that international law should be identified with recourse to social facts alone. According to their view, excluding moral considerations from legal reasoning tends to produce international stability, insofar as it avoids the proliferation of inter-State disputes. For the non-positivist, however, the exclusion of moral considerations from legal reasoning is wrongheaded, either because they believe normative positivists to be mistaken about the allegedly destabilising effects of moral reasoning,[58] or because they believe identifying international legal norms to be impossible on the basis of social facts alone. In what follows, we examine a few reasons why one might reject legal positivism wholesale and adopt a non-positivist approach instead.

I. INSUFFICIENT CONSENSUS

Central to the positivism of Hart, Raz, and others is the notion that legal validity turns on the existence of one or more rules of recognition. This claim can also be put in the following terms: within any given legal order, the norms of that order are ultimately determined in relation to the convergent behaviours and attitudes of law-applying officials. The social facts that such officials treat as being sources of law *become* sources *for that reason*.[59] Within international law, the relevant legal officials include State representatives and international adjudicative bodies, to name two examples. One possible reason for rejecting this view is that international law lacks sufficient convergence in official attitude or behaviour, meaning that no rule of recognition can exist within that legal order.[60] So, for instance, although it might be true that the text of a particular bilateral investment treaty[61] is binding on its State Parties because of their consent to be bound by that text, it nonetheless remains the case that the binding force of *pacta sunt servanda* (English: 'agreements must be kept')[62] requires explaining and there is little to no consensus at the international level as to

---

56 Alex Green, 'The Precarious Rationality of International Law: Critiquing the International Rule of Recognition' (2022) 22(8) German Law Journal 1613, 1626.

57 Ronald Dworkin, *Law's Empire* (Hart 1986) 114–130, 238–258. The distinction as presented here may elide non-positivism and 'soft' positivism, which accepts that moral reasoning can indeed form part of legal reasoning but only to the extent that moral norms are 'incorporated' within the law by norms that are themselves determined ultimately and exclusively by social facts. For more on soft positivism, see Eleni Mitrophanous, 'Soft Positivism' (1997) 17(4) Oxford Journal of Legal Studies 621.

58 Nahuel Maisley, 'Better to See International Law This Other Way: The Case Against International Normative Positivism' (2021) 12(2) Jurisprudence 151.

59 Green (n 56) 1619–1620.

60 Ibid 1627–1633.

61 On investment law, see Hankings-Evans, § 23.1, in this textbook.

62 On treaty law, see Fiskatoris and Svicevic, § 6.1, in this textbook.

the precise status of that principle (e.g. whether it is a general principle[63] of law or custom).[64]

II. 'RATIONAL' DETERMINATION AND SOCIAL FACTS

Another doubt about rules of recognition concerns the mechanics of how such rules supposedly 'fix' the content of international law. Even if the attitudes and behaviours of international legal officials are sufficiently convergent for rules of recognition to exist, it is unclear *why* these attitudes and behaviours should be treated as determining international law.[65] Why, in other words, should rules of recognition function in the way that positivists claim they do? According to a broadly Hartian view of legal validity, the cumulative attitudes and behaviours of legal officials fix to the content of international law *by definition*. However, given what many non-positivists consider to be the plausible assumption that there must be a *rational explanation* for why legal norms exist in the way and with the content that they do, it is not obvious *why* official attitudes and behaviour should be treated this way.[66] For example, if we are asked to explain why *pacta sunt servanda* holds within international relations, it seems highly unsatisfactory to answer, 'because the relevant people believe that it does'. This concern arises because the attitudes and practices of legal officials are social facts, with no necessary normative implications, and therefore cannot provide reasons why international law should be viewed one way rather than another.[67] Importantly, this critique is inapplicable to normative positivism, which holds that facts about political morality can explain why ultimate and exclusive recourse to a particular set of social facts should be observed.[68] Nonetheless, concerns about the 'rationality' of positivism remain applicable to its purely analytical variants.

BOX 3.1.2 Example: 'Rational' Determination and Social Facts – An Imaginary Tribunal

Imagine that an international tribunal ('the Tribunal') were to deliver judgment in an ongoing case according to an absurd method: they flip a coin. When doing so, imagine the Tribunal holds that immediately prior to their decision to proceed in this manner, all the usual rules of law determination – the application of treaty texts, customary practices, and so on – were undoubtedly relevant. But all that changed, the Tribunal says, the second before their decision to resort to coin flipping was made. Clearly, the Tribunal is wrong, but why?

---

63 On general principles of law, see Eggett, § 6.3, in this textbook.

64 On customary international law, see Stoica, § 6.2, in this textbook.

65 Mark Greenberg, 'Hartian Positivism and Normative Facts: How Facts Make Law II' in Scott Hershovitz (ed), *Exploring Law's Empire: The Jurisprudence of Ronald Dworkin* (OUP 2006) 273.

66 Mark Greenberg, 'How Facts Make Law' (2004) 10 Legal Theory 157, 164.

67 Greenberg (n 65).

68 Green (n 56) 1626–1627.

The State that lost the coin toss might object that the Tribunal wrongly ignored the relevant social facts. No prior item of State practice or expression of *opinio juris*, nor any academic or judicial commentary, mentioned that coin flipping would suddenly become the way to resolve complex legal disputes. The Tribunal, this losing State might say, is just ignoring international law. But the Tribunal could respond that this objection is mistaken because, at the moment when coin flipping became the correct way to resolve disputes, every legal rule that was previously applicable, including the 'old' rules for identifying international law, became irrelevant. They might also say that any current and continuing legal trends that suggest otherwise are simply mistakes: all legal orders, after all, contain at least some mistaken decisions. How can the losing State answer them?

Analytical legal positivists have no real answer to this question because everything our absurd imaginary tribunal says is logically consistent with the fact that international disputes used to be resolved in the 'normal way'. This holds because established legal trends, including the established attitudes and behaviour of legal officials, are social facts with no intrinsic normative implications of their own. By themselves such facts leave open the question of which standards they support and which standards they do not.

Once again, the point is not that such arguments are plausible: obviously they are ridiculous. The question is what makes them ridiculous. Non-positivists and normative positivists both have clear answers as to why: the Tribunal in this case is acting illegitimately and exceeding its authority by adopting a standard for the resolution of disputes that undermines the international rule of law. But that answer includes a value judgment – that the international rule of law is something worth promoting and defending – so it is unavailable to anyone who believes that legal argument is a matter of social facts alone.

III. THE 'POSITIVE' NON-POSITIVIST CASE

Finally, one might wish to appeal directly to political morality within legal reasoning for more positive reasons. In the first place, on the assumption that either of the first two critiques presented above are true, then reliance upon more than just social facts alone is inevitable when identifying international law. This being so, there is no point, or so the argument might go, in pretending otherwise. It is preferable to be transparent about one's reliance upon political morality, instead of obscuring it behind a positivist veneer. Alternatively, one might believe that direct recourse to moral considerations within legal reasoning would be conducive to the promotion of global justice, if for no other reason than it focuses attention on the most morally salient aspects of a given international dispute.[69] Considerations of this sort have motivated a range of contemporary non-positivist scholarship, both in relation to international law in general[70] and as regards more discrete regimes, such as the law of statehood,[71] international trade law,[72] or the law of human rights.[73]

D. CONCLUSION

This section has sought to summarise legal positivism and its different aspects, as well as its main critiques. However, positivists and non-positivists scholars have argued for centuries about the merits and faults of these theories, going far beyond international law. This section can merely be an introduction to these discussions, and interested students of international law can explore them further through the readings provided below.

BOX 3.1.3 Further Readings and Further Resources

Further Readings

- E Başak, 'Legal Positivism' in *Elgar Encyclopedia of Human Rights* (Edward Elgar 2022) 412

- HLA Hart, *The Concept of Law* (2nd edn, OUP 1994)

- H Kelsen, *Pure Theory of Law* (M Knight, trans., 2nd edn, University of California Press 1967)

- J Raz, *The Authority of Law: Essays on Law and Morality* (2nd edn, OUP 2009)

- R Dworkin, *Law's Empire* (Hart 1986)

Further Resources

- Başak Etkin and Kostia Gorobets, 'Episode 3: Adil Haque on International Law and Morality' (*Borderline Jurisprudence*, 30 April 2021) <https://podcasts.apple.com/gb/podcast/episode-3-adil-haque-on-international-law-and-morality/id1561575704?i=1000519437534> accessed 14 August 2023

---

69 John Tasioulas, 'Customary International Law and the Quest for Global Justice' in Amanda Perreau-Saussine and James Murphy (eds), *The Nature of Customary Law* (CUP 2007) 326–329.

70 Fernando Teson, *A Philosophy of International Law* (Perseus 1998); Ronald Dworkin, 'A New Philosophy for International Law' (2013) 41(1) Philosophy & Public Affairs 2.

71 Alex Green, *Statehood as Political Community: International Law and the Emergence of New States* (CUP 2023).

72 Oisin Suttle, *Distributive Justice and World Trade Law: A Political Theory of International Trade Regulation* (CUP 2018).

73 George Letsas, *A Theory of Interpretation of the European Convention on Human Rights* (OUP 2007).

- Başak Etkin and Kostia Gorobets, 'Special Episode "Joseph Raz and International Law: An Unfinished Journey" ' (*Borderline Jurisprudence*, 25 August 2022) <https://podcasts.apple.com/gb/podcast/special-episode-joseph-raz-and-international-law/id1561575704?i=1000577334459> accessed 14 August 2023

- Başak Etkin and Kostia Gorobets, 'Episode 15: Başak Çalı on Authority, Interpretivism, and Human Rights' (*Borderline Jurisprudence*, 4 November 2022) <https://podcasts.apple.com/gb/podcast/episode-15-ba%C5%9Fak-%C3%A7al%C4%B1-on-authority-interpretivism-and/id1561575704?i=1000585098146> accessed 14 August 2023

- Başak Etkin and Kostia Gorobets, 'Episode 19: Alex Green on Natural Law, Statehood and International Law' (*Borderline Jurisprudence*, 7 April 2023) <https://podcasts.apple.com/gb/podcast/episode-19-alex-green-on-natural-law-statehood-and/id1561575704?i=1000607861316> accessed 14 August 2023

§ § §

§ 3.2 THIRD WORLD APPROACHES TO INTERNATIONAL LAW

SUÉ GONZÁLEZ HAUCK

BOX 3.2.1 Required Knowledge and Learning Objectives

Required knowledge: Approaches

Learning objectives: Understanding the main tenets that unite TWAIL thought while getting a glimpse of the pluralities of TWAIL engagement with international law.

A. INTRODUCTION

This section introduces Third World Approaches to International Law (TWAIL), a movement within international legal scholarship trying to reshape international law in a way that centres people who have suffered the consequences of colonialism. The section introduces the notions of Third World and Global South and briefly recapitulates the trajectory of TWAIL as a movement. It delves deeper into some of the most influential analyses of how international law has been and continues to be shaped by colonialism and introduces some of the methodologies employed by TWAIL scholars.

B. POINTS OF DEPARTURE AND TWAIL TRAJECTORIES

I. INTRODUCTION TO THE CONCEPTS OF THE THIRD WORLD AND THE GLOBAL SOUTH

The term *Third World* originates from the time of the bipolar Cold War opposition between the First World, comprising the member States of the North Atlantic Treaty Organization (NATO), and the Second World, organised in the Warsaw Pact, in the second half of the 20th century. The Third World rallied not only around the idea of non-alignment but also around a shared history of being subjected to European colonialism. As a politically institutionalised project, the Third World took shape in several conferences, of which the Afro-Asian meetings in Bandung[74] in 1955 and in Cairo in 1961, the inaugural conference of the Non-Aligned Movement in Belgrade in 1961, and the Tricontinental Conference in Havana in 1966 stand out.[75] Today, the term *Third World*

---

74 For an in-depth engagement with the Bandung conference from a TWAIL perspective, see Luis Eslava and others (eds), *Bandung, Global History, and International Law: Critical Pasts and Pending Futures* (CUP 2017).

75 Vijay Prashad, *The Darker Nations: A People's History of the Third World* (New Press 2008).

has been partially replaced by the term *Global South*. This latter term bears less direct links to the Cold War bloc opposition and points instead at a critique of the kind of neoliberal globalisation that gained traction in the 1990s after the collapse of the Soviet Union.

II. TRAJECTORIES OF TWAIL AS A MOVEMENT

TWAIL as a rubric for an academic movement emerged in Harvard in 1996.[76] To acknowledge the intellectual tradition within which scholars who started calling themselves TWAIL scholars in the 1990s were working, Antony Anghie and BS Chimni coined the terms 'TWAIL I' and 'TWAIL II'. With the term TWAIL I, Anghie and Chimni referred to scholars like Georges Abi-Saab, F Garcia-Amador, RP Anand, Mohammed Bedjaoui, and Taslim O Elias, the first generation of international law scholars from newly independent States, who grappled with the exclusions that a Eurocentric and colonial international law had produced.[77] TWAIL II scholars started building on the legacy of the aforementioned scholars while further developing the analytical tools necessary to engage with international law from a Third World perspective. This meant taking a critical stance towards some of the main tenets of TWAIL I thought. TWAIL II scholars shifted their attention and normative commitment from the post-colonial State to the people living in the Third World, which allowed for analyses that could take into account the violence within post-colonial States as well as conflicts generated by class, caste, race, and gender.[78] Additionally, the shift from TWAIL I to TWAIL II meant a shift in general attitudes regarding the role of colonialism in international law. While TWAIL I scholars had treated colonialism as an aberration, which could be broken with and remedied by using and slightly modifying the techniques of the existing international legal order, TWAIL II scholars turned to the history and theory of international law to show how colonialism has been a central and defining feature of the formation of international law.[79]

C. TWAIL ENGAGEMENTS WITH THE COLONIAL LEGACIES OF INTERNATIONAL LAW

The main aspect that unites TWAIL scholarship despite the heterogeneity of the movement is the shared endeavour of grappling with international law's colonial legacies.[80] Several influential TWAIL authors, including Antony Anghie, Sundhya Pahuja, and, most recently, Ntina Tzouvala have examined the structure of international

---

76 Luis Eslava, 'TWAIL Coordinates' (*Critical Legal Thinking*, 2 April 2019) <https://criticallegalthinking. com/2019/04/02/twail-coordinates/> accessed 25 August 2023.

77 Antony Anghie and BS Chimni, 'Third World Approaches to International Law and Individual Responsibility in Internal Conflicts' (2003) Chinese JIL 77, 79 et seq.

78 Ibid 82.

79 Ibid 84.

80 Usha Natarajan and others, 'Introduction: TWAIL – On Praxis and the Intellectual' (2016) 37 Third World Quarterly 1946.

legal arguments through history to show how colonial and racist thought animates international law. Anghie argues that it is the dynamic of difference which generates the concepts and dichotomies that are fundamental to the formation of international law.[81] By *dynamic of difference*, Anghie refers to the conceptual tools positivist international lawyers deployed to, first, postulate a gap between the civilised European and the uncivilised non-European world and, second, to construct and employ techniques to bridge this gap (i.e. to civilise the uncivilised, to engage in the civilising mission).[82] The civilising mission, the idea that non-European peoples are savages, barbaric, backward, and violent, and that European peoples thus must educate, convert, redeem, develop, and pacify – in short, civilise – them has been used to justify continued intervention by European countries and other countries of the Global North (or the West) in Third World countries.[83]

Pahuja emphasises that international law constructs its own subjects and objects. It does not merely rely on a number of foundational notions, such as the State, the international, or the law. Nor does it merely apply to objects external to it, like the economy. Rather, through definitions that make categorial cuts between what is inside and outside certain categories, international law produces these categories even though it is deemed to be founded on them.[84] As the production of international law's foundational concepts has occurred through the colonial encounter and through the particular contexts of several imperial and post-imperial projects, the shape these concepts gained is determined by these very particular contexts. Simultaneously, however, international law posits the legal categories it produces as universally true. It is the interplay between international law's self-formation in (post)colonial contexts and international law's universalising gestures that produce what Pahuja calls international law's critical instability.[85] 'The instability is "critical" in both senses of the word, for it is simultaneously a threat to the reach and existence of international legality and an essential, generative dimension of it'.[86] Pahuja's work has focused on how the potential offered by this critical instability, a potential of pointing out international law's shortcomings in terms of its own aspirations towards universal justice and thus using international law in emancipatory ways, has been repeatedly contained by a ruling rationality.

A key dimension of that rationality is the position of development and economic growth vis-à-vis international law. The combination of the promise offered by international law's critical instability and the subsumption by the ruling rationality of efforts to take up that promise explains international law's dual quality, or its puzzling tendency to exhibit both imperial and counter-imperial dimensions.[87]

---

81 Antony Anghie, *Imperialism, Sovereignty and the Making of International Law* (CUP 2005) 9.
82 Ibid 37, 56.
83 Anghie and Chimni (n 77) 85.
84 Sundhya Pahuja, *Decolonising International Law: Development, Economic Growth and the Politics of Universality* (CUP 2011) 26.
85 Ibid 25 et seq.
86 Ibid 25; Cf. Peter Fitzpatrick and Patricia Tuitt, 'Introduction' in Peter Fitzpatrick and Patricia Tuitt (eds), *Critical Beings: Race, Nation and the Global Legal Subject* (Ashgate Press 2003) xi–xx, xi.
87 Pahuja (n 84) 25.

Ntina Tzouvala focuses on the standard of civilisation as a set of argumentative patterns, which oscillate between two modes of distinguishing between the West and the rest. The first is what she calls the 'logic of biology'. It is based on biological racism and the insurmountable barriers it erects against colonised and formerly colonised peoples gaining equal rights and obligations under international law. The second, the 'logic of improvement' in Tzouvala's terminology, replaces definitive exclusion with conditional inclusion, offering peoples of the Third World a prospect for gaining equal rights and obligations. The condition for gaining such equal recognition, as Tzouvala argues, has been capitalist transformation.[88]

D. TWAIL METHODOLOGIES

TWAIL scholars employ a variety of methodologies and engage in various inter- and intradisciplinary conversations. Among this variety of methodologies, approaches informed by critical legal history stand out, as well as approaches employing critical political economy. Additionally, TWAIL is cross-fertilised by approaches focusing on other systems of oppression that intersect with the system on which TWAIL scholarship mainly focuses (i.e. colonialism). Thus, TWAIL engagements with critical scholarship on race and racism as well as TWAIL feminisms deserve explicit attention.

The focus on history is one of the main characteristics of TWAIL scholarship. 'History matters', as Luis Eslava reaffirms as the first of five TWAIL coordinates, which characterise the movement.[89] The particular appreciation of history stems from TWAIL's aim of transforming international law. Understanding the past is a necessary prerequisite for transforming the present and the future.[90] TWAIL histories have pointed out the Eurocentric nature of existing histories of international law. They have focused on the co-constitution of international law and imperialism as well as on histories of Third World resistance, of alternative projects and movements.

Besides history, the second methodological orientation central to TWAIL is an engagement with political economy, especially Marxism, which will be treated elsewhere in this textbook in more detail.[91]

In recent years, TWAIL scholarship has started to engage more directly not only with colonialism but with racism as the structure that has served to legitimise and entrench colonial domination, thus engaging in an active dialogue with critical scholarship on race and racism.[92] Critical scholarship on race and racism, which includes but is not

---

88 Ntina Tzouvala, *Capitalism as Civilisation: A History of International Law* (CUP 2020) 1–7.

89 Eslava (n 76).

90 BS Chimni, 'The Past, Present and Future of International Law: A Critical Third World Approach' (2007) 8 Melbourne Journal of International Law 499, 500.

91 See Bagchi, § 3.4, in this textbook.

92 James T Gathii, 'Writing Race and Identity in a Global Context: What CRT and TWAIL Can Learn from Each Other' (2021) 67 UCLA Law Review 1610; E Tendayi Achiume and Aslı Ü Bâli, 'Race & Empire in

limited to Critical Race Theory, is mainly concerned with the social construction of races and racial hierarchies and with how these hierarchies have been used to justify exclusion, exploitation, and domination. Drawing also on critical scholarship on race and racism, TWAIL feminisms place additional emphasis not only on colonialism and racism but also on the patriarchy as systems of oppression.[93]

E. CONCLUSION

TWAIL scholarship is characterised by a dynamic and transformative perspective that challenges the Eurocentric foundations of international law. By centring the experiences of those who have borne the brunt of colonialism, TWAIL scholars illuminate the enduring impacts of historical injustices on the global legal landscape. The evolution from TWAIL I to TWAIL II signifies a shift in focus from post-colonial States to marginalised populations, acknowledging the complexities of class, caste, race, and gender within these contexts. Through critical examinations of international law's colonial legacies and its reliance on exclusionary concepts, TWAIL scholars have unveiled the intricate interplay between law, domination, and resistance. Employing historical analysis, political economy, as well as feminist and critical race analysis, TWAIL provides a multifaceted toolkit for understanding and reshaping international law toward greater justice.

BOX 3.2.2 Further Readings

Further Readings

- JT Gathii, 'The Promise of International Law: A Third World View (Including a TWAIL Bibliography 1996–2019 as an Appendix)' (2020) 114 Proceedings of the ASIL Annual Meeting 165

- R Kapur, *Gender, Alterity and Human Rights: Freedom in a Fishbowl* (Edward Elgar 2018)

- U Natarajan and others, 'Introduction: TWAIL – On Praxis and the Intellectual' (2016) 37 Third World Quarterly 1946

- A Anghie, *Imperialism, Sovereignty and the Making of International Law* (CUP 2005)

---

§ § §

International Law at the Intersection of TWAIL & CRT' (*TWAILR: Reflections*, 30 July 2021) <https://twailr. com/race-empire-in-international-law-at-the-intersection-of-twail-crt/> accessed 26 August 2023.

93 Ratna Kapur, *Gender, Alterity and Human Rights: Freedom in a Fishbowl* (Edward Elgar 2018); J Oloka-Onyango and Sylvia Tamale, ' "The Personal Is Political", or Why Women's Rights Are Indeed Human Rights: An African Perspective on International Feminism' (1995)17 HRQ 691; Vasuki Nesiah, 'Toward a Feminist Internationality: A Critique of US Feminist Legal Scholarship' (1993) 16 Harvard Women's Law Journal 189.

§ 3.3 FEMINIST AND QUEER THEORY
VERENA KAHL AND TAMSIN PHILLIPA PAIGE

BOX 3.3.1 Required Knowledge and Learning Objectives

Required knowledge: Approaches; History of International Law

Learning objectives: Understanding feminist and queer approaches and their particular relevance for public international law.

A. INTRODUCTION

This section introduces feminist and queer theories and their relevance for public international law. It departs from the male and heterosexual standard and a gender-biased international legal order as the common baseline for queer and feminist deconstruction. By pointing out the commonalities of feminist and queer theory, the contribution underscores the utility and necessity of a consolidated approach. Common terms and concepts are then connected to some of the manifestations and specific examples of feminist and queer theory in international law.

Feminist and queer approaches form part of a diverse field of schools of thought, which observe, analyse, and criticise public international law from a particular perspective and, coming from this specific theoretical foundation, seek to deconstruct its object of analysis. In this regard, feminist and queer theory aims at the deconstruction of a perceived neutral or natural international legal order that rests on a dominating masculine and heterosexual standard.[94]

Different approaches in feminist and queer theory share a common baseline: international law has been predominantly developed and shaped by (white, cis, heterosexual) men and has been built on the assumption that men and masculinity are the (societal) norm.[95] While this norm and public international law have been perceived as neutral, they neglect categories deviating from this standard and exclude them as 'the other'.[96] People who deviate from the norm relating to sex, gender, or sexuality have their perspectives and interests constantly ignored.[97] Public international law, like domestic law, exhibits a clear gender bias.[98] This gender bias, elevating the masculine to the norm, functions like a 'veiled representation and projection of a masculine which

---

94 Hilary Charlesworth and Christine Chinkin, *The Boundaries of International Law – A Feminist Analysis* (Manchester University Press 2000) 60.

95 Ibid ix, 2.

96 Ibid x.

97 Ibid 2–4, 60.

98 Ibid ix.

takes itself as the unquestioned norm, the ideal representative without any idea of the violence that this representational positioning does to its others'.[99]

B. COMMON TERMS AND CONCEPTS

I. SEX AND GENDER

Sex and gender are two interconnected concepts crucial to feminist and queer theory. *Sex* refers to biological differences between men and women construed as binary categories related to bodies.[100] *Gender* describes the cultural and social imprinting of distinctions made on the basis of sex.[101] Gender is seen as a fluid concept[102] and rejects biological determinism embodied in the concept of sex,[103] challenging the binary understanding of sex and opening up a broader range of identities beyond woman and man.[104] The complexity of gender identity arises from the 'dynamic relationship between the body and identity which gives rise to multiple possible alignments, which can change over time, or even from moment to moment'.[105] However, the same complexity applies to the oversimplified category of sex, as biology itself unveils the existence of a variety of sexes beyond the socially constructed dualism.[106] The idea that sex is a natural and immutable characteristic has been increasingly challenged[107] for having constructed, contingent and political dimensions.[108] Consequently, the distinction between sex and gender itself has been questioned.[109] Queer and feminist approaches have attempted to denaturalise sex and gender, assuming that they 'should both be understood as the effects of performative and reiterative gender norms . . . which materialise, naturalise, regulate, and discipline sexed bodies and identifications'.[110]

---

99 Elisabeth Grosz, *Volatile Bodies: Toward a Corporeal Feminism* (Indiana UP 1994) 188.

100 See e.g. Charlesworth and Chinkin (n 94) 3–4; Dianne Otto, 'Queering Gender [Identity] in International Law' (2015) 33 Nordic Journal of Human Rights 299, 300–302. For a predominantly biological understanding of sex, see *Corbett v Corbett* [1971] 2 All ER 33; Margaret Davies, 'Taking the Inside Out: Sex and Gender in the Legal Subject' in Ngaire Naffine and Rosemary J Owens (eds), *Sexing the Subject of Law* (LBC Information Service 1997) 25, 31; Alison Blunt and Jane Willis, *Dissident Geographies: An Introduction to Radical Ideas and Practice* (Pearson Education 2000) 92.

101 Joan W Scott, 'Gender: A Useful Category for Historical Analysis' (1986) 91 American Historical Review 1053, 1053 et seq.; Davies (n 100) 25, 31; Blunt and Willis (n 100) 92.

102 Gina Heathcote, *Feminist Dialogues on International Law: Success, Tensions, Futures* (OUP 2019) 3. See also Blunt and Willis (n 100) 93.

103 Otto (n 100) 299, 300; Scott (n 101) 1053, 1054.

104 Ibid 299, 300 f.

105 Ibid 299, 300.

106 Claire Ainsworth, 'Sex Redefined: The Idea of 2 Sexes Is Overly Simplistic' (*Scientific American*, 22 October 2018) <www.scientificamerican.com/article/sex-redefined-the-idea-of-2-sexes-is-overly-simplistic1/> accessed 25 August 2023.

107 See Davies (n 100) 25, 30 ff.

108 Cf. Ibid 25, 30 ff, articularly 32. See also Charlesworth and Chinkin (n 94) 4; Jane Flax, 'Postmodernism and Gender Relations in Feminist Theory' (1987) 12 Signs 621, 635 et seq.

109 Cf. Blunt and Willis (n 100) 93 ff.

110 Otto (n 100) 299, 300 et seq; cf. Judith Butler, *Gender Trouble: Feminism and the Subversion of Identity* (Routledge 1990) 25.

Despite the aim of inclusivity and diversity beyond traditional understandings of masculinity and femininity,[111] gender has often been used as a synonym for 'women',[112] including in public international law. Gender-based analyses have primarily focused on women, neglecting gender discrimination experienced by individuals with diverse gender identities.[113] Attempts to deconstruct the category of women in international law have not sufficiently challenged the rigidity and fixation of gender meanings at the international level.[114] For instance, the Convention on the Elimination of all forms of Discrimination Against Women (CEDAW), in its articles 1 and 5 in particular, fails to distinguish between sex and gender, reinforcing a dualistic perspective of men/women.[115] This perpetuates the male standard as the norm, upholding a gender binary and hierarchy even within a project aimed at endorsing the full humanity of women.[116] Such international protection mechanisms measuring women's experiences against the male standard harm women worldwide, particularly in the Global South,[117] and reinforce gender and cultural essentialism by defining women as 'victim subject'.[118] International law's predominant and persisting recognition of and holding on to dominant binary and oversimplified categories therefore ignores the many signs of gender and bodily diversity present across centuries, continents, and cultures.[119]

II. FEMINIST AND QUEER THEORY

1. Feminism and Feminist Theory

Despite controversies and disagreement within feminist thought, the common aim is to analyse, challenge, and change gendered power relations in all spheres of life to achieve human liberty for all genders.[120] Black, revolutionary feminists, such as bell hooks,[121]

---

111 Charlesworth and Chinkin (n 94) 3.

112 Cf. Scott (n 101) 1053, 1056.

113 Cf. Otto (n 100) 299, 300.

114 Cf. Brenda Cossman, 'Gender Performance, Sexual Subjects and International Law' (2002) 15 Canadian Journal of Law and Jurisprudence 281, 284.

115 See, inter alia, Darren Rosenblum, 'Unsex CEDAW, or What's Wrong with Women's Rights' (2011) 20(2) Columbia Journal of Gender and Law 98; Otto (n 100) 299, 302. See, by contrast, possible advantages of silence in form of non-definition of terms like 'gender' as described in Juliana Santos de Carvalho, 'The Powers of Silence: Making Sense of the Non-Definition of Gender in International Criminal Law' (2022) 35 LJIL 963–985.

116 Cf. Otto (n 100) 299, 302.

117 Cf. Ibid.

118 Ratna Kapur, 'The Tragedy of Victimisation Rhetoric: Resurrecting the "Native" Subject in International/Postcolonial Feminist Legal Politics' (2002) 15 Harvard Human Rights Journal 1.

119 Cf. Aoife M O'Connor and others, 'Transcending the Gender Binary under International Law: Advancing Health-Related Human Rights for Trans★ Populations' (2022) 50(3) The Journal of Law, Medicine & Ethics 409.

120 Blunt and Willis (n 100) 90; Flax (n 108) 621, 622; Charlesworth and Chinkin (n 94) 61; Miriam Schneir, *The Vintage Book of Historical Feminism* (Vintage 1996) xi.

121 bell hooks, *Ain't I a Woman: Black Women and Feminism* (South End Press 1981); bell hooks, *Feminist Theory: From Margin to Center* (South End Press 1984); bell hooks, *Feminism Is for Everybody: Passionate Politics* (Pluto Press 2000).

Barbara Smith,[122] Patricia Hill Collins,[123] and Kimberlé Crenshaw,[124] have contributed to a more inclusive (re)definition of feminism and feminist theory by emphasising intersectionality and diversity in experiences of discrimination. Indigenous feminism[125] highlights decolonisation, indigenous sovereignty, and indigenous women's rights within indigenous life and culture.[126] To embrace the diversity of feminist voices, Sandra Harding asks feminists to give up 'the goal of telling "one true story"', but instead to embrace 'the permanent partiality of feminist inquiry', thereby seeking 'a political and epistemological solidarity in our oppositions to the fiction of the naturalized, essentialized, uniquely "human" and to the distortions, perversions, exploitations, and subjugations perpetrated on behalf of this fiction'.[127]

2. Feminist Approaches to International Law

Feminist approaches to international law use feminist theory 'to show how the structures, processes, and methodologies of international law marginalize women by failing to take account of their lives or experiences'.[128] These approaches lift the veil of an international legal order perceived as neutral and objective and reveal its underlying male standard constructed as the 'norm' and the 'normal', which results in a power imbalance and hierarchy between men and women and materialises in the silence of international law regarding women's experiences and interests.[129] They demonstrate that international law is a 'thoroughly gendered system'.[130] According to Charlesworth and Chinkin, feminist analyses of international law fulfil two main tasks. First, they deconstruct the values underlying the international legal system, challenging their

---

122 Barbara Smith, 'Racism in Women's Studies' (1979) 5(1) Frontiers: A Journal of Women's Studies 48–49.

123 Margaret L Andersen and Patricia Hill Collins, *Race, Class and Gender: An Anthology* (10th edn, Wadsworth Cengage Learning 2020).

124 Kimberlé Crenshaw, 'Demarginalizing the Intersection of Race and Sex: A Black Feminist Critique of Antidiscrimination Doctrine, Feminist Theory and Antiracist Politics' (1989) University of Chicago Legal Forum 139–167.

125 Joyce A Green, *Making Space for Indigenous Feminism* (Fernwood Publication 2007); Cheryl Suzack and others, *Indigenous Women and Feminism: Politics, Activism, Culture* (UBC Press 2010); Aileen Moreton-Robinson, *Talkin' Up to the White Woman: Indigenous Women and Feminism* (University of Queensland Press 2002); Rosalva Aída Hernández Castillo, 'The Emergence of Indigenous Feminism in Latin America' (2010) 35(3) Signs 539–545; Heidi Sinevaara-Niskanen, 'Crossings of Indigenousness, Feminism, and Gender' (2010) 18(3) NORA – Nordic Journal of Feminist and Gender Research 217–221; Rebecca Tsosie, 'Indigenous Women and International Human Rights Law: The Challenges of Colonialism, Cultural Survival, and Self-Determination' (2010) 15(1) UCLA Journal of International Law and Foreign Affairs 187–237.

126 Celeste Liddle, 'Intersectionality and Indigenous Feminism: An Aboriginal Woman's Perspective' (*The Postcolonialist*, 25 June 2014) <http://postcolonialist.com/civil-discourse/intersectionality-indigenous-feminism-aboriginal-womans-perspective/> accessed 25 August 2023.

127 Sandra Harding, *The Science Question in Feminism* (Cornell University Press 1986) 193.

128 Christine Chinkin, 'Feminism, Approach to International Law' (*Max Planck Encyclopedia of International Law*, October 2010) <https://opil.ouplaw.com/view/10.1093/law:epil/9780199231690/law-9780199231690-e701> accessed 25 August 2023.

129 Charlesworth and Chinkin (n 94) 60.

130 Hilary Charlesworth, Christine Chinkin, and Shelley Wright, 'Feminist Approaches to International Law' (1991) 85 AJIL 613, 615.

claim to rationality and objectivity.[131] Second, feminist approaches seek to reconstruct international law by redefining its core concepts 'in a way that they do not support or reinforce the domination of women by men'.[132] Importantly, voices in feminist approaches to international law have diversified, with many leading icons stemming from the Global South.[133]

3. Queerness and Queer Theory

Queerness has a complex history as a term used to pejoratively label those who deviate from societal norms and expectations of heterosexuality.[134] The term has been reclaimed by the QUILTBAG+ community (Queer, Unsure, Intersex, Lesbian, Trans★, Bisexual, Asexual/Aromantic/Agender, Gay, plus others outside these categories and heteronormative classification) as both a generalised shorthand for the community at large and an individualised identity for those within the community who do not feel comfortable with the constraints of more specific identity descriptors.[135] In this way, queer acts as a generalised or collective (descriptive) noun but also an individualised (identity) noun. Queer also operates as a verb, in that 'queering' denotes the act of questioning and interrogating underlying (heteronormative) assumptions that underpin the subject of enquiry and the normative approach to the thing that is being queered.[136] Technically, *queer* can also be used as an adjective; however, as the adjective use of queer is irreversibly tied to the pejorative use, it has rightly fallen out of common vernacular.

4. Queer Approaches to International Law

Queer approaches to international law seek to include experiences and identities outside the cis/het standard, particularly illustrated in the granting of equal rights and prohibition of discrimination on the basis of sexuality and sexual identity.[137] In addition, Dianne Otto understands 'queering of international law' more broadly than traditional approaches of norm inclusion.[138] In this sense, queer theory fundamentally

---

131 Cf. Charlesworth and Chinkin (n 94) 60.

132 Ibid 61.

133 Ratna Kapur, *Gender, Alterity and Human Rights: Freedom in a Fishbowl* (Edward Elgar 2018); Adrien Wing, 'Global Critical Race Feminism Post 9–11: Afghanistan' (2002) 10 Washington University Journal of Law and Policy (2002) 19; J Oloka-Onyango and Sylvia Tamale, '"The Personal Is Political", or Why Women's Rights Are Indeed Human Rights: An African Perspective on International Feminism' (1995) 17(4) HRQ 691; Rosalva Aída Hernández Castillo, 'The Emergence of Indigenous Feminism in Latin America' (2010) 35(3) Signs 539.

134 Annamarie Jagose, *Queer Theory: An Introduction* (Melbourne University 2013) 9.

135 Ibid; Wayne Morgan, 'Queer Law: Identity, Culture, Diversity, Law' (1995) 5 Australasian Gay and Lesbian Law Journal 1, 5; Gabrielle Simm, 'Queering CEDAW? Sexual Orientation, Gender Identity and Expression and Sex Characteristics (SOGIESC) in International Human Rights Law' (2020) 29 Griffith Law Review 374, 376.

136 Simm (n 135).

137 Dianne Otto, '"Taking a Break" from "Normal": Thinking Queer in the Context of International Law' (2007) 101 Proceedings of the ASIL Annual Meeting 119, 119 et seq.

138 Ibid 120.

challenges and criticises the regime of what is considered as 'normal' with regard to human sexuality.[139] In the words of Otto, queer theory to international law is '"taking a break" from the politics of hetero-normative injury, and imagines human sexuality as much more diverse and shifting'.[140] Quite similar to the deconstructionist approach of feminism, queer theory makes 'visible the [hetero]sexual ordering that is taken for granted as an underpinning of the "normal" system of international law' and discloses heterosexuality as the 'basic model for all dominant systems of societal relations'.[141] When heterosexuality is seen as the preferred, natural, normal form of sexuality, it not only shapes how society considers '"normal" interpersonal and familial relationships', but it also forms the (presumed) basis for our perception of community in general and thereby dictates our understanding of 'all forms of "normal" community, including that encompassed by the "normal" nation-state, international law's primary subject'.[142] In essence, queer approaches to international law unveil how international law 'provides a conduit for the micromanagement and "disciplining" of everyday lives, including sexual pleasure, despite its many rules purporting to leave these matters in the domestic realm of jurisdiction'.[143]

5. Frictions and Intersections of Feminist and Queer Theory to International Law

There is much to be said for a joint presentation of feminist and queer approaches to international law. Especially considering the open, fluid concept of gender and the need to break down and overcome the heteronormative binary of both sex and gender, a critical analysis of international law from a one-sided feminist or queer perspective would remain patchy and incomplete. Still, constructive dialogues between feminist and queer theory have been the exception. According to Gina Heathcote, this is due to the fact that 'mainstream feminist approaches to international law are yet to incorporate queer and trans scholarship into feminist accounts'[144] and have mostly ignored the dialogue commenced by queer approaches.[145] Instead, feminist approaches have – intentionally or unintentionally, for pragmatic or other reasons[146] – largely built on the heteronormativity and cisgenderism inherent in the structures they seek to criticise, resulting in the 'invisibility of individuals who do not neatly fit into the normalized gender binary' and reproducing the 'fear of undermining heteronormative social structures'.[147] In contrast, moving beyond dualism and asymmetry would allow 'to tell a story

---

139 Ibid.
140 Ibid.
141 Ibid.
142 Ibid.
143 Ibid.
144 Heathcote (n 102) 21.
145 Cf. Ibid.
146 Otto (n 100) 299, 306.
147 Tamsin Phillipa Paige, 'The Maintenance of ~~International Peace and Security~~ Heteronormativity' in Dianne Otto (ed), *Queering International Law: Possibilities, Alliances, Complicities, Risks* (Routledge 2018) 91, 107.

of marginality that has not yet been told',[148] drawing an inclusive picture of discriminatory experiences without 'losing the precarious spaces that have been carved out for addressing women's human rights abuses'.[149]

III. STRUCTURAL DISCRIMINATION

During the last two decades, international human rights institutions have increasingly referred to the phenomenon of structural injustices through the lens of the concept of structural discrimination.[150] Structural discrimination refers to discrimination rooted in grown and therefore pre-existing structures and inequalities of society.[151] It occurs when the rules, norms, and policies of a society's major(ity) institutions impose and produce disproportionately disadvantageous and unjust outcomes for the members of certain salient social groups.[152] Discrimination is thereby introduced into often unconscious societal routines and patterns of attitudes and behaviour that create and maintain discriminatory practice,[153] which are largely perceived as neutral, because their negative outcome – the differential and/or harmful effect on certain groups – is usually not intended.[154] As Pincus highlights, the 'key element in structural discrimination is not the intent but the effect of keeping minority groups in a subordinate position'.[155] In the context of gender inequality, MacKinnon has described structural discrimination as 'the systematic relegation of an entire group of people to a condition of inferiority'.[156] Structural discrimination is inscribed in

---

148 Cossman (n 114) 281, 289.

149 Otto (n 100) 299, 309.

150 See, inter alia, UN Economic and Social Council, Integration of the human rights of women and a gender perspective: violence against women, Report of the Special Rapporteur on violence against women, its causes and consequences, Yakin Ertürk, Mission to Mexico, 13 January 2006, UN Doc. E/CN.4/2006/61/ Add.4, para 13; IACtHR, Case of González and others ('Cotton Field') v. Mexico (Preliminary Objection, Merits, Reparations and Costs), Judgment, 16 November 2009, Series C No. 205, paras 134, 450; Committee on the Elimination of Racial Discrimination, General Recommendation No. 34, Racial discrimination against people of African descent, 30 September 2011, UN Doc. CERD/C/GC/34, paras 5–7; Committee on the Elimination of Discrimination against Women, General Recommendation No. 30 on women in conflict prevention, conflict and post-conflict situations, 18 October 2013, UN Doc. CEDAW/C/GC/30, paras 77, 79.

151 See Elisabeth Veronika Henn, *International Human Rights Law and Structural Discrimination: The Example of Violence against Women* (Springer 2018) 1.

152 Cf. Andrew Altman, 'Discrimination' (*Standford Encyclopedia of Philosophy*, First Published 1 February 2011, last substantive revision 20 April 2020) <https://plato.stanford.edu/entries/discrimination/#OrgInsStrDis> accessed 9 August 2022. See also Fred L Pincus, 'From Individual to Structural Discrimination' in Fred L Pincus and Howard J Ehrlich (eds), *Race and Ethnic Conflict: Contending Views on Prejudice, Discrimination, and Ethnoviolence* (2nd edn, Routledge 2018) 122.

153 See Mirjana Najcevska, 'Structural Discrimination – Definition, Approaches and Trends' (2010) <www.ohchr.org/EN/Issues/Racism/IntergovWG/Pages/Session8.aspx> accessed 25 August 2023.

154 See Fred L Pincus, 'From Individual to Structural Discrimination' in Fred L Pincus and Howard J Ehrlich (eds), *Race and Ethnic Conflict: Contending Views on Prejudice, Discrimination, and Ethnoviolence* (2nd edn, Routledge 2018) 122.

155 Ibid.

156 Catharine A McKinnon, *Feminism Unmodified: Discourse on Life and Law* (Harvard University Press 1987) 41.

international law, resulting in the invisibility and underrepresentation of non-cis male individuals in institutions,[157] structural gender-based violence,[158] or persisting racism in international law (education).[159]

IV. INTERSECTIONALITY

While bell hooks had already described interlocking webs of oppression beforehand,[160] it was Kimberlé Crenshaw who coined and finally introduced the concept of intersectionality into feminist theory. Her work 'Demarginalizing the Intersection of Race and Sex: A Black Feminist Critique of Antidiscrimination Doctrine, Feminist Theory and Antiracist Politics' can be read as a critique of both feminist and anti-racist movements for their one-sided focus on the most privileged members of the respective group.[161] According to Crenshaw, the 'single-axis analysis' results in anti-racist strategies that tend to focus on gender privileged persons (men) and a women's movement which puts a spotlight on class-privileged women associated with a certain race,[162] namely white, Western, heterosexual, middle- and upper-class women.[163] This leads to the marginalisation of 'those who are multiply burdened and obscures claims that cannot be understood as resulting from discrete sources of discrimination'.[164] Building upon this, intersectionality has been commonly defined as 'the complex, cumulative way in

---

157 Stéphanie Hennette Vauchez, 'Gender Balance in International Adjudicatory Bodies' (*Max Planck Encyclopedia of International Law*, July 2019) <https://opil.ouplaw.com/display/10.1093/law-mpeipro/e2699.013.2699/law-mpeipro-e2699> accessed 25 August 2023; Priya Pillai, 'Women in International Law: A Vanishing Act?' (*Opinio Juris*, 3 December 2018) <http://opiniojuris.org/2018/12/03/women-in-international-law-a-vanishing-act/> accessed 25 August 2023; Josephine Jarpa Dawuni, 'Why the International Law Commission Must Address Its Gender and Geography Diversity Problem' (*Opinio Juris*, 1 November 2021) <https://opiniojuris.org/2021/11/01/why-the-international-law-commission-must-address-its-gender-and-geography-diversity-problem/> accessed 25 August 2023.

158 Claudia Card, 'Rape as a Weapon of War' (1996) 11(4) Women and Violence 5; Henn (n 151) particularly 13–44; Misty Farquhar, 'Structural Violence in the Queer Community: A Comparative Analysis of International Human Rights Protections for LGBTIQ+ People' (2021) 13(12) Inquiries Journal; Natalie E Serra, 'Queering International Human Rights: LGBT Access to Domestic Violence Remedies' (2013) 21(3) Journal of Gender, Social Policy & the Law 583; International Criminal Court, 'Policy on the Crime of Gender Persecution' (7 December 2022) <www.icc-cpi.int/sites/default/files/2022-12/2022-12-07-Policy-on-the-Crime-of-Gender-Persecution.pdf>.

159 E Tendayi Achiume and James Thuo Gathii, 'Introduction to the Symposium on Race, Racism, and International Law' (2023) 117 AJIL Unbound 26; Mohsen Al Attar, '"I Can't Breathe": Confronting the Racism of International Law' (*AfroconomicsLAW*, 2 October 2020) <www.afronomicslaw.org/2020/10/02/i-cant-breathe-confronting-the-racism-of-international-law/>; Anna Spain Bradley, 'International Law's Racism Problem' (*Opinio Juris*, 4 September 2019) <http://opiniojuris.org/2019/09/04/international-laws-racism-problem/>

160 hooks (n 121) 5.

161 Crenshaw (n 124) 139, 140.

162 It is important to underscore at this point that 'race' – just as the terms 'sex' and 'gender' – is a socially constructed concept. See, for example, Ian F Haney López, 'The Social Construction of Race' (1994) 29 Harvard Civil Rights–Civil Liberties Law Review 1.

163 Crenshaw (n 124) 139, 140; Chandra Talpade Mohanty, 'Under Western Eyes: Feminist Scholarship and Colonial Discourses' in Chandra Talpade Mohanty and others (eds), *Third World Women and the Politics of Feminism* (Indiana University Press 1991) 51, 70.

164 Crenshaw (n 124) 139, 140.

which the effects of multiple forms of discrimination . . . combine, overlap, or intersect especially in the experiences of marginalized individuals or groups'.[165]

The Beijing Declaration as an outcome of the Fourth World Conference of Women in 1995 can be seen as an early beginning of intersectionality feeding into international law.[166] Both concept and terminology of intersectionality found their way into international documents particularly at the intersection of gender and race,[167] examples of which are the adoption of the Durban Declaration and Action Programme of the World Conference Against Racism, Racial Discrimination, Xenophobia Related Intolerance in 2001[168] and General Recommendation No. 25 of the Committee on the Elimination of Racial Discrimination.[169] CEDAW has endorsed intersectionality in several of its General Recommendations.[170] Intersectionality has also come to play a vital role in the adjudication of international human rights law, particularly with regard to violations of anti-discrimination norms, and has consequently found its way into the jurisprudence of regional human rights monitoring bodies.[171]

C. PROBLEMS THAT FEMINIST AND QUEER THEORY SEEKS TO ADDRESS

I. FEMINIST ENGAGEMENT WITH INTERNATIONAL LAW

There is a valid argument that the drafting and entry into force of CEDAW in 1979 and 1981 marked the beginning of feminist approaches to international law.[172] However, feminist scholarship only gained traction a decade later with the foundational article

---

165 Merriam-Webster Dictionary, 'Intersectionality' <www.merriam-webster.com/dictionary/intersectionality> accessed 9 August 2022.

166 Even though the term 'intersectionality' was not explicitly mentioned in the declaration, the corresponding plan for action stated 'that women face barriers to full equality and advancement because of such factors as their race, age, language, ethnicity, culture, religion or disability, because they are indigenous women or because of other status'. Beijing Declaration and Platform for Action, adopted at the Fourth World Conference on Women, 27 October 1995, Platform for Action, para 45.

167 See Abigail B Bakan and Yasmeen Abu-Laban, 'Intersectionality and the United Nations World Conference Against Racism' (2017) 38(1) Atlantis 220, particularly 221 and 231.

168 Durban Declaration and Programme of Action, adopted at the World Conference Against Racism, Racial Discrimination, Xenophobia and Related Intolerance, 8 September 2001, Programme of Action para 54(a). See also a detailed discussion in Abigail B Bakan and Yasmeen Abu-Laban, 'Intersectionality and the United Nations World Conference Against Racism' (2017) 38(1) Atlantis 220, particularly 221 and 231.

169 CERD, General Recommendation XXV on gender-related dimensions of racial discrimination, 20 March 2000, particularly para 3.

170 See, for example, CEDAW, General Recommendation No. 28 on the core obligations of States parties under article 2 of the Convention on the Elimination of All Forms of Discrimination against Women, 16 December 2010, para 18, and CEDAW, General recommendation No. 25, on article 4, paragraph 1, of the Convention on the Elimination of All Forms of Discrimination against Women, on temporary special measures, 2004, para 12.

171 Johanna Bond, *Global Intersectionality and Contemporary Human Rights* (Oxford University Press 2021), particularly chapter 4 on 'Intersectionality and Human Rights within Regional Human Rights Systems' 78–129.

172 Convention on the Elimination of All Forms of Discrimination against Women 1979 (1249 UNTS 13).

'Feminist Approaches to International Law' by Charlesworth, Chinkin, and Wright.[173] While this development coincided with third wave feminism (most distinctively characterised by the work of Butler and incorporating intersectionality following Kimberlé Crenshaw's work),[174] the approach taken by feminist international law academics was shaped by their education in second wave feminism. This can be seen in the construction of CEDAW and in how Charlesworth et al. define the goal of feminism as being 'to capture the reality of women's experience or gender inequality'.[175]

This tendency of the feminist tradition in international law to follow second wave feminism, which is much more grounded in biological determinism and the gender binary than third wave feminism, is evident in the UN's gender mainstreaming programs[176] and the Gender Legislative Index,[177] which focus on cisgender women as the subject of arguments for equality, rather than addressing the cultural social structures that perpetuate inequality, such as the heteropatriarchy.

The outcome of this focus on women as subjects rather than on social structures has led to two separate approaches within feminist interventions in international law. The first embraces Crenshaw's call for intersectionality in its analysis[178] and the fact that women's experiences of the impacts of law are shaped by various intersecting forms of marginalisation, including race, class, sexuality, and disability.[179] The second approach, often criticised as 'White Feminism', embraces Catharine MacKinnon's call for considering women as a single unified and universal political category that disregards questions of race, class, and so on when advocating for equality.[180] Proponents of this approach believe that it creates a stronger argument for women's equality, but ignore that the focus of the approach is often the interests of white, straight, Western women.

Feminist interventions into international law were successful in getting International Criminal Law and International Humanitarian Law to treat armed conflict sexual violence as a crime against the victim's personhood rather than military discipline as it had historically been treated.[181] This success led to the UN Security Council's Women,

---

173 Hilary Charlesworth, Christine Chinkin, and Shelly Wright, 'Feminist Approaches to International Law' (1991) 85 AJIL 613.

174 Butler (n 110); Crenshaw (n 124) 139.

175 Hilary Charlesworth, Christine Chinkin, and Shelley Wright, 'Feminist Approaches to International Law' (1991) 85 AJIL 613.

176 Tamsin Phillipa Paige and Joanne Stagg, 'Well-Intentioned But Missing the Point: The Australian Defence Force Approach to Addressing Conflict-Based Sexual Violence' (2020) 29 Griffith Law Review 468, 471–472.

177 Ramona Vijeyarasa, 'What Is Gender-Responsive Legislation? Using International Law to Establish Benchmarks for Labour, Reproductive Health and Tax Laws That Work for Women' (2020) 29 Griffith Law Review 334.

178 Crenshaw (n 124) 139.

179 Heathcote (n 102) 21.

180 Catharine MacKinnon, 'From Practice to Theory, or What Is a White Woman Anyway?' (1991) 4 Yale Journal of Law and Feminism 13, 20–22.

181 *The Prosecutor v Jean-Paul Akayesu (Trial Judgement)* [1998] International Criminal Tribunal for Rwanda ICTR-96-4-T; *Prosecutor v Anto Furundžija (Appeals Chamber Judgement)* [2000] International Criminal Tribunal for

Peace, and Security agenda and the expansion of UN Women as a sub-agency of the UN.[182]

II. HOW QUEER THEORY IN INTERNATIONAL LAW DIFFERS FROM FEMINISM

Queer theory grew out of third wave feminism, in particular the work of Butler and Sedgwick,[183] with a much less cohesive equality agenda than feminism. Queer theory is inherently broad (and is mostly inclusive but not without its problems) but tends to focus upon QUILTBAG+ subjects and to explore advocating for equality through an intersectional lens. Queer theory, at its core, is an embrace of curiosity and questioning – generally from a framework of understanding that the law and normative assumptions that are brought to law and social practice are culturally dependent social constructions rather than natural and inevitable.[184] The easiest space to see this distinction between feminist approaches to international law and queer theory approaches to international law is in examination of the project of gender mainstreaming within UN projects. Feminist approaches to international law, while often critical of the details, have treated this introduction of idea and process into every UN body (and numerous State foreign affairs and defence departments) as a net good. Queer theory approaches to international law, while acknowledging the improvements that adding gender mainstreaming has produced, have heavily critiqued how the process of gender mainstreaming has led to the use of gender being an euphemism for women, how it has normalised and reinforced the (white) cis/het masculine subject as the un-gendered normal to which all other expressions of humanity must be compared, and how the process has reproduced bio-essentialist views of sex and gender along regressive heteronormative lines within international legal discourse.

There is a tension created within feminist and queer theory approaches to international law where the perfect can be the enemy of the good. This tension is often referred to as the 'double-bind'.[185] This idea of the double-bind broadly posits that advocates for change and equality suffer pressures from those outside governmental institutions not to compromise in questions of equality, while also suffering pressures from within the institution that require accepting an improvement that is less than ideal

---

the Former Yugoslavia IT-95-17/1; *Prosecutor v Zejnil Delalic, Zdravko Mucic (aka 'Pavo'), Hazim Delic, and Esad Landzo (aka 'Zenga') (Appeals Chamber Judgement)* [2001] International Criminal Tribunal for the Former Yugoslavia IT-96-21.

182 UNSC Res 1325 (2000); UNSC Res 1820 (2008); UNSC Res 1888 (2009); UNSC Res 1889 (2009); UNSC Res 1960 (2010); UNSC Res 2106 (2013); UNSC Res 2122 (2013); UNSC Res 2242 (2015); UNSC Res 2467 (2019); UNSC Res 2493 (2019).

183 Judith Butler, *Gender Trouble: Feminism and the Subversion of Identity* (Routledge 1990); Eve Kosofsky Sedgwick, *Tendencies* (Duke University Press 1993).

184 Dianne Otto, 'Introduction: Embracing Queer Curiosity' in Dianne Otto (ed), *Queering International Law: Possibilities, Alliances, Complicities, Risk* (Routledge 2017).

185 Faye Bird, ' "Is This a Time of Beautiful Chaos?": Reflecting on International Feminist Legal Methods' (2020) 28 Feminist Legal Studies 179.

in the alternative to no improvement. It is because of these competing pressures that feminism and queer theory requires advocates inside governmental institutions to push for change and accept compromise, and advocates outside of governmental institutions to hold those inside the institutions to account and drive them to continue advocating for better equality.

Overall, feminist and queer theory seek the same thing: equality. This is achieved better by marginalised groups working together for the betterment of all, and that is something that is known and acknowledged by the majority of feminist and queer theory advocates in international law.

D. CONCLUSION

Public international law suffers from a clear gender bias and was built on and therefore permeated by a male and heterosexual standard that serves as a basis for structural discrimination of all deviations from this standard. The de- and reconstruction of public international law therefore requires a holistic approach that unites feminist and queer approaches despite persisting differences and frictions. Sex and gender are core concepts to feminist and queer theory, which due to cultural baggage, oversimplification, and modes of application have also led to exclusionary approaches, particularly within the feminist discourse, that perpetuate the very discriminatory structures feminist and queer theory seeks to disclose and abolish. Both terms therefore require careful consideration in their use, taking into account both their social and normative imprint as well as the fluidity, complexity, and multiplicity of (gender) identities. The analysis of structural discrimination that queer and feminist theory seeks to address requires an intersectional perspective to disclose complex experiences of discrimination and to put a spotlight on the perspectives of marginalised individuals and groups where several forms of discrimination overlap. International law itself is permeated by structural discrimination, which requires more (feminist and queer) quantitative and qualitative (intersectional) research.

BOX 3.3.2 Further Readings and Further Resources

Further Readings

- H Charlesworth and C Chinkin, *The Boundaries of International Law – A Feminist Analysis* (Manchester University Press 2000)

- K Crenshaw, 'Demarginalizing the Intersection of Race and Sex: A Black Feminist Critique of Antidiscrimination Doctrine, Feminist Theory and Antiracist Politics' (1989) University of Chicago Legal Forum 139

- R Kapur, *Gender, Alterity and Human Rights: Freedom in a Fishbowl* (Edward Elgar 2018)

- D Otto, *Queering International Law: Possibilities, Alliances, Complicities, Risks* (Routledge 2018)

- S Harris Rimmer and K Ogg, *Research Handbook on Feminist Engagement with International Law* (Edward Elgar 2019)

Further Resources

- Catherine Amirfar and Kal Raustiala, 'Episode 39: Feminist Theories of International Law, 30 Years On' (*ASIL International Law Behind the Headlines*) <www.asil.org/resources/podcast/ep39> accessed 25 August 2023

- Başak Etkin and Kostia Gorobets, 'Episode 18: Tamsin Paige on Sociology of International Law, Queerness, and Pastry' (*Borderline Jurisprudence*, 3 March 2023) <https://open.spotify.com/show/7rlKzpmKoFmmOoXmL9Glkq> accessed 25 August 2023

- Kimberlé Crenshaw, 'The Urgency of Intersectionality' (*Ted Talk*, 14 November 2016) <www.ted.com/talks/kimberle_crenshaw_the_urgency_of_intersectionality/transcript> accessed 25 August 2023

- Sina Rahmani, 'Ratna Kapur on "Gender and Human Rights: Success, Failure or New Imperialism?" (2016)' (*The East Is a Podcast*, 16 February 2021) <https://eastisapodcast.libsyn.com/ratna-kapur-gender-and-human-rights-success-failure-or-new-imperialism-2016> accessed 25 August 2023

- ILGA Europe, 'Trans Inclusion in the Women's Movement' (*The Frontline*, 31 March 2023) <www.ilga-europe.org/podcast/the-frontline-trans-inclusion-in-the-womens-movement/> accessed 25 August 2023

§ § §

§ 3.4 MARXISM

KANAD BAGCHI

BOX 3.4.1 Required Knowledge and Learning Objectives

Required knowledge: Third World Approaches to International Law

Learning objectives: Understanding how Marxist literature can illuminate the theory and practise of international law, its relationship to other approaches, the different academic contributions on the subject, and the possible direction of future scholarship in this area.

A. INTRODUCTION

Marxism is a broad church: 'splits, disagreements, and denunciations'[186] within it are routinely common. No wonder that many of its tenets have been misinterpreted by both Marxists and non-Marxist scholars, associating Marxist thought with reductionism, economic determinism,[187] and a certain complicity in authoritarian rule. Ironically, Marx himself had vehemently decried being called a Marxist.[188] To write about a Marxist legal approach is equally difficult, given that Marx and Engels did not have much to say about the law, let alone international law.

Yet, generations of Marxist scholars have drawn from Marx's insights into society and history to explain a number of propositions about law and, more recently, about international law. Marxists have challenged international law's fundamental claims about promoting peace, prosperity, equality, or progress. Even while maintaining this critique, Marxist legal theory has pointed to ways in which law can and should be instrumentalised towards progressive ends mindful of its limits for emancipation. In what follows, I reflect upon five distinct perspectives that Marxist scholars have brought to the disciplinary understandings of the history and present of international law. Additionally, I also highlight some of the voids within Marxist legal theory and how recent scholarship has made important strides to fill those voids.

B. MARXISM AS APPROACH AND CRITIQUE

The use of 'approach' rather than 'method' is a conscious choice. Marxist theory rarely conforms to the idea of a singular method of approaching law. The Marxist tradition

---

186 Robert Knox, 'Marxist Approaches to International Law' in Anne Orford, Florian Hoffmann, and Martin Clark (eds), *The Oxford Handbook of the Theory of International Law* (OUP 2016) 307.

187 Economic determinism is the idea that all social and political phenomenon are fully determined by economic relationships.

188 See Karl Marx and Jules Guesde, 'The Programme of the Parti Ouvrier' (1880) <www.marxists.org/archive/marx/works/1880/05/parti-ouvrier.htm#n5> accessed 25 August 2023.

is a theory about the *totality* of social forms and relationships among individuals, rather than a specific set of propositions about the law. To invoke a Marxist lens is to view the world and society as an endless set of inter-relationships, where one phenomenon is always connected to the other. This means that ideas, institutions, and human agency need to be understood as part of an integrated whole that is both dynamic and also beholden to history and past structures.[189] How we think about the law will depend on how we think about the determining elements of social relationships more broadly. Moreover, Marxism continues to evolve, even as it registers critique, new ways of thinking, and a continuing to push against its own traditions. Confining Marxist theory to a pre-determined set of propositions or institutional boundaries is not only misguided but also deeply depoliticising. 'Approaches' in this sense keeps that space open to be constantly revisited and challenged.

A Marxist critique is a structural critique, not aimed at individual instances of exploitation alone, but at a reflection on the material structures of society at a *systemic* level, which make such exploitation part of the ordinary and mundane. It is also an internal critique of the system, which exposes the inner contradictions of its operating logic. Law, then, is to be viewed as a social practice with its own internal formal logic containing a set of argumentative structures that give stability to dominant interests and power. It probes us to think about law and international law not as a fragmented, insular, and detached body of rules, but as part of a larger social and economic infrastructure, within which it is embedded and takes its form. Finally, Marxism is not simply a set of theoretical escapades, but a call for radical political action to *change* existing structures of political economy.[190] It is inherently an emancipatory praxis, the aim of which is to 'create space for interpretive rules and strategies that contribute to the welfare of the subaltern classes'.[191] Marxism therefore, does not draw an overtly strict boundary between theory and practice, acknowledging that one is necessarily dependent on the other.

C. FIVE MARXIST PERSPECTIVES ON INTERNATIONAL LAW

Despite their long and influential pedigree, Marxist approaches to international law, largely remained in the margins of the discipline, even within critical circles. Yet, in the last decades, Marxist scholarship in international law has witnessed a revival. Many of our contemporary crises, whether that be the War on Terror, rising inequality, financial crisis, climate change, racial injustice, violence against women and indigenous communities, or the rise of authoritarian populism, have brought to the fore capitalism's worse consequences. Alongside that, many of the contemporary social movements, including the farmers' protests in India, the Black Lives Matter movement, or the

---

189 Andrea Bianchi, *International Law Theories: An Inquiry into Different Ways of Thinking* (OUP 2016) 84.

190 Karl Marx, *Theses on Feuerbach* (1845).

191 BS Chimni 'An Outline of a Marxist Course on Public International Law' (2004) 17 LJIL 1, 4.

Palestinian struggle against imperialist violence, have been mobilised using Marxist language. Increasingly, the visible inter-connectedness of local events with the global structures of political economy have called into question the role of international law in the (re)production of worldwide dispossession and alienation. Marxist concepts such as class, ideology, economic base, and commodification carry tremendous explanatory potential in laying bare the systemic forces at work, which naturalise the historical legacies of this unequal and violent order of things.

I. INTERNATIONAL LAW AS A MATERIAL PHENOMENON

Marxist theory asserts that all social relations need to be understood in their historical-material context. This means that law, like other social forms of regulation, is rooted in 'the material conditions of life', which are the so-called base, the 'real foundation, on which arises a legal and political superstructure'.[192] Legal relations reflect larger economic processes within society. However, the relationship between law and the economic structure is neither static nor unidirectional. To the contrary, the relationship of the base/superstructure is highly contingent, co-constitutive and even contradictory – a point that is routinely forgotten. The task of Marxist legal scholarship is to ask how this relationship plays out in concrete situations.

Unlike liberal accounts of the discipline, a historical-material perspective locates the rise of international law within the consolidation of global capitalism. In this, the story of capital, although it begins in Europe, travels to the rest of the world through colonial expansion and imperial violence.[193] *Primitive accumulation*, the resolutely violent and coercive enterprise of 'divorcing the producer from the means of production',[194] becomes the chief means of encounter between capitalist Europe and the non-capitalist world. For Marx, colonial expansion and the 'extirpation, enslavement and entombment' of the native population was not only indispensable for capitalist accumulation, but was a natural consequence of it.[195] International law, including its rules concerning trade and commerce, the doctrine of sovereignty, and the legal standard of civilisation become central to this project of worldwide domination and subjugation.

Thus, from a Marxist perspective, imperialism and colonial expansion is a *material* phenomenon at the heart of which lies the need for capital to constantly expand 'over the whole surface of the globe'.[196] This requires forcibly dispossessing native populations and transforming non-capitalist societies into the image of capitalist modernity. As Rosa Luxemburg argued, 'Capitalism must always and everywhere fight a battle of annihilation

---

192 Karl Marx, 'Preface to a Contribution to the Critique of Political Economy' (1859).

193 See González Hauck, § 1, in this textbook.

194 Karl Marx, *Capital: A Critique of Political Economy*, vol 1, 'Chapter Twenty-Six: The Secret of Primitive Accumulation' (1867).

195 Karl Marx, *Capital: A Critique of Political Economy*, vol 1, 'Chapter Thirty-One: Genesis of the Industrial Capitalist' (1867).

196 Karl Marx and Friedrich Engels, *Manifesto of the Communist Party* (1848).

against every non-capitalist form that it encounters'.[197] Imperialism in a Marxist sense, then, is 'the political expression of the accumulation of capital'[198] which works to efface all traditional forms of economic and cultural organisation and turn them into social spaces that would be safe and productive for capital.[199] Similarly, the distinction between civilised and uncivilised and corresponding denial of sovereignty to the latter from the realm of 19th-century European international law was not only about racial supremacy or domination, but was centrally rooted in the logic of capitalism. Equal sovereignty for the colonies could only come through Western capital, the creation of a centralised bureaucracy, and through modern forms of political organisation.[200] Realisation of statehood under international law became synonymous with violent capitalist transformation.

Viewing international law through a materialist lens points to the persistence of the civilising mission, even as the language of racial difference has diminished. It allows us to witness modern international law as a continuation of past practices of 'exclusion and conditional inclusion' of the non-Western world.[201] The post–World War II international legal order, purportedly based on international rule of law and self-determination, did not fundamentally alter the imperial nature of international law, but marked the shift to neo-colonialism, tying the Third World to the economic dependence of former colonial powers and the institutions that they controlled.[202] International law and international institutions, through structural adjustment and conditionality, market liberalisation, promotion of rule of law, and protection of foreign investment, disciplined and remodelled the Global South. The IMF and the World Bank, among others, promote monetary stability, free capital mobility, disciplined finance, and a shrinking of the public sector, under the pretext of the seemingly neutral concept of good governance. David Harvey calls this 'accumulation by dispossession' to refer to the accelerated ways in which capital inhabits every non-capitalist space, leaving in its wake mass poverty, social stratification, forced migration, and land dispossession.[203] Accumulation by dispossession is primitive accumulation in the neo-liberal age aided by the privatisation and commodification of natural resources. Modern international investment law, especially BITs,[204] entrench the power of foreign capital, while the WTO prescribes harmonised rules, subjects State autonomy to international adjudication, and legalises the international protection of property rights.[205]

---

197 Rosa Luxemburg, *The Accumulation of Capital*, 'Chapter 27: The Struggle Against Natural Economy' (1913) <https://www.marxists.org/archive/luxemburg/1913/accumulation-capital/> accessed 12 December 2023.
198 Ibid.
199 Robert Knox, 'A Critical Examination of the Concept of Imperialism in Marxist and Third World Approaches to International Law' (PhD thesis, London School of Economics and Political Science 2014); Robert Knox, 'Imperialism, Hypocrisy and the Politics of International Law' (2022) 3 TWAIL Review 25.
200 Ntina Tzouvala, *Capitalism as Civilisation: A History of International Law* (CUP 2020).
201 Ibid.
202 Kwame Nkrumah, *Neo-Colonialism: The Last Stage of Imperialism* (Thomas Nelson & Sons 1965) x; BS Chimni, *International Law and World Order: A Critique of Contemporary Approaches* (CUP 2017) 496.
203 David Harvey, *The New Imperialism*, 'Chapter 4: Accumulation by Dispossession' (OUP 2003).
204 See Hankings-Evans, § 23.1, in this textbook
205 Kate Miles, *The Origins of International Investment Law: Empire, Environment and the Safeguarding of Capital* (CUP 2013).

The logic of Marx's primitive accumulation as a gateway to both imperial expansion and capitalist transformation is also writ large in the continuing forms of settler-colonial practices across the world, where dispossession and expropriation of indigenous land and territory is legally and constitutionally sanctioned. It allows us to conceptualise the relationship between international law, capitalism, and imperialism as a permanent process and not one that ought to be confined simply to the pre-history of the discipline. International law as a material phenomenon contests many of the idealistic portrayals of the discipline, which trace its contours to mythical accounts of benign trade between private individuals, ideas about denouncing war, human rights, or peace.[206] Instead, Marxist accounts of the field have spent considerable efforts in grounding these ideas about international law within a historically specific and materially influenced conception of evolution, where it is indistinguishable from violence and expropriation. As Antony Anghie argued, international law is imperialism all the way down and much like the birth of capital in Marx's analysis, international law also comes into the world dripped in 'blood and dirt'.[207]

II. INTERNATIONAL LAW AS A CLASS PROJECT

Class is the organising principle of society in the Marxist tradition. Marx famously remarked that '[t]he history of all hitherto existing society is the history of class struggles', between those who own the means of production and those whose only means of subsistence is their labour power.[208] All aspects of social relationships, including those that make up the economic base, constantly evolve through these struggles, which are often expressed through the law.[209] Law is the means through which class conflict is mediated, and, more fundamentally, it is in the process of engaging with the law that class consciousness takes its concrete form. The law reflects and consolidates the interests of dominant classes but also shapes the form and content of the struggle. The outcomes are therefore never predetermined.

Classes extend beyond domestic borders. With the consolidation of the neo-colonial project in the 1970s and the accelerating trend towards hyper-globalisation, class formations too acquired a different dimension. Capital accumulation now relied on a 'globalized regime of exploitation and waged labour'.[210]

Marxist scholars, especially Rasulov and Chimni,[211] pointed to the emergence and consolidation of a transnational capitalist class (TCC) – a dispersed, yet influential

---

206 See González Hauck, § 1, in this textbook.

207 Karl Marx and Friedrich Engels, 'Manifesto of the Communist Party': Chapter I – Bourgeois and Proletarians (1848).

208 Ibid.

209 Bill Bowring, 'Marxist International Law Methodology?' in Rossana Deplano and Nicholas Tsagourias (eds), *Research Methods in International Law* (Edward Elgar 2021).

210 Akbar Rasulov, 'The Nameless Rapture of the Struggle': Towards a Marxist Class-Theoretic Approach to International Law' (2008) 19 FinnishYBIL 243, 268.

211 BS Chimni, 'Prolegomena to a Class Approach to International Law' (2010) 21(1) EJIL 57.

fraction of capitalist classes from advanced capitalist countries and the Third World. TCC works closely with international institutions to create a 'functional unified global economic space' where restrictions to capital movement can be flattened.[212] On the flip side, a transnational oppressed class (TOC) comprising social groups that are disenfranchised from the means of production came to be gradually consolidated, building coalitions with different oppressed groups using both legal and political means to push against the TCC.

In this constellation, international law becomes a site of class struggle between the TCC and TOC, promoting class consciousness and providing its constitutive structure. This is most visible in the struggle for environment, bio-diversity, development-related displacement, and the like, where interests of capital compete with the rights of labour, indigenous communities, and agricultural workers. These antagonisms play out through overtly capitalist institutions such as the WTO, the World Bank, and the IMF, but also through institutions such as the International Labour Organization, which one might otherwise think works to correct the power imbalance between capital and labour.[213] The 'emerging bourgeois imperial international law' uses the rhetoric of universal human rights and rule of law while entrenching the material and ideational primacy of capitalist classes.[214]

A class approach to international law helps navigate the black box of the State and international institutions by identifying the dominant groups which benefit from the system of international law.[215] It also helps foreground a more granular story of resistance by TOC to capitalist accumulation and directs our focus to new actors in the global arena. From social movements to civil society organisations espousing the cause of TOC, international law is made and re-made in different terrains.

III. INTERNATIONAL LAW, IDEOLOGY, AND THE CRITIQUE OF UNIVERSALITY

Law then becomes, sustains, and stabilises particular interests as universal ones. In the Marxist tradition, this is law acting as an ideological form, which domesticates resistance and class conflict by depoliticising legal relationships and rationalising conceptual categories.[216] Ideology, in the words of Susan Marks, plays a 'key role in legitimating exploitation' precisely by representing capitalist social relations as natural and permanent.[217] Relationships of domination and exploitation are delineated as

---

212 BS Chimni, 'International Institutions Today: An Imperial Global State in the Making' (2004) 15(1) EJIL1 9.

213 Mai Taha, 'Reading "Class" in International Law: The Labor Question in Interwar Egypt' (2016) 25(2) Social & Legal Studies 567.

214 Chimni (n 191).

215 An important work here is by Claire Cutler in analysing the rise of transnational finance class. Claire Cutler, *Private Power and Global Authority: Transnational Merchant Law in the Global Political Economy* (CUP 2003).

216 Karl Marx, 'Preface to a Contribution to the Critique of Political Economy' (1859).

217 Susan Marks (ed), *International Law on the Left: Re-examining Marxist Legacies* (CUP 2008) 292; See also the work of Claire Cutler, who uses the concept of 'hegemony' drawn from Italian Marxist Antonio Gramsci

pertaining to the individual sphere rather than as systemic outcomes. In other words, a focus on ideology exposes the abstracting character of the law, which flattens differences of power, even while projecting exchange as transpiring between free and equal participants.

It is not difficult to see how ideology critique provides a useful lens to the work of international law, especially in the context of deeply political conflicts. From humanitarian intervention to economic conditionalities and the War on Terror, capitalist States and international institutions have routinely invoked international law to justify a particular idea of liberation and freedom.[218] Sundhya Pahuja has shown that notions of development, when prescribed in universalistic terms, carry with them the prescription for particular kinds of economic and political arrangements, which mirrors the Western bureaucratic-State apparatus essential for capital accumulation.[219] International law, by focusing on domestic roots of poverty and conflict in the Third World, detracts attention from the systemic patterns of capitalist exploitation and violence at the heart of core-periphery relationships. The growing infrastructure of international adjudication and the increase in specialised forums of dispute resolution add another layer of depoliticisation to social conflicts concerning land, environment, and property. Even the concept of democracy promoted by international law sidesteps crucial questions of entrenched social hierarchy and inter-group domination, while privileging a narrow set of indicators and benchmarks to assess participation.[220]

To point to the ideological character of international law probes us to think about the fact that social arrangements need not be the way they are. If existing social relations seem inevitable or natural, it is but the result of repeated ideas and rhetorical processes that legitimise and order such structures. But one should also be mindful of the fact that even though historical relations are contingent, they are not always open to change. Quoting Susan Marks once again, 'just as things do not have to be as they are, so too history is not simply a matter of chance and will', meaning that human agency, while paramount for resistance and change, always operates within the 'logics of a system'.[221] In other words, as much as one ought to be sceptical of historical necessity, meaningful transformation can only transpire through a clear-headed understanding of the false contingency and limits of individual action.

---

to argue that law helps in projecting private interests as societal ones. Claire Cutler, 'Gramsci, Law, and the Culture of Global Capitalism' (2005) 8(4) Critical Review of International Social and Political Philosophy 527–542.

218 See for instance, Hilary Charlesworth, 'Feminist Reflections on the Responsibility to Protect' (2010) 2(3) GR2P 232–249.

219 Sundhya Pahuja, *Decolonising International Law: Development, Economic Growth and the Politics of Universality* (CUP 2011).

220 Susan Marks, *The Riddle of All Constitutions: International Law, Democracy, and the Critique of Ideology* (OUP 2003).

221 Susan Marks, 'False Contingency' (2009) 62(1) Current Legal Problems 1–21, 10.

IV. INTERNATIONAL LAW AS COMMODITY FORM

For Marx, capital makes commodities out of everything, but, most crucially, capital expands by commodifying labour power. The process entails abstracting the individual from the product of its own labour for surplus value and alienating labour from the very means of production. With the spread of capitalism, commodification extends to every aspect of life, mediated, of course, through legal relationships. Capitalist relations, then, are marked by an endless collection of commodities connected through an endless set of legal relations.[222]

Commodification and the abstracting/individualising character of the law was central to the work of Soviet jurist Evgeny Pashukanis. Drawing from Marx's insight that commodities are but the elementary form of wealth,[223] Pashukanis argued that, in a capitalist society, relations between individuals based on property rights are homologous to abstract commodities, which are traded. Just as for commodities to be exchanged, each party much recognise the other as an equal owner of property in an abstract sense, so too does the law treat those parties as equal bearers of rights.[224] Law treats individuals as abstract, neutral entities, detached from the material conditions in which they exist. This makes it seem like exchange is between two equals, while the law invisibilises and 'permits real inequality'. Pashukanis illustrated that sovereign entities in their relationship to one another precisely operate as owners of property (read: territory) with each possessing equal rights and obligations. This formal equality in status eludes, however, the reality 'that they are unequal in their significance and their power'.[225] It is in this context that Pashukanis characterised international law as 'the legal form of the struggle of the capitalist states among themselves for domination over the rest of the world'.[226]

The crucial question that arises is how are disputes then resolved between two formally equal sovereigns? What is the nature of the legal form that makes certain claims trump others? This is where China Miéville[227] extended Pashukanis' commodity theory to argue that the legal form inherent in international law is that of coercion. Exchange implies ownership and ownership is primarily about the right, mostly exercised through law, to exclude others.[228] In a deeply unequal world, what this means is that powerful states are able to shape the order and content of legal norms through economic and military force. Because 'coercion is at the heart of the commodity form'[229] and

---

222 China Miéville, 'The Commodity-Form Theory of International Law' in Susan Marks (ed), *International Law on the Left: Re-examining Marxist Legacies* (CUP 2008) 107.

223 Karl Marx, *Capital Vol I: 'Part I: Commodities and Money – Chapter One: Commodities'* (1867).

224 Evgeny Pashukanis, *The General Theory of Law and Marxism*, 'Chapter IV: Commodity and the Subject' (1924).

225 Evgeny Pashukanis, *International Law* (1925).

226 Ibid.

227 China Miéville, *Between Equal Rights: A Marxist Theory of International Law* (Brill 2005).

228 Taken from Marina Velickovic's extremely lucid way of expanding Pashukanis. See Marina Velickovic, 'A Marxist Account of the Individual in International Law' (Draft presented for the conference on 'Individual in International Law, Heidelberg 2021). On file with the author.

229 Miéville (n 227) 126.

international law mediates commodity exchange, violence is central to it: 'between equal rights, force decides'.

To suggest, then, that international law furthers a rules-based order and is counterpoised to power and brute force is misleading. Instead, as Miéville poignantly put it, '[t]he chaotic and bloody world around us is the rule of law'.[230]

The commodity form theory provides a singularly persuasive historical account of why and how law developed the way it did and what makes legal relations the perfect infrastructure for capitalism's expansion. Claire Cutler has applied the commodity form theory to illustrate the nature of the WTO and GATS in the commodification of public commons,[231] while Grietje Baars reflects on the nature of law as a 'congealing' devise for capitalist relations. Their work also centres the role of corporation as a tool for imperialist expansion.[232]

V. INTERNATIONAL LAW AS EMANCIPATION

For Marx, legal struggles and the pursuit of human rights although conditioned by capitalist relations did not mean that they ought to be repudiated. Indeed, Marx expended considerable attention to the law as a means of working class struggle in his elaborate description on the length of the working day, which was won on a legal terrain.[233] Law was important in providing the oppressed classes with the means to push back against capitalist expansion. Similarly, in his work 'On the Jewish Question', which is often cited to bring home the point that Marx was disillusioned with the potential of equal rights, Marx had only advanced a limited critique of *formal* legal equality. For him, political emancipation through law and legal rights was deeply individualising and alienating and thus cannot be an end in itself, but only a means towards engendering larger social changes beyond what the law could provide.

Law and the legal form, therefore, in the Marxist tradition exhibit a dual character, which, even while constraining the possibility of deep structural transformation, provides an important, albeit limited, form of social emancipation through concrete legal struggles. These legal struggles, then, must go hand in hand with more demanding political interventions. It is not a choice between Reform or Revolution but about how these two paths can have always coexisted. Understanding the role of law in the reproduction of capitalist relations and also as a means to resist some of its worst excesses alludes to its relative autonomy. Both Chimni and Marks thus hold on to the possibility of international law acting as a shield against powerful states. Chimni argues for a

---

230 Ibid 319.

231 Claire Cutler, 'Toward a Radical Political Economy Critique of Transnational Economic Law' in Susan Marks (ed), *International Law on the Left: Re-examining Marxist Legacies* (CUP 2008).

232 Grietje Baars, *The Corporation, Law, and Capitalism: A Radical Perspective on the Role of Law in the Global Political Economy* (Haymarket Books 2020); see also González Hauck, § 7.7, in this textbook.

233 For a good description, see Igor Shoikhedbrod, *Revisiting Marx's Critique of Liberalism: Rethinking Justice, Legality and Rights* (Palgrave 2019).

'radicalism with rules' where international law should be viewed as a site of contestation rather than a mere reflection or consolidation of the interests of dominant classes. Bill Bowring goes one step further in situating human rights and international law's relationship to past revolutions as evidence of the emancipatory role that law can play.[234]

Robert Knox provides a useful lens to navigate through this duality of rejection and embrace of international law. Given that the use of legal means comes with the danger of legitimising the existing order of social relations, law should only be used for short-term *tactical* purposes, as a 'mere tool to be discarded when not useful'.[235] Knox terms this engagement with the law 'principled opportunism' to put forth the point that international law should be pursued for progressive purposes not because it is law but because it aids a larger political commitment to fundamentally transform existing society. This would eventually provide the path for what Marina Veličković calls the 'planned obsolescence of international law' (i.e. the law's gradual disappearance altogether).[236] But before that happens, the task of radical critique and practise through international law must continue, even when we realise that any utopian hopes of wholesale transformation are ultimately constrained by the legal form.

D. EXCLUSIONS AND ABSENCES IN MARXIST LEGAL SCHOLARSHIP

Despite the growing cohort of scholars writing within the Marxist tradition in international law and sharpening its conceptual tools, the general project of Marxism has been unable to fully shed its blinkers and unwilling sometimes to reorient its own constitutive categories in the light of other modes of struggles that cut across various axes of social divisions. The project of building solidarity across different resistance movements has not always been forthcoming.

This is perhaps most visible in the way Marxist legal scholars have privileged the category of class as the most important marker of social division, ignoring how race, gender, sexuality, and caste play an equally important role in the chain of production, distribution, and thus also exploitation. Marxism has maintained a distance with other critical tradition such as TWAIL, CLS, Critical Race Theory, and also feminist approaches to international law in its singular focus that material conditions are unrelated to how cultural or gender stratifications co-constitute the capitalist mode of production.[237] Despite its emphasis on the *totality* of social relations, Marxist scholars have

---

234 Bill Bowring, *The Degradation of the International Legal Order? The Rehabilitation of Law and the Possibility of Politics* (Routledge 2008).

235 Robert Knox, 'Marxism, International Law, and Political Strategy' (2009) 22 LJIL 413–436, 433.

236 Marina Veličković, 'Planned Obsolescence of International Law: On Contingency and Utopian Possibilities' (*Völkerrechtsblog*, 17 June 2021) <https://voelkerrechtsblog.org/de/planned-obsolescence-of-international-law/> accessed 25 August 2023.

237 Akbar Rasulov, ' CLS and Marxism: A History of an Affair' (2014) 5(4) Transnational Legal Theory 622–639.

themselves advanced an understanding of individuals abstracted from deep structural and social markers of community. As Knox points out, within the Marxist discourse, race and racism 'tend to be understood as counterposed to processes of capitalist accumulation'.[238] No wonder that these exclusions are reflected in some of the 'mainstream' iterations of Marxist legal scholarship (including this one) which are produced by men, with a relative absence of women, trans, or even black writings on the subject.

Equally, this dissonance is sustained by critical scholars in other traditions who mechanically associate the writings of Marx and the Marxist project with that of structural determinism and Eurocentrism. In some influential quarters of TWAIL, for instance, Marx is portrayed to be irrelevant to Third World decolonial struggles.[239] These interventions, of course, overlook not just the fact that Marx himself was alive to the conditions of colonialism and expropriation of native peoples as central to Western capitalist expansion, but also generations of Third World Marxist scholars and anti-colonial movements which applied, modified, and even stretched Marxist theory to local conditions and experiences of domination and imperialist expansion.[240] For the latter, reading Marx has always been about how under conditions of capitalist accumulation, racialisation, gender, and caste-based stratifications are crucial determinants of what constitutes the material conditions of life.

In contemporary times however, many Marxists and equal number of TWAILers, feminist theorists, and critical race scholars have moved beyond traditional class variants of historical materialism to underscore the multifaceted nature of capitalist oppression, which straddles race, patriarchy, and culture. For instance, Knox's recent scholarship has highlighted that the concepts of value and race are but two side of the same coin and that any materialist mode of analysis needs to consider them together.[241] Similarly, Chimni's integrated Marxist analysis, which supplements issues of class with that of social feminist and post-colonial theory, has been received approvingly both within the TWAIL and Marxist communities.[242] Tzouvala, in her materialist history of the concept of civilisation, addresses how particular conceptions of race, gender, and sexuality operated as tropes for European international lawyers to infantilise, racialise, and feminise non-Western communities while laying the groundwork for capitalist expansion.[243] Her work is also instrumental in bringing together insights

---

238 Robert Knox, 'Valuing Race? Stretched Marxism and the Logic of Imperialism' (2016) 4LRIL 81, 100.

239 Mohsen al Attar, 'Teaching Karl Marx About Third World Approaches to International Law' (*Opinio Juris*, 7 February 2022) <https://opiniojuris.org/2022/02/07/teaching-karl-marx-about-third-world-approaches-to-international-law/> accessed 25 August 2023.

240 Knox (n 238); Umut Özsu, 'Determining New Selves: Mohammed Bedjaoui on Algeria, Western Sahara, and Post-Classical International Law' in Jochen von Bernstorff and Philipp Dann (eds), *The Battle for International Law: South-North Perspectives on the Decolonization Era* (OUP 2019) 341–357. Noura Erakar and John Reylonds, 'We Charge Apartheid? Palestine and the International Criminal Court' (2021) TWAILR Reflections 33.

241 Knox (n 238).

242 Chimni (n 202) 440–550.

243 Ntina Tzouvala, *Capitalism as Civilisation: A History of International Law* (CUP 2020); James Thuo Gathii, 'Imperialism, Colonialism, and International Law' (2007) 54(4) Buffalo Law Review 1013.

from indeterminacy in the CLS tradition with a Marxist framework of capitalism and its contradictions. Ruth Fletcher's work is equally inspiring in thinking through Pashukanis' commodity form theory from a feminist perspective to foreground the role of social reproduction within notions of value in commodity exchange.[244] These and many other voices have in some sense made Marxist analysis of law and international law respond to and reflect on the many dimensions of social relationships that continue to change, evolve, and transform under the conditions of global capitalist accumulation.[245] Here the emphasis is not that class analysis ought to be displaced, but that 'class realizes itself and becomes embodied through gender, race, sexuality'.[246] This is the direction that future Marxist international legal scholarship must embrace.

BOX 3.4.2 Further Readings

Further Readings

- P Connell and U Özsu (eds), *Research Handbook on Law and Marxism* (Elgar 2021)

- Law and Political Economy Project, 'Revival and Renewal of Marxist Approaches' <https://lpeproject.org/conferences/revival-and-renewal-of-marxist-approaches/> accessed 25 August 2023

- C Miéville, *October: The Story of the Russian Revolution* (Verso 2017)

---

§ § §

---

244 Ruth Fletcher, 'Legal Form, Commodities and Re-Production: Reading Pashukanis' (2013) Queen Mary School of Law Legal Studies Research Paper No. 158.

245 For a very helpful summary of Marxist work in international law, see Robert Knox, 'Marxist Approaches to International Law Bibliography' (*Oxford Bibliographies*, 2018) <www.oxfordbibliographies.com/view/document/obo-9780199796953/obo-9780199796953-0163.xml> accessed 25 August 2023.

246 Marks (n 220) 5.

4

CHAPTER 4
METHODS
SUÉ GONZÁLEZ HAUCK, MAX MILAS, SILVIA STEININGER, AND TAMSIN PHILLIPA PAIGE

INTRODUCTION
SUÉ GONZÁLEZ HAUCK

BOX 4.1 Required Knowledge and Learning Objectives

Required knowledge: None

Learning objectives: Understanding what research methods are in general and knowing enough basics about different research methods employed in international law to understand the sections on specific methods.

BOX 4.2 Interactive Exercises

Access *interactive exercises for this chapter*[1] by positioning your smartphone camera at the dot-filled box, also known as a QR code.

Figure 4.1 QR code referring to interactive exercises.

A. INTRODUCTION

As explained in the previous chapter on approaches to international law, methods are the practices of doing research in application of a theory or the roadmaps to guide the research process.[2] In contrast to other disciplines, academic conventions in legal

---

1 https://openrewi.org/en-projects-project-public-international-law-methodology/
2 Cf. Steven R Ratner and Anne-Marie Slaughter, 'Appraising the Methods of International Law: A Prospectus for Readers' (1999) 93 AJIL 291, 292.

DOI: 10.4324/9781003451327-5

scholarship do not always call for an explicit engagement with method. This can make legal scholars uncomfortable when asked to articulate their methods explicitly.[3] However, the only way to ensure that what you are producing is scholarship and not just a random collection of thoughts and opinions is to be clear and transparent about the questions you are asking, the material you are examining, and the process you are employing to ensure a systematic examination of said material. This introductory section reflects on different uses of the term 'method', offers an entry-level account of what it means to choose your research question, data, and method in the narrower sense, and provides a glimpse into differences between doctrinal, critical, and interdisciplinary methods. The following sections, then, provide further insights into case analysis and interdisciplinary methods.

B. WHAT IS METHOD?

The term 'method' can be understood in a broader sense to encompass the entire research process or in a narrower sense to refer specifically to the systematic examination of the material.[4] The first two steps of the research process, defining the research question and gathering relevant material (or 'data'), are often referred to as the research design. Unease among legal scholars when it comes to methods is not only caused by the fact that lawyers often are not explicitly trained in methods, but also because descriptions of methods – including this one – create the (often false) impression that the research process is neatly organised into sequential steps. Presenting the employed method as if it followed clear steps from the beginning is important, because it allows other researchers to appreciate and evaluate the research. However, if you feel like you are constantly jumping between choosing which theorists to rely on, which data to gather and how, changing your research question as you go along, you are not alone. It is perfectly normal to switch between different steps and re-adjust the research question even during the analysis phase. The key factor is to have a flexible and transparent system in place that can be adjusted as needed, rather than conducting research in a random or haphazard manner, as that would undermine its integrity and validity.

Furthermore, distinguishing between terms like *method, methodology, approach*, and *theory* is not always straightforward. Not only do people use these terms in various ways, but even when attempting to adhere to a specific distinction, there is often overlap and interplay among them. In the context proposed here, methodology refers to a set of epistemological and ontological assumptions, while theory or approach stems from these assumptions and provides a theoretical framework. Method, on the other hand, describes the practical application of the theory – a roadmap for addressing a specific

---

3   Eliav Lieblich, '"You Keep on Using That Word" – On Methods in (International) Legal Scholarship (Part I)' (*Opinio Juris*, 21 March 2022) <http://opiniojuris.org/2022/03/21/symposium-on-early-career-international-law-academia-you-keep-on-using-that-word-on-methods-in-international-legal-scholarship-part-i/> accessed 26 August 2023.

4   Cf. Sundhya Pahuja, 'Methodology: Writing About How We Do Research' in Rossana Deplano and Nicholas Tsagourias (eds), *Research Methods in International Law: A Handbook* (Edward Elgar 2021) 63–64.

research question using the chosen theoretical framework. However, it is important to note that theory and method influence each other. They are interconnected elements that shape and inform the research process.[5]

By acknowledging the non-linear nature of research and the overlapping nature of terms like method, methodology, approach, and theory, scholars can adopt a more flexible and adaptive mindset. This allows researchers to embrace the iterative nature of the research process – at least in qualitative research, where adjustments and refinements are made based on emerging insights and findings. The goal is to establish a systematic and transparent process that ensures the rigour and credibility of the research while remaining open to modifications and adaptations as necessary.

C. RESEARCH DESIGN AND METHOD

I. IDENTIFYING A RESEARCH QUESTION

To embark on a research project, it is essential to identify a research question.[6] Having a research question differs from having a general area of interest. You may start with a topic you are interested in, perhaps because you see something happening in the world and you want to understand it in order to be able to change it, for example, violence at the European, US, or Australian borders. To narrow down your focus, you need to explore existing literature and identify the questions that other scholars have asked within this topic. While conducting literature searches on platforms like Google or Google Scholar can be a starting point, it is more advisable to use library catalogues for a comprehensive and ethical approach. As you delve into the literature, it is crucial to recognise that you will never read everything that has been written on a topic. To discern which bodies of literature to focus on, you should actively choose the conversations you want to engage with and contribute to. This coincides with identifying and refining your research question. Different conversations may encompass distinct sets of questions. For instance, one set of questions may revolve around determining the legality of the behaviour of the Greek coastguard in preventing people from reaching European shores. Another set of questions may explore how international law enables border violence, examine how people resist such violence, where the law creates or leaves space for such resistance, and how resistance is, in turn, usurped by dominant narratives. By choosing which conversations to actively engage in, you can gauge when you have read enough. It is acceptable to have a cursory overview of conversations you are not directly engaging with, but you should thoroughly immerse yourself in the conversations you wish to contribute to, ensuring you have something

---

5   Cf. Eliav Lieblich, '"You Keep on Using That Word" – On Methods in (International) Legal Scholarship (Part II)' (*Opinio Juris*, 22 March 2022) <http://opiniojuris.org/2022/03/22/symposium-on-early-career-international-law-academia-you-keep-on-using-that-word-on-methods-in-international-legal-scholarship-part-ii/> accessed 26 August 2023.

6   For an excellent instruction on this, see Pahuja (n 4) 67 et seq.

new or insightful to add. Additionally, a point of saturation can be reached when you consistently encounter the same references in new literature, indicating that you have covered a significant portion of the existing scholarship.

II. CHOOSING YOUR DATA

Once you have (provisionally) formulated your research question, the next step is to gather the relevant material that will aid in answering it. This involves selecting the data, that is, gathering the body of information that you will later analyse to answer your research question. Even though the term 'data' evokes numerical information, it can actually be any kind of information, including court cases, legal writings, archival materials, interviews, field notes, or information retrieved from pre-existing databases. It is important to note that the process of choosing your data is intertwined with the iterative development of your research question and with the choice of method in the narrower sense.

III. METHOD

In the narrower sense, method refers to the systematic practices used to analyse the selected data in a transparent and structured manner. This stage involves applying the chosen theoretical framework to the data to answer the research question effectively. Methodological choices may vary depending on the nature of the research project, ranging from quantitative methods for statistical analysis to qualitative approaches for textual or interpretive analysis. It is crucial to articulate your method clearly, ensuring that your research process remains rigorous and well founded.

D. DOCTRINAL, CRITICAL, AND INTERDISCIPLINARY METHODS IN INTERNATIONAL LAW

Doctrinal scholarship is the classical method employed in legal research to identify and interpret legal norms by analysing existing case law and engaging with the works of other doctrinal scholars. This approach emphasises the examination of legal principles and doctrines to understand 'what the law is'. Methodological soundness, in this context, consists in employing argumentative structures that can convince the target audience of the claim's 'legal correctness'.[7] Within doctrinal scholarship, case analysis stands out as one of the most important methods.[8] By closely examining judicial decisions, legal researchers gain insights into the development, interpretation, and application of legal rules.

---

7   Martti Koskenniemi, 'Methodology of International Law' (*Max Planck Encyclopedia of International Law*, November 2007) <https://opil.ouplaw.com/display/10.1093/law:epil/9780199231690/law-9780199231690-e1440> accessed 26 August 2023, para 1.

8   See Milas, § 4.1, in this textbook.

In contrast to doctrinal scholarship, critical scholarship focuses on questioning and critiquing the underlying assumptions of legal doctrine and practice. It delves into how the law is embedded in, upholds, and operates within societal structures, how it distributes material resources, consolidates power dynamics, legitimises violence, and perpetuates domination.

Interdisciplinary methods can be utilised in both doctrinal and critical legal scholarship.[9] Integrating insights from other disciplines, such as sociology, anthropology, political science, or economics, can enrich the understanding of legal phenomena. This interdisciplinary approach allows legal scholars to analyse the law in a broader societal context, uncover hidden power dynamics, and explore alternative perspectives.

E. CONCLUSION

Understanding and employing the methods behind public international law research is crucial for producing rigorous and insightful scholarship. Although the research process may not adhere strictly to a linear sequence of steps, articulating your research question, consciously choosing your data, and implementing a structured analysis are essential elements of methodological soundness. The following sections on case analysis and interdisciplinarity provide more concrete examples of the multitude of methods that can be employed for international legal research.

BOX 4.3 Further Readings

Further Readings

- S Pahuja, 'Methodology: Writing About How We Do Research' in Rossana Deplano and Nicholas Tsagourias (eds), *Research Methods in International Law: A Handbook* (Edward Elgar 2021) 60

- R Deplano and N Tsagourias (eds), *Research Methods in International Law: A Handbook* (Edward Elgar 2021)

- E Lieblich, 'How to Do Research in International Law? A Basic Guide for Beginners', 62 Harvard Journal of International Law (2021) 42

---

§ § §

---

9   See Steininger and Paige, § 4.2, in this textbook.

§ 4.1 CASE ANALYSIS

MAX MILAS

> ### BOX 4.1.1 Required Knowledge and Learning Objectives
>
> **Required knowledge**: None
>
> **Learning objectives**: Evaluating the relevance of cases in international law; researching international cases; applying cases depending on role and objective.

A. INTRODUCTION

Cases are not only a 'subsidiary means for the determination of rules of law' in international law (article 38(1)(d) ICJ Statute[10]), but also an influential means of communication in legal practice and research. For this reason, it is even more surprising that all popular public international law textbooks include a section on the relevance of cases[11] but none on how to engage with judicial decisions. This section attempts to change that by discussing the relevance of cases, presenting tools to research cases, and introducing methods to use cases in international law. In doing so, this section aims to guide students through exams, term papers, and moot courts in which case law analysis is key.

B. RELEVANCE OF CASES IN INTERNATIONAL LAW

According to the traditional reading, cases[12] are one of the four main sources to determine rules of international law.[13] Both judges and scholars of international law deal extensively with prior domestic and international decisions. Finding and analysing cases is therefore one of the main tasks of international lawyers.

---

10 Statute of the International Court of Justice (adopted 17 December 1963, entered into force 31 August 1965) 993 UNTS 33.

11 James Crawford, *Brownlie's Principles of Public International Law* (8th edn, OUP 2012) 37–41; Malcolm N Shaw, *International Law* (8th edn, CUP 2017) 81–83; Gleider I Hernández, *International Law* (OUP 2019) 32–53, 305–316; Jan Klabbers, *International Law* (3rd edn, CUP 2021) 40–42, 155–181.

12 On judicial decisions as sources of international law, see Kunz, Lima, and Castelar Campos, § 6.4, in this textbook.

13 On sources of international law, see Eggett, Introduction to § 6, and the following sections on specific sources of international law in this textbook.

I. DECISIONS OF INTERNATIONAL ADJUDICATIVE BODIES

On a strict reading of article 38(1)(d) ICJ Statute, judicial decisions are only subsidiary sources of international law.[14] At first glance, the absence of a formal concept of precedent confirms this reserved importance.[15] This, however, belies the realities of international law. Courts base their decisions on previous cases to build a coherent system,[16] scholars use cases to adjust their approaches to the realities of international law, and commissions use cases when codifying law.[17] This applies not only to judicial decisions but also to decisions of quasi-judicial bodies.[18]

International law involves different types of applicants and procedures.[19] In most proceedings before international courts like the ICJ and the International Tribunal for the Law of the Sea (ITLOS),[20] two States[21] are in dispute. Private parties can file complaints against States before international human rights courts[22] and investment protection tribunals.[23] Additionally, prosecutors can file cases against individuals before international criminal courts.[24] Finally, international organisations[25] and States can seek advisory opinions from international tribunals.

Cases consist of up to four parts. Preliminary objections address the court's jurisdiction, the plaintiff's ability to bring the case to trial (standing), and other admissibility requirements. Under merits, courts present their reasoning and the result of the case. Under reparations, most courts specify the consequences of their judgment (e.g. reversal of measures, payment of reparations). Under interpretation, courts may, at the request of the applicant, clarify how a judgment is to be interpreted and whether the respondent has fulfilled their obligations.

---

14 Article 38(1)(d) provides that 'The Court . . . shall apply: subject to the provisions of Article 59, judicial decisions . . ., as subsidiary means for the determination of rules of law'; see also *Cameroon v Nigeria*: Equatorial Guinea intervening) [Preliminary Objections] 275 (ICJ) [28].

15 Article 59 of the ICJ Statute, article 46(1) ECHR, articles 68(1) ACHR, article 33(2) Statute of the International Tribunal for the Law of the Sea.

16 The ICJ often argues with well-established case law. See *United States Diplomatic and Consular Staff in Tehran (United States v Iran)* [1980] ICJ Rep 3 [33].

17 The ILC heavily relied on the ICJ's decision in *Gabčíkovo-Nagymaros Project (Hungary v Slovakia)* [1997] ICJ Rep 7 to codify the state of necessity in its Draft Articles on Responsibility of States for Internationally Wrongful Acts; see ILC, 'ARSIWA Commentaries' (2001) article 25, paras 11, 15, 16, 20.

18 The ICJ even considered the Human Rights Committees' interpretation of the ICCP in its *Ahmadou Sadio Diallo (Republic of Guinea v Democratic Republic of the Kongo)* (Preliminary Objections) [2007] ICJ Rep 582 [66].

19 On dispute settlement in international law, see Choudhary, § 12, in this textbook.

20 On the law of the sea in general, see Dela Cruz and Paige, § 15, in this textbook.

21 On States, see Green, § 7.1, in this textbook.

22 On international human rights courts, see Milas, § 21.1, in this textbook.

23 On international investment law, see Hankings-Evans, § 23.1, in this textbook.

24 On international criminal law, see Ciampi, § 22, in this textbook.

25 On international organisations, see Baranowska, Engström, and Paige, § 7.3, in this textbook.

II. DOMESTIC CASES IN INTERNATIONAL LAW

Even though domestic court decisions are also covered by article 38(1)(d) ICJ Statute,[26] international courts rarely cite them. While international decisions are usually cited to ensure a supposed uniformity of the international legal order, the use of domestic decisions often serves to prove customary international law[27] and to secure States' acceptance. By discussing domestic decisions, courts signal to States that their legal traditions are being taken seriously.[28]

Studies on citation practices of international courts and textbooks show a bias towards cases from Australia, Canada, China, France, Israel, South Africa, the United Kingdom, and the United States, whereas cases from jurisdictions outside the Global North are scarcely cited.[29]

Admittedly, there are plausible reasons for this: in some cases, only decisions from certain jurisdictions will exist, decisions in English are easy to understand for most international lawyers, many databases contain only judgments from these jurisdictions, and the style of reasoning of these courts is similar to the style of reasoning taught in international law departments around the world.[30] However, this prevalence of English-language decisions in citations is not inevitable, but the result of historical inequalities within the international system. Over the past 400 years, European States have imposed their legal systems on countries on every continent. Today, English is the working language in international institutions, and English-language publications are expected by international law scholars in many regions of the world.[31] Considering these colonial roots of the bias in favour of English-language decisions, a thorough research on domestic decisions should not only try to use decisions of a certain group of States but instead should strive for representativeness.[32]

---

26 Mads Andenas and Johann Ruben Leiss, 'The Systemic Relevance of "Judicial Decisions" in Article 38 of the ICJ Statute' (2017) 77 HJIL 907, 951–952, 958, 966.

27 *Jurisdictional Immunities of the State* (*Germany v Italy*: Greece intervening) [2012] ICJ Rep 99 [64, 68, 71–75, 76, 78, 83, 85, 90, 96, 118]; see also International Law Commission, 'Identification of Customary International Law' (2016) UNGA A/CN.4/691.

28 *Arrest Warrant of 11 April 2000* (*Democratic Republic of the Congo v Belgium*) [2002] ICJ Rep 3 [56–58].

29 Katerina Linos, 'How to Select and Develop International Law Case Studies: Lessons from Comparative Law and Comparative Politics' (2015) 109 AJIL 475, 476; Erik Voeten, 'Borrowing and Nonborrowing Among International Courts' (2010) 39 Journal of Legal Studies 547, 558–568; Anthea Roberts, *Is International Law International?* (Vol 1, OUP 2017) 167–172.

30 Linos (n 29) 476.

31 Odile Ammann, 'Language Bias in International Legal Scholarship: Symptoms, Explanations, Implications and Remedies' (2022) 33 European Journal of International Law 821; Justina Uriburu, 'Between Elitist Conversations and Local Clusters: How Should We Address English-Centrism in International Law?' (*Opinio Juris*, 2 November 2020) <http://opiniojuris.org/2020/11/02/between-elitist-conversations-and-local-clusters-how-should-we-address-english-centrism-in-international-law/> accessed 26 July 2023.

32 Andenas and Leiss (n 26) 965.

BOX 4.1.2 Advanced: Case Selection

Including all countries of the world in the research of domestic court decisions is neither feasible in terms of time nor valuable in terms of insights. Instead, students may strive for theoretically informed sampling. This requires a three-step approach: first, students define their object of interest as precisely as possible (e.g. State practice regarding prosecuting institutionalised mass atrocities). Second, students search for States that faced similar problems in their history. Third, students group the relevant States by 'legal families', geographic region, economic and political systems, and their position within international power structures. Last, students select a representative State from each possible combination for their analysis. The reasons for selection should be presented transparently.[33]

C. RESEARCHING CASES IN INTERNATIONAL LAW

Generally, case law analyses have two different starting points. In the first type of question, students are asked to respond to a general question of international law. Students can only answer this question convincingly if they also engage with international and domestic cases.

BOX 4.1.3 Example: General Question of International Law

Are entry restrictions against foreigners permissible under international law if they serve to combat the COVID-19 pandemic?

In the second type of question, students must answer a case-specific question. Although this question seems to refer only to one case, students can only answer this question persuasively if they also consider comparable cases.

BOX 4.1.4 Example: Case-Specific Question

Why did the ICJ reject State responsibility of Serbia and Montenegro for acts in Srebrenica in the Bosnian Genocide Case?

---

33 Linos (n 29) 479–480.

Thus, for both types of questions, students must find the applicable case law for persuasive reasoning. For this, students can resort to libraries and online databases.

I. FINDING CASES IN LIBRARIES

The most obvious but also the most challenging sources for researching case law are law reports. Their main advantage is that they reflect the case law comprehensively and authentically. The major disadvantage, however, is that law reports are often only available in print. The following list provides an overview of the most common law reports in international law:

- Covering almost all fields of case law in international law:
  - International Law Reports (CUP)
  - Oxford Reports on International Law
- Covering international case law from 1929 to 1945: Annual Digest of Public International Law Cases
- Decisions of the International Court of Justice: UN Summaries of Judgments, Advisory Opinions and Orders of the International Court of Justice
- International arbitral and judicial awards: United Nations Reports of International Arbitral Awards
- Decisions of UN judicial bodies: United Nations Juridical Yearbook
- Law of the sea: ITLOS Annual Reports
- Cases in the European human rights system: Tim Eicke (ed.), *European Human Rights Reports.*

Many international law journals also contain sections summarising and assessing cases. However, they contain only a sample of current decisions, and they focus usually on analysing individual aspects of cases. For this reason, journals are recommended sources of inspiration for case law analysis only after students have already found the relevant cases.

II. FINDING CASES IN ONLINE DATABASES

Nowadays, online databases exist for almost all international courts. Most of these databases enable machine-readable research and parsing of case law. This allows students to filter case law by terms, topics, rules, and years to find the most relevant cases as quickly as possible. For this reason, online databases should usually be the starting point for case law research. To avoid mistakes in quoting and citing, students may use the court's own databases for citations and footnotes. For initial research, third-party databases are better suited. These databases often contain more precise options for filtering. The following table provides an overview of online databases for international courts, tribunals, commissions, and committees:

Comprehensive databases	International courts	Human rights bodies	Economic law bodies
WorldCourts	Permanent Court of International Justice: Series A for Judgments until 1930, Series B for Advisory Opinions until 1930, and Series A/B for Judgments, Orders and Advisory Opinions from 1931	University of Minnesota, Human Rights Library for almost all international human rights adjudicative bodies	International Commercial Law: Case Law on UNCITRAL Texts database
World Legal Information Institute	International Court of Justice: List of All Cases database	UN human rights system: • UN Treaty Body Database • OHCHR Jurisprudence Database for United Nations Treaty Bodies • UN Human Rights Bodies Database	International Centre for Settlement of Investment Disputes: ICSID database
JusMundi	International criminal courts: ICC Legal Tools Database	ECtHR's HUDOC database for the European human rights system	International trade dispute settlement bodies: WTO Dispute Documents database
Max Planck Encyclopedias of International Law	International Tribunal for the Law of the Sea: ITLOS Document Search	Inter-American human rights system: • IACmHR's Reports on Cases • Judgments of the IACtHR database • Loyola of Los Angeles International and Comparative Law Review's Inter-American Court of Human Rights Project database • IUSLAT Database on the Inter-American human rights system • SUMMA Database on the Inter-American human rights system	Intellectual Property Law: WIPO Lex

Comprehensive databases	International courts	Human rights bodies	Economic law bodies
World Court Digest		African human rights system: • Cases of the African Court on Human and Peoples' Rights • Communications of the African Commission on Human and Peoples' Rights • Database and commentary on jurisprudence of the African Court on Human and Peoples' Rights • African Human Rights Case Law Analyser	

To use databases effectively, students may think of key phrases that precisely describe the problem. Sometimes, the relevant phrases already emerge from the questions. Our first example asks about the legality of entry restrictions under international law, so that students could search for keywords like 'entry restrictions' and their synonyms. However, this is usually not sufficient to find all relevant cases. Students may also search for secondary literature in parallel, using search engines, library catalogues, encyclopedias, search engines of the major international law publishers, and international law blogs.[34] After this secondary literature review, students can gain a deeper understanding of the legal issues and refine their keywords accordingly.

For instance, our second example asks solely about the lack of State responsibility of Serbia and Montenegro. Searching for the broad term 'State responsibility' would be tedious and yield irrelevant results. Instead, students may first read the relevant case (Bosnian Genocide Case) and literature to identify key legal issues. After this, they can narrow down their search to specific phrases like 'effective control' and 'overall control'.

As international adjudicative bodies draw inspiration from decisions outside their own system, students should also look for comparable problems and decisions in other fields of international law.[35] Throughout the research process, students may repeat their research several times using adjusted keywords as their knowledge increases.

---

34 E.g. AfricLaw, Afronomics, EJIL: Talk!, Just Security, Lawfare, Legal Form, Opinio Juris, TWAILR, Voelkerrechtsblog.
35 See section B.

D. USING CASES IN INTERNATIONAL LAW

To apply the cases, students should first understand the case and then determine the relevance of the case for their assignment and argument.

I. UNDERSTANDING CASES

Case analysis starts with reading, annotating, and summarising it (at least in thought). However, the reading as well as objects of markings and summaries differ depending on the position and task of the student.

In international law, two distinct types of tasks require case analysis. In one case, students must analyse cases strictly from a doctrinal perspective. This applies particularly to moot courts and when students have to write a case brief or solve a case from a judge's standpoint. The focus of analysis should be on locating the cases in the broader context of the relevant field of international law. Students can criticise decisions that deviate from the established canon of the field. In most instances, however, students should focus on distinguishing cases or establishing exceptions and qualifications to rules derived from judgments. In the other case, students can analyse cases not only doctrinally but also disruptively. This occurs when students analyse cases not as (imaginary) members of an institution (be it as applicant/respondent or as a judge) but as external observers (e.g. in a critical case analysis). In this task, students should also locate the case in the broader context of the relevant field of international law. However, the analysis does not end there. Instead, students can analyse the case in light of decisions from other fields of international law, critical methodological approaches (e.g. Third World Approaches to International Law[36]), or interdisciplinary[37] insights. These two types of tasks represent two extreme positions of case analyses. In between, there is a continuum of tasks that combine elements from both types.

1. Reading and Annotating a Case

Before reading the case for the first time, students may ensure that they understand the assignment, as the type of task influences the approach of case analysis. In a second step, students can use the techniques of 'skimming' and 'scanning'[38] to obtain a first overview of the case. Skimming offers a first glimpse of the overarching content of the judgment. Instead of reading the entire judgment or entire paragraphs, students should focus on the title, date of the decision, parties, subheadings, and the first and last sentences of sections. Scanning helps to locate relevant passages within the judgment for further reading. Students can use subheadings and first and last sentences of sections identified during skimming to read only the relevant passages for answering the task. For example,

---

36 On Third World Approaches to International Law, see González Hauck, § 3.2, in this textbook

37 On interdisciplinarity, see Steininger and Paige, § 4.2, in this textbook.

38 BBC Teach Skillswise, 'Reading: Skimming and Scanning' <www.bbc.co.uk/teach/skillswise/skimming-and-scanning/zd39f4j> accessed 26 July 2023.

if students are only interested in the legal reasoning, they may bypass parts describing the facts and the proceedings. In a third step, students may read and annotate the case. Annotations help to create a visual structure for easy reference later.

In the final step of reading and annotating, students may consider rereading the case to review their annotations and prevent mistakes or oversights. Depending on the assignment, it might be useful to read not only the case itself but also case summaries. Many courts provide these summaries themselves, but also journals or encyclopaedias of international law contain case summaries. By supplementing one's own thoughts with thoughts from other lawyers, one's own idea of the case can be verified.

2. Summarising a Case

After several readings of the case, the case can be summarised at least in thought, and for some assignments, in writing. As a rule, this step is not only relevant for examiners but also for students. The case summary should comprehensively, but briefly, present the most important aspects of the case. Only by this step can students verify whether they have really understood the case. In addition, it serves to recall the case later without much effort. Thus, the case summary, in addition to the case reading, is a key prerequisite for using cases in international law.

II. DETERMINING THE RELEVANCE OF A CASE

Before students apply the case, they should determine the relevance of the case for their assignment. Judgments that, at first glance, support one's argumentation should not be used for one's reasoning without hesitation. Likewise, cases that contradict one's own argumentation at first glance are not a final farewell to one's own reasoning. Instead, cases can be evaluated from doctrinal and critical perspectives before they are presented. The appropriate combination of doctrinal and critical evaluation depends on the assignment at hand and cannot be determined in the abstract.

1. Approaching Cases Doctrinally

From a doctrinal perspective, when students want to determine the relevance of the case to their assignment and argument, they must first determine the case's applicability to the assignment. In addition, they may consider obiter dicta and individual opinions.

a) Distinguishing Cases

Before classifying a case as supporting or opposing their reasoning, students may answer two questions. First, do the facts of the case correspond to the facts of the assignment (so-called factual distinguishing)? Students must carefully compare the facts of the case and the assignment's facts to identify similarities that allow the rule to be applied or differences that hinder it. Second, the legal elaborations in the case may contain hidden qualifications or exceptions that preclude the application of a seemingly fitting case or that justify applying an apparently unsuitable case (so-called legal distinguishing). Finally, reasoning in old cases can also be displaced by new legal developments. Crafting a persuasive argument involves acknowledging the cursory fit or lack thereof, and then explaining why the case does or does not fit. Avoid characterising a case as mistaken; instead, rely on factual and legal distinguishing to support your argument.[39]

b) Obiter Dicta

Legal interpretations of courts that are not relevant for deciding the case (so-called *obiter dicta* [Latin: 'incidentally said']) may also be considered in analysing cases. For example, the ICJ defined *opinio juris* (Latin: 'legal opinion') in an obiter dictum in *North Sea Continental Shelf*[40] and defined obligations *erga omnes* (Latin: 'towards all') for the first time in an obiter dictum in *Barcelona Traction*.[41] In both instances, the legal reasoning was not relevant to the outcome of the case, and yet both obiter dicta continue to shape the international legal order to this day. However, even though no formal rule of precedent exists in international law, obiter dicta often exert less persuasive authority on other judicial bodies and should therefore be treated cautiously. For example, ITLOS in *Delimitation of the Maritime Boundary in the Bay of Bengal* refused to apply an obiter dictum of the ICJ in *Territorial and Maritime Dispute between Nicaragua and Honduras in the Caribbean Sea*.[42]

c) Individual Opinions

Many domestic legal systems and almost all international adjudicative bodies (e.g. article 57 ICJ Statute) allow judges to attach individual opinions to the majority decision if they disagree with the majority's reasoning (so-called concurring opinion) or result (so-called dissenting opinion).[43] Although individual opinions are not enforceable, they can contribute to developing legal standards. Individual opinions can assist in interpreting the majority opinion.[44] Concurring opinions often clarify or generalise the court's reasoning,[45] facilitating its application to similar cases. Dissenting opinions not only reveal the rationale for the majority opinion but also offer criticism.

---

39 Michael Y Liu and others, A Guide to the Philip C Jessup International Law Moot Court Competition (Chinese Initiative on International Criminal Justice 2014) 16; David M Scott and Ukri Soirila, 'The Politics of the Moot Court' [2021] European Journal of International Law 1089–1092.

40 *North Sea Continental Shelf Cases (Federal Republic of Germany v Denmark; Federal Republic of Germany v Netherlands)* (Judgement) [1969] ICJ Rep 3 [77].

41 *Barcelona Traction, Light and Power Company, Limited (Belgium v Spain)* (Preliminary Objections) [1964] ICJ Rep 6 [33].

42 *Territorial and Maritime Dispute between Nicaragua and Honduras in the Caribbean Sea (Nicaragua v Honduras)* [2007] ICJ Rep 659 [319]. *Dispute Concerning Delimitation of the Maritime Boundary Between Bangladesh and Myanmar in the Bay of Bengal (Bangladesh/Myanmar)* [2007] ITLOS Rep 4 (ITLOS) [384].

43 See article 57 Statute of the ICJ, article 45(2) ECHR, article 14.3 DSU, article 30 Statute of the ITLOS.

44 Rainer Hofmann, 'Separate Opinion: International Court of Justice (ICJ)' (*Max Planck Encyclopedia of International Procedural Law*, February 2018) <https://opil.ouplaw.com/display/10.1093/law-mpeipro/e3414.013.3414/law-mpeipro-e3414> accessed 26 August 2023, para 48.

45 ICJ, 'Comments of the International Court of Justice on the Report of the UN Joint Inspection Unit on "Publications of the International Court of Justice"' (1986) UN Doc A/41/591/Add.l para 11.

2. Approaching Cases Critically

From a critical perspective, it is much more difficult to recommend generally accepted approaches. However, one common feature of many critical approaches is to view cases as social facts rather than legal ones. Critical approaches address, among other aspects, the sociological conditions of human decision-making in adjudicative bodies, (post-)colonial imprints and effects of decisions, the political economy, and ecological consequences of judgments. While the application of these perspectives requires an engagement with their basic methodological assumptions,[46] they usually enrich a case law analysis enormously by unmasking the supposed neutrality of doctrinal methods. Examples of critical engagement with cases include the 'feminist judgment movement',[47] 'trashing' in the sense of critical legal studies,[48] and 'Reading Back, Reading Black'.[49] In other chapters, this textbook provides insights into how to employ interdisciplinary,[50] (post-)colonial,[51] feminist,[52] and Marxist[53] approaches to legal thinking.

E. CONCLUSION

This section has attempted to provide students with an introduction to case analyses. (Un-)fortunately, it is up to students, along with their teachers and practitioners of international law, to ensure that case analyses in the future no longer only consider decisions from colonising legal systems. This will require a challenging but also rewarding engagement with foreign legal systems, possibly including the learning of new languages (for this, Anglophone readers may feel particularly encouraged, while students from the Global South may refer to the peculiarities of their legal systems and traditions), and the critical questioning of traditional citation practices and case analysis techniques. While this process is time-intensive, it will not only promise novel insights but also serve to counteract the exclusion of the majority of States from the process of creating and developing international law, thereby contributing to fulfilling international law's universalist potential.

---

46 On different approaches to international law, see González Hauck and Kahl, Introduction to § 3, in this textbook.

47 L Hodson and T Lavers, *Feminist Judgments in International Law* (Hart 2019); Troy Lavers and Loveday Hodson, 'Feminist Judgments in International Law' (*Völkerrechtsblog*, 24 April 2017) <https://voelkerrechtsblog.org/feminist-judgments-in-international-law/> accessed 20 June 2023.

48 Mark G Kelman, 'Trashing' (1984) 36 Stanford Law Review 293.

49 I Bennett Capers, 'Reading Back, Reading Black' (2006) 35 Hofstra Law Review article 2.

50 On interdisciplinarity, see Steininger and Paige, § 4.2, in this textbook.

51 On TWAIL, see González Hauck, § 3.2, in this textbook.

52 On feminist approaches to international law, see Kahl and Paige, § 3.3, in this textbook.

53 On Marxist approaches to international law, see Bagchi, § 3.4, in this textbook.

BOX 4.1.5 Further Readings and Further Resources

Further Readings

- G Acquaviva and F Pocar, 'Stare Decisis' (*Max Planck Encyclopedia of Public International Law*) <https://opil.ouplaw.com/display/10.1093/law:epil/9780199231690/law-9780199231690-e1683?prd=MPIL> accessed 26 August 2023

- M Andenas and JR Leiss, 'The Systemic Relevance of "Judicial Decisions" in Article 38 of the ICJ Statute' (2017) 77 HJIL 907

- E Bjorge and CA Miles (eds), *Landmark Cases in Public International Law* (Hart 2017)

- K Linos, 'How to Select and Develop International Law Case Studies: Lessons from Comparative Law and Comparative Politics' (2015) 109 AJIL 475

- M Shahabuddeen, *Precedent in the World Court* (CUP 1996)

Further Resources

- UC Hastings Law, 'International Law Research Guide: Analysis of International Law', <https://libguides.uchastings.edu/international-law/analysis> accessed 26 July 2023.

- NYU Law, 'International Law: General Sources: General Tools for Finding Cases on International Law' <https://nyulaw.libguides.com/c.php?g=773832&p=5975599> accessed 26 July 2023.

- The University of Melbourne, 'Finding International Cases', <https://unimelb.libguides.com/internationallaw/caselaw> accessed 26 July 2023.

§ § §

§ 4.2 INTERDISCIPLINARITY

SILVIA STEININGER AND TAMSIN PHILLIPA PAIGE

BOX 4.2.1 Required Knowledge and Learning Objectives

Required knowledge: None

Learning objectives: This section introduces law students to the basics of interdisciplinarity in public international law. Students will learn about the main strands of interdisciplinary scholarship and the most prominent methodological tools available. They will be able to fully grasp the benefits and challenges of adopting an interdisciplinary perspective on international law and receive helpful practical guidance in creating their own interdisciplinary legal research projects.

A. BASICS FOR INTERDISCIPLINARITY IN PUBLIC INTERNATIONAL LAW

The call for 'interdisciplinarity' has become a staple in international legal research. It 'can be seen everywhere, ranging from funding calls, research agendas, grant applications, conference themes and internet blogs to rhetorical manoeuvres'.[54] Yet, the more interdisciplinarity gained in popularity, the fuzzier its meaning became. To move between disciplines comes with benefits and challenges. In this section, we want to sketch the basics for what interdisciplinarity means, why it is useful, and how to start an interdisciplinary research project.

I. WHAT IS INTERDISCIPLINARITY?

Interdisciplinarity denotes research projects aiming at synthesising and harmonising knowledge and methods from multiple disciplines into a coherent whole.[55] It contrasts with intradisciplinarity, which describes working within the boundaries of one single discipline. Interdisciplinarity requires that the assumptions between two or more disciplines do not contradict each other. It necessitates a strong, substantial, and methodological understanding of those disciplines. Most international legal scholarship takes the form of transdisciplinary or multidisciplinary research, the latter describing persons from different disciplines working together on a common project, each drawing

---

54 Nikolas M Rajkovic, 'Interdisciplinarity' in Jean d'Aspremont and Sahib Singh (eds), *Concepts for International Law* (Edward Elgar 2019) 490.

55 See also Moti Nissani, 'Fruits, Salads, and Smoothies: A Working Definition of Interdisciplinarity' (1995) 29 Journal of Educational Thought 121.

on their own disciplinary knowledge and expertise. Transdisciplinarity attempts to create a unitary common framework among two or more disciplines, to find common research questions, harmonise definitions, and identify explanations that stretch over the scope of just one disciplinary horizon.

Critics argue that the emergence of *x-disciplinarity* (inter-, intra-, trans-, and multi-disciplinarity)[56] dilutes disciplinary boundaries, threatens the idea of a specialised profession, and challenges legal autonomy.[57] In fact, disciplines are not academic silos but overlap and interact with each other. International law suits itself to interdisciplinary approaches, as many research questions necessitate at least a contextual understanding. Nevertheless, 'interdisciplinarity is a politically charged activity in itself'.[58] Interdisciplinary approaches might reproduce, disguise, or even strengthen existing power relations. Adopting an interdisciplinary research agenda and methodological toolbox further requires, for instance, access to methodological training or resources such as specific programs, which might exacerbate structural inequalities in academia. Interdisciplinarity can thus rupture disciplinary gatekeeping and democratise the creation of new knowledge on fundamental questions of international law, but also create additional barriers and adopt a marketised logic.[59]

II. WHY DO INTERDISCIPLINARY RESEARCH?

Doctrinal scholarship adopts an internal viewpoint, taking the perspective of an insider to law, a law student, a professor, or practitioner, who was trained and socialised into the legal community. Such insiders participate in legal discourse, are preoccupied with legal arguments, and are decision oriented. In contrast, interdisciplinary scholarship promotes an external view of law. It usually takes the perspective of the outsider, who observes the processes, structures, and norms of international law in action. Interdisciplinary research allows to ask questions that go beyond the internal logic of law. It does not limit itself to how the law is, but also why the law has been applied in a certain way, and how it should be in the future. Interdisciplinary approaches can illuminate previously overlooked underlying patterns and structures, thus benefiting critical engagement with international law and providing support for improvement via interpretation or further development of the law.[60]

---

56 Outi Korhonen, 'From Interdisciplinary to x-Disciplinary Methodology of International Law' in Rossana Deplano and Nicholas Tsagourias (eds), *Research Methods in International Law* (Edward Elgar 2021) 345.

57 Martti Koskenniemi, 'Letter to the Editors of the Symposium' (1999) 93 AJIL 351.

58 Jan Klabbers, 'The Relative Autonomy of International Law or the Forgotten Politics of Interdisciplinarity' (2004) 1 Journal of International Law and International Relations 35.

59 Outi Korhonen, 'Within and Beyond Interdisciplinarity in International Law and Human Rights' (2017) 28 EJIL 625.

60 Sanne Taekema and Bart van Klink, 'On the Border: Limits and Possibilities of Interdisciplinary Research' in Bart van Klink and Sanne Taekema (eds), *Law and Method. Interdisciplinary Research into Law* (Mohr Siebeck 2011) 7.

III. HOW TO DO INTERDISCIPLINARY RESEARCH

There are countless options to analyse international law from an interdisciplinary perspective and we will give you more insights in the following section. However, in general, one can distinguish between five steps.

To begin, familiarise yourself with the respective approaches, their underlying epistemological considerations, fundamental concepts, and classic influential authors. It is helpful to map existing interdisciplinary engagement with international law. This is important not only to assess the state of the discipline and the topics that are being discussed, but also to identify the respective community, which underpins the respective research project. One can thereby learn how to approach the same topic from different angles, how to transpose fundamental concepts to the study of international law, and how to get socialised into the respective academic and writing style.

Second, in contrast to doctrinal research, interdisciplinary research embraces a more transparent and open structure. In general, the scholar will first identify the research question(s) and possible hypotheses and counterhypotheses before analysing the data. That does not mean that the availability and access to source material cannot guide the respective research design, but it means that the data does not predetermine the research questions. This is different to doctrinal research, in which the identification of structures and the categorisation of cases is a major research aim in itself.

Third, it is important to justify the research design transparently. Interdisciplinary scholarship often includes an explicit methodology section, justifying, among other things, why this particular approach is useful for the study of international law, how this influences the research question(s), which factors guide the identification of hypotheses, what were the criteria required for the selection of research units, which methodologies are going to be applied, how the data is being gathered, and what the limitations of this particular method are. At this stage, you can also identify how the project relates to existing research or conflicting approaches and clearly limit the research agenda.

Fourth, collect the necessary data using comparative research designs, archival work, or other qualitative and quantitative approaches, which will be highlighted in section C. This step might take significant time and require additional resources. It is also heavily reliant on factors outside of the control of the respective researcher, such as access to sources, for instance archives and interview partners.

Finally, evaluate the data with respect to the aforementioned research question. This often includes giving a systematic overview and highlighting particularly interesting or unexpected factors. Hypotheses can be confirmed or refuted. Moreover, it is possible to consider some possible explanations for particular outcomes, reaffirm the limitations of the results, or identify options to expand on the research in future projects.

B. TYPES OF INTERDISCIPLINARY SCHOLARSHIP IN INTERNATIONAL LAW

I. INTERNATIONAL LAW AND HISTORY

Combining international law and history is a very popular form of interdisciplinarity. Prime examples of this type of scholarship can be found in the work of Arnulf Becker Lorca,[61] James Crawford,[62] Martti Koskenniemi,[63] and Anne Orford.[64] Scholars engaging historical enquiries of international law often aim to disrupt accepted narratives that established alleged 'legal truths'.[65] The historiographical turn in international law has also significantly emphasised researching the history of international law in non-Western regions and peripheries. This includes not only a renewed emphasis on questions of imperialism[66] and colonialism,[67] but also on regional and inter-civilisational perspectives.[68]

II. INTERNATIONAL LAW AND SOCIOLOGY

The primary goal of legal sociology is 'to provide insight into an understanding of the law through an empirical study of its practice'.[69] It finds inspiration in the works of Pierre Bourdieu, Émile Durkheim, and Max Weber. In the last two decades, research on sociological perspectives in international law has particularly focused on the practice of international lawyers as a legal profession,[70] the evolution, proliferation, and authority of international courts,[71] the practices of international adjudicators,[72] as well as the

---

61 Arnulf Becker Lorca, *Mestizo International Law: A Global Intellectual History 1842–1933* (CUP 2015).

62 James Crawford, *The Creation of States in International Law* (2nd edn, OUP 2006).

63 Martti Koskenniemi, *The Gentle Civilizer of Nations: The Rise and Fall of International Law 1870–1960* (CUP 2001).

64 Anne Orford, *International Law and the Politics of History* (CUP 2021).

65 For recent examples, see Cristian Van Eijk, 'Unstealing the Sky: Third World Equity in the Orbital Commons' (2022) 47 Air and Space Law 25; Mark Chadwick, *Piracy and the Origins of Universal Jurisdiction: On Stranger Tides?* (Brill/Nijhoff 2019); Tamsin Paige, 'Piracy and Universal Jurisdiction' (2013) 12 Macquarie Law Journal 131.

66 Antony Anghie, *Imperialism, Sovereignty and the Making of International Law* (CUP 2005).

67 Ntina Tzouvala, *Capitalism as Civilisation: A History of International Law* (CUP 2020).

68 Juan Pablo Scarfi, *The Hidden History of International Law in the Americas: Empire and Legal Networks* (OUP 2017); James Thuo Gathii, 'Africa' in Bardo Fassbender and Anne Peters (eds), *The Oxford Handbook of the History of International Law* (OUP 2015) 943; Lauri Mälksoo, *Russian Approaches to International Law* (OUP 2015); Onuma Yasuaki, 'When Was the Law of International Society Born – An Inquiry of the History of International Law from an Intercivilizational Perspective' (2000) Journal of the History of International Law 1.

69 Tamsin Phillipa Paige, *Petulant and Contrary: Approaches by the Permanent Five Members of the UN Security Council to the Concept of 'threat to the Peace' under Article 39 of the UN Charter* (Brill/Nijhoff 2019) 33.

70 Jean d'Aspremont and others (eds), *International Law as a Profession* (CUP 2017).

71 Mikael Rask Madsen, 'From Cold War Instrument to Supreme European Court: The European Court of Human Rights at the Crossroads of International and National Law and Politics: The European Court of Human Rights' (2007) 32 Law & Social Inquiry 137.

72 Salvatore Caserta and Mikael Rask Madsen, 'The Situated and Bounded Rationality of International Courts: A Structuralist Approach to International Adjudicative Practices' (2022) 35 LJIL 931.

emergence and structure of legal fields, for instance in international economic law[73] and international criminal law.[74]

III. INTERNATIONAL LAW AND POLITICAL SCIENCE

Political science perspectives on international law focus on the 'development, operation, spread, and impact of international legal norms, agreements, and institutions'.[75] They expand the study of international law to investigate the role of political organisation, government, and structures upon which international law relies. The most prominent political science approach to international law is international relations.[76] With the proliferation of international cooperation, the end of realist Cold War politics, and the rise of the US-backed liberal internationalist world order, a vocal community of IL–IR scholars emerged in the 1990s.[77] Prominent IL–IR research strands focus on compliance with international law,[78] questions of legality and legitimacy,[79] the emergence of norms[80] and their contestation,[81] and the proliferation of international courts.[82]

IV. INTERNATIONAL LAW AND LITERATURE

The general goal of International Law and Literature is to use literature to advance understandings of international law either through academic scholarship or through works of fiction. Classic examples of using works of fiction to discuss concepts of international law and justice are the work of China Miéville[83] and *The Reader* by Bernhard Schlink.[84] When engaging in academic approaches to International Law and Literature, authors tend to do one of three things with the literature aspect of this scholarship: (1) use works of fiction to explain and make accessible concepts of

---

73 Moshe Hirsch, 'The Sociology of International Economic Law: Sociological Analysis of the Regulation of Regional Agreements in the World Trading System' (2008) 19 EJIL 277.

74 Mikkel Jarle Christensen, 'The Professional Market of International Criminal Justice: Divisions of Labour and Patterns of Elite Reproduction' (2021) 19 Journal of International Criminal Justice 783.

75 Emilie M Hafner-Burton, David G Victor and Yonatan Lupu, 'Political Science Research on International Law: The State of the Field' (2012) 106 AJIL 47.

76 Basak Cali (ed), *International Law for International Relations* (OUP 2009), Jeffrey L Dunoff and Mark A Pollack, 'International Law and International Relations. Introducing an Interdisciplinary Dialogue' in Jeffrey L Dunoff and Mark A Pollack (eds), *Interdisciplinary Perspectives on International Law and International Relations. The State of the Art* (CUP 2013).

77 Kenneth W Abbott, 'Modern International Relations Theory: A Prospectus for International Lawyers' (1989) 14 Yale Journal of International Law 335; Robert O Keohane, 'International Relations and International Law: Two Optics' (1997) 38 HILJ 487; Anne-Marie Slaughter, Andrew S Tulumello and Stepan Wood, 'International Law and International Relations Theory: A New Generation of Interdisciplinary Scholarship' (1998) 92 AJIL 367.

78 Beth A Simmons, 'Compliance with International Agreements' (1998) 1 Annual Review of Political Science 75.

79 Jutta Brunnee and Stephen J Toope, *Legitimacy and Legality in International Law. An Interactional Account* (CUP 2013).

80 Martha Finnemore and Kathryn Sikkink, 'International Norm Dynamics and Political Change' (1998) 52 IO 887.

81 Antje Wiener, *Contestation and Constitution of Norms in Global International Relations* (CUP 2018).

82 Karen Alter, *The New Terrain of International Law: Courts, Politics, Rights* (Princeton University Press 2014).

83 China Miéville, *The City & the City* (Macmillan 2009).

84 Bernhard Schlink, *The Reader* (Vintage International 1995).

international law to non-experts or to illustrate a point of international law to fellow legal scholars,[85] (2) use works of literature as conceptual data to explore societal responses to international law,[86] or (3) use literature as a tool of jurisprudence in order to develop legal theory on particular issues.[87]

V. INTERNATIONAL LAW AND ECONOMICS

The economic analysis of international law emerged in the 2000s[88] but builds on the more established domestic Law and Economics literature starting from the 1960 in US academia.[89] It applies economic theory, in particular rational choice approaches, to problems of international law. The core assumption is the rational actor model. Economic analysis of international law assumes that States are self-interested and decide among alternatives to maximise their gains. The economic approach to international law[90] has been focused on different modes of treaty making,[91] the design of specific clauses such as treaty exits,[92] international dispute settlement,[93] and the legitimacy of customary international law.[94]

A more recent but rapidly growing strand of economic analysis of international law is formed under the umbrella of Law and Political Economy (LPE).[95] This research

---

85 See for instance, Kenneth Anderson, 'Space Law Update – US Won't Build Death Star, Also Does Not Support Blowing Up Planets' (*Opinio Juris*, 12 January 2013) <http://opiniojuris.org/2013/01/12/space-law-update-us-wont-build-death-star-does-not-support-blowing-up-planets/> accessed 25 August 2023; Australian Red Cross, 'Game of Thrones: Violations of and Compliance with International Humanitarian Law' (Australian Red Cross 2019); Stephen Bainbridge, 'Was the Alderaan Incident Consistent with Just War Theory' (*ProfessorBainbridge.com*, 6 June 2005) <www.professorbainbridge.com/professorbainbridgecom/2005/06/was-the-alderaan-incident-consistent-with-just-war-theory.html> accessed 25 August 2023; Kevin Jon Heller, 'The Problem with "Crossing Lines"' (*Opinio Juris*, 25 June 2013) <http://opiniojuris.org/2013/06/24/the-problem-with-crossing-lines/> accessed 25 August 2023.

86 Tamsin Phillipa Paige, 'Zombies as an Allegory for Terrorism: Understanding the Social Impact of Post-9/11 Security Theatre and the Existential Threat of Terrorism Through the Work of Mira Grant' (2021) 33 Law and Literature 119.

87 Mark Bould and China Miéville (eds), *Red Planets: Marxism and Science Fiction* (Pluto Press 2009).

88 Jeffrey L Dunoff and Joel P Trachtman, 'Economic Analysis of International Law' (1999) 24 Yale Journal of International Law 1.

89 Herbert Hovenkamp, 'Law and Economics in the United States: A Brief Historical Survey' (1995) 19 Cambridge Journal of Economics 331; George L Priest, *The Rise of Law and Economics. An Intellectual History* (Routledge 2020).

90 Anne van Aaken, Christoph Engel, and Tom Ginsburg, 'Public International Law and Economics. Symposium Introduction' (2008) 1 University of Illinois Law Review 1.

91 Kenneth W Abbott and Duncan Snidal, 'Hard and Soft Law in International Governance' (2000) 54 IO 421.

92 Laurence R Heifer, 'Exiting Treaties' (2005) 91 Virginia Law Review 1579.

93 Andrew T Guzman, 'International Tribunals: A Rational Choice Analysis' (2008) 157 University of Pennsylvania Law Review 171.

94 Jack L Goldsmith and Eric A Posner, 'A Theory of Customary International Law' (1999) 66 University of Chicago Law Review 1113.

95 Alberta Fabbricotti (ed), *The Political Economy of International Law: A European Perspective* (Edward Elgar 2016). However, see critically on whether this constitutes interdisciplinary research, John Haskell and Akbar Rasulov, 'International Law and the Turn to Political Economy' (2018) 31 LJIL 243.

investigates how international law creates wealth and inequality[96] and upholds neoliberal hegemony,[97] but also how it might 'contribute to understanding and transforming centre – periphery patterns of dynamic inequality in global political economic life'.[98]

VI. INTERNATIONAL LAW AND PSYCHOLOGY

International Law and Psychology was developed in the 2010s and primarily adopts insights of behaviouralism and cognitive psychology. Behaviouralism complements the economic approach by demonstrating that individuals' actions are often not determined by the maximum utility of rational choice but are influenced by several biases.[99] To understand how those biases influence the behaviour of individuals, behaviouralists often rely on experiments. Behaviouralist insights have been applied to treaty design,[100] treaty interpretation,[101] international trade disputes,[102] bilateral investment treaties,[103] legal theory,[104] international humanitarian law,[105] and how to incentivise compliance via rewards.[106]

VII. INTERNATIONAL LAW AND ANTHROPOLOGY

Anthropology and international law attempts to understand the social and cultural contexts of international law, often via ethnographical fieldwork.[107] Anthropological perspectives can be applied to legal norms notwithstanding if they take the form of hard or soft law, written text or oral order.[108] They focus on how individuals and communities as well as non-State actors, corporations, organisations, and so forth create and interact with international law also along transnational lines[109] and in specific local contexts.[110] Anthropological perspectives have been applied to understand how human

---

96 Katharina Pistor, *The Code of Capital: How the Law Creates Wealth and Inequality* (Princeton University Press 2019).

97 Nina Tzouvala, 'International Law and (the Critique of) Political Economy' (2022) 121 South Atlantic Quarterly 297.

98 David Kennedy, 'Law and the Political Economy of the World' (2013) 26 LJIL 7.

99 Anne van Aaken and Tomer Broude, 'The Psychology of International Law: An Introduction' (2019) 30 EJIL 1225.

100 Jean Galbraith, 'Treaty Options: Towards a Behavioral Understanding of Treaty Design' (2013) 53 Virginia Journal of International Law 309.

101 Anne van Aaken, 'The Cognitive Psychology of Rules of Interpretation in International Law' (2021) 115 AJIL Unbound 258.

102 Tomer Broude, 'Behavioral International Law' (2015) 163 University of Pennsylvania Law Review 1099–1157.

103 Lauge N Skovgaard and Emma Aisbett, 'When the Claim Hits: Bilateral Investment Treaties and Bounded Rational Learning' (2013) 65 World Politics 273.

104 Anne van Aaken, 'Experimental Insights for International Legal Theory' (2019) 30 EJIL 1237.

105 Tomer Broude and Inbar Levy, 'Outcome Bias and Expertise in Investigations Under International Humanitarian Law' (2019) 30 EJIL 1303.

106 Anne van Aaken and Betül Simsek, 'Rewarding in International Law' (2021) 115 AJIL 195.

107 Sally Engle Merry, 'Anthropology and International Law' (2006) 35 Annual Review of Anthropology 99. See also Gerhard Anders, 'Anthropology and International Law' Oxford Bibliographies (OUP 2021); Annelise Rise, 'Introduction to the Symposium on The Anthropology of International Law' (2021) 115 AJIL Unbound 268.

108 Miia Halme-Tuomisaari, 'Toward a Lasting Anthropology of International Law/Governance' (2016) 27 EJIL 235.

109 Sally Engle Merry, 'Anthropology, Law, and Transnational Processes' (1992) 21 Annual Review of Anthropology 357.

110 Ricarda Rösch, 'Learning from Anthropology. Realizing a Critical Race Approach to (International) Law' (*Voelkerrechtsblog*, 19 February 2018) <doi:10.17176/20180219-174436> accessed 25 August 2023.

rights have spread globally while also being clearly affected by local dynamics,[111] how social movements engaged with struggles over international law,[112] interactions between indigenous law and international law,[113] the role of professionals such as lawyers and judges,[114] and case studies of different legal institutions and regimes, for instance in international criminal justice.[115]

VIII. INTERNATIONAL LAW AND LINGUISTICS

International Law and Linguistics aims to uncover the meaning of legal provisions by examining how it is being used or understood by different actors.[116] This includes the study of different languages[117] and translation issues.[118] Insights of the linguistic analysis of international law are used to understand the drafting, interpretation, and application of legal norms in treaties and jurisprudence.[119] For instance, discourse analysis and text linguistics examines the legal text and its surrounding context. Studies of historical linguistics and etymology investigate how particular terms have been historically developed and interpreted. Corpus linguistics and computational linguistics aim at handling large amounts of texts to understand the use of certain words or collocations. In international law, linguistic insights have been applied to the interpretation of international legal norms,[120] the use of references in the decisions of international courts and tribunals,[121] and citation practices in general.[122] Another important strand

---

111 Sally Engle Merry, 'Transnational Human Rights and Local Activism: Mapping the Middle' (2006) 108 American Anthropologist 38; Karen Engle, 'From Skepticism to Embrace: Human Rights and the American Anthropological Association from 1947–1999' (2001) 23 HRQ 536.

112 Boaventura de Sousa Santos and César A Rodriguez-Garavito (eds), *Law and Globalization from Below: Towards a Cosmopolitan Legality* (CUP 2005).

113 Paulo Ilich Bacca, 'Indigenizing International Law, Part 1: Learning to Learn from Below' (Blog of the APA, 23 August 2019) <https://blog.apaonline.org/2019/08/23/indigenizing-international-law-part-1-learning-to-learn-from-below/> accessed 25 August 2023.

114 Yves Dezalay and Bryant Garth (eds), *Lawyers and the Construction of Transnational Justice* (Routledge 2012).

115 Richard Ashby Wilson, *Writing History in International Criminal Trials* (CUP 2012).

116 Ulf Linderfalk, 'Introduction: Language and International Law' (2017) 86 NJIL 119.

117 Clara Chapdelaine-Feliciati, 'The Semiotic Puzzle: Authentic Languages & International Law' (2020) 5 International Journal of Legal Discourse 317.

118 Markus Beham, 'Lost in Translation. Varying German-Language Versions of International Treaties and Documents' (*Voelkerrechtsblog*, 17 June 2019) <doi:10.17176/20190617-232607-0> accessed 25 August 2023; Jean d'Aspremont, 'International Law, Universality, and the Dream of Disrupting from the Centre' (2018) 7 ESIL Reflections 1; Jacqueline Mowbray, 'The Future of International Law: Shaped by English' (*Voelkerrechtsblog*, 18 June 2014) <https://voelkerrechtsblog.org/the-future-of-international-law-shaped-by-english/> accessed 25 August 2023.

119 Benedikt Pirker and Jennifer Smolka, 'International Law and Linguistics: Pieces of an Interdisciplinary Puzzle' (2020) 11 Journal of International Dispute Settlement 501.

120 Ingo Venzke, *How Interpretation Makes International Law. On Semantic Change and Normative Twists* (OUP 2012).

121 See for instance, Antje Wiener and Philip Liste, 'Lost without Translation? Cross-Referencing and a New Global Community of Courts' (2014) 21 Indiana Journal of Global Legal Studies 263; Silvia Steininger, 'What's Human Rights Got to Do with It? An Empirical Analysis of Human Rights References in Investment Arbitration' (2018) 31 LJIL 33; Wayne Sandholtz, 'Human Rights Courts and Global Constitutionalism: Coordination Through Judicial Dialogue' (2021) 10 Global Constitutionalism 439.

122 Wolfgang Alschner and Damien Charlotin, 'The Growing Complexity of the International Court of Justice's Self-Citation Network' (2018) 29 EJIL 83.

of research critically reflects on the language(s) in which international law claims universality[123] and challenges the Anglocentrism of international law.[124]

IX. INTERNATIONAL LAW AND OTHER APPROACHES

It is essential to point out that there is also a multitude of other types of interdisciplinary approaches to international law and legal research. These have been particularly popular in new fields of legal research, for instance in the areas of climate research, animal studies, or technology and data science. In general, for interactions with philosophy, you can find inspiration in the chapter on positivism, while critical approaches explained in this book such as TWAIL, Marxism, and feminism and queer theory, also suit themselves to interdisciplinary research agendas.

C. METHODS OF INTERDISCIPLINARY INTERNATIONAL LAW SCHOLARSHIP

While traditional legal scholarship mainly advocates for the doctrinal method, the toolbox of interdisciplinary approaches offers a wider variety of methods to study international law. In the following, we propose the four main methodological 'baskets': comparative method, archival research, qualitative method, and quantitative method. Those four methodological baskets are not mutually exclusive but can be combined with each other and with classical doctrinal approaches.

I. COMPARATIVE METHOD

Comparison can be generally understood as a method which aims at contrasting two or more research units to identify parallels and differences. Interdisciplinary research puts significant emphasis on justifying the design of a comparison. After identifying the research question, the respective scholar generally justifies the comparability of the respective research units.[125] The respective research units are called a *case*. The notion of case here is broader than its general use in international law.[126] A 'case' in interdisciplinary scholarship can be a judgment, an institution, a court, or even a legal system as such. For instance, comparative international law has focused on understanding how and why national legal cultures differ in their engagement with international law.[127] In particular, when there is only a small number of research units,

---

123 Anthea Roberts, *Is International Law International Law* (OUP 2017).

124 Justina Uriburu, 'Between Elitist Conversations and Local Clusters: How Should We Address English-Centrism in International Law?' (*Opinio Juris*, 2 November 2020) <http://opiniojuris.org/2020/11/02/between-elitist-conversations-and-local-clusters-how-should-we-address-english-centrism-in-international-law/> accessed 25 August 2023.

125 See also, Ran Hirschl, 'The Question of Case Selection in Comparative Constitutional Law' (2005) 53 American Journal of Comparative Law 125.

126 For discussion of case analysis, see Milas, § 4.1, in this textbook.

127 Anthea Roberts and others (eds), *Comparative International Law* (OUP 2018).

interdisciplinary scholars aim to provide a thick description of the respective institutions or legal regimes, highlighting similarities and differences, and, if possible, how the researcher aims to account for potential divergences.

In the social sciences, most comparisons adopt an inductive method, originally developed by John Stuart Mill in his 1843 book *A System of Logic*, to illustrate their causal research hypotheses. This means that they account for an outcome (the dependent variable) as well as possible explanatory factors (the independent variable[s]). This is also called the 'most different' or 'most similar' cases design. In the former, the two or more cases are different in every relevant characteristic except for the outcome and the explanatory factor; in the latter, everything between the two cases is similar except for the explanation and the outcome. Charles Tilly further distinguishes four types of comparative analysis, namely individualising, universalising, variation-finding, and encompassing.[128]

II. ARCHIVAL RESEARCH

Given the overlap of historical enquiry to other forms of interdisciplinary research, references to archival material will often crop up in various types of interdisciplinary research and even doctrinal research. The purpose of archival research is a search 'for materials that might flesh out the stories and histories of modern rhetoric and composition we were presenting'.[129] The biggest question related to archival research is the decision about what to include (and perhaps more importantly what to exclude) from a piece of research.[130] Because this is an issue for all forms of empirical research, this will be dealt with in more detail below; however, a general guide is that for something to be excluded there needs to be a defensible basis for that decision – if something is relevant to the topic, credible in terms of its origins, as within an acceptable tolerance of verifiability, it likely should be included in the work.

III. QUALITATIVE RESEARCH METHODS

Qualitative research focuses on an (often hermeneutical) interpretation of texts. These texts could range from ethnographic observation, interviews, free text answers in surveys, or, historical transcripts (e.g. official meetings or speeches).[131] The respective

---

128 Charles Tilly, *Big Structures, Large Processes, Huge Comparisons* (Russell Sage Foundation 1984).

129 Alexis E Ramsey and others, 'Introduction' in idem (eds), *Working in the Archives: Practical Research Methods for Rhetoric and Composition* (Southern Illinois University Press 2010) 1.

130 Jennifer Clary-Lemon, 'Archival Research Processes: A Case for Material Methods' (2014) 33 Rhetoric Review 381, 385.

131 Carl F Auerbach and Louise B Silverstein, *Qualitative Data: An Introduction to Coding and Analysis* (New York University Press 2003) 3; For examples of the authors, see Tamsin Phillipa Paige, 'The Impact and Effectiveness of UNCLOS on Counter-Piracy Operations' (2017) 22 Journal of Conflict & Security Law 97 (based on interviews); Silvia Steininger, 'What's Human Rights Got to Do with It? An Empirical Analysis of Human Rights References in Investment Arbitration' (2018) 31 LJIL 33 (based on references in investment awards); Tamsin Phillipa Paige, 'Zombies as an Allegory for Terrorism: Understanding the Social Impact of

number of texts depends on the research question. In general, the gathered texts should at least constitute a representative sample to guarantee validity, reliability, and objectivity of the resulting analysis. After gathering enough text data, the texts are analysed following a previously identified method to identify patterns, arguments, or frames. Qualitative research methods enable a researcher to understand *why* a phenomenon is occurring.[132] This can be contrasted with quantitative investigations focused on establishing what is occurring. The value of qualitative studies as a supplement to doctrinal analysis is how it permits an understanding of why certain elements of doctrinal law have been developed, or how they play out when implemented on the ground.[133]

IV. QUANTITATIVE RESEARCH METHODS

Quantitative research methods are based on numerical data, which generally means large numbers of texts or codes in international law, for instance from legislation, treaties, or jurisprudence.[134] Hence, a major challenge of quantitative methods concerns the collection of data, either manually or through computational methods. For beginners, it is advisable to use existing databases, either from international courts, international organisations, or academic research projects. Quantitative research methods can be generally differentiated in four types. First, descriptive research aims at identifying patterns and structures in the data without necessarily having a hypothesis before data collection. Second, correlation-aimed research seeks to determine the extent of a relationship between two or more variables using statistical data. Third, causality-focused research attempts to establish cause-effect relationships among the variables in the data. Fourth, experimental research investigates the cause-effect relationship in a study situation in which an effort is made to control for all other variables except one. In international law, quantitative methods have been applied to the jurisprudence of international courts,[135] as well as legal regimes which feature a large number of legal instruments such as international human rights[136] or investment law.[137]

Post-9/11 Security Theatre and the Existential Threat of Terrorism Through the Work of Mira Grant' (2020) 33 Law & Literature 119 (based on literary texts and an interview); Silvia Steininger, 'Creating Loyalty: Communication Practices in the European and Inter-American Human Rights Regimes' (2022) 11 Global Constitutionalism 161 (based on interviews).

132 Roger Cotterrell, *Law, Culture and Society: Legal Ideas in the Mirror of Social Theory* (Ashgate 2006) 130–131; Moshe Hirsch, 'The Sociology of International Economic Law: Sociological Analysis of the Regulation of Regional Agreements in the World Trading System' (2008) 19 EJIL 277, 280.

133 Moshe Hirsch, 'The Sociology of International Law: Invitation to Study International Rules in Their Social Context' (2005) 55 University of Toronto Law Journal 891, 893; Paige (n 69) 34.

134 Wolfgang Alschner, Joost Pauwelyn, and Sergio Puig, 'The Data-Driven Future of International Economic Law' (2017) 20 Journal of International Economic Law 217.

135 Urska Sadl and Henrik Palmer Olsen, 'Can Quantitative Methods Complement Doctrinal Legal Studies? Using Citation Network and Corpus Linguistic Analysis to Understand International Courts' (2017) 30 LJIL 327.

136 Kevin L Cope, Cosette D Creamer, and Mila Versteeg, 'Empirical Studies of Human Rights Law' (2019) 15 Annual Review of Law and Social Science 155.

137 Daniel Behn, Ole Kristian Fauchald, and Malcolm Langford (eds), *The Legitimacy of Investment Arbitration. Empirical Perspectives* (CUP 2022).

D. PITFALLS AND CHALLENGES

I. FINDING THE RIGHT METHOD FOR YOUR RESEARCH QUESTION

Doctrinal law scholars are notoriously bad at articulating their methodology, often stating 'I just read some stuff and then I analyse it'.[138] In this dominantly doctrinal academic culture, interdisciplinary research in law is referred to under the broad umbrella of 'socio-legal' research.[139] One of the biggest hurdles faced by this broad and inclusive categorisation is that it doesn't provide clarity on what the interdisciplinary research is doing and which particular method should be applied. The range of methods available to interdisciplinary scholars is extensive and cannot be covered here in full.[140] The key to understanding what method is most appropriate for the question you are trying to address in your research is familiarising yourself with the other disciplines you are working with and the methods that are employed within that space. No method is inherently correct or incorrect for a particular research question – the key lies in how you justify both the theory and method you are bringing to your question and articulating why that method is being used and not a different one.[141] That said, one should be wary of scholarship that defines itself by the method rather than the research question.

II. SELECTION BIAS

Selection bias is when, deliberately or accidentally, you use a dataset that is incomplete. It renders your argument void, because the data you used was not reliable or meaningful. Data-driven research must include all data, even data that may undercut the primary thesis, because otherwise it is incomplete and therefore is without value.[142] This often goes against many legal researchers' instincts, because legal training still largely focuses on advocacy. In advocacy, focusing on the evidence that support your argument is appropriate and necessary. Another, wider shift when moving from a legal mindset to a data mindset consists in the following: lawyers think in terms of absolutes rules, data-driven research seeks to demonstrate tendencies.

III. UNDERSTANDING EXTERNAL DATA

Broadly speaking, the data source is considered external if the data was not gathered by the researchers themselves. When using external data sources, it is important to establish

---

138 Tamsin Paige, 'Let's Talk About [Sociology], Baby . . . Let's Talk About All the Good Things and the Bad Things That May Be' (*Opinio Juris*, 17 July 2020) <http://opiniojuris.org/2020/07/17/lets-talk-about-sociology-baby-lets-talk-about-all-the-good-things-and-the-bad-things-that-may-be/> accessed 25 August 2023.

139 Dawn Watkins and Mandy Burton, 'Introduction' in Dawn Watkins and Mandy Burton (eds), *Research Methods in Law* (2nd edn, Routledge 2018) 4.

140 Dawn Watkins and Mandy Burton (eds), *Research Methods in Law* (2nd edn, Routledge 2018); Rossana Deplano and Nikolaos K Tsagourias (eds), *Research Methods in International Law: A Handbook* (Edward Elgar 2021).

141 Fiona Cownie and Anthony Bradney, 'Socio-Legal Studies: A Challenge to the Doctrinal Approach' in Dawn Watkins and Mandy Burton (eds), *Research Methods in Law* (2nd edn, Routledge 2018) 46.

142 Ian Dobinson and Francis Johns, 'Legal Research as Qualitative Research' in Dawn Watkins and Mandy Burton (eds), *Research Methods in Law* (2nd edn, Routledge 2018) 34.

the accuracy and integrity of the data, while also acknowledging (or highlighting) any weaknesses that may exist with the dataset. It is also important to justify why the use of an external dataset in this instance is the most appropriate approach to addressing the question at hand. An example of how to manage these questions can be found in the second part of chapter 2 of Paige's study on UN Security Council decision-making in relation to threat to the peace.[143]

IV. PERSONAL CONSTRAINTS (TIME, SKILLS, RESOURCES)

The most significant factor when considering personal constraints is time. In a 2013 seminar on doing interdisciplinary research, renowned sociologist of law Angela Melville noted that the best approach to assessing time constraints in empirical research was to generate a realistic timeline and then triple it,[144] because no planning accounts for all the unexpected hurdles that crop up when doing empirical work. The other main constraint to consider is access: Will you have access to the dataset? Will you have access to sufficient interview participants to have a complete dataset? Will you have access to enough resources to continue data gathering until you have reached data saturation? Will you physically be able to get access to the relevant participants themselves? All of these questions need to be considered in the research design phase, and all of the complications that arise around these issues are why any empirical work will take three times longer than you expect.

BOX 4.2.2 Further Readings

Further Readings

- E Lieblich, 'How to Do Research in International Law? A Basic Guide for Beginners', 62 Harvard Journal of International Law (2021) 42–67

- S Dothan, 'A Guide to Quantitative Legal Research', iCourts Working Paper Series No. 221 (2020)

- S Pahuja, 'Practical Methodology: Writing About How We Do Research' in Rossana Deplano and Nicholas Tsagourias (eds), *Research Methods in International Law* (Edward Elgar 2021) 60

- Siddharth Peter de Souza and Lisa Hahn, 'The Socio-Legal Lab: An Experiential Approach to Research on Law in Action' (*Free Interactive Visual Workbook*) <https://openpresstiu.pubpub.org/socio-legal-lab> accessed 25 August 2023

---

§ § §

---

143 Paige (n 69) 38–42.
144 Angela Melville, 'Qualitative Methods' (Early Career Research Workshop: Socio-Legal Scholarship, ANU College of Law, 14 February 2013).

PART II
GENERAL INTERNATIONAL LAW

5

CHAPTER 5
INTERNATIONAL LAW AND DOMESTIC LAW

RAFFAELA KUNZ

BOX 5.1 Required Knowledge and Learning Objectives

Required knowledge: Positivism; Enforcement; Sources

Learning objectives: Understanding the questions arising in the interaction between domestic and international law, the dominant theories conceptualising the relationship between the legal orders, practical questions arising for domestic courts, and the relevance of domestic courts in the international legal order.

BOX 5.2 Interactive Exercises

Access *interactive exercises for this chapter*[1] by positioning your smartphone camera at the dot-filled box, also known as a QR code.

Figure 5.1 QR code referring to interactive exercises.

A. INTRODUCTION

How to conceptualise the relationship between international and domestic (or municipal) law is an old question in international legal scholarship. Yet, interactions between the two bodies of law give rise to lively debates until today. The conceptualisation of the relationship is closely connected to fundamental questions: it is tied to the very concept of law one has and mirrors the structural changes of

---

1   https://openrewi.org/en-projects-project-public-international-law-interaction/

DOI: 10.4324/9781003451327-7

international law over time.[2] From the perspective of domestic law, it touches upon issues as crucial as the separation of powers and the democratic legitimacy of the law. In times of global governance, with encounters between domestic and international law increasing, the question has arisen whether new conceptualisations are required.

This chapter aims to give an overview of questions arising when domestic and international law meet. It first presents the classic theories conceptualising the relationship between domestic and international law and their limitations to then discuss some practical questions domestic courts face when applying international law. Finally, it also touches upon the application of domestic law by international courts and discusses several contemporary debates.

B. CONCEPTUALISING THE RELATIONSHIP

I. THE CLASSICAL THEORIES AND THEIR LIMITS

1. Starting Point

Traditionally, there are two main theories conceptualising the relationship between international and domestic law: monism and dualism. Their main difference is that monism understands international and domestic law as one legal order, whereas dualism starts from the idea of two separate legal orders. Today, one might argue that the legal reality rather resembles a dualist conception. While international law asserts its primacy over domestic law and requires to be followed in good faith,[3] it leaves it up to the States to decide about the specific modalities to do so. International obligations thus stop 'short at the outer boundaries of the State machinery'.[4] In this sense, international law may 'insert its demands in the box, requiring certain results to come out of it; however, it cannot determine how these results are reached within the box'.[5]

States' 'freedom of implementation' is limited by the fact that they cannot invoke their domestic law to justify the non-fulfilment of their obligations.[6] Article 3 of the Articles on the Responsibility of States for Internationally Wrongful Acts[7] makes clear that the characterisation of an act as internationally wrongful 'is not affected by the characterization of the same act as lawful by internal law'. The non-achievement of the

---

2 Cf. also Pierre Mary Dupuy, 'International Law and Domestic (Municipal) Law' (*Max Planck Encyclopedia of International Law*, April 2011) para 1.

3 Articles 26 and 27 Vienna Convention on the Law of Treaties (adopted 23 May 1969, entered into force 27 January 1980) 1155 UNTS 331(VCLT).

4 ILC, 'Report of the Commission to the General Assembly on the Work of Its Twenty-Ninth Session' (9 May–29 July 1977), UN Doc A/32/10 [18].

5 Ward Ferdinandusse, 'Out of the Black Box? The International Obligation of State Organs' (2003) 29 Brooklyn Journal of International Law 45, 48.

6 Articles 26 and 27 VCLT.

7 ILC, 'Responsibility of States for internationally wrongful acts (53rd session 23 April–1 June and 2 July–10 August 2001) UN Doc A/RES/56/83 Annex.

required result thus leads to the responsibility of the State on the international plane.[8] Yet, given that the international order to a large extent lacks centralised enforcement mechanisms, it is domestic actors and among them chiefly domestic courts which play a primordial role in bringing international law to life. This decentralised application of the law is necessarily less uniform than at the domestic level.

Dualism and monism address the question how international law becomes *valid* within the domestic legal system (i.e. how it becomes binding law within the domestic sphere). This question is distinct from the question of the position of international law within the *norm hierarchy* or the question whether international law is *directly applicable* by domestic courts and authorities, as discussed below. Given that, in practice, these latter questions are often more relevant than the formal validity of international law, the monism/dualism controversy has been criticised as 'unreal, artificial and strictly beside the point'.[9] Moreover, today neither of the two theories is ever fully realised. Even dualist States often recognise the immediate binding force of some rules of international law; conversely, in monist States, courts often reserve the right not to apply international law in certain cases, as will be discussed below. Nonetheless, the theories continue to play a role in international legal practice and discourse.

2. Dualism

Dualism starts from the idea that international law and domestic law are two distinct legal orders and highlights the autonomy of both systems. As Heinrich Triepel, the founder of dualism, has put it, international and domestic law are like 'two circles that at most touch, but never intersect'.[10] According to this view, for an international legal norm to become valid in the domestic system, it needs to be 'translated' to the domestic sphere through an act of 'transformation'. States following a dualist model include Germany, the United Kingdom, India, and Israel.

Among the dualist States, a further distinction is necessary. In the first group of States, including Germany, formal parliamentary approval through a legislative act is sufficient for the transformation of international law.[11] In the second group, a treaty can only be applied after having been implemented through substantive legislation. An example is the *Human Rights Act*[12] in the United Kingdom, which implements the European Convention of Human Rights (currently again subject to reform discussions).[13] In this case, the law that is applied domestically is not the treaty itself but rather the domestic legislation that implements it.

---

8 On State responsibility, see Arévalo-Ramírez, § 9, in this textbook.

9 Gerald Fitzmaurice, 'The General Principles of International Law Considered from the Standpoint of the Rule of Law' (1957) 92 RdC 71.

10 Heinrich Triepel, *Völkerrecht und Landesrecht* (First Published 1899, Aalen 1958) 111.

11 Basic Law 1949 article 59(2).

12 Human Rights Act 1998.

13 See on the government's reform proposal Colm O'Cinneide, 'Having Its (Strasbourg) Cake, and Eating It: The UK Government's Proposals for a New "Bill of Rights"' (*Völkerrechtsblog*, 26 January 2022) <doi:10.17176/20220126-180053-0>

3. *Monism*

Contrary to dualism, monism considers international and domestic law to be one single legal order. According to Hans Kelsen, the most prominent proponent of monism, both international and domestic law derive their validity from one basic norm (German: 'Grundnorm').[14] The main difference between monism and dualism in practice is that in monist States, international law does not need to be transformed into domestic law to acquire validity. In other words, international norms become automatically valid upon adoption. But Kelsen went even further, considering that any domestic rule contradicting international law is void. While dualism can therefore be described with Triepel as two separate circles, a pyramid with international law on top best represents monism.

Examples of monist States include the Netherlands, Switzerland, China, and many Latin American countries.

II. CURRENT DEBATES: IS DUALISM MORE DEMOCRATIC THAN MONISM?

On the international plane, the executive branch remains the main actor, including for the conclusion of treaties. This differs from the domestic realm, with designated law-making bodies in place for law-making processes. The ratification process (i.e. involving the legislative branch before a treaty becomes domestically binding law) is to some extent a compromise allowing to involve the democratically elected body in the process. However, many argue that this is no longer sufficient considering the significant structural changes that international law has undergone. Classical international law was primarily focused on inter-State issues. This has changed significantly, with virtually every area now subject to international regulation. Wolfgang Friedman famously described this process as a transformation from a 'law of coexistence' to a 'law of cooperation'.[15] Today some even employ the term 'global administration' to describe the dense web of international regulation in place, blurring established boundaries between the domestic and the international as well as public and private spheres.[16] This development has increased concerns about the democratic legitimacy or a 'political deficit'[17] of large parts of the law governing today's societies.

Dualism, which entails a stronger involvement of legislative bodies, is sometimes portrayed as more democratic than monism. By way of example, in Switzerland,

---

14 Hans Kelsen, 'Pure Theory of Law' (Max Knight, trans., 2nd edn, University of California Press 1967). On the 'Grundnorm', see Etkin and Green, § 3.1, in this textbook.

15 Wolfgang Friedman, *The Changing Structure of International Law* (Columbia University Press 1964). See also Joseph Weiler, 'The Geology of International Law' (2004) 64 HJIL 547; Bruno Simma, 'From Bilateralism to Community Interest International Law' (1994) 250 RdC 217.

16 For an overview, see Benedict Kingsbury and Nico Krisch, 'The Emergence of Global Administrative Law' (2005) 68 LCP 15.

17 Isabelle Ley, 'Opposition in International Law – Alternativity and Revisibility as Elements of a Legitimacy Concept for Public International Law' (2015) 28 LJIL 717, 720.

known for its strong direct democratic tradition, a parliamentary motion in 2014 (unsuccessfully) requested a shift from monism to dualism, arguing that this would strengthen the democratic legitimacy of the Swiss legal order.[18] In the UK, in earlier discussions about the legal modalities of Brexit, it was argued that dualism 'may save the United Kingdom from Brexit'.[19] The core of the argument was that leaving the European Union would alter the UK's domestic law, necessitating parliamentary involvement. Also some domestic courts have displayed a 'dualist reflex' in recent years (see C.II.).

However, dualism's democratic potential is overrated. Legislation transforming treaties must align with the corresponding international obligations, reflecting the principle that States must not invoke domestic norms to deviate from international law. Legislative discretion is therefore inherently limited. Conversely, in monist States like Switzerland, there are discussions about whether parliament needs to be involved in treaty withdrawal, especially for important treaties.[20] This suggests that neither dualism nor monism provides satisfactory answers to all challenges and tensions arising in times of global governance, where concerns over the legitimacy of the law have intensified. Consequently, some argue that a different conceptualisation is needed and that domestic actors should be accorded a certain degree of flexibility when applying international law (see C.II.).

C. INTERNATIONAL LAW
IN DOMESTIC COURTS

I. QUESTIONS DETERMINING THE ROLE OF INTERNATIONAL LAW

Because of the decentralised nature of the international legal system, in practice it is often domestic actors and, among those, chiefly domestic courts that apply and implement international law. Until not so long ago, domestic courts were rather reluctant in this regard. The reason was that the international arena was considered to be the exclusive realm of the executive branch.[21] This prompted the *Institut de Droit International* in 1993 to state that it was necessary 'to strengthen the independence of national courts in relation to the Executive and to promote better knowledge of

---

18 Parliamentary motion No 14.3221, 'Dualismus statt Monismus' (21 March 2014) <www.parlament.ch/de/ratsbetrieb/suche-curia-vista/geschaeft?AffairId=20143221> accessed 21 August 2023.

19 Julian Ku, 'How Dualism May Save the United Kingdom from Brexit' (*OpinioJuris*, 3 November 2016) <https://opiniojuris.org/2016/11/03/how-dualism-may-save-the-united-kingdom-from-brexit/> accessed 21 August 2023.

20 See e.g. Nina Blum, Vera Nägeli, and Anne Peters, 'Die verfassungsmäßigen Beteiligungsrechte der Bundesversammlung und des Stimmvolkes an der Kündigung völkerrechtlicher Verträge' (2013) 114 ZBl 527.

21 Eyal Benvenisti, 'Reclaiming Democracy: The Strategic Uses of Foreign and International Law by National Courts' (2008) 102 AJIL 241; Eyal Benvenisti and George W Downs, *Between Fragmentation and Democracy: The Role of National and International Courts* (CUP 2017) 105.

international law by such courts'.[22] Today the situation has changed. Following the significant increase in international regulation leading to substantial overlaps with issues previously falling in the *domaine réservé* (French: 'exclusive domain') of States, domestic courts started to engage with international law more frequently. Today, they regularly decide on cases involving international law and are even considered to play a gap-filling role in the decentralised international legal order, to large extent lacking centralised enforcement mechanisms. By applying international law in the cases before them, domestic courts bring international law to life and contribute to enforcing it. In line with Georges Scelle's theory of *dédoublement fonctionnel* (French: 'functional splitting'),[23] domestic judges thus not only fulfil a judicial function at the domestic level; they also have an international judicial function.[24] They thus arguably contribute to strengthening the international rule of law.[25] In recent years, due to the increased activity of international tribunals and the regulatory activities of international organisations, domestic courts not only deal with international treaties and custom, but they increasingly also have to decide cases in which international judicial decisions or secondary rules play a role.[26] Recently, cases in which domestic courts contradict their international counterparts or refuse to apply international law seem to occur more frequently (see C.II.).

In practice, besides the question whether international law has gained *validity*, there are a number of other questions that determine if courts can become active as 'enforcers' of international law and, consequently, the role international law may effectively play in the domestic sphere. To begin with, some questions are considered *non-justiciable* (i.e. not in the competence of courts to decide). By way of example, in some States, primarily the US and the UK, the 'act of State doctrine' still applies. According to this doctrine, which is related to State immunity, handling international affairs falls within the exclusive ambit of the executive branch, and thus certain issues fall outside of what courts can decide.[27]

Another question also concerning the separation of powers, in this case towards the legislative branch, is the question whether international law is *directly applicable* ('self-executing'). Under this doctrine, courts or administrative agencies test if they are allowed to apply an international legal provision directly, that is,

---

22 Institut de droit international, 'The Activities of National Judges and the International Relations of their State' (7 September 1993) <www.idi-iil.org/app/uploads/2017/06/1993_mil_01_en.pdf> accessed 21 August 2023.

23 Georges Scelle, 'Le phénomène juridique du dédoublement fonctionnel' in Walter Schätzel and Hans-Jürgen Schlochauer (eds), *Rechtsfragen der Internationalen Organisation. Festschrift für Hans Wehberg* (Verlag Klostermann 1956) 324.

24 Yuval Shany, 'Dédoublement fonctionnel and the Mixed Loyalties of National and International Judges' in Filippo Fontanelli, Giuseppe Martinico, and Paolo Carrozza (eds), *Shaping Rule of Law Trough Dialogue: International and Supranational Experiences* (Europa Law 2010) 29.

25 André Nollkaemper, *National Courts and the International Rule of Law* (OUP 2011).

26 On judicial decisions and resolutions of international organisations as sources of law, see Kunz, Lima, and Castelar Campos, § 6.4, in this textbook.

27 Fausto de Quadros and John Henry Dingfelder Stone, 'Act of State Doctrine' (*Max Planck Encyclopedia of International Law*, April 2021) paras 1, 6.

without the need for further specification or implementation through legislative or administrative measures.[28] Even though the question under which conditions international law is directly applicable primarily is a question of domestic law, as confirmed by the ICJ in *Avena*,[29] courts around the globe have developed similar criteria.[30] Among these criteria, the *precision* of a norm is often decisive.[31] This is because if a norm is imprecise, it is considered incomplete and in need of implementation, or indeed being 'executed', before it can be applied to concrete cases.

Finally, a question which is highly relevant in practice concerns the *rank* of international law within the domestic norm hierarchy.[32] This question becomes relevant in cases of norm conflicts between international and domestic law which occur frequently and in times of globalisation arguably even more so, as discussed in the next section. If domestic law prevails in such a case, international law will remain ineffective. However, domestic courts have found ways to avoid conflicts, such as through the consistent interpretation of domestic law in light of international law.[33]

II. RECENT DEVELOPMENTS: 'BACKLASH' AGAINST INTERNATIONAL LAW?

In the decentralised international legal system, great hope is being placed on domestic courts. Yet, over the last years, there seems to be an increasing number of cases in which domestic courts explicitly refuse to apply international law and/or follow judgments of international courts. These cases have sometimes been called cases of 'principled resistance'.[34] To be sure, it is not a new phenomenon that domestic courts clarify that, while they are open to international law and willing to contribute to its enforcement, there are certain limits. In Europe, many high courts have reserved the right to 'defend' a certain constitutional core against the 'intrusion' of European and international law, with the *Solange I* case of the German Federal Constitutional Court being a famous example.[35]

---

28 Karen Kaiser, 'Treaties, Direct Applicability' (*Max Planck Encyclopedia of International Law*, February 2013) para 1.

29 *Request for Interpretation of the Judgment of 31 March 2004 Case Concerning Avena and Other Mexican Nationals (Mexico v. United States of America)* (Judgment) [2009] ICJ Rep 3 [44].

30 Yuji Iwasawa, 'Domestic Application of International Law' (2016) 378 RdC 9, 157–158.

31 Ibid 172.

32 On norm hierarchy, see Eggett, § 6.D., in this textbook.

33 On consistent interpretation, see Nollkaemper (n 25) chapter 7.

34 Fiona de Londras and Kanstantsin Dzehtsiarou, 'Mission Impossible? Addressing Non-Execution Through Infringement Proceedings in the European Court of Human Rights' (2017) 66 ICLQ 467. For a critical answer, see Alice Donald, 'Tackling Non-Implementation in the Strasbourg System: The Art of the Possible?' (*EJIL: Talk!*, 28 April 2017) <www.ejiltalk.org/tackling-non-implementation-in-the-strasbourg-system-theart-of-the-possible/> accessed 21 August 2023. See also Marten Breuer, '"Principled Resistance" to ECtHR Judgments: Dogmatic Framework and Conceptual Meaning' in Marten Breuer (ed), *Principled Resistance to ECtHR Judgments – A New Paradigm?* (Springer 2019).

35 (1974) BVerfGE 37, 271 BvL 52/71 (German Constitutional Court); for more examples, see Peters, 'The Globalization of State Constitutions' in Janne E Nijman and André Nollkaemper (eds), *New Perspectives on the Divide between National and International Law* (OUP 2007) 266–267.

Yet, the number and diversity of these cases seem to be growing.[36] Today, they seem to span many jurisdictions and issue areas of international law. Much-discussed examples include the Italian Constitutional Court, which in 2014 decided that the implementation of the judgment of the International Court of Justice in the *Jurisdictional Immunities* case[37] would among other things violate the Italian constitution. It declared the law implementing the judgment to be unconstitutional, and, as a consequence, the ICJ judgment has not been implemented to this date.[38] In human rights law, examples include the Argentinian Supreme Court, which in 2017 refused to follow the Inter-American Court of Human Rights in the case of *Fontevecchia and D'Amico*,[39] and the Russian Constitutional Court, which even developed a certain 'control of constitutionality' of judgments of the European Court of Human Rights (later translated into legislation).[40]

In many cases courts rely on constitutional norms, including fundamental rights, when refusing to follow international law.[41] Rather than violating the rule of law, they thus seem to believe that they act in the interest of the rule of law. While these cases are often perceived as a setback or 'backlash' against international law, this suggests that the reality is more complicated.[42] To be sure, in some cases the invocation of constitutional law might simply be a pretext not to follow an undesired international norm. Overall, however, it is undeniable that with the massive growth of international regulation in quantitative terms and the proliferation of international courts, clashes between legal orders have simply become more frequent.[43] Domestic courts can thus find themselves in a dilemma: on the one hand, they are 'servants' to international law within the domestic realm and act as pivotal safeguards for its effectiveness. On the other hand, they remain 'answerable to the dictates of applicable domestic law'.[44]

There are no simple answers to this dilemma. To give precedence to the domestic constitution as a matter of principle might not be the best solution in times of global governance. A more flexible approach, allowing to balance the different rights and

---

36 On this in more detail, see Raffaela Kunz, 'Judging International Judgments Anew? The Human Rights Courts Before Domestic Courts' (2019) 30 EJIL 1129.

37 *Jurisdictional Immunities of the State (Germany v. Italy: Greece intervening)* (judgment) [2012] ICJ Rep 99.

38 See on this stalemate Valentina Volpe, Anne Peters, and Stefan Battini (eds), *Remedies against Immunity? Reconciling International and Domestic Law after the Italian Constitutional Court's Sentenza 238/2014* (Springer 2021).

39 (2017) 368/1998 (34-M)/CS1 (Supreme Court Argentina).

40 (2015) 21-P/2015 (Constitutional Court Russia).

41 See also Fulvio Palombino, 'Compliance with International Judgments: Between Supremacy of International Law and National Fundamental Principles' (2015) 75 HJIL 503; Stefano Battini, 'E costituzionale il diritto internazionale?' (2015) 3 Giornale di diritto amministrativo 367; Anne Peters, 'Supremacy Lost: International Law Meets Domestic Constitutional Law' (2009) 3 ICL Journal 170.

42 See e.g. Mikael Rask Madsen, Pola Cebulak, and Micha Wiebusch, 'Backlash against International Courts: Explaining the Forms and Patterns of Resistance to International Courts' (2018) 14 JLC International 197.

43 See also Kunz (n 36) 1157; Nico Krisch, 'Pluralism in International Law and Beyond' in Jean d'Aspremont and Sahib Singh (eds), *Concepts for International Law. Contributions to Disciplinary Thought* (Edward Elgar 2019) 691.

44 Rosayln Higgins, 'National Courts and the International Court of Justice' in Mads Adenas and Duncan Fairgrieve (eds), *Tom Bingham and the Transformation of the Law: A Liber Amicorum* (2009) 417.

interests at stake in each case, might better fit today's complex legal reality. In some cases, the application of international law might lead to more just outcomes even if domestic law stands in the way, for example the reopening of a domestic court ruling if the underlying procedure violated human rights standards even if domestic law does not foresee such a possibility. On the other hand, in some situations the application of international law may lead to unreasonable outcomes.[45] This reflects a more pluralist vision of legal orders: today's complex legal situation has prompted scholars to suggest new conceptualisations of the relationship between international and domestic law, conceptualisations that recognise multiple legal systems with competing claims to authority and no clear point of reference.[46]

D. DOMESTIC LAW IN INTERNATIONAL COURTS

Domestic courts as State organs contribute to fulfil the international legal duties of their States when applying international law. Conversely, international courts cannot be said to contribute to fulfilling a broader duty when engaging with domestic law. Against this background, it is not surprising that international courts have been reluctant to apply domestic law. The Permanent Court of International Justice has famously stated that 'municipal laws are merely facts which express the will and constitute the activities of States'.[47]

Today, however, it is well recognised that domestic law also plays a role on the international plane. This is obvious when it comes to the creation of international law: domestic legislation is at the heart of general principles of law,[48] and the decisions of domestic courts may constitute State practice, thus contributing to the formation of customary international law.[49] It has furthermore been argued that 'domestic law is sometimes a necessary component in the functioning of an international rule itself: the determination of nationality for the purposes of diplomatic protection or the definition of the rights of a shareholder are prime examples'.[50]

But the relevance of domestic law on the international plane does not end there. It has been shown that the structural changes of international law, moving away from

---

45 See Kunz (n 36) in more detail and with further references.

46 For an overview, see Krisch (n 43).

47 *Certain German Interests in Polish Upper Silesia* (Merits) PCIJ Rep Series A No. 7.

48 On general principles, see Eggett, § 6.3, in this textbook.

49 See, for example, ILC, 'Second Report on the Identification of Customary International Law, Michael Sir Wood, Special Rapporteur' (Sixty-Sixth Session, 5 May–6 June and 7 July–8 August 2014) UN Doc A/CN.4/672, para 34; Philip M Moremen, 'National Courts Decisions as State Practice: A Transjudicial Dialogue?' (2006) 32 North Carolina Journal of International Law 259; Wolfgang Friedmann, 'The Use of "General Principles" in the Development of International Law' (1963) 57 AJIL 279. On customary international law, see Stoica, § 6.2, in this textbook.

50 Daniel Peat, *Comparative Reasoning in International Courts and Tribunals* (CUP 2019) 51.

purely inter-State issues towards more and more areas previously only regulated by domestic law, has not only led to a more frequent application of international law by domestic actors, but more generally has had the consequence that 'the line between domestic and international law is increasingly blurred, with legal concepts, rules and principles crossing freely between the two spheres'.[51] Today, just as international law plays a role for domestic courts, the same is true the other way around. While inter-State courts, such as the ICJ, are still cautious in relying on domestic law, in other areas of law, domestic law is an integral part of the legal system, such as in the 'margin of appreciation' doctrine of the European Court of Human Rights (ECtHR).[52] This doctrine allows the Court to take into account developments at the domestic level; only if there is a certain consensus among member States will it intervene. The ECtHR has furthermore made it clear that the interpretation and development of the Convention standards is a joint endeavour, a 'shared responsibility' between domestic courts and the ECtHR.[53] In some cases, it has even been criticised for allegedly 'giving in' to domestic actors in the face of political pressure, risking to lose credibility.[54]

E. CONCLUSION

The question how the relationship between domestic law and international law should be conceptualised, and how concrete cases of conflict between the two bodies of law should be resolved, remains live and practically relevant until today. This chapter has shown that in times of global governance, domestic and international law are not neatly separated legal orders, but rather strongly intertwined and mutually influential. With the body of international law growing quantitatively and expanding into more issue areas previously regulated solely by domestic law, the legal reality has become more complex. Seeking to provide clarity and stability, some domestic courts have started to develop new criteria on how to deal with international law. One common thread is that they give precedence to the domestic constitution. While it seems to be too far-reaching to see this as a 'backlash' against international law, it is questionable whether the approach is suited to today's legal reality. A more flexible approach, reflecting pluralist conceptualisations of the relationship between legal orders, although less clear than strict conflict rules and hierarchies, might fit better, for it allows to balance the different rights and interests at stake in each case.

---

51 Ibid 3.

52 See on this in detail ibid.

53 ECtHR, 'Implementation of the Judgments of the European Court of Human Rights: A Shared Judicial Responsibility?' (31 January 2014) <www.echr.coe.int/Documents/Seminar_background_paper_2014_ENG. pdf> accessed 21 August 2023; Janneke Gerards, 'The European Court of Human Rights and the National Courts: Giving Shape to the Notion of "Shared Responsibility"' in Jenneke Gerards and Joseph Fleuren (eds), *Implementation of the European Convention of Human Rights and of the Judgments of the ECtHR in National Case-Law* (Intersentia 2014).

54 European Court of Human Rights, *Hutchinson v The United Kingdom* (Judgement) [2017] App No 57592/08, Dissenting Opinion of Judge Pinto de Albuquerque [38].

BOX 5.3 Further Readings and Further Resources

Further Readings

- A Nollkaemper, *National Courts and the International Rule of Law* (OUP 2011)

- M Rask Madsen, P Cebulak, and M Wiebusch, 'Backlash Against International Courts: Explaining the Forms and Patterns of Resistance to International Courts' (2018) 14 JLC International 197

- R Kunz, 'Judging International Judgments Anew? The Human Rights Courts Before Domestic Courts' (2021) 30 EJIL 1129

Further Resources

R Kunz, A Chehtman, and K O'Reagan, 'From Compliance Partners to Gatekeepers? The Role of Domestic Courts in Interpreting and Enforcing IHRL' (*Bonavero Discussion Group*, 9 March 2021) <www.law.ox.ac.uk/events/compliance-partners-gatekeepers-role-domestic-courts-interpreting-and-enforcing-ihrl> accessed 29 August 2023

§ § §

6

CHAPTER 6
SOURCES OF INTERNATIONAL LAW

CRAIG EGGETT, TAXIARCHIS FISKATORIS,
MARKO SVICEVIC, VICTOR STOICA,
RAFFAELA KUNZ, LUCAS CARLOS LIMA,
AND BERNARDO MAGESTE CASTELAR CAMPOS

INTRODUCTION
CRAIG EGGETT

BOX 6.1 Required Knowledge and Learning Objectives

Required knowledge: Nature and Purpose of International Law; Approaches to International Law

Learning objectives: Understanding the nature of sources in international law and the relationship between the sources.

BOX 6.2 Interactive Exercises

Access *interactive exercises for this chapter*[1] by positioning your smartphone camera at the dot-filled box, also known as a QR code.

Figure 6.1 QR code referring to interactive exercises.

---

1   https://openrewi.org/en-projects-project-public-international-law-sources-of-international-law/

DOI: 10.4324/9781003451327-8

A. INTRODUCTION

The topic of the 'sources' of international law is essentially concerned with one central, and rather basic, question: how are international legal rules made? Despite the foundational nature of this question, there are few areas of international legal scholarship that have generated such long-running and fierce debate. Questions about the sources of international law have always been central to international legal discourse, and understanding the language of the sources remains critical for all actors wishing to engage with the international legal system. This chapter introduces some broader questions about the sources of international law, with the aim of setting the scene for the examination of the individual sources discussed in the following chapters.

B. THE CONCEPT OF A 'SOURCE' OF INTERNATIONAL LAW

As a preliminary point, it is useful to consider the precise meaning of 'source', as some authors have used the term to describe a range of foundational aspects and processes of the international legal system. Some scholars have understood this term to cover the origins and rationale of international law as such.[2] The use of the term 'source' to include the background and objectives of a rules-based international order is broader and rather unconventional.[3] More commonly, sources doctrine is concerned with the processes through which international legal rules are created.[4] These processes are, and should continue to be, subject to discussion and critique. As parts of the foundation of international law, they should be continually revisited to ensure they reflect the modern objectives of the legal system.

I. SOURCES AND THE INTERNATIONAL LEGAL SYSTEM

The international legal system, like all legal systems, is composed of primary and secondary rules.[5] Primary rules are those that create obligations, grant rights, or change a legal situation. Examples include the prohibition of the use of force, rules on human rights, and provisions that set conditions for membership to international organisations. Conversely, secondary rules are those that regulate the creation, modification, and application of those rules. Examples include rules on the interpretation of treaties and the law of State responsibility. The rules on the sources of international law are a category of secondary rules; they set out the criteria for the creation of other international rules. The presence and operation of secondary rules is indispensable for the existence and functioning of the international legal system. As such, when searching for answers to questions about the sources, it is

---

2   Percy Corbett, 'The Consent of States and the Sources of the Law of Nations' (1925) 6 BYIL 20, 29–30.

3   See, for example, Randall Lesaffer, 'Sources in the Modern Tradition: The Nature of Europe's Classical Law of Nations' in Samantha Besson and Jean d'Aspremont (eds), *The Oxford Handbook on the Sources of International Law* (OUP 2017).

4   Samantha Besson, 'Theorizing the Sources of International Law' in Samantha Besson and John Tasioulas (eds), *The Philosophy of International Law* (OUP 2010) 170.

5   Herbert Hart, *The Concept of Law* (OUP 1994) 94.

necessary to confront difficult questions about the foundations of international law as a normative order. In turn, the theory and practice of the sources plays a role in shaping international law as a legal system. In other words, there is a co-constitutive and mutually influential relationship between the sources of international law and the international legal system.[6] Sources questions touch on issues such as the functions of different international actors, including the continued dominance of States as participants in the legal system, and the relationship between international legal norms.

II. CATEGORIES OF SOURCES?

There is a tendency to attempt to delineate between different categories of sources of international law. Most commonly, authors have distinguished between formal and material sources of law.[7] The formal sources of international law provide criteria against which the validity of a prospective rule is to be judged. If these criteria are fulfilled, there is a valid and legally binding rule of the system. An example is the procedure for the formation of a treaty as reflected in the Vienna Convention on the Law of Treaties.[8] Conversely, material sources do not in and of themselves create binding legal rules, but may provide evidence for the existence of such rules and their content. Examples include some resolutions of international organisations, the output of the International Law Commission (ILC), and judicial decisions.[9]

Others suggest a division between primary and secondary (or subsidiary) sources. This distinction is also drawn using the terms 'formal' and 'material' sources of law.[10] Both sets of labels delineate between, on the one hand, the *criteria* for the creation of binding rules and, on the other, the *evidence* for the fulfilment of such criteria. It should be noted with caution that the use of the terms 'primary' and 'secondary' *sources* in this way is distinct from the description of primary and secondary *rules* referred to above, which refers to categorisation of different functions of rules. It is also important to note that this use of primary and secondary should not be taken to imply a formal and strict hierarchy between the sources as may be implied from such use in other legal systems. The question of hierarchy between sources and norms is considered below.

C. ARTICLE 38 ICJ STATUTE

Article 38 of the Statute of the International Court of Justice (ICJ) is the traditional, and perhaps inevitable, starting point for an examination of the sources of international law.

---

6 Gleider Hernández, 'Sources and the Systematicity of International Law: A Co-Constitutive Relationship?' in Besson and d'Aspremont (n 3).

7 Malcolm Shaw, *International Law* (7th edn, CUP 2014) 51; Patrick Dailler, Mathias Forteau, and Alain Pellet, *Droit International Public* (8th edn, LGDJ 2009) 124–125.

8 Vienna Convention on the Law of Treaties (adopted 23 May 1969, entered into force 27 January 1980) 1155 UNTS 331; on the law of treaties, see Fiskatoris and Svicevic, § 6.1, in this textbook.

9 On sources beyond article 38 ICJ statute, see Kunz, Lima, and Castelar Campos, § 6.4, in this textbook.

10 For a critique of these terms, see Bhupinder Chimni, 'Customary International Law: A Third World Perspective' (2018) 112 AJIL 1.

As evidenced by the opening sentence, this provision is, strictly speaking, the *lex arbitri* (Latin: 'applicable law') provision of the ICJ. That being said, article 38 has traditionally been viewed as an authoritative statement of the sources of international law.[11] This provision is composed of three main parts. First, article 38(1)(a)–(c) sets out the (formal or primary) sources of international law: treaties, customary international law, and general principles of law. Second, article 38(1)(d) sets out the 'subsidiary means' for the determination of international rules. Third, article 38(2) allows for the Court to resolve a dispute before it on the basis of (a form of) equity, should the parties agree.

On the traditional understanding of international law, States play the dominant role in the formation of international rules and an initial reading of article 38 seems to confirm this. Indeed, the mainstream view has traditionally been that States are not bound by international rules unless they have consented to them.[12] While it is clear that States remain prominent actors in international law-making,[13] it can now be legitimately questioned whether the creation of rules remains the sole prerogative of States.

Article 38(1)(d)'s reference to 'subsidiary means' reflects the aforementioned distinction between formal and material sources. These 'means' are not sources of binding rules themselves but can provide evidence that the conditions set out in (one of the) formal sources have been fulfilled. This is confirmed by the reference to article 59 ICJ statute, which states that the decisions of the Court have 'no binding force except between the parties and in respect of that particular case'. As will be explained below, that judicial decisions are not generally binding as such does not mean that the jurisprudence of international courts and tribunals does not play an important role in shaping the international legal system.

The reference to *ex aequo et bono* (Latin: 'according to the right and the good') in article 38(2) identifies the possibility that a dispute before the Court may be settled on the basis of equitable considerations, should the parties agree. This is a reference to a specific form of equity free from interaction with legal norms.[14] To date, this provision has never been invoked before the ICJ.

Article 38 ICJ Statute has long been revered as an authoritative statement of the sources of international law. While it is clear that this provision is central to any doctrine sources, it should not be read in isolation. It is important to both question what is generally accepted as part of the mainstream position on the sources[15] and to consider what international law-making looks like beyond the text of article 38.[16]

---

11 Gleider Hernández, *The International Court of Justice and the Judicial Function* (OUP 2014) 31; Godefridus van Hoof, *Rethinking the Sources of International Law* (Kluwer 1983) 82.

12 On consent, see Gonzàlez Hauck, § 2.2, in this textbook.

13 On States as main subjects of international law, see Green, § 7.1, in this textbook.

14 For an overview, see Vaughn Lowe, 'The Role of Equity in International Law' (1989) 12 AYIL 54.

15 See, for example, the contributions of Mónica García Salmones-Rovira and Upendra Baxi regarding the 'anti-formalist tradition' in Besson and d'Aspremont (n 3).

16 For an excellent overview of the multifaceted nature of international law-making, see Christine Chinkin and Alan Boyle, *The Making of International Law* (OUP 2007).

D. HIERARCHY IN THE SOURCES OF INTERNATIONAL LAW

At first sight, it may appear that the sources listed in article 38(1)(a)–(c) ICJ Statute are listed in a specific order, denoting a hierarchy between them. This is not the case. There can be multiple rules that have similar or identical content, but emanate from different sources of international law. For example, in the *Nicaragua* case, the Court confirmed the parallel existence of customary and treaty rules regarding the use of force.[17] This question of a hierarchy between the sources is separate from that of hierarchical relationships between international *norms*. While there are clear examples of normative hierarchies, a rule will not prevail over another *because of its source*. The question of a hierarchy between the sources is also separate from the question of the role and importance of the different sources of international law more generally. For example, much of international law-making is done by States through concluding treaties. There are now thousands of bilateral and multilateral treaties covering a broad range of topics. Conversely, it may be possible to argue that many of the fundamental rules of general application are custom or general principles.

Broadly speaking, there are three aspects of international law that are referred to as evidence of hierarchical relationships between norms: article 103 UN Charter,[18] *jus cogens* (Latin: 'peremptory norms') and obligations *erga omnes* (Latin 'towards all'). It may be argued that article 103 UN Charter functions as a 'supremacy clause', elevating the Charter to a hierarchically superior position in the international legal system.[19] While at first sight this seems to be the case, it should be noted that the practical effect of this provision is largely limited to the obligation to comply with UN Security Council resolutions contained in article 25, as there are few other specific and concrete obligations in the Charter. It should also be borne in mind that this provision functions more as a rule of precedence, very different to the consequences of a norm's *jus cogens* status, for example.

Jus cogens norms are clear example of hierarchy in international law. These peremptory rules of international law are defined as rules 'from which no derogation is permitted'.[20] In the event of a conflict between a rule of *jus cogens* and another international rule, the *jus cogens* rule prevails and the other rule is void.[21] Further, articles 40 and 41 of ARSIWA impose additional obligations on States in the event of serious violations of *jus cogens* norms,[22] including a requirement to cooperate to bring about the end of the

---

17 *Military and Paramilitary Activities In and Against Nicaragua (Nicaragua v United States of America)* (Merits) [1986] ICJ Rep 14 [178].

18 Charter of the United Nations (adopted 26 June 1945, entered into force 24 October 1945) 1 UNTS XVI.

19 Dinah Shelton, 'International Law and "Relative Normativity"' in Malcolm Evans (ed), *International Law* (4th edn, OUP 2014) 157.

20 VCLT 1969 (n 10) article 53.

21 Ibid articles 53 and 64.

22 ILC, 'Responsibility of States for Internationally Wrongful Acts (53rd session 23 April–1 June and 2 July–10 August 2001) UN Doc A/RES/56/83 Annex.

jus cogens violation and an obligation not to recognise as lawful any situation created as a result of such a violation. Established *jus cogens* norms include the prohibitions on genocide, slavery, torture, and racial discrimination.[23]

Obligations *erga omnes* are defined as those owed 'towards the international community as a whole', with the result that 'all States can be held to have a legal interest in their protection'.[24] This seems to confirm the importance of such obligations, yet this concept does not imply a hierarchy between these and other norms. The label '*erga omnes*' serves to denote only an expansion in potential scope of actors who can invoke violation of the rule. This is a purely procedural device, which facilitates the enforcement of international rules which may not necessarily involve an injured State or to increase the likelihood of enforcement of rules deemed to be substantively important.[25] Obligations *erga omnes* do not prevail over other rules of international law in the same way as *jus cogens* rules.

E. CONCLUSION

This chapter has explored the foundations of the doctrine of the sources in international law. In doing so, it has explained that the primary objective of this doctrine is to distinguish between rules that are part of the corpus of international law and those that are not. It has been explained that article 38 ICJ Statute constitutes an essential starting point for an account on the sources of international law, yet it does not paint a full picture. The relationships between international norms and their sources are complex and will be taken up further in subsequent chapters.

BOX 6.3 Further Reading

Further Reading

- S Besson and J d'Aspremont, *The Oxford Handbook of the Sources of International Law* (OUP 2017).

- C Chinkin and A Boyle, *The Making of International Law* (OUP 2007).

- H Thirlway, *The Sources of International Law* (OUP 2014).

---

§ § §

---

23 See, generally, the ILC's work on the topic: ILC, 'Fourth Report on Peremptory Norms of General International Law (Jus Cogens) by Dire Tladi, Special Rapporteur' 71st Session (29 April–7 June and 8 July–9 August 2019) UN Doc A/CN.4/727.

24 *Barcelona Traction, Light and Power Company Limited (Belgium v Spain)* (Preliminary Objections, Second Phase) [1970] ICJ Rep 3 [33].

25 Shelton (n 19) 140.

§ 6.1 TREATY LAW

TAXIARCHIS FISKATORIS AND MARKO SVICEVIC

BOX 6.1.1 Required Knowledge and Learning Objectives

Required knowledge: History of International Law; Consent; Subjects and Actors; States

Learning objectives: Being able to define the term 'treaties' as sources of international law; being familiar with the key characteristics of treaties and how they are negotiated, drafted, and interpreted; understanding how treaties enter into force, and, conversely, how they are terminated or invalidated, and understanding what reservations are.

A. INTRODUCTION

Article 38(1) of the Statute of the International Court of Justice (ICJ) names 'conventions, whether general or particular, establishing rules expressly recognized by . . . states' as the first source of public international law. More commonly known as 'treaties', they represent the most trusted and least controvertible avenue for States to express their consent to international legal rules.[26] The United Nations (UN) Treaty Collection, which registers and publishes lists of treaties in accordance with article 102 of the UN Charter, records over 250,000 treaties.[27]

The basic international instrument of treaty law is the 1969 Vienna Convention on the Law of Treaties (VCLT), which is the focus of this chapter.[28] This chapter will therefore define what treaties are, how they are negotiated and drafted, how they may be invalided or terminated, and how they are to be interpreted.

As of March 2023, the VCLT has been ratified by 116 States.[29] Most of its provisions have codified pre-existing customary international law, while other provisions have generated new custom.[30] The VCLT only 'applies to treaties between States' (article 1).

---

26 Statute of the International Court of Justice (adopted 26 June 1945, entered into force 24 October 1945) 1 UNTS XVI. On consent, see González Hauck, § 2.2, in this textbook.

27 See *United Nations Treaty Collection* <https://treaties.un.org/pages/overview.aspx?path=overview/overview/page1_en.xml> accessed 8 August 2023. See also article 102, Charter of the United Nations (adopted 26 June 1945, entered into force 24 October 1945) 1 UNTS XVI.

28 Vienna Convention on the Law of Treaties (adopted 23 May 1969, entered into force 27 January 1980) 1155 UNTS 331 (VCLT).

29 United Nations Treaty Series, *Vienna Convention on the Law of Treaties* <https://treaties.un.org/Pages/showDetails.aspx?objid=080000028003902f&clang=_en> accessed 9 August 2023.

30 Rudolf Bernhardt, 'Treaties' in Rudolf Bernhardt (ed), *Encyclopedia of Public International Law* (7th edn, Elsevier Science Publishers 1984) 459, B.V.

The rules regulating treaties between States and international organisations, and between international organisations have also been imprinted in a convention, which has not yet entered into force.[31] A third international convention with direct relevance to treaty law is the Vienna Convention on Succession of States in Respect of Treaties, which is in force but poorly ratified.[32] All three have been drafted by the International Law Commission (ILC). The ILC is also responsible for several non-binding instruments which contribute to the overall study and scope of the law of treaties, such as the 2011 'Draft Articles on the Effects of Armed Conflicts on Treaties',[33] the 2016 'Draft Conclusions on Subsequent Agreements and Subsequent Practice in Relation to the Interpretation of Treaties',[34] and the 2017 'Draft Guide to Provisional Application of Treaties'.[35]

B. THE NATURE AND CHARACTER OF TREATY LAW

I. TREATY LAW IN CONTEXT AND OF THE TIMES

Treaty law forms part and parcel of the 'nuts and bolts' of international law. As such, it is interwoven with almost every field of international law. For example, while treaties are traditionally concluded between States, the role of non-State actors, broadly speaking, has increasingly brought about new questions. Non-governmental organisations,[36] although without legal capacity to conclude treaties, have, and continue to play, a growing role in the drafting and negotiating of treaties.[37] Likewise, as entities capable of legal personality, questions arise as to what extent non-governmental organisations derive obligations under treaty law, such as universal and regional human rights treaties.

It is also worth noting that treaty law, although its progressive development and codification enhances clarity, is not without controversy and ambiguity. Worthy of recollection is the fact that at the time the VCLT was negotiated and eventually adopted, not all States we see today were independent. Any consideration of the VCLT

---

31 UNGA 'Vienna Convention on the Law of Treaties between States and International Organizations or between International Organizations' (adopted 21 March 1986, not yet in force) UN Doc A/CONF.129/15 ('VCLTIO').

32 Vienna Convention on Succession of States in Respect of Treaties (adopted 23 August 1978, entered into force 6 November 1996) 1946 UNTS 3.

33 ILC, 'Draft Articles on the Effects of Armed Conflicts on Treaties' (2011) II(2) U.N.Y.B.I.L.C. 107.

34 ILC, 'Draft Conclusions on Subsequent Agreements and Subsequent Practice in Relation to the Interpretation of Treaties' (2018) II(2) U.N.Y.B.I.L.C. 24.

35 ILC, 'Draft Guidelines and Draft Annex Constituting the Guide to Provisional Application of Treaties' in (2021) II(2) U.N.Y.B.I.L.C.

36 On non-governmental organisations, see He Chi, § 7.6, in this textbook.

37 See for example Maiara Giorgi, 'The Role of Non-Governmental Organizations in the Process of International Treaty Making' (2019) 19 AMDI 153; Kal Raustiala, 'NGOs in International Treaty-Making' in Duncan B Hollis (ed), *The Oxford Guide to Treaties* (2nd edn, OUP 2020) 173.

as a treaty regulating other treaties must therefore bear in mind its historical context. By this token, it has been pointed out that applying a purely positivist approach to the VCLT would marginalise its role in international law.[38]

These difficult issues more often than not transcend the VCLT itself, plaguing by extent the entirety of the law of treaties. Consider for example the effect of treaty-making before the era of human rights and the adoption of the VCLT. The partitioning of Africa was in many ways effected through treaty law. Despite what were in fact treaties which ultimately laid claim to territory and to the detriment of peoples of that territory, they were not necessarily directed at the various peoples they were negotiated with, but rather as 'legal' symbols against rival European powers.[39] While it is oftentimes easy to dismiss these practices and the corresponding effects of treaty law as relegated to the pages of history, the potential for these effects remains today.[40] Indeed, while a fundamental principle of treaty law is that treaties are to be negotiated and implemented in good faith, there remain numerous cases even today where the law of treaties has fallen short of this expectation.

II. DEFINING TREATIES

Article 2(1)(a) VCLT defines a treaty as 'an international agreement concluded between States in written form and governed by international law, whether embodied in a single instrument or in two or more related instruments and whatever its particular designation' (article 2(1)(a) VCLT).

1. An International Agreement Concluded Between States

'Every State possesses capacity to conclude treaties'.[41] Although reference is made in the VCLT exclusively to States, the definition of treaties extends to international organisations.[42] Until such a time as the 1986 VCLTIO enters into force, which is admittedly very similar to the VCLT, such treaties are based on other sources of international law, in particular customary international law.[43]

Of course, it is not States as such but their *representatives* that conclude treaties. In order to be able to legally and validly do so, the State must have provided them with a document bestowing 'full powers' (article 2(1)(c) VCLT). Such a document is unnecessary for heads of State, heads of government, ministers of foreign affairs, and

---

38 See e.g. European Commission for Democracy Through Law, 'Human Rights Treaties and the Vienna Convention on the Law of Treaties – Conflicts or Harmony' (7–8 October 2005, Coimbra) CDL-UD(2005)014rep.

39 Saadia Touval, 'Treaties, Borders and the Partition of Africa' (1966) 7(2) JAH 280.

40 Baron FM van Asbeck, 'International Law and Colonial Administration' (1953) 39 Transactions of the Grotius Society 5, 8. See also broadly, Antony Anghie, 'The Evolution of International Law: Colonial and Postcolonial Realities' (2006) 27(5) TWQ 739.

41 Article 6 VCLT.

42 On international organisations, see Baranowska, Engström, and Paige, § 7.3, in this textbook.

43 Alina Kaczorowska, *Public International Law* (4th edn, Routledge 2010) 89–90. See also article 3(b) VCLT.

on specific occasions for other high-ranking State representatives, such as heads of diplomatic missions (article 7(2) VCLT). A State may exceptionally endorse and validate the acts of an unauthorised representative *ex post facto* (article 8 VCLT).

2. In Written Form

For an international agreement to be called a treaty, it must be in written form, but not necessarily on paper. This is exactly the feature that renders treaties the most predictable and hence reliable source of public international law. Oral international agreements are not treaties as per the VCLT, but they may still have legal effects.[44]

3. Whether Embodied in a Single Instrument or in Two or More Related Instruments

Treaties are usually contained in a single document, but they do not need to be. Exchange of letters (diplomatic notes), and even records of meetings between State representatives may constitute treaties if the intention of the parties was to create through them binding effects under international law.[45]

4. Governed by International Law

The intention to establish obligations and/or rights under international law is a key requirement. States (and international organisations) are free to sign contractual agreements governed by national law (e.g. for leasing an embassy's premises), which cannot be considered treaties. They are also free to enter international agreements not giving rise to obligations and/or rights under international law. Such agreements are often called 'Memoranda of Understanding' (MoUs). However, one should not pay too much attention to the headline of an agreement, as MoUs may be proper treaties if the intention of the parties to give them binding effect under international law can be discerned. This intention must be manifest within the text and context of the treaty.

5. Whatever Its Particular Designation

If an international agreement fulfils the above four characteristics, it is a treaty from a legal point of view, whatever its name. Some of the most common names attached to a treaty are 'convention', which is usually the name given to treaties prepared within an international organisation (e.g. UN Convention on the Law of the Sea; European Convention on Human Rights); 'protocol', which is in most cases a treaty that supplements a pre-existing treaty with additional rights or obligations (e.g. Additional Protocols to the 1949 Geneva Conventions on International Humanitarian Law); 'charter', which is the label preferred for the constitutive treaties of international organisations (e.g. UN Charter); the term may also designate a document setting

---

44 Article 3 VCLT; article 3 VCLTIO and Anthony Aust, 'Vienna Convention on the Law of Treaties (1969)' *Max Planck Encyclopedia of International Law* (March 2023) para 12. See also broadly, Kelvin Widdows, 'On the Form and Distinctive Nature of International Agreements' (1981) 7(1) Aust YBIL 114.

45 See Jan Klabbers, 'Qatar v. Bahrain: The Concept of "Treaty" in International Law' (1995) 33(3) AdV 361.

out rights or privileges (e.g. EU Charter of Fundamental Rights, African Charter on Humans and Peoples' Rights); and the treaty establishing an international court or tribunal is often called a 'statute' (e.g. ICJ Statute; ICC Statute).

The word 'covenant' originates in religious scripts and traditionally refers to a solemn promise to engage in or refrain from a specified action. In international law it is used in the title of two major human rights conventions: International Covenant on Civil and Political Rights (ICCPR) and the International Covenant on Economic, Social and Cultural Rights (ICESCR).[46] The label 'pact', more common during the inter-war period, seems to connote a deal, that is not only legally but also morally binding (e.g. 1928 Kellogg-Briand Pact for Renunciation of War as an Instrument of National Policy). Finally, the term 'agreement' is used as an umbrella term covering both treaties and other instruments not meeting the VCLT criteria. In a narrow sense, an agreement is usually employed for treaties of a technical or administrative character.

III. CLASSIFICATION OF TREATIES

Treaties establishing mutual rights and obligations between two parties are classified as *bilateral*. The great bulk of international treaties are bilateral in nature, with extradition treaties being one example.[47] A *multilateral* treaty is, on the other hand, a binding international agreement between many parties.[48] A treaty between more than two but still not many parties can also be classified as *plurilateral*.

Most bilateral and plurilateral treaties merely create mutual rights and/or obligations for their parties, similarly to typical contracts of domestic law (contractual treaties). Although multilateral treaties also establish binding rights and/or obligations, most of them may eventually create, modify, elucidate, and stabilise, or progressively develop international law more generally (law-making treaties).[49] To be sure, several multilateral treaties purport to do so. The distinction between 'contractual treaties' and 'law-making treaties' is not always obvious.

IV. OBSERVANCE AND APPLICATION OF TREATIES

The whole branch of international treaty law is premised on the fundamental legal principle of *pacta sunt servanda* (Latin: 'agreements must be respected'). Article 26 VCLT enunciates that '[e]very treaty in force is binding upon the parties to it and must be

---

46 International Covenant on Civil and Political Rights (adopted 16 December 1966, entered into force 23 March 1976) 999 UNTS 171; International Covenant on Economic, Social and Cultural Rights (adopted 16 December 1966, entered into force 3 January 1976) 999 UNTS 3.

47 E.g. Extradition Treaty Between the Argentine Republic and the Republic of Peru (11 June 2004) 2446 UNTS 259.

48 See e.g. the African Charter on Human and Peoples' Rights (adopted 27 June 1981, entered into force 21 October 1986) 1520 UNTS 217.

49 See Catherine Brölmann, 'Law-Making Treaties: Form and Function in International Law' (2005) 74 Nordic Journal of International Law 383.

performed by them in good faith'. A change of government does not release the State from its treaty obligations, unless the new government can raise a valid ground for the termination of the treaty, as discussed below. Besides, '[a] party may not invoke the provisions of its internal law as justification for its failure to perform a treaty' (article 27 VCLT).

The flip side to that is the principle *pacta tertiis nec nocent nec prosunt* (Latin: 'agreements neither injure nor benefit third parties'). This is enshrined in article 34 VCLT, according to which a 'treaty does not create either obligations or rights for a third State without its consent'. When parties to a treaty intend to impose an obligation on third parties, the latter must accept the obligation in writing (article 35 VCLT). If a treaty provision acquires the status of a customary rule of international law, it then becomes binding on third parties, even without their expressed consent.[50]

The question of whether treaties are directly binding on individuals or other non–State actors is of marked importance in the context of international human rights law and international criminal law, but has yet to be doctrinally settled.[51] Finally, unless otherwise agreed by their parties, treaties do not apply retroactively.[52]

C. TREATY-MAKING

I. DRAFTING AND NEGOTIATION

Before adopting a bilateral treaty, States normally hold a series of meetings of diplomats and legal experts who negotiate and draft the terms of the treaty. Multilateral treaties, especially 'law-making treaties', are negotiated at international conferences, usually summoned by international organisations. At international conferences, where negotiations are more difficult due to the number of participants, States often debate based on optional draft texts prepared by committees of experts, such as the ILC. The drafting process of a treaty may take many years. States are free to decide the place, time frames, setup, and rules of procedure of a conference. The VCLT only stipulates that, unless participants decide otherwise, the minimum requirement for the adoption of the text of a treaty at an international conference is a two-thirds majority of the 'States present and voting'.[53] In practice, States resort to voting only if consensus appears impossible.

II. SIGNATURE

Successful negotiations conclude with the adoption of the text of the treaty and its recognition as authentic and definitive.[54] The most common way for authenticating

---

50 See article 38 VCLT; on customary international law, see Stoica, § 6.2, in this textbook.
51 See Christine Chinkin, *Third Parties in International Law* (OUP 1993); Marko Milanović, 'Is the Rome Statute Binding on Individuals? (And Why We Should Care)' (2011) 9 JICJ (2011) 21.
52 Article 28 VCLT.
53 Article 9(2) VCLT.
54 Article 10 VCLT.

the finalised text of a treaty is its signature. Signing a treaty is an expression of a government's intention to render the treaty binding for its State in due course. Nonetheless, the signature alone seldom establishes the consent of States to be bound by the treaty and an additional step is required (see next section).[55] Binding agreements from the point of signature are called 'treaties in simplified form' or 'executive agreements'. They mostly concern bilateral matters of technical nature or of minor importance. It is still debated whether such treaties are legally or politically binding. Ordinarily, it is evident from the text of the treaty when no further steps are required.

The signature entails the legal obligation of the signatory 'to refrain from acts which would defeat the object and purpose of a treaty' until the ratification of the treaty, or until the signatory 'shall have made its intention clear not to become a party to the treaty' (article 18 VCLT). This interim obligation is vague and open to contradictory interpretations.[56]

III. CONSENT TO BE BOUND

As a matter of rule, States establish on the international plane their consent to be bound by a treaty through the acts of 'ratification', 'acceptance', 'approval', or 'accession', although 'any other [agreed] means' are an option (articles 2(1)(b) and 11 VCLT).

A second step after signature offers the required time to reconsider the treaty, eventually to submit it to parliamentary scrutiny and approval, or to enact respective legislation. It may take many years between signature and ratification, as there are no general time limits, unless the treaty specifies them. After all, States are under no obligation to ratify a treaty that they have signed.

Ratification of bilateral treaties occurs through the exchange of documents called 'instruments of ratification', which are issued by the competent authorities of the contracting States. A mere mutual notification of completion of all domestic procedures that give effect to the treaty may in routine cases replace the ceremonial exchange of instruments.

Treaties remain commonly open for signature until an arranged date. States that did not exist or sign the treaty before that date can still adhere to the treaty if the treaty or its parties allow it.[57] The international act with which a State avails itself of the opportunity to become a party to a treaty previously adopted by another is called 'accession'. It consists of an expression to be bound by a treaty and hence has the same legal effect as ratification.[58] It usually happens after the treaty has entered into force, but, depending on the treaty, it can also take place before.

---

55 Article 12 VCLT.

56 See Paul Gragl and Malgosia Fitzmaurice, 'The Legal Character of Article 18 of the Vienna Convention on the Law of Treaties' (2019) 68(3) ICLQ 699.

57 Article 15 VCLT.

58 See article 2(1) VCLT.

> ## BOX 6.1.2 Advanced: Acceptance, Approval
>
> The acts of 'acceptance' and 'approval' equally establish at the inter-State level the consent of States to assume treaty obligations and rights. In other words, they do not differ from 'ratification' from a legal perspective. Their difference is basically one of preferred terminology, the terms 'acceptance' and 'approval' being mostly used by States without a constitutional duty of treaty ratification. Besides, some constitutions provide for the possibility to accept a treaty by a mere executive action, before all domestic procedures for a formal ratification have been completed. When international organisations express their consent to be bound by a treaty, the term 'act of formal confirmation' replaces the word 'ratification'.

Ratification, acceptance, approval, or accession of multilateral treaties is accomplished with the deposit of the respective instruments with the depositary.[59] The depositary is one or more States, an international organisation, or the secretary-general of an international organisation, especially the UN.[60] The depositary is normally designated by the treaty, among others to keep custody of the original text of the treaty, to collect all documents or communications relating to it, and inform respectively all parties concerned.[61]

IV. ENTRY INTO FORCE

Ratification does not signify an immediate assumption of the obligations and/or rights emanating from the treaty, which only begins when the treaty enters into force. After the ratification and before the entry of the treaty into force, States must still 'refrain from acts which would defeat the object and purpose of a treaty', provided that such entry into force is not unduly delayed (article 18(b) VCLT). Although it is very infrequent, States that have ratified a treaty may freely withdraw their consent to be bound before the treaty becomes operative. There may also be transitional clauses, dealing for instance with the permissibility of reservations, that take effect from the adoption of the treaty, as discussed below. Most treaties contain a clause specifying when and how they will come into force.[62]

---

59 Article 16 VCLT.
60 Article 76 VCLT.
61 Articles 76–79 VCLT. See for example article 110(2) UN Charter.
62 E.g. article 308(1) UN Convention on the Law of the Sea: 'This Convention shall enter into force 12 months after the date of deposit of the sixtieth instrument of ratification or accession'.

BOX 6.1.3 Advanced: Entry Into Force Clauses

Although there are several variations, such clauses typically stipulate a minimum number of ratifications (and sometimes accessions) necessary to trigger the entry into force. Some of them contain additional conditions, such as a list of specific States that must figure on the ratifications table, or an additional short period of time to elapse after the last required ratification. In absence of such a clause and of a related agreement by the signatories, the treaty cannot take effect before all of them have ratified it. This is to guarantee a certain degree of reciprocity.

Bilateral treaties often enter into force at the time the two parties exchange the ratification instruments, while treaties in simplified form can readily come into force immediately after signature. In case of an accession, the treaty enters into force for the acceding party on the date of the deposit of the accession instrument, or after a short period of time, if there was a corresponding provision with respect to the initial entry into force of the treaty.[63]

V. REGISTRATION AND PUBLICATION

Article 102 UN Charter requires that 'every treaty and every international agreement entered into by any Member of the United Nations . . . shall as soon as possible be registered with the Secretariat and published by it'. Registration and publication with the UN Treaty Series is meant to eradicate the conflictual dynamic of secret diplomacy and to enable public access. The UN Charter warns that unregistered international agreements cannot be invoked before any organ of the UN, including the ICJ (article 102(2)). However, the practice of UN organs is less strict than the rule.

Registration should not be confused with a deposit of a ratification instrument with the UN Secretary-General. Treaties and international agreements can only be registered with the UN after their entry into force. The registration and publication duty extends to cases of treaty amendments. The registration by just one party to the treaty is adequate, while multilateral treaties are registered by their depositary.[64] The UN does not impose any time constraints for registration. More importantly, 'non-registration or late registration . . . does not have any consequence for the actual validity of the agreement, which remains no less binding upon the parties'.[65] Vice versa, the act of registration cannot turn a non–binding international agreement into a binding treaty.

---

63 Article 24(3) VCLT.

64 Article 77 VCLT; on the institution of the 'depositary' see supra C.III.

65 Case Concerning Maritime Delimitation and Territorial Questions between Qatar and Bahrain *(Qatar v Bahrain) (Jurisdiction and Admissibility)* [1994] ICJ Rep 112 para 29.

VI. ALTERATIONS

1. Amendments

An amendment is a change of one or more treaty provisions, usually with the aim of updating or enhancing the treaty regime. Given that amendments affect all parties to the treaty, they must obtain the consent of parties to be bound by the amended provision. Thus, amendments are negotiated, signed, ratified, brought into force, registered, and published. Some treaties require unanimity for an amendment to pass. If amendments can pass with a majority, parties that do not express their consent to be bound by the amendment remain bound by the previous provision, in conformity with the principles *pacta tertiis nec nocent nec prosunt* and *pacta sunt servanda*.[66] However, new parties acceding the treaty must accept the treaty as amended.[67] Between the parties that have ratified the amendments or acceded the amended treaty, and those that have not ratified them, it is the old provision that remains effective. The more parties to a treaty, the more difficult its amendment. This is why many multilateral treaties lay down specific amendment procedures and requirements, which may deviate from the above canon.

2. Reviews and Revisions

Some treaties provide an alternative 'review' or 'revision' procedure, which refers to updating the whole or parts of the treaty at a new diplomatic conference with the participation of all parties. Review or revision takes place after a provided number of years, or following a majority vote.[68]

3. Modifications

Furthermore, 'two or more of the parties to a multilateral treaty may conclude an agreement to modify the treaty as between themselves alone if: (a) the possibility of such a modification is provided for by the treaty; or (b) . . . not prohibited by the treaty' (article 41 VCLT). The original treaty provisions remain applicable between those few parties and all other parties. The modification must not affect the rights and/or rights of other parties under the treaty, and must not be incompatible with the object and purpose of the treaty as a whole.[69]

D. TERMINATION AND INVALIDITY OF TREATIES

I. TERMINATION AND SUSPENSION

A treaty may be terminated or suspended in several situations. The termination permanently releases the parties from any obligation to perform the treaty.[70] The

---

66　Article 40(4) VCLT.
67　Article 40(5) VCLT.
68　See for instance article 109 UN Charter or article 123 ICC Statute.
69　Article 41 VCLT.
70　Articles 70 and 72 VCLT.

suspension releases them from their treaty obligations temporarily. However, the termination 'does not affect any right, obligation or legal situation of the parties created through the execution of the treaty prior to its termination' (article 70(1)(b) VCLT). It is also immaterial when there exists a parallel customary rule of international law, which continues being biding on States. Besides, '[d]uring the period of the suspension the parties shall refrain from acts tending to obstruct the resumption of the operation of the treaty' (article 72(2) VCLT).

1. Consent Based

A treaty may be terminated or suspended with the consent of all its parties.[71] Likewise, if all parties to a treaty adopt a new substitute treaty, the earlier treaty impliedly loses its effect.[72] However, the old treaty remains effective if not all its parties adhere to the new one.

Should only some of the parties no longer intent to be bound by a treaty, they may denounce it or withdraw from it, but only if such a possibility is expressly allowed, implied by the nature of the treaty, or predicated on the established consensual intention of the parties.[73] In any event, a party wishing to exit a treaty must give notice of its intention at least one year in advance.[74] The term 'denunciation' is mostly used with reference to bilateral treaties, whereas 'withdrawal' usually describes the retreat from a multilateral treaty, which continues being in force among the rest of its parties.

There is also the possibility that the treaty itself contains an expiration date, or a clear goal, the achievement of which terminates the agreement. Nonetheless, a treaty does not terminate merely because it has not reached the required ratifications number for its entry into force.[75]

2. After a Material Breach of the Treaty

The operation of a treaty can also be terminated or suspended because of its material breach. The VCLT defines a material breach as '(a) a repudiation of the treaty not sanctioned by the present Convention; or (b) the violation of a provision essential to the accomplishment of the object or purpose of the treaty' (article 60(3) VCLT).

A material breach, regardless of its gravity, does not in itself terminate or suspend the treaty. It only entitles innocent parties to pursue the termination or suspension of the treaty in whole or in part, in accordance with a predetermined procedure.[76] The consequences of a material breach depend on the bilateral or multilateral nature of the treaty.[77] A breach of a multilateral treaty is more probable to temporarily render

---

71 Articles 54 and 57 VCLT.
72 Article 59 VCLT.
73 See article 56 VCLT.
74 Article 56(2) VCLT.
75 Article 55 VCLT.
76 Articles 60 and 65–68 VCLT.
77 Article 60 VCLT.

the treaty ineffective between the injured and the defaulting State, rather than lead to a comprehensive termination of the treaty.

The party that breached the treaty cannot invoke its own wrongdoing to terminate or suspend the treaty. Neither can a party pursue the termination or suspension of a treaty invoking the material breach of another treaty.[78] Besides, 'treaties of a humanitarian character', including human rights treaties, cannot be terminated or suspended on such grounds (article 60(5) VCLT). If a material breach of a treaty causes harm to a State, secondary rules of State responsibility apply, irrespective of whether the harmed State pursues the termination or suspension of the breached treaty.[79]

3. Due to a Fundamental Change of Circumstances

On demand of several drafting States, the VCLT did not exclude the termination of or withdrawal from a treaty due to a fundamental change of circumstances which has rendered the execution of treaty obligations unexpectedly onerous or unfair. However, to keep it in line with the primordial principle of the sanctity of treaties (*pacta sunt servanda*), the VCLT sets a high threshold for the application of the so-called *rebus sic standibus* (Latin: 'so long as things stand') clause.[80] The ICJ has also consistently upheld a very restrictive approach.[81]

Such a pleading can only be made if cumulatively (1) the change is fundamental; (2) could not have been foreseen; (3) has 'radically' transformed the extent of obligations still to be performed under the treaty into something different from what originally agreed; and (4) the specific circumstances at the time of the conclusion of the treaty constituted an essential basis of the consent of the parties to be bound by the treaty.

Additionally, this ground of termination is inapplicable to treaties establishing a boundary. 'A boundary established by treaty thus achieves a permanence which the treaty itself does not necessarily enjoy'.[82] It is furthermore unavailable to any party that induced the fundamental change by not performing its duties towards the other treaty parties.[83]

4. Due to Supervening Impossibility of Performance

A less controversial ground for termination/withdrawal is 'the permanent disappearance or destruction of an object indispensable for the execution of the treaty', which unexpectedly renders its performance not simply onerous or unfair, but impossible.[84] If the supervening impossibility of performance is temporary, it can only lead to the suspension of the treaty.

---

78 *Case Concerning the Gabčíkovo-Nagymaros Project (Hungary v Slovakia)* (Merits) [1997] ICJ Rep 7 para 106.
79 On State responsibility, see Arévalo-Ramírez, § 9, in this textbook.
80 Article 62 VCLT.
81 *Gabčíkovo-Nagymaros* (n 52) para 104.
82 *Case Concerning the Territorial Dispute (Libyan Arab Jamahiriya v Chad)* (Merits) [1994] ICJ Rep 6 para 73; see also article 11 Vienna Convention on Succession of States in Respect of Treaties.
83 Article 62(2) VCLT.
84 Article 61(1) VCLT.

Once again, if a party contributed to the occurrence of such a situation, it cannot itself pursue the termination/suspension of the treaty on this ground.[85] The submergence of an island under the sea level, or the natural desiccation of a river as an effect of climate change, may be scenarios giving rise to such a termination/suspension ground.

5. Armed Conflicts

The VCLT sets forth that

> [t]he severance of diplomatic or consular relations between parties to a treaty does not affect the legal relations established between them by the treaty except insofar as the existence of diplomatic or consular relations is indispensable for the application of the treaty.
>
> (article 63 VCLT)

However, the effects of armed conflicts on treaties fall outside the scope of the Convention.[86] The ILC has attempted, to prepare a set of non-binding Draft Articles on the matter.[87] The general principle is that the outbreak of an international armed conflict, or a non-international armed conflict in which governmental authorities take part, may terminate or suspend a treaty as between States parties to the conflict or as between a State party to the conflict and a State that is not — but not necessarily.[88]

However, there are a number of treaties, 'the subject matter of which involves an implication that they continue in operation, in whole or in part, during armed conflict'.[89] Such are, by way of illustration, multilateral 'law-making treaties', treaties creating permanent regimes, especially treaties establishing boundaries, treaties for the international protection of human rights, treaties on international criminal justice, treaties relating to the international protection of the environment or to international watercourses and aquifers, treaties creating international organisations, treaties relating to diplomatic and consular relations, treaties relating to the international settlement of disputes, and of course treaties regulating the conduct of hostilities.[90]

6. Other Grounds

Article 64 VCLT foresees an additional termination ground, namely the emergence of a new peremptory norm of general international law (*jus cogens*).[91] In such an event, 'any existing treaty which conflicts with that norm becomes void and terminates' (articles 64 and 44(3) VCLT).

---

85 Article 61(2) VCLT.
86 Article 73 VCLT.
87 ILC, 'Draft Articles on the Effects of Armed Conflicts on Treaties' (2011) II(2) *Yearbook of International Law Commission* 107.
88 Ibid articles 2(b) and 3 ILC Draft Articles on the Effects of Armed Conflicts on Treaties.
89 Ibid article 7.
90 Ibid annex.
91 On the concept of *jus cogens*, see article 53 VCLT; see also Eggett, § 6 and Stoica, § 6.2.D.I., in this textbook.

Article 42 VCLT suggests that the enumerated termination/suspension grounds are exclusive. However, it is debatable whether by means of customary international law, or as forms of implied consent, desuetude or obsolescence constitute additional grounds. The former refers to a consistent practice of the parties to a treaty that runs counter to their treaty obligations. The latter refers to the expiration of the treaty through disuse. Another debatable termination ground is the full performance of a treaty when the treaty itself does not explicitly provide for such eventuality. Finally, it is only logical that a bilateral treaty comes to an end when one of the two State parties loses its international legal personality, unless of course there is a successor State.

II. INVALIDITY

Under specific circumstances, treaties may lose their validity, although this occurs very rarely. Invalidity has different legal consequences compared to termination. While the latter releases the parties from their treaty obligations from the point of the termination on, invalidity exonerates the injured parties from the legal effects from the point of conclusion of the treaty. Practically, acts having been performed in execution of a void treaty before its invalidation may need to be reversed.[92] However, claims of reversal cannot be made by a party that has generated the grounds for the invalidity.[93]

1. Absolute Grounds for Invalidity

The VCLT enumerates three absolute grounds for invalidity, which automatically render the treaty null and void. First, a treaty is void when the consent of a State to be bound by the treaty has been a product of coercion of a representative of a State through acts or threats directed against him or her.[94] Second, a treaty is void when the consent is a product of coercion of the State itself by the illegal threat or use of force 'in violation of the principles of international law embodied in the Charter of the United Nations' (article 52 VCLT). The last words exclude any legal threat or use of force after an authorisation of the UN Security Council or in self-defence.[95] Only military use of force gives rise to invalidity. A treaty cannot be invalidated if a State has been compelled, say, under the pressure of economic sanctions, or the political pressure from a former coloniser.[96] Third, a treaty is void if, at the time of its conclusion, it conflicted with an existing *jus cogens* rule.[97]

2. Relative Grounds for Invalidity

The VCLT also lists five relative grounds for invalidity. They do not immediately nullify the treaty, but rather give a State the right to retrospectively annul its consent to be

---

92 Article 69(2) VCLT.
93 Article 69(3) VCLT.
94 Article 51 VCLT.
95 On the use of force, see Svicevic, § 13, in this textbook.
96 'Declaration on the Prohibition of Military, Political and Economic Coercion in the Conclusion of Treaties' annexed to the 'Final Act of the Vienna Conference on the Law of Treaties' UN Doc A/CONF.39/26.
97 Article 53 VCLT. On *jus cogens*, see also Eggett, § 6 and Stoica, § 6.2.D.I., in this textbook.

bound by that treaty. This would practically mean the nullification of a bilateral treaty, or a withdrawal of the victim State from a multilateral treaty with retrospective effect. In the latter scenario, though, the rights and obligations of other treaty parties would remain unaffected.[98] Contrary to the consequences of absolute grounds, there is the possibility for severing the clauses to which the relative grounds are related, instead for nullifying the whole treaty.[99]

Relative grounds are the following:

(a) A 'manifest' violation of 'fundamental' internal law provisions regarding competence to conclude treaties (article 46(1) VCLT). The VCLT goes on to clarify that '[a] violation is manifest if it would be objectively evident to any State conducting itself in the matter in accordance with normal practice and in good faith' (article 46(2) VCLT). The term 'fundamental' points to constitutional or equivalent rules.
(b) Omission by a State representative to observe specific restrictions on authority to express the consent of their State, on the precondition that the other negotiating parties had been duly notified (article 47 VCLT).
(c) An error that 'relates to a fact or situation which was assumed by [the affected] State to exist at the time when the treaty was concluded and formed an essential basis of its consent to be bound by the treaty' (article 48(1) VCLT). Had the error been foreseeable or caused by the affected State itself, it cannot be invoked as a ground for invalidity. The same is true if the error relates only to the wording of treaty text (articles 48(2) and 48(3) VCLT).
(d) Fraudulent conduct of another negotiating State (article 49 VCLT).
(e) Corruption of a representative of the affected State, directly or indirectly by another negotiating State (article 50 VCLT).[100]

E. RESERVATIONS TO TREATIES

I. RESERVATIONS

Article 2(1)(d) VCLT defines a reservation as

> a unilateral statement, however phrased or named, made by a State, when signing, ratifying, accepting, approving or acceding to a treaty, whereby it purports to exclude or to modify the legal effect of certain provisions of the treaty in their application to that State.

Reservations are one way in which States express their disagreement with certain provisions and exclude their legal effect. States disagreeing with one or several

---

98 Article 69(4) VCLT.
99 Article 44(4) VCLT.
100 Article 50 VCLT.

provisions with may thus nonetheless adopt and ratify the treaty without compromising its entirety. For such reasons, reservations provide a compromise whereby, especially for multilateral treaties, they can achieve widespread adoption and acceptance by numerous States.[101]

While reservations are a useful tool for States in excluding or modifying a treaty's legal effects, there are certain cases where reservations are prohibited. This concerns three situations:

- If the reservation is incompatible with the object and purpose of a treaty;
- If the reservation is prohibited by the treaty; or
- If the treaty provides only for specified reservations and the reservation in question falls beyond the scope of such specified reservation.[102]

These limitations are for the most part reasonable. For example, reservations which are incompatible with the object and purpose of a treaty could render the very logic behind the treaty void.

Where a treaty expressly provides for reservations, there is no need for other States party to the treaty to accept the reservation made by one of the State parties.[103] In some cases, however, State parties to a treaty may need to accept reservations. If, for example, there is a limited number of negotiating States and the object and purpose of the treaty requires its application to all the parties as an essential condition of their consent, then reservations made to such treaty need to be accepted by all parties.[104] Another scenario where reservations need to be accepted is where the treaty in question is a constituent instrument of an international organisation, in which case a competent organ of that organisation needs to accept the reservation.[105]

Reservations and objections to reservations may be withdrawn at any time and do not require the consent of any State which had previously accepted such reservation.[106]

Some treaties explicitly prohibit reservations. For example, article 25 of the Kyoto Protocol provides that '[n]o reservations may be made to this Protocol'.[107] Another example is article 120 of the Rome Statute of the International Criminal Court.[108]

---

101 Kaczorowska (n 43) 98.
102 Cf. article 19 VCLT.
103 Article 20(1) VCLT.
104 Article 20(2) VCLT.
105 Article 20(3) VCLT.
106 Article 22 VCLT.
107 Kyoto Protocol to the United Nations Framework Convention on Climate Change (adopted 11 December 1997, entered into force 16 February 2005) 2303 UNTS 162.
108 Rome Statute of the International Criminal Court (adopted 17 July 1998, entered into force 1 July 2002) 2187 UNTS 3.

II. INTERPRETATIVE DECLARATIONS

Another unilateral statement which a State can make when joining a treaty is an interpretative declaration. Interpretative declarations are statements in which a State indicates or clarifies what it understands to be the scope or nature of specific treaty provisions. Interpretative declarations do not modify the provisions of a treaty but may later be followed by other States in how they too interpret certain provisions of that treaty.

Beyond the standard interpretative declaration, a State may also make a conditional interpretative declaration. Such a declaration signals that a State does not wish to be bound by certain provisions unless a specific interpretation is accorded to those provisions. Conditional interpretative declarations are therefore subject to the same rules as reservations.[109]

The distinction between reservations, interpretative declarations, and conditional interpretative declarations in practice is often not clear-cut. States sometimes use ambiguous language when entering these unilateral statements, ultimately making it difficult to determine their intention.

F. INTERPRETATION OF TREATIES

I. INTERPRETATIVE AUTHORITIES

As with many other areas of treaty law, the interpretation of treaties is no simple task. As a body of provisions usually drafted and negotiated over long periods of time, and which apply to numerous States with binding legal effect, the interpretation of treaties is one of the most crucial aspects concerning the law of treaties.

One of the starting points in discussing treaty interpretation is precisely who has the authority to interpret treaties. Given that treaties are legal texts distinct from the domestic laws of States, it is necessary to understand both who may interpret them and precisely how they are to be interpreted. In principle, every application of a treaty implies interpretation; it would not be possible to apply the provisions of a treaty without first reading and interpreting its provisions.[110] On this basis, all entities concerned with the treaty in question engage in its interpretation. Actors who have the competence to interpret treaties and their provisions besides States include international organisations, international courts, and domestic courts.

---

109 ILC, 'Guide to Practice on Reservations to Treaties' (2911) II(2) *Yearbook of the International Law Commission* 26.

110 Oliver Dörr, 'Chapter 31' in Oliver Dörr and Kirsten Schmalenbach (eds), *Vienna Convention on the Law of Treaties: A Commentary* (2nd edn, Springer 2018) 567–568.

II. GENERAL RULE OF INTERPRETATION

Article 31 VCLT provides the general rule of interpretation of treaties. It reflects customary international law and embodies a multifaceted approach to interpreting treaties.[111] Treaties are first and foremost to be interpreted in good faith, and the ordinary meaning of terms are to be used in context and in light of a treaty's object and purpose.[112] The interpretation of a treaty includes its context, which in addition to the main text, preamble, and annexes also includes other agreements which relate to the treaty made between the parties in connection with the treaty, or an instrument made between one or more parties in connection with the treaty accepted by other parties as an instrument to the treaty.

In addition, context includes subsequent agreements and practice of State parties regarding the interpretation of a treaty. This may clarify how they interpret it and even indicate that they consider such an interpretation effective for purposes of applying its provisions. It also makes perfect sense that given the wording of article 31(1), special meaning is given to terms only if the parties so intended. In practice, most treaties usually start with a section defining terms used with the treaty, in this way clarifying how such terms are not only understood in the context of the treaty, but how they are applied throughout its provisions.

One of the reasons behind the interpretation of treaties suggested by article 31 is that, naturally by examining the very text and context of a treaty, it is presumed that a treaty constitutes an authentic expression of the intentions of its parties.[113] Only by examining the treaty itself can one ascertain the intention of its drafters.

III. SUPPLEMENTARY MEANS OF INTERPRETATION

Beyond the general rule of interpretation, article 32 VCLT provides supplementary means of interpretation. Certain elements may thus be used in furthering the precise meaning of provisions if the application of the general rules prove unsatisfactory (to the extent that ambiguities remain or the application of article 31 leads to manifest absurdity or unreasonableness). They thus carry less weight because they are in effect meant to complement and clarify the application of article 31.[114]

Supplementary means of interpretation under article 32 most commonly include the preparatory work of a treaty, including documents related to negotiation history between the State parties and drafting history of the treaty. Preparatory works are usually available to the negotiating parties, thereby excluding unilateral sources and

---

111 Chang-Fa Lo, *Treaty Interpretation under the Vienna Convention of the Law of Treaties: A New Round of Codification* (Springer 2017) 39–44.

112 Article 31(1) VCLT.

113 Dörr (n 84) 620–624.

114 Oliver Dörr, 'Article 32' in Oliver Dörr and Kirsten Schmalenbach (eds), *The Vienna Convention on the Law of Treaties: A Commentary* (2nd edn, Springer 2018) 618.

confidential sources, that may not necessarily have been introduced or made available to other negotiating States parties.[115]

IV. OTHER METHODS OF TREATY INTERPRETATION

In addition to those rules of interpretation mentioned above, there exist a number of methods of treaty interpretation.[116]

- Teleological interpretation: requires that the meaning of words and terms be interpreted in light of the object and purpose of a treaty. In such cases, a teleological interpretation aims to give effect to the overall aims and objectives of a treaty.
- Systematic interpretation: requires a treaty to be interpreted with the ordinary meaning of words and that all parts of a treaty as well as corresponding documents produced between the parties be taken into account. Such documents would include the negotiation and drafting history of a treaty.
- Textual interpretation: requires that the ordinary meaning of words be used to interpret treaties, that such meaning be clear, and that upon interpretation does not lead to unreasonable or absurd outcomes.

It is worth mentioning that other methods of interpretation may differ from those found in the VCLT. There is no concrete position as to which method one should adopt when interpreting treaties. Some authors take the VCLT as a point of departure, whereas others consider either the complementary or exclusive position of other methods of interpretation.

G. CONCLUSION

Treaty law remains one of the most fundamental fields within international law, interwoven with almost every other branch of international law. At its core, treaty law, most notably as represented within the VCLT, governs the application rules to international treaties. Although treaties remain the most conclusive evidence of international cooperation, they are not without controversy. The very nature of treaties, their negotiation and drafting, invalidation and termination, continue to give rise to various debates in international law. Equally so, the very interpretation of treaties in international law remains a delicate art. The law of treaties has also been a changing field. While in the past it was a transaction of rights and duties between States, today organisations and actors without legal capacity may too engage with treaty law (be it in negotiation, drafting, or conclusion). Finally, it is worth keeping in mind that treaty law's approach in time means it has oftentimes contributed to problems in the past. Treaty-making before the advent of human rights serves as just one example of this, where treaty law enabled the subdivision and claiming of land and the arbitrary separation of peoples across these lands.

---

115 Ibid 620–624.
116 See also Kaczorowska (n 43) 124–126.

BOX 6.1.4 Further Readings

Further Readings

- O Dörr and K Schmalenbach (eds), *Vienna Convention on the Law of Treaties: A Commentary* (2nd edn, Springer 2018)

- R Gardiner, *Treaty Interpretation* (2nd edn, OUP 2017)

- DB Hollis (ed), *The Oxford Guide to Treaties* (2nd edn, OUP 2017)

- R Kolb, *The Law of Treaties: An Introduction* (Edward Elgar 2016)

- B Mulamba Mbuyi, *Droits des Traités Internationaux: Notes de Cours à l'Usage des étudiants en Droit* (L'Harmattan 2009)

§ § §

§ 6.2 CUSTOMARY INTERNATIONAL LAW

VICTOR STOICA

BOX 6.2.1 Required Knowledge and Learning Objectives

Required knowledge: History of International Law; Nature and Purpose of International Law; Consent

Learning objectives: Understanding what customary international law as a source of international law is, and who directly and indirectly contributes towards its formation and identification.

A. INTRODUCTION

Customary international law is unwritten; it is tacit agreement. Prior to World War II, it represented the main mechanism through which international law was created. It has been argued that the current framework of customary international law is, to a certain degree, the result of a rather regionalised State practice.[117] This practice became 'general' by colonial domination and European resistance towards efforts of newly independent States in the 1950s and 1960s to participate in the custom-making and codification process on their own terms.[118]

Today, customary international law is no longer the primary, but remains one of the most important, sources along with treaties. In times of crisis of classic treaty-making, it is arguably even of renewed relevance, by offering binding rules irrespective of hyper-political treaty negotiations. Article 38(1) of the Statute of the International Court of Justice (ICJ)[119] is essential for understanding the meaning and content of customary international law, which rests on the implied consent of States.[120]

There is much controversy around the concept, which is closely connected to the unwritten nature of customary law and the way it comes into being. Because of its State-centredness, the legitimacy of customary international law may seem debatable.[121] One of the main reasons for this rather convoluted understanding is that, as opposed to treaties, the formation of customary international law does not follow a predictable path or an

---

117 Patrick Kelly, 'Customary International Law in Historical Context' in Brian Lepard (ed), *Reexamining Customary International Law* (CUP 2017) 47.

118 On the history of international law, see González Hauck, § 1, in this textbook.

119 Statute of the International Court of Justice (adopted 17 December 1963, entered into force 31 August 1965) 993 UNTS 33.

120 Vincy Fon and Francesco Parisi, 'Stability and Change in International Customary Law' (2009) 17 Supreme Court Economic Review 279. On consent, see González Hauck, § 2.2, in this textbook.

121 John Tasioulas, 'Opinio Iuris and the Genesis of Custom: A Solution to the "Paradox"' (2007) 26 Aust YBIL 199.

exact and regulated procedure. It may seem that customary international law blooms slowly and appears abruptly. While the traditional view is that the creation of custom essentially entails a substantial amount of time to pass for its creation, recent doctrine has also acknowledged the possibility for the creation of an 'instant custom',[122] in certain emerging domains such as space law. The United Nations General Assembly, through is Resolutions, is also regarded as a main contributor to the creation of instant customs.[123]

Over the last years, efforts to codify customary international law and systematise its identification have certainly contributed to its understanding. Worth mentioning are the International Law Commission's (ILC) Draft conclusions on Identification of Customary International Law[124] and the ILA Statement of Principles Applicable to the Formation of General Customary International Law.[125] The same is true for the jurisprudence of the ICJ.

The aim of this chapter is to give an overview of how customary law as one of the sources of international law is formed and identified. By doing so, it will also touch upon some of the contemporary controversies revolving around customary international law.

B. CONSTITUTIVE ELEMENTS OF CUSTOMARY LAW

I. GENERAL PRACTICE

1. Actions and Active Doing

The first element required to form custom is general practice. What is primarily relevant is *State* practice.[126] States are abstract entities, with no material form through which they could manifest their activities. High officials, such as Heads of State or Ministers, municipal courts or legislative bodies may be viewed as the limbs through which States act and develop practice. However, not all actions performed by States may create custom.

One classic example for the formation of customary international law is maritime law, which was 'almost entirely customary international law'.[127] Not only physical acts (such

---

122 Michael Sharf, 'Seizing the Grotian Moment: Accelerated Formation of Customary International Law in Times of Fundamental Change' (2010) 43 Cornell International Law Journal 440, 445–446.

123 Ibid.

124 ILC, 'Draft Conclusions on Identification of Customary International Law, with Commentaries' (70th session, 30 April–1 June and 2 July–10 August 2018) UN Doc A/73/10 122–156.

125 Committee on Formation of Customary (General) International Law, 'Final Report of the Committee. Statement of Principles Applicable to the Formation of General Customary International Law' in International Law Association Report of the Sixty-Ninth Conference (London 2000).

126 Draft Conclusion 4 (n 8) 130. See also *Military and Paramilitary Activities in and Against Nicaragua (Nicaragua v USA)* (Merits) [1986] ICJ Rep 14 [184].

127 Richard Barns and others, 'The Law of the Sea: Progress and Prospects' in David Freestone and others (eds), *The Law of the Sea. Progress and Prospects* (OUP 2006) 22; see also *North Sea Continental Shelf (Federal Republic of*

as the exercise of fishing rights or the seizure of foreign vessels) may constitute practice, but also *legal acts*.[128] Illustratively, if States enact legislation to protect fish within 200 miles off their coasts, there is potential for the creation of a rule of customary international law.[129]

The distinctions between State practice and *opinio juris* are not always clear-cut, leading to difficult questions in practice. Yet, this should not be regarded as negative, especially since the way States act continues to diversify.[130]

2. Inaction and Not-Doing (Acquiescence)

Sometimes, omissions may also represent State practice, for the silence of States can be interpreted as *approval*.[131] A State's inaction, thus, sometimes has legal effects. Unsurprisingly, this has given rise to controversy. The ICJ has greatly contributed to clarifying the circumstances under which this is the case. In the *Temple of Preah Vihear* case, the Court made clear that inaction may only be read as approval or *acquiescence* if 'the circumstances called for some reaction, within a reasonable period'.[132] The ICJ confirmed its findings in other judgments and held that 'silence may also speak, but only if the conduct of the other State calls for a response'.[133] The ILC provides further examples of omissions that may lead to the creation of custom: 'abstaining from instituting criminal proceedings against foreign State officials; refraining from exercising protection in favour of certain naturalized persons; and abstaining from the use of force'.[134] Doctrine confirms that only the omissions which are clear in their scope may constitute relevant practice.[135] Omissions must, thus, be carefully interpreted in order to determine the true intention of the State that did not perform a particular action.

3. Statements

Regarding the value of public statements of States, different opinions exist. Some argue that they should rather be considered under the subjective element, *opinio juris*.[136]

Germany v Denmark; Federal Republic of Germany v the Netherlands) (Judgment) [1969] ICJ Rep 3. On the law of the sea, see Dela Cruz and Paige, § 15, in this textbook.

128 Laurence Boisson de Chazournes, 'Qu'est-ce que la Pratique en Droit International?' in Société française pour le droit international, *La pratique et le droit international: Colloque de Genève* (Pedone 2004).

129 Ibid.

130 María Vásquez Callo-Müller and Iryna Bogdanova, 'What Is the Role of Unilateral Cyber Sanctions in the Context of the Global Cybersecurity Law-Making?' (*Völkerrechtsblog*, 10 May 2022) <https:// voelkerrechtsblog.org/what-is-the-role-of-unilateral-cyber-sanctions-in-the-context-of-the-global-cybersecurity-law-making/> accessed 10 August 2023.

131 Draft Conclusion 6 (n 124) 133.

132 *Case concerning the Temple of Preah Vihear (Cambodia v Thailand)* (Merits) [1962] ICJ Rep 6.

133 *Sovereignty over Pedra Branca/Pulau Batu Puteh, Middle Rocks and South Ledge (Malaysia v Singapore)* (Judgment) [2008] ICJ Rep 12 [121].

134 Draft Conclusions (n 124) 133.

135 Maurice H Mendelson, 'The Formation of Customary International Law' (1998) 272 RdC 155, 207.

136 Anthony D'Amato, *The Concept of Custom in International law* (Cornell UP 1971) 49; Anthea Roberts, 'Traditional and Modern Approaches to Customary International Law: A Reconciliation' (2001) 95 AJIL 757.

According to a more progressive view, statements (especially those of high officials) may constitute State practice. In support of this, certain scholars point out that some 'important acts of state behaviour, such as recognition of another state, do not need a physical act'.[137] It has been argued that what matters is that statements may constitute either State practice or *opinio juris* depending on the relevant contextual circumstances.[138] For example, a statement of a head of State or a foreign minister, which are the actors representing the State on the international plane, may constitute practice.[139]

4. What Does 'General' Mean?

A crucial question that arises is how widespread a practice must be. A universalist perspective would mean that 'all or almost all of the nations of the world engage in it'.[140] Even if this view has certain merit, it is nearly impossible to determine if more than 190 States have engaged in a certain practice.[141] Further, practice is rarely virtually homogenous.[142]

The ILC opted for a pragmatic but abstract solution, stating that for practice to be general, it must be 'sufficiently widespread and representative as well as consistent'.[143] This three-pronged standard is lower; it does not require unanimity or even majority.

a) Sufficiently Widespread

Widespread practice is generally understood as 'existing or happening in many places and/or among many people'.[144] The ICJ has not defined the concept, nor did the ILC, which quotes the *North Sea Continental Shelf* cases, in which the ICJ concluded that the practice in question must be 'both extensive and virtually uniform',[145] or 'settled practice'.[146] These standards are not universal, nor were they relevant in all cases in which the application of customary international law was at stake. The only clarification provided is that practice is sufficiently widespread when it is not 'contradictory or

---

137 Jorg Kammerhofer, 'Uncertainty in the Formal Sources of International Law: Customary International Law and Some of Its Problems' (2004) 15 EJIL 526.

138 Mendelson (n 135) 206.

139 Ibid.

140 Jack Landman Goldsmith, 'A Theory of International Law' (1999) University of Chicago Law School, John M Olin Law & Economics Working Paper No. 63, 7 <https://papers.ssrn.com/sol3/papers.cfm?abstract_id=145972> accessed 16 August 2023.

141 Ibid.

142 Niels Petersen, 'The International Court of Justice and the Judicial Politics of Identifying Customary International Law' (2017) 28 EJIL 377.

143 Draft Conclusion 8 (n 124) 135.

144 'Widespread', *Cambridge Advanced Learner's Dictionary & Thesaurus* (CUP) <https://dictionary.cambridge.org/dictionary/english/widespread> accessed 17 August 2023.

145 *North Sea Continental Shelf* (n 27) [74].

146 Ibid [77].

inconsistent'.[147] It would then seem that the first criterion is defined through what it is not. In other words, practice may be widespread if it is not limited.

b) Sufficiently Representative

Representative practice is generally understood as 'typical of, or the same as, others in a larger group of people or things'.[148] At first glance, it might seem that the concept of 'representative' has common features with the concept of 'widespread', especially because the number of entities participating in the creation of custom is relevant in both cases. However, in comparison, representative practice is rather qualitative, whereas widespread practice is quantitative.

The ICJ has not addressed what 'representative' means. According to the ILC, it must take into consideration the 'various interests at stake and/or the various geographical regions'.[149] Therefore, for practice to be representative, the approach of certain States has more weight than others.

c) Consistency

Consistency is generally understood as 'the quality of always behaving or performing in a similar way, or of always happening in a similar way'.[150] This standard implies that practice should manifest stability over time.[151] As such, if the behaviour of States fluctuates over time, it would be difficult to identify a general practice.[152] The question, here, is whether there is a need for uniformity of practice (complete consistency) for the formation of custom or whether a lower standard suffices.

In the *Nicaragua* case, the ICJ found that complete consistency is not required and that the corresponding practice may not be in 'absolute conformity with the rule'.[153] The 'virtual uniformity' concept used in the *North Sea Continental Shelf* is also relevant here, even if the period of time in which it is developed is short.[154]

II. ACCEPTED AS LAW (*OPINIO JURIS*)

For general practice to become custom, it needs, furthermore, to be performed *out of a sense of a legal obligation*. The ICJ confirmed that States must feel that they are respecting

---

147 Ibid.

148 'Representative', *Cambridge Advanced Learner's Dictionary & Thesaurus* (CUP) <https://dictionary.cambridge. org/dictionary/english/representative> accessed 17 August 2023.

149 Draft Conclusion 8 (n 124) 135.

150 'Consistency', *Cambridge Advanced Learner's Dictionary & Thesaurus* (CUP) <https://dictionary.cambridge.org/ dictionary/english/consistency> accessed 17 August 2023.

151 Fon and Parisi (n 120) 283.

152 Ibid.

153 *Military and Paramilitary Activities in and Against Nicaragua* (n 126) [186].

154 *North Sea Continental Shelf* (n 127) [74].

a legal obligation.[155] This criterion is the subjective element of customary international law, *opinio juris*.

How does one determine what an abstract entity such as a State believes? Unsurprisingly, this element of custom is controversial. The ILC sheds some light on the tools that may evidence *opinio juris*, such as 'public statements made on behalf of states; official publications; diplomatic correspondence; decisions of national courts; treaty provisions; and conduct in connection with resolutions adopted by an international organisation or intergovernmental conference'.[156]

The distinction between acts (such as the ones enumerated above) that confirm the perception of States to be bound by legal obligations and those evidencing actions out of courtesy is also not clear. The ICJ, in the *North Sea Continental Shelf* cases, confirmed that 'there are many international acts, e.g. in the field of ceremonial and protocol, which are performed almost invariably, but which are motivated only by considerations of courtesy, convenience or tradition, and not by any sense of legal duty'.[157] As such, 'it is difficult to determine what states believe as opposed to what they say'.[158]

These uncertainties regarding a precise way *opinio juris* should be determined have led certain authors to conclude that the subjective element should be less relevant,[159] and that practice should be at the forefront of identifying customary international law. Nevertheless, it is rather generally accepted that 'while *opinio juris* confers the legal bindingness of custom, practice, it is argued, can be understood as what provides custom with normative content'.[160] In other words, while practice provides what the norm contains, *opinio juris* is what confers to that norm its binding character. *Opinio juris* is, thus, essential for the creation of customary international law.

C. WHO IS BOUND BY CUSTOM?

I. THE PERSISTENT OBJECTOR

The 'persistent objector' doctrine captures situations in which a State expressly objects to a rule of customary international law when that rule is in the process of formation. It provides that, in these cases, said rule will not be applicable to that State.

---

155 Ibid.

156 Draft Conclusion 6 (n 8) 133.

157 *North Sea Continental Shelf* (n 18) [77].

158 Roberts (n 136) 757.

159 Pierro Mattei-Gentili, 'The Quest for Opinio Juris: An Analysis of Customary Law, from Hart's Social Rules to Expectations and Everything in the Middle' (2020) 34 Noesis 89.

160 Maiko Meguro, 'Distinguishing the Legal Bindingness and Normative Content of Customary International Law' (2017) 6(11) ESIL Reflection <https://esil-sedi.eu/post_name-1149/> accessed 16 August 2023.

The timing of contestation is relevant, because potential objections of States which are performed after customary international law was formed are no longer relevant. In other words, States that did not object during the formation of custom must comply with the created rules. The role of the consistent objector doctrine is to respect States' sovereignty and protect them from the imposition of rules against their will; yet, if the support for the new rule is sufficiently widespread, 'the convoy of the law's progressive development can move forward without having to wait for the slowest vessel'.[161]

II. SPECIALLY AFFECTED STATES

The 'specially affected States' doctrine aims to take into account the fact that some States were 'particularly involved in the relevant activity or most likely to be concerned with the alleged rule'.[162] For example, the rise of the level of seas and oceans imply significant threats to small island States for multiple reasons, such as the concentration of people and infrastructure present in coastal areas.[163] These States may be considered as specially affected for the creation and identification of customary international law related to sea level rise.

This is not to argue that the specially affected States are the only ones that contribute to the creation of customary international law in a particular field. Rather, their practice should carry more weight than the practice of States that are not in the same position.

D. SPECIAL CUSTOMARY INTERNATIONAL LAW

I. *JUS COGENS* NORMS

Jus cogens norms, or the peremptory norms of public international law, are rules 'accepted and recognized by the international community as a whole . . . from which no derogation is permitted'.[164] They thus reside at the top of the hierarchy of norms. While the legal justification of *jus cogens* is not entirely clear, one explanation is that they are created through custom. In other words, some customary norms 'are considered so vital that they cannot be contracted out of by individual states'.[165]

---

161 International Law Association (n 125) 28.

162 Draft Conclusions (n 124).

163 Rosanne Martyr-Koller and others, 'Loss and Damage Implications of Sea-Level Rise on Small Island Developing States' (2021) 50 COSUST 245.

164 Article 53 VCLT. On *jus cogens*, see Eggett, § 6, in this textbook.

165 Roozbeh Baker, 'Customary International Law in the 21st Century: Old Challenges and New Debates' (2010) 21 EJIL 177.

II. REGIONAL CUSTOMARY INTERNATIONAL LAW

At the opposite end of the spectrum rests regional (or particular) customary international law. By way of example, the Arbitral Tribunal in the Eritrea/Yemen Arbitration recognised the possibility of a custom to exist on a regional or even a bilateral basis,[166] practice which may be based upon a need for 'respect for regional legal traditions'.[167] In the *Asylum* case, the ICJ accepted the possibility of regional customs to exist, even if in the case at hand it concluded that the Colombian government did not prove the existence of such a rule.[168] In a later case, the Court emphasised the relevance of practice between two States.[169] Subsequent practice can also be taken into account when determining the content of customary norms. In its *Nicaragua* judgment, the Court appeared to agree that regional customary international law, 'particular to the inter-American legal system',[170] exists.

E. CONCLUSION

Beyond the general assertion that custom exists of two elements, State practice and accompanying *opinio juris*, there are no clear, universally applicable, and fixed rules for the creation of customary international law. However, the lack of such parameters is not in itself a disadvantage, given the ever-evolving nature of international law. Customary international law is characterised by agility and has the potential to address multiple legal frameworks: it may be regional or global, it may be confirmed through treaties or detached from them, and it may be general or special. Consequently, flexibility in the identification of customary law may appear suitable, as it reflects the ever-changing developments of international law and policy.

The role of the ICJ in identifying customary law is essential:

> Customary law, being vague and containing gaps compared with written law, requires precision and completion about its content. This task, in its nature being interpretative, would be incumbent upon the Court. The method of logical and teleological interpretation can be applied in the case of customary law as in the case of written law.[171]

Even though custom does not anymore occupy the place it historically has, it remains important. It is a fragile source and should be carefully addressed by international courts and tribunals, policy makers, and all actors playing on the scene of international relations.

---

166 *Government of the State of Eritrea and Government of the Republic of Yemen (Phase Two: Maritime Delimitation)* (2002) 119 ILR 417, 448.
167 Draft Conclusion 16 (n 124) 154.
168 *Colombian-Peruvian asylum case (Colombia v Peru)* (Judgment) [1950] ICJ Rep 266 [277].
169 *Case concerning Right of Passage over Indian Territory (Portugal v India)* (Merits) [1960] ICJ Rep 6 [44].
170 *Military and Paramilitary Activities in and against Nicaragua* (n 26) [199].
171 *North Sea Continental Shelf (Federal Republic of Germany v Denmark; Federal Republic of Germany v the Netherlands)* (Dissenting Opinion of Judge Tanaka) [1969] ICJ Rep 172.

BOX 6.2.2 Further Readings

Further Readings

- J Crawford, *Chance, Order, Change: The Course of International Law, General Course on Public International Law* (Brill 2014)

- J D'Aspremont, *International Law as a Belief System* (CUP 2017)

- A Roberts, *Is International Law International?* (OUP 2017)

- H Lauterpacht, *The Function of Law in the International Community* (OUP 2011)

§ § §

§ 6.3 GENERAL PRINCIPLES

CRAIG EGGETT

BOX 6.3.1 Required Knowledge and Learning Objectives

Required knowledge: Sources of International Law; Subjects and Actors; Positivism; Consent

Learning objectives: Understanding the background to article 38(1)(c) ICJ Statute and how general principles can be identified; understanding what general principles (can) do in international law.

A. INTRODUCTION

Article 38(1) of the Statute of the International Court of Justice's (ICJ) list of generally accepted sources of international law concludes with sub-paragraph (c)'s 'general principles of law recognised by civilised nations'.[172] That the final three words of this provision are to be discarded is clear, yet doing so is just the beginning of thorough engagement with general principles in international law.[173] This source of law has received considerably less attention than treaties and customary law, and there are few unequivocally recognised examples of general principles. Article 38(1)(c) has never been explicitly relied on by the ICJ as a basis of a decision. The discourse on general principles received a significant boost when, in 2017, the International Law Commission (ILC) decided to include the topic on its programme.[174] This chapter aims to provide an overview of the core aspects of the ongoing discussion on general principles in international law. It is structured around three main questions: (1) What kind of norms are general principles? (2) How are they ascertained? and (3) What functions do they perform? These questions overlap to an extent, yet they provide a basic logical structure to examine general principles and their place in the international legal system.

---

172 Statute of the International Court of Justice (adopted 17 December 1963, entered into force 31 August 1965) 993 UNTS 33.

173 For a discussion of the broader issue of reference to 'civilisation' in this provision, and in international law more generally, see Sué González Hauck, 'All Nations Must Be Considered to Be Civilized: General Principles of Law between Cosmetic Adjustments and Decolonization' (*Verfassungsblog*, 21 July 2020) <https://verfassungsblog.de/all-nations-must-be-considered-to-be-civilized/> accessed 9 August 2023; Ntina Tzouvala, *Capitalism as Civilisation* (CUP 2020) chapter 1.

174 The overview of the ILC's work on general principles can be found here: ILC, 'Analytical Guide to the Work of the International Law Commission' <https://legal.un.org/ilc/guide/1_15.shtml> accessed 9 August 2023.

B. THE NATURE OF GENERAL PRINCIPLES

I. HISTORY AND ORIGINS OF GENERAL PRINCIPLES IN INTERNATIONAL LAW

Both the wording and history of the ICJ Statute confirm that general principles have a role as applicable law in the settlement of disputes. The drafting of article 38 ICJ Statute is based on the corresponding provision of the PCIJ Statute, which contains identical wording, yet the history extends further back than the drafting of the PCIJ Statute.[175] For example, references to 'principles' as a source of applicable law were included in the Arbitral Procedure Regulations 1875,[176] the First Hague Convention establishing the PCA,[177] and the Convention Relative to the Creation of an International Prize Court 1907.[178] While differing in their precise construction, the references to 'principles' illustrates that early practice recognised a role for a source of international law beyond treaties and custom. Even early arbitral practice suggested a role for general principles in international law. Examples are the *Walfish Bay Boundary* case[179] or the *Pious Fund* case,[180] in which the Tribunal found that the principle of *res judicata* (Latin: 'a matter judged'), which has its origins in domestic systems and Roman law, was applicable in international law and so governed the decision in question.[181]

The original draft of article 38 referred to 'the *rules* of international law as recognised by the legal conscience of civilized nations'.[182] This formulation represents a departure from some earlier references to 'principles of justice and equity'. The members of the Advisory Committee debated the role that this third source of law would play and the powers that it would grant to the Court.[183] Throughout the discussions of the Advisory Committee, there was broad agreement

---

175 For an overview, see Imogen Saunders, *General Principles as a Source of International Law: Article 38(1)(c) of the Statute of the International Court of Justice* (Hart 2021) 21–38.

176 Institute de Droit International, *Projet de règlement pour la procédure arbitrale internationale* [1875] Vol 1, article 22 (referring to 'principles of law which are applicable by virtue of the rules of international law).

177 Convention (I) on Pacific Settlement of International Disputes (adopted 29 July 1899, entered into force 4 September 1900) 187 CTS 410, article 48.

178 Convention Relative to the Creation of an International Prize Court 1907 (signed 18 October 1907) 205 CTS 381, article 7 (referring to 'general principles of justice and equity').

179 *Walfish Bay Boundary Case (Germany v Great Britain)* [1911] 11 RIAA 263.

180 *The Pious Fund Case (United States of America v Mexico)* [1902] 9 RIAA 1.

181 Ibid 7–10.

182 Permanent Court of International Justice: Advisory Committee of Jurists, *Procès-verbaux of the Proceedings of the Committee* (Van Langenhuysen Brothers 1920) 13th Meeting, 306.

183 See the *Procès-verbaux* of the 13th, 14th, and 15th meetings. For an overview, see, for example, Saunders (n 175) 38–46; Ole Spiermann, 'The History of Article 38 of the Statute of the International Court of Justice: "A Purely Platonic Discussion?"' in Samantha Besson and Jean d'Aspremont (eds), *The Oxford Handbook on the Sources of International Law* (OUP 2017) 170–173.

that the purpose of this provision was to make available to the Court a source of applicable law that could be relied upon in the absence of any applicable treaty or customary rules. The legal nature of general principles as a source of applicable law was apparent from the outset.

II. GENERAL PRINCIPLES, RULES, AND OTHER NORMS

A central issue is whether general principles, in and of themselves, can be a source of obligations in international law. The decision to use the term 'principle' in place of the original 'rule' could suggest that general principles are a different kind of norm, distinct from concrete rules of law. Indeed, there are authors who argue that general principles are broader and vaguer norms that do not impose direct obligations but provide a more general framework for the interpretation and application of rules and discretion to judges.[184] In a similar vein, some would argue that general principles have natural law overtones[185] and links to broader values or moral considerations.[186] Conversely, some authors would argue that general principles, like the other sources of law, are capable of granting rights and imposing obligations.[187] There are others, still, that view general principles as some sort of in-between; as a type of transitory norm between values and concrete rules[188] or as a form of 'inchoate custom'.[189] Despite these contrasting positions, it seems clear that international courts and tribunals view themselves as being capable of recognising rights and obligations beyond treaties and customary law. A prominent example of this is the development of many procedural rules of international law, which courts and tribunals have frequently recognised as general principles owing to their presence in domestic law and foundation in certain established 'legal maxims'.[190]

---

184 See, for example, Ulf Linderfalk, 'General Principles as Principles of International Legal Pragmatics: The Relevance of Good Faith for the Application of Treaty Law' in Mads Andenas and others (eds), *General Principles and the Coherence of International Law* (Brill/Nijhoff 2019).

185 Igno Venzke, *How Interpretation Makes International Law: On Semantic Change and Normative Twists* (OUP 2012) 25 (claiming that the approach of the ICJ to general principles has clear natural law overtones).

186 See, for example, *South West Africa Cases (Ethiopia v South Africa; Liberia v South Africa)* (Second Phase) (Judgment) [1966] ICJ Rep 6, Reply of Ethiopia and Liberia [271]

187 Beatrice Bonafé and Paolo Palchetti, 'Relying on General Principles in International Law' in Catherine Brölmann and Yannick Radi (eds), *Research Handbook on the Theory and Practice of International Lawmaking* (Edward Elgar 2016) 165–168; Alain Pellet, 'Article 38' in Andreas Zimmermann and Christian Tams (eds), *The Statute of the International Court of Justice: A Commentary* (2nd edn, OUP 2012) 251; Craig Eggett, *General Principles as Systemic Elements of International Law* (PhD Thesis, Maastricht University 2021) chapter III.

188 Roman Kwiecień, 'General Principles of Law: The Gentle Guardians of Systemic Integration of International Law' (2017) 37 PolishYIL 235, 242.

189 Olufemi Elias and Chin Lim, 'General Principles of Law, Soft Law and the Identification of International Law' (1997) 28 NYIL 3, 35.

190 For an overview, see Mathias Forteau, 'General Principles of International Procedural Law' (*The Max Planck Encyclopedia of International Procedural Law*, January 2018) <https://opil.ouplaw.com/display/10.1093/law-mpeipro/e3544.013.3544/law-mpeipro-e3544> accessed 9 August 2023.

> ## BOX 6.3.2 Advanced: Rules and Principles in International Law
>
> International lawyers will frequently debate whether something is part of international law; that is, whether it is a legal norm that regulates a given situation or dispute. In doing so, they deploy a range of terms to help delineate the different kinds of norms at play. 'Rules' and 'principle' are two of the most common such terms. While these terms may mean slightly different things to different people, and indeed the Court saw no relevance to the terminology at all in *Gulf of Maine*,[191] these terms can be used to draw a distinction between concrete norms that impose rights and obligations (rules) and those that underlie the system and influence the interpretation of rules (principles). If such a distinction is accepted, it may be more accurate to describe general principles in the sense of article 38(1)(c) as a category of *rules* of international law.[192]

It can be a challenge to demarcate general principles from other categories of norms. First, the differentiation with custom can be particularly difficult to identify.[193] Both are unwritten sources of (typically) general application. Further, it seems perfectly possible that there could exist customary rules and general principles that have similar or identical content, as has been recognised in the case of treaty and customary rules.[194] Yet, there are key differences in both the ascertainment and functions of custom and general principles. While custom is anchored in the practice and views of States, the formation of general principles involves a more pronounced role for courts and tribunals in the examination of domestic systems and notions of legal logic.

As for *jus cogens*, the ILC expressed support for the idea that general principles of law could attain *jus cogens* status.[195] However, it should be noted that the label *jus cogens* denotes a certain elevated status that can be assigned to a norm, regardless of its source, and not a source of law in and of itself.

---

191 *Delimitation of the Maritime Boundary in the Gulf of Maine Area (Canada v United States of America)* (Judgment of a Chamber) [1984] ICJ Rep 246 [79].

192 On this view, see Craig Eggett, 'The Role of Principles and General Principles in the "Constitutional Processes" of International Law' (2019) 66(2) NILR 197; Eggett (n 187) chapter III.

193 On custom, see Stoica, § 6.2, in this textbook.

194 *Military and Paramilitary Activities In and Against Nicaragua (Nicaragua v United States of America)* (Merits) [1986] ICJ Rep 14 [178]. See also ILC, 'Text of the draft conclusions provisionally adopted by the Drafting Committee on first reading' 74th Session (24 April–2 June and 3 July–4 August 2023) UN Doc A/CN.4/L.982, draft conclusion 11.

195 ILC, 'Second Report on Peremptory Norms of General International Law (*jus cogens*) by Dire Tladi, Special Rapporteur', 69th Session (1 May–2 June and 3 July–4 August 2017) UN Doc A/CN.4/706 52; 49 49 and draft conclusion 5.3.

Finally, it seems that there is a close relationship between general principles and notions such as equity, justice, and the values of the international community. It is commonly recognised that there exist certain basic values upon which the international legal system is built,[196] such as peace and security,[197] respect for human rights and humanity,[198] and sustainable development.[199] These broad values, it has been argued, may lead to the creation of general principles of law.[200] Indeed, it seems logical that support for a general principle may be evidenced by its consonance with the basic objectives of the system as a whole and with fundamental ideas of legal logic.

C. IDENTIFYING GENERAL PRINCIPLES

We turn now to the more practical question of how to identify a general principle. The text of the ICJ Statute itself provides little guidance on how to identify a general principle. It is broadly agreed that the term 'civilised nations' should be discarded.[201] Indeed, the ILC has confirmed that the phrasing 'is anachronistic and should no longer be employed. In today's world, all nations must be considered to be civilized'.[202] Going further, in a Separate Opinion in *North Sea Continental Shelf*, Judge Ammoun asserted that the term 'is incompatible with . . . the United Nations Charter'.[203] Once the term 'civilised nations' is discarded, two issues remain: (1) Whose recognition is relevant? and (2) How can it be determined that there is sufficient recognition of a general principle?

I. RECOGNITION BY THE 'COMMUNITY OF NATIONS'

The issue of whose recognition is relevant for the identification of a general principles touches upon a fundamental question in international law, namely, is the creation of

196 Otto Spijkers, *The United Nations, the Evolution of Global Values and International Law* (Intersentia 2011); Louis Henkin, 'International Law: Politics, Values and Functions General Course on Public International Law' (1990) 216 RdC.

197 Hersch Lauterpacht, 'The Grotian Tradition in International Law' (1946) 23 BYIL 1, 51; Hans Kelsen, *Peace Through Law* (University of North Carolina Press 1944).

198 Antonio Cassese, 'A Plea for a Global Community Grounded in a Core of Human Rights' in Antonio Cassese (ed), *Realizing Utopia* (OUP 2012).

199 Alexander Orakhelashvili, *The Interpretation of Acts and Rules in Public International Law* (OUP 2008) 182.

200 See, for example, Ginevra le Moli, 'The Principle of Human Dignity in International Law' in Andenas and others (n 184).

201 See, for example, Charles Kotuby Jr. and Luke Sobota, *General Principles of Law and International Due Process: Principles and Norms Applicable in Transnational Disputes* (OUP 2017) 22; Giorgio Gaja, 'General Principles of Law' (*The Max Planck Encyclopedia of Public International Law*, April 2020) <https://opil.ouplaw.com/display/10.1093/law:epil/9780199231690/law-9780199231690-e1410> accessed 9 August 2023 para 2.

202 ILC, Second report on general principles of law by Marcelo Vázquez-Bermúdez, Special Rapporteur (72nd Session 27 April–5 June and 6 July–7 August 2020) Un Doc A/CN.4/741 2.

203 *North Sea Continental Shelf Cases (Germany v Denmark; Germany v Netherlands)* (Judgment) [1969] ICJ Rep 3, Separate Opinion of Judge Ammoun, 132.

international law solely the prerogative of States? The ILC seemed to stay broadly in line with a traditional position: 'For a general principle of law to exist, it must be recognized by the community of nations'.[204] The Commission explained that it adopted this phrase because of its use in article 15(2) of the ICCPR,[205] which, because of the widespread membership of this treaty, signifies broad acceptance of this terminology.[206]

II. METHODOLOGY FOR THE RECOGNITION OF GENERAL PRINCIPLES

Many of the ILC draft conclusions on general principles are concerned with the approach to be taken when identifying these norms. The approach set out by the Commission is predicated on an initial distinction between two categories of norms, 'those: (a) that are derived from national legal systems; (b) that may be formed within the international legal system'.[207] This distinction is consonant with previous accounts of general principles of law,[208] and the ILC differentiates between the approaches to the ascertainment of each of these categories.

1. General Principles Derived From National Systems

Similar to previous attempts,[209] the ILC sets out a two-stage approach to this category of general principles, first ascertaining 'the existence of a principle common to the various legal systems of the world' and then 'its transposition to the international legal system'.[210]

The first of these steps is anchored in the idea that comparative law serves as a foundation for the ascertainment of general principles in international law.[211] The Commission claims that this need not involve the examination of every legal system of the world. Instead, it proposed a more 'pragmatic' approach involving consideration of a representative sample of both the 'different legal families and the regions' of the world.[212] Indeed, such an approach would be a welcome departure from the practice

---

204 ILC Draft Conclusions (n 194) draft conclusion 2.

205 International Covenant on Civil and Political Rights (adopted 16 December 1966, entered into force 23 March 1976) 999 UNTS 171.

206 ILC Second Report (n 202) 13.

207 ILC Draft Conclusions (n 194) draft conclusion 3.

208 See, for example, Catherine Redgwell, 'General Principles of International Law' in Stefan Vogenauer and Stephen Weatherill (eds), *General Principles of Law: European and Comparative Perspectives* (Hart 2017) 9; Patrick Dailler, Mathias Forteau and Alain Pellet, *Droit International Public* (8th edn, LGDJ 2009) 380 et seq.; Charles Rousseau, *Principes généraux du Droit International Public, Vol. I (Sources)* (Pedone 1944) 891.

209 Fabián Raimondo, *General Principles of Law in the Decisions of International Criminal Courts and Tribunals* (Brill/Nijhoff 2008) 62–74; Miles Jackson, 'State Instigation in International Law: A General Principle Transposed' (2019) 30(2) EJIL 391.

210 ILC Draft Conclusions (n 194) draft conclusion 4.

211 For an exploration, see Jaye Ellis, 'General Principles and Comparative Law' (2011) 22 EJIL 949.

212 ILC Second Report (n 202) 28.

of courts and tribunals when engaging in comparative law, as there has typically been reliance on just a handful of predominantly European legal systems.[213]

Second, there is an additional step of transposition into international law. As was noted in the *South West Africa Advisory Opinion*, rules of domestic law are not transposed 'lock, stock and barrel, ready-made and fully equipped' into international law.[214] According to the ILC, '[a] principle common to the various legal systems of the world may be transposed to the international legal system in so far as it is compatible with that system'.[215] A prospective general principle must be compatible with the fundamental principles of international law, such as sovereignty or basic principles in certain fields like law of the sea.[216] Further, it is necessary that 'the conditions exist to allow the adequate application of the principle in the international legal system. This serves to ensure that the principle can properly serve its purpose in international law, avoiding distortions or possible abuse'.[217] This requirement seems logical given the fundamental differences in the nature and structure of international law – as a decentralised and horizontal legal system – when compared with national systems.

2. General Principles Formed Within the International Legal System

When it comes to the identification of general principles with origins in the international legal system, the ILC states that 'it is necessary to ascertain that the community of nations has recognised the principle as intrinsic to the international legal system'.[218] This is the case if (1) it is widely recognised in treaties and other international instruments, (2) it underlies a general treaty or customary rule, or (3) it is inherent in the basic features and fundamental requirements of the international legal system.[219] The first two of these indicate a close relationship between general principles and the other sources listed in article 38 ICJ Statute, suggesting that the repeated reference to a norm in treaty law or custom can in turn create a general principle. As for the final alternative, the ILC provided examples such as *uti possidetis juris* (Latin: 'as you possess under law'), or the requirement that States consent to jurisdiction.[220]

Evidence for the existence of a general principle can be found in a range of different instruments and other sources. Further, the ILC specifically reiterates the role of the

---

213 See, for example, the approaches taken by some individual ICJ judges: *Certain Phosphate Lands in Nauru (Nauru v Australia)* (Preliminary Objections) [1992] ICJ Rep 240, Separate Opinion of Judge Shahabudeen, 285; *Oil Platforms (Islamic Republic of Iran v United States of America)* (Judgment) [2003] ICJ Rep 161, Separate Opinion of Judge Simma.

214 *International Status of South West Africa* case (Advisory Opinion) [1950] ICJ Rep 128, 148.

215 ILC Draft Conclusions (n 194) draft conclusion 6.

216 ILC Second Report (n 202) [75]–[84].

217 Ibid 85.

218 ILC Draft Conclusions (n 194) conclusions 7.1.

219 ILC Second Report (n 202) [122]–[158].

220 Ibid 146–158.

subsidiary means – judicial decisions and academic teachings – in the determination of general principles of both categories.[221]

D. THE FUNCTIONS OF GENERAL PRINCIPLES

Already at the drafting stage of article 38, it was suggested that general principles would have primarily a role to play where there was no applicable treaty or customary rule. This 'gap-filling' function is also a prevalent feature of scholarly accounts on general principles.[222] The ILC confirmed that the 'essential function'[223] of general principles was to avoid situations of *non liquet* (Latin: 'it is not clear').[224]

In addition, general principles contribute to the coherence of the international legal system,[225] a function that has also been advanced in literature.[226] The Commission elaborated that general principles, 'may serve, *inter alia*: (a) to interpret and complement other rules of international law; (b) as a basis for primary rights and obligations, as well as a basis for secondary and procedural rules'.[227] The first of these functions seems to follow logically from the references to the links between general principles and the other sources of law in the context of ascertainment. In this regard, the ILC makes explicit reference to the rules of systemic interpretation referred to in article 31(3)(c) VCLT,[228] confirming that this provision's reference to 'rules of international law' includes general principles.[229] Finally, the ILC's confirmation that general principles can form a basis for both primary and secondary rules is consonant with the aforementioned legal nature of general principles as source of international law. It should be noted that it is in the development of secondary procedural rules that general principles have been identified as the most relevant. Scholarly accounts of general principles couple them with 'international due process'[230] and 'procedural' norms,[231] and international practice confirms that courts and tribunals most frequently make reference to general principles when attempting to answer a procedural question not covered by treaty or customary rule.[232]

---

221 ILC Draft Conclusions (n 194) draft conclusions 8 and 9.

222 Hugh Thirlway, *The Sources of International Law* (OUP 2014) 125; Pellet (n 187) 290; Elias and Lim (n 189) 35–37; Kotuby and Sobota (n 201) 35.

223 ILC, Third report on general principles of law by Marcelo Vázquez-Bermúdez, Special Rapporteur (73rd Session 18 April–3 June and 4 July–5 August 2022) UN Doc A/CN.4/753 [108].

224 Ibid 39–41.

225 ILC Draft Conclusions (n 194) draft conclusion 11.2.

226 See, generally, the contributions in in Andenas and others (n 184); Eggett (n 187) 149–155.

227 ILC Draft Conclusions (n 194) draft conclusion 11.2.

228 Vienna Convention on the Law of Treaties (adopted 23 May 1969, entered into force 27 January 1980) 1155 UNTS 331, 8 ILM 679.

229 ILC Third Report (n 223) [124].

230 Kotuby and Sobota (n 201).

231 Forteau (n 190).

232 See, for example, Eggett (n 187) chapter V.

> ## BOX 6.3.3 Example: Pushing the Boundaries of International Law: Judge Cançado Trindade
>
> The recognition that general principles can serve as a basis of primary rules indicates significant potential for general principles as a means to expand and modernise the international legal system. If courts and tribunals, particularly the ICJ, embrace this function, it could be that general principles of law serve as a basis of rights and obligations where treaty law and custom do not.[233] The late Judge Antonio Augusto Cançado Trindade was an enthusiastic advocate of such a role for general principles, explaining that these norms could serve as a basis for the progressive development of international law to meet contemporary global challenges such as climate change and the protection of human rights.[234]

E. CONCLUSION

This section has provided an overview of the basic conceptual aspects of general principles as a source of international law, in light of ongoing debates about their place in the international legal system. General principles are a recognised source of international law and there are many potential instruments and concepts that can be consulting during their ascertainment. It remains to be seen what exactly the full potential of these norms will be, but there is scope for greater reliance on general principles to enhance the functioning of the international legal system as a whole.

> ## BOX 6.3.4 Further Reading
>
> **Further Reading**
>
> - M Andenas and others (eds), *General Principles and the Coherence of International Law* (Brill/Nijhoff 2019).
>
> - B Cheng, *General Principles of Law as Applied by International Courts and Tribunals* (CUP 1953).
>
> - C Eggett, 'The Role of Principles and General Principles in the "Constitutional Processes" of International Law' (2019) 66(2) NILR 197.
>
> - I Saunders, *General Principles as a Source of International Law: Article 38(1) (c) of the Statute of the International Court of Justice* (Hart 2021).

§ § §

---

233 Ibid.

234 See, for example, *Pulp Mills on the River Uruguay (Argentina v Uruguay)* (Judgment) [2010] ICJ Rep 14, Separate Opinion of Judge Cançado Trindade.

§ 6.4 OTHER SOURCES

RAFFAELA KUNZ, LUCAS CARLOS LIMA, AND BERNARDO MAGESTE CASTELAR CAMPOS

BOX 6.4.1 Required Knowledge and Learning Objectives

Required knowledge: Consent; Enforcement; Sources; Treaty Law; Customary International Law

Learning objectives: Understanding the secondary sources of international law as listed in article 38 of the ICJ Statute and the limits of the catalogue of formal sources in times of global governance; understanding the role of non-State subjects – such as international organisations – in today's processes of norm production.

A. INTRODUCTION

Besides treaty law, customary international law and general principles of law, article 38 of the Statute of the International Court of Justice (ICJ)[235] lists two 'subsidiary means for the determination of rules of law', namely judicial decisions and 'the teachings of the most highly qualified publicists of the various nations'. The word 'subsidiary' has predominantly been interpreted as meaning that judicial decisions and teachings are not formal sources themselves, but rather serve as *evidence* of the existence of the three formal sources.[236] In light of this, it has been argued that the term *auxiliaire* used in the French version more adequately describes the function of jurisprudence and doctrine.[237] Rather than providing guidance in a subordinate way if the formal sources give no clear answer, these two means serve as tools to elucidate the existence of norms of international law.

However, the distinction between formal sources and subsidiary means is not as clear-cut as often portrayed. For instance, while judicial decisions are listed as 'subsidiary means', it is becoming increasingly recognised that in light of the indeterminacy of the law, international norms only come to life once applied in concrete cases. Indeterminacy not only refers to the fact that international legal obligations are often phrased in vague terms, leaving room for divergent interpretations. More fundamentally, language as such is indeterminate, and meaning is only established through interpretation.[238]

---

235 Statute of the International Court of Justice (adopted 17 December 1963, entered into force 31 August 1965) 993 UNTS 33.

236 Alain Pellet and Daniel Müller, 'Art. 38' in Andreas Zimmermann and others (eds), *The Statute of the International Court of Justice: A Commentary* (OUP 2019) para 338.

237 Ibid.

238 Ingo Venzke, *How Interpretation Makes International Law: On Semantic Change and Normative Twists* (OUP 2012) 66.

Consequently, judicial decisions undoubtedly play a considerable role in clarifying and thus also making international law.[239]

It is also well-established today that further sources exist beyond the 'list' contained in article 38. Unilateral declarations are recognised as further 'traditional' source of international law. More recently, acts of international organisations, so-called secondary law, and soft law have become increasingly relevant. Both play a crucial role in today's globalised world. The aim of this chapter is to give an overview of these 'other' sources and discuss some of the consequences of the 'pluralisation' of the sources doctrine in international law.

B. SUBSIDIARY SOURCES (ARTICLE 38(1)(D) ICJ STATUTE)

I. JUDICIAL DECISIONS

1. International Judicial Decisions as Sources of Law

When an international court or tribunal renders a judicial decision, it becomes binding upon the parties to the dispute. While the bindingness of a specific judicial decision can be traced to the parties' consent,[240] the general obligation to respect judicial decisions stems from the principle of *pacta sunt servanda* (Latin: 'agreements must be kept').[241] An international judicial decision creates *lex inter partes* (Latin: 'law between the parties'). The extent to which that decision can create law for the community as a whole is up to debate. Since international judicial decisions are an unavoidable part of the judicial legal system and might perform distinct functions within different legal regimes (e.g. trade law, human rights law, international criminal law), it is not possible to generalise the role of decisions as sources of international law.[242]

The Advisory Committee of Jurists responsible for drafting the Statute of the Permanent Court of International Justice had to address the status of judicial decisions. A proposal to include 'international jurisprudence as a means for the application and development of law'[243] as applicable law was dismissed. Instead, judicial decisions were placed alongside the teachings of publicists in a secondary position.

Article 38(1)(d) of the ICJ Statute prescribes that the ICJ ('the Court'), responsible for deciding in accordance with international law, shall apply judicial decisions as subsidiary

---

239 Armin von Bogdandy and Ingo Venzke, 'Beyond Dispute: International Judicial Institutions as Lawmakers' Special Issue (2011) 12 GLJ 979.

240 On consent, see González Hauck, § 2.2, in this textbook.

241 On *pacta sunt servanda*, see Fiskatoris and Svicevic, § 6.1.B.IV., in this textbook.

242 ILC, 'Report of the International Law Commission on the Work of its 72nd Session' (26 April–4 June and 5 July–6 August 2021) UN Doc A/76/10, Annex 'Subsidiary means for the determination of rules of international law'.

243 Procès-verbaux [1920] 306.

means for the determination of rules of law. Additionally, the subsidiary application of judicial decisions concerning the other three main sources envisaged in article 38 (treaties, custom, and general principles) is subject to article 59, stating that a decision of the Court 'has no binding force except between the parties and in respect of that particular case'.

Nonetheless, in a legal order predominantly characterised by decentralised methods of normative production, judicial decisions play an important role. While 'the Court, as a court of law, cannot render judgment sub specie *legis ferendae* [Latin: 'of the law to be made'], or anticipate the law before the legislator has laid it down',[244] judicial decisions significantly shape the law in certain fields. As put by one author, 'there has long been no room for doubt that international law has become very much a case law'.[245] This has promoted scholarly debate about judicial decisions as formal sources of international law. While some find this position unjustifiable,[246] others defend nuanced approaches like 'quasi-formal'[247] sources, attributing different degrees of normativity to judicial decisions, depending on the field. Less debatable is the fact that judicial decisions are highly authoritative[248] within the international legal discourse. While States, international organisations, and other subjects might disagree with a judicial decision, it is binding upon the parties and serves as a guide to the other members of the community as the most appropriate way to perceive the rule.

The importance of judicial decisions can be observed not only through the legal value attributed to them by courts or tribunals but also through their impact on the work of codification performed by the International Law Commission (ILC),[249] the practice of States, or eventually how certain decisions were transformed into treaty law. An illustrative example in this regard can be found in the field of the law of the sea, in which the ICJ considerably shaped questions such as regarding maritime delimitation.[250]

However, it is not always possible to identify areas clearly developed on account of judicial decisions. Judicial decisions also exert more subtle, informal influence on the legal field, initiating debates or forming a repository of arguments that become unavoidable to understand the development of a certain field of international law.

---

244 *Fisheries Jurisdiction Case (United Kingdom v Iceland)* (Merits) [1974] ICJ Rep 53.

245 Robert Jennings, 'What Is International Law and How Do We Tell It When We See It?' (1981) 37 SJIR 41.

246 Alain Pellet, 'Decisions of the ICJ as Sources of International Law?' in *Gaetano Morelli Lectures Series* (International and European Papers 2018).

247 Gerald Fitzmaurice, 'Some Problems Regarding the Formal Sources of International Law' in F.M. van Asbeck and others (eds), *Symbolae Verzijl* (Martinus Nijhoff 1958).

248 On this issue, see e.g. Luigi Condorelli, 'L'autorité de la décision des juridictions internationales permanente' in Luigi Condorelli (ed), *L'optimisme de la raison* (IREDIES Pedone 2016) 45.

249 On this topic, see Fernando Lusa Bordin, 'Reflections of Customary International Law: The Authority of Codification Conventions and ILC Draft Articles in International Law' (2014) 63 ICLQ 535.

250 Vaughan Lowe and Antonios Tzanakopoulos, 'The Development of the Law of the Sea by the International Court of Justice' in Christian J Tams and James Sloan (eds), *The Development of International Law by the International Court of Justice* (OUP 2013) 177.

2. The Authority of a Court's Own Case Law

As seen above, international court decisions, in principle, only bind the parties to the dispute. Consequently, international courts, unlike many of their domestic counterparts, are not legally bound to their own previous decisions. There is no formal rule of precedent (Latin: *stare decisis*) in international law.[251] However, a closer look at the jurisprudence of international courts reveals judicial bodies' tendency to refer authoritatively to their previous decisions, either to reinforce the interpretation of a given rule or as a shortcut to the legal reasoning previously espoused. In both cases, the court or tribunal contributes to the consolidation of such a rule, apart from the possibility of developing the content of the law. The ICJ stated in 2015 that while its past decisions are not binding on it, 'it will not depart from its settled jurisprudence unless it finds very particular reasons to do so'.[252]

This presumption in favour of adhering to past decisions gives the assurance to future litigants that similar situations will be treated similarly and reaffirms important legal values such as equality, predictability, clarity, and, to a certain extent, uniformity, and consistency of international law. Overall, the protection of these values reinforces the legitimacy of an international court and the perception of preservation of the equality of the parties. This might be a good explanation why different international courts follow a similar path of self-reference and refer to their previous decisions or even decisions of other international courts.[253]

3. The Authority of Other Courts' Case Law

Since every international court and tribunal was designed with a unique purpose and according to specific contextual and social needs, the decisions they render do not carry the same weight. In this regard, there appears to exist a presumption that a certain tribunal's first duty is to pay tribute to its own case law before looking beyond its premises. Nonetheless, international courts increasingly draw on external precedents,

---

251 See, for instance, Mohamed Shahabuddeen, *Precedent in the World Court* (CUP 2010); Mathias Forteau, 'Les décisions juridictionnelles comme précédent' in Société Française pour le Droit International (ed), *Le précédent en droit international* (Pédone 2016); Makane Moïse Mbengue, 'Precedent' in Jean d'Aspremont and Sahib Singh (eds), *Concepts for International Law* (Edward Elgar 2019) 708. For a more recent reading of the phenomenon, see James Devaney, 'The Role of Precedent in the Jurisprudence of the International Court of Justice: A Constructive Interpretation' (2022) 35 LJIL 641.

252 *Application of the Convention on the Prevention and Punishment of the Crime of Genocide (Croatia v Serbia)* (Merits) [2015] ICJ Rep 3.

253 See, for instance, Eric De Brabandere, 'The Use of Precedent and External Case Law by the International Court of Justice and the International Tribunal for the Law of the Sea' (2016) 15 LPICT 24; Yonatan Lupu and Erik Voeten, 'Precedent in International Courts: A Network Analysis of Case Citations by the European Court of Human Rights' (2012) 42 BJPolS 413; *The 'Grand Prince' Case (Belize v France)*, (Prompt Release, Judgment of 20 April 2001) ITLOS Reports 78; *M/V 'Louisa' Case (Saint Vincent and the Grenadines v. Kingdom of Spain)* (Judgment of 28 May 2013) ITLOS Reports 81; WTO, United States Import Prohibition of Certain Shrimp and Shrimp Products (12 October 1998) WT/DS58/AB/R 67; *Al-Adsani v United Kingdom*, Judgment, European Court of Human Rights App no 35763/97 (21 November 2001) [60–61].

a phenomenon called 'cross-fertilisation'.[254] The reference to the case law of other courts follows a logic of speciality, meaning that the specific function of a judicial body places it in a privileged position for the identification, application, and interpretation of certain rules. In this regard, the ICJ has observed that

> [w]hen the court is called upon . . . to apply a regional instrument for the protection of human rights, it must take due account of the interpretation of that instrument adopted by the independent bodies which have been specifically created, if such has been the case, to monitor the sound application of the treaty in question.[255]

Cross-fertilisation has acted as a counterforce to the tendencies of fragmentation in international law, since it is highly capable of promoting harmony between international courts on very specific and often contentious issues. Earlier jurisprudence of a given tribunal may inform future judges of other courts when deciding disputes involving similar factual backgrounds or the ascertainment and interpretation of the same norms. A clear example is the use of regional human rights courts' case law by the ICJ when it is called upon to resolve disputes relating to human rights.[256] In these situations, the findings of the 'external' case law are applied directly as a secondary source of international law (i.e. as authoritative statements of what the law is). Finally, courts also rely on each other regarding procedural questions, including the delimitation of jurisdiction, the conduct of ancillary proceedings, or the behaviour of the parties. This situation reveals not precisely the import of legal 'findings' of an external case law, but a recognition of certain judicial practices as legal rules binding the court given their compatibility with statutory norms and other sources of procedural law (rules of procedure, for instance).[257]

4. Decisions of Municipal Courts

Article 38(1)(d) ICJ Statute does not differentiate between decisions of international courts and municipal courts. Judicial decisions in general may be considered as a subsidiary source of law and as means for the identification of other sources of law.[258] However, some particularities of the decisions of municipal courts may be observed in considering them as sources of international law.

Contrary to decisions of international courts, those of municipal courts can rarely create obligations binding other States and international organisations, partly due

---

254 Karin Oellers-Frahm, 'Multiplication of International Courts and Tribunals and Conflicting Jurisdiction – Problems and Possible Solutions' (2001) 5 UNYB 67; Tullio Treves, 'Fragmentation of International Law: The Judicial Perspective' (2007) 23 Comunicazionie studi 821.

255 *Ahmadou Sadio Diallo (Rep. of Guinea v. Democratic Republic of Congo)* (Merits) [2010] ICJ Rep. 639.

256 Antônio Augusto Cançado Trindade, 'The Continuity of Jurisprudential Cross-Fertilization in the Case-Law of International Tribunals in their Common Mission of Realization of Justice' in *The Global Community Yearbook of International Law and Jurisprudence* (OUP 2019) 247.

257 Chiara Giorgetti, 'Cross-Fertilisation of Procedural Law Among International Courts and Tribunals: Methods and Meanings' in Arman Sarvarian and others (eds), *Procedural Fairness in International Courts and Tribunals* (BIICL 2015) 223.

258 André Nollkaemper, *National Courts and the International Rule of Law* (OUP 2011).

to the rules of immunity.[259] They may, however, have international legal effects in two situations. First, decisions of municipal courts may be binding on other actors of international law, such as individuals, non-State actors, movements of national liberation, and transnational companies.[260] Therefore, decisions of municipal courts may have different degrees of normativity or authority in international law.[261] Second, decisions of municipal courts may be considered part of the elements of the formation of customary international law. This is not the same thing as to affirm that decisions of municipal courts are able to 'create' international law. Rather, they can contribute to the identification of an emergent rule of customary nature if their content resonates with other samples of practice which, *in toto*, amount to sufficient consensus concerning its legal character. In the *Jurisdictional Immunities of the State* case of 2012, the ICJ considered that judgments of national courts would have particular significance in determining the existence of an international custom conferring immunity on States and the scope and extent of such rule. Such decisions were not analysed alone but considered together with statements made by States in the ILC and during the adoption of the *Convention on Jurisdictional Immunities of States and Their Property* as relevant State practice.[262] However, priority is given to decisions of international courts over decisions of municipal courts in the determination of the existence of an international custom. In the *Lotus* case, for example, the PCIJ only considered decisions of domestic courts after recognising that there were no international decisions to assist in the recognition of the existence of an international norm dealing with the criminal jurisdiction of States in cases of collisions on the high seas.[263]

There are differences between varying types of municipal court decisions. Final decisions of higher courts have greater weight than decisions of lower courts in the identification of other sources of law. In the *Arrest Warrant* case, for instance, the ICJ analysed specifically decisions of national higher courts, such as those of France and the United Kingdom, as State practice to consider the existence of exceptions to the immunity from criminal jurisdiction to Ministers of Foreign Affairs, together with national legislation.[264]

The role of decisions of municipal courts is even further enhanced when it comes to the identification of general principles of law, since their very conceptual framing encompasses the 'recognition' by municipal legal orders.[265] The assessment of decisions of national courts is part of the comparative analysis of national

---

259 On immunities, see Walton, § 11, in this textbook.

260 See for instance *Filártiga v. Peña-Irala*, 630 F.2d 876 (2nd Cir. 1980).

261 Nollkaemper (n 258) 255.

262 *Jurisdictional Immunities of the State (Germany v Italy: Greece intervening)* (Merits) [2012] ICJ Rep 99, 123. See also ILC, 'Draft conclusions on identification of customary international law' (2018) UN Doc A/73/10 4.

263 *Lotus (France v Turkey)*, (Merits) PCIJ Rep Series A 10 No 28.

264 *Arrest Warrant of 11 April 2000 (Democratic Republic of the Congo v Belgium)* (Merits) [2002] ICJ Rep 2.

265 On general principles, see Eggett, § 6.3, in this textbook.

legal systems necessary to determine the existence of a general principle of law. Nevertheless, this element should be considered together with the assessment of national laws and other materials.[266]

Decisions of municipal courts might also be authoritative within the international legal discourse in several areas. For instance, cases such as the *Schooner Exchange* (1812) of the US Supreme Court,[267] *Reference Re Secession of Quebec* (1998) from the Supreme Court of Canada,[268] and *In Re Pinochet* (1999) from the House of Lords of the United Kingdom[269] are often mentioned in the legal literature to refer to exceptions to the rule of sovereign immunity, the content of the right to self-determination, and the existence of universal jurisdiction, respectively.

II. TEACHINGS OF THE MOST HIGHLY QUALIFIED PUBLICISTS

Article 38(1)(d) lists 'the teachings of the most highly qualified publicists of the various nations' as second subsidiary means to identify the content of international law. Today, the word 'scholars' would likely replace the word 'publicists'. Often, the literature makes a clear-cut distinction between law-making and scholarly writing. In this view, the role of those writing about international law, as opposed to those making the law, is limited to systematising and providing a better understanding of the law. As one scholar put it, '[i]t is obviously not a question of "doctors" dictating the law, but of their influence on its better understanding'.[270]

Yet, in reality, the line between law-making and scholarly writing – and in general, between formal and informal sources of international law – is not as clear-cut. In times when the formal sources of international law were much less well documented, scholars played a central role in gathering legal materials, and by doing so arguably also in separating between law and non-law. With the increasing availability of State practice and legal materials in other ways, this role became less relevant. Nonetheless, scholars still wield considerable influence. Particularly in newer or evolving fields of international law, such as cyberspace law,[271] many legal questions are unsolved and courts and other actors applying the law thus turn to the existing literature for guidance and clarification. They also contribute to international law-making through collective bodies and expert groups, often mandated by States.[272] For instance, the ILC was established by the UN General Assembly (UNGA) with the task of progressively

---

266 UNGA 'General Principles of Law: Text of the draft conclusions provisionally adopted by the Drafting Committee on first reading' (12 May 2023) UN Doc A/CN.4/L.982 2, Draft Conclusion 5.

267 *The Exchange v McFaddon* [1812] 11 US (7 Cranch) 116.

268 *Reference re Secession of Quebec* [1998] 2 SCR 217.

269 *R, ex parte Pinochet v Bartle and ors*, Appeal, [1999] UKHL 17.

270 Manfred Lachs, 'Teachings and Teaching of International Law' (1976) 151 RdC 161, 212.

271 On international law in cyberspace, see Hüsch, § 19, in this textbook.

272 See on the distinction between State-empowered and other categories of publicists Sandesh Sivakumaran, 'The Influence of Teachings of Publicists on the Development of International Law' (2017) 66 ICLQ 1, 4.

developing and codifying international law (article 1 of the statutes of the ILC).[273] According to article 2(1) of its statute, the ILC shall consist of 'persons of recognized competence in international law', which, in practice, has often included scholars. Some of the ILC's work has proven to be highly authoritative and influential, such as the famous *Articles on the Responsibility of States for Internationally Wrongful Acts*, which today provide the starting point for most discussions on State responsibility.[274] Examples of non–State-sponsored expert groups who proved to be highly authoritative include the group who drafted the *San Remo Manual on International Law applicable to Armed Conflicts at Sea*[275] or, more recently, the *Tallinn Manuals*[276] on the application of international law to cyberspace.

Repeatedly, attempts were undertaken to 'measure' the influence of scholars on international law. One method to do so is to look at citations by international courts. However, this method is not particularly reliable.[277] For example, the ICJ only rarely cites scholarly writings, but there is broad agreement that the influence of scholars on the 'World Court' is greater than it appears.[278] The same is true for other courts and institutions. More important than the direct reception, citation, and influence of scholarship are the manifold indirect ways in which scholars shape and contribute to international law. This begins in the classroom where scholars teach future practitioners, but scholars certainly also exert a certain influence by criticising, systematising, and ordering the body of international law – a role that has been described as one of 'grammarians' within the international legal system.[279]

C. SOURCES BEYOND THE ICJ STATUTE

I. SOFT LAW

1. Definition

Soft law refers to those norms in the international legal order that lack legal bindingness. What makes soft norms nonetheless *legal* and distinguishes them from

---

273 Statute of the International Law Commission, UNGA Res 174 (II) (21 November 1974) (last amended 18 November 1981). For a recent debate on the role of the ILC the symposium on Völkerrechtsblog, 'The International Law Commission as an Interpreter of International Law?' <https://voelkerrechtsblog.org/symposium/the-role-of-the-ilc/> accessed 20 July 2023.

274 ILC, 'Responsibility of States for Internationally Wrongful Acts' (53rd session 23 April–1 June and 2 July–10 August 2001) UN Doc A/RES/56/83 Annex.

275 See e.g. San Remo Manual on International Law Applicable to Armed Conflicts at Sea, 12 June 1994 (1995) 309 IRRC 583.

276 Michael Schmitt (ed), *Tallinn Manual on the International Law Applicable to Cyber Warfare* (CUP 2013); Michael Schmitt (ed), *Tallinn Manual 2.0 on the International Law Applicable to Cyber Operations* (CUP 2017).

277 Sivakumaran (n 272).

278 Pellet and Müller (n 236).

279 Gleider Hernández, 'The Responsibility of the International Legal Academic. Situating the Grammarian within the "Invisible College"' in Jean d'Aspremont and others (eds), *International Law as a Profession* (CUP 2017).

other normative systems is that they contain behavioural guidelines that go beyond purely political or moral declarations.[280] According to a narrow view, soft law can only emanate from subjects of international law.[281] Examples include non-binding agreements between States, such as the Global Compact for Migration;[282] non-binding outcomes of inter-State conferences such as in the field of the environment the 1972 *Stockholm Declaration*[283] and the 1992 *Rio Declaration*;[284] acts of international organisations lacking bindingness such as the resolutions of the UNGA; and codes of conducts adopted by States or international organisations, for example in international economic law[285] or humanitarian law.[286] A wider definition of soft law also includes acts of actors not possessing international legal personality or whose status is not entirely clear, such as self-regulatory instruments of businesses or NGOs.[287] This definition overlaps with what some describe as 'informal law-making'.[288] Such a wider view is preferable – there are countless examples of legislative attempts outside of the traditional diplomatic fora and involving actors other than formal subjects of international law that shape today's international legal reality.[289]

2. Function and Contemporary Debates

With its defining features, soft law not only falls outside of the category of article 38 ICJ Statute; it seems to fall outside of the category of law altogether. It has therefore caused long-standing and controversial debates in international scholarship. While some praise its flexibility, which might be better suited to adjust to a fast-changing world than formal and slow treaty-making processes, others deem soft law to be undemocratic, a threat to the authority of the law, or simply 'redundant'.[290]

Yet, today it seems undeniable that soft law is 'relevant to international law in some way'.[291] On the one hand, it is well recognised that soft law may exert some quasi-legal

---

280 Anne Peters and Anna Petrig, *Völkerrecht* (Schulthess 2020) 48.

281 Daniel Thürer, 'Soft Law' (*Max Planck Encyclopedia of International Law*, March 2009) para 8.

282 Global Compact for Safe, Orderly and Regular Migration (adopted 19 December 2018 UNGA Res 73/195).

283 'Report of the United Nations Conference on the Human Environment' (Stockholm 5–16 June 1972) UN Doc A/CONF.48/Rev.1.

284 'Report of the United Nations Conference on Environment and Development' (Rio de Janeiro 3–14 June 1992) UN Doc A/CONF.151/26 (Vol I).

285 OECD, *OECD Guidelines for Multinational Enterprises on Responsible Business Conduct* (OECD 2023).

286 See e.g. San Remo Manual on International Law Applicable to Armed Conflicts at Sea (n 275).

287 See e.g. Oversight Board, 'Meta Oversight Board Charter' (February 2023) <https://oversightboard.com/attachment/494475942886876/> accessed 10 August 2023.

288 Joost Pauwelyn, Ramses A Wessels, and Jan Wouters (eds), *Informal International Lawmaking* (OUP 2012).

289 See the numerous cases studies in Joost Pauwelynn and others, *Informal International Lawmaking: Case Studies* (Torkel Opsahl Academic EPublisher 2013).

290 Jan Klabbers, 'The Redundancy of Soft Law' (1996) 65 Nordic Journal of International Law 167. For a good overview of the debate, see Jean d'Aspremont and Tanja Aalberts, 'Which Future for the Scholarly Concept of Soft International Law? Editors' Introductory Remarks' (2012) 25 LJIL 309.

291 Jaye Ellis, 'Shades of Grey: Soft Law and the Validity of Public International Law' (2012) 25 LJIL 313, 318.

effects: soft standards can 'harden' over time – they may be taken up in a later treaty or mature into *opinio juris* and therefore catalyse the formation of customary international law. Another way soft law becomes legally relevant is as a guideline for interpretation of 'hard' law, with UNGA resolutions being an important example.[292]

On the other hand, soft standards can have rather 'hard' and tangible consequences despite not being legally binding. Because of the factual relevance of soft law, in some States such as Switzerland, attempts are being undertaken to introduce stronger parliamentary oversight for soft law instruments, traditionally reserved to formal treaty-making.[293] Currently, the relevance of soft law even seems to increase. Several studies have constated a 'treaty fatigue' and shown that the conclusion of treaties over the last years has stagnated.[294] By way of example, while in the period between 1950 and 2000, each decade around 35 new multilateral treaties were concluded, this number significantly dropped in the following decade and currently even stopped.[295] Given the difficulties to reach consensus on binding obligations, the relevance of soft instruments arguably grows.

Regardless of its advantages and disadvantages, what seems clear today is 'that soft law is a reality and instrument of contemporary governance that cannot be wished away'.[296] The importance of soft standards not only evidences the pluralisation of the sources of international law, but also of the *actors* behind these instruments.[297] The concept of soft law is thus a prime example showing that both the classic notions of sources *and* of actors in international law do not fully capture the international legal reality anymore.

II. ACTS OF INTERNATIONAL ORGANISATIONS

Acts or resolutions of international organisations are often listed among possible sources of international law besides the traditional categories of sources listed in article 38(1) ICJ Statute. This consideration reflects the growing importance of the activities and acts of international organisations in times of global governance.[298]

New procedures of collective action within international organisations have been developed in an approach paralleling the law-making process of domestic law. For

---

292 Rossana Deplano, *Empirical and Theoretical Perspectives on International Law: How States Use the UN General Assembly to Create International Obligations* (CUP 2022).

293 For an overview, see Anna Petrig, 'Democratic Participation in International Lawmaking in Switzerland After the "Age of Treaties"' in Helmut Aust and Thomas Kleinlein (eds), *Encounters Between Foreign Relations Law and International Law* (CUP 2021) 180.

294 Joost Pauwelyn, Ramses A Wessel, and Jan Wouters, 'When Structures Become Shackles: Stagnation and Dynamics in International Lawmaking' (2014) 25 EJIL 733, 739; see also Jan Wouters, 'International Law, Informal Law-Making, and Global Governance in Times of Anti-Globalism and Populism' in Heike Krieger, Georg Note, and Andreas Zimmermann (eds), *The International Rule of Law: Rise or Decline?* (OUP 2019).

295 Wouters (n 294) 251.

296 D'Aspremont and Aalberts (56) 309.

297 On the pluralisation of actors in international law, see Engström, introduction to § 7, in this textbook.

298 On international organisations, see Baranowska, Engström, and Paige, § 7.3, in this textbook.

instance, the UN Security Council (UNSC) adopted a new form of procedure creating general obligations for all States to prevent the commission or the financing of terrorist acts.[299] It is possible to consider, therefore, that a new way of creating international rules beyond the classic means has emerged from the operation of international organisations, especially the United Nations. On the other hand, such characterisation presents some problems, as discussed in the following.

1. Acts of International Organisations as a Distinct Source of International Law

a) Acts of International Organisations as Formal Source of International Law

Acts of international organisations can serve as a formal source of rights and obligations depending on the actor concerned. They can be divided into two categories. The first consists of acts by organs of the organisation externally directed to States or other organisations, such as recommendations, declarations, or decisions. The second type includes internal measures by organs of the organisation in fulfilment of their functions according to the constitutive instrument, determining for instance the budget of the organisation, the creation or composition of an organ, and other procedural aspects. As this second type of act may establish rights and obligations in the internal law of organisations for different organs, individuals, and entities, it may be considered a formal source of law for such actors. This is the case of the decisions of the United Nations Dispute Tribunal, which are binding upon the parties of disputes opposing individuals and the UN Secretary-General or a specialised agency.[300]

The first type of instrument may be considered as a distinct formal source of international law creating legal obligations for the parties concerned.[301] Member States are obliged to comply with binding resolutions by virtue of an obligation assumed through the constitutive treaty, not because such resolutions create direct obligations for them. This is the case of decisions of the UNSC based on article 25 and Chapter VII of the UN Charter[302] and some acts emanating from the European Union based on article 288 of the Treaty on the Functioning of the European Union.[303] In this sense, it could be argued that the normative force of resolutions of international organisations is linked to conventional obligations created by treaties, a traditional source of international law.

It is claimed that the UNSC on some occasions has adopted a sort of 'law-making procedure' by imposing general obligations to all UN member States regarding

---

299 UNSC Res 1373 (28 September 2001) UN Doc S/RES/1373.

300 UNGA Res 62/253 (17 March 2009) UN Doc A/RES/62/253 (Statute of the United Nations Dispute Tribunal) article 11(3). See also *Effect of Awards of Compensation Made by the United Nations Administrative Tribunal* (Advisory Opinion) [1954] ICJ Rep 47.

301 On the formal/material distinction, see Eggett, § 6.B.II., in this textbook.

302 Charter of the United Nations (adopted 26 June 1945, entered into force 24 October 1945) 1 UNTS 16, articles 25 and 39–51.

303 Consolidated version of the Treaty on the Functioning of the European Union [2012] OJ C326/47, article 288.

specific matters. In general, the Council adopts decisions binding on the UN member States which are instrumental to deal with a situation characterised by it as a threat to the peace, a breach of the peace or an act of aggression, according to article 39 of the UN Charter.[304] In some resolutions, nonetheless, the UNSC seem to have stated obligations of abstract nature, that is, not limited to a particular situation or dispute, such as general obligations concerning the suppression of terrorist acts[305] and the limitation of certain types of weapons.[306] In such cases, the UNSC appears to impose on member States obligations that are found in conventions to which they have not necessarily expressed their consent. Since such obligations have general application and are not limited to a particular situation or dispute, they appear to have been the result of a law-making process by the UNSC. Yet in this case, the resolutions do not act as formal sources of obligations since their binding force is based on the action of the UNSC under Chapter VII of the UN Charter, although their legality in relation to the Charter and the powers of the UNSC may be questioned.[307]

b) Acts of International Organisations as Material Source of International Law

Resolutions of international organisations can be viewed not merely as formal sources of obligations but also as evidence of the existence of a rule of customary international law. In such cases, these resolutions function as material sources of international law.[308]

The ICJ occasionally analyses UNGA Resolutions to determine the existence of a rule of customary international law,[309] considering that although not binding, they may 'provide evidence important for establishing the existence of a rule or the emergence of an *opinio juris*'.[310] Such an approach was adopted in the *Nicaragua* case, where the Court interpreted the consent of the United States and Nicaragua expressed at the moment of the adoption of UNGA Resolution 2625 (24 October 1970, establishing the Friendly Relations Declaration)[311] as 'an acceptance of the validity of the rule or set of rules declared by the resolution'.[312]

UNGA Resolutions are also sometimes considered to reflect legal rules of international law due to the almost universal representation of the international

---

304 Stefan Talmon, 'The Security Council as World Legislature' (2005) 99 AJIL 175–193.

305 UNSC Res 1373 (28 September 2001) UN Doc S/RES/1373.

306 UNSC Res 1540 (28 April 2004) UN Doc S/RES/1540.

307 James Crawford, 'Chance, Order, Change: The Course of International Law' (2013) 365 RdC 17, 312–313.

308 On the formal/material distinction, see Eggett, § 6.B.II., in this textbook.

309 On customary international law, see Stoica, § 6.2, in this textbook.

310 *Legality of the Threat or Use of Nuclear Weapons* (Advisory Opinion) [1996] ICJ Rep 226, 254–255 [para 70].

311 UNGA Res 2625 (XXV) (24 October 1970).

312 *Military and Paramilitary Activities in and against Nicaragua (Nicaragua v United States of America)* (Merits) [1986] ICJ Rep 14, 99–100 [para 188].

community of States in the organ. Instances include other declarations besides the Friendly Relations Declaration,[313] such as the Universal Declaration of Human Rights of 1948,[314] the Declaration on the Granting of Independence to Colonial Countries and Peoples of 1960,[315] and the Declaration of Legal Principles Governing the Activities of States in the Exploration and Uses of Outer Space of 1963.[316] In the *Chagos* Advisory Opinion, the ICJ found that the Declaration on the Granting of Independence to Colonial Countries and Peoples 'has a declaratory character with regard to the right to self-determination as a customary norm' and clarified the content and scope of the right to self-determination, representing a 'defining moment in the consolidation of State practice on decolonization'.[317]

Resolutions may also be relevant in the interpretation of international treaties and even constitute subsequent practice for the purpose of treaty interpretation.[318] In the *Whaling* case, for instance, the ICJ considered that resolutions from the International Whaling Commission may be relevant for the interpretation of the International Convention for the Regulation of Whaling when adopted by consensus or by a unanimous vote, even not having a binding effect.[319]

2. Acts of International Organisations Beyond the Concept of Legal Source of Rights and Obligations

The classic definition of sources of international law may be insufficient to apprehend the legal significance of acts of international organisations to international law as they can hardly be considered as an independent category of sources of international law for not being able to create autonomously rights and obligations for States. Traditionally, it is recognised that acts of international organisations usually are the result of a political compromise that does not intend to create legal obligations by itself. This understanding is shared by the practice of the ICJ, which often rejects the claim that resolutions create legal obligations for States that consent to them. For instance, in the *Nicaragua* case, the Court rejected the claim that a resolution of the Meeting of Consultation of Ministers of Foreign Affairs of the Organization of American States had established a legal obligation for Nicaragua regarding its domestic policy.[320] In the *Access to the Pacific Ocean* case of 2012, the Court rejected the claim that resolutions

---

313 UNGA Res 2625 (XXV) (24 October 1970).

314 UNGA Res 217A (III) (10 December 1948).

315 UNGA Res 1514 (XV) (14 December 1960).

316 UNGA Res 1962 (XVIII) (13 December 1963).

317 *Legal Consequences of the Separation of the Chagos Archipelago from Mauritius in 1965* (Advisory Opinion) [2019] ICJ Rep 95 [paras 150–153].

318 Michael C Wood, The Interpretation of Security Council Resolutions (1998) 2 Max Planck Yrbk UN L 73–95, 91–92.

319 *Whaling in the Antarctic (Australia v Japan: New Zealand intervening)* [2014] ICJ Rep 226, 248 [para 46]. See also *Nicaragua* (n 78) [para 188].

320 *Nicaragua* (n 78) [para 261].

adopted by the General Assembly of the Organisation of the American States had created a legal obligation for Chile to negotiate Bolivia's access to the Pacific Ocean, even if adopted with its consent.[321]

Nevertheless, the legal importance of resolutions of international organisations goes beyond the legal effects traditionally assigned to them. Often such acts affect the behaviour of States and other international actors even without the establishment of legally binding rules, which may be observed in the context of the role of international organisations in global governance. It is increasingly common for international organisations to adopt resolutions containing standards, practices, and procedures which provide a normative framework for the exercise of public authority in several areas of international law regardless of their binding character. Such acts, which often are classified as 'soft law', sometimes are preferred over traditional sources of international law for the facility in their creation and flexibility. This may be seen, for instance, in the regulatory function of the food standards issued by the Codex Alimentarius Commission, the Code of Conduct for Responsible Fisheries of the UN Food and Agriculture Organisation (FAO), and the OECD Guidelines for Multinational Enterprises, all of which with significant regulatory form even without binding character.[322] Another important example concerns the role of the World Health Organization (WHO) in global health governance, especially regarding the COVID-19 pandemic. The coordination between public and private international actors in the fight against the virus was done by the WHO not only through binding rules provided for by the International Health Regulations (2005) but also by temporary and non-binding recommendations adopted on advice of an Emergency Committee composed by experts of different fields.[323]

III. UNILATERAL DECLARATIONS

Besides soft law and acts of international organisations, unilateral declarations are often discussed as a further source beyond article 38 of the ICJ Statute. The question is whether declarations States make towards other States or the international community, for example a promise to act in a certain way, may deploy *legal* effects. In other words, can States be legally bound by statements or announcements they made? In the *Nuclear Tests* case,[324] the ICJ has answered this question in the positive under certain conditions, deducing the legal bindingness from the principle of *good faith*, a general principle under article 38(1)(c) ICJ Statute. In this case, the ICJ among other things had to determine whether France was

---

321 *Obligation to Negotiate Access to the Pacific Ocean (Bolivia v Chile)* (Merits) [2018] ICJ Rep 507, 562 [para 171].

322 See in special the analysis of such regulations by Gefion Schuler and others (eds), *The Exercise of Public Authority by International Institutions: Advancing International Institutional Law* (Springer 2010).

323 Armin von Bogdandy and Pedro Villarreal, 'International Law on Pandemic Response: A First Stocktaking in Light of the Coronavirus Crisis' (2020) MPIL Research Paper 07/2020. See also Mateja Steinbrück Platise, 'The Changing Structure of Global Health Governance' in L Vierck, P Villarreal, and A Weilert (eds), *The Governance of Disease Outbreaks* (Nomos 2017) 83–111.

324 *Nuclear Tests Case (Australia v. France)* (Merits) [1974] ICJ Rep. 253. See already *Legal Status of Eastern Greenland (Denmark v. Norway)* PCIJ Ser A/B No 53.

bound by its announcements in various public statements to refrain from carrying out further atmospheric nuclear tests in the South Pacific region. In order not to deduce legal effects from merely political statements, the ICJ developed three criteria:

- The declaration must have been made by the competent authority in a framework that indicates seriousness;
- The declaration must be sufficiently specific; and
- It must indicate the intention to be legally bound.[325]

A specific form is not required according to the Court; this means that also oral statements can deploy legal effects. Also further unilateral acts of States can deploy certain legal effects, as discussed in other chapters. By way of example, the protesting State under the persistent objector doctrine can avoid being legally bound by emerging customary international law;[326] also acts of recognition by States may deploy legal effects.[327]

D. CONCLUSION

This chapter has shown that further sources of international law beyond article 38 of the ICJ Statute exist, and that they are in fact highly relevant. In times of global governance, the decisions of international courts, resolutions of international organisations, and soft law regulate many aspects of our lives. This pluralisation of the sources of international law to some extent reflects the pluralisation of its actors. This development challenges the formal distinction between law and non-law, showing that 'the universe of norms is larger than the universe of law'[328] and once more raising the fundamental question: is it international law or not, and does it even matter?[329] According to voices from the New Haven School, what ultimately counts is the influence of norms on behaviour of States, and not their form.[330] However, as important as informal sources of international law might be, the distinction between law and non-law is certainly not entirely redundant. Even though international courts might take other sources into account, they rule on the basis of formal law. The pluralisation of the sources of international law also leads to new challenges for the democratic legitimisation of international law, as the debate in Switzerland about stronger parliamentary involvement in the process of adopting soft law shows.[331] Even though touching upon some of the oldest debates in international law, the sources doctrine certainly has not lost any of its currency.

---

325 *Nuclear Tests Case* (n 90) [paras 42–46]. See also ILC, 'Guiding Principles Applicable to Unilateral Declarations of States Capable of Creating Legal Obligations (Final Outcome)' UN Doc A/61/10 para 176.

326 On the persistent objector doctrine, see Stoica, § 6.2.C.II., in this textbook.

327 On recognition, see Green, § 7.1.C.I.1., in this textbook.

328 See Jost Pauwelyn, 'Is It International Law or Not, and Does it Even Matter?' in Joost Pauwelyn, Ramses Wessel, and Jan Wouters (eds), *Information International Lawmaking* (OUP 2012) 125.

329 Ibid.

330 See e.g. Monica Hakimi, 'The Work of International Law' (2017) 58 Harvard International Law Journal 1.

331 See above n 293.

BOX 6.4.2 Further Readings

Further Readings

- S Besson, 'Theorizing the Sources of International Law' in S Besson and J Tasioulas (eds), *The Philosophy of International Law* (OUP 2010).

- G Guillaume, 'The Use of Precedent by International Judges and Arbitrators' (2011) 2(1) JILDS 5.

- C Tams, 'The World Court's Role in the International Law-Making Process' in J Delbrück and others (eds), *Aus Kiel in die Welt: Kiel's Contribution to International Law. Essays in Honour of the 100th Anniversary of the Walther Schücking Institute for International Law* (Duncker und Humblot 2014).

- A Tzanakopoulos, 'Domestic Judicial Lawmaking' in C Brölmann and Y Radi (eds), *Research Handbook on the Theory and Practice of International Lawmaking* (Edward Elgar 2016).

- G Hernández, 'International Judicial Lawmaking', in C Brölmann and Y Radi (eds), *Research Handbook on the Theory and Practice of International Lawmaking* (Edward Elgar 2016).

§ § §

7

CHAPTER 7
SUBJECTS AND ACTORS

VILJAM ENGSTRÖM, ALEX GREEN,
RAGHAVI VISWANATH, GRAŻYNA BARANOWSKA,
TAMSIN PHILLIPA PAIGE, JENS T. THEILEN,
JULIANA SANTOS DE CARVALHO, VERENA KAHL,
HE CHI, SUÉ GONZÁLEZ HAUCK, ANNE PETERS,
AND RAFFAELA KUNZ

INTRODUCTION
VILJAM ENGSTRÖM

BOX 7.1 Required Knowledge and Learning Objectives

Required knowledge: History of International Law, Sources of International Law

Learning objectives: Understanding the interrelations between the concepts of legal subject and legal personality; the evolution of the concepts of legal subject and legal personality; and the expansion and pluralisation of acknowledged actors in international law.

BOX 7.2 Interactive Exercises

Access *interactive exercises for this chapter*[1] by positioning your smartphone camera at the dot-filled box, also known as a QR code.

Figure 7.1 QR code referring to interactive exercises.

---

1 https://openrewi.org/en-projects-project-public-international-law-subjects-and-actors-in-international-law/

DOI: 10.4324/9781003451327-9

A. INTRODUCTION

Any legal system defines who can possess rights and obligations in it. This is also the case for international law. This chapter identifies States as the paramount subjects of international law, with international organisations possessing legal personality alongside States. Our conception of the sphere of actors that can have a regulatory function at the international level has broadened beyond these two subjects to include for example individuals, non-governmental organisations, corporations, animals, and cities. This chapter introduces the challenge that this poses to the conventional conception of subjects of international law.

B. SUBJECTS OF INTERNATIONAL LAW

I. STATES AND INTERNATIONAL ORGANISATIONS AS PRIMARY SUBJECTS

The main subjects of international law are States[2] and international organisations.[3] States are commonly considered the original subjects of international law. Out of States and international organisations, States are undoubtedly the main subjects, which follows from the central role of State consent for the creation of international law. States can be considered the main source of international law also because one characterising feature of international organisations is that they consist of States as their constituents. A particular feature of the international legal system is that it lacks a central legislator (compared to domestic law). For this reason, international legal persons are also commonly considered to possess the capacity to create international law. In other words, the capacity to have rights/obligations under international law is a defining feature of being an international legal person.

The notion of a legal person as such can be traced back to the publications of Gottfried Wilhelm von Leibniz in the late 17th century, whereas Emer de Vattel's Le Droit des Gens (1758) is considered to have expanded the moral personality of the State to also cover the international dimension.[4] In practice, 'legal subject' and 'legal person' are commonly used as synonyms. However, they need not be identical. To be a subject can be characterised as possessing an academic label, whereas personality is a status conferred by the legal system.[5] There are also diverging views as to whether the capacity to create international legal obligations should be a necessary attribute for legal personality to begin with.[6]

---

2   On States, see Green, § 7.1, in this textbook.
3   In this context meaning 'intergovernmental organisations'. On international organisations, see Baranowska, Engström, and Paige, § 7.3, in this textbook.
4   Catherine Brölmann and Janne Nijman, 'Legal Personality as a Fundamental Concept of International Law' in Jean d'Aspremont and Sahib Singh (eds), *Concepts for International Law – Contributions to Disciplinary Thought* (Edward Elgar 2017).
5   Jan Klabbers, 'The Concept of Legal Personality' (2005) 11 Ius Gentium 35.
6   Roland Portmann, *Legal Personality in International Law* (CUP 2010).

The international legal personality of international organisations was confirmed by the ICJ in 1949 in the *Reparation for Injuries* case.[7] However, the Court made clear that the 'legal personality and rights and duties [of international organisations] are [not] the same as those of a State'.[8] No automatic set of rights or legal powers can be derived from the possession of personality as such. Instead, the nature and extent of rights of organisations depend on 'the needs of the community'.[9] Some common powers that organisations do possess are, however, the capacity to conclude treaties, to acquire and dispose of property, and to institute legal proceedings.[10]

This does not mean that the legal personality of organisations is categorically 'lesser' in the sense that the rights and obligations of organisations could never be more extensive than those of States. The paradigm example is the monopoly on authorisation of use of force possessed by the United Nations.[11]

II. CLASSICAL SUBJECTS 'IN THE GREYZONE'

In addition to States and international organisations, some actors are commonly identified at the fringes of legal subjectivity. Among such actors are for example national liberation movements, which may have a role as a de facto government, have the capacity to conclude international agreements, and possess rights and obligations under international humanitarian law. The Holy See is also considered to possess international legal personality, being a party to multiple treaties, having concluded diplomatic relations, and governing a defined territory, all of which can be considered elements of statehood.[12] Also governments in exile, as well as self-governing territories, may exercise functions that indicate the possession of limited legal personality.[13] Actors of international law can, in other words, enjoy legal personality to various degrees.

C. THE EXPANDING SPHERE OF ACTORS OF INTERNATIONAL LAW

I. THE ERODING DISTINCTION BETWEEN SUBJECTS AND OBJECTS

The concept of international legal personality has always been subject to debate. Today, as more and more actors have the capacity to possess rights and duties in international law, the question arises whether this also affects (or should affect) the conventional

---

7 *Reparation for Injuries Suffered in the Service of the United Nations* (Advisory Opinion) [1949] ICJ Rep 174.

8 Ibid 178.

9 Ibid 179.

10 See for example IMF Articles of Agreement (adopted 22 July 1944, entered into force 27 December 1945) 2 UNTS 39, articles IX(2) and VII(2).

11 Robert Kolb, *An Introduction to the Law of the United Nations* (Hart 2010). On the UN, see Baranowska, Engström, and Paige, § 7.3, in this textbook.

12 On criteria for statehood, see Green, § 7.1, in this textbook.

13 See e.g. James Crawford, *Brownlie's Principles of Public International Law* (8th edn, OUP 2012) 123–125.

divide between subjects and 7,2 objects of international law. The position of the individual is a classical debate in this respect, with Georges Scelle already in the early 20th century positioning individuals as international legal subjects.[14] Along with the proliferation of international human rights, humanitarian, and criminal law, the status of the individual in international law has been increasingly elevated.[15] Another actor the position of which is in change is that of animals.[16] Animals are considered rights holders,[17] and several countries have in their civil codes gone beyond treating animals as mere 'things'.[18] This has also generated calls for acknowledging at least a limited legal personality of animals.[19]

II. THE PLURALISATION OF ACTORS OF INTERNATIONAL LAW

In addition to being legal subjects and possessing international legal personality, States and international organisations are undoubtedly also 'actors' of, and 'participants' in, the international legal system. Rosalyn Higgins in 1994, building on the ideas of the so-called New Haven School, preferred to approach international law as a dynamic process of decision-making that through 'interaction of demands by various actors, and State practice in relation thereto . . . leads to the generation of norms and the expectation of compliance in relation to them'.[20] In this 'actor conception', the importance of the notion of legal personality as a threshold for the creation of international law is reduced.[21] A realisation of the limits of the conventional subjects doctrine goes hand in hand with globalisation and the consequent surge in the institutionalisation of international cooperation.[22] A State-centred image of international law is considered overly narrow both in respect of the actors that it acknowledges as well as the instruments and acts that it considers relevant.

A 'regulatory' or 'governance' layer is steadily thickening, developed through institutional regimes, atop the constitutional and legislative layer.[23] This emergence of new political arenas and actors is sometimes addressed as the 'post-national condition', taking hold of the fact that the pluralisation of actors and the corresponding

---

14 Georges Scelle, *Précis de Droit des Gens, Principes et Systématique* (1932) Vol I, introduction, le milieu intersocial.

15 On individuals, see Theilen, § 7.4, in this textbook.

16 On animals, see Peters, § 7.8, in this textbook.

17 Cass R Sunstein and Martha C Nussbaum (eds), *Animal Rights: Current Debates and New Directions* (OUP 2005).

18 Birgitta Wahlberg, 'Animal Law in General and Animal Rights in Particular' (2021) 67 Scandinavian Studies in Law 13.

19 David Favre, 'Living Property: A New Status for Animals within the Legal System' (2010) 93 Marquette Law Review 1021.

20 Rosalyn Higgins, *Problems and Process: International Law and How We Use It* (Clarendon Press 1994).

21 Roland Portmann, *Legal Personality in International Law* (CUP 2010).

22 Richard Collins, 'Mapping the Terrain of Institutional Lawmaking: Form and Function in International Law' in Elaine Fahey (ed), *The Actors of Postnational Rule-Making* (Routledge 2016); Janne E Nijman, *The Concept of International Legal Personality: An Inquiry into the History and Theory of International Law* (TMC Asser Press 2004).

23 Richard Collins, *The Institutional Problem in Modern International Law* (Hart 2016) 235; Jean d'Aspremont (ed), *Participants in the International Legal System: Multiple Perspectives on Non-State Actors in International Law* (Routledge 2011).

proliferation of new forms of regulatory acts also suggests that the role of the nation State is under change.[24]

This development does not solely take place outside of the realm of States and international organisations. A phenomenon known as 'agencification' concerns the establishment of international bodies that are not based on international agreements but on decisions of international organisations. This includes, for example, subsidiary bodies established by the UN General Assembly (e.g. UNEP and UNDP), but also bodies established jointly by organisations (e.g. the WFP or the Codex Alimentarius Commission).[25] Also in the European Union agencies (e.g. the Maritime Safety Agency and the European Fisheries Control Agency) have become new sources of authority.[26] Agencies in the EU have separate legal personality,[27] whereas the situation among agencies in international law in general is more varied.

Whereas agencies display an institutional relationship to the founding organisation(s), a pluralisation of actors in international law also goes further than that practice. Under labels such as 'post-national rule-making',[28] 'global administrative law',[29] 'exercise of public authority',[30] and 'informal international lawmaking',[31] interest has been turned to less formalised forms of international collaboration. These approaches bring into focus actors such as the G20, the ISO, and ICANN, and explore the performance of their tasks, their role in global governance, the regulatory impact of their activities, and the potential status of their acts as sources of international law.[32] As part of this, also domestic authorities become of interest,[33] including cities,[34] which can bear rights and obligations and play a role in implementing international law.[35]

---

24 Damian Chalmers, 'Post-Nationalism and the Quest for Constitutional Substitutes' (2000) 27 Journal of Law and Society 178.

25 Edoardo Chiti and Ramses A Wessel, 'The Emergence of International Agencies in the Global Administrative Space' in Richard Collins and Nigel D White (eds), *International Organizations and the Idea of Autonomy: Institutional Independence in the International Legal Order* (Routledge 2011).

26 Elspeth Guild and others, *Implementation of the EU Charter of Fundamental Rights and Its Impact on EU Home Affairs Agencies: Frontex, Europol and the European Asylum Support Office* (2011), Report to the European Parliament's Committee on Civil Liberties, Justice and Home Affairs; Deirdre Curtin, *Executive Power of the European Union: Law Practices, and the Living Constitution* (OUP 2009).

27 European Parliamentary Research Service, EU Agencies, Common Approach and Parliamentary Scrutiny (2018).

28 Elaine Fahey (ed), *The Actors of Postnational Rule-Making: Contemporary Challenges of European and International Law* (Routledge 2016).

29 Benedict Kingsbury, 'The Concept of Law in Global Administrative Law' (2009) 20 European Journal of International Law 23, 20–23.

30 Armin von Bogdandy and others, *The Exercise of Public Authority by International Institutions: Advancing International Institutional Law* (Springer 2010).

31 Joost Pauwelyn, Ramses Wessel, and Jan Wouters, *Informal International Lawmaking* (OUP 2012).

32 On soft law and sources beyond article 38 ICJ statute, see Kunz, Lima, and Castelar Campos, § 6.4, in this textbook.

33 See e.g. Lorenzo Casini, 'Domestic Public Authorities within Global Networks: Institutional and Procedural Design, Accountability, and Review' in Pauwelyn and others (n 31).

34 Helmut Aust and Janne E Nijman (eds), *Research Handbook on International Law and Cities* (Edward Elgar 2021).

35 Yishai Blank, 'International Legal Personality/Subjectivity of Cities' in Aust and Nijman (n 34).

There are merits and demerits with this development at large, as well as in respect of particular actors (discussed more in detail in the subsequent chapters). This broadening of the scope of international law to include a varied range of actors also raises question marks concerning the conventional squaring of the notions of 'subject of international law' and 'international legal personality'.[36] At any rate it seems clear that the conventional doctrine of international legal personality can be inadequate or even an obstacle to discussing other actors than States or international organisations from a legal perspective.[37]

BOX 7.3 Advanced: Regulatory Pluralism

There are many ways in which a regulatory function or effect may arise of acts which in themselves do not create formal legal obligations. Acknowledging such an effect builds on a conception of legally binding rules as only one aspect of the international regulatory framework. 'Regulation' in this sense refers to all rules, standards, or principles that govern conduct by public and/or private actors.[38] This development has by no means been incidental but is rather the result of an active push. For example, the preamble of the Rio Declaration sets 'the goal of establishing new and equitable global partnership through the creation of new levels of cooperation among States, key sectors of societies and people', and Agenda 21 states that these global partnerships are intended to be inclusive of all thinkable non-State actors. In a regional setting, for example the EU's approach to its macro-regions (such as the Mediterranean and the Baltic Sea), explicitly builds upon using existing funds, institutions, and legislation 'more strategically and imaginatively'.[39]

D. CONCLUSION

This chapter has positioned States and international organisations as the conventional legal subjects of international law. Out of these two, States are the legal subjects par excellence, as State consent is needed for the creation of international legal obligations, including the establishment of organisations. An increasingly expanding set of actors, however, are acknowledged as performing a regulatory function in the international legal system. This development reveals the evolutionary nature of the subject/object

---

36 Gerd Droesse, *Membership in International Organizations: Paradigms of Membership Structures, Legal Implications of Membership and the Concept of International Organization* (TMC Asser 2020).

37 Nijman (n 22).

38 Nupur Chowdhury and Ramses A Wessel, 'Conceptualising Multilevel Regulation in the EU: A Legal Translation of Multilevel Governance?' (2012) 18 ELJ 335, 337–338, and Joost Pauwelyn, 'Informal International Law-Making: Framing the Concept and Research Questions' in Pauwelyn and others (n 31) 13.

39 Commission, 'Report concerning the added value of macro-regional strategies' COM (2013) 468 final, 2.

dichotomy for capturing a regulatory function and effect. The following sub-chapters will further expand on the status and function in international law of a set of actors not traditionally thought of as international legal subjects.

BOX 7.4 Further Readings

Further Readings

- F Johns (ed), *International Legal Personality* (Ashgate 2010)

- E Fahey (ed), *The Actors of Postnational Rule-Making: Contemporary Challenges of European and International Law* (Routledge 2016)

- Special Issue: *Legal Personality* (2005) 11 Ius Gentium

- Special Issue: *The Exercise of Public Authority by International Institutions* (2008) 9(11) GLJ

- RA Wessel, 'Decisions of International Institutions: Explaining the Informality Turn in International Institutional Law' (Conference Paper 2014)

---

§ § §

§ 7.1 STATES

ALEX GREEN

BOX 7.1.1 Required Knowledge and Learning Objectives

Required knowledge: Sources of International Law; Subjects and Actors in International Law; Founding Myths

Learning objectives: Understanding the history, nature, and contemporary context of Statehood; the law of State creation; the principles of State continuity and extinction; the status of contemporary States; and the typical legal consequences of Statehood.

A. INTRODUCTION

As quipped by Thomas Baty, international law, 'it is universally agreed . . . has something to do with States'.[40] Although States are no longer the *only* subjects of international law (if indeed they ever were), they remain some of the most important and powerful. Moreover, in the absence of a global government, States constitute some of the most important institutional actors within the international legal order in terms of law creation, interpretation, application, and enforcement. To quote James Crawford, the laws of 'Statehood are of a special character, in that their application conditions the application of most other international law rules'.[41] Given the importance and complexity of these laws, conceptual clarity is essential.

To that end, we must distinguish three sets of questions about States. The first set is *existential*, concerning the conditions necessary for new States to arise (creation), endure (continuity), and become destroyed (extinction).

Questions surrounding the existence of States are some of the most politically charged within international law. This controversy can be found not only in relation to the various national and regional independence movements that are, at the time of writing, active around the world,[42] but also, for example, within the unique challenges posed by the global climate crisis and its implications for the survival of many States at risk from rising sea levels.[43]

---

40 Thomas Baty, *The Canons of International Law* (J. Murray 1930) 1.

41 James Crawford, *The Creation of States in International Law* (OUP 2006) 45.

42 Anne Bayefski (ed), *Self-Determination in International Law: Quebec and Lessons Learned* (Kluwer Law International 2000); Julie Dahlitz (ed), *Secession and International Law: Conflict Avoidance – Regional Appraisals* (Asser 2003); Marcelo Kohen (ed), *Secession: International Law Perspectives* (CUP 2006).

43 Carolin König, *Small Island States & International Law: The Challenge of Rising Seas* (Routledge 2023).

The second set covers the *essence* of statehood, or to put this another way, the *concept of statehood* itself. These are by far the most challenging to answer, encompassing political philosophy and sociology as well as international law, and implicate issues of justice, equality, and sovereignty. The third set concerns questions of *entitlement*, encompassing the 'juridical consequences' of statehood, in terms of the characteristic rights and powers that States possess.

One might also add a further set of questions, pertaining to the characteristic *obligations* that States hold. However, given the extent to which this implicates the law of international responsibility,[44] this chapter will focus exclusively upon *existential, essential*, and *entitlement*-based questions. Before proceeding, however, brief consideration must be given to the emergence of contemporary statehood, such that these three sets of questions can be placed in their proper historical context.

B. THE NATURE AND HISTORY OF MODERN STATEHOOD

The traditional story about the dawn of modern States is that they first emerged from the 1648 Peace Settlements of Münster and Osnabrück, collectively known as the 'Peace of Westphalia'.[45] According to Leo Gross, these settlements 'undoubtedly promoted the laicization of international law by divorcing it from any particular religious background, and the extension of its scope so as to include, on a footing of equality, republican and monarchical States'.[46] This story is so inaccurate as to be effectively mythological.[47] Not only is the 'Westphalian myth' problematically Eurocentric, but States of some kind or another have existed within Europe itself since ancient times.[48]

Westphalia is nonetheless instructive, albeit because it tells us more about the attitudes of those propagating the story than it does about historical reality.[49] Particularly illuminating are historical attempts to draw retroactive lines of conceptual continuity from the early United Nations (UN) period,[50] back through the 'nation-States' of the late 19th and early 20th centuries,[51] to some mythologised point at which 'States [were recognised as] units in an international society with mutual rights and obligations'.[52] This ideological move is best understood as an attempt to legitimate the principle of

---

44 On international responsibility, see Arévalo-Ramírez, § 9, in this textbook.

45 Gerard Mangone, *A Short History of International Organization* (McGraw-Hill 1954) 100.

46 Leo Gross, 'The Peace of Westphalia, 1648–1948' (1948) 42 AJIL 20, 26.

47 On international law's founding myths, see González Hauck, § 1, in this textbook.

48 See generally Christian Reus-Smith, *The Moral Purpose of the State: Culture, Social Identity, and Institutional Rationality in International Relations* (Princeton UP 1999).

49 Andreas Osiander, 'Sovereignty, International Relations, and the Westphalian Myth' (2001) 55 Int'l Org. 251, 264–266.

50 On the UN, see Baranowska, Engström, and Paige, § 7.3.D., in this textbook.

51 On the 19th century, see González Hauck, § 1, in this textbook.

52 Percy H Winfield, *The Foundations and the Future of International Law* (CUP 1942) 18.

sovereign equality that predominates within international legal doctrine today
(see below). It is perhaps ironic that such legitimising narratives not only risk a
naturalistic fallacy (because history alone *justifies* nothing) but are also unnecessary, since
the normative merits of sovereign equality can be assessed on their own terms.[53]

Beyond Westphalia, two more recent legal-historical developments merit attention. First,
there is the conceptual decoupling of *statehood* from *nationhood*. Second, there is the
transition from viewing the (non-)existence of statehood as an issue of *social fact* to one
of *legal status*. Taking the first, the link between statehood and identifiable nations was
pushed most vociferously during the inter-war period.[54] That connection has survived, at
least to some extent, within particular branches of contemporary political philosophy and
is most neatly captured by David Miller's claim that '"nation" must refer to a community
of people with an *aspiration* to be politically self-determining, and "State" must refer to
the set of political institutions that they may aspire to possess for themselves'.[55] Whatever
the merits of this definition for philosophical purposes, it is legally inaccurate. There
are many plurinational and multinational States, whose existence and normative value
cannot be reduced to their supervenience upon one nation.[56]

Taking the second point, it was once typical to regard Statehood as a 'pre-legal'
sociological fact, rather than a matter of legal status. Lassa Oppenheim famously opined
that '[t]he formation of a new State is . . . a matter of fact, not law',[57] his words being
echoed, for example, by Abba Eban on behalf of the State of Israel.[58] In a similar vein,
Hersch Lauterpacht argued that, although States lack legal personality until they are
recognised by other members of the international community, they have an existence
prior to recognition, which, whilst not entirely 'pre-legal' in character, corresponds to
the existence of factually effective governance over a discrete portion of the globe.[59]
More recent scholarship departs from such views, with James Crawford most clearly
expressing what is now the more-or-less orthodox position that

> [a] state is not a fact in the sense that a chair is a fact; it is a fact in the sense in which
> it may be said a treaty is a fact: that is, a legal status attaching to a certain state of
> affairs by virtue of certain rules or practices.[60]

This view is wholly supported by the analysis that follows.

---

53 Steven Ratner, *The Thin Justice of International Law: A Moral Reckoning of the Law of Nations* (OUP 2015) 212,
   219; Alex Green, 'A Political Theory of State Equality' (2023) 14(2) TLT 178, 179.
54 This general position was most famously articulated by Woodrow Wilson, then President of the United States,
   in a speech to Congress on 8 January 1918, in which he disclosed his 'Fourteen Points'.
55 David Miller, *On Nationality* (OUP 1995) 19.
56 Roger Merino, 'Reimagining the Nation-State: Indigenous Peoples and the Making of Plurinationalism in
   Latin America' (2018) 31(4) LJIL 773.
57 Lassa Oppenheim, *International Law* (Vol 1, 1st edn, Longmans, Green 1905) 264; (Vol 1, 9th edn, Longman
   1992) 677.
58 UNSC Verbatim Record (27 July 1948) UN DOC S/PV/339, 29–30.
59 Hersch Lauterpacht, *Recognition in International Law* (CUP 1947) 6, 26–30.
60 Crawford (n 41) 5.

C. EXISTENTIAL QUESTIONS: CREATION, CONTINUITY, AND EXTINCTION

I. CREATION

1. The Law of Recognition

Whether an entity is recognised as a State or not is of supreme practical importance. Although it is conceivable that non-recognised entities might nonetheless possess statehood, an absence of recognition typically means that the entity in question will not be treated as a State by those members of the international community that refuse to recognise it as such. If non-recognition is total, many of the benefits consequent upon statehood (see below) will not in practice be available to that entity. Moreover, since international law lacks any centralised authority for determining its State subjects, the international community of States must fulfil this function collectively through practices of *mutual* recognition. Given these points, questions of foreign recognition can often be highly controversial: for example, the State of Israel, amongst others, famously refuses to recognise the State of Palestine, largely in an attempt to ensure its (alleged) non-existence.

a) Recognition of Governments and Recognition of States

The law of recognition can be split into those principles that govern the recognition of *States* and those that, instead, concern the recognition of *governments*. Strictly speaking, the latter does not form part of the law of statehood. Where one State has recognised another, it will be legally estopped from acting on the basis that the recognised entity is *not* a State, at least until it can be demonstrated that recognition has been effectively withdrawn.[61] Changes in government, including under belligerent occupation (see below), do not ordinarily alter this position. Moreover, the very concept of 'governments-in-exile', and the effective representation of States before international organisations,[62] assumes a schism between the two. The distinction between the recognition of States and the (non-)recognition of particular governments is therefore of considerable importance. The essence of that distinction is between States as abstract legal entities, understood in the terms canvassed below, and governments as (1) the political institutions in place within those entities and/or (2) the collection of individuals who administer those institutions.[63] For example, although very few States have established formal diplomatic relations with the current Taliban government of Afghanistan, there is little doubt that Afghanistan itself remains a State under international law.

---

61 Jean Charpentier, *Le Reconnaissance Internationale et L'Evolution du Droit des Gens* (Pedone 1956) 217–225.

62 On international organisations, see Baranowska, Engström, and Paige, § 7.3, in this textbook.

63 To this extent, the distinction here differs from the most common distinction between 'States' and 'governments' within political philosophy, which is that between governance institutions, on the one hand, and governing individuals or groups, on the other. See, for example Allen Buchanan, *Justice, Legitimacy, and Self-Determination: Moral Foundations for International Law* (OUP 2004) 281.

b) The 'Great Debate'

Another fundamental distinction that needs to be drawn concerns the 'great debate' that surrounds the question of whether recognition is *declaratory* or whether it *constitutes* Statehood, in the sense of imbuing erstwhile non-State entities with that status.[64]

This disagreement holds between those who believe recognition to be merely declarative of already existing statehood, and those who believe recognition instead constitutes (or 'creates') that status. The debate, at its most fundamental level, concerns the nature of statehood itself. According to the most extreme version of the declaratory view, recognition is a purely political act that signifies little more than a willingness to engage in full diplomatic relations.[65] On the most uncompromising version of the constitutive view, statehood itself exists only relatively speaking, which is to say only *between* entities that recognise the statehood of each other.[66] Both views are, according to general consensus, mistaken. Contemporary proponents of the declaratory view typically hold that, although statehood is not legally contingent upon receiving foreign recognition, recognition is nonetheless probative because existing States bear primary legal responsibility for identifying new States as a matter of customary international law.[67] Conversely, contemporary proponents of the constitutive view often hold that although widespread recognition is not always *necessary* for State creation, it can be *sufficient*, with recognition itself representing just one means through which statehood can be conferred.[68]

In light of this moderation, it may seem odd that the 'great debate' is still presented in such terms. One explanation may be the insistence in some quarters that 'the declaratory view is generally more consistent with the practice of States',[69] as well as the less controversial claim that '[a]mong writers the declaratory doctrine, with differences in emphasis, predominates'.[70] Logically speaking, there is no necessary dichotomy, at least not between more moderate variants of both views. It is entirely consistent to hold, for example, that foreign recognition has *both* probative value *and* constitutive effect in relation to State creation. Moreover, there is no logical obstacle to Statehood arising *without* widespread foreign recognition in some cases and nonetheless arising (at least partly) *because of* recognition in others.

The better view is that widespread foreign recognition can indeed have constitutive effect but that it is insufficient for statehood to arise.[71] Recognition *bolsters* nascent

---

64 Crawford (n 41) 26.

65 See, for instance, Ian Brownlie, *Principles of Public International Law* (6th edn, OUP 2003) 89–90.

66 Robert Redslob, 'La reconnaissance de l'état comme sujet de droit international' (1934) 13(2) Revue de Droit International 429, 430–431.

67 Crawford (n 41) 27.

68 See for example Jure Vidmar, *Democratic Statehood in International Law: The Emergence of States in Post-Cold War Practice* (Hart 2013) 238.

69 Ratner (n 53) 186.

70 Crawford (n 41) 25.

71 Alex Green, *Statehood as Political Community: International Law and the Emergence of New States* (CUP 2024) chapter 4.

statehood: where one or more antecedents of Statehood are in doubt, widespread recognition can act as a legal counterweight, 'pulling' towards the conclusion that a new State has emerged.[72]

c) The Collective Duty of Non-recognition

The importance of recognition is such that there are circumstances under which it should not be extended. Within political philosophy, a lively debate persists over precisely when, normatively speaking, nascent entities should not be recognised as possessing statehood.[73] Insofar as international law is concerned, established States will have a duty *not* to recognise nascent entities when their emergence is attended by serious international illegalities. These are, namely, violations of the norms underlying the procedural principles canvassed below: self-determination, territorial integrity, and the prohibition on the threat or use of force. In practice, violation of the second norm (territorial integrity) is typically attended by violation of the first (self-determination) or third (the prohibition on force). Nonetheless, all three contribute towards the normative foundations of collective non-recognition in justificatory terms.

BOX 7.1.2 Example: Independence of Southern Rhodesia

Southern Rhodesia declared independence from the United Kingdom on 11 November 1965 under the moniker 'Rhodesia'. Controlled by a white minority, and unopposed militarily by the United Kingdom, it was condemned by the UN Security Council (UNSC) and the UN General Assembly (UNGA) for its racial segregation and widespread ethnic discrimination. (See UNSC resolutions 217 (1965), 253 (1968), and 277 (1970); and UNGA resolutions 2022 (XX), 5 November 1965 and 2024 (XX), 11 November 1965.) Crucially, despite swiftly gaining 'effective' government in the sense described below, international refusal to recognise either entity was essentially total. Southern Rhodesia no longer exists, following the 1979 Lancaster House Agreement and the resulting independence of the Republic of Zimbabwe on 18 April 1980.

---

2. The Antecedents of Statehood

Accepting the above, particular conditions must be fulfilled before any plausible claim can be made that a new State has emerged. These conditions are best understood as the factual 'antecedents' of statehood and constitute, in effect, a collection of paradigmatic

---

72 This explains, for instance, the emergence of Bosnia and Herzegovina, which is generally accepted to have emerged in the absence of effective governmental control, and also the more-or-less uncontroversial statehood of the Principality of Monaco, which for some considerable time lacked important indicators of political independence. See Alex Green, 'Successful Secession and the Value of International Recognition' in Jure Vidmar, Sarah McGibbon, and Lea Raible (eds), *Research Handbook on Secession* (Edward Elgar 2023).

73 See, for example, the arguments and references within Buchanan (n 63) 266–288.

properties that new States must possess.[74] These antecedents are often treated as providing a *definition* of statehood.[75]

While the historical roots are within customary international law,[76] the antecedents are most famously referenced within article 1 of the 1933 Montevideo Convention on the Rights and Duties of States.[77] These 'Montevideo criteria' were once considered dispositive; however, this is no longer the case.[78] Making adjustments for contemporary practice and scholarship, a more accurate list of factual antecedents reads as follows: (1) a permanent population; (2) a more or less defined territory; (3) an effective government; and (4) relative political independence.[79]

Although all four antecedents are important for State creation, they do not operate as a set of strictly necessary conditions. In some cases, one or more antecedents may be present to a lesser extent than usual and, nonetheless, State creation may still occur. The most commonplace circumstances are where statehood is widely recognised despite the absence of effective governance. In such circumstances, that recognition arguably has a partly constitutive role. A holistic judgment in relation to any given case is thus necessary.

a) A Permanent Population

This antecedent requires there to be a more or less identifiable body of people who are habitually resident upon the territory of the nascent State. Various justifications for this have been posed, however most agree that (1) States are concerned with governance and (2) governance requires an identifiable group of 'the governed'.[80] In contemporary law, there are no limitations upon the size of this group. Tuvalu and the Republic of Nauru, which have populations of under 1 million, are no less States than the Republic of India and the People's Republic of China, which have populations well in excess of 1 billion. Historically, this point was not so clear. As recently as the early 20th century, some smaller States, such as the Grand Duchy of Luxembourg and the Principality of Liechtenstein, were considered by several larger entities to be of dubious international status, largely on the basis of their relative size.[81] Moreover, although numerous 'micro-States' have now joined the UN, they were once excluded from the League of

---

74 Green (n 71) chapter 3.

75 For example: Matthew Craven, 'Statehood, Self-Determination, and Recognition' in Malcolm D Evens (ed), *International Law* (4th edn, OUP 2014) 216–226.

76 *Deutsche Continental Gas-Gesellschaft v Polish State* (1929) 5 A.D. 11, 15.

77 Montevideo Convention on the Rights and Duties of States, adopted at Montevideo (26 December 1933, entered into force 26 December 1934).

78 Thomas Grant, 'Defining Statehood: The Montevideo Convention and Its Discontents' (1998) 37 Columbia Journal of Transnational Law 403.

79 The fourth Montevideo criterion, the 'capacity to enter into relations with other States', is best viewed as either an element of effective government and political independence or as a legal consequence of Statehood, rather than an antecedent of that status.

80 Green (n 71) chapter 3.

81 Craven (n 75) 218.

Nations on the basis of their size.[82] A survey of more contemporary practice, however, shows conclusively that in 'modern' international law size does not matter.[83]

One other important point to note is that the presence or absence of a permanent population for the purposes of State creation does *not* require exclusive ties of *nationality* between that population and the nascent entity. Nationality is determined in relation to the domestic laws of established States, or else by treaty.[84] It follows from this that an entity must possess statehood, or at least an analogous international status,[85] *before* nationality can arise in relation to it. To avoid any transitional issues arising from State creation by secession or devolution (see below), the position in contemporary international law appears to be that, absent any contrary agreement, nationality of a new State automatically arises in relation to the people habitually resident upon its territory.[86]

b) A More or Less Defined Territory

States are territorial entities, traditionally delineated with reference to their inhabitable land but with consequent entitlements to any internal waters, territorial sea, and to the airspace above this 'horizontal' territory. This means that some more or less determinate land-based territorial unit must be identifiable in relation to which a nascent State can be said to exist. This point has been put somewhat more extremely by some, such as Philip Jessup, who commented in his capacity as representative of the United States 'that one cannot contemplate a State as a kind of disembodied spirit'.[87]

However, that territory does not have to be either contiguous or of any particular size. The Republic of Indonesia, which comprises around 17,500 separate islands,[88] is no less a State than the Republic of Kenya or the Republic of Bulgaria, whilst even very small territorial units can be subject to plausible statehood claims.[89] Furthermore, the existence of disputes over the status or extent of the territory in question will not prevent statehood from arising.[90] One illustrative example is that of the State of Israel,

---

82 Benedict Kingsbury, 'Sovereignty and Inequality' (1998) 9 EJIL 599, 607.

83 Crawford (n 41) 52.

84 *Nottebohm Case (second phase) (Liechtenstein v. Guatemala)* (Merits) [1955] ICJ Rep 4 [23].

85 One clear example of this is the Republic of China (Taiwan), which while not formally recognised as a State itself has functioning nationality laws that *are* recognised by a preponderance of other States.

86 Crawford (n 41) 53. See also *Acquisition of Polish Nationality* (Advisory Opinion) [1923] PCIJ Rep Series B No 7.

87 UNSC Verbatim Record (2 December 1948) UN DOC S/PV/383, 11.

88 Indonesia, 'Identification of Islands and Standardization of Their Names' 11th UN Conference of the Standardization of Geographical Names (New York 8–17 August 2017) (30 June 2017) UN DOC E/CONF.105/115/CRP.115.

89 Thomas Franck and Paul Hoffman, 'The Right of Self-Determination in Very Small Places' (1976) 8(3) New York University Journal of International Law and Politics 331, 383–384. See also Jorri Duursma, *Fragmentation and the International Relations of Micro-States: Self-Determination and Statehood* (CUP 1996) 117.

90 See, for example: *Monastery of Saint-Naoum* (Advisory Opinion) [1924] PCIJ Rep Series B No 9 and *Question of Jaworzina* (Advisory Opinion) [1923] PCIJ Series B No 8, both of which assume this point; and *North Sea Continental Shelf* (Merits) [1969] ICJ Rep 3, 32 and *Case Concerning the Territorial Dispute (Libyan Arab Jamahiriya v. Chad)* (Merits) [1994] ICJ Rep 6, 22, which both confirm the point, at least in relation to disputed boundaries.

which was admitted to the UN on 11 May 1949 notwithstanding ongoing disputes as to *both* the extent of its territorial limits *and* the soundness of its claim to hold any territory at all in a lawful manner.[91]

c) An Effective Government

According to several orthodox views, the requirement of effective government is central to State creation.[92] Indeed, Crawford goes so far as to suggest that the territorial antecedent itself is little more than a specification of the fact that 'effective government' means 'effective governmental control over a more or less defined territory'.[93] Whether or not this is true, it is clear that effectiveness holds considerable sway over the emergence of statehood in the ordinary course of events. In the case of the Republic of Finland, which seceded from the Russian Empire in 1917, the prevalence of 'revolution and anarchy' was held to have prevented the new State from arising until May 1918.[94] Such cases have often been argued to be paradigmatic.[95]

Two questions nonetheless persist in relation to the effectiveness antecedent. The first is what precisely makes a government 'effective': what are the conditions (or 'desiderata') of effectiveness and how, as a result, does the law of statehood conceptualise governance? Call this the 'purposive' question. The second concerns the *extent to which* government must be effective, no matter what 'effectiveness' may mean in purposive terms. Call this the 'variability' question. Both questions have more or less orthodox answers, which are characterised by Crawford in the following terms:

> to be a State, an entity must possess a government or a system of government in general control of its territory, to the exclusion of other entities . . . [and] international law lays down no specific requirements as to the nature and extent of this control, except that it include some degree of maintenance of law and order and the establishment of basic institutions.[96]

What does seem clear is that, purposively speaking, 'effective' government does not imply democracy, nor does it require a demonstrable capacity to achieve the full and speedy protection of basic human rights.[97] In terms of variability, it seems that at least in some circumstances, such as those where statehood goes effectively unopposed, the requirement that government establish 'some degree of maintenance of law and order' might be extremely thin. For example, when the Kingdom of Belgium was forced to grant independence in 1960 to what is now the Democratic Republic of Congo (DRC), the latter swiftly suffered several secession movements within its territory, an

---

91 UNGA Res 273 (III) (11 May 1949); UNSC Res 70 (4 March 1949) UN DOC S/RES/1280.
92 Crawford (n 41) 55.
93 Ibid 52, 56.
94 *Aaland Islands Case* (1920) L.N.O.J. Spec. Supp. No. 3 [8]-[9].
95 See generally: Thomas Baty, 'Can an Anarchy Be a State?' (1934) 28(3) AJIL 444.
96 Crawford (n 41) 56.
97 Vidmar (n 68) 39, 65, 241–242.

upsurge in endemic violence, and a continued Belgian military presence.[98] Nonetheless, the DRC was quickly recognised to be an independent State.[99]

d) Relative Political Independence

Nascent States must demonstrate an absence of foreign *domination*,[100] which is distinguishable from both the absence of foreign political *influence* and the absence of *dependence* upon foreign infrastructure. For example, no serious doubt pertains as to the independence of the Principality of Liechtenstein, notwithstanding the fact that (out of logistical necessity) it makes use of Austrian prisons rather than maintaining its own. Such cases can be usefully contrasted with the erstwhile foreign policy of Great Britain, which historically claimed an entitlement to bind its Dominions, for instance, to the 1924 Treaty of Lausanne without their permission. Such asymmetric authority claims constitute foreign – in this case, colonial – domination par excellence.[101]

Non-domination can be assessed both formally and de facto. Formally, independence will be in doubt where another State makes a legally plausible authority claim over the territory in question, whether that claim of right concerns the internal affairs or the foreign relations of the affected entity.[102] In de facto terms, the question is whether there exists substantial external control over the governmental functions or territory of the nascent entity by some other State. For example, the purported creation of the State of Manchuria (Manchukuo) by the erstwhile Empire of Japan in 1932 was generally denied recognition on the basis that Manchukuo was, in fact, a 'puppet' State lacking de facto independence.[103] As this also demonstrates, in circumstances where formal independence is apparent but de facto independence is lacking, the latter should be considered the more probative.

3. Procedural Principles

Plausible claims to statehood may nonetheless fail if the nascent entity violates one of three procedural principles, which, in combination with the cumulative effects of recognition, mediate the process of State creation. Before canvassing the principles, it must be stressed once more that they are not generally considered to be absolute disqualifiers for the creation of new States.[104] In each case, holistic judgment is required. However, it is highly likely that a failure to satisfy even one procedural principle will result in statehood *not* accruing. Moreover, violation of one of these three is characteristically sufficient to trigger the duty of collective non-recognition.

---

98 Thomas Kanza, *Conflict in the Congo: The Rise and Fall of Lumumba* (Penguin Books 1972) 78, 109, 192; UNGA Res 1599 (XV) (15 April 1961).

99 UNSC Res 142 (7 July 1960) UN DOC S/RES/142; UNGA Res 1480 (XV) (20 September 1960).

100 Green (n 71) chapter 3.

101 Crawford (n 41) 71–72.

102 Ibid.

103 *Sino-Japanese Dispute – Advisory Committee of the Special Assembly, Resolution of 24 February 1933*: LNOJ Sp Supp no 101/1, 87.

104 Cf. Green (n 71) chapter 4.

a) 'Negative' Self-Determination

There is a strong legal presumption against State creation where this would result in the formal disenfranchisement or political subordination of large sections of a territory's extant population. This presumption is a function of collective self-determination as an underlying value of contemporary international law.[105] In addition to weighing against State creation in circumstances where this 'negative' requirement of self-determination is breached, the emergence of an entity in violation of this principle operates as a trigger for the duty of collective non-recognition. This can be seen most clearly in the alleged emergence of the Turkish Republic of Northern Cyprus, as well as in the unsuccessful attempts, by the apartheid government of South Africa, to create the Bantustans of Transkei,[106] Bophuthatswana,[107] Venda,[108] and Ciskei.[109]

BOX 7.1.3 Example: Northern Cyprus

Northern Cyprus emerged in 1974 under a Turkish Cypriot administration with military support from the Republic of Turkey (*Loizidou and Cyprus (intervening) v Turkey*, Merits, [1996] ECHR 70, paras 16–23). Its creation resulted in some 211,000 Greek Cypriots being displaced from the North, whilst those who remained faced severe restrictions upon their liberty, most notably in terms of freedom of movement (*Cyprus v Turkey*, Merits, App no 25781/94, (2002) ECHR 2001-IV, paras 28–48). These dispossessions and restrictions caused mass disenfranchisement, which resulted in collective non-recognition under the auspices of the UNSC (UNSC resolutions: 541, 18 November 1983; and 550, 3 May 1984). To date, only Turkey recognises the statehood of this entity.

---

b) The Presumption in Favour of Territorial Integrity

This presumption is a function of the entitlements that established States enjoy to (1) continue to possess territory to which they are legally entitled and (2) administer that territory free from the wrongful interference of other States.[110]

The importance of this principle reinforces the application of the other procedural principles. By virtue of the presumption that established States will remain whole, greater weight is placed upon any illegality occasioning State creation. This can be seen,

---

105 Crawford (n 41) 128–131. On self-determination, see Bak-McKenna, § 2.4, in this textbook.

106 Status of Transkei Act 100 of 1976.

107 Status of Bophuthatswana Act 89 of 1977.

108 Status of Venda Act 107 of 1979.

109 Status of Ciskei Act 110 of 1981.

110 See also UNGA 2625 (XXV) (24 October 1970) UN DOC A/RES/25/2625, principle 5; *Military and Paramilitary Activities in and against Nicaragua (Nicaragua v. United States of America)* (Merits) [1986] ICJ Rep 14, paras 191–193; Conference on Security and Co-operation in Europe. Final Act, Helsinki 1975, article IV.

for example, in the response of the international community to the Russian Federation's unlawful recognition of the so-called Donetsk People's Republic and Luhansk People's Republic in the Donbas region of Ukraine in 2022.[111]

Furthermore, it entails that international law grants no entitlement to secession (the creation of new States via *unilateral* departures from 'parent' entities).[112] The orthodox argument is that only erstwhile colonies possessed a *right* to independent statehood and that, following the decolonisation movement, no entities now exist to which such a right might apply.[113] Instead, following the International Court of Justice in its advisory opinion on the *Accordance with International Law of the Unilateral Declaration of Independence in Respect of Kosovo*,[114] this line of argument maintains that international law (1) generally *permits* secession but accords no entitlement to secede, but (2) will nonetheless hold secession unlawful when it is occasioned by violations of self-determination or the prohibition on the use of force.[115] This arrangement protects territorial integrity, according to some scholars, because the absence of a right to secession means that nascent entities must prove either that their independence was *granted* by their 'parent' State or that they exhibit the antecedents of Statehood to such an extent (and for such a length of time) that the practical reality of their Statehood cannot be cogently denied.[116]

As a result, grants of independence have considerable importance. Such grants characteristically occur through devolution (the creation of new States via the *consent* of parent entities).[117] Where this consent is provided, no issues of territorial integrity arise. In this respect, consent places new States in an analogous normative position to those arising from the *dissolution* of their predecessors. In both cases, the territorial integrity of the erstwhile sovereign no longer pertains.

c) The Prohibition on the Threat or Use of Force

This prohibition is enshrined in article 2(4) of the UN Charter.[118] Attempts to create States through the unlawful use of force will trigger duties of collective non-recognition. This is justified not only by the importance of ensuring that unlawful force does not benefit States that use it but also by the need to uphold the territorial integrity of affected State from the attacks of foreign belligerents. Evidence for this duty

---

111 See, for example: *Statement by Ambassador Martin Kimani, during the Security Council Urgent Meeting on the Situation in Ukraine*, 21 February 2022, para 2; *Prime Minister's statement on Ukraine (United Kingdom)*, 22 February 2022, HC Deb 22 February 2022, Vol 709, col 173; *Statement of Mélanie Joly, Minister of Foreign Affairs (Canada)*, 21 February 2022, Ottawa, Ontario, Global Affairs Canada, para 3.

112 *Reference re Secession of Quebec*, 1998 SCJ No 61 [155].

113 Crawford (n 41) 415.

114 [2010] ICJ Rep 403 [436]-[438].

115 Marko Milanovic, 'A Footnote on Secession' (*EJIL: Talk!*, 26 October 2017) <www.ejiltalk.org/a-footnote-on-secession/> accessed 28 February 2022.

116 Vidmar (n 68) 52–53.

117 Crawford (n 41) 330–373. Devolution, in this sense, should not be confused with any internal devolution of governmental power that stops short of granting independent statehood.

118 On the use of force, see Svicevic, § 13, in this textbook.

can be found, for example, in the international response to the Russian Federation's 2022 military invasion of Ukraine, which purported to be for the purpose of securing 'remedial' independence for the so-called Donetsk People's Republic and Luhansk People's Republic within the Donbas region.[119]

Some have suggested that unilateral foreign intervention might be permissible to secure regional secession in response to mass atrocities conducted by a parent State.[120] One example might be the People's Republic of Bangladesh (or East Pakistan as it was then known), which gained generally recognised independence despite unilateral military intervention by the Republic of India.[121] However, even those who argue in favour of a right to remedial secession typically stop short of arguing that India's unilateral intervention was lawful as a result.[122] A more credible view is that evidence of mass atrocities renders international countermeasures short of unilateral military intervention permissible. It is also possible that the international community may, at the same time, come under an 'imperfect' obligation to provide military support for independence under the auspices of the UNSC but that the lawfulness of military intervention would be contingent on an authorising resolution being adopted.[123]

II. CONTINUITY AND EXTINCTION

1. The Presumption of Continuity

States are, in general, far harder to destroy than they are to create. This is so because there exists, as a matter of customary international law, a strong but rebuttable presumption of State *continuity*, which serves to ensure relative geopolitical stability.[124] Nonetheless, States can and do become extinct. This happens when the antecedents of Statehood become absent to such an extent and for such a length of time that it no longer remains plausible to hold that an independent entity exists. However, the threshold for this occurring is, due to the presumption in favour of continuity, extremely high. An effective government, for example, may remain absent for

---

119 Decree of the President of the Russian Federation, 21 February 2022, No. 71, 'On the recognition of the Donetsk People's Republic'; Decree of the President of the Russian Federation, 21 February 2022, No. 72, 'On the recognition of the Luhansk People's Republic'.

120 Green (n 71) chapter 4; Robert McCorquodale, 'Self-Determination: A Human Rights Approach' (1994) 43 ICLQ 857, 880.

121 Jean JA Salmon, 'Naissance et Reconnaissance du Bangladesh' in *Multitudo legum, ius unum: Melanges en honneur de Wilhelm Wengler* (Interrecht 1973) 478–480.

122 Green (n 71) chapter 4.

123 Following UNGA Res 337 (V) (3 November 1950), the General Assembly may make recommendations for the adoption of sanctions but cannot, by itself, authorise military action, see Rebecca Barber, 'What Can the UN General Assembly Do About Russian Aggression in Ukraine?' (*EJIL: Talk!*, 26 February 2022) <www.ejiltalk.org/what-can-the-un-general-assembly-do-about-russian-aggression-in-ukraine/> accessed 28 February 2020. See on humanitarian intervention Svicevic, § 13.E.II.2., in this textbook.

124 See the detailed, if somewhat historical, review of State practice provided by Krystyna Marek in her *Identity and Continuity of States in International Law* (Librairie E. Droz 1954) 15–126; and also Crawford (n 41) 671–673, 700–701, 715–717.

many years without the extinction of the State in question. In a similar vein, even considerable changes in territory, or the total loss of de facto independence due to belligerent obligation, will not ordinarily result in the extinction of the affected State.[125] It is indicative that only eight States became extinct in the period between 1945 and 2005, whilst within the same period 128 new States came into being.[126] One important example of extinction is the former Socialist Federal Republic of Yugoslavia, the dissolution of which resulted – following protracted conflict, complicated by considerable international intervention – in the emergence of what are now Bosnia and Herzegovina, the Republic of Croatia, Montenegro, the Republic of North Macedonia, the Republic of Serbia, and the Republic of Slovenia, as well as the partially recognised Republic of Kosovo.[127]

2. Extinction and Succession

If a State does become extinct, its space on the map will not remain empty for long. Should a new State arise within the territory of an extinct entity, we must then ask whether the newcomer will be a 'successor' to the former State.[128] Already existing States can also succeed others, either where an establish entity absorbs the territory of an extinct community, or where two or more established States merge to form a new entity.[129] More generally, succession to existing rights and obligations is possible following secession or devolution, as well as, historically speaking, decolonisation. The question arising is whether the new entity in fact succeeds to the obligations of the previous one. Unfortunately, the 'law of State succession' (such as it is) forms little more than an area of legal controversy concerning what happens when the statehood of one entity is displaced by that of another.[130] There is no 'overriding principle, or even a presumption, that a transmission or succession of legal rights and duties occurs in a given case'.[131]

In general, only the following propositions hold with any degree of certainty. First, where a successor State emerges but its predecessor State endures (e.g. within circumstances of decolonisation), succession to treaties is not possible, with the notable exception of boundary treaties, which govern the extent of the new entity's extant borders.[132] Second, successor States are not liable for their predecessor's international wrongdoing unless they have by conduct adopted the unlawful activity in question.[133] Third, membership of international organisations characteristically does not pass

---

125 Crawford (n 41) 673–678, 688–690.

126 Ibid 715–716.

127 For a detailed discussion of this process, see Vidmar (n 68) 66–111, 117–136, 176–184.

128 Daniel P O'Connell, *The Law of State Succession* (CUP 1956) 3–6.

129 James Crawford, *Brownlie's Principles of Public International Law* (8th edn, OUP 2012) 423.

130 Arman Sarvarian, 'Codifying the Law of State Succession: A Futile Endeavour?' (2016) 27(3) EJIL 789.

131 Ibid.

132 Arnold McNair, *The Law of Treaties* (OUP 1961) 592, 600–601, 629, 655.

133 *Robert E Brown (United States v. Great Britain)* (1923) 6 R.I.A.A. 120; *Redward and Others (Great Britain) v. United States (Hawaiian Claims)* (1925) 6 R.I.A.A. 157; *Lighthouses Arbitration between France and Greece (France v Greece), Claims No 11 and 4* (1956) 23 I.L.R. 81. On State responsibility and attribution, see Arévalo-Ramírez, § 9, in this textbook.

to succeeding States, although special accommodation can be made and the matter ultimately rests with the constitution or charter of the relevant organisation.[134] Succession to treaty obligations is now partially governed by the 1978 Vienna Convention on Succession of States in respect of Treaties, although only 23 States have both signed and ratified that Convention. As such, it is typically necessary to proceed by examining discrete customary principles and treaty arrangements that may or may not govern particular State successions. To take one example, the 1919 Treaty of St Germain-en-Laye covered the inheritance of public debts by the successor States to the Austro-Hungarian monarchy, while there is a generally accepted customary presumption, to take another example, that ownership of public property on the territory of a successor State is passed to that successor.[135]

Most importantly for present purposes, *succession* is both conceptually distinct from the *continuity* and *identity* of States and mutually exclusive with those two things. Where a State is identical with some prior entity, issues of succession do not arise. In cases of continuity and identity – and not in circumstances of succession – every single entitlement and obligation of a State can be *presumed* to endure through time. One example is Russia, considered to be identical with the former Soviet Union.

3. Continuity and the Climate Crisis

One particularly troubling possibility caused by the contemporary law of continuity and extinction is the existential threat posed to Small Island Developing States (SIDS) by the global climate crisis.[136] Several SIDS may well suffer *legal extinction* due to human-caused climate change.[137] On an 'austere view' of State continuity, the total loss of their territory, if physically irrecoverable, would result in a loss of statehood, rendering the erstwhile population of affected SIDS stateless.[138] Currently, several SIDS, including Vanuatu and Tuvalu, are taking steps to combat the austere view as part of an overall attempt to address the long-term harms they stand to suffer from the global climate crisis.[139]

---

134 See generally: Konrad Bühler, 'State Succession, Identity/Continuity and Membership in the United Nations' in Pierre Eisemann and Martti Koskenniemi (eds), *State Succession: Codification Tested against the Facts* (Brill Nijhoff 1997). On international organisations, see Baranowska, Engström, and Paige, § 7.3, in this textbook.

135 *Appeal from a Judgment of Hungaro-Czechoslovak Mixed Arbitral Tribunal (Czechoslovakia v. Hungary)*, 1933 P.C.I.J. (ser. A/B) No. 61 [237].

136 Declaration on Preserving Maritime Zones in the Face of Climate Change-related Sea-Level Rise (51st Pacific Islands Forum, 6 August 2021) <www.forumsec.org/2021/08/11/declaration-on-preserving-maritime-zones-in-the-face-of-climate-change-related-sea-level-rise/> accessed 10 August 2023. On climate law, see Viveros-Uehara, § 17, in this textbook.

137 Kate Pucell, *Geographical Change and the Law of the Sea* (OUP 2019) 228–229; Carolin König, *Small Island States & International Law. The Challenge of Rising Seas* (Routledge 2023) chapter 3.

138 Alex Green, '*The Creation of States* as a Cardinal Point: James Crawford's Contribution to International Legal Scholarship' (2022) 40(1) AYBIL 68, 82–83.

139 'Vanuatu to Seek International Court Opinion on Climate Change Rights' (*The Guardian*, 26 September 2021) <www.theguardian.com/world/2021/sep/26/vanuatu-to-seek-international-court-opinion-on-climate-change-rights> accessed 21 February 2022.

D. QUESTIONS OF ESSENTIALITY: SOVEREIGNTY AND EQUALITY

I. THE BASIC QUESTION

Different academic disciplines may ask 'what States are' for different reasons, not all of which will be strictly relevant to international law. Within legal and political philosophy, for example, the essence of statehood is typically interrogated in relation to its purpose. In this way, Allen Buchanan characterises States as the units of human social and political organisation responsible for securing justice via the protection of fundamental human rights.[140] Purely legal accounts of statehood are typically articulated in two ways (although these sometimes overlap). They either reflect the antecedents of statehood, on the basis that statehood reduces to a particular kind of effective territorial governance, or they list 'the exclusive and general legal characteristics of States'.[141]

However, some have developed discrete understandings of statehood based on philosophically informed reconstructions of international legal doctrine.[142] These reconstructions are unique insofar as they each reinterpret the law of statehood in light of particular philosophical principles, whilst at the same time constructing the full account of those principles with reference to contemporary law.[143] Substantively, such work characterises statehood *as it exists within contemporary law* in terms of political community,[144] legitimate governance,[145] or republicanism.[146] Notwithstanding the insights offered by such approaches, I stick to more 'mainstream' doctrinal work in what follows.

II. SOVEREIGN STATEHOOD AS STATUS AND CAPACITY

Sovereignty can be an unhelpfully opaque legal concept, due to the controversial place it holds within domestic law, normative philosophy, and contemporary political rhetoric. Internationally, 'sovereignty' is often used as synonym for statehood itself ('a sovereign State'), as shorthand for the minimal degree of political independence necessary for statehood to arise or endure, or else to express the residual liberty that States possess when they are not otherwise legally bound.[147] Moreover, 'sovereignty' can

---

140 Buchanan (n 63) 98–105, 235–238, 247–249.

141 Crawford (n 41) 40–41.

142 Green (n 71); Fernando Tesón, *A Philosophy of International Law* (Westview Press 1997) 57–66; Mortimer Sellers, *Republican Principles in International Law: The Fundamental Requirements of a Just World Order* (Palgrave Macmillan 2006) 33–37, 95–103.

143 They mirror, to this extent, the work of Ronald Dworkin (and others) within domestic/municipal jurisprudence, see Dworkin, *Law's Empire* (Hart 1986) 56–72, 87–88, 250–256.

144 Green (n 71).

145 Tesón (n 144).

146 Sellers (n 144).

147 Kamal Hossain, 'State Sovereignty and the United Nations Charter' (MS DPhil d 3227, Oxford 1964).

not only be used to articulate claims of territorial title ('sovereignty *over* territory') but also as a catch-all for the complete set of legal capacities and entitlements that States characteristically possess.[148]

Historic usage tended to link sovereignty to the existence of an identifiable sovereign.[149] In the words of Thomas Hobbes, such an entity 'consisteth the Essence of the Common-wealth'; which (to define it,) is

> One Person, of whose Acts a great Multitude, by mutuall Covenants one with another, have made themselves every one the Author, to the end he may use the strength and means of them all, as he shall think expedient, for their Peace and Common Defence.[150]

This historic insistence upon the right of sovereigns to act 'as [they] shall think expedient',[151] created within both philosophy and law 'a tendency to associate with [sovereignty] . . . the idea of a person above the law whose word is law for his inferiors or subjects'.[152]

An important contemporary implication of this is the common but mistaken belief that sovereign statehood entails *legally unlimited* authority.[153] This has caused some international lawyers to pose as a 'dilemma' the question, 'Can the existence of rules binding upon States be reconciled with the very notion of sovereignty?'[154] Much like the old theological paradox of whether an omnipotent God can create a stone that He is incapable of lifting,[155] this line of enquiry asks, for example, whether 'sovereign States' can 'truly' possess the capacity to bind themselves via treaty. If we say 'yes', then they can become legally bound, which undermines their 'unlimited' authority, whereas if we say 'no', then that authority is *also* undermined, since they cannot then have the authority to bind themselves.[156]

The answer to this 'dilemma' lies in rejecting the belief that sovereignty implies unlimited authority. Rather than being inconsistent with legal obligation, State authority is itself an aspect of international law and therefore must possess legally defined limits.[157] This holds because the sovereignty of any single State *because it*

---

148 Crawford (n 41) 32.

149 John Austin, *The Province of Jurisprudence Determined* (John Murray 1832) Lecture VI. On international law's founding myths, see González Hauck, § 1, in this textbook.

150 Thomas Hobbes, *Leviathan or the Matter, Forme, and Power of a Common-Wealth Ecclesiastical and Civil* (Andrew Crooke 1651), chapter XVII ('The Definition of a Common-wealth').

151 Cf. David Dyzenheus, 'Hobbes and the Legitimacy of Law' (2001) 20(5) Law and Philosophy 461.

152 HLA Hart, *The Concept of Law* (2nd edn, OUP 1994) 221.

153 On one interpretation, this notion grounded the ruling of the Permanent Court in *The Lotus* (supra n 111).

154 Jan Klabbers, 'Clinching the Concept of Sovereignty: Wimbledon Redux' (1999) 3 ARIEL 345, 348.

155 Thomas Aquinas, *Summa Theologica*, Book 1, Question 25, article 3.

156 Timothy Endicott, 'The Logic of Freedom and Power' in Samantha Besson and John Tasioulas (eds), *The Philosophy of International Law* (OUP 2010) 246.

157 Ibid 246–252. On jurisdiction, see González Hauck and Milas, § 8, in this textbook.

is a State necessarily implies the equal sovereignty of all others. In a world where more than one State exists, freedom from obligation and wholly unlimited authority thus becomes illogical.[158] 'Sovereignty' thus means no more nor less than the full set of legal capacities ordinarily associated with statehood. To put this another way, to be sovereign for the purposes of international law means to have the *status* of an established State. In concrete terms, this has two implications. First, that the acquisition and maintenance of sovereignty turns on the law that governs the creation, continuation, and extinction of States, even though this law may then be supplemented by other principles such as human rights. Second, 'sovereignty as status and capacity' means that sovereignty implies the entitlements canvassed below in addition to the *obligations* necessary to secure those entitlements by all States on a formally equal basis.

III. SOVEREIGN EQUALITY IN AN UNEQUAL WORLD

Although States possess *formal* equality,[159] in almost all other respects they are staggeringly unequal.[160] For example, extensive scholarship exists on disparities of international power,[161] within which considerable attention is paid to the inequalities of global influence created by the existence of the so-called Great Powers.[162] States are also unequal, to take another example, in terms of their size (both geographically and demographically), their access to natural resources, and qualitatively, in terms of their democratic credentials and their compliance with international human rights standards.[163] Moreover, some have coastlines whilst some are landlocked, whilst others govern unique ecosystems, cultural sites, and indigenous communities.[164] In light of this, it is difficult to imagine a group of 'equals' with *less equality* than contemporary States. Fortunately for present purposes, to invoke equality is, conceptually speaking, to *preclude* total sameness. If two things are identical, in the

---

158 Henry Shue, 'Limiting Sovereignty' in Jennifer Welsh (ed), *Humanitarian Intervention and International Relations* (OUP 2004) 16.

159 See, for example: Charter of the United Nations (adopted 26 June 1945, San Francisco, entered into force 24 October 1945) 1 UNTS XVI, article 2; Benedict Kingsbury, 'Sovereignty and Inequality' (1998) 9 EJIL 599, 600; *Questions Relating to the Seizure and Detention of Certain Documents and Data (Timor-Leste v. Australia)* (Order of 3 March 2014) [2014] ICJ Rep 147, paras 26–28; *Jurisdictional Immunities of the State (Germany v. Italy: Greece intervening)* (Merits) [2012] ICJ Rep 99, para 57; and *Arrest Warrant of 1 1 April 2000 (Democratic Republic of the Congo v. Belgium)* (Merits) [2002] ICJ Rep 3 [62]-[71].

160 Philip Jessup, 'The Equality of States as Dogma and Reality' (1945) 60(4) PSQ 527, 528.

161 See, for example: Michael Byers, *Custom, Power and the Power of Rules: International Relations and Customary International Law* (CUP 2009); James Crawford, *Chance, Order, Change: The Course of International Law, General Course on Public International Law* (Brill 2014); Jack Goldsmith and Eric Posner, *The Limits of International Law* (OUP 2007).

162 Gerry Simpson: 'The Great Powers, Sovereign Equality and the Making of the United Nations Charter' (2000) 21 Aust YBIL 133; *Great Powers and Outlaw States: Unequal Sovereigns in the International Legal Order* (CUP 2009); 'Great Powers and Outlaw States Redux' (2012) 43 NYIL 83.

163 Sean Murphy, 'Democratic Legitimacy and the Recognition of States and Governments' (1999) 48 ICLQ 545, 556; Gregory Fox and Bradley Roth, 'Democracy and International Law' (2001) 27 Review of International Studies 327, 337.

164 On indigenous peoples, see Viswanath, § 7.2, in this textbook.

sense that they are completely indiscernible, then they are not equal but entirely the same.[165] The formal equality of States should therefore be understood in terms of *normative* equality, which is to say an *equality of status*. To paraphrase the philosopher Thomas Nagel, States are formally equal in that they hold the same place within the 'normative community' of international law.[166] The content of that status is controversial, being connected to the philosophical as well as the legal essence of States;[167] however, its *implications* are reasonably clear and encompass the full incidents of sovereignty (canvassed above).[168]

E. QUESTIONS OF ENTITLEMENT: THE JURIDICAL CONSEQUENCES OF STATEHOOD

I. AUTONOMY AND SECURITY ENTITLEMENTS

The entitlements that protect the autonomy and security of States correspond to their right to continue to exist *as* States, which is to say as 'sovereign' members of the international community. For this reason, several of these entitlements correspond, in a more or less direct manner, to the existential conditions for the creation and continuation of Statehood, canvassed above.[169]

1. Territorial Integrity

As canvassed in the section 'The Presumption in Favour of Territorial Integrity', the principle of territorial integrity is a fundamental constituent of the United Nations Charter system, referenced in article 2(4) of that text and therefore very often linked to the prohibition on the threat and use of force within international relations. These elements support the proposition that States are legally protected from incursions into their territory by other States, both in existential terms and insofar as such incursions generate recoverable loss. Moreover, the operation of territorial integrity within the law of State creation is to present a normative hurdle that seceding entities must in some manner overcome. In this manner, established States are entitled not only to continue to exist within their extant territorial boundaries but also to do so free from military or paramilitary interference from other States.

---

165 Bertrand Russell, *An Inquiry into Meaning and Truth* (George Allen and Unwin 1972) 97–102.
166 Thomas Nagel, 'Personal Rights and Public Space' (1995) 24(2) Philosophy & Public Affairs 83, 85.
167 Green (n 71).
168 Focusing upon the consequences of sovereign equality, rather than upon the essence of statehood itself, is sufficient for present purposes but does risk a certain artificiality. Without deeper philosophical reflection, this view may amount only to the tautologous proposition that 'States are equal in view of their statehood', which is admittedly rather unhelpful.
169 Green (n 71) chapter 3.

2. Political Independence

The right to political independence, protected by the principle of non-intervention, mirrors the right to territorial integrity in that it not only concerns an established State's right to continue to exist but its right to freedom from foreign domination. It is also, to this extent, the corollary of independence as an antecedent of statehood, representing the right of States, once fully independent, to remain so. Although States are entitled to be free from the *domination* of foreign governments, they are not entitled to freedom from the political *influence* of other States. To take just one example, interference in governmental elections, be it covert or otherwise, constitutes a breach of the non-intervention principle (and a violation of political independence),[170] whereas exerting purely diplomatic influence upon domestic policy does not.

In practice, applying the non-intervention principle faces greatest practical difficulties when determining the practise line between foreign domination and mere influence. Although the threat or use of force, for example, represents a clear violation of that principle, the International Court of Justice (ICJ) in the *Nicaragua* case explicitly recognised the possibility that 'indirect' action supporting subversive activities within another State may violate that principle as well.[171]

This was affirmed in 2005, when the ICJ cited the principle of non-intervention when passing judgment against the Republic of Uganda for supporting rebel forces in the Democratic Republic of the Congo. The Court held that 'the principle of non-intervention prohibits a State "to intervene, directly or indirectly, with or without armed force, in support of an internal opposition in another State"'.[172]

In each case, the relevant questions are first whether the alleged intervention was coercive or subversive in nature – thereby amounting to an attempt at foreign domination – and then whether any available defences are available, such as the implied consent of the complainant State. Given the commonplace conflation of independence with sovereignty,[173] it is necessary to remark upon several other things that do *not* frustrate political independence. First, the opposability of international obligations against a State in no way undermines its legal independence.[174] Second, membership within international organisations, including those with institutions capable of issuing binding directives upon their members, in no way abrogates the independence of States

170 Michael Schmitt and Liis Vihul (eds), *Tallin Manual 2.0 on the International Law Applicable to Cyber Operations* (CUP 2017) 312 Rule 66; Michael Schmitt, 'Foreign Cyber Interference in Elections: An International Law Primer, Part I' (*EJIL: Talk!*, 16 October 2020) <www.ejiltalk.org/foreign-cyber-interference-in-elections-an-international-law-primer-part-i/> accessed 28 February 2022.

171 *Military and Paramilitary Activities in and against Nicaragua (Nicaragua v. United States of America)* (Merits) [1986] ICJ Rep 14.

172 *Armed Activities on the Territory of the Congo (Democratic Republic of the Congo v. Uganda)* (Merits) [2005] ICJ Rep 168.

173 Hossain (n 149).

174 Supra n 73 (at 131).

belonging to such organisations.[175] Notwithstanding the rhetoric surrounding 'Brexit', it is trite international law that membership of the European Union in no way affected the political independence of the United Kingdom.[176] Third, domestic constitutional arrangements, even those settled upon under direction from foreign powers, pose no necessary threat to political independence *unless* the arrangements in question establish unilateral claims of right or general authority over the domestic or foreign affairs of the affected State.[177] As above, the presence or absence of foreign domination, be it formal or de facto, is determinative of independence and not the existence of bilateral or even multilateral commitments amongst juridical equals.

3. Freedom to Choose Political, Social, Economic, and Cultural Systems

Contemporary statehood does not require particular forms of government and so does not depend, for example, upon the presence of democratic institutions, the provision of social security, or the separation of church and State.[178]

The general applicability of this principle is borne out, perhaps, by the fact that UN membership does not turn upon, for example, the presence of democratic institutions within the applicant entity.[179] The only nuance to be noted here is that other branches of international law, such as the international law of human rights, can and do regulate the *manner in which* governance is undertaken. Freedom to choose a political system, to this extent, excludes the freedom to choose one that violates fundamental human rights norms, at least to the extent that the State in question is party to the relevant international human rights law treaties.[180]

4. Permanent Sovereignty Over Natural Resources

Established States have exclusive rights to exploit any natural resources falling within their territory, which includes any onshore resources and any located within their territorial sea.[181] This general rule, which arguably sits 'downstream' from both territorial integrity and the freedom States enjoy to establish their own economic systems, is most clearly expressed within Principle 21 of the 1972 Stockholm Declaration,[182] which references a State's

---

175 Crawford (n 41) 70–71.

176 Ibid.

177 Green (n 71) chapter 3.

178 [1986] ICJ Rep 14 [263].

179 Whilst the United Nations Charter frequently uses the word 'State' in an idiosyncratic manner – and therefore sometimes may not entail much for the status of the 'State' it references – membership decisions pursuant to article 4(1) broadly reflect the notion that members must be States under international law, see Higgins (n 20) 11–57.

180 On human rights law, see Ciampi, § 21, in this textbook.

181 Ricardo Pereira, 'The Exploration and Exploitation of Energy Resources in International Law' in Karen E Makuch and Ricardo Pereira (eds), *Environmental and Energy Law* (Blackwell 2012) 199. On the law of the sea, see Dela Cruz and Paige, § 15, in this textbook.

182 'Report of the United Nations Conference on the Human Environment' (Stockholm 5–16 June 1972) UN Doc A/CONF.48/Rev.1.

sovereign right to exploit their own resources pursuant to their own environmental policies, and the responsibility to ensure that activities within their jurisdiction or control do not cause damage to the environment of other States or of areas beyond the limits of national jurisdiction.

This formulation was also adopted, in slightly modified form, within Principle 2 of the 1992 Rio Declaration.[183] As argued by Sundhya Pahuja, there is some concern that permanent sovereignty over natural resources, which was originally developed to safeguard postcolonial States against foreign economic exploitation immediately following decolonisation, has in fact led to the protection and elevation of the foreign investor as a subject of international law to the expense of domestic populations of those States.[184]

II. ENTITLEMENTS OF STANDING

If the entitlements listed above cover the rights of States to exercise the capacities ordinarily associated with the term 'sovereignty', then the entitlements now at issue protect their position as equal members of the international community. Such entitlements of standing might be conceived as rights to participate on certain terms within the international legal order,[185] and include, amongst other things, principles of sovereign immunity, the law of diplomatic and consular relations, and the immunity of States from the compulsory jurisdiction of international courts and tribunals. Since other chapters in this volume address these elements in greater detail than would be possible here, the remainder of this chapter will focus instead upon two further entitlements of standing.

1. Legal Personality

Legal personality is the capacity to exist within (legally enforceable) juridical relations: to hold certain rights, duties, powers, liabilities, and so on.[186] The precise relationship between statehood and legal personality has been subject to some controversy. According to Lassa Oppenheim, '[t]he equality before International Law of all member-States of the Family of Nations is an invariable quality derived from their international personality'.[187] This order of derivation is highly misleading. Properly construed, legal personhood is a *consequence* of statehood and not its logical antecedent.

The fact that legal personality follows from statehood (and not the other way around) is best demonstrated by the direction of analysis adopted in the *Reparation*

---

183 'Report of the United Nations Conference on Environment and Development' (Rio de Janeiro 3–14 June 1992) UN Doc A/CONF.151/26 (Vol I).

184 Sundhya Pahuja, *Decolonising International Law: Development, Economic Growth and the Politics of Universality* (CUP 2011) 95–171. On international investment law, see Hankings-Evans, § 23.1, in this textbook.

185 Ratner (n 53) 190–197.

186 See, for example: Neil MacCormick, *Institutions of Law: An Essay in Legal Theory* (OUP 2007) 77–100. On legal personality in international law, see Engström, § 7, in this textbook.

187 Lassa Oppenheim, *International Law: A Treatise* (Hersch Lauterpacht ed, Vol I, 6th edn, Longman 1947) 238.

for Injuries advisory opinion, in which the International Court of Justice grounded the legal personality of the UN upon an enquiry into *nature and function* of that organisation.[188] Importantly, within the context of identifying whether or not the UN had personality sufficient to bring a claim for damage done to that organisation, the Court characterised the undoubted capacity of *States* to bring analogous claims as being facilitative of consensual dispute resolution 'between two political entities, equal in law, similar in form, and both the direct subjects of international law'.[189] The *essence* of States, in other words, as 'political entities' equally subject to international law is what grounds *their* legal personality (which, after all, consists in little more than the capacity to hold rights and duties such as those at issue in the opinion itself).[190]

2. The Powers to Create and Apply International Law

Whether or not States are the only entities capable of creating and applying international law, they remain crucially important institutions for law creation and application within the global legal order.[191]

Fortunately, none of this creates insuperable difficulties because the statehood of most entities within the international community is reasonably clear. The point, for present purposes, is that statehood itself imparts these important 'jurisgenerative' capacities,[192] meaning that important normative questions arise surrounding the authority and legitimacy of State-made international law.[193] According to some scholars, international law should differentiate between States when it comes to their impact upon international law-making and application. Suggestions include, for example, (1) that democratically legitimate States should have to consent to putative international norms before those norms become opposable against them, whilst non-democratic States should have no such option;[194] and (2) that States which fail routinely to observe fundamental human rights principles should have their jurisgenerative capacities suspended or curtailed.[195] Whatever the merits of these views in normative terms, they do not reflect contemporary international doctrine, which makes no such discriminations.

---

188 *Reparation for Injuries Suffered in the Service of the United Nations* (Advisory Opinion) [1949] ICJ Rep 174, 178–180.

189 Ibid 177–178.

190 'Personality', to this extent, is distinct from 'personhood', which is arguably more substantive, see Ngaire Naffine, 'Who Are Law's Persons? From Cheshire Cats to Responsible Subjects' (2003) 66(3) MLR 346.

191 On the State-centredness of law-making in international law, see Eggett, § 6, in this textbook.

192 This phrase is taken from: Robert M Cover, 'The Supreme Court, 1982 Term – Forward: *Nomos* and Narrative' (1983) 97 Harvard Law Review 4.

193 See generally: Carmen Pavel, *Law Beyond the State* (OUP 2021).

194 Samantha Besson, 'State Consent and Disagreement in International Law-Making: Dissolving the Paradox' (2016) 29(2) LJIL 289.

195 Patrick Capps, *Human Dignity and the Foundations of International Law* (Bloomsbury 2009) 264–268.

F. CONCLUSION

States are some of the most powerful actors within the international legal system. They are also, in a range of other ways, central to the functioning of that normative order. Nonetheless, the idea of Statehood remains both complex and contested. Questions persist surrounding the law that governs their creation, continuity, and extinction, as well as their fundamental nature and entitlements. This is, however, hardly surprising. Just as States remain some of the most powerful entities on Earth, so too do they remain some of the most complex. As a result, when approaching the State within international law, the careful student and practitioner is best advised to take these issues one at a time, rather than seeking a one-size-fits-all, ultimate view of what States truly are and how, according to the law that governs international relations, they should be treated.

BOX 7.1.4 Further Readings and Further Resources

Further Readings

- J Crawford, *The Creation of States in International Law* (OUP 2006).

- J Duurmsa, *Fragmentation and the International Relations of Micro-States: Self-Determination and Statehood* (CUP 1996).

- A Green, *Statehood as Political Community: International Law and the Emergence of New States* (CUP 2024).

- C König, *Small Island States & International Law the Challenge of Rising Seas* (Routledge 2023).

- J Vidmar, *Democratic Statehood in International Law: The Emergence of States in Post-Cold War Practice* (Hart 2013).

Further Resources

- Başak Etkin and Kostia Gorobets, 'Episode 19: Alex Green on Natural Law, Statehood and International Law' (*Borderline Jurisprudence*, 7 April 2023) <https://podcasts.apple.com/gb/podcast/episode-19-alex-green-on-natural-law-statehood-and/id1561575704?i=1000607861316> accessed 8 August 2023.

---

§ § §

§ 7.2 INDIGENOUS PEOPLES

RAGHAVI VISWANATH

BOX 7.2.1 Required Knowledge and Learning Objectives

Required knowledge: Decolonisation; Sources of International Law; States

Learning objectives: Understanding how international law has come to comprehend indigeneity and indigenous peoples and the underlying logic; learning about the rights afforded to indigenous peoples and the ways in which this may be limiting; familiarising oneself with indigenous epistemologies and their growing relevance to legal research and law-making.

A. INTRODUCTION

International law, as Ntina Tzouvala notes, is constituted by argumentative patterns around the 'standard of civilization'. This oscillates between a 'logic of biology' invoking blatantly racist notions of a supposedly natural 'backwardness' of peoples deemed to be 'uncivilised' and a 'logic of improvement', invoking more subtle but equally racist notions of inferiority combined with the promise of conditional inclusion in the family of 'civilised nations'.[196] This discourse manifests violently in international law's engagement with indigenous peoples. As colonialism expanded in the 16th century, those whose lands were encroached were labelled 'indigenous', 'native', 'Indian', or 'tribal', each term constructed to convey their supposed lower degree of civilisation.[197]

The association of the term 'Indians' to indigenous communities in the Americas was a misattribution by Christopher Columbus in 1492, who erroneously thought he had reached India.[198] Columbus' encounter with the Arawaks was a telling example of the drastically different worldviews of the native Arawaks and the Europeans.[199] 'They believe very firmly', Columbus wrote, 'that I, with these ships and people, came from the sky'.[200] This assumption of intellectual and biological superiority bred dismissal of 'Native Americans' humanity. People like Vespucci and Winthrop dehumanised indigeneity to justify European invasion of indigenous lands.[201]

---

196 Ntina Tzouvala, *Capitalism as Civilisation* (CUP 2020).

197 Antony Anghie, *Imperialism, Sovereignty, and the Making of International Law* (CUP 2005).

198 See González Hauck, § 1, in this textbook.

199 Peter Carroll, *The Free and the Unfree: A Progressive History of the United States* (Penguin 2001) 35–36.

200 'First Encounters in the Americas' (*Facing History*, 1 August 2017) <www.facinghistory.org/resource-library/first-encounters-americas> accessed 16 July 2023.

201 Ibid.

This civilisational discourse permeated the vestiges of international law and became the bedrock of modern international law. Early proponents of international law such as Vitoria infamously remarked that while 'Indians were capable of holding rights and dominion over land', they were 'unfit to found or administer a lawful state up to the standard required by human and civil claims'.[202] To Vitoria, sovereign status was contingent on conforming to Christian norms. Grotius, similarly, introduced the 'terra nullius' doctrine.[203] By the application of 'terra nullius', land was considered vacant if it was not occupied by Christians.[204] 'Vacant' land could be defined as 'discovered', and as a result sovereignty, title, and jurisdiction over such lands could be claimed. As criticism of the doctrine mounted after the world wars, the doctrine fell into disuse, but the afterlives of its biological logic remained. Case in point is the trusteeship model that was devised to justify the widespread colonialism from the late 18th century onwards and later codified in Chapter XII of the UN Charter.[205]

These narratives excluded indigenous peoples from recognition under State regimes. International law's State-centredness sidelined them as actors. Illustratively, no indigenous peoples were consulted during the making of the International Covenant on Civil and Political Rights and the International Covenant on Economic, Social, and Cultural Rights.[206] It was only as formal decolonisation processes started to succeed in the 1960s that indigenous peoples started gaining visibility, but even then, they remained trapped in State-created grammars of sovereignty and national borders.

This chapter traces the historical struggles of indigenous peoples to be recognised as actors in international law. It introduces readers to indigenous peoples' encounters with international law, and the ways in which international law has responded to indigenous demands for legal status and sovereignty. It also traces the continuities between historical discourses and contemporary logics. The discussion then zooms into specific debates surrounding the identification of indigenous peoples and the contestations relating to rights enjoyed by indigenous peoples. The final part focuses on indigenous resistance to material and epistemic gatekeeping in international law.

B. INDIGENOUS PEOPLES AND THE STATE

Until the 1900s, international law adhered tightly to a European grammar of statehood.[207] As the club of statehood begrudgingly opened to members outside of

---

202 Ronald Takaki, *A Different Mirror: A History of Multicultural America* (Back Bay Books 2008) 34.

203 On Grotius and Vitoria, see González Hauck, § 1, in this textbook.

204 'Challenging Terra Nullius' (*National Library of Australia*) <www.nla.gov.au/digital-classroom/senior-secondary/cook-and-pacific/cook-legend-and-legacy/challenging-terra> accessed 16 July 2023.

205 On the world wars and their aftermath in terms of colonial reorganisation, see González Hauck, § 1, in this textbook.

206 International Covenant on Civil and Political Rights 1966 (adopted 16 December 1966, entered into force 23 March 1976), 999 UNTS 171; International Covenant on Economic, Social, and Cultural Rights 1966 (adopted 16 December 1966, entered into force 3 January 1976), 993 UNTS 3.

207 Ian Brownlie, *Principles of Public International Law* (4th edn, OUP 1990) 88–91 (discussing theories of recognition of statehood).

Europe,[208] international law's vocabulary evolved. In 1945, upon the setting up of the United Nations (UN), human rights, even in their rudimentary form, fiercely tugged at the statist form of international law.[209] However, it was not long before human rights were also fashioned by States as components of their prerogative. The early successes of decolonisation only effected a change in hands without disrupting these rubrics of statehood. As Kodjoe notes, the 'salt water thesis' ensured that decolonisation was not made available to enclaves of indigenous communities living within independent States.[210] The thesis posited that only colonies located across the 'salt-water' (or the ocean) could gain independence without disrupting the territorial integrity of existing nation-States, while independence for domestic non-self-governing territories had the potential to cause a severe disruption.[211] The first effort to codify indigenous peoples' rights, which was Convention No. 107 of 1957, adopted within the International Labour Organization (ILO), only paid lip service to the material ways in which indigenous peoples' demands militate against State sovereignty.[212] Convention 107 was adopted with a view to 'redress the isolation and marginalisation of indigenous peoples and to ensure that indigenous peoples benefited from development programmes'.[213] It follows Tzouvala's 'logic of improvement', which describes that certain actors were only seen as entitled to limited personhood, contingent on the Eurocentric and capitalist moulds of personhood. Rather than 'indigenous peoples', the Convention uses the term 'indigenous *populations*'. It thus employs a grammar of assimilation – cultural and legal – of indigenous identity within State units, and dresses this in the rhetoric of recognition of indigeneity.[214]

The tussle between indigeneity and statehood continued well until the 1990s. This was the period during which ILO's Convention No. 169 concerning Indigenous and Tribal peoples in Independent Countries was adopted in response to the 'developments in the situation of indigenous peoples', presumably related to the social capital acquired by the global indigenous peoples' movement in the 1970s.[215] The Convention was predicated on the need to consult indigenous peoples in development-related decisions. The Convention was more alive to the colonialist undertones of categories such as 'semi-tribal populations', unlike its predecessors.[216] Still, States expressed

---

208 On decolonisation, see González Hauck, § 1, in this textbook.

209 Helene Ruiz Fabri, 'Human Rights and State Sovereignty: Have the Boundaries Been Significantly Redrawn?' in P Alston and E MacDonald (eds), *Human Rights, Intervention, and the Use of Force* (OUP 2008) 33.

210 Wentworth Ofuatey-Kodjoe, *The Principle of Self-Determination in International Law* (Nellen 1977) 115, 119.

211 Audrey Jane Roy, *Sovereignty and Decolonization: Realizing Indigenous Self-Determination at the United Nations and in Canada* (thesis submitted to Cornell University 1998).

212 Indigenous and Tribal Populations Convention (adopted 26 June 1957, entered into force 2 June 1959), 328 UNTS 247.

213 Alexandra Xanthaki, 'The ILO Conventions' in Xanthaki (ed), *Indigenous Rights and United Nations Standards: Self-Determination, Culture and Land* (CUP 2007).

214 James Anaya, *Indigenous Peoples in International Law* (OUP 1996).

215 Convention No. 169 Concerning Indigenous and Tribal Peoples in Independent Countries (adopted 27 June 1989, entered into force 5 September 1991) 28 ILM 1832.

216 International Labor conference (75th session), Replies received and Commentaries' in International Labor Conference, Partial Revision of the Indigenous and Tribal Peoples Convention, 1957 (No. 107), Report VI(2), Question 9, 16–17 (Geneva 1988).

much apprehension about the use of terms traditionally associated with independent statehood, such as 'territory' and self-determination. States like Canada and United States feared that self-determination would enable invocations of external secession, thereby threatening State sovereignty.[217]

Even as the delegation of statehood function to non-State actors increased in contemporary times, it only facilitated a change of hands from imperial offices to postcolonial authorities, as Usha Natarajan rightly notes.[218] Postcolonial States, supported by international organisations like the World Bank, implemented industrial projects to meet economic growth metrics, without considering marginalised communities.[219] The vocabulary of development finds legs both in the Global North(s) as in the Global South(s) and compounds to displace indigenous communities. This is best illustrated by the fact that 40% of indigenous communities are displaced by development projects in India alone.[220] The focus on development started to push indigenous demands of sovereignty to the fringes, making small of the deeply spiritual, cultural, social, and economic relationship that indigenous peoples share with land.[221]

Development was also framed as 'removed' from the indigenous worldview, which the State frames as an interest in the preservation of the 'primitive'. Marooma Murmu writes about how indigenous dance and music – which are indeed central to indigenous existence – give birth to urban romanticised stereotypes of indigenous peoples as the 'Other'.[222] This rhetoric of backwardness is repeatedly invoked to remove indigenous peoples from decision-making spaces.

C. IDENTIFYING INDIGENOUS PEOPLES

In the 1960s, as formal decolonisation efforts succeeded,[223] consciousness of indigenous peoples' special cultural identity and their relationship with land grew. International indigenous mobilisation became more systematic and visible. The capstone was the International Non-Governmental Organization Conference on Discrimination

---

217 David Meren, 'Safeguarding Settler Colonialism in Geneva: Canada, Indigenous Rights, and ILO Convention No. 107 on the Protection and Integration of Indigenous Peoples (1957)' (2021) 102(2) CHR 102, 106.

218 Usha Natarajan, 'Decolonization in Third and Fourth Worlds: Synergy, Solidarity and Sustainability Through International Law' in Sujith Xavier and others (eds), *Decolonizing Law: Indigenous, Third World and Settler Perspectives* (Routledge 2021).

219 Sutapa Chattopadhyay, 'Postcolonial Development State, Appropriation of Nature, and Social Transformation of the Ousted Adivasis in the Narmada Valley, India' (2014) 25(4) Capitalism, Nature, Socialism 65, 74.

220 Sriram Parasuraman, *The Development Dilemma: Displacement in India* (Palgrave Macmillan 1999).

221 Irene Watson, 'Sovereign Spaces, Caring for Country, and the Homeless Position of Aboriginal Peoples' (2009) 108(1) South Atlantic Quarterly 27, 29; Lucy Claridge, 'Landmark Ruling Provides Major Victory to Kenya's Indigenous Endorois' (2010) Minority Rights Group International <https://minorityrights.org/wp-content/uploads/old-site-downloads/download-1009-Download-full-briefing-paper.pdf> accessed 16 July 2023.

222 Maroona Murmu, 'There Is No Caste Discrimination in West Bengal?' (*Radical Socialist*, 8 July 2019) <www.radicalsocialist.in/articles/national-situation/865-there-is-no-caste-discrimination-in-west-bengal> accessed 16 July 2023.

223 On decolonisation, see González Hauck, § 1, in this textbook.

against Indigenous Populations in the Americas in 1977,[224] where Western indigenous representatives discussed strategies to forge a transnational indigenous front and a set of sovereignty demands. From the late 1980s onwards, indigenous peoples won consultative status at several UN forums. This mobilisation started to bear fruit, with the UN starting to take steps to recognise indigeneity. The first of such steps was Special Rapporteur Martinez Cobo's report, which noted that indigenous populations were descendants of those who inhabited territories before settlers arrived. Such populations were known to have a distinct social, economic, and cultural identity– typically tied to their ancestral land.[225] Its focus, however, was on peoples disenfranchised by settler colonialism, understood as the occupation of territory and resources by foreign peoples and the displacement of indigenous legal orders.[226]

Scholars were quick to show that the Cobo conditions were misplaced for communities in Africa and Asia.[227] Since African colonies were fully occupied before colonisation, imperial force was exerted through what Kenyan scholar Ngugi wa Thiong'o calls the 'cultural bomb' that 'annihilate[s] a people's belief in their names, in their languages, in their environment, in their heritage of struggle, in their unity, in their capacities and ultimately in themselves', thus 'mak[ing] them want to identify with that which is furthest removed from themselves'.[228] This hybrid form of colonialism benefited the African elites, who led decolonisation movements and were able to successfully occupy the positions of authority previously held by imperialists. Because of this complicated model of colonialism, tracing indigeneity in Africa is far from easy. Most people can draw links with pre-colonial inhabitants.[229] The same is true of indigeneity in Asia, where everyone has an equal claim to being indigenous.[230]

In response, more reflexive definitions of indigeneity emerged. In 1989, ILO Convention No. 169 utilised the term 'peoples'.[231] Peoples was a nod to the autonomy of indigenous communities and their demands for political and legal sovereignty. The Convention also differentiated between tribal peoples and indigenous peoples, with the former being units that are socially and culturally distinct from the majority and

224 Ingrid Washinawatok, 'International Emergence: Twenty-One Years at the United Nations Symposium' (1998) 3 City University of New York Law Review 41.
225 UNCHR Thirty-sixth session, 'Final report submitted by Special Rapporteur Jose Martinez Cobo' (30 September 1983) E/CN.4/Sub.2/1983/21/Add.8; Chidi Oguamanam, 'Indigenous Peoples and International Law: The Making of a Regime' (2004) 30 Queen's Law Journal, 348, 352.
226 Adelaja O Odukoya, 'Settler and Non-Settler Colonialism in Africa' in Samuel Ojo Oloruntoba and Toyin Falola (eds), The Palgrave Handbook of African Politics, Governance and Development (Palgrave Macmillan 2018).
227 Kealeboga Bojosi and George Mukundi Wachira, 'Protecting Indigenous Peoples in Africa: An Analysis of the Approach of the African Commission on Human and People's Rights' (2006) 6 African Human Rights Law Journal 382.
228 Ngugi Thiong'o, Petals of Blood (Penguin Books 1977).
229 Dorothy Hodgson, 'Comparative Perspectives on the Indigenous Rights Movement in Africa and the Americas' (2002) 104(4) American Anthropologist 1037, 1041.
230 Bhangya Bhukya and Sujatha Surepally, 'Unveiling the World of the Nomadic Tribes and Denotified Tribes: An Introduction' (2021) 56 Economic and Political Weekly 36.
231 Convention 169, article 2.

organised by customary rules of clanship and being.[232] The UN Working Group on Indigenous Populations adopted a different approach and, in 1993, chose not to define indigeneity because 'historically, indigenous peoples have suffered, from definitions imposed by others'.[233]

Nonetheless, indigeneity holds powerful social meaning. It has become 'a shared experience of loss of forests, alienation of land, displacements by development projects, and much more',[234] allowing for cross-border indigenous mobilisation.

D. RIGHTS OF INDIGENOUS PEOPLES

I. NATURE OF RIGHTS-HOLDERS

Efforts to garner international recognition of indigenous identity have predominantly employed the vocabulary of rights. However, formal recognition of indigenous peoples' rights was slow. ILO Convention No. 107 of 1957 recognised the economic, social, and cultural rights of indigenous peoples. Yet, these rights were contingent on the assimilation of indigenous peoples into the dominant population, and they were individual rights by design. Article 27 of the ICCPR[235] on cultural rights, for instance, has been widely criticised for exclusively recognising cultural rights of 'persons' belonging to minorities, instead of groups as a whole.[236] Moreover, the *travaux préparatoires* of the Covenants suggests that the term 'minorities' was understood in a restrictive sense as well-defined stable groups that enjoyed a distinct culture and were numerically disadvantaged.[237] The cultural rights protections granted to minorities were not intended to even mildly threaten majority regimes.[238] It has been suggested that indigenous peoples were deliberately kept removed from the drafting of the Covenants because States feared 'that this might cause political destabilization' and lend credibility to secession demands.[239] With time, there was gradual recognition of the collective dimension of indigenous peoples' rights, an important step being international jurisprudence acknowledging this dimension.[240]

---

232 Ibid.

233 UNCHR (Sub-Commission), 'Report by Erica-Irene Daes on the Protection of the heritage of indigenous peoples' (1997) E/C'N.4/Sub.2/1995/26.

234 Gladson Dungdung, 'The Pathalgari Movement for Adivasi Autonomy: A Revolution of India's Indigenous Peoples' (*IWGIA*, 11 March 2022) <www.iwgia.org/en/india/4613-the-pathalgari-movement-for-adivasi-autonomy-a-revolution-of-india%E2%80%99s-indigenous-peoples.html> accessed 16 July 2023.

235 International Covenant on Civil and Political Rights (adopted on 16 December 1966, entered into force 23 March 1976), 999 UNTS 171.

236 Rudiger Wolfrum, 'The Protection of Indigenous Peoples in International Law' (1999) 59 HJIL 371.

237 Commission of Human Rights (6th session), (1950) A/2929, paragraph 184; 8th session (1952), 9th session (1953).

238 UNGA, 'Report of the Third Committee' UNGAOR 16th session, UN Doc. A/5000 (1961), paragraph 123.

239 Rebecca Tsosie, 'Tribalism, Constitutionalism, and Cultural Pluralism: Where Do Indigenous Peoples Fit within Civil Society?' (2003) 5 University of Pennsylvania Journal of Constitutional Law 357, 376.

240 Lubicon Band in *Ominayak v. Canada* CCPR/C/38/D/167/1984 (1990), Ayyamas in *Poma Poma v. Peru*, CCPR/C/95/D/1457/2006 (2009), Sami of the Nordic countries in *Lansman v. Finland*, CCPR/

II. SELF-DETERMINATION

The recognition of self-determination has been tied to the recognition of 'peoples'.[241] In the specific context of indigenous peoples, the 2007 UN Declaration on the Rights of Indigenous Peoples (UNDRIP) clarified that the right to self-determination does not include secession.[242] States like Australia, New Zealand, Canada, and the United States did not sign the Declaration, citing their discomfort with recognising the right to self-determination of indigenous peoples. Although these States have now reversed their position, their discomfort with self-determination has not dampened. Tribunals have continued to be uncomfortable with recognising indigenous peoples' right to external self-determination. The *Poma Poma v Peru* case before the Human Rights Committee is a case in point.[243] The Committee declared the case to be inadmissible, arguing that self-determination was not an individual right as required by the Optional Protocol. Similarly, in the other cases where self-determination has been invoked, the Committee has chosen instead to situate the facts within other rights.

III. RIGHTS OF NATURE

Recognition of indigeneity challenges the anthropocentric grammar of rights. In several indigenous cosmologies, humans are only custodians and symbiotic partners within nature. Inspired by these epistemologies, the Ecuadorian Constitution codified the rights of Pacha Mama, the Andean earth goddess as known in the Quichua and Aymara indigenous languages, in 2008.[244] The Constitution now commits to protecting the *sumak kawsay* (the 'good way of living'), which also reinforces the State's obligations towards restoration and preservation of the functions of nature.[245] States like Bolivia and Uganda have followed suit.[246] Importantly, the Bolivian Constitution does not entrench the rights *of nature*, but frames such rights as stewardship of humans towards nature and 'other living

---

C/52D/511/1992 (1994).; *Centre for Minority Rights Development (CEMIRIDE) on behalf of the Endorois Community v. Kenya*, Comm. No. 276/2003, Afr. Comm'n on Human & Peoples' Rights (2009). See also Elizabeth Ashamu, 'Centre for Minority Rights Development (Kenya) and Minority Rights Group International on Behalf of Endorois Welfare Council v Kenya: A Landmark Decision from the African Commission' (2011) 55(2) Journal of African Law 300, 311.

241 On self-determination, see Bak McKenna, § 2.4, in this textbook.

242 Jackie Hartley, Paul Joffe, and Jennifer Preston (eds), *Realizing the UN Declaration on the Rights of Indigenous Peoples: Triumph, Hope, and Action* (Purich 2010); and Sheryl Lightfoot, *Global Indigenous Politics: A Subtle Revolution* (Routledge 2018), notably chapter 2.

243 *Poma Poma v. Peru*, CCPR/C/95/D/1457/2006 (2009), 13.

244 Constitucion de 2008, República del Ecuador (ECD) <https://pdba.georgetown.edu/Constitutions/Ecuador/english08.html> accessed 16 July 2023.

245 María Valeria Berros, 'The Constitution of the Republic of Ecuador: Pachamama Has Rights' (*Environment & Society Portal*, 2015) <www.environmentandsociety.org/arcadia/constitution-republic-ecuador-pachamama-has-rights> accessed 16 July 2023.

246 'Rights of Nature gain ground in Uganda's Legal System' (*Gaia Foundation*, 2019) <https://gaiafoundation.org/rights-of-nature-gain-ground-in-ugandas-legal-system/> accessed 16 July 2023.

things'.[247] Rights of nature are contained in another statute.[248] In India, rights of nature are recognised in a patchwork of judicial pronouncements.[249] In other States, rivers and national parks have been recognised as legal persons. Case in point is the Whanganui River in New Zealand,[250] and the legal status of the Sukhna River near India's northeast border with Nepal.[251] Such a reorientation is intended to better serve claims against polluting projects that threaten to damage ecologies. However, the retention of the language of rights – often alien to indigenous epistemologies – still allows balancing exercises in favour of extractivist projects and is furthermore sometimes used for 'whitewashing' purposes.[252]

IV. RIGHT TO FREE, PRIOR, AND INFORMED CONSENT

The right to free, prior, and informed consent is chiefly concerned with the quality of consent given by communities before development projects are implemented. Free denotes the lack of intimidation or coercion, prior refers to consent taken well in advance of a project, and informed refers to the range of facts offered (nature, size, impact, permissions of project) prior to obtaining consent.[253] The mode of obtaining consent must be aligned with the customary laws of indigenous peoples. Although typically consent is understood as an obligation of conduct, there are some regimes which stress 'obtaining' consent, turning it into an obligation of result.

V. INDIGENOUS RIGHT TO LAND

Historically, sovereignty was understood as a conceptual instrument to reclaim lands and natural resources. The right to land was initially situated within the rubric of property rights. However, property rights hinge on grammars of individuality, ownership, and saleability. For indigenous peoples, the relationship to land is one of spirituality, less one of ownership.[254]

---

247 Paola Villavicencio Calzadilla and Louis J Kotzé, 'Living in Harmony with Nature? A Critical Appraisal of the Rights of Mother Earth in Bolivia' (2018) 7(3) TEL 397, 402.

248 Law 071 of the Rights of Mother Earth, 21 December 2010 (BO) <http://181.224.152.72/~embajad5/wp-content/uploads/2017/12/rights-of-mother-earth.pdf> accessed 16 July 2023.

249 See the Madras High Court's decision covered here: Katie Surma, 'Indian Court Rules That Nature Has Legal Status on Par with Humans – and That Humans Are Required to Protect It' (*Inside Climate*, 4 May 2022) <https://insideclimatenews.org/news/04052022/india-rights-of-nature/> accessed 16 July 2023.

250 Whanganui River Deed of Settlement, 5 August 2014 <www.govt.nz/treaty-settlementdocuments/whanganui-iwi> accessed 16 July 2023. For a discussion, see Catherine I Magallanes, 'Reflecting on Cosmology and Environmental Protection: Maori Cultural Rights in Aotearoa New Zealand' in Anna Grear and Louis J Kotzé (eds), *Research Handbook on Human Rights and the Environment* (Edward Elgar 2015), 274, 291.

251 *Sukhna Enclave Residents Welfare Association and Ors. v. State of Punjab and Ors.*, CWP No.18253 of 2009 & other connected petitions, High Court of Punjab and Haryana.

252 Paola Villavicencio Calzadilla and Louis J Kotzé, 'Living in Harmony with Nature? A Critical Appraisal of the Rights of Mother Earth in Bolivia' (2018) 7(3) TEL 397.

253 OHCHR, 'Free, Prior and Informed Consent of Indigenous Peoples' (2015) <www.ohchr.org/sites/default/files/Documents/Issues/IPeoples/FreePriorandInformedConsent.pdf> accessed 16 July 2023.

254 Alexandra Xanthaki, 'Indigenous Rights and United Nations Standards: Self-Determination, Culture and Land' in Alexandra Xanthaki (ed), *Indigenous Rights and United Nations Standards* (CUP 2007), chapter 5.

Today, land is increasingly being read into cultural rights. In General Comment No. 23, the UN Human Rights Committee observed that 'culture manifests in various forms, including a particular way of life associated with the use of land resources'.[255] The draft general comment on the right to land also confirms this linkage.[256]

VI. FOURTH WORLD APPROACHES TO INTERNATIONAL LAW

The 'Fourth-World' movement (FWAIL)[257] was born out of the failure of TWAIL[258] to combat the predatory role that international law plays in perpetuating violence against indigenous peoples. Fourth World approaches question the basic assumptions underlying international law, including the idea of the State being an impartial guarantor, the dominance of the English and French languages as the vernacular of international law, or even the criteria based on which personhood is recognised. Fourth World approaches push for the recognition of non-anthropocentric personhoods – of land, of nature, of ancestors, and of ecosystems. Such approaches also expose the colonial motivations behind diminishing the personhood of indigenous peoples. At its root, this opposition stems from a basic difference in epistemology. That is, they highlight the fact that there are different ways of thinking about international law and all these different ways are equally credible and valid.

VII. FRAMEWORK OF RELATIONALITY

Indigenous epistemologies – while incredibly diverse – share certain tenets, the first of which is relationality. 'Relationality' has been coined in answer to the individual-focus of Western liberalism. It centres the relationships each knowledge producer shares with their kin and with nature.[259]

In fact, extractivism demands and sometimes even imposes relationships, eroding the reality of relationships and therefore also the principle of relationality.[260] In practical terms, relationality requires a serious introspection of one's positionality and privilege, and understanding how to surrender and *listen* to indigenous co-collaborators. From a position of doing, the researcher moves to a position of listening. Listening, not only in the biological sense, but as Cahill notes, listening in the affective sense.[261]

---

255 CCPR General Comment No. 23: article 27 (Rights of Minorities), (1994) CCPR/C/21/Rev.1/Add.5.
256 CESCR Draft General Comment No. 26: Land and Economic, Social and Cultural Rights, (2022) E/C.12/ GC/26.
257 The term has been coined by George Manuel and Michael Posluns. See George Manuel and Michael Posluns, *The Fourth World: An Indian Reality* (Minnesota Press 1974)
258 On TWAIL, see González Hauck, § 3.2, in this textbook.
259 Lauren Tynan, 'What Is Relationality? Indigenous Knowledges, Practices and Responsibilities with Kin' (2021) 28(4) Cultural Geographies 597, 602.
260 Linda Tuhiwai Smith, *Decolonizing Methodologies: Research and Indigenous Peoples* (Zed Books 2012); Eve Tuck and Wayne Yang, 'Decolonization Is Not a Metaphor' (2012) 1(1) Decolonization: Indigeneity, Education & Society 1.
261 Caitlin Cahill, 'The Personal Is Political: Developing New Subjectivities Through Participatory Action Research' (2007) 14(3) Gender, Place & Culture 267, 272.

VIII. SACRED AND SECULAR

Spirituality is central in indigenous worldviews, informing rationality and meaning-making.[262] All relationships and all beings are endowed with spirituality – whether it is the land or one's knowledge. Spirituality, in Western legal discourse, is often romanticised and treated as less than scientific.[263] In their piece, Townsend and Townsend critique how indigenous elders' articulations of their spiritual relationships with territory and nature were not seen as relevant to more scientific assessments about territory apportionment and environmental rights for which an external expert was invited.[264]

IX. RECIPROCITY AS EPISTEMOLOGY

Several indigenous epistemologies rest on the notion of reciprocity. As Kovach notes,

> they say that we traditionally knew about portal, the doorway, how to get knowledge and that it was brought to the people by sharing, by community forums, by sitting in circles, by engaging in ceremony, by honouring your relationship to the spirit. When we do that, the spirit will reciprocate and we will be given what we are needed.[265]

Reciprocity applies to insiders and outsiders and those in-between. Indigenous cultures – unlike Western epistemologies – do not attach neutrality to people situated outside indigenous cultures. They see all worlds as being interconnected and each individual and community responsible for changes affecting peoples everywhere. Internal positions are equally problematised. As Linda Tuhiwai-Smith notes, insiders often take their familiarity for granted. However, indigenous epistemologies pin critical reflexivity on insiders, too.[266] These ideals are not only embedded in stories and myths, but also in songs, rituals, and dance.[267]

E. CONCLUSION

This chapter illuminates how international law was born out of and profited from the violent dispossession of indigenous peoples. It also examines the long-standing struggles

---

262 Ross Hoffman, 'Respecting Aboriginal Knowing in the Academy' (2013) 9(3) AlterNative: An International Journal of Indigenous Peoples 189.

263 Virginius Xaxa, 'Decolonising Tribal Studies in India' (*Raiot,* 2021) <https://raiot.in/decolonising-tribal-studies-in-india-prof-virginius-xaxa/> accessed 16 July 2023.

264 Dina Lupin Townsend and Leo Townsend, 'Epistemic Injustice and Indigenous Peoples in the Inter-American Human Rights System' (2021) 35(2) Social Epistemology 147.

265 Margaret Kovach, *Indigenous Methodologies: Characteristics, Conversations and Contexts* (University of Toronto Press 2009), 41; Kathleen Absolon, *Kaandossiwin: How We Come to Know* (Fernwood 2011) 55.

266 Linda Smith, *Decolonizing Methodologies* (University of Otago Press 1999) 13.

267 Shay Welch, *The Phenomenology of a Performative Knowledge System: Dancing with Native American Epistemology* (Springer International 2019); Sowvendra Shekhar Hansda, *The Adivasi Will Not Dance: Stories* (Speaking Tiger 2017).

organised by indigenous peoples to gain personhood in international law. In so doing, it also highlights the incongruities within the global fraternity of indigenous peoples. The later parts of the chapter unpack the bundle of rights that indigenous peoples enjoy. This discussion also shows how certain rights such as the right to land often clash with indigenous ways of thinking, because they place emphasis on materiality and individuality over spirituality.

BOX 7.2.2 Further Readings

Further Readings

- C Oguamanam, 'Indigenous Peoples and International Law: The Making of a Regime', (2005) 30 QLJ 348

- S Lightfoot, 'The Declaration on the Rights of Indigenous Peoples' in Sheryl Lightfoot (ed), *Global Indigenous Politics* (Routledge 2016)

- K Absolon, *Kaandossiwin: How We Come to Know: Indigenous Re-Search Methodologies* (Fernwood 2022)

- SH Venne, *Our Elders Understand Our Rights: Evolving International Law Regarding Indigenous Peoples* (Theytus 1998)

- J Anaya, *Indigenous Peoples Under International Law* (2nd edn, OUP 2004)

---

§ § §

§ 7.3 INTERNATIONAL ORGANISATIONS

GRAŻYNA BARANOWSKA, VILJAM ENGSTRÖM, AND TAMSIN PHILLIPA PAIGE

BOX 7.3.1 Required Knowledge and Learning Objectives

Required knowledge: Sources of International Law; Subjects and Actors in International Law; States

Learning objectives: Understanding the concept of international organisation; varieties of international organisations and their categorisation; organisations as actors in international law and as international legal persons; the autonomous nature of international organisations; concepts of legal personality and legal powers/competences; main features of the United Nations and its structure and function; the law of the United Nations and the fundamental principles of public international law in the UN Charter.

A. INTRODUCTION

It has been said that everything we do is today in one way or another dealt with by an international organisation. International organisations have become an established way of structuring inter-State relations, today outnumbering, in any definition, the number of States. This chapter identifies basic features of international organisations, highlights elements of their autonomy, and explains fundamental concepts relating to organisations. It also introduces the United Nations (UN) as the paramount organisation of the international legal system.

B. IDENTIFYING AN INTERNATIONAL ORGANISATION

I. DEFINING AN INTERNATIONAL ORGANISATION

While international organisations influence many aspects of our life – they regulate our food,[268] how we travel,[269] and who delivers our mail[270] – defining them appears challenging. The ILC's Draft articles on the responsibility of international organisations defines international organisations as established by a treaty or another instrument governed by international law and possessing international legal personality. The Draft

---

268 Food and Agriculture Organization of the United Nations <www.fao.org/home/en> accessed 18 June 2023.

269 World Tourism Organization <www.fao.org/home/en> accessed 18 June 2023.

270 Universal Postal Union <www.upu.int/en/Home/> accessed 18 June 2023.

articles further stipulate that such organisations may include other entities as members in addition to States.[271]

Several characteristics can be identified that – while not providing an exhaustive definition – provide a 'useful point of departure' for identifying international organisations. These include (1) being created by States, (2) being based on a treaty, and (3) consisting of at least one organ with a distinct will. All these characteristics are fluid and raise further discussion. For example, international organisations can be jointly created by States and international organisations; not all organisations are based on a treaty but, for example, a decision of the UN General Assembly (UNGA) or domestic parliaments.[272]

II. CATEGORISING INTERNATIONAL ORGANISATIONS

1. Intergovernmental – Supranational – Non-governmental

International organisations are traditionally understood to consist of States. As such, a defining feature of international organisations as actors in international law is that they are 'intergovernmental'. The notion 'intergovernmental' can also be used to indicate a distinction to other forms of organisations. As a point of departure, an intergovernmental organisation does not limit the sovereignty of States.[273] Although the constituent instrument of an intergovernmental organisation is a treaty, and as such may contain certain obligations for the member States (e.g. financial obligations), most organisations cannot adopt legally binding decisions. One exception is the UN, discussed below. However, the UN would still not qualify as a supranational organisation.

Supranational organisations differ from intergovernmental organisations in respect of their regulatory authority. The European Union is currently the only example of a truly supranational organisation, exercising a range of law-making, adjudicative, and enforcement powers.[274] As stated by the Court of Justice of the European Union, by becoming members, States have created an organisation of 'unlimited duration, having its own institutions, its own personality, its own legal capacity and capacity of representation on the international plane and, more particularly, real powers stemming from a limitation of sovereignty or a transfer of powers'.[275] This 'limitation' means that EU legislative measures can have direct effect in the legal orders of EU member States.

A common way to distinguish between organisations is to scrutinise the body of law that governs the organisation's activities: only those entities are international organisations that are governed by international law. Consequently, organisations whose activities are

---

271 ILC, 'Responsibility of States for Internationally Wrongful Acts' (53rd session 23 April–1 June and 2 July–10 August 2001) UN Doc A/RES/56/83 Annex.

272 Jan Klabbers, *An Introduction to International Organizations Law* (CUP 2022) 6–12.

273 On sovereignty, see Green, § 7.1, in this textbook.

274 Peter L Lindseth, 'Supranational Organizations' in Jacob Katz Cogan, Ian Hurd, and Ian Johnstone (eds), *The Oxford Handbook of International Organizations* (OUP 2016).

275 Case 6/64 *Flaminio Costa v E.N.E.L* [1964] ECR 585, 593.

governed by domestic law are considered non-governmental organisations.[276] By way of examples, the International Committee of the Red Cross is governed by Swiss law, and Amnesty International by British law. Membership in non-governmental organisations is also withheld for individuals. This does not mean that non-governmental organisations would not perform important tasks in the practice of international law. This reflects the trend of increasingly recognising an ever more diverse set of actors.[277] Moreover, organisations can transition from non-governmental to intergovernmental.

BOX 7.3.2 Example: Transition From Non-governmental to Intergovernmental

The International Commission on Missing Persons was initially established in Sarajevo in 1996 to help to account for missing persons during the Yugoslavian wars. The Commission gradually expanded its mandate and sphere of activities. Eventually, its status changed in 2014, when five States signed a treaty and conferred upon it the status of an intergovernmental organisation.[278]

---

2. Global/Open – Non-global/Closed

Another useful distinction can be made between global and non-global organisations. In global or open organisations all States are eligible to become members, such as the UN or the World Health Organization. To the contrary, non-global or closed organisations restrict their membership in one way or another. Examples include regional organisations such as the Organization of American States and the African Union, organisations based on a common background such as the Organisation of Islamic Cooperation or Organisation Internationale de la Francophonie, or organisations where membership is restricted to a particular function, such as the Organization of the Petroleum Exporting Countries or the North Atlantic Treaty Organization.

BOX 7.3.3 Example: Membership in Closed Organisations

The restricted membership of closed organisations need not be carved in stone. For example, Armenia, Azerbaijan, and Georgia were initially found ineligible to partake in the Council of Europe as they were considered geographically part of Asia. Nevertheless, they were eventually admitted at the turn of the century.[279]

---

276 Klabbers (n 275) 7. On NGOs, see He Chi, § 7.6, in this textbook.
277 On the pluralisation of actors, see Engström, § 7, in this textbook.
278 Agreement on the status and functions of the International Commission on Missing Persons (adopted 15 December 2014, entered into force 14 May 2015) article 1(1) stating: 'The International Commission on Missing Persons is hereby established as an international organisation'.
279 Henry G Schermers and Niels Blokker, *International Institutional Law* (Brill/Nijhoff 2018) 57–59.

3. Political – Technical

While most international organisations are established to perform a specific function, the limited scope and nature of the tasks of some organisations make them appear as dealing with predominantly technical issues. For example, the Universal Postal Union regulates global postal services. Instead of diplomats, States usually delegate experts to meetings of such organisations. By contrast, 'political' organisations may discuss any matter of global governance, and State delegations usually consist of diplomats and politicians, the paradigm example being the UNGA (further discussed below). At the same time, the distinction between political and technical organisations can be difficult to uphold.[280]

BOX 7.3.4 Example: Technical Versus Political Organisations

Seemingly technical questions can turn out to be intensely political. The Universal Postal Union's tasks may be thought of as rather technical. However, in 2019 the United States threatened to withdraw from the Union claiming that China is taking advantage of its developing country status within the organisation.[281]

C. INTERNATIONAL ORGANISATIONS AS AUTONOMOUS ACTORS

I. LEGAL PERSONALITY

Although international organisations have been created by treaty already since the late 19th century, it was only with the creation of the League of Nations and the International Labour Organization that the issue of legal personality of organisations came to be discussed.[282] International organisations are established legal subjects of international law.[283] This was confirmed by the ICJ in the Reparation for Injuries Advisory Opinion in 1949.[284]

The legal personality of organisations has two dimensions: personality in domestic law and in international law. The constituent treaties of international organisations commonly contain a provision granting the organisation legal personality under the

---

280 Schermers and Blokker (n 282) 62–63.

281 'Trump Pulls US Out of UN Postal Scheme on China Price Concerns' (*The Guardian*, 17 October 2018) <www.theguardian.com/us-news/2018/oct/17/trump-universal-postal-union-withdraw-foreign-postal-rates> accessed 8 August 2023.

282 On treaties, see Fiskatoris and Svicevic, § 6.1, in this textbook. On the history of international organisations, see Bob Reinalda, *Routledge History of International Organizations: From 1815 to the Present Day* (Taylor & Francis 2009)

283 On the concept of legal subject, see Engström, § 7, in this textbook.

284 *Reparation for Injuries* (n 7).

domestic law of its member States.[285] Like all provisions of the constituent instrument, this grant of domestic legal personality only applies in relation to the members of the organisation. Explicit provisions on international legal personality, on its part, is a rarity especially in open international organisations, whereas such provisions may be found in closed organisations.[286]

While the question of legal personality may seem rather theoretical, in practice the absence of legal personality has proved problematic as it can prevent an organisation, for example, from concluding agreements or renting buildings.[287] Due to the lack of legal personality, for example, the Organization for Security and Co-operation in Europe has faced several practical obstacles.[288]

II. COMPETENCES/POWERS

The question of personality and powers are so closely intertwined that they may sometimes be difficult to distinguish from one another. This has to do with the fact that the exercise of powers is an inherent element by which legal personality manifests itself.[289] An organisation performs its tasks by exercising legal powers. As these powers are organisation specific, they can range from being very limited to exceeding the powers of its member States. There are very few organisations that can make decisions that become directly binding on member States (basically the European Union, and the UN Security Council [UNSC]). Most exercises of powers, in other words, gain their regulatory impact through other means.[290]

The main source of the legal powers of an organisation is the conferral or attribution by members as provided in its constituent instrument.[291] The basic rule governing acts of organisations is that they must remain within the confines of their attributed powers.[292] This principle is explicit for example in the Treaty on the European Union, article 5.[293] Similar provisions are explicit in constituent instruments of several organisations.

---

285 See for example Charter of the United Nations 1945 (adopted 26 June 1945, entered into force 24 October 1945) 1 UNTS XVI article 104; Consolidated version of the Treaty on the Functioning of the European Union, OJ C 326 (adopted 13 December 2007, entered into force 26 October 2012) (TFEU) article 335.

286 See for example TFEU (n 19), article 47, and Agreement Establishing the African Development Bank (adopted 4 August 1963, entered into force 10 September 1964) 510 UNTS 3, article 10.

287 Schermers and Blokker (n 282).

288 Jan Klabbers, 'Institutional Ambivalence by Design: Soft Organizations in International Law' (2001) 70 *NJIL* 403; Isabelle Ley, 'Legal Personality for the OSCE?: Some Observations at the Occasion of the Recent Conference on the Legal Status of the OSCE' (*Völkerrechtsblog*, 8 August 2016) <https://voelkerrechtsblog. org/legal-personality-for-the-osce/> accessed 8 August 2023.

289 Klabbers (n 275).

290 José E Alvarez, *International Organizations as Law-Makers* (OUP 2005).

291 Dan Sarooshi, *International Organizations and Their Exercise of Sovereign Powers* (OUP 2007).

292 *Jurisdiction of the European Commission of the Danube* (Advisory Opinion), PCIJ Rep Series B No 14, 64.

293 Article 5 states: '1. The use of Union competences is governed by the principles of subsidiarity and proportionality. 2. Under the principle of conferral, the Union shall act only within the limits of the

In addition to explicitly conferred powers, organisations can also exercise
such 'implied powers' as are necessary for the performance of their duties.[294]
An express embodiment of this idea can be found in the Treaty on the
Functioning of the European Union, article 352.[295] The element of attribution/
conferral emphasises that organisations do not, unlike States, possess a general
competence (also called the 'principle of speciality'). However, the 'necessities
of international life' may reveal the need for the exercise of implied powers that
are not expressly provided for in the constituent instrument.[296] As long as an act
of an organisation is necessary for achieving the purpose of the organisation, and
there is political agreement on that necessity, such an act is not *ultra vires* (Latin:
'beyond the powers'). The two doctrines are tools for constructing and adjusting
the functions and tasks of organisations in accordance with the desires of their
membership.[297]

The commonality of certain powers, such as the capacity to conclude treaties and to
bring international claims, has tempted some academics to locate those powers in the
mere possession of legal personality. There is a bulk of powers, in this logic, that have
become customary, which means that as soon as an organisation comes into existence,
it would enjoy those powers.[298] In the 'inherent powers approach' organisations are
potentially free, like States, to perform any sovereign act which they are in a practical
position to perform.[299] In practice, claims to inherent powers are more common in
the context of international courts and tribunals. However, the distinction to implied
powers is in this practice not always consistent.[300] In the context of international
organisations, the more common position is that particular powers cannot be derived
from the mere possession of legal personality.

III. OTHER ASPECTS OF THE AUTONOMY OF INTERNATIONAL ORGANISATIONS

While legal powers may be the most visible way by which organisations assert an
autonomy, it is not the only expression of it. Organisations and their employees enjoy

---

competences conferred upon it by the Member States in the Treaties to attain the objectives set out therein'.
Consolidated version of the Treaty on European Union (adopted 13 December 2007, entered into force 26
October 2012) OJ C 326.

294 *Reparation for Injuries* (n 7).

295 Article 352(1) TFEU (n 19) states: 'If action by the Union should prove necessary, within the framework of
the policies defined in the Treaties, to attain one of the objectives set out in the Treaties, and the Treaties have
not provided the necessary powers, the Council . . . shall adopt the appropriate measures'.

296 *Legality of the Use by a State of Nuclear Weapons in Armed Conflict* (Advisory Opinion) [1996] ICJ Rep 66.

297 Viljam Engström, *Constructing the Powers of International Institutions* (Martinus Nijhoff 2012).

298 On customary law, see Victor Stoica, § 6.2, in this textbook.

299 As argued by Finn Seyersted, *Common Law of International Organizations* (Martinus Nijhoff 2008).

300 Viljam Engström, 'Article 4. Legal Status and Powers of the Court' in Mark Klamberg (ed), *The Commentary
on the Law of the International Criminal Court* <https://cilrap-lexsitus.org/en/clicc/4> accessed 8 August 2023.

immunities which secure a degree of physical autonomy.[301] To act independently of any particular State interest and free from political pressure, organisations and staff commonly enjoy those immunities that are necessary for the performance of the functions of the organisation.[302] In respect of membership, the autonomy of organisations expresses itself, for example, through a right to include and exclude States. There is no automatic right of States to become members in any organisation of choice. Also membership rights, such as the right to participate in the work of organs and/or the right to vote, can be restricted by the organisation.[303]

BOX 7.3.5 Example: Losing Membership Rights

A member that acts in breach of the constituent instrument of an organisation may be expelled from that organisation. As a reaction to the Russian aggression against Ukraine in 2022, the Committee of Ministers of the Council of Europe decided on the 16 March 2022 to exclude the Russian Federation as of that date from the organization (in anticipation of which The Russian Fedaration withdrew from the organisation the preceding day).[304] Although the same mechanism exists in the UN Charter,[305] it has never been used. Instead, the UN has used other means towards States that act in violation of the Charter, such as withholding credentials.[306]

D. THE UNITED NATIONS

I. OVERVIEW

The core goal of the UN is the maintenance of peace. The horrors of World War I and World War II are reflected in the preamble of the UN Charter, its foundational treaty, where the first stated aim of the organisation is 'to save succeeding generations from the scourge of war, which twice in our lifetime has brought untold sorrow to [human]

---

301 On immunities, see Walton, § 11, in this textbook.
302 And as defined in separate treaties. See for example UN Charter (n 288), article 105(1), and Convention on the Privileges and Immunities of the United Nations (adopted 13 February 1946, entry into force 17 September 1946, 1 UNTS 15.
303 UN Charter (n 288), article 19.
304 Council of Europe, 'The Russian Federation Is Excluded from the Council of Europe' (16 March 2022) <www.coe.int/en/web/portal/-/the-russian-federation-is-excluded-from-the-council-of-europe> accessed 8 August 2023.
305 Article 6 of the UN Charter stating: 'A Member of the United Nations which has persistently violated the Principles contained in the present Charter may be expelled from the Organization by the General Assembly upon the recommendation of the Security Council'.
306 Viljam Engström, 'Credentials and the Politics of Representation: What's in It for the UN?' (*EJILtalk*, 11 October 2021) <www.ejiltalk.org/credentials-and-the-politics-of-representation-whats-in-it-for-the-un/> accessed 9 August 2023.

kind'.[307] This overarching goal is further reflected in article 1(1) of the Charter, where it is stated that the purpose of the UN is 'to maintain international peace and security'.[308] Article 1 defines as goals of the UN in the following terms: maintenance of peace by collective measures and settlement of disputes; development of friendly relations, equal rights and self-determination; promoting human rights; and international cooperation.[309] Whereas the primary goal of maintaining peace is a prerogative of the UN main bodies, as stated by the ICJ in its *Nuclear Weapons* opinion,[310] in the pursuit of the broader set of goals the UN not only works through the core organisation but also the broader UN system.

II. THE DRAFTING HISTORY AND LEGAL STATUS OF THE CHARTER

The term 'United Nations' was first coined on 1 January 1942 in the 'Declaration by United Nations',[311] which pledged to uphold the purposes and principles of the Atlantic Charter (a joint statement between Churchill and Roosevelt on 14 August 1941).[312] At the close of World War II, this term became the basis of the new organisation to replace the League of Nations. The UN was formed through the drafting of the UN Charter at the San Francisco Conference in April 1945, with 50 nations present, and Poland signing once a government was formed to constitute the 51st original member State.[313] As of June 2023, the UN has 193 member States.[314] The volume of membership gives it near universal status, and also gives rise to a strong argument that the principles enshrined in the Charter should be considered customary law. The Charter is a multilateral treaty, binding upon its member States, that creates a permanent venue for diplomatic relations. The UN Charter establishes the basic structure and procedures of the organisation. The most forceful tool at the disposal of the UN is the binding nature of Chapter VII resolutions by the UNSC, when it finds that there is a threat to international peace.[315] Today the organisation's main areas of work are international peace and security, the protection of human rights, humanitarian aid, sustainable development and climate action, and upholding international law.

---

307 UN Charter (n 288), preamble.
308 UN Charter (n 288), article 1(1).
309 UN Charter (n 288), article 1(2)–(4).
310 *Legality of the Use* (n 299).
311 Dag Hammarskjöld Library, '1942–26 Nations Declare Themselves United' <https://un-library.tumblr.com/post/108736439924/1942-26-nations-declare-themselves-united> accessed 24 January 2022.
312 Dag Hammarskjöld Library, '1941 – A Special Relationship Helps Forge the Beginnings of the United Nations' <https://un-library.tumblr.com/post/108647995769/1941-a-special-relationship-helps-forge-the> accessed 24 January 2022.
313 United Nations, 'The San Francisco Conference' <www.un.org/en/about-us/history-of-the-un/san-francisco-conference> accessed 24 January 2022.
314 United Nations Treaty Collection, 'Status of Charter of the United Nations and the Statute of the International Court of Justice' <https://treaties.un.org/pages/ViewDetails.aspx?src=IND&mtdsg_no=I-1&chapter=1&clang=_en> accessed 24 January 2022.
315 On 'Chapter VII determinations' see Svicevic, § 13, in this textbook.

BOX 7.3.6 Advanced: The Charter as a Global Constitution

The UN Charter is sometimes characterised as a world constitution.[316] The argument builds on the fact that article 103, which grants the UN Charter precedence over conflicting obligations of member States, elevates the status of the Charter to a superior source of international law. Interestingly, article 2(6) of the Charter also states that 'the Organization shall ensure that states which are not Members of the United Nations act in accordance with these Principles'. Yet, there are also profound problems with the idea of global constitutionalism.[317] Article 2(6) can also be considered to contradict the fundamental principle of the Law of Treaties whereby '[a] treaty does not create either obligations or rights for a third State without its consent'.[318]

III. THE LAW OF THE UNITED NATIONS

Article 2 is one of the most important provisions of the Charter, as it lists the principles that the UN and its members States commit to respect. These principles have been reproduced and further defined in the Declaration on Principles of International Law concerning Friendly Relations and Cooperation among States (1970).[319] Given the near-universal membership of the UN, these principles are often referred to as the fundamental principles of international law and international relations.[320] Some of them can even be considered *peremptory* norms.[321] These principles are:

- Sovereign equality
- Fulfilment of obligations in good faith
- Peaceful settlement of disputes
- Prohibition on the use of force
- Non-intervention in internal affairs
- The duty to cooperate
- The right of self-determination of peoples.[322]

---

316 See for example: Bardo Fassbender, *The United Nations Charter as the Constitution of the International Community* (Martinus Nijhoff 2009); Ronald St. John Macdonald, 'The International Community as a Legal Community' in Ronald St. John Macdonald and Donald M Johnston (eds), *Towards World Constitutionalism – Issues in the Legal Ordering of the World Community* (Brill 2005).

317 See Christine Schwöbel, 'Situating the Debate on Global Constitutionalism' (2010) 8 I-CON 611.

318 Vienna Convention on the Law of Treaties (adopted 23 May 1969, entered into force 27 January 1980) 1155 UNTS 331, article 34. On the law of treaties, see Fiskatoris and Svicevic, § 6.1, in this textbook.

319 UNGA Res 2624 (XXV) (24 October 1970).

320 Paola Gaeta, 'The Fundamental Principles Governing International Relations' in Paola Gaeta, Jorge E Viñuales, and Salvatore Zappalá (eds), *Cassese's International Law* (OUP 2020).

321 On *jus cogens* and hierarchy in international law, see Eggett, § 6, in this textbook.

322 For an overview, Kolb (n 11). For discussions of the principles, see e.g. Tamsin Phillipa Paige, *Petulant and Contrary: Approaches by the Permanent Five Members of the UN Security Council to the Concept of 'Threat to the*

III. THE GENERAL ASSEMBLY

The UNGA is the primary organ of diplomatic relations within the UN and was
established to be the principal forum for multilateral negotiations. Article 9 of the
Charter grants all UN member States representation in the UNGA. The UNGA meets
annually from September to December to discuss issues on its agenda. In addition, the
UNGA can meet in special sessions and emergency special sessions.[323] Articles 10 to
17 outline the scope of the UNGA's functions and powers, with voting and procedure
set out in articles 18 to 22. Most voting in the UNGA requires a simple majority,
whereas voting on 'important matters' (such as the membership of the non-permanent
members of the UNSC, membership of the Human Rights Council, membership of
the Economic and Social Council, or the budget of the UN) requires a two-thirds
majority.[324] All voting in the UNGA is done on a 'one member, one vote' basis.[325]

Apart from the annual sessions, most of the work of the UNGA is conducted by six
committees that it oversees. These are Disarmament and International Security (First
Committee); Economic and Financial (Second Committee); Social, Humanitarian and
Cultural (Third Committee); Special Political and Decolonisation (Fourth Committee);
Administrative and Budgetary (Fifth Committee); and Legal (Sixth Committee). Each
member State of the UN may assign one person to each committee.[326] The committees,
for example, prepare draft resolutions to the UNGA.

It is important to note that UNGA resolutions, with the exception of budgetary
matters under article 17, are not formally legally binding.[327] In terms of legal status
they can, however, be considered expressions of State practice and/or *opinio
juris*, thus supporting the formation of customary law.[328] UNGA resolutions may
themselves gain the status as customary law, as for example in the case of the
Universal Declaration of Human Rights.[329] An important function of the UNGA as
a permanent multilateral diplomatic forum is the ability to request advisory opinions
from the ICJ, thereby contributing to the development of the articulation of the
current status of international law.[330]

Peace' under Article 39 of the UN Charter (Brill/Nijhoff 2019); Simon Chesterman, 'An International Rule of
Law?' 56 American Journal of Comparative Law 331, 357; Gerry J Simpson, *Great Powers and Outlaw States:
Unequal Sovereigns in the International Legal Order* (CUP 2004) 5; James Crawford, *The Creation of States in
International Law* (2nd edn, Clarendon Press; OUP 2006) 126. On the distinction between rules and principles,
see Eggett, § 6.3.B.II., in this textbook.

323 UN Charter (n 288), article 20.
324 UNGA Rules of Procedure of the General Assembly, UN Doc A/520/Rev 15 (1984) paras 82–95.
325 UN Charter (n 288), article 18(1).
326 Rules of Procedure (n 327) para 38.
327 The Charter of the UN label GA decisions as recommendations, UN Charter (n 288), chapter IV.
328 On customary law, see Stoica, § 6.2, in this textbook.
329 On human rights, see Ciampi, § 21, in this textbook.
330 UN Charter (n 288), article 96.

IV. THE SECURITY COUNCIL

The UNSC is the executive body of the UN, charged with the primary responsibility for the maintenance of international peace and security.[331] The UNSC is made up of five permanent members (China, France, Russia, the UK, and the US) and ten non-permanent members who are elected by the UNGA for two years at a time.[332] The composition of the non-permanent members is fixed: five members from African and Asian States, one from Eastern European States, two from Latin American States, and two from Western European and other States.[333] The special role of the UNSC is reflected in its structure, the binding nature of its resolutions, and the right of veto granted to the permanent members of the UNSC.

Unlike the UNGA, the UNSC sits permanently and meets whenever necessary to discuss any situation that falls within its mandate (the maintenance of international peace and security). When making decisions, the UNSC has the option to make recommendations with relation to any situation under Chapter VI (Pacific Settlement of Disputes) of the Charter. Resolutions made under Chapter VII of the Charter (Action with Respect to Threats to the Peace, Breaches of the Peace, and Acts of Aggression) are binding upon all member States of the UN by virtue of article 25 of the Charter.

The threshold for UNSC action according to article 39 of the Charter is the finding of 'the existence of any threat to the peace, breach of the peace, or act of aggression'. Voting in the UNSC on any resolution (Chapter VI or Chapter VII) is governed by article 27 of the Charter. In all other than procedural decisions, this must, according the the Charter, include the concurring vote of all permanent members. This requirement has become colloquially known as the veto power (although the word `veto' is not mentioned in the Charter as such). Practice has however developed a divergent interpretation of the text of the Charter according to which abstention from voting by a permanent member does not prevent the adoption of a decisions.[334] A Chapter VII resolution is the only generally accepted exception (beside self-defence) to the prohibition on the use of force found in article 2(4) of the UN Charter.[335]

---

331 UN Charter (n 288), article 24(1).

332 UN Charter (n 288), article 23.

333 UNGA A/RES/1990 (XVIII) (17 December 1963).

334 Kolb (n 11).

335 On the system of collective security, see Svicevic, § 13, in this textbook.

BOX 7.3.7 Example: Limits to UNSC Powers

A claim has been made that 'the Security Council may basically decide or do anything it wishes and it will remain within the limits of the legal framework for its action'.[336] The interpretation of what can be considered a 'threat to the peace, breach of the peace, or act of aggression', triggering the article 39 threshold, has indeed expanded.[337] While UNSC decisions must be consistent with the purposes and principles of the Charter, the UNSC has for example relied upon its implied powers in order to establish criminal tribunals.[338] The UNSC has also made decisions obliging UN member States to undertake legislative measures domestically, hereby assuming something of a role of a 'world legislature'.[339]

V. THE SECRETARIAT

The UN Secretariat is set up under articles 97 to 101 of the Charter, and operates as the administrative arm of all UN activities. The Secretary-General is appointed by the GA, upon the recommendation of the UNSC. The SG (awkwardly referred to as 'he' in the Charter) is responsible for overseeing all the activities of the Secretariat, and reporting annually to the GA on the activities of the UN. The SG is also charged with bringing before the UNSC any matter that may threaten the maintenance of international peace and security. The Secretariat itself is made up of a number of departments that cover the broad functions of the UN each with a specific focus, acting on direction from the UNSC, the GA, and other UN bodies (e.g. the Human Rights Council, or the Economic and Social Council).

VI. OTHER UN BODIES

1. The Economic and Social Council

The Economic and Social Council is established under article 61 of the Charter, and is made up of 54 members of the UN elected for three-year terms by the GA. The role of the Economic and Social Council is to conduct studies and reports with respect to international economic, social, cultural, educational, health, and related matters

---

336 Inger Österdahl, Threat to the Peace: *The Interpretation by the Security Council of Article 39 of the UN Charter* (Iustus 1998) 98.

337 Christopher J Le Mon and Rachel S Taylor, 'Security Council Action in the Name of Human Rights: From Rhodesia to the Congo' (2004) 10 U.C. Davis Journal of International Law & Policy 197, 207; Paige (n 325) 20; Daniel Pickard, 'When Does Crime Become a Threat to International Peace and Security?' (1998) 12 Florida Journal of International Law 1, 19–20.

338 *Prosecutor v Tadic* (Decision on the Defence Motion for Interlocutory Appeal on Jurisdiction) (1995) ICTY IT-94-1-AR-72.

339 Stefan Talmon, 'The Security Council as World Legislature' 2005 (99) AJIL 175–93. On 'law-making' resolutions, see Kunz, Lima, and Castelar Campos, § 6.4 D.II.1 in this textbook.

and to make recommendations to the GA on the basis of those reports, as well as recommendations for the purpose of promoting respect and observance of human rights.

2. The Trusteeship Council

The Trusteeship Council was established under article 86 of the Charter and charged with overseeing the administration of UN trust territories. The Trusteeship Council suspended operations on 1 November 1994, a month after the last remaining UN trust territory, Palau, gained independence. While its abolishing has been proposed, it may also experience a revival due to climate change events.[340]

3. The International Court of Justice

The International Court of Justice (ICJ) was established under article 92 of the UN Charter, and the annexed statute of the ICJ.[341] The ICJ was established as a successor to the Permanent Court of International Justice.

BOX 7.3.8 Advanced: The Effectiveness of the UN

The UN meets criticism from many directions. The UNSC in particular is, for example, accused of applying double standards and selectivity. The UN has also been accused for failing to deliver on the maintenance of international peace and security, such as preventing the genocide in Rwanda.[342] The Russian aggression against Ukraine has recently highlighted anew the structural problem of the veto power of permanent members in the UNSC, which can render the Council incapable of acting. While the shortcomings of the Charter have been subject of debate at least since the Cold War, the veto power was at the time of the UN's establishment a prerequisite for granting a monopoly for authorisation of use of force to the UNSC.[343] Whereas the UN at the time of its establishment was strongly focused on the prevention of war, it is nowadays engaged in activities across societal sectors.[344] While many of the criticisms towards the UN are valid, the UN still remains 'the go-to forum in a time of crisis, and is likely to remain so well into the future'.[345]

---

340 Dag Hammarskjöld Library, 'Proposals Related to the Reform of the Trusteeship Council' <https://research.un.org/en/docs/tc/reform> accessed 18 June 2023.

341 Statute of the International Court of Justice (adopted 26 June 1945, entered into force 24 October 1945) 1 UNTS XVI. On peaceful settlement of disputes, see Choudhary, § 12, in this textbook.

342 See generally, Paige (n 325).

343 Peter Nadin, 'United Nations Security Council 101' (*Our World*, United Nations University, 15 April 2014) <https://ourworld.unu.edu/en/united-nations-security-council-101> accessed 8 August 2023.

344 Kolb (n 11); Sir Brian Urquhart, 'The Role of the United Nations in a Changing World' (UN Audiovisual Library 2008) <https://legal.un.org/avl/ls/Urquhart_UN_1.html> accessed 8 August 2023.

345 Nadin (n 342).

E. CONCLUSION

This chapter has provided an overview of international organisations as subjects of international law. In characterising and classifying organisations, the role of State consent was noted as central both for the establishment of an organisation and for delimiting it, for example, from non-governmental organisations. One of the defining features of international organisations is their autonomy from their member States. While this autonomy may take various forms, the conferral of legal personality upon an organisation, and its exercise of legal powers, are undoubtedly crucial features. The second part of the chapter introduced the UN as the primary example of a global/ open organisation with an openly political agenda. The UN Charter assumes a special position among legal sources of public international law, and the UNGA and the Security Council are important venues for bringing States together in addressing global challenges. Although the international legal system today acknowledges a range of non-State actors,[346] international organisations have retained their central role as venues for State collaboration in global governance.

BOX 7.3.9 Further Readings and Further Resources

Further Readings

- FA Chittharanjan, *Principles of the Institutional Law of International Organizations* (2nd edn, CUP 2005)

- R Kolb, *An Introduction to the Law of the United Nations* (Bloomsbury 2010)

- J Klabbers, *An Introduction to International Organizations Law* (CUP 2022)

- HG Schermers and NM Blokker, *International Institutional Law: Unity Within Diversity* (6th edn, Martinus Nijhoff 2018)

Further Resources

- The United Nations system chart: https://www.un.org/en/delegate/page/un-system-chart

- The United Nations Dag Hammarskjöld Library: https://www.un.org/en/library

- The United Nations treaty collection: https://treaties.un.org/

---

§ § §

---

346 On the pluralisation of international law, see Engström, § 7, in this textbook.

§ 7.4 INDIVIDUALS

JENS T. THEILEN

BOX 7.4.1 Required Knowledge and Learning Objectives

Required knowledge: Subjects and Actors in International Law

Learning objectives: Understanding the development of individuals'
   international legal personality, and being able to critically assess the narratives
   of progress that often accompany it.

A. INTRODUCTION

The role of individuals in international law is complex, contested, and shifting. Whether
and what kind of international legal personality individuals possess,[347] in particular, is a
much-debated topic that is poised between somewhat technical definitions and doctrinal
debates on the one hand and implications for the very foundations of the international
legal order on the other. Any stance on individuals' international legal personality or
subjecthood[348] presumes a definition of how such subjecthood is constituted, which in
turn reveals a particular theoretical outlook on international law. The dominant position
as a matter of legal doctrine seems to be that international legal personality is the capacity
to occur rights and duties under international law.[349] On that account, the question
becomes, empirically, whether and to what extent such rights and duties have, in fact,
been imparted upon individuals and, conceptually, what this means for the subjecthood
of individuals under international law, especially in relation to the prototypical
subject of international law on traditional accounts – the State.[350] This section will
trace the different steps of what the chapter calls the standard narrative regarding the
position of individuals before questioning, by reference to the related field of global
constitutionalism, whether it should be considered a narrative of progress.

B. ORIGINS OF INDIVIDUALS' INTERNATIONAL LEGAL PERSONALITY

To legitimise the international legal personality of individuals, some authors point
to history: at the very origins of international law,[351] it is said, no distinctions were

---

347 On subjecthood in international law generally, see Engström, § 7, in this textbook.
348 For the purposes of this chapter, the terms are used interchangeably, as they often have been since Reparation
   for Injuries Suffered in the Service of the United Nations (Advisory Opinion) [1949] ICJ Rep 174, 179.
349 See Engström, introduction to § 7, in this textbook.
350 On the State, see Green, § 7.1, in this textbook.
351 On international law's founding myths, see González Hauck, § 1, in this textbook.

made between the subjecthood of individuals and communities such as States. Many
proponents of individuals' international legal personality point to the writings of the
Spanish theologian Francisco de Vitoria, particularly his treatise *De Indis* (published
posthumously in 1557) on the relations between the Spanish and the indigenous
peoples they conquered during their transatlantic voyages.[352] Vitoria is said to have
established 'natural law as the universal law of all humanity', including individuals
among its subjects.[353] He is summarised as arguing 'that the Native Americans in the
territories conquered by Spain and Portugal had rights and claims under both public
law and private law, just like Christians' – hence implicitly recognising individuals
including indigenous persons as subjects under international law without distinction, for
example, between 'private' and 'public' wars.[354]

These celebratory tones[355] are misleading, however. Vitoria's ostensibly humane
characterisation of indigenous persons as possessing reason led them to be bound, on
his account, to the principles of international law: 'it is precisely *because* the Indians
possess reason that they are bound by *jus gentium*', as Antony Anghie, one of the leading
scholars associated with the Third World Approaches to International Law (TWAIL),[356]
has put it.[357] But the content of *jus gentium* mirrored Spanish norms and cast alternate
social practices as uncivilised.[358] Inevitably, the colonised peoples were held to have
violated the international norms they now found themselves subject to, which, in turn,
legitimated their conquest and other forms of violence against them.[359] This illustrates
that legal subjecthood can fulfil a variety of functions, not all of them benign.

C. FROM STATE-CENTRIC TO HUMAN-CENTRIC INTERNATIONAL LAW

Classical legal positivism brought with it a State-centric view of international law.[360]
The orthodox position regarding international legal personality at the beginning of
the 20th century was aptly summed up by Lassa Oppenheim, one of the most famous

---

352 Franciscus de Victoria, *De Indis et de Iure Belli Relectiones* (Ernest Nys ed., Carnegie Institution of Washington 1917).

353 Christopher Barbara, 'International Legal Personality: Panacea or Pandemonium? Theorizing About the Individual and the State in the Era of Globalization' (2007) 12 ARIEL 17, 32.

354 Anne Peters, *Beyond Human Rights. The Legal Status of the Individual in International Law* (CUP 2016) 11–12.

355 See e.g. Antônio Augusto Cançado Trindade, 'The Emancipation of the Individual from His Own State: The Historical Recovery of the Human Person as Subject of the Law of Nations' (2006) Revista do IBDH 11, 12.

356 On TWAIL, see González Hauck, § 3.2, in this textbook.

357 Antony Anghie, *Imperialism, Sovereignty and the Making of International Law* (CUP 2004) 20.

358 On the fusion of civilisation and legal personality, see also Rose Parfitt, 'Theorizing Recognition and International Personality' in Anne Orford and Florian Hoffmann with Martin Clark (eds), *The Oxford Handbook of the Theory of International Law* (OUP 2016) 583, 586; on how the 'Third World individual' was written out of international law, see Vincent O Nmehielle, 'A Just World Under Law: An African Perspective on the Status of the Individual in International Law' (2006) 100 ASIL Proceedings 252, 255.

359 On indigenous peoples and how Vitoria's argument still resonates toady, see Viswanath, § 7.2, in this textbook.

360 On positivism, see Etkin and Green, § 3.1, in this textbook.

positivist international lawyers: 'Since the law of nations is based on the common consent of individual States, and not of individual human beings, States solely and exclusively are subjects of international law'.[361] Individuals were said to be 'objects' rather than 'subjects' of international law.[362] On this view, even when treaties or other sources of international law seemed to provide rights to individuals, they were, in fact, not granted to the individuals themselves but rather to their State of nationality. It was only through the mediation of the State that the individual could appear on the international scene – provided that their State of nationality was willing to engage on their behalf, for example by exercising diplomatic protection but also, potentially, by the use of force. This was particularly relevant in the case of foreign investments, where – despite protest by Latin American States in particular[363] – it was increasingly regarded as legitimate for the investor's home State to intervene on their behalf in cases of expropriation or public debt.

Over the course of the 20th century, the exclusively State-centred position lost ground significantly. Various academic accounts already argued that the individual should be considered international law's 'ultimate unit' and 'in that capacity a subject of international law'.[364] In the decades that followed the Second World War, human rights came to be seen as an increasingly important sub-field of international law,[365] and a vast number of human rights treaties were concluded. This 'proliferation' or 'inflation'[366] of individual rights also includes fields which were traditionally viewed as merely the purview of States, such as consular relations.[367] In the famous *LaGrand* case, the ICJ was seized of a dispute regarding consular law: two German nationals, the LaGrand brothers, had been sentenced to death in the United States without being informed of the possibility of contacting and communicating with the consular post of their State of nationality. Germany contended that this entailed not only a breach of its own rights, but also those of the LaGrand brothers themselves. In its 2001 judgment, the ICJ concluded that

---

361 Lassa Oppenheim, *International Law: A Treatise* (Longmans, Green 1912) 19.

362 For an overview and criticism, see George Manner, 'The Object Theory of the Individual in International Law' (1952) 46 AJIL 428; see also PK Menon, 'The Legal Personality of Individuals' (1994) 6 Sri Lanka Journal of International Law 127, noting that non-Western territories, too, were considered 'objects'; for further reflections on objects (and their relation to subjects) in international law, see the contributions in Jessie Hohmann and Daniel Joyce (eds), *International Law's Objects* (OUP 2018).

363 See Kate Miles, *The Origins of International Investment Law. Empire, Environment and the Safeguarding of Capital* (CUP 2013) 47 et seq.; Fabia Fernandes Carvalho Veçoso, 'Resisting Intervention through Sovereign Debt: A Redescription of the Drago Doctrine' (2020) 1 TWAIL Review 74; Arnulf Becker Lorca, *Mestizo International Law. A Global Intellectual History 1842–1933* (CUP 2014) 62 et seq., 145 et seq.

364 Hersch Lauterpacht, 'The Subjects of the Law of Nations' in Elihu Lauterpacht (ed), *International Law. Being the Collected Papers of Hersch Lauterpacht. Volume 2* (CUP 1975) 487, 526–527; see also Georges Scelle, *Précis de droit des gens: principes et systématique* (Recueil Sirey 1932) 42.

365 On the history of human rights, see Samuel Moyn, *The Last Utopia. Human Rights in History* (Belknap 2012); Jessica Whyte, *The Morals of the Market: Human Rights and the Rise of Neoliberalism* (Verso 2019). On human rights, see Ciampi, § 21, in this textbook.

366 For a critique of the 'inflation objection', see Jens T Theilen, 'The Inflation of Human Rights: A Deconstruction' (2021) 34 LJIL 831.

367 On diplomatic and consular relations, see Arévalo Ramírez, § 10, in this textbook.

Article 36, paragraph 1 [of the Vienna Convention on Consular Relations], creates individual rights, which, by virtue of Article I of the Optional Protocol [of that Convention], may be invoked in this Court by the national State of the detained person.[368]

Besides this landmark judgment and the field of human rights as the paradigm of individual rights, proponents of individuals' international legal personality point to developments in many other fields of international law, including but not limited to humanitarian law, the law of the sea, and economic law.[369] The field of investment law, previously the poster child of individuals being perceived on the international legal scene only when mediated through action of their home State, now provides a prime example of individuals not only being accorded their own rights under international law, but of participating in the law-making process through 'State contracts' between investors and host States and of individuals enforcing their rights before arbitral tribunals. Thus, in some cases individual rights also include standing to bring cases before regional or international courts or other quasi-judicial bodies. This possibility is seen by some authors as in turn enshrined within international law as an individual right of petition and characterised as 'the most luminous star in the universe of human rights' and an expression of the individual as the 'ultimate subject' of international law.[370]

In terms of duties, too, there have been clear developments since the Second World War. Already in its immediate aftermath, the Military Tribunal at the trials of Nuremberg noted that 'International Law imposes duties and liabilities upon individuals as well as upon States'.[371] Today, the field of international criminal law has spread to a number of other contexts.[372] Most notably, the Rome Statute brought the International Criminal Court (ICC) into being at the turn of the century – although it has to be said that the duties which the Rome Statute imposes have, in practice, fallen only on some individuals, particularly those from Africa, while others seem exempt.[373]

---

368 *LaGrand (Germany v United States of America)* [2001] ICJ Rep 466 [77]; confirmed in *Avena and other Mexican Nationals (Mexico v United States of America)* [2004] ICJ Rep 12; see also previously *The Right to Information on Consular Assistance in the Framework of the Guarantees of the Due Process of Law* Advisory Opinion OC-16/99 (IACtHR, 1 October 1999).

369 See on humanitarian law Dienelt and Ullah, § 14, in this textbook; on law of the sea, Dela Cruz and Paige, § 15, in this textbook; on economic law, Hankings-Evans, § 23, in this textbook. For overviews of the status of individuals in these fields, see e.g. Peters (n 356); Kate Parlett, *The Individual in the International Legal System. Continuity and Change in International Law* (CUP 2011); Astrid Kjeldgaard-Pedersen, *The International Legal Personality of the Individual* (OUP 2018).

370 Cançado Trindade (n 357) 23.

371 International Military Tribunal (Nuremberg), judgment of 1 October 1946, in: The Trial of German Major War Criminals. Proceedings of the International Military Tribunal sitting at Nuremberg, Germany, Part 22, 446–447.

372 On international criminal law, see Ciampi, introduction to § 22, in this textbook.

373 For this aspect but also broader and more complex critiques of the ICC from a TWAIL perspective, see John Reynolds and Sujith Xavier, '"The Dark Corners of the World". TWAIL and International Criminal Justice' (2016) 14 JICJ 959; Asad G Kiyani, 'Third World Approaches to International Criminal Law' (2016) 109 AJIL Unbound 255; for an assessment of African States' response, see Dorothy Makaza, 'Towards Afrotopia: The AU Withdrawal Strategy Document, the ICC, and the Possibility of Pluralistic Utopias' (2017) 60 GYIL 481.

This brief overview has merely scratched the surface; a great many other legal developments could be mentioned. Taking them all together, it is easy to understand why the dominant position on the international legal personality of individuals has shifted: if legal personality is understood as the capacity to have international rights and duties, then the sheer volume of individual rights and duties under modern international law makes the recognition of individual subjecthood inevitable by implication. Denying international legal personality to individuals entirely has, accordingly, become a minority position based on highly restrictive readings of international law and additional prerequisites for legal personality such as significant participation in international law-making processes.[374]

Debates now rage, rather, on the question of how to qualify individuals' subjecthood. One position is that States continue to be the primary subjects of international law, and that individuals' international legal personality is partial and derivative – in other words, restricted to those rights and duties that States have bestowed upon them by way of treaties and other sources of international law.[375] On the other hand, the idea that individuals rather than States are in some sense the 'primary', 'principal', 'original', or 'natural' subjects of international law is gaining ground and can increasingly be viewed as the new orthodoxy.[376]

Proponents of both views typically tell the story of international legal personality's development over the last century or so as a success story: from being on the fringes of international law in the heyday of legal positivism, the individual has now emerged as a subject of international law in its own right, forming part of the overall 'humanisation' of international law.[377] In this narrative, the individual's international legal personality merges into a claim about the normative importance of the human being which, it is implied, makes for a more just and ethical international legal order. State-centrism has thus become a pejorative concept, whereas its critics associate themselves 'with a progressive and enlarged angle of vision'.[378]

---

374 E.g. Alexander Orakhelashvili, 'The Position of the Individual in International Law' (2001) 31 CWIJL 241.

375 Parlett (n 371) 359–360; Petra Perišić, 'Some Remarks on the International Legal Personality of Individuals' (2016) 49 CILJSA 223; this view is often traced back to *Reparation for Injuries Suffered in the Service of the United Nations* (n 1) which was not, however, specifically concerned with individuals; see e.g. Menon (n 364) 148–150.

376 Peters (n 356); Cançado Trindade (n 357); Janne Elisabeth Nijman, *The Concept of International Legal Personality: An Inquiry into the History and Theory of International Law* (Asser 2004); Sinthiou Estelle Buszewski, 'The Individual, the State and a Cosmopolitan Legal Order' in Norman Weiß and Jean-Marc Thouvenin (eds), *The Influence of Human Rights on International Law* (Springer 2015) 201; though combining his approach with a more formal conception of subjecthood, Roland Portmann, *Legal Personality in International Law* (CUP 2010) 273 also tends in this direction 'in the context of international crimes and fundamental human rights'.

377 E.g. Rein A Mullerson, 'Human Rights and the Individual as Subject of International Law: A Soviet View' (1990) 1 EJIL 33, 35.

378 Susan Marks, 'State-Centrism, International Law, and the Anxieties of Influence' (2006) 19 LJIL 339, 339–340.

D. INDIVIDUALISATION, HUMANISATION, AND GLOBAL CONSTITUTIONALISM

It is worth pausing here to ask ourselves why the increasing individualisation of international law is, often without further reasoning, seen as progressive in this way. After all, there is a long line of critique, reaching back at least to Karl Marx and further developed, for example, in Marxist perspectives[379] and critiques of human rights,[380] that problematises individualisation as giving way to egoism and self-interest, disregarding 'species-life' in society, and constituting a set of social relations that prevent emancipation.[381] Feminist critique,[382] too, has long grappled with the ambiguities of individual rights and the 'standing' that comes with them: 'rights secure our standing as individuals even as they obscure the treacherous ways in which that standing is achieved and regulated', thus forming part of historically specific power structures and entrenching subordination even as they offer limited redress.[383]

Part of the answer to the continuing popularity of individuals as subjects of international law presumably lies simply in the positive feelings that speaking of an 'international law for humankind' evokes.[384] It is associated, for example, with a 'substantive core' of 'flesh and blood' for international law.[385] Given the affective impact that the 'humanisation' of international law seems to invoke, debates over the international legal personality of individuals in such terms may function primarily as a placeholder for broader debates on the nature and ultimate function of international law as such.[386] This hypothesis is confirmed by the connection often drawn between the international legal personality of individuals and the constitutionalisation of international law.[387] The field of global constitutionalism is itself a broad church, but can be summarised as an attempt to give meaning and legitimacy to international law by understanding it as a constitutional order imbued with certain foundational values. Particular emphasis tends to be placed

---

379 See Bagchi, § 3.4, in this textbook.
380 See Ananthavinayagan and Theilen, § 21.8, in this textbook.
381 Karl Marx, 'On the Jewish Question' in Robert C Tucker (ed), *The Marx-Engels Reader* (Norton 1978) 26; see also Anthony Carty, 'International Legal Personality and the End of the Subject: Natural Law and Phenomenological Responses to New Approaches to International Law' (2005) 6 MJIL 534, 551–552 on individualism and 'collective life' with reference to international legal personality.
382 See Kahl and Paige, § 3.3, in this textbook.
383 Wendy Brown, 'Suffering Rights as Paradoxes' (2000) 7 Constellations 230, 238.
384 Cançado Trindade (n 357) 25; see also Nijman (n 378) 473.
385 Barbara (n 355) 47.
386 On this connection, see also Nehal Bhuta, 'The Role International Actors Other Than States Can Play in the New World Order' in Antonio Cassese (ed), *Realizing Utopia. The Future of International Law* (OUP 2012) 61.
387 E.g. Anne Peters, 'Are We Moving Towards Constitutionalization of the World Community?' in Antonio Cassese (ed), *Realizing Utopia. The Future of International Law* (OUP 2012) 122 and 129; for a critical overview, see Astrid Kjeldgaard-Pedersen, 'Global Constitutionalism and the International Legal Personality of the Individual' (2019) 66 NILR 271; Ekaterina Yahyaoui Krivenko, *Rethinking Human Rights and Global Constitutionalism* (CUP 2017) 19 et seq.

on the 'holy trinity' of human rights, democracy and the rule of law[388] – all associated, in some way, with individuals.

But if the approaches share ground in this way, they are also open to similar objections. Global constitutionalism has been rightly criticised for the active neglect of its own history, particularly colonialism, slavery, and their legacies[389] – in much the same way as the colonial origins of individuals' international legal personality are commonly glossed over, as described above. Another crucial shortcoming of global constitutionalism is the way in which it reinscribes liberal values as universal, including the liberal distinction between politics and economics. Indeed, global constitutionalism tends to take the market as a given and to relegate economic matters to the private sphere, untouched by the public law principles it propounds for international law – thus legitimising structures of global capitalism and shielding them from democratic contestation.[390]

A similarly liberal outlook on economic matters is also often implied, although rarely made explicit and certainly not politicised, in the insistence on international legal personality of individuals. It shines through, for example, in the analogisation of the individual under international law to 'a global *bourgeois* in the dual sense of an economic actor and bearer of so-called unpolitical international rights that secure his or her personal freedom and development'.[391] The individual here becomes individual-as-free-economic-actor. Simultaneously, most proponents of individuals as the primary subjects of international law relegate market structures and economic matters to the unquestioned background in much the same way as global constitutionalists – for example, the complex economic phenomenon of globalisation and the social relations of racialised and gendered exploitation that accompany it are reduced to a manifestation of humans' ostensible nature as 'social animals', with an emphasis on communication and technological innovation.[392]

Against this backdrop, it becomes vital to question which individuals are ascribed international legal personality, and which of them stand to profit from it. While the rhetoric of humanisation and of 'flesh and blood' leads us to equate the individual and the human being, the technical meaning of 'individuals' on most accounts is by

---

388 Mattias Kumm and others, 'How Large Is the World of Global Constitutionalism?' (2014) 3 Global Constitutionalism 1, 3.

389 Vidya Kumar, 'Towards a Constitutionalism of the Wretched. Global Constitutionalism, International Law and the Global South' (*Völkerrechtsblog*, 27 July 2017) <doi:10.17176/20170727-141227> accessed 10 August 2023.

390 Sigrid Boysen, 'Postcolonial Global Constitutionalism' in Anthony F Lang and Antje Wiener (eds), *Handbook on Global Constitutionalism* (2nd edn, Edward Elgar forthcoming); from broader critiques of global constitutionalism, see also Christine EJ Schwöbel, *Global Constitutionalism in International Legal Perspective* (Martinus Nijhoff 2011).

391 Peters (n 356) 553 (emphasis in original); see also Oliver Dörr, '"Privatisierung" des Völkerrechts' (2005) 60 JZ 905, 908, considering *Marktbürgerrechte* (literally 'rights of market citizens') in the law of regional integration as a reference point for individual rights.

392 Barbara (n 355) 44–46.

no means restricted to natural persons. As the inclusion of investment law alongside other fields in which the rights of individuals are enshrined in international law shows, the term also includes juridical persons constituted by private law under its ambit – and it is notable that investment law, commonly acknowledged as particularly important to the entrenchment of imperialist, capitalist structures through international law,[393] forms one of the crucibles in which the international legal personality of individuals was forged. For that matter, human rights doctrine likewise recognises juridical persons as bearers of 'human' rights.[394] Although transnational corporations tend to be discussed separately under the rubric of international legal personality,[395] then, there is a significant but underacknowledged area of overlap with discussions of the international legal personality of individuals and their (economic) rights. The ostensible humanisation of international law of which individual subjecthood is said to form part thus turns out to include the kind of economic freedom that underlies a liberal capitalist order which serves the interests of corporations in the Global North.

E. CONCLUSION

The doubts canvassed above are intended to contextualise the debates on individuals' international legal personality, not to argue against it – States are no more 'natural' candidates for international legal personality than individuals,[396] and no less entangled with civilisational hierarchies and the structures of global capitalism. In any case, that individuals possess some form of subjecthood under international law is nowadays almost indisputable. Its form and extent hinges not only on one's definition of international legal personality but also on various precommitments as to the nature and ultimate function of international law. What stands out about the new orthodoxy emphasising the development from State-centric to human-centric international law, however, is its self-presentation as a narrative of progress – a characterisation which not only elides the downsides of individualisation and the politics of claiming primary subjecthood for individuals, including juridical persons, but also delegitimises broader doubts about the concept of international legal personality as such.[397] Against this narrative of progress, it is worth asking: why individualise, which 'individuals', and who profits from approaching international law in this way?

---

393 Kate Miles, *The Origins of International Investment Law. Empire, Environment and the Safeguarding of Capital* (CUP 2013); David Schneiderman, *Investment Law's Alibis. Colonialism, Imperialism, Debt and Development* (CUP 2022); Muthucumaraswamy Sornarajah, 'Mutations of Neo-Liberalism in International Investment Law (2011) 3 Trade, Law and Development 203.

394 See critically Anna Grear, 'Challenging Corporate "Humanity": Legal Disembodiment, Embodiment and Human Rights' (2007) 7 HRLR 511. On human rights doctrine, see Milas, § 21.1, in this textbook.

395 See González Hauck, § 7.7, in this textbook.

396 See also Portmann (n 378) 274.

397 For a starting point on such doubts, see Rose Parfitt (n 360) 599.

BOX 7.4.2 Further Readings

Further Readings

- A Peters, *Beyond Human Rights. The Legal Status of the Individual in International Law* (Cambridge University Press 2016)

- SE Buszewski, 'The Individual, the State and a Cosmopolitan Legal Order' in N Weiß and J-M Thouvenin (eds), *The Influence of Human Rights on International Law* (Springer 2015) 201

- A Kjeldgaard-Pedersen, 'Global Constitutionalism and the International Legal Personality of the Individual' (2019) 66 NILR 271

- VO Nmehielle, 'A Just World Under Law: An African Perspective on the Status of the Individual in International Law' (2006) 100 ASIL Proceedings 252

- A Grear, 'Challenging Corporate "Humanity": Legal Disembodiment, Embodiment and Human Rights' (2007) 7 HRLR 511

§ § §

§ 7.5 WOMEN

JULIANA SANTOS DE CARVALHO
AND VERENA KAHL

BOX 7.5.1 Required Knowledge and Learning Objectives

Required knowledge: Feminism and Queer Theory; Individuals; Human Rights
Law; International Criminal Law

Learning objectives: Understanding how women have been included as subjects
of international law; how they have contributed to the development of
international legal practice; and taking stock of (some) persisting challenges
to gender equality in the field.

A. INTRODUCTION

Despite the well-documented (white) masculine dominance,[398] women have long
been a part of international law both as subjects of international legal instruments and
as agents within the profession. This chapter aims to give a brief overview of how
women are addressed in international law and their contributions to the field. It first
introduces international legal instruments that recognise and advance women's rights
internationally. The chapter then addresses the persisting widespread invisibility of
women as active designers and interpreters of international law and casts a spotlight on
selected women as key actors and active agents of and within public international law.

B. WOMEN AS SUBJECTS
OF INTERNATIONAL LAW

Women have long been the subject of different international legal instruments, either
as a central group category for the norms in question or as a specially protected group
within a larger framework of rights and protection. International law's attention to
women is mainly owed to the continuous activism from international and transnational
coalitions of different women's movements and civil society,[399] and has encompassed a
great variety of sub-fields in the international legal order.

---

398 Hilary Charlesworth, Christine Chinkin, and Shelley Wright, 'Feminist Approaches to International Law'
(1991) 85 AJIL 613.

399 See, among others, Jane Addams, Emily Greene Balch, and Alice Hamilton, *Women at the Hague: The
International Congress of Women and Its Results* (Garland 1972); Devaki Jain, *Women, Development, and the UN:
A Sixty-Year Quest for Equality and Justice* (Indiana UP 2005); Katherine M Marino, *Feminism for the Americas:
The Making of an International Human Rights Movement* (University of North Carolina Press 2019); Rebecca

Perhaps one of the most emblematic inclusions of women as subjects of international law is contained in the UN Charter. In its preamble, the Charter introduces among the UN's objectives the equal rights of men and women.[400] Additionally, in article 8, the Charter makes explicit that the UN's principal and subsidiary organs are to follow the equality between men and women in their functioning.[401]

Similarly, the Universal Declaration of Human Rights (UDHR)[402] in its article 2 reiterates the right of all individuals, without distinction as to their sex,[403] to fully enjoy the human rights set out in the Declaration. Further, article 16 of the UDHR recognises the right of men and women of full age to marry and found a family.

The International Covenant on Civil and Political Rights (ICCPR), establishes that State parties are to respect all individuals' civil and political rights irrespective of their sex.[404] Article 3 indicates explicitly that States need to ensure that men and women will enjoy the rights enshrined in the document equally.[405] Similarly, articles 4(1), 23(2), 24, 25, and 26 contain provisions protecting individuals from discrimination on the basis of their sex.[406] Mirroring these provisions, articles 2(2) and 3 of the International Covenant on Economic, Social and Cultural Rights also establish equality provisions for men and women in relation to the rights established therein.[407] Additionally, article 7(a) (i) requires States to ensure equal pay for equal work,[408] something that is also ensured

---

Adami and Dan Plesch (eds), *Women and the UN: A New History of Women's International Human Rights* (Routledge 2021); Giusi Russo, *Women, Empires, and Body Politics at the United Nations, 1946–1975* (University of Nebraska Press 2023).

400 Charter of the United Nations 1945 (adopted 26 June 1945, entered into force 24 October 1945) 1 UNTS XVI.

401 Ibid article 8.

402 Although non-binding in character, the UDHR has been understood as having been (partially) solidified as international custom. See, for instance, John Humphrey, 'The Universal Declaration of Human Rights: Its History, Impact and Judicial Character' in BG Ramcharan (ed), *Human Rights. Thirty Years After the Universal Declaration* (Martinus Nijhoff 1979) 21–37; Hurst Hannum, 'The UDHR in National and International Law' (1998) HHR 144, 147–149.

403 In this article, we understand sex as also being socially constructed (see Judith Butler, *Gender Trouble: Feminism and the Subversion of Identity* [Routledge 1999] 1–32; Brenda Cossman, 'Gender Performance, Sexual Subjects and International Law' [2002] 15 CJLJ 281; Dianne Otto, 'Queering Gender [Identity] in International Law' [2015] 33 NJHR 299).

404 International Covenant on Civil and Political Rights (adopted 16 December 1966, entered into force 23 March 1976) 999 UNTS 171.

405 Given ICCPR's article 3 central focus on gender equality, it is important to note that some State Parties have explicitly made reservations or interpretative declarations on this regard, namely Bahrain (reservation), Liechtenstein (declaration), Monaco (declaration), Kuwait (declaration), and Qatar (reservation).

406 State Parties have also issued declarations and reservations to these ICCPR articles. For a full list, see <https://treaties.un.org/Pages/ViewDetails.aspx?chapter=4&clang=_en&mtdsg_no=IV-4&src=IND#29> accessed 11 August 2023.

407 International Covenant on Economic, Social and Cultural Rights (adopted 16 December 1966, entered into force 3 January 1976) 999 UNTS 3. The State Parties that have made reservations or interpretative declarations on article 3 of the ICESCR are Kuwait and Qatar.

408 Some States have issued reservations to postpone the application of this provision, namely Barbados and the UK.

by the International Labour Organization (ILO) Convention 100 (Equal Remuneration Convention) of 1951.[409]

Going beyond equality clauses, international legal instruments also add special protective provisions for women. In this regard, for instance, article 6(3) of the ICCPR prohibits the execution of capital punishment on pregnant women. Additionally, several ILO conventions establish specific protective measures for women, such as the Maternity Convention (first established in 1919, with the latest revised variant in 2000),[410] night work,[411] plantation work,[412] among others.

However, perhaps one of the most comprehensive legal regimes of special rights and protection accorded to women have been those elaborated by the Commission on the Status of Women (CSW). Established by the UN Economic and Social Council in 1946,[413] the CSW was fundamental for the drafting and adoption of several international conventions on women's rights,[414] including the 1979 Convention on the Elimination of All Forms of Discrimination against Women (CEDAW).[415] CEDAW provisions encompass a variety of issues, including, but not limited to, equality before the law and within cultural practices, access to education, political rights, equal representation in national governments and international bodies, specific rights for rural women, and economic and social benefits, among others. Nevertheless, it bears noting that the CEDAW is one of the universal human rights instruments with the most significant number of State reservations.[416]

The CEDAW also has an Optional Protocol with 115 States parties.[417] This document establishes a monitoring Committee, competent to receive and consider communications concerning alleged Convention violations. Moreover, article 8 enables the Committee to conduct an inquiry procedure when it receives 'reliable information indicating grave or systematic violations by a State Party'.[418]

---

409 Convention (No. 100) concerning equal remuneration for men and women workers for work of equal value (adopted 29 June 1951, entered into force 23 May 1953) 165 UNTS 303 (C100).

410 Convention (No. 183) concerning the revision of the Maternity Protection Convention (adopted 15 June 2000, entered into force 7 February 2002) 2181 UNTS 253 (C183).

411 ILO Night Work Convention 1990 (No. 171) (adopted 26 June 1990, entered into force 4 January 1995) (C171).

412 Convention (No. 110) concerning conditions of employment of plantation workers (adopted 24 June 1958, entered into force 1960) 348 UNTS 275 (C110).

413 UN Economic and Social Council resolution 11(II), *Commission on the Status of Women*, E/RES/11(II) (21 June 1946).

414 Most notably, see Convention on the Political Rights of Women (adopted 31 March 1953, entered into force 7 July 1954) 193 UNTS 135; Convention on the Nationality of Married Women (adopted 20 February 1957, entered into force 11 August 1958) 309 UNTS 65.

415 Convention on the Elimination of all forms of Discrimination Against Women (adopted 18 December 1979, entered into force 3 September 1982) 1249 UNTS 13 (CEDAW).

416 Seo-Young Cho, 'International Women's Convention, Democracy, and Gender Equality' (2014) 95 SSQ 719.

417 Optional Protocol to the Convention on the Elimination of all forms of Discrimination Against Women (adopted 6 October 1999, entered into force 22 December 2000) 2131 UNTS 83.

418 Ibid article 8.

Other noteworthy special instruments adopted on women's rights are those concerning the regional systems of human rights, such as the 2003 Maputo Protocol on the Rights of Women in Africa,[419] the 1994 Inter-American Convention on the Prevention, Punishment and Eradication of Violence Against Women,[420] and the Convention on preventing and combating violence against women and domestic violence (Istanbul Convention).[421]

Aside from international human rights, women have been particularly included in international criminal law. Most notably, the Rome Statute of the International Criminal Court (ICC) includes gender as a protected category for the crime of persecution,[422] recognises women as a specific vulnerable group to specific international crimes,[423] and indicates that gender equality and expertise should count in the selection of judges for the ICC.[424]

Despite its contested legal status,[425] the Women, Peace and Security (WPS) agenda of the UN Security Council is also considered an influential set of documents that reinforce existing legal obligations of parties to armed conflicts concerning the rights and specific needs of women and girls. Initiated by the unanimously adopted Resolution 1325 (2000),[426] and comprising nine different sister resolutions under the same rubric,[427] the WPS agenda encompasses several issues relating to women and girls during and after conflict settings, such as prevention and protection against conflict-related sexual violence (CRSV), increased participation of women in peace processes, and specific measures to ensure the specific needs of women and girls in humanitarian relief. The fact that women have often been depicted merely as victims of conflict-related sexual violence, as mothers, or as peacemakers has been criticised.[428]

---

419 Protocol to the African Charter on Human and People's Rights on the Rights of Women in Africa (Maputo Protocol) (adopted 11 July 2003, entered into force 25 November 2005).

420 Inter-American Convention on the Prevention, Punishment and Eradication of Violence against Women ('Convention of Belém do Pará', adopted 9 June 1994, entered into force 5 March 1995) 33 ILM 1534.

421 The Council of Europe Convention on Preventing and Combating Violence against Women and Domestic Violence (adopted 11 May 2011, entered into force 1 November 2022) CETS 210.

422 Rome Statute of the International Criminal Court (adopted 17 July 1998, entered into force 1 July 2002) 2187 UNTS 3, article 7(3).

423 More specifically, these are enslavement and forced pregnancy when committed as a crime against humanity. See Rome Statute articles 7(2)(c) and 7(2)(f).

424 Ibid 36(8)(a), 36(8)(b).

425 Christine Chinkin, *Women, Peace and Security and International Law* (CUP 2022) chapter 2.

426 UN Security Council resolution 1325 (2000), S/RES/1325(2000) (31 October 2000).

427 These are resolutions 1820(2008), 1888(2009), 1889(2009), 1960(2010), 2106(2010), 2122(2013), 2242(2015), 2467(2019), 2493(2019).

428 Hilary Charlesworth, 'Feminist Methods in International Law' (1999) 93 AJIL 379, 381; Dianne Otto, 'The Exile of Inclusion: Reflections on Gender Issues in International Law over the Last Decade' (2009) 10 MJIL 11; Dianne Otto, 'Feminist Approaches to International Law' in Anne Orford and Florian Hoffmann (eds), *The Oxford Handbook of the Theory of International Law* (OUP 2016) 496; Christine Chinkin, 'Gender and Armed Conflict' in Andrew Clapham and Paola Gaeta (eds), *The Oxford Handbook of International Law in Armed Conflict* (Vol 1, OUP 2014); Nicola Pratt, 'Reconceptualizing Gender, Reinscribing Racial-Sexual Boundaries in International Security: The Case of UN Security Council Resolution 1325 on "Women, Peace and Security"' (2013) 57 ISQ 772.

C. WOMEN AS AGENTS OF INTERNATIONAL LAW

I. EXPLAINING THE INVISIBILITY OF WOMEN IN INTERNATIONAL LAW

Systematic and structural discrimination[429] and marginalisation of women in all their diversity has had yet another effect: the invisibility and non-recognition of women as active agents in international law. Various factors are said to have contributed to this, including the public-private divide,[430] behavioural stereotypical gender roles, power imbalances and corresponding lack of or aggravated access to financial resources, land and property, and educational institutions and offices.[431]

BOX 7.5.2 Advanced: The Public-Private Divide

The approach of the public-private divide, following Western political and legal philosophy,[432] explains the structural discrimination of women in the context of socio-political spheres: based on stereotyped gender roles, women are associated with and relegated to a domestic, private, and devalued sphere, while men are rather assigned to a public, political, and economic sphere, which, among others, influences the distribution of work and professions within the dominant gender dichotomy.[433] The function of the State and international law as a gendered system have been associated with the public sphere and therefore described as 'operating in the . . . male world'.[434] While the public-private divide, in combination with discrimination-related lack of or limited access to resources, education, and offices, may to a certain extent

---

429 On structural discrimination, see Kahl and Paige, § 3.3, in this textbook.

430 For an emblematic example, see Cynthia Enloe who underscored that '[g]overnments . . . need wives who are willing to provide their diplomatic husbands with unpaid services so these men can develop trusting relationships with other diplomatic husbands. They need a steady supply of women's sexual services to convince their soldiers that they are manly [and] depend on ideas about masculinized dignity and feminized sacrifice to sustain [a] sense of autonomous nationhood'. Cynthia Enloe, *Bananas, Beaches, and Bases: Making Feminist Sense of International Politics* (Pandora Press 1989) 196–197.

431 See, inter alia, Caroline ON Moser, 'Planning in the Third World: Meeting Practical and Strategic Gender Needs' (1989) 17(11) World Development 1799, 1801, 1803, 1812–1813; Maxine Molyneux, 'Mobilization without Emancipation? Women's Interests, State and Revolution in Nicaragua' (1985) 11(2) Feminist Studies 227, 232–233.

432 For the distinction made between *polis* (public sphere) and *oikos* (private sphere) in ancient Greece, see Margaret Thornton, 'The Cartography of Public and Private' in Margaret Thornton (ed), *Public and Private: Feminist Legal Debates* (OUP 1995) 2–4.

433 Ibid 2–3; similarly, inter alia, Rebecca Grant, 'The Sources of Gender Bias in International Relations Theory' in Rebecca Grant and Kathleen Newland (eds), *Gender and International Relations* (Indiana UP 1991) 8, 11–12.

434 Hilary Charlesworth and Christine Chinkin, *The Boundaries of International Law – A Feminist Analysis* (Manchester UP 2000) 56. See also the connection between sovereign men and sovereign States in V. Spike Peterson and Anne Sisson Runyan, *Global Gender Issues* (Avalon 1993) 34.

explain the absence and invisibility of women agents in international law, the Western character of the concept and its (necessarily) oversimplified categories neglect the discriminatory patterns and corresponding struggles of women across spheres, particularly those of the Global South, that also contribute to the complex combination of factors that drive the persisting prevention, invisibility, and non-recognition of women agents of international law.[435]

The structural discrimination, which manifests itself differently depending on the specific situation of a woman,[436] continues in the denial of or difficult access to and participation in international institutions, key positions, and corresponding law- and decision-making processes. It is also worth mentioning that the struggles caused by and the fight against patriarchal structures also tie up important resources, such as money, time, and energy, that could otherwise be invested differently.[437] Invisibility therefore refers to all those women of diverse backgrounds that could not participate in the 'game' of international law in the first place.[438] This absence of women in the international sphere is also reflected in their continuous underrepresentation in important and influential international legal institutions, such as the ILC[439] or international courts and tribunals.[440] No woman has been nominated UN Secretary-General so far.[441]

---

435 See, inter alia, Susan B Boyd, *Challenging the Public/Private Divide: Feminism, Law, and Public Policy* (University of Toronto Press 1997).

436 On intersectionality, see Kahl and Paige, § 3.3, in this textbook.

437 As Rebecca Solnit underscored: 'Think of how much more time and energy we would have to focus on other things that matter if we weren't so busy surviving'. *Men Explain Things To Me* (Haymarket Books 2014) 35.

438 See, by way of illustration, the tragic story of Shakespeare's fictional sister described by Virginia Woolf. Virginia Woolf, *A Room of One's Own* (Hogarth Press 1929) 39–41.

439 From 1947 until 2022, there were seven women at the ILC compared to 229 men. See Priya Pillai, 'Symposium on Gender Representation: Representation of Women at the International Law Commission' (*Opinio Juris*, 7 October 2021) <http://opiniojuris.org/2021/10/07/symposium-on-gender-representation-representation-of-women-at-the-international-law-commission/> accessed 11 August 2023. See also Lorenzo Gradoni, 'Still Losing: A Short History of Women in Elections (and By-Elections) for the UN International Law Commission' (*EJIL: Talk!*, 25 November 2021) <www.ejiltalk.org/still-losing-a-short-history-of-women-in-elections-and-by-elections-for-the-un-international-law-commission/> accessed 11 August 2023.

440 See the description of women representation in international courts with further sources in Catherine Kessedjian, 'Gender Equality in the Judiciary – With an Emphasis on International Judiciary' in Elisa Fornalé (ed), *Gender Equality in the Mirror: Reflecting on Power, Participation and Global Justice* (Brill 2022) 195, 201. See also Nienke Grossman, 'Sex on the Bench: Do Women Judges Matter to the Legitimacy of International Courts?' (2012) Chicago Journal of International Law 647; Leigh Swigart and Daniel Terris, 'Who Are International Judges?' in Cesare PR Romano, Karen J Alter, and Yuval Shany (eds), *The Oxford Handbook of International Adjudication* (OUP 2014) 619.

441 On the topic, see Heather Barr, 'Time for a Female UN Secretary-General? Guterres Reelection Run Shouldn't Deter Nominations of Qualified Women' (*Human Rights Watch*, 2 March 2021) <www.hrw.org/news/2021/03/02/time-female-un-secretary-general> accessed 11 August 2023.

In addition, international law has also fostered patterns of overseeing, ignoring, and denying adequate recognition to those women that *have* been active designers of the international legal order, often precisely despite the very difficult conditions they faced.[442] Invisibility and non-recognition of women agents in the realm of international law is also owed to a patriarchal system that operates in invisibility itself.[443]

The mechanism that fuels invisibility of these women agents can particularly be observed where international law is taught, described, analysed, and criticised. Trailblazing women in international law are largely absent in universities' classrooms in comparison to their men colleagues. The 'classics of international law' seldom include contributions of women. These 'classics' go beyond the eponymous series edited by James Scott,[444] as they refer to preselected works, which are considered contributions of such significance that they are regularly addressed in seminars, lectures, and academic publications. Besides losing valuable contributions to the development of international law, the resulting invisibility and recognition of women's contributions also lead to a presumption of their nonexistence and a lack of role models for younger women.

Recently, some important scholarly projects have tried to break the glass ceiling in favour of the visibility and recognition of women as active agents and designers of international law, such as the works of Rebecca Adami and Dan Plesch[445] as well as Immi Tallgren.[446]

II. TRAILBLAZING WOMEN IN INTERNATIONAL LAW

Despite the aforementioned hurdles, women have made important contributions to the development of international law in different roles, such as diplomats, judges, scholars, lawyers, and active members of civil society. Nevertheless, it is important to highlight that white, Western women have notably gained more recognition than their racialised and Global South counterparts. We thus aim at modestly correcting this bias by foregrounding the diverse set of women who have contributed to substantial landmarks of contemporary international law.

In this sense, while Eleanor Roosevelt has become much more visible in her efforts to encourage the adoption of the UDHR, Dominican Minerva Bernardino was crucial in her promotion of the rights of women in the document.[447] Bernardino, along with

---

442 Nancy Fraser has described such cultural injustice as being rooted 'in social patterns of representation, interpretation, and communication'. Nancy Fraser, *Justice Interruptus: Critical Reflections on the 'Postsocialist Condition'* (Routledge 1997) 14.

443 Mary Becker, 'Patriarchy and Inequality: Towards a Substantive Feminism' (1999) University of Chicago Legal Forum 21.

444 See James Brown Scott, *Classics of International Law* (volumes I and II, Carnegie Institution 1912).

445 Rebecca Adami and Dan Plesch, *Women and the UN: A New History of Women's International Human Rights* (Routledge 2022).

446 Immi Tallgren (ed), *Portraits of Women in International Law: New Names and Forgotten Faces?* (OUP 2023).

447 Johannes Morsink, 'Women's Rights in the Universal Declaration' (1991) 13(2) HRQ 229.

other Latin American diplomats, such as the Brazilian Bertha Lutz and Mexican Amalia González Caballero de Castillo Ledón, have also had an important role in the inclusion of women's rights during the negotiations of another landmark international legal document: the UN Charter. Both Bernardino and Lutz were active in the drafting process of the Charter, especially in their work of including crucial wording on the equality of men and women.[448] An equally outstanding international figure of that time is Hansa Mehta from India, the only woman delegate to the UN Commission on Human Rights besides Eleanor Roosevelt in 1947.[449] The change in the wording of article 1 of the Universal Declaration from 'All men are born free and equal' to 'All human beings are born free and equal' is to her merit.[450]

Even before the birth of the UN System, as early as 1889, Bertha von Suttner formulated her (at that time) very progressive thoughts on peace and the international legal order in her bestselling anti-war novel, *Die Waffen nieder!* She envisaged an international legal order with international institutions, international jurisdiction, and peaceful cooperation among States. Suttner was the first woman to participate as an observer at the First Hague Peace Conference (in 1899) and the first woman to be awarded the Nobel Peace Prize (in 1912).[451] Nearly a century before, another trailblazing woman, a feminist, abolitionist playwright fought against discrimination of women and publicly opposed slavery in the context of the French revolution: Olympe de Gouges.[452] As a response to the 1789 Declaration of the Rights of Man and of the Citizen, she published a 'Declaration of the Rights of Women and of the Female Citizen', advocating for equal rights and challenging male authority and oppression of women.

Nowadays, outstanding women from the Global South and their important contributions to international law are gaining more and more attention, such as Navanethem Pillay, Hauwa Ibrahim, Xue Hanqin, Unity Dow, Taghreed Hikmat, and Cecilia Medina Quiroga, besides many others.

This is only a very limited selection and therefore a very incomplete list of many trailblazing women and their important contributions to international law across different times and cultures. (Re)discovering the contributions of women to international law is still the subject of ongoing scholarly research and discussion.

---

448 Elise Dietrichson and Fatima Sator, 'The Latin American Women: How They Shaped the UN Charter and Why Southern Agency Is Forgotten' in Rebecca Adami and Daniel Plesch (eds), *Women and the UN: A New History of Women's International Human Rights* (Routledge 2022).

449 United for Human Rights, 'Meet the Women Who Shaped the Universal Declaration of Human Rights' <www.humanrights.com/news/2021-news-meet-the-women-who-shaped-the-universal-declaration-of-human-rights.html> accessed 12 August 2023.

450 Khushi Singh Rathore, 'Excavating Hidden Histories: Indian Women in the Early History of the United Nations' in Rebecca Adami and Daniel Plesch (eds), *Women and the UN: A New History of Women's International Human Rights* (Routledge 2022).

451 See e.g. Janne Elisabeth Nijman, 'Bertha von Suttner: Locating International Law in Novel and Salon' in Immi Tallgren (ed), *Portraits of Women in International Law: New Names and Forgotten Faces?* (OUP 2023).

452 See e.g. Anne Lagerwall and Agatha Verdebout, 'Olympe de Gouges: Beyond the Symbol' in Immi Tallgren (ed), *Portraits of Women in International Law: New Names and Forgotten Faces?* (OUP 2023) 56.

D. CONCLUSION

This chapter has demonstrated that, despite the structural gender bias and barriers in the international legal field, women have been a significant part of international law – both as subjects of international legal instruments and as agents contributing to the development of the international legal order. However, there is still a long way to go to achieve full gender equality and meaningful inclusion in the international legal order. Women – especially those positioned within an intersectional background of discrimination and oppression – still face structural marginalisation in the international legal field, despite their continued relevance for the profession. As such, striving for gender equality and the recognition of women's contribution to international law is still an important and much needed endeavour.

BOX 7.5.3 Further Readings and Further Resources

Further Readings

- R Adami and D Plesch, *Women and the UN: A New History of Women's International Human Rights* (Routledge 2022)

- R Adami, *Women and the Universal Declaration of Human Rights* (Routledge 2019)

- H Charlesworth and C Chinkin, *The Boundaries of International Law: A Feminist Analysis*, With a New Introduction (Manchester University Press 2022)

- I Tallgren (ed), *Portraits of Women in International Law: New Names and Forgotten Faces?* (OUP 2023)

Further Resources

- 'Calendar on Outstanding Women of International, European and Constitutional Law' <www.jura.uni-hamburg.de/forschung/institute-forschungsstellen-und-zentren/iia/kooperationen-projekte/womencalendar.html>

- 'Women and War: A Feminist Podcast' <www.rsc.ox.ac.uk/research/women-war-a-feminist-podcast>

---

§ § §

§ 7.6 NONGOVERNMENTAL ORGANISATIONS

HE CHI

> **BOX 7.6.1** Required Knowledge and Learning Objectives
>
> **Required knowledge**: Subjects of International Law; Sources of International Law; International Organisations; International Human Rights Law
>
> **Learning objectives**: Understanding the role of NGOs in international law and different lenses to appraise their functions.

A. INTRODUCTION

Nongovernmental organisations (NGOs) are generally not regarded as formal subjects of international law. However, these actors are active and vital in today's international order. Indeed, one cannot miss the headlines occupied by the several prominent NGOs in the global media: Amnesty International, Save the Children, Doctors Without Borders/Médecins Sans Frontières (MSF), and Transparency International.

NGOs are often hailed as a crucial force to legitimise international law, a forum to voice the concerns of the global civil society, or even the vanguards of a post-sovereigntist, cosmopolitan world. In recent years, however, the world has witnessed criticism against NGOs.[453] This chapter will turn from descriptive to normative to examine NGOs' role in international law.

B. WHAT ARE NONGOVERNMENTAL ORGANISATIONS?

I. DEFINITION

NGOs are generally defined as 'groups of persons or societies, freely created by private initiative, that pursue an interest in matters that cross or transcend national borders and are not profit-seeking'.[454] However, this definition cannot provide meaningful information about NGOs' nature, organisation, and function. NGOs as a social phenomenon are complex.

---

453 See Kenneth Anderson and David Reiff, 'Global Civil Society: A Skeptical View' in Marlies Glausis, Mary Kaldor, and Helmut Anheier (eds), *Global Civil Society* (SAGA 2004) 35.

454 Steve Charnovitz, 'Nongovernmental Organizations and International Law' (2006) 100 AJIL 348, 350.

So, what exactly is an NGO? First, it is an organisation made by individuals. It gathers people in one group, regardless of its organisational structure. Second, an NGO is independent of the government. This distinguishes it from international organisations and is one of its most salient features.[455] However, this feature is blurred as government-organised nongovernmental organisations (GONGOs) have emerged recently.[456] Third, an NGO is not-for-profit,[457] relying on voluntary contributions from external parties to ensure its existence. Its operation creates intangible results, such as environmental protection, charity, hobbies or interest groups, human rights, and legal or economic communities.

II. FROM LOCAL TO INTERNATIONAL: NGOS IN THE GLOBAL DOMAIN

We are living in a globalised era. Nevertheless, since people tend to focus on the things around them, civil society has traditionally been local oriented. The earliest form of NGOs that spanned continents was religious groups and secret organisations.[458] The British and Foreign Anti-Slavery Society, established in London in 1839, is often considered the earliest modern NGO.[459]

In the 19th century, we witnessed a boom in the amount and scope of NGOs. The Union of International Associations sought to compile a complete record of NGOs, making the 19th century the starting point of 'globalisation' for NGOs.[460] The development of NGOs on the international stage was not a linear but rather a cyclical process. The NGO sector has been profoundly shaped by the global environment brought out by the end of the Cold War, technological advancement, and globalisation.

C. THE LEGAL STATUS OF NGOS IN INTERNATIONAL LAW

The legal status of NGOs, along with other non-State actors, has been subject to continuous debate. The focus of the discussion centres around the fact that NGOs, according to dominant accounts, do not hold international legal personality. Even though

---

455 On international organisations, see Baranowska, Engström, and Paige, § 7.3, in this textbook.

456 See Reza Hasmath, Timothy Hildebrandt, and Jennifer YJ Hsu, 'Conceptualizing Government-Organized Non-Governmental Organizations' (2019) 15 JCS 267. See also Fiona McGaughey, 'From Gatekeepers to GONGOs: A Taxonomy of Non-Governmental Organizations Engaging with United Nations Human Rights Mechanisms' (2018) 36 NQHR 111.

457 It is debatable whether NGOs include profit-making organisations. In this chapter, the author tends not to have those profit-making organisations and focuses on those not-for-profit.

458 See Steve Charnovitz, 'Two Centuries of Participation: NGOs and International Governance' (1997) 18 MJIL 184.

459 Charles Chatfield, 'Intergovernmental and Non-Governmental Associations to 1945' in Jackie Smith, Charles Chatfield, and Ron Pagnucco (eds), *Transnational Social Movements and Global Politics: Solidarity Beyond the State* (Syracuse UP 1997) 21.

460 See Thomas Davies, 'Understanding Non-Governmental Organizations in World Politics: The Promise and Pitfalls of the Early "Science of Internationalism"' (2017) 23 EJIR 884.

non-State actors thus occupy an 'inferior' position compared to States, one cannot neglect that the roles played by these actors are becoming increasingly significant.[461]

I. THE UN SYSTEM

In article 71, the UN Charter stipulates that 'the Economic and Social Council may make suitable arrangements for consultation with non-governmental organisations which are concerned with matters within its competence'.[462]

For many, this article signified a great leap forward in democracy on the international stage and initiated an exciting institutional linkage between States and NGOs. It is the first time NGOs can occupy an official place and make their voices heard in an international organisation dominated by States. All NGOs participating in the work of the UN Economic and Social Council, based on the working field and competence, are classified into three types: general consultative status, special consultative status, and roster status.[463]

With the consultative status, NGOs can participate in conferences convened by the UN, including meetings convened by the ECOSOC, its subsidiary bodies, and various UN human rights organs.

More recently, a participatory relationship has been proposed to integrate NGOs even more actively in the day-to-day working of the UN system, moving beyond the consultative status stipulated in article 71.[464] One of the reasons for the UN's welcoming attitude towards NGOs might be that the UN and NGOs can achieve a kind of 'mutual legitimacy', concretising each other's role in the State-centric international society.[465]

II. REGIONAL BODIES

Following the UN, the Organization of American States (OAS), in its Charter of 1948, laid out several provisions concerning NGOs. The Council of Europe established formal working relationships with NGOs as early as 1951.[466] It distinguished international and domestic NGOs and gave the former participatory

---

461 On States, see Green, § 7.1, in this textbook; on the pluralisation of international legal personhood, see
   Engström, introduction to § 7, in this textbook.
462 The Charter of the United Nations (signed on 26 June 1945, entered into force 24 October 1954) 1 UNTS
   XVI.
463 UN ECOSOC 'Consultative Relationship between the United Nations and Non-Governmental
   Organizations' Res 1996/31 (25 July 1996) 60–61.
464 UNGA 'We the Peoples: civil society, the United Nations and global governance: Report of the Panel of
   Eminent Persons on United Nations – Civil Society Relations' UN Doc A/58/817(2004).
465 See Peter Willets, 'The Cardoso Report on the UN and Civil Society: Functionalism, Global Corporatism, or
   Global Democracy?'(2006) 12 Global Governance 305.
466 CoE 'Relations with International Organizations, Intergovernmental and Non-governmental' Res(51)30
   F(3 May 1951).

and later partnership status. One notable point is that in 1999, the general assembly of the OAS established a commission for civil society participation in the OAS activities within the permanent council and a guideline for civil society participation.[467] One salient feature of NGO participation in the OAS system is its term used. 'Civil society' rather than 'NGO' is used frequently, symbolising an optimistic attitude toward the NGOs, and attaches a progressive narrative towards the role of NGOs in the international arena. This mentality can be summarised as treating NGOs as a force for good.[468]

The African Union (AU) is unique in its relationship with civil society organisations (CSOs).[469] Only some NGOs have been granted observer status, but no explicit legal basis was provided to entitle NGOs to work with the AU at the general level.[470] Article 22 of the Constitutive Act on the AU established an Economic, Social, and Cultural Council (ECOSOCC).[471] The ECOSOCC is an advisory body comprising different social and professional groups. Although the aim and purpose of the ECOSOCC are expansive, what comes with this expansiveness is the vagueness. Evaluating NGOs' roles and actual positions in the AU is challenging. In the meantime, Africa has also been an important place of activity for Western NGOs, which has led to controversial debate.[472]

D. THE ROLE OF NGOS IN INTERNATIONAL LAW

I. INTERNATIONAL LAW-MAKING

NGOs have been increasingly influential in international law-making as a response to concerns about a democracy deficit in international law, for it can supplement the State-centrism of international law and bring more voices into legislative processes. For one, they can influence agenda-setting in international affairs.[473] For example, in the Convention on Biological Diversity drafting process,[474] the World Conservation Union intensely participated in discussing and wording several vital articles and successfully

---

467 OAS 'Guidelines for Participation by Civil Society Organizations in OAS Activities' CP/RES 759 (1217/99) (15 December 1999).

468 See George Kaloudis, 'Non-Governmental Organisations: Mostly a Force for Good' (2017) 34 IJWP 81.

469 In the AU document, 'civil society organisation' (CSO) is the preferred usage. However, CSO primarily refers to NGOs, and the author uses the two terms interchangeably.

470 On the African human rights system, see Rachovitsa, § 21.3, in this textbook.

471 Constitutive Act of the African Union (adopted 11 July 2000, enter into force 26 May 2001) 2158 UNTS I-37733.

472 See Usman A Tar, 'Civil Society and Neoliberalism' in E Obadare (ed), *The Handbook of Civil Society in Africa* (Springer 2014) 253–270.

473 Peter M Haas, 'Introduction: Epistemic Communities and International Policy Coordination (1992) 46 IO 3.

474 Convention on Biological Diversity (adopted 5 June 1992, enter into force 29 December 1993) 1760 UNTS 79.

integrated its agenda into the Convention.[475] In some instances, NGOs can even join in the drafting process directly. In negotiating the Ottawa Treaty of the Prohibition of Anti-Personnel Mines,[476] the International Campaign to Ban Landmines followed through.[477] Occasionally, NGOs may furthermore directly join government delegations as counsels or delegates. This happened in negotiating the Rome Statute of the International Criminal Court.[478] Finally, NGOs also engage in advocacy. Even when excluded from the negotiation process, NGOs can exert influence as pressure groups, demonstrating before venues.

II. ADMINISTRATION OF INTERNATIONAL AFFAIRS

NGOs also engage with the daily routines of international affairs. Many international organisations enlist NGOs to provide professional opinions on the issues or discuss policies and documents. In the UN system, various working groups work with relevant NGOs. For example, in the UN Global Compact Initiative,[479] NGOs have been pioneers in taking advantage of the voluntary code of conduct to induce good behaviour of transnational corporations in human rights and the environment. The tripartite decision-making structure in the International Labour Organization gives NGOs critical outlets to participate in global labour rights management.[480] As an NGO specialising in standards-making, the International Organization for Standardization (ISO) provides a case in point of NGOs' role in the administration of international affairs.[481]

Some NGOs are particularly worth mentioning. These are the International Committee of the Red Cross (ICRC); the International Union for Conservation of Nature (IUCN), the Global Fund to Fight AIDS, Tuberculosis and Malaria; Gavi, the Vaccine Alliance (Gavi), and the World Anti-Doping Agency (WADA). The particularity of these NGOs is that they have a hybrid character, and they all share a mission of international interest. To a certain extent, especially in the case of the ICRC,

---

475 Erik B Bluemel, 'Overcoming NGO Accountability Concerns in International Governance' (2005) 31 Brooklyn Journal of International Law 141, 162.

476 The Convention on the Prohibition of the Use, Stockpiling, Production, and Transfer of Anti-Personnel Mines and on Their Destruction (adopted December 3 1997, entered into force on March 1 1999) 2056 UNTS 211.

477 Williams and Goose, 'The International Campaign to Ban Landmines' in Maxwell A Cameron, Brian W Tomlin, and Robert J Lawson (eds), *To Walk without Fear: The Global Movement to Ban Landmines* (OUP 1998) 20.

478 See Michael J Struett, *The Politics of Constructing the International Criminal Court: NGOs, Discourse, and Agency* (Palgrave Macmillan 2008).

479 Peter J Spiro, 'New Global Potentates: Nongovernmental Organizations and the Unregulated Marketplace' (1996) 18 Cardozo Law Review 962.

480 See Sergey Ripinsky and Peter Van Den Bossche, *NGO Involvement in International Organizations: A Legal Analysis* (British Institute of International and Comparative Law 2007) 67–69.

481 See Karsten Ronit and Volker Schneider, 'Global Governance Through Private Organisations' (1999) 12 Governance 243.

they are deemed as having legal personality and enjoy the privilege of immunity.[482] The reasons for this are closely connected to the functions these institutions played in the administration of international affairs.

III. INTERNATIONAL LAW ENFORCEMENT

Enforcement of international law has long been dubbed as the 'vanishing point of international law'.[483] However, this defect of problematic enforcement can be remedied by the 'soft' enforcement which NGOs lead. With the help of modern information technology, NGOs worldwide can cause a 'boomerang effect' that can equip them with the necessary civil power – public opinion – to compel or even coerce States into compliance.[484]

One can observe these trends in human rights and environmental protection in particular. In the Montreal Protocol on Substances That Deplete the Ozone Layer, NGOs are implicitly tasked to monitor State parties' compliance. If they find any treaty breach, they can notify the secretariat, thus ensuring a quick sanctioning process.[485] In the human rights field, by issuing shadow reports and adopting the 'naming and shaming' strategy, human rights NGOs can pressure States to comply with relevant human rights norms. In the meantime, some judicial or quasi-judicial mechanisms have opened the door to NGOs.[486] For example, in the WTO dispute settlement mechanism, NGOs may submit amicus curiae opinions to assist in resolving trade disputes.[487] NGOs may press States to conform to relevant international standards through domestic litigation.

E. A CRITICAL APPRAISAL OF NGOs IN INTERNATIONAL LAW

Some scholars praise NGOs as the vanguard of global democracy.[488] Acting individually, NGOs have allowed ordinary people to make their voices heard worldwide. NGOs are leading a 'global association revolution'.[489] Organisations such as Greenpeace, Amnesty International, Human Rights Watch, and the recent Nobel Peace Prize winner

---

482 The ICRC stands alone among NGOs for it attains *sui generis* status as a subject of international law.

483 On enforcement, see Quiroga Villamarín, § 2.3, in this textbook.

484 See Margaret E Keck and Kathryn Sikkink, *Activists Beyond Borders: Advocacy Networks in International Politics* (Cornell University Press 1998).

485 Elizabeth P Barratt-Brown, 'Building a Monitoring and Compliance Regime Under Montreal Protocol' (1991) 16 Yale Journal of International Law 564.

486 See Robyn Eckersley, 'A Green Public Sphere in the WTO? The Amicus Curiae Interventions in the Transatlantic Biotech Dispute' (2007) 13 EJIL 329.

487 See Michelle Ratton Sanchez, 'Brief Observations on the Mechanisms for NGO Participation in the WTO' (2006) 4 Sur 103.

488 See Jan Aart Scholte, 'Global Governance, Accountability, and Civil Society' in Jan Aart Scholte (ed), *Building Global Democracy: Civil Society and Accountable Global Governance* (CUP 2011) 1–40.

489 Lester M Salamon, 'The Rise of the Nonprofit Sector' (1994) 73 Foreign Affairs 109.

International Campaign to Abolish Nuclear Weapons are fighting at the forefront for world peace, a sustainable environment, and human rights. NGOs are not powerless actors protesting in the corner. Constituting the main body of Global Civil Society (GCS), NGOs gained legitimacy and potency to occupy streets, block unfavourable bills, and criticise governments.

However, NGOs, or GCS, have ambiguities. First, GSC is not a bounded 'non-governmental' space but a means of making global politics governable in particular ways. In this regard, NGOs, States, and markets are closely intertwined and mutually constituting. Second, by being nongovernmental, one may presume that NGOs are neutral actors; however, occasionally, NGOs represent certain social groups' interests and potent groups. Third, against NGOs' progressive and empowering image, NGOs also engage in power struggles and cannot escape tensions and contradictions as they try to transform politics.[490]

The term 'NGOisation' is commonly used among many social movements, activist networks, and academics to refer to the institutionalisation, professionalisation, depoliticisation, and demobilisation of movements for social and environmental change.[491] As many scholars have pointed out, NGOisation is a relatively new phenomenon that concurred with the outgrowth of neoliberalism, or, put another way, NGOisation is a 'symptom' desired by neoliberal ideology. Some scholars put it directly: 'The greater the devastation caused by neoliberalism, the greater the outbreak of NGOs'.[492] Only by following the path of NGOisation do some NGOs gain the organising imperative and internal momentum to participate in the world struggle under the disguise of non-government, impartiality, and independence.

F. CONCLUSION

The case of NGOs has provided us with a vivid example to observe the perils of international law. By embracing NGOs or the more intriguing term 'Global Civil Society' without a second thought, international lawyers celebrate the advent of a more democratic, inclusive, and cosmopolitan international law, which can bring hope for a murky world dominated by greedy, aggressive, and violent States. NGOs are caring agents for the sake of humanity, but they can also be shrewd groups with the sheer aim of attracting donors and fulfilling formal obligations, which is far from the real needs of the weak. NGOs are also part of a world of struggle.[493] As international lawyers, we must note the losses and gains that are present in this struggle.

---

490 See Sangeeta Kamat, 'The Privatization of Public Interest: Theorizing NGO Discourse in a Neoliberal Era' (2004) 11 RIPE 156.

491 See Aziz Choudry and Dip Kapor (eds), *NGOization: Complicity, Contradiction, and Prospects* (Zed Books 2013).

492 Arundhati Roy, 'Help That Hinders' (2004) *Le monde diplomatique* (English Edition).

493 See David Kennedy, *A World of Struggle: How Power, Law, and Expertise Shape Global Political Economy* (Princeton UP 2016).

BOX 7.6.2 Further Readings

Further Readings

- A Lindblom, *Non-governmental Organizations in International Law* (CUP 2005)

- BK Woodward, *Global Civil Society in International Lawmaking and Global Governance: Theory and Practice. Queen Mary Studies in International Law* (Vol. 2, Martinus Nijhoff 2010)

- B Reinalda, M Noortmann, and B Arts (eds), *Non-State Actors in International Relations* (Ashgate 2001)

- D Chandler, *Constructing Global Civil Society: Morality and Power in International Politics* (Palgrave Macmillan 2004)

- J Keane, *Global Civil Society?* (CUP 2003)

§ § §

§ 7.7 CORPORATIONS

SUÉ GONZÁLEZ HAUCK

BOX 7.7.1 Required Knowledge and Learning Objectives

Required knowledge: History, Subjects, and Actors

Learning objectives: Understanding the role corporations have played in the creation of international law; having a cursory knowledge of corporations' rights and obligations under contemporary international law.

A. INTRODUCTION

Corporations are entities endowed with legal personality separate from their owners. The International Court of Justice (ICJ) recognised corporations' separate legal personality in *Barcelona Traction*[494] and *Ahmadou Sadio Diallo*.[495] This distinct legal identity empowers corporations to own assets, conclude contracts, acquire rights, and assume obligations in their own name.[496] Under international law, corporations enjoy various rights, notably property, freedom of establishment and movement, and access to markets. A whole branch of international law – international investment law – is devoted to securing the rights of corporations.[497] In contrast, international law imposes only minimal obligations on corporations. This chapter retraces historical factors shaping corporations' international legal status, examines their role as ostensibly private entities with often public functions, highlights key corporate rights in international law, and briefly surveys ongoing efforts for corporate legal accountability.

B. HISTORY OF INTERNATIONAL LAW AND THE CORPORATION

One of the key tenets of mainstream international law is that the State is the sole 'natural' subject of international law and that granting rights to or, especially, imposing obligations on other actors requires specific rules.[498] This means that the commonly

---

494 *Case Concerning the Barcelona Traction, Light, and Power Company, Limited* (Belgium v Spain) (Second Phase) (Judgment) [1970] ICJ Rep 3 [33], [38].

495 *Ahmadou Sadio Diallo (Republic of Guinea v Democratic Republic of the Congo)* (Preliminary Objections) (Judgment) [2007] ICJ Rep 582 [61].

496 Peter T Muchlinski, 'Corporations in International Law' (*Max Planck Encyclopedia of International Law*, June 2014) para 2.

497 See Hankings-Evans, § 23.1, in this textbook.

498 On States, see Green, § 7.1, in this textbook; on subjects and actors in international law more generally, see Engström, Introduction to § 7, in this textbook.

held position is that corporations can only be held accountable under national jurisdictions.[499] A glance at the history of modern international law shows that this narrative is, at best, incomplete.

The emergence of international law is inextricably linked to chartered companies, that is, commercial organisations endowed with special privileges by States, usually through a royal charter.[500] At the beginning of the 17th century, two particularly influential colonial empires, the Dutch and the British, founded the Dutch East India Company (Vereenigde Oost-Indische Compagnie, VOC) and the British East India Company, respectively. Both companies exhibited features that became typical of modern corporations: they were endowed with permanent capital, legal personhood, and tradable shares, and their governance structures allowed for separation between ownership and management and for limited liability for shareholders and for directors.[501]

The memoranda Hugo Grotius crafted for the VOC[502] influenced international trade law and the international law of the sea,[503] as well as central doctrines of international law, including sovereignty and subjects.[504] To justify the VOC's seizure of foreign vessels, Grotius extended just war concepts to ostensibly private entities like the VOC, thus granting them public sovereign powers.[505] The structure of international law Grotius put forward, therefore, is one in which the chartered company is a central actor and subject.[506] Chartered companies concluded contracts with local authorities and established titles over territory.[507] Incrementally, the VOC used such contracts to claim trade monopolies and the right to punish violations of these claimed monopoly rights, including by conquest. These claims and the resulting forcible actions resulted in hollowing out the sovereign rights of local authorities.[508]

A new model of cross-border business enterprise started to emerge with the Industrial Revolution. New modes of transport like railroads and steamboats and new modes of communication like the telegraph made it possible and capitalism's inherent drive for

---

499 Muchlinski (n 495) para 7.

500 Tony Webster, 'British and Dutch Chartered Companies' (*Oxford Bibliographies*) <www.oxfordbibliographies. com/display/document/obo-9780199730414/obo-9780199730414-0099.xml> accessed 25 August 2023.

501 Oscar Gelderblom and others, 'The Formative Years of the Modern Corporation: The Dutch East India Company VOC 1602–1623' (2013) 73 The Journal of Economic History 1050.

502 See González Hauck, § 1.B.II., 1.C.II., in this textbook.

503 Koen Stapelbroek, 'Trade, Chartered Companies, and Mercantile Associations' in Bardo Fassbender and Anne Peters (eds), *The Oxford Handbook of the History of International Law* (OUP 2013) 338, 347.

504 José-Manuel Barreto, 'Cerberus: Rethinking Grotius and the Westphalian System' in Martti Koskenniemi and others (eds), *International Law and Empire: Historical Explorations* (OUP 2017) 149, 156.

505 Barreto (n 503) 156 et seq.; Richard Tuck, *The Rights of War and Peace: Political Thought and International Order from Grotius to Kant* (OUP 1999) 85; Eric Wilson, 'The VOC, Corporate Sovereignty and the Republican Sub-Text of *De iure praedae*' (2005–2007) 26–28 Grotiana 310.

506 Barreto (n 503) 158.

507 Stapelbroek (n 502) 341.

508 Ibid 350.

expansion made it necessary for businesses to establish permanent subsidiaries in other countries. This was mainly focused on resource extraction like mining companies, but not limited to them. In the second half of the 19th century, starting with the British New Company Law of 1844, many States, including France, the United States, Germany, and Japan established laws allowing for the free incorporation of private companies.[509] This turn from chartered companies to private corporations entailed a shift in how business enterprises were perceived: from vehicles of State power to entities operating separately from the State.[510]

C. THE CORPORATION AND THE PUBLIC-PRIVATE DIVIDE

Exploring the role of corporations in international law naturally involves delving into the well-known distinction between public and private law. International law's 'public' nature arises from its focus on sovereignty and States. On the flip side, corporations are typically considered private entities.[511] However, corporations wield considerable public power, not only by leveraging their economic power to pressure governments, but also in ways that can be seen as expressions of autonomous regulatory force or governance. Corporations create transnational rules and regulations through their business practices, contractual agreements, and private dispute resolution mechanisms.[512] They can shape the interpretation of established legal norms, particularly when official judicial or public interpretative guidance is absent – a common situation in international law.[513] Adding to this complexity is the prevalence of modern-day public-private partnerships, where public State entities collaborate with private, often foreign, investors. These partnerships often involve entrusting functions like utility service provision to private parties.[514]

D. RIGHTS OF CORPORATIONS UNDER INTERNATIONAL LAW

A corporation's links to a State via incorporation or through the centre of administration establishes corporate nationality. Corporations have the rights granted to the nationals of the parties under Treaties of Friendship, Commerce, and Navigation or under Bilateral Investment Treaties (BITs).[515] The traditional way of enforcing these rights is through diplomatic protection.[516] Establishing the link of nationality between

---

509 Doreen Lustig, *Veiled Power: International Law and the Private Corporation, 1886–1981* (OUP 2020) 15.

510 Ibid 16.

511 Lustig (n 508) 2–3.

512 Dan Danielsen, 'Corporate Power and Global Order' in Anne Orford (ed), *International Law and its Others* (CUP 2006), 86–88.

513 Ibid.

514 Muchlinski (n 495) para 3.

515 Ibid para 9.

516 See Arévalo-Ramírez, § 10, in this textbook.

the corporation and the State willing to exercise diplomatic protection can be difficult, especially for transnational entities.[517]

The most important international case concerned with the legal personality and the nationality of corporations is the *Barcelona Traction* case. Barcelona Traction, incorporated in Canada, had subsidiaries there and in Spain, holding bonds and facing financial issues due to the Spanish Civil War.[518] Belgium, among other States, intervened on behalf of their shareholding nationals. The ICJ held the Belgian claims on behalf of the Belgian shareholders to be inadmissible, holding that States could only bring forward claims in the name of shareholders if the corporation had seized to exist or if the State of incorporation lacked the capacity to take action on its behalf.[519] The ICJ explored 'lifting the corporate veil' (i.e. allowing legal claims both on behalf of and against shareholders directly), but decided this was only possible under exceptional circumstances, mirroring domestic law practices for fraud or malfeasance.[520] Additionally, the ICJ affirmed that corporations' nationality should be established based on incorporation and registered office, not on a genuine link test,[521] differing from the *Nottebohm* case's standards for individuals.[522]

Corporations also enjoy rights that they can directly enforce under international law. The most important of these rights are conferred on corporations under international investment law. Corporations can bring claims derived from BITs or other international investment treaties against host States directly before specialised investment tribunals.[523] Despite not being *human*, corporations are also recognised as bearers of human rights within the European human rights system.[524] Some international legal scholars have pushed for a broader recognition of corporate 'human' rights through broad interpretations of the term 'everybody', which human rights treaties often use to describe rights holders.[525] More critical voices have raised concerns that corporate human rights contradict the very idea of human rights and pointed towards them as an illustration of the structural liaison between human rights and capitalism.[526]

---

517 Muchlinski (n 495) para 14.

518 Stephan Wittich, 'Barcelona Traction Case' (*Max Planck Encyclopedia of Public International Law*, May 2007) para 1.

519 *Barcelona Traction* (n 493) [61].

520 Ibid [56–58].

521 Ibid [56].

522 *Nottebohm Case* (Second Phase) (Judgment) [1955] ICJ Rep 4 [23].

523 See Hankings-Evans, § 23.1, in this textbook.

524 Silvia Steininger and Jochen von Bernstorff, 'Who Turned Multinational Corporations into Bearers of Human Rights? On the Creation of Corporate 'Human' Rights in International Law' in Ingo Venzke and Kevin Jon Heller (eds), *Contingency in International Law: On the Possibility of Different Legal Histories* (OUP 2021) 283–284; Marius Emberland, *The Human Rights of Companies. Exploring the Structure of ECHR Protection* (OUP 2006). On the European human rights system, see Theilen, § 21.4, in this textbook.

525 Lucien J Dhooge, 'Human Rights for Transnational Corporations' (2007) 16 Journal of Transnational Law and Policy 197.

526 Steininger and von Bernstorff (n 523); Grietje Baars, *The Corporation, Law and Capitalism. A Radical Perspective on the Role of Law in the Global Political Economy* (Brill 2019); Turkuler Isiksel, 'The Rights of Man and the Rights of the Man-Made: Corporations and Human Rights' (2016) 38 HRQ 294; Anna Grear, 'Challenging Corporate Humanity: Legal Disembodiment, Embodiment and Human Rights' (2007) 7 HRLR 511.

E. OBLIGATIONS OF CORPORATIONS UNDER INTERNATIONAL LAW

International law imposes only minimal obligations on corporations. The rise of the Business and Human Rights movement, however, has pushed for corporate accountability for human rights abuses.[527] The adoption of the United Nations Guiding Principles on Business and Human Rights (UNGPs) is one of the main achievements of this movement, outlining the responsibility of corporations to prevent, address, and remedy human rights violations in their activities.[528] International soft law instruments like the UNGPs, although not legally binding, may exert influence on corporate behaviour.[529] An open-ended working group within the United Nations is currently tasked with developing a legally binding treaty on business and human rights.[530]

Domestic law mechanisms also play a role in holding corporations accountable. The United States Alien Tort Statute (ATS) grants foreign citizens the ability to sue in US federal courts for (at least some) violations of customary international law, including human rights abuses, committed outside the US.[531] In recent years, jurisdictions like the European Union, France, and Germany have introduced legislation imposing due diligence obligations on corporations to ensure their operations do not contribute to human rights abuses or environmental harm.[532]

F. CONCLUSION

Corporations have been a central actor in international law since its inception and they continue to shape international law well beyond their purportedly 'private' role. They enjoy a variety of rights under international law, most importantly the right to own property and other rights conferred on them under international investment law, and can even bring claims before international courts and tribunals. Their rights are still to be matched by international legal obligations. Even though the Business and Human Rights movement has successfully pushed for national legislation imposing due diligence obligations on corporations and for soft law instruments outlining corporations' human rights obligations, no binding international legal rules in this regard have yet been accepted.

---

527 See e.g. Surya Deva and David Birchall (eds), *Research Handbook on Human Rights and Business* (Edward Elgar 2020).

528 United Nations Human Rights – Office of the High Commissioner, *Guiding Principles on Business and Human Rights* (United Nations 2011).

529 On soft law, see Kunz, Lima, and Castelar Campos, § 6.4.C.I., in this textbook.

530 Olivier de Schutter, 'Towards a New Treaty on Business and Human Rights' (2015) 1 BHRJ 41.

531 Anthony J Bellia and Bradford R Clark, 'The Alien Tort Statute and the Law of Nations' (2011) University of Chicago Law Review 445.

532 Christopher Patz, 'The EU's Draft Corporate Sustainability Due Diligence Directive: A First Assessment' (2022) 7 BHRJ 291; Philip Nedelcu and Stefan Schäferling, 'The Act on Corporate Due Diligence Obligations in Supply Chains – An Examination of the German Approach to Business and Human Rights' (2021) 64 GYBIL 443.

BOX 7.7.2 Further Readings and Further Resources

Further Readings

- D Lustig, *Veiled Power: International Law and the Private Corporation, 1886–1981* (OUP 2020)

- G Baars, *The Corporation, Law and Capitalism. A Radical Perspective on the Role of Law in the Global Political Economy* (Brill 2019)

- D Danielsen, 'Corporate Power and Global Order' in Anne Orford (ed), *International Law and Its Others* (CUP 2006) 85

Further Resources

- Sundhya Pahuja, 'The Changing Place of Corporation in International Law' (Hersch Lauterpacht Memorial Lecture, 2018) <www.sms.cam.ac.uk/media/2696888> accessed 25 August 2023

- 'Laureate Research Program Global Corporations and International Law' <www.lpgcil.org/> accessed 25 August 2023

§ § §

§ 7.8 ANIMALS

ANNE PETERS

BOX 7.8.1 Required Knowledge and Learning Objectives

Required knowledge: Subjects and Actors

Learning objectives: Understanding the status of animals as objects rather than subjects of international law; getting an overview of the relevant legal regimes that protect animal collectives as natural resources or commodified endangered species; understanding possible advantages of the concept of personhood in international law.

A. INTRODUCTION

International law as it stands has not only failed to acknowledge non-animal personhood but has overall paid very little attention to non–human animals (in the following: animals) at all and is inconsiderate of animal needs. Animals are not international legal persons (subjects). Both the legal status of animals and the regulation of how humans should treat them lies in the *domaine réservé* (French: 'reserved domain') of States. As this chapter shows, the domestic shield is only gradually and selectively punctuated by some international or EU norms, often only soft ones. International (and European) law is most developed with regard to wildlife, or attached to transboundary constellations (international animal trade and livestock transport), or to animals outside national jurisdiction (in the High Seas). The chapter argues that recognising legal personhood of animals would signal that they 'count' in international law and would convey the message that animals are intrinsically valuable.

B. WILD ANIMALS: STATUS AND PROTECTION

Wild animals are commodified under international law (just as under domestic laws) and are qualified as natural resources.[533] They therefore fall both under the States' 'permanent sovereignty over natural resources'[534] and under the self-determination of

---

533 See article XX(g) General Agreement on Tariffs and Trade (signed 30 October 1947, provisionally applied 1 January 1948) 55 UNTS 194 and WTO, *United States: Import Prohibition of Certain Shrimp and Shrimp Products – Report of the Appellate Body* (12 October 1998) WT/DS58/AB/R [131]. See also article V(1) of the Revised African Convention on the Conservation of Nature and Natural Resources (adopted 11 July 2003, entered into force 23 July 2016) <https://au.int/en/treaties/african-convention-conservation-nature-and-natural-resources-revised-version> accessed 22 June 2023; article 77(4) United Nations Convention on the Law of the Sea (signed 10 December 1982, entered into force 16 November 1982) 1833 UNTS 397.

534 UNGA Res 1803 (14 December 1962) UN Doc A/RES/1803; *Armed Activities on the Territory of the Congo (Democratic Republic of the Congo* v. *Uganda)* (Judgment) [2005] ICJ Rep 168 [244].

peoples over natural resources.[535] The legal consequence of this status is that each State has the 'sovereign' right to exploit its 'own' resources pursuant to its own environmental and developmental policies. The interests of the animals themselves play no role here.

The status as a resource under the sovereignty of the territorial or range State and for disposal of its people is mitigated but not eliminated by universal and regional treaties on species conservation, trade in endangered species, habitat protection, and biodiversity. In these regimes, very few groups of animals (belonging to certain species) are the objects of protection and conservation, or otherwise indirectly benefit from ecological measures. The overarching paradigm is one of human stewardship over nature and its elements.

BOX 7.8.2 Advanced: Tensions Between Conservation and Exploitation

Under the purview of these regimes, the tension between conservation and human interests constantly comes up in the meetings or conferences of the parties. The intensification of international habitat and species conservation law would be more acceptable for humans in the Global South if wildlife protection included also the restoration of wild animals in Europe and North America that were extinguished by human civilisation. Scholars have read out such an obligation out of article 8(f) of the Biodiversity Convention, but with no acceptance in State practice so far.[536]

The international legal status of animals in areas beyond national jurisdiction (especially in the High Seas) is different but equally inconsiderate to the interests of the animals themselves. Marine life was here historically regarded as *res nullius* (Latin: 'nobody's thing', open to acquisition and exploitation by all). After the experience of over-exploitation and risk of depletion, the concept of *res communis* (or *res communis omnium* or *res omnium*; Latin: 'thing of the [entire] community'), that is, common property, emerged for wildlife in international spaces.[537] More recent scholarly concepts are wildlife as a global 'common concern',[538] 'common heritage',[539] and 'global

---

535 Common article 1(2) of the UN Human Rights Covenants (International Covenant on Economic, Social and Cultural Rights (adopted 16 December 1966, entered into force 3 January 1976) 999 UNTS 3 and International Covenant on Civil and Political Rights (adopted 16 December 1966, entered into force 23 March 1976) 999 UNTS 171); article 21 of the African Charter on Human and Peoples' Rights (adopted 27 June 1981, entered into force 21 October 1986) 1520 UNTS 217.

536 Convention on Biological Diversity (opened for signature 5 June 1992, entered into force 29 December 1993) 1760 UNTS 79. Arie Trouwborst, Jens-Christian Svenning, 'Megafauna Restoration as a Legal Obligation: International Biodiversity Law and the Rehabilitation of Large Mammals in Europe' (2022) 31 RECIEL 182.

537 Kemal Baslar, *The Concept of the Common Heritage of Mankind in International Law* (Martinus Nijhoff 1998) 312.

538 Werner Scholtz, 'Animals in International Law (Book Review)' (2023) 117 AJIL 386, 387.

539 Rachelle Adam and Joan Schaffner, 'International Law and Wildlife Well-Being: Moving from Theory to Action' (2017) 20 Journal of International Wildlife Law and Policy 1, 14.

environmental resource',[540] up to biodiversity as a 'global public good'.[541] These novel qualifications were first applied to wild animals in areas beyond national jurisdiction, and later also to wildlife inside national jurisdictions.

These concepts are valuable answers to problems of global distributive justice and inter-generational fairness. However, the aspiration of justice is still limited to humans, and not directed toward the animals themselves. The principal legal consequence of all these categories remains identical: States are (at most) obliged to manage the animals (as living resources) in a cooperative and sustainable way, to secure their common exploitation by humans, including their killing. Moreover, the focus is still almost exclusively on the protection of species as a group and not on the welfare of animals as suffering individuals. Although animal welfare may be promoted as a side effect of species conservation, both goals often stand in tension (e.g. when combating 'invasive species'). Finally, all new international law-based labels still treat animals as things as opposed to persons.

This would change with the recognition of wild animals' right to property or to sovereignty, or other fundamental rights (see on animal rights below). From the property perspective, groups of wildlife should become collective owners of the territory where the groups live or roam. The property (including overlapping and joint property) would be managed by a human trustee who is obliged to act in the best interest of the animal owners.[542]

Alternatively, wild animal sovereignty[543] or wild animal self-determination[544] could be acknowledged. From that perspective, the injustice of human encroachment into wild animal habitats resembles the injustice of colonisation.[545] This injustice needs to be acknowledged and as far as possible remedied through restoration and other measures directed at facilitating and re-enabling wild animal flourishing.[546]

C. CONCERN FOR ANIMAL HEALTH AS AN INTERNATIONAL PRINCIPLE

Animal health is the core mandate of the World Organisation for Animal Health (WOAH), founded under the name OIE in 1924.[547] It is also a main topic of the

---

540 Michael Glennon, 'Has International Law Failed the Elephant?' (1990) 84 AJIL 1, 34.

541 Edith Brown Weiss, 'Establishing Norms in a Kaleidoscopic World: General Course on Public International Law' (2018) 396 RdC 46, 112.

542 John Hadley, *Animal Property Rights: A Theory of Habitat Rights for Wild Animals* (Lexington Books 2015); Karen Bradshaw, *Wildlife as Property Owners: A New Conception of Animal Rights* (University of Chicago Press 2020).

543 On sovereignty, see Green, § 7.1, in this textbook.

544 On self-determination, see Bak McKenna, § 2.4, in this textbook.

545 On consent and colonialism, see González Hauck, § 2.2.B., in this textbook.

546 Sue Donaldson and Will Kymlicka, *Zoopolis* (OUP 2011) Chapter 6.

547 International Agreement for the Creation at Paris of an International Office for dealing with Contagious Diseases of Animals, with annexed Organic Statutes (signed 25 January 1924, entered into force 17 January 1925) 57 LNTS 135.

SPS Agreement,[548] which spells out the WTO members' obligations under GATT in relation to sanitary or phytosanitary measures and the application of the exception in favour of 'animal . . . health' (article XX(b) GATT). Animal health has become a prominent issue since the Covid-19 pandemic. It is one of the three elements in the One Health approach. 'One Health' signals that the health of humans, non-human animals, and the planet are interdependent and indivisible and must therefore be protected in a holistic way. This approach is pursued by an alliance of now four international organisations and programmes (WHO, FAO, WTO, UNEP).[549] It is also proposed as a principle of the draft treaty on pandemic preparedness currently under negotiation at the WHO.[550] However, the attention paid by these regimes to animal health, and the main motivation of the One Health approach has until now been purely anthropocentric, namely to prevent zoonoses and to safeguard human health and food security.

D. ANIMAL WELFARE AS A CUSTOMARY NORM OR GENERAL PRINCIPLE

Animal welfare (i.e. the well-being of animal individuals) has so far been addressed only very scarcely and in an ancillary fashion in some species conservation treaties.[551] Gradually, the international institutions entrusted with animal species conservation or animal health have begun to pay more attention to animal welfare and have even stretched their mandates in that direction.[552]

Notably, chapters with animal welfare standards have since 2002 been inserted into the (soft) animal health codes issued regularly by the WOAH and are regularly updated.[553]

---

548 Agreement on the Application of Sanitary and Phytosanitary Measures (signed 15 April 1994, entered into force 1 January 1995) 1867 UNTS 493.

549 'Memorandum of Understanding between the Food and Agriculture Organization of the United Nations and the World Organisation for Animal Health and the World Health Organization and the United Nations Environment Programme, Cooperation to Combat Health Risks at the Animal-Human-Ecosystems Interface in the Context of the "One-Health" Approach and including Antimicrobial Resistance' (29 April 2022) <www.woah.org/app/uploads/2023/06/20220317-mou-quadripartite-en.pdf> accessed 20 June 2023; 'One Health Joint Plan of Action (2022–2026): Working Together for the Health of Humans, Animals, Plants and the Environment' (14 October 2022) <www.who.int/publications/i/item/9789240059139> accessed 20 June 2023.

550 Art. 5 of the 'Proposal for negotiating text of the WHO Pandemic Agreement' (A/INB/7/3) of 30 October 2023 <https://apps.who.int/gb/inb/pdf_files/inb7/A_INB7_3-en.pdf>

551 See e.g. article VII(7)(c) of the Convention on International Trade in Endangered Species of Wild Fauna and Flora (signed 3 March 1973, entered into force 1 July 1975) 993 UNTS 243.

552 International Whaling Commission, 'The Florianópolis Declaration on the Role of the International Whaling Commission in the Conservation and Management of Whales in the 21st Century' (17 September 2018) Res. 2018–5 (Florianópolis Declaration), preamble, 3rd indent. See also International Whaling Commission, Intersessional Working Group on Welfare 'Progress on the Welfare Action Plan' (2022) Doc. No. WKMWI/68/5.1/01.

553 Last: WOAH, 'Terrestrial Animal Health Code' (31st edn, August 2023) (TAHC); 'Aquatic Animal Health Code' (25th edn, August 2023) (AAHC) <www.woah.org/en/what-we-do/standards/codes-and-manuals/> accessed 8 December 2023, reflecting the revisions at the 90th General Session (May 2023).

In 2022, the UN Environmental Assembly adopted a resolution 'Animal Welfare—Environment—Sustainable Development Nexus'.[554] This is the first mentioning of 'animal welfare' by a UN body. It seems to manifest at a 'One Welfare' approach, in extension of the One Health approach.

A WTO Panel acknowledged 'that animal welfare is a matter of ethical responsibility for human beings in general'[555] and that animal welfare is 'a globally recognized issue'.[556] This was confirmed by the WTO Appellate Body.[557] Animal welfare has thus become part of 'public morals'. Under that heading, animal welfare considerations allow States to deviate from obligations to liberalise trade under article XX(a) GATT and parallel provisions in bilateral and regional trade agreements. Concern for animal welfare is also a legitimate objective for limiting the exercise of international human rights (e.g. the right to property and contract, and freedom of research).[558]

Recent formal expressions of commitment to animal welfare seem to manifest the formation of a relevant *opinio juris* (Latin: 'legal opinion').[559] This might constitute one building block for the formation of an international customary norm.[560] Such pronouncements might also demonstrate a convergence upon a 'general principle of law' (article 38(c) ICJ Statute) that is widespread in the domestic legal systems and transposable to international law.[561]

However, a widespread relevant legal practice on respect for animal welfare is lacking. Around 50% of States have no animal protection legislation.[562] Against the background of wide variations in national legislation, the exact contours of the putative customary rule or of a general principle of international law are unclear. The hard core of a

---

554 UNEA resolution 'Animal welfare – Environment – Sustainable Development Nexus' (2 March 2022) UNEP/EA.5/L.10/rev.1.

555 WTO, *European Communities: Measures Prohibiting the Importation and Marketing of Seal Products – Reports of the Panel*, WT/DS400/R and WT/DS401/R (25 November 2013) [7.409].

556 *Ibid* [7.420].

557 WTO, *European Communities: Measures Prohibiting the Importation and Marketing of Seal Products – Reports of the Appellate Body*, WT/DS400/AB/R and WT/DS401/AB/R (22 May 2014) [5.201].

558 See the explicit reference to the protection of morals in article 10(2) of the Convention for the Protection of Human Rights and Fundamental Freedoms (European Convention on Human Rights, as amended) (ECHR) on freedom of expression, which includes freedom of research.

559 See with regard to whales *Whaling in the Antarctic (Australia v Japan, New Zealand intervening)* (Judgment, Separate Opinion of Judge Cançado Trindade) [2014] ICJ Rep 348 [9].

560 On customary international law, see Stoica, § 6.2, in this textbook.

561 Michael Bowman, 'The Protection of Animals Under International Law' (1989) 4 CJIL 487; Michael Bowman, Peter Davies, and Catherine Redgwell, *Lyster's International Wildlife Law* (2nd edn, CUP 2010) 680; Katie Sykes, '"Nations Like Unto Yourselves": An Inquiry into the Status of a General Principle of International Law on Animal Welfare' (2011) 49 Canadian Yearbook of International Law 3. On general principles, see Eggett, § 6.3, in this textbook.

562 GAL Association, 'Animal Legislations in the World at National Level' <www.globalanimallaw.org/database/national/index.html> accessed 20 June 2023.

possibly emerging universal principle (in one of the mentioned 'forms') seems to be only a prohibition of deliberate and wanton cruelty against animals.

E. PATHS TO FUTURE INTERNATIONAL ANIMAL PERSONHOOD

International legal personhood could be conferred on animals explicitly or even implicitly by treaty, and it could emerge as a customary rule, or as a general principle of international law. International law is particularly open to the personhood of non-humans – with States being the main persons in this legal order. The circle of international legal persons has never been closed but has been continuously expanded.[563] There is no intrinsic conceptual barrier against assigning legal personality to animals.

The concomitant change of the status of animals from 'things' ('objects') to 'persons' ('subjects') under international law would even match the status change of humans in international law that was triggered by legal developments after 1918 and completed only after 1945. In the early 20th century – when the idea of international legal personhood was first sharply conceptualised – humans were relegated to the realm of things, they were explicitly and adamantly qualified as 'objects', not 'subjects' of international law, by influential scholars.[564]

The currently booming case law on animal personhood in domestic law might in the long run give rise to a general principle of animal personhood that could then enter into the realm of international law (article 38(1)(c) ICJ Statute), provided that it is sufficiently widespread and transposable to the international legal order. The extant case law has been produced only by courts in the Global South, with Latin American courts being front runners. This regional concentration might actually facilitate the spread of the underlying principle. Its universalisation would be less suspect of legal imperialism, because it would travel in the opposite direction than the traditional legal migration that has almost always flowed from the North-Western legal orders (backed by economic and political power) to the South. However, such a maturation of animal personhood into a general principle in international law is not yet in sight and is not very likely.

Alternatively, animals could potentially benefit from the highly dynamic legislation and case law recognising Rights of Nature in all world regions, again mostly in the Global South.[565] It is not unlikely that these domestic developments will in the future give rise to a general principle of Rights of Nature. Then, it would be possible that

---

563 On the pluralisation of subjecthood in international law, see Engström, § 7.C., in this textbook.
564 See Heinrich Triepel, *Völkerrecht und Landesrecht* (Verlag von CL Hirschfeld 1899) 20–21; Lassa von Oppenheim, *International Law – A Treatise* (Ronald F Roxbourgh ed, 3rd edn, Longmans, Green 1920) Vol 1, Peace, para 290. On the individual in international law, see Theilen, § 7.4, in this textbook.
565 See UNGA 'Harmony with Nature: Report of the Secretary General' (26 July 2019) UN Doc A/74/236.

the animals which form part of nature would also be elevated to a rights-holder under international law, with a right to exist in integrity and flourish.[566] This would at the same time constitute an international legal personhood of animals, even if only a so-called partial one.

Animal international personhood would – unlike the international legal personhood of international organisations – not be an extension of States, but would rather feed on the moral pedigree of the personhood of humans. In this context, personhood appears to be more than a purely technical juridic device. It would signal that animals 'count' in international law and would convey the message that animals are intrinsically valuable. However, animals would always need some form of political and legal representation by humans to vindicate their legal status and rights if these are challenged or infringed.

F. CONCLUSION

Non-human animals are still far away from being recognised as international legal persons. More even, international law has up to now been a mixed blessing for them. Public international law treaties, due to their focus on animal species conservation, suffer not only from an animal welfare gap but even risk to pit animal species survival against individual animal welfare. Recent steps in the direction of upgrading the status and the interests of animals in international law are the expansion of regimes and institutional activity to cater for animal welfare, the Rights of Nature movement, and the insertion of the One Health principle into international governance.

These observations allow the conjecture that an overarching international norm of 'animal *protection*' is emerging. This emerging norm seems to encompass both the conservation of wild animals against extinction and the safeguarding of welfare and rights of individual animals of all groups (domestic, wild, and liminal) against suffering.[567]

If developed (much) further along these lines, international law in the Anthropocene might cater for the interests of animals to live in peace, even without enjoying the status of international legal persons. Importantly, however, the relevant international norms must be properly applied and implemented in the first place by national and local authorities. The need to design and monitor such domestic implementation warrants a global animal law approach.

---

566 This consequence has been drawn for the law of Ecuador by Constitutional Court of Ecuador, *Mona Estrellita, Sentencia* No. 253–20-JH/22, 27 January 2022.

567 Katie Sykes, 'Globalization and the Animal Turn: How International Trade Law Contributes to Global Norms of Animal Protection' (2016) 5 TEL 55–79.

BOX 7.8.3 Further Readings

Further Readings

- C Blattner, *Protecting Animals Within and Across Borders: Extraterritorial Jurisdiction and the Challenges of Globalization* (OUP 2019)

- M Bowman, P Davies, and C Redgwell, *Lyster's International Wildlife Law* (2nd edn, CUP 2010)

- A Peters, *Animals in International Law* (Brill 2021)

- W Scholtz (ed), *Animal Welfare and International Environmental Law* (Edward Elgar 2019)

- S Stucki, *One Rights: Human and Animal Rights in the Anthropocene* (Springer 2022)

§ § §

§ 7.9 CITIES

SUÉ GONZÁLEZ HAUCK AND RAFFAELA KUNZ

BOX 7.9.1 Required Knowledge and Learning Objectives

Required knowledge: Subjects and Actors, History of International Law

Learning objectives: Understanding how cities and other local governments shape and are shaped by international law.

A. INTRODUCTION

Although having played a role in shaping the global economy and international order,[568] cities are not among the traditional subjects of international law. Globalisation has sparked renewed interest in the concept of the 'Global City'.[569] Today, cities are vital sites for global concerns such as human rights, environmental sustainability, economic development, and inequality.[570] Some international instruments explicitly recognise cities as important actors. For example, the Paris Agreement recognises the importance of the subnational and local levels (articles 7(2) and 11(2)).[571] Transmunicipal networks like Local Governments for Sustainability and C40 address climate change mitigation, partly bridging gaps left by inconsistent commitments from national governments, notably the US.[572] Within the UN system, the United Nations Human Settlements Programme (UN-HABITAT) is devoted to issues of urbanisation and of people's lives in cities. Additionally, cities play a prominent role within the UN Sustainable Development Goals (SDGs), SDG 11 being devoted to inclusive, safe, resilient, and sustainable cities.[573] Cities are the spaces where international law plays out in people's everyday lives, where international norms are implemented, enforced, and challenged.[574] Given cities' role as hubs for social movements, studying them is crucial for engaging with international law

---

568 A Claire Cutler, *Private Power and Global Authority: Transnational Merchant Law in the Global Political Economy* (CUP 2003) 112 et seq.

569 Saskia Sassen, *The Global City – New York, London, Tokyo* (2nd edn, Princeton University Press 2001); Diane E Davis, 'Cities in Global Context: A Brief Intellectual History' (2005) 29 International Journal of Regional and Urban Research 92.

570 Janne E Nijman, 'The Future of the City and the City and the International Law of the Future' in Sam Muller and others (eds), *The Law of the Future and the Future of Law* (Torkel Posahl Academic 2011) 213.

571 Paris Agreement (adopted 12 December 2015, entered into force on 4 November 2016) 3156 UNTS 79.

572 Kelsey Coolidge, 'Cities and the Paris Agreement' in Vesselin Popovski (ed), *The Implementation of the Paris Agreement on Climate Change* (Routledge 2019) 263–282; Anél du Plessis, 'Climate Change Law and Sustainable Development' in Aust and Nijman (n 34) 187; Jolene Lin, 'The Role of Transnational City Networks in Environmental Governance' in Aust and Nijman (n 34) 201–213.

573 Helmut Philipp Aust and Anél du Plessis (eds), *The Globalisation of Urban Governance* (Routledge 2019).

574 Luis Eslava, *Local Space, Global Life. The Everyday Operation of International Law and Development* (CUP 2015); Luis Eslava, 'Istanbul Vignettes: Observing the Everyday Operation of International Law' (2014) 2 LRIL 3.

'from below'.[575] This section provides a concise overview of how cities have increasingly become subjects of international regulation and how they shape international law. At the same time, it urges caution against romanticising cities' roles.

B. DEFINITION AND LEGAL STATUS OF CITIES

Cities are defined by characteristics like population density, spatial expansion, diverse socio-economic activities, and land use.[576] Some interpretations equate cities with other forms of local governments, understood as subnational entities authorised to govern various matters.[577] Currently, cities lack recognition as subjects of international law or international legal personality.[578] Examples of cities apart from city States gaining international status independently are few, such as the Free City of Danzig and the International City of Tangiers, placed under international administration.[579] The starting point under international law is that cities are State organs and thus remain 'hidden behind the veil or the "black box" of their state'.[580] The status as State organs has international legal consequences. First, cities are bound by the international obligations of their mother State. If their conduct is not consistent with those obligations, this is attributed to the State (article 4 of the Articles on State Responsibility).[581] Second, their behaviour counts as State practice and may thus contribute to the formation of customary international law.

Cities' growing international role suggests rethinking their status as mere State organs. Arguably, cities' engagement with international law today is such that they gained international legal personality.[582] Arguments supporting this view include the dense web of agreements local governments conclude among themselves in the form of

---

575 Balakrishnan Rajagopal, *International Law from Below: Development, Social Movements, and Third World Resistance* (CUP 2003).

576 United Nations Human Settlements Programme (UN-HABITAT), 'What Is a City?' (2020) <https://unhabitat.org/sites/default/files/2020/06/city_definition_what_is_a_city.pdf> accessed 11 August 2023.

577 Yishai Blank, 'International Legal Personality/Subjectivity of Cities' in Aust and Nijman (n 34) 105.

578 Ibid; Chrystie Swiney, 'The Urbanization of International Law and International Relations: The Rising Soft Power of Cities in Global Governance' (2020) 41 Michigan Journal of International Law 227, 234; Anirudh Vijay and Jamia Millia Islamia, 'A Case for the International Legal Status of Cities and Local Sub-National Governments' (2019) Novum Jus 165, 167.

579 Yishai Blank, 'The City and the World' (2006) 44 Columbia Journal of Transnational Law 875, 886.

580 Blank, 'International Legal Personality/Subjectivity of Cities' in Aust and Nijman (n 34) 107.

581 ILC, 'Responsibility of States for Internationally Wrongful Acts (53rd session 23 April–1 June and 2 July–10 August 2001) UN Doc A/RES/56/83 Annex; see also James Crawford and Murielle Mauguin, 'Les collectivités territoriales non-étatiques et le droit international de la responsabilité' in Société française pour le droit international (ed), *Les collectivités territoriales non-étatiques dans le système juridique international* (Pedone 2002) 157; Katja Creutz, 'Responsibility' in Aust and Nijman (n 34). On State responsibility, see Arévalo-Ramírez, § 9, in this textbook.

582 For an overview, see Blank, 'International Legal Personality/Subjectivity of Cities' (n 35) 106–114; On international legal personhood and the pluralisation of subjects of international law, see Engström, Introduction to § 7, in this textbook.

transnational networks, with the field of climate change law being only the most prominent example.[583] International organisations as well started to 'go local' and cooperate with cities.[584] In some cases, cities forge direct links with international organisations that can be considered international obligations.[585] Furthermore, cities in many instances symbolically ratify treaties and enforce them, sometimes in response to their governments' inaction, such as in the case of 'sanctuary cities'[586] in the field of migration law or the activities of the C40 network to combat climate change mentioned in the introduction. Another often-mentioned development concerns cities' increasing involvement in proceedings before international courts, mostly in the area of international trade and economic law, with standing before international courts being another element of international legal personality.[587]

C. CITIES AND SPECIFIC SUBJECT AREAS

I. CITIES AND SUSTAINABLE DEVELOPMENT

Cities play a pivotal role in pursuing 'sustainable development'.[588] The 1972 Stockholm Declaration states that local governments, not just national ones, 'bear the greatest burden for large-scale environmental policy and action within their jurisdictions' (paragraph 7 of its preamble).[589] Principle 15 directly addresses cities, asserting that 'planning must be applied to human settlements and urbanization to avoid adverse environmental effects while maximizing social, economic, and environmental benefits for all'. Another milestone is Agenda 21, adopted at the 1992 'Earth Summit' in Rio de Janeiro.[590] This document mentions local authorities throughout, with article 28.2(a) setting a key objective for them to create a 'local Agenda 21'. In 2000, the World Bank introduced the 'Cities in Transition' guideline document, outlining a 'new strategy for an urbanizing world'.[591] This strategy envisions sustainable cities that are liveable, competitive, well governed, and financially solvent. Together with the 2002

---

583 For an overview, see David Gordon and Michele Acuto, 'If Cities Are the Solution, What Are the Problems? The Promise and Perils of Urban Climate Leadership' in Craig Johnson, Noah Toly, and Heike Schroeder (eds), *The Urban Climate Challenge – Rethinking the Role of Cities in the Global Climate Regime* (Routledge 2015).

584 See the overview in Jacob Katz Cogan, 'International Organizations and Cities' in Aust and Nijman (n 34).

585 See Michael Riegner, 'Development Cooperation and the City' in Aust and Nijman (n 34), using the example of the World Bank.

586 See e.g. Rose Cuisine Villazor and Pratheepan Gulasekaram, 'Sanctuary Networks' (2019) 103 Minnesota Law Review 1209.

587 Moritz Baumgärtel, 'Dispute Settlement' in Aust and Nijman (n 34).

588 Ileana M Porras, 'The City and International Law: In Pursuit of Sustainable Development' (2009) 36 Fordham Urban Law Journal 537; On sustainable development, see Poorhashemi, § 16.D.III., in this textbook.

589 'Report of the United Nations Conference on the Human Environment' (Stockholm 5–16 June 1972) UN Doc A/CONF.48/Rev.1.

590 'Report of the United Nations Conference on Environment and Development' (Rio de Janeiro 3–14 June 1992) UN Doc A/CONF.151/26 (Vol I).

591 Christine Kessides, *Cities in Transition: World Bank Urban and Local Government Strategy* (World Bank Group 2000); cf. Luis Eslava and George Hill, 'Cities, Post-Coloniality and International Law' in Aust and Nijman (n 34) 77; 82.

Johannesburg Declaration[592] and, notably, the 2007 UN-HABITAT International Guidelines on Decentralisation and the Strengthening of Local Authorities,[593] these documents constitute what Luis Eslava and George Hill call 'international urban law'.[594] Eslava and Hill offer examples of how this international urban law, applied specifically to cities in the Global South, can adversely affect local communities. For instance, in Rio de Janeiro, a World Bank–backed land-titling initiative forcibly displaced slum-dwellers.[595] Similarly, in Ulaanbaatar, an Asian Development Bank project implementing the World Bank's above-stated vision had a disciplining impact on local life without considering Ulaanbaatar's unique circumstances.[596]

In some instances this approach arguably bears resemblance to the 'indirect rule' model implemented during the late colonial period and particularly within the League of Nations' Mandate System.[597] In contrast to this top-down approach, there are instances of community-led, bottom-up projects originating within marginalised communities themselves. These projects aim to achieve social inclusion by reclaiming a portion of the city's economic and political capital for its residents, especially those living in informal urban settlements.[598]

II. CITIES AND HUMAN RIGHTS

Another important field concerns human rights law, originating in the human rights cities movement in the late 1990s.[599] Today communities around the globe gather at human rights cities meetings and engage with human rights in diverse forms.[600] In addition, there are numerous examples of local authorities adopting specific human rights treaties despite – or because of – their local governments refusing to do so.[601] An example is San Francisco, which ratified the Convention on the Elimination of All Forms of Discrimination against Women.[602] Another area where cities actively engage with human rights law often against contrary State policies is the protection of migrants.[603]

---

592 Report of the World Summit on Sustainable Development (Johannesburg 26 August–4 September 2002) UN Doc A/CONF.199/20.

593 United Nations Human Settlements Programme (UN-HABITAT), *International Guidelines on Decentralisation and the Strengthening of Local Authorities* (2007).

594 Eslava and Hill (n 593) 82.

595 Ibid 84.

596 Ibid 86.

597 Eslava, *Local Space, Global Life* (n 576) 20.

598 Maria Clara Dias and Luis Eslava, 'Horizons of Inclusion: Life Between Laws and Developments in Rio de Janeiro' (2013) 44 IALR 177, 182.

599 Barbara Oomen, Martha Davis, and Michele Grigolo (eds), *Global Urban Justice – The Rise of Human Rights Cities* (CUP 2016); Michele Grigolo, *The Human Rights City – New York, San Francisco, Barcelona* (Routledge 2019).

600 Martha Davis, 'Finding International Law "Close to Home": The Case of Human Rights Cities' in Aust and Nijman (n 34) 227–228.

601 For an overview, see Barbara Oomen and Moritz Baumgärtel, 'Frontier Cities: The Rise of Local Authorities as an Opportunity for International Human Rights Law' (2018) 29 EJIL 607, 616–617.

602 Stacy Laira Lozner, 'Diffusion of Local Regulatory Innovations: The San Francisco CEDAW Ordinance and the New York City Human Rights Initiative' (2008) 104 CLR 768.

603 Oomen and Baumgärtel (n 600) 617–619.

D. CONCLUSION

These brief elaborations have shown that cities occupy an important space on the international scene. Some even argue that they should be recognised as new subjects of international law. This position, however, has not yet entered the mainstream discourse. The city thus provides another example illustrating that the narrow category of subjects of international law does not capture all actors that play a role in the international legal order. In the current discourse, cities often form part of a progress narrative and are described as forces for good, strengthening international law from the bottom up and stepping in when governments fail to act in the interest of the local population. Yet, it is important to keep in mind that recognising the personhood of cities under international law would not be a positive development per se. Examples show that cities, just as any other actor holding power over people, may engage in discriminatory practices against minorities[604] or participate in upholding (national and global) economic inequalities.[605] While cities certainly shape international law, the internationalisation of the city also has repercussions for cities, exerting pressure to conform to an internationalised model of what a sustainable city should look like, which often runs counter to the needs and perspectives of marginalised local populations and echoing colonial models of indirect rule. Cities remain, however, important hubs for contestation, resistance, and community organising, which grapple with the contradictions that come with the internationalisation of cities.

BOX 7.9.2 Further Readings and Further Resources

Further Readings

- HE Aust and JE Nijman (eds), *Research Handbook on International Law and Cities* (Edward Elgar 2021)

- HE Aust and A du Plessis (eds), *The Globalisation of Urban Governance* (Routledge 2019)

- L Eslava, *Local Space, Global Life. The Everyday Operation of International Law and Development* (CUP 2015)

Further Resources

- China Miéville, *The City & the City* (Novel) (Macmillan 2009)

- Benjamin Barber, 'If Mayors Ruled the World' (*TedX Talks*) <www.youtube.com/watch?v=3BJgmV7GRVc> accessed 14 August 2023

§ § §

---

604 Patrick Lukusa Kadima, 'Afro-Phobia and the Law: How Has the South African Judiciary Responded to Cases of Afro-Phobia' (LLB dissertation, University of the Witwatersrand 2019).

605 Yishai Blank, 'Urban Legal Autonomy and (de) Globalization' (2020) 79 Raison Politique 57.

8

CHAPTER 8
JURISDICTION

SUÉ GONZÁLEZ HAUCK AND MAX MILAS

BOX 8.1 Required Knowledge and Learning Objectives

Required knowledge: History of International Law, States, International
Organisations

Learning objectives: Understanding the histories and functions of jurisdiction;
the difference between domestic and international jurisdiction; jurisdiction in
specialised fields of international law; how jurisdiction is used as a means of
exercising power.

BOX 8.2 Interactive Exercises

Access *interactive exercises for this chapter*[1] by positioning your smartphone
camera at the dot-filled box, also known as a QR code.

Figure 8.1 QR code referring to interactive exercises.

A. INTRODUCTION

Jurisdiction assigns an actor the authority to speak on behalf of the law. The Latin
origin of the term *juris dicere* (Latin: 'speaking law') illustrates this.[2] However, when an
individual is granted the right to speak from a position of authority, this simultaneously
restricts others from doing so.[3] International law confirms this (dis-)empowering
function of jurisdiction. Jurisdiction demarcates distinct realms: one domestic

---

1 https://openrewi.org/en-projects-project-public-international-law-subjects-and-actors-in-international-law/
2 Shaun McVeigh and Shaunnagh Dorsett, 'Questions of Jurisdiction' in Shaun McVeigh (ed), *Jurisprudence of
Jurisdiction* (Routledge 2007) 3.
3 Sué González Hauck and others, 'Jurisdiction – Who Speaks International Law?' (2022) 82 HJIL 289, 290.

DOI: 10.4324/9781003451327-10

jurisdiction from another, domestic from international, and one international sphere of competence from another.[4] Jurisdiction entitles States to exercise power within their territory by means of legislative, executive, and judicial authority. It can be exercised by the legislative (especially parliaments), executive (especially administrations) and judicial (especially courts) branches. International law reflects this threefold nature of jurisdiction by distinguishing between jurisdiction to prescribe, enforce, and adjudicate. The use of one term, jurisdiction, to describe different demarcations often leads to misunderstandings. However, these are inherent in the breadth – or 'multivalent'[5] nature – of the concept.

Jurisdiction generally describes a triangular relationship between a holder of authority, the share of the world to which this authority relates, and the creator or source of authority.[6] This chapter examines this triangular relationship, first, by focusing on the historical developments that shaped each side of the triangle as they relate to international law; second, by presenting the rules of international jurisdiction, which mainly authorise the State and relate to the concept of territory; and third, by shedding some light on varying concepts of community as sources of jurisdictional authorisation or entitlement.

B. HISTORICAL EVOLUTION OF JURISDICTION

In the Roman Republic, *iuris dictio* (Latin: 'the speech of the law') denoted the role of an official to judge in a matter.[7] Central to this concept was the principle of personality, wherein jurisdiction encompassed both the authority of an officeholder to make legally binding decisions and an individual's ability to invoke the law.[8] This principle necessarily led to pluralistic legal arrangements, where one person could be subject to multiple bodies of rules stemming from different authorities.[9]

The development of the modern notion of jurisdiction in the 16th and 17th centuries was intimately linked to the development of territorial sovereignty.[10] It was Jean Bodin's idea of sovereignty as absolute authority over a population that sparked authors like Pierre Ayrault to develop early versions of territorial jurisdiction.[11]

---

4 Ibid.

5 Asha Kaushal, 'The Politics of Jurisdiction' (2015) 78 MLR 759, 791.

6 Gregor Noll, 'Theorizing Jurisdiction' in Anne Orford and Florian Hoffmann (eds), *The Oxford Handbook of the Theory of International Law* (OUP 2016) 600, 601.

7 Louise Hodgson, *Res Publica and the Roman Republic: 'Without Body or Form'* (OUP 2017) 31, 83 et seq.

8 Kaius Tuori, 'The Beginnings of State Jurisdiction in International Law Until 1648' in Stephen Allen and others (eds), *The Oxford Handbook of Jurisdiction in International Law* (OUP 2019) 25–39, 28.

9 Kaius Tuori, 'The Beginnings of State Jurisdiction in International Law until 1648' in Stephen Allen and others (eds), *The Oxford Handbook of Jurisdiction in International Law* (OUP 2019) 25–39, 28.

10 Stuart Elden, *The Birth of Territory* (University of Chicago Press 2013).

11 Stéphane Beaulac, 'The Lotus Case in Context: Sovereignty, Westphalia, Vattel, and Positivism' in Stephen Allen and other (eds), *The Oxford Handbook of Jurisdiction in International Law* (OUP 2019) 40–58, 46, citing

During this period, jurisdiction's progression on the European continent retained elements of personal and religious dimensions. The Spanish and Portuguese concepts of jurisdiction were embedded in religious ideas of natural law, distinguishing between particular and local forms of worldly jurisdiction and the universal jurisdiction of the Catholic Church. The main argument that Spanish *conquistadores* (Spanish: 'conquerors') deployed to justify the subjugation of the indigenous population in the 'New World' was this universal Papal jurisdiction.[12]

The concept of jurisdiction in international law was subsequently formed by Alberico Gentili and by Hugo Grotius. Grotius developed the concept of 'freedom of the seas'[13] on behalf of the Dutch East India Company.[14] The main argument in his work *Mare Liberum* served to counter British and Spanish claims of exclusivity over the Atlantic and to legally facilitate the economic exploitation of the oceans by the Dutch East India Company.[15] The construction of jurisdiction-free spaces thus enabled European colonial powers to pursue their interests unhindered and seemingly legitimised by international law.[16]

The development of jurisdiction in the 19th century was marked by increasing formalisation, which had two main consequences. First, on the European continent, jurisdiction was now exclusively tied to territory. Second, formal colonial governments and bureaucracies replaced chartered companies as the protagonists of colonial appropriation, which resulted in the 'formalisation of empire' and included the imposition of strict territorial boundaries.[17] In the colonies, semi-colonial territories, and other territories subject to Western hegemony, the newly established Western model of exclusive territorial State jurisdiction was defended by dismissing and supplanting non-Western laws as unsystematic.[18]

Even though the Western model of jurisdiction was imposed on colonised territories, jurisdiction in the colonies differed from jurisdiction on the European continent. After all, the colonies were built on inequality and on – at best – relative sovereignty

---

Pierre Ayrault, *L'Ordre, formalité et instruction judiciaire, dont les anciens Grecs et Romains ont usé és accusations publiques* (Michel Sonnius 1588).

12 Nurfadzilah Yahaya, 'The European Conception of Jurisdiction in the Colonies' in Stephen Allen and others (eds), *The Oxford Handbook of Jurisdiction in International Law* (OUP 2019) 60. See also González Hauck, § 1.C.I., in this textbook.

13 Hugo Grotius, *The Freedom of the Seas or the Right Which Belongs to the Dutch to Take Part in the East Indian Trade* (Ralph van Deman MaGoffin, trans., OUP 1916) 24 et seq.

14 Martine Julia van Ittersum, 'Grotius: The Making of a Founding Father of International Law' in Anne Orford and Florian Hoffmann (eds), *The Oxford Handbook of the Theory of International Law* (OUP 2016) 82, 84–85.

15 Yahaya (n 12) 61.

16 Ibid 66.

17 Ibid 62–63.

18 Ibid 64–65; Werner Menski, *Hindu Law: Beyond Tradition and Modernity* (OUP 2003); John Strawson, 'Islamic Law and English Texts' in Eve Darian-Smith and Peter Fitzpatrick (eds), *Laws of the Postcolonial* (University of Michigan Press 1999); Bernard Cohn, *Colonialism and Its Forms of Knowledge: The British in India* (Princeton UP 1996).

of peoples in the South, whereas jurisdiction on the European continent relied on sovereign equality and non-intervention.[19] In addition, colonial jurisdiction relied on an intricate web of privileges and exceptions, epitomised in various forms of extraterritorial jurisdictions like treaty ports, concessions, garrisons, and protectorates, all of which served the primary objective of protecting commercial interests.[20]

These extraterritorial jurisdictions, with their links to the 'standard of civilisation', encapsulated the essence of legal imperialism.[21] The interplay between jurisdiction and colonial imperialism underscores its pivotal role in shaping legal paradigms on the global stage.

C. TERRITORIES OF JURISDICTION

International law uses jurisdiction for three key functions. It demarcates domestic jurisdictions from each other, distinguishes domestic jurisdiction from international jurisdiction, and separates international jurisdictions from each other. The concept of territory is central to each of these types of demarcations, in the sense that territorial sovereignty is generally presented as the rule and exercising jurisdiction without territory is seen as the exception.

I. THE CONCEPT OF TERRITORY

The concept of territory is not innately tied to jurisdiction. Instead, the relationship between jurisdiction and territory is contingent upon the specific decisions made in the context of specific social, economic, and political constellations.

Additionally, territory itself is not just naturally 'there'. Although it may be tempting to reduce territory to geographical expanse due to its physical underpinnings, a closer examination reveals that territory is a social institution,[22] shaped and constantly reshaped through cultural, social, and political practices.[23]

Understanding the contingent nature of territorial jurisdiction and the social character of territory itself provides insight into the phenomenon of 'jurisdiction without territory', exercising jurisdiction without a physical presence. This has historically taken three forms,

---

19 Antony Anghie, *Imperialism, Sovereignty, and the Making of International Law* (CUP 2005).

20 Yahaya (n 12) 69.

21 Ibid; Turan Kayaoglu, *Legal Imperialism: Sovereignty and Extraterritoriality in Japan, the Ottoman Empire, and China* (CUP 2014) 6; Daniel S Margolies and others (eds), *The Extraterritoriality of Law: History, Theory, Politics* (Routledge 2019).

22 John Agnew, 'The Territorial Trap: The Geographical Assumptions of International Relations Theory' (1994) 1 RIPE 53; Stuart Elden, *The Birth of Territory* (University of Chicago Press 2003) 3; Péter D Szigeti, 'The Illusion of Territorial Jurisdiction' (2017) 52 Texas International Law Journal 369, 372.

23 N Brenner, 'Urban Governance and the Production of New State Spaces in Western Europe, 1960–2000' (2004) 11 RIPE 447, 447.

which still exist in some way today.[24] The first is the direct exercise of extraterritorial jurisdiction by a State, seen in the informal empire created by imperial Western powers through the capitulation or consular regimes in semi-colonies.[25] This can be seen today in agreements such as the State of Forces Agreement signed by the US.[26] The second is the exercise of jurisdiction by private firms, historically seen in chartered companies like the Dutch and the British East India Companies, and now in multinational corporations that construct transnational non-State governance systems where they hold authority.[27] The third is jurisdiction exercised by international organisations, such as the Mandate System of the League of Nations, the Trusteeship system under the United Nations, and, in the present, International Territorial Administration.[28]

II. DOMESTIC JURISDICTION

1. Types of Domestic Jurisdiction

Jurisdiction entitles States to exercise power within their territory by means of legislative, executive, and judicial authority. In this respect, jurisdiction is an important component of State sovereignty.[29] Standard types of jurisdiction are thus jurisdiction to prescribe, jurisdiction to enforce, and jurisdiction to adjudicate.[30]

Prescriptive jurisdiction allows States to stipulate rules that govern the relationship between humans, institutions, corporations, animals, things, and the environment. States can enforce these rules by relying on their enforcement jurisdiction.[31] Finally, States may also provide for judicial or quasi-judicial procedures for the observance and enforcement of prescribed rules or legal relations between subjects according to their adjudicative jurisdiction.[32] International law contains rules that deviate from this basic freedom of States to prescribe, enforce, and adjudicate, depending on the area of law and the subjects concerned.

States always have jurisdiction within their territory unless explicitly prohibited.[33] This view is primarily based on the infamous *Lotus* case, in which the PCIJ held that – in

---

24 Bhupinder S Chimni, 'The International Law of Jurisdiction: A TWAIL Perspective' (2022) 35 LJIL 29, 35.

25 Eliana Augusti, 'From Capitulations to Unequal Treaties: The Matter of an Extraterritorial Jurisdiction in the Ottoman Empire' (2011) 4 JCLS 285, 290.

26 Kal Raustiala, *Does the Constitution Follow the Flag?* (OUP 2009) 138–140.

27 On corporations and international law, see González Hauck, § 7.7, in this textbook.

28 Ralph Wilde, *International Territorial Administration How Trusteeship and the Civilizing Mission Never Went Away* (OUP 2008)

29 Malcolm N Shaw, *International Law* (8th edn, CUP 2017) 483.

30 Bernard H Oxman, 'Jurisdiction of States' (*Max Planck Encyclopedia of Public International Law*, November 2007) <https://opil.ouplaw.com/display/10.1093/law:epil/9780199231690/law-9780199231690-e1436> accessed 22 August 2023, para 3.

31 Cedric Ryngaert, 'The Concept of Jurisdiction in International Law' in Alexander Orakhelashvili (ed), *Research Handbook on Jurisdiction and Immunities in International Law* (Edward Elgar 2015) 57.

32 Ibid 58.

33 Ibid 51.

the absence of a prohibition – international law permits States to exercise jurisdiction.[34] States can even enact laws and render judgments that govern conduct outside their territory.[35] However, these laws cannot be enforced provided there is no permission.[36] The permission can be based on treaties[37] between the States concerned or on customary international law.[38]

The three key principles of international law on jurisdiction can be traced back to the three components of Statehood: territory, population, and government.[39] First, States can exercise jurisdiction if an act takes place on their territory.[40] Second, they can exercise jurisdiction if their nationals act or are affected by an act on or outside their national territory.[41] Third, States can exercise jurisdiction if the act at least affects their effective exercise of State power.[42]

While this third principle is generally accepted, the specific definition is highly contested. According to the widest 'effects doctrine', propounded particularly by the United States, any effect is sufficient.[43] On the other side is the narrowest view, which requires impairment of the internal or external security of the State.[44] By way of conciliation, others demand at least a reasonable exercise of jurisdiction[45] or a genuine link between the State and the act giving rise to its jurisdiction.[46] However, this question cannot be answered in the abstract. Instead, the specifics of each field of international law must be considered.

2. Domestic Jurisdiction in Domains

a) Criminal Jurisdiction

In criminal law,[47] five grounds for jurisdiction were developed in the 19th century. According to the territorial principle, States may exercise jurisdiction over crimes committed on their territory. This applies both to crimes initiated on a State's own territory but finalised on foreign territory and to crimes initiated on foreign territory and finalised on a State's own territory.[48] From the perspective of jurisdiction, ships and

---

34 *The Case of the SS 'Lotus' (France v Turkey)* [1927] PCIJ Series A No 10 1 19.

35 Ibid.

36 Ibid 18.

37 On international treaties, see Fiskatoris and Svicevic, § 6.1, in this textbook.

38 On customary international law, see Stoica, § 6.2, in this textbook.

39 Jan Klabbers, *International Law* (3rd edn, CUP 2021), Chapter 5: Jurisdiction, Powers, and Immunities: Five Principles.

40 James Crawford, *Brownlie's Principles of Public International Law* (9th edn, OUP 2019) 442.

41 Ibid 443–445.

42 Ibid 446.

43 Ibid 447.

44 Ibid 446.

45 Ryngaert (n 31) 62–64.

46 Shaw (n 29) 516.

47 On international criminal law, see Ciampi, § 22, and the following sub-chapters in this textbook.

48 Crawford (n 40) 442–443.

aircrafts are part of the national territory of the flag or registering State and are thus subject to the territorial principle.[49]

Based on nationality, States may exercise criminal jurisdiction if the offence is committed by (active personality principle) or against (passive personality principle) one of their citizens.[50] According to the protective principle, States may exercise jurisdiction over crimes committed on foreign territory by foreigners if the offence threatens the national security or comparable interests of that State.[51] States of the Global North in particular invoke this principle to penalise irregular migration.[52] According to the universal principle, States may exercise criminal jurisdiction even though none of the four principles presented justifies jurisdiction, if the crime affects fundamental interests of the international community.[53] The principle applies in particular to piracy, slavery, genocide, crimes against humanity, war crimes, and torture.[54]

These five principles of jurisdiction must be distinguished from the enforcement of international criminal law. The five principles establish the jurisdiction of the State to enforce domestic criminal law, whereas the norms of international criminal law enable the enforcement of international law.[55] These specific grounds of jurisdiction in international criminal law cannot simply be transferred to other specialised fields of international law. Instead, the special rules of the respective field are decisive.

b) Civil Jurisdiction

Compared to criminal jurisdiction, States assume greater discretion for civil jurisdiction.[56] Ultimately, it is up to the respective State to define its civil jurisdiction. This results in differing practices. In common law countries, jurisdiction is often based on the territorial principle. Accordingly, States assert their jurisdiction as soon as a natural person enters their State's territory or a legal person registers (parts of) a company on its territory. Civil law countries often seek to establish jurisdiction in the State where the defendant resides.[57] Because of these wide possibilities it seems reasonable that States should be free to exercise their civil jurisdiction within the framework of the general rules of jurisdiction of international law.[58]

---

49 Ibid 448–450.

50 Ibid 443–446.

51 Ibid 446.

52 Ibid.

53 Ibid 451.

54 Ibid 452.

55 Ibid 451, 454–455.

56 Shaw (n 29) 488.

57 Crawford (n 40) 455–458.

58 Michael Akehurst, 'Jurisdiction in International Law' (1972) 46 BYBIL 145, 177; Frederick A Mann, 'The Doctrine of Jurisdiction in International Law' (1964) 111 RdC 49–51; Derek W Bowett, 'Jurisdiction: Changing Patterns of Authority Over Activities and Resources' (1983) 53 BYBIL 1, 3–4.

c) Immunity Law and Jurisdiction

Immunity law determines in which cases States cannot exercise their jurisdiction. It thus reflects the core idea according to which States may exercise jurisdiction unless it is prohibited by international law. Immunity law – as jurisdiction itself – serves to protect the sovereign equality of States.[59] Immunities from jurisdiction derive from State immunity, head of State immunity, and diplomatic immunity.[60] State immunity prohibits a State from exercising jurisdiction to enforce and to adjudicate over another State and its property.[61] According to the immunity of heads of States doctrine,[62] 'holders of high-ranking office in a State . . . enjoy immunities from jurisdiction in other States'.[63] Diplomatic immunity serves to protect the effective exercise of diplomatic functions by prohibiting the receiving States from enforcing laws and adjudicating against the diplomatic missions, the personnel of diplomatic missions, and the archives and communication of diplomatic missions of the sending State.[64]

d) Other Specialised Fields of International Law

Jurisdictional issues are also relevant in other fields of international law. In some cases, customary international law or international treaties prohibit the establishment of sovereignty over a territory (so-called common heritage of humankind), so that no State may exercise territorial jurisdiction. This applies in particular to Antarctica,[65] outer space,[66] and the high seas.[67] In other fields of international law, several States can simultaneously claim jurisdiction over a matter. For example, the internet[68] enables the exchange of communications and other data across borders. A typical data processing operation begins in one State, ends in another, and often has a global impact. States respond to this part of globalisation by relying on the nationality principle, the territoriality principle, or (a broad interpretation of) the protective principle as known from criminal law.[69]

---

59 Shaw (n 29) 523.

60 On immunities, see Walton, § 11, in this textbook.

61 Peter-Tobias Stoll, 'State Immunity' (*Max Planck Encyclopedia of Public International Law*, April 2011) <https://opil.ouplaw.com/display/10.1093/law:epil/9780199231690/law-9780199231690-e1106> accessed 22 August 2023, para 1.

62 On immunities of heads of States, see Walton, § 11, in this textbook.

63 *Arrest Warrant of 11 April 2000 (Democratic Republic of the Congo v Belgium)* [2002] ICJ Rep 3 [51], [54]–[55]. On immunities of heads of States, see Walton, § 11, in this textbook.

64 Rosanne van Akebeek, 'Immunity, Diplomatic' (*Max Planck Encyclopedia of Public International Law*, May 2009) <https://opil.ouplaw.com/display/10.1093/law:epil/9780199231690/law-9780199231690-e1055> accessed 22 August 2023, paras 1, 3. On diplomatic relations, see Arévalo-Ramírez, § 10, in this textbook.

65 The Antarctic Treaty (adopted 1 December 1959, entered into force 23 June 1961) 402 UNTS 71, article 4.

66 Treaty on principles governing the activities of States in the exploration and use of outer space, including the moon and other celestial bodies (adopted 27 January 1967, entered into force 10 October 1967) 610 UNTS 205 (OST), article II.

67 United Nations Convention on the Law of the Sea (opened for signature 10 December 1982, entered into force 16 November 1994) 1833 UNTS 397, article 86.

68 On international law in cyberspace, see Hüsch, § 19, in this textbook.

69 Oxman (n 30) paras 31–32; Johann-Christoph Woltag, 'Internet' (*Max Planck Encyclopedia of Public International Law*, September 2010) <https://opil.ouplaw.com/display/10.1093/law:epil/9780199231690/law-9780199231690-e1059?rskey=kNSxKR&result=1&prd=MPIL accessed 22 August 2023>, paras 17–20.

On waters,[70] jurisdictional overlaps may also occur, for example, between the State in which a ship is registered, the State whose citizens are on the ship, and the State in whose waters the ship is navigating. While the first two cases can already be resolved with the general principles of jurisdiction, modern maritime law divides the waters jurisdiction of States into three geographical zones. The sovereign zone includes the internal waters of a State, the territorial sea, and the archipelagic waters of a State. In this zone, a State may exercise its territorial jurisdiction exclusively, although other States have the right of innocent passage. The zone of sovereign rights includes the contiguous zone and the exclusive economic zone. In this zone, a State has the right to explore, exploit, conserve, and manage the environment. The territorial jurisdiction therefore lies with the coastal State. However, other States may also use this zone, provided that in doing so they do not interfere with any interests of the coastal State. On the high seas, no State may exercise territorial jurisdiction;[71] it remains territorially unoccupied.[72] Similarly to the maritime jurisdiction, States can also exercise exclusive territorial jurisdiction within the airspace above their territory, which includes territorial waters.[73] Vertically, however, this territorial jurisdiction is limited by customary law[74] on outer space[75] and international treaties[76] granting States the right to fly across the territory of another State.[77]

The flip side of jurisdiction are certain obligations. In international environmental law,[78] States have an obligation to ensure that activities within their territory do not cause damage in areas beyond their jurisdiction.[79] In international human rights law,[80] jurisdictional clauses state responsibility extraterritorially.

III. INTERNATIONAL JURISDICTION

While States[81] may claim jurisdiction based on their territory or population, international organisations[82] lack this possibility. Instead, they derive their power

---

70 On the law of the sea, see Dela Cruz and Paige, § 15, in this textbook.

71 Dolliver Nelson, 'Maritime Jurisdiction' (*Max Planck Encyclopedia of Public International Law*, January 2010) paras 55–58.

72 *The Case of the SS 'Lotus' (France v Turkey)* [1927] PCIJ Series A No 10 1 25.

73 Convention on International Civil Aviation (adopted 7 December 1944, entered into force 4 April 1947) 15 UNTS 295, article 2.

74 On customary international law, see Stoica, § 6.2, in this textbook.

75 Stephan Hobe, 'Airspace' (*Max Planck Encyclopedia of Public International Law*, May 2019) <https://opil.ouplaw.com/display/10.1093/law:epil/9780199231690/law-9780199231690-e1138?rskey=WX8mzC&result=1&prd=MPIL> accessed 22 August 2023, paras 9–13. On space law, see Kansra, § 20, in this textbook.

76 On international treaties, see Fiskatoris and Svicevic, § 6.1, in this textbook.

77 Hobe (n 75) para 16.

78 On international environmental law, see Poorhashemi, § 16, in this textbook.

79 *Case concerning Pulp Mills on the River Uruguay (Argentina v Uruguay)* [2010] Rep 14 (ICJ) [204–205]; see also Declaration on the Human Environment, UNGA Res 2994 (XXVII), 2995/XXVII and 2996/XXII (15 December 1972), Principle 21.

80 On recurring themes in human rights doctrine, see Milas, § 21.1, in this textbook.

81 On States, see Green, § 7.1, in this textbook.

82 On international organisations, see Baranowska, Engström, and Paige, § 7.3, in this textbook.

to speak from their founding treaties.[83] By way of example, article 1 of the WHO Constitution stipulates that the WHO shall promote global health. Similarly, international courts[84] base their jurisdiction on the treaties establishing them. For some courts, however, this is not sufficient to exercise jurisdiction. Instead, States must additionally consent to the jurisdiction of the court for contentious cases (*ratione materiae*).[85]

IV. OVERLAPPING JURISDICTIONS

The principles of the law of jurisdiction discussed above shape all fields of international law. However, each field derives specific rules from these principles to address its own particularities. At first glance, this produces a confusing, sometimes contradictory web of jurisdictional concepts. At the same time, the various fields of international law also face differing challenges that can hardly be resolved appropriately through uniform sets of rules. Often, more than one State may exercise jurisdiction in more than one field of international law based on more than one principle.[86] Similarly, several international organisations and courts often claim jurisdiction over the same matters.[87] In this respect, the fragmentation of jurisdiction in international law is evidence of 'the social complexity of a globalizing world'.[88]

D. JURISDICTION, POLITICS, AND PRACTICAL AUTHORITY

To understand jurisdiction beyond the purportedly neutral and technical rules, it is necessary to focus on how jurisdictional rules both rely on and shape political communities. To be given the authority to speak in the name of the law means being authorised to speak for the political community constituted and bound by this law.[89] Not only is jurisdiction intimately linked both to the constitution of a community and to the constant reorganisation of the varying attachments between the members of this community, but jurisdiction can also be used as a lens through which the meeting of communities and power struggles between them can be redescribed as a meeting of laws. Sundhya Pahuja adopts this latter approach to jurisdiction to redescribe the

---

83 Klabbers (n 39).

84 On international courts, see Choudhary, § 12, in this textbook.

85 Shabtai Rosenne, 'International Court of Justice (ICJ)' (*Max Planck Encyclopedia of Public International Law*, June 2006) paras 62–72. On consent, see González Hauck, § 2.2, in this textbook.

86 Oxman (n 30) para 10.

87 August Reinisch, 'International Courts and Tribunals, Multiple Jurisdiction' (*Max Planck Encyclopedia of Public International Law*, April 2021) <https://opil.ouplaw.com/display/10.1093/law:epil/9780199231690/law-9780199231690-e41?rskey=tVEzhz&result=1&prd=MPIL> accessed 23 August 2023.

88 ILC, 'Fragmentation of International Law: Difficulties Arising from the Diversification and Expansion of International Law – Report of the Study Group of the International Law Commission' UN Doc A/CN.4/L.682 and Add.1, para 222.

89 Kaushal (n 5) 760.

relationship between international law and its 'others', notably communities whose ways of life are dismissed by international law – particularly the 'development' project that came to replace the 'civilising mission' in the pursuit of deeming laws and forms of community that do not align with the needs of capitalism as mere 'traditions' or 'customs', which are not deemed to be on the same plane as 'law'.[90] Pahuja's approach to international law as the law of jurisdictional encounter allows, in particular, to see the relationship between claims to land made by colonising States under international law and indigenous claims to land as a relationship of rival jurisdictions.[91] This redescription allows us not only to see communities and laws that the classical account of international law has dismissed as 'backward' as being on the same plane as international law; it also offers a way of giving 'primacy to practical questions of authority, and to how the organisation of lawful relations takes place'.[92]

E. CONCLUSION

This chapter presented the doctrinal principles of jurisdiction, which shape almost all aspects of modern international law, within a critical framework informed both by the genealogy of jurisdiction and by an account of the material realities of jurisdiction as a reflection and tool of resource distribution. The chapter began by observing that jurisdiction assigns an actor the authority to speak in the name of the law. By conferring this right on one, it is at the same time denied to others. It is this simultaneously empowering and disenfranchising function of jurisdiction that, in the history of international law, is closely linked to colonial oppression and postcolonial exercise of power, but also to emancipatory movements that have struggled for a right to speak. However, there is nothing to suggest that jurisdiction will not continue to be used for inclusion and exclusion within the international system. A purely neutral, doctrinal perspective on jurisdiction will therefore never be able to capture the full potential of this concept.

BOX 8.3 Further Readings and Further Resources

Further Readings

- S Allen and others (eds), *The Oxford Handbook of Jurisdiction in International Law* (OUP 2019)

- BS Chimni, 'The International Law of Jurisdiction: A TWAIL Perspective' (2002) 35 LJIL 29

- A Kaushal, 'The Politics of Jurisdiction' (2015) 78 MLR 759

---

90 Sundhya Pahuja, 'Laws of Encounter: A Jurisdictional Account of International Law' (2013) 1 LRIL 6366.
91 Ibid 67.
92 Ibid 68.

- S Pahuja, 'Laws of Encounter: A Jurisdictional Account of International Law' (2013) 1 LRIL 63

- Nicole Roughan, *Authorities. Conflicts, Cooperation and Transnational Legal Theory* (OUP 2013) 262

- C Ryngaert, *Jurisdiction in International Law* (OUP 2015)

Further Resources

- 'EJIL: The Podcast! Episode 17 – "What's Wrong with the International Law on Jurisdiction?" '

- *Red Notice* (Directed by Rawson Marshall Thurber, Netflix 2021)

- *The Mosquito Coast* (Directed by Justin Theroux and Rupert Wyatt, Apple TV+ 2021)

- *Stateless* (Directed by Emma Freeman and Jocelyn Moorhouse, Netflix 2020)

- Sundhya Pahuja and Shaun McVeigh, 'Who Speaks International Law?' (*Völkerrechtsblog*, 4 September 2021) <https://voelkerrechtsblog.org/who-speaks-international-law-sundhya-pahuja-and-shaun-mcveigh-in-conversation/> accessed 21 August 2023

- Tendayi Achiume, 'Race, Borders and Jurisdiction' (*Völkerrechtsblog*, 4 September 2021) <https://voelkerrechtsblog.org/race-borders-and-jurisdiction/> accessed 21 August 2023

§ § §

9

CHAPTER 9
STATE RESPONSIBILITY
WALTER ARÉVALO-RAMÍREZ

BOX 9.1 Required Knowledge and Learning Objectives

Required knowledge: Sources; Subjects

Learning objectives: Understanding the regime of State responsibility and the steps to establish the consequences of an internationally wrongful act.

BOX 9.2 Interactive Exercises

Access *interactive exercises for this chapter*[1] by positioning your smartphone camera at the dot-filled box, also known as a QR code.

Figure 9.1 QR code referring to interactive exercises.

A. INTRODUCTION

Responsibility is the necessary corollary of a right. All rights of an international character involve international responsibility. Responsibility results in the duty to make reparation if the obligation in question is not met.[2]

(Max Huber)

Max Huber's famous statement makes clear that responsibility for internationally wrongful acts is a fundamental principle of international law, dealing with the consequences of breaches of international obligations. Since the first half of the 20th century, there has been a growing interest in the development and codification of the principles of State responsibility, reinforced by the emergence of permanent courts and

---

1 https://openrewi.org/en-projects-project-public-international-law-state-responsibility/
2 *Spanish Zone of Morocco Claims (Spain v United Kingdom)* (1925) 2 RIAA 615.

DOI: 10.4324/9781003451327-11

tribunals and the discussions regarding reparations that followed the two world wars. The issue was taken up at the 1930 Hague Codification Conference,[3] but the participating States were unable to reach an agreement. Later, the issue was selected as one of the first topics to be dealt with by the International Law Commission (ILC).[4]

Starting in 1956, the ILC focused efforts on developing a series of articles on State responsibility, taking as a reference pre-existing case law, State practice, and doctrine. Finally, in 2001 the ILC approved the Draft Articles on State Responsibility for Internationally Wrongful Acts (ARSIWA) and submitted the text to the UN General Assembly.[5] The original intention to translate the draft into a binding treaty never materialised. However, despite being commonly called 'draft' articles, great parts of the substantive content of the ARSIWA reflects customary international law and the articles are widely applied in practice.

This chapter analyses the concept of State responsibility. Following the structure proposed by the ILC, it discusses the elements required for the invocation of State responsibility and explores the consequences of established internationally wrongful acts.

B. THE CONCEPT OF INTERNATIONALLY WRONGFUL ACTS

I. THE NOTION OF 'OBJECTIVE RESPONSIBILITY' IN INTERNATIONAL LAW

Article 1 ARSIWA establishes the general principle of State responsibility. It states: 'Every internationally wrongful act of a State entails the international responsibility of that State'.[6] The direct relationship between a wrongful act and responsibility has been classified as a form of *objective* responsibility, since it is not dependent on elements such as negligence, guilt, or other forms of subjective responsibility.[7]

State responsibility is the set of new legal relationships and obligations that emerge between subjects of international law once an internationally wrongful act is attributed to a State.[8] The content of these possible new obligations consists of the consequences of the wrongful act and varies from case to case, as will be further discussed below.

---

3   Codification Conference, The Hague, 13 March to 12 April 1930. League of Nations Official Journal, Special Supplement, No. 92, 9.

4   James Crawford, *State Responsibility: The General Part* (CUP 2013) Part I.

5   ILC, 'Responsibility of States for Internationally Wrongful Acts (53rd session 23 April–1 June and 2 July–10 August 2001) UN Doc A/RES/56/83 Annex.

6   James Crawford, *The International Law Commission's Articles on State Responsibility: Introduction, Text and Commentaries* (CUP 2002) 32.

7   Ibid 77.

8   James Crawford, 'The ILC's Articles on Responsibility of States for Internationally Wrongful Acts: A Retrospect' (2002) 96 AJIL 874.

II. ELEMENTS OF AN INTERNATIONALLY WRONGFUL ACT

The elements of an internationally wrongful act can be understood as part of a two-tier test to establish State responsibility. In the first step, the internationally wrongful act is established; the second step consists of reviewing whether the conduct can be justified, as discussed below.

An internationally wrongful act is defined in article 2 ARSIWA as a conduct consisting of an act or omission that it is attributable to a State and constitutes a breach of a binding international obligation of a State at that time. The concept of 'act' was chosen by the ILC so as not to introduce concepts such as international 'crime' or 'offence', which could be confused with concepts of domestic law or international criminal law.[9]

Establishing State responsibility implies identifying (1) conduct, consisting of an action (positive acts against a primary obligation) or omission (e.g. failures to takes measures,[10] or any inaction that breaches a primary obligation) (2) that is attributable to a State by different criteria of individuals or groups that can be linked to the State as agents or subjects under their control, and (3) is a breach of an international obligation of that State, emanating from any primary rule that can be represented in any source of international law, from treaties to customary law, including obligations included in peremptory rules of international law (*ius cogens*).[11]

It is fundamental to highlight that 'harm' or 'damage' are not constitutive elements of the notion of an international wrongful act. A breach of a treaty can occur without harm (e.g. breaching a boundary treaty by an unauthorised movement of troops, without harming the territory of the neighbour State). It is noteworthy that in space law a regime of strict liability has emerged for dangerous activities in outer space.[12]

C. ATTRIBUTION

I. GENERAL PRINCIPLE

Attribution of conduct to a State implies a legal exercise whereby the conduct of an organ, a person, or a group of persons is imputed on that State, in accordance with criteria determined by international law. The State will thus be considered as the author of that act and the legal consequences will fall on it, without prejudice to the legal consequences that may also fall on the material author of the act or fact emanating from other regimes.

---

9 Crawford, *The International Law Commission's Articles on State Responsibility* (n 5) 111.

10 *Corfu Channel Case (UK v Albania)* (Assessment of Compensation) [1949] ICJ Rep 4.

11 Crawford, *The International Law Commission's Articles on State Responsibility* (n 5) 31.

12 Convention on International Liability for Damage Caused by Space Objects (adopted 29 November 1971, entered into force 1 September 1972) 610 UNTS 205. On space law, see Kansra, § 20, in this textbook.

In principle, the State is responsible only for wrongful acts of its organs and agents. Except in the cases expressly provided for, the acts of private persons are not attributable to the State under international law. However, not every conduct of organs and agents of the State is imputable to the State. Moreover, in exceptional situations, the State may be held responsible for acts of private persons. Public international law provides for several cases in which the conduct of certain individuals and organs is considered attributable to the State, as explained below.

II. ATTRIBUTABLE CONDUCT

1. Conduct of State Organs

Article 4 ARSIWA provides that the conduct of any State organ, whatever its position or function within the State, is considered an act of that State. In this sense, the concept of responsibility extends to any State entity, whether it exercises executive, legislative, judicial, or even commercial functions, at the central, regional, local or even federal government level.

The domestic law of the State plays a fundamental role in establishing whether a given entity constitutes a State organ for the purposes of international responsibility. However, the conduct of institutions exercising public functions is attributable to the State even if under domestic law such institutions are considered independent or autonomous.

According to article 5 ARSIWA, the conduct of any person or entity empowered by domestic law of a State to exercise public functions is attributed to the State, if the person or entity acts in that capacity. This is a *functional* criterion, since it refers to the function exercised by the individual or entity, regardless of whether it is structurally considered an organ of the State or not. In the *Hyatt* case, the authority given by Iran to a non-governmental entity to suggest enterprises for expropriation was considered an element of public authority.[13] Therefore, the State may be held liable for the wrongful conduct of parastatal entities or public, semi-public, or even private companies provided that (1) they are empowered by domestic law to exercise certain public or regulatory functions and (2) the act is related to the exercise of the assigned public or regulatory function.[14]

Article 6 provides that the conduct of an organ of a State in the service of another State with its consent and acting under its authority and control shall be attributable to the receiving State, as long as the organ is acting in the exercise of public functions of the State at whose disposal it is placed. For example, the Privy Council, a body of advisors to the British monarch, has occasionally acted as a judicial body of last resort at the disposal of several Commonwealth States. In such cases, the decisions of the Privy Council are attributable to the receiving State and not to the United Kingdom, from which the Privy Council originates.

---

13 *Hyatt International Corporation v Iran* (1985) 9 Iran-USCTR 72.

14 Michael Feit, 'Responsibility of the State Under International Law for the Breach of Contract Committed by a State-Owned Entity' (2010) 28 Berkeley Journal of International Law 142.

In any of the cases envisaged above, the conduct will be equally attributable to the State even if the person, organ, or entity has exceeded its competence or contravened its instructions or the domestic law of the State. Thus, article 7 ARSIWA provides that to the extent that the organ, person, or entity has acted in its official capacity, the State may not invoke the alleged violation of its instructions or the improper, illegitimate, or excessive exercise of public functions as circumstances for interrupting the link of attribution of the conduct to a State. However, if the conduct of the organ, person or entity is totally outside its official functions (i.e. *ultra vires*), such conduct will not be attributable to the State.

2. Conduct of Factual Organs of a State

Article 8 ARSIWA provides for a control criterion according to which the conduct of a person or group of persons acting on the instructions or under the direction or control of the State is a de facto State organ. Their behaviour is considered attributable to the State even though from an administrative point of view it is not an organ within its official structure.

For example, in the case of an armed conflict, the internationally wrongful act of a paramilitary group fighting against government armed forces may give rise to the international responsibility of a third State if the group acts under its control.[15] Similarly, semi-public or even private companies may be attributable to the State when they act on the instruction or control of that State. The mere ownership of an enterprise by the State does not necessarily imply that the acts of the enterprise are attributable to the State, except in cases where the enterprise has exercised public powers, in accordance with article 5 of the Draft Articles.

Several criteria regarding the threshold of control needed to attribute conduct of private entities to a State have emerged from the practice of international courts: while the International Court of Justice (ICJ) has developed a strict notion of 'effective control',[16] the International Criminal Tribunal for the Former Yugoslavia (ICTY) developed an overall criterion that does not require direct, effective knowledge or control of every act committed by the entity and the direction of its goals.[17]

3. Attribution in the Absence of a State

Article 9 ARSIWA provides for the case in which, exceptionally, due to a revolution, armed conflict or foreign occupation, the regular State organs are absent or prevented from acting. In such a case, the conduct of persons or groups of persons exercising public functions shall be attributable to the State.[18]

---

15 Veronika Holker and Walter Arévalo Ramírez, 'La Responsabilidad Internacional y la Jurisdicción Especial para la Paz en Colombia Frente a la Corte Penal Internacional' in Carlos Escobar Uribe (ed), *Gobernanza Global y Responsabilidad Internacional del Estado Experiencias en América Latina* (Universidad del Bosque 2019).

16 *Military and Paramilitary Activities in and against Nicaragua (Nicaragua v USA* (Merits) [1986] ICJ Rep 14.

17 *Prosecutor v Duško Tadić* (Judgment) ICTY-94-1-A (15 July 1999).

18 Tania Bonilla Matiz and Walter Arévalo Ramírez, 'Responsabilidad Internacional del Estado por Hechos Internacionalmente Ilícitos, Obligaciones Internacionales Emanadas del Sistema Interamericano de Derechos

Article 10 of the Draft Articles provides that if an insurrectional movement succeeds in becoming the new government of a State, its conduct shall be attributable to that State. Furthermore, should the insurrectional movement succeed in establishing a new State, its conduct shall be attributable to the new State. If the insurrectional movement fails to take over the government of the State or in creating a new State, its acts shall not be attributable to the State, without prejudice to other criteria of attribution under the Draft Articles, for instance, if the insurrectional movement acts under the control of a third State under article 8 ARSIWA.

Article 11 contains a residual criterion, according to which the conduct of a person or entity that is explicitly or implicitly recognised and adopted by the State as its own shall be attributable to that State, even if none of the above-mentioned criteria of attribution are met. Therefore, the attribution of the conduct to the State will be determined by a subsequent act of that State recognising or adopting such conduct as its own.

4. Responsibility in Connection With Acts of Another State

In principle, each State is responsible for its own conduct. Nonetheless, there are three exceptional situations in which a State is held responsible for an internationally wrongful act committed by another State, without prejudice to the international responsibility of the State committing the wrongful act.

First, a State which aids or assists another State in the commission of an internationally wrongful act is internationally responsible, provided that (1) the State has knowledge that its aid or assistance will contribute to the commission of an internationally wrongful act, (2) the aid or assistance is given with the intent to facilitate the commission of the wrongful act, and (3) the assisting State is also bound by the obligation breached, so that the conduct of the assisted State would have been equally wrongful had it been committed directly by the assisting State (article 16 ARSIWA).

Second, a State directing and controlling another State in the commission of an internationally wrongful act is internationally responsible, provided that (1) the controlling State has knowledge of the wrongful character of the act, and (2) the controlling State is also bound by the obligation breached (article 17 ARSIWA). For example, in case of military occupation where the organs of the occupied State act under the direction and control of the occupying State, the occupying State is vicariously liable, without prejudice to the direct responsibility of the occupied State.

Finally, article 18 provides for the responsibility of a State which coerces another State to commit an internationally wrongful act, that is, which exercises force or violence against another State to cause the coerced State to breach an international obligation.

Humanos y Procesos de Justicia Transicional: Entre el Cumplimiento y la Colisión' in Carlos Mauricio López-Cárdenas (ed), *Reflexiones Sobre el Sistema Interamericano de Derechos Humanos* (Editorial Universidad del Rosario 2020).

The coercing State shall be held solely responsible towards the third State provided that it acted with knowledge of the circumstances of the wrongful act and that the act would have constituted an internationally wrongful act of the coerced State.

D. CIRCUMSTANCES PRECLUDING WRONGFULNESS

I. GENERAL PRINCIPLE

In certain situations, the breach of an obligation may be excused and some of the consequences of such breach avoided. These so-called circumstances precluding wrongfulness are of general application, that is, they apply to obligations arising from any source of international law.

Furthermore, the circumstances precluding wrongfulness only exclude the wrongfulness of the act but are not exemptions from responsibility. This implies that they do not exempt the State from the obligation to repair the damages caused by the conduct that would have been unlawful if the circumstances precluding wrongfulness had not arisen, nor do they destroy the existence and continuity of the international obligation, to which the State covered by the cause must return as soon as possible.

II. THE CIRCUMSTANCES PRECLUDING WRONGFULNESS

1. Consent

Article 20 ARSIWA provides that a State may obtain the consent of another State which, in the absence of such permission, would constitute a wrongful act. To be valid, consent must be given by State authorities who are authorised to represent the State and bind it internationally.

Consent is not required to be given through an instrument as the one where the principal obligation arises, such as a treaty, and may extend both before and during the occurrence of the allegedly wrongful conduct. The limits of the consent granted by the State must be respected. Otherwise, independent wrongful acts will be established. For example, in the case of a permit to cross the airspace to attend to a specific situation, if unauthorised overflights were to take place subsequently, each of these would constitute an autonomous wrongful act.

2. Self-Defence

Wrongfulness is excluded if a State breaches its international obligations in the exercise of an act of self-defence under article 2(4) of the UN Charter,[19] whether

---

19 Charter of the United Nations (signed 26 June 1945, entered into force 24 October 1945) 1 UNTS XVI. On self-defence, see Svicevic, § 13, in this textbook.

against the State from which it is repelling an attack or against third States (article 21 ARSIWA).[20]

Self-defence as a circumstances precluding wrongfulness has certain limits.[21] On the one hand, for the circumstance to be valid, the State invoking it must comply with all the substantive and procedural elements described in the UN Charter on self-defence and the general prohibition of the use of force.[22] Likewise, acts carried out in the context of self-defence must respect international humanitarian law.[23]

3. Countermeasures

Countermeasures are reactive actions against a State's wrongful conduct, which seek to compel it to return to compliance with a breached obligation. They consist of measures that seek to have a sufficient effect on the State that has breached an obligation, so that it ceases its non-compliance. They have been described as legal reprisals or sanctions in some proceedings.[24] In the choice of these measures, obligations in force between the two States in question may be breached. An example is the enactment of a tax bill, otherwise prohibited by a free trade agreement, to induce the other State party to return to compliance with its obligations.[25]

Countermeasures are a circumstance excluding wrongfulness if they meet certain requirements: they need to be proportionate, temporary, and to be lifted once the breach has ceased. Furthermore, they may not constitute measures of armed force and must be reversible in nature and not punitive in character.[26]

4. Force Majeure

Force majeure is characterised especially by the presence of an invincible, uncontrollable, and involuntary element that compels the State to perform a conduct that is contrary to what is required of it by an international obligation. Article 23 ARSIWA, by recognising an 'irresistible force' or an 'unforeseen event' beyond the control of the State, accepts that both natural and human-made causes may constitute circumstances of force majeure, such as an avalanche, an earthquake, or an armed attack on a portion of the territory.

---

20 Walter Arévalo Ramírez, 'Responsabilidad Internacional del Estado por Hechos Internacionalmente Ilícitos: Las Causales de Exclusión de Ilicitud, su Contenido y Escenarios de Aplicación' in Ricardo Abello Galvis (ed), *Derecho Internacional: Varias Visiones un Maestro: Liber Amicorum en Homenaje a Marco Gerardo Monroy Cabra* (Editorial Universidad del Rosario 2015).

21 Jean-Marc Thouvenin, 'Circumstances Precluding Wrongfulness in the ILC Articles on State Responsibility: Self-Defence' in James Crawford and others (eds), *The Law of International Responsibility* (OUP 2010).

22 On self-defence, see Svicevic, § 13, in this textbook.

23 *Legality of the Threat or Use of Nuclear Weapons* (Advisory Opinion) (1996) ICJ Rep 226.

24 *Case Concerning the Air Services Agreement of 27 March 1946 (US v France)* (1979) 54 ILR 303.

25 *Archer Daniels Midland Company and Tate & Lyle Ingredients Americas, Inc. v. United Mexican States*, ICSID Case No ARB(AF)/04/5, Award (21 November 2007).

26 Thomas M Franck, 'On Proportionality of Countermeasures in International Law' (2008) 102 AJIL 715.

These circumstances, apart from being unforeseeable (or difficult to foresee or avoid) must create a situation where it is materially impossible to perform an international obligation, and not only make its performance more difficult.[27] A circumstance where the State invoking it has directly contributed to the existence of the circumstance will not be admissible as force majeure. Nor does it exempt from the damage generated by the action; it only exempts from its wrongfulness, such as the damage caused by the ships of a State that are dragged to a foreign port by an irresistible storm.

5. Distress

In the case of distress, article 24 ARSIWA recognises the voluntary and conscious action to take a measure contrary to an international obligation to save lives in a situation of maximum danger and urgency. The circumstance has been mostly invoked in cases of ships and aircrafts that, in the face of mechanical failures or meteorological threats, enter the territory of another State without permission seeking shelter from the weather or other emergencies that threaten the loss of the ship and the lives on board. The circumstance of distress cannot be invoked if the measure taken to safeguard the lives of the persons on board generates a greater danger. Likewise, the circumstance of distress is invalidated if the situation of distress is the result of the negligence of the State, such as the lack of aircraft maintenance.

6. Necessity

Article 25 ARSIWA provides that necessity may not be invoked unless the act from which wrongfulness is sought to be excluded (1) is the only way for the State to safeguard an essential interest against a grave and imminent peril and (2) does not seriously affect an essential interest of another State. This is the only circumstance identified by the ILC that begins with a prohibition on its invocation. This is due to the delicate legal and political consequences of the indeterminacy of the concept 'essential interest of the State' at the heart of the circumstance. In the case of a recent economic crisis in Argentina, resolving the claims of different foreign investors against the State, some arbitral tribunals admitted and at the same time others rejected that Argentina invoked that its economic stability was an 'essential interest' to justify violations of obligations regarding the protection of foreign investment.[28]

E. INVOCATION OF STATE RESPONSIBILITY

The international responsibility of a State arises when the conditions analysed above are met. However, to give effect to such responsibility, it must be invoked by the injured State or another subject of international law entitled to that effect. Who is entitled

---

27 Crawford, *The International Law Commission's Articles on State Responsibility* (n 5).

28 Walter Arévalo Ramírez and Laura Garcia, 'El Estado de Necesidad en el Arbitraje de Inversión: su Invocación Consuetudinaria y Convencional en los Arbitrajes Enron, Sempra, CMS, LG&E y Continental ante el Centro Internacional de Arreglo de Diferencias Relativas a Inversiones (CIADI)' (2017) 17 AMDI 469.

to invoke of a breach or in other words enjoys standing depends on the nature of the obligation. Article 42 ARSIWA illustrates that in the case of bilateral treaties, the standing lies in the injured State party. In a multilateral treaty or an obligation owed to a group of States, the standing lies on any State that has been specially affected by the breach, or the breach has affected its position for further compliance of the obligation. Finally, in the case of peremptory norms of international law (*ius cogens*), recent cases such as the *Genocide* case show that any State could bear a legitimate interest to invoke the breach.[29]

F. CONSEQUENCES OF STATE RESPONSIBILITY

Article 28 of the Draft Articles reflects the general principle that an internationally wrongful act produces legal consequences. The responsible State will be subject to several obligations, without prejudice to the legal consequences provided for under other regimes. By way of example, in case of a serious breach of a treaty, the injured State will be entitled to terminate or suspend the treaty.[30]

I. CESSATION AND NON-REPETITION

Besides the obligation to make reparation as discussed in the next section, article 30 ARSIWA provides two additional obligations of the responsible State. First, the responsible State must cease its wrongful conduct. The obligation will arise only if the wrongful act is of a continuing or composite nature and the breached norm remains in force despite its violation by the responsible State.

Second, the responsible State may be obliged to provide adequate assurances and guarantees of non-repetition of its wrongful conduct when this is deemed necessary for the purpose of restoring confidence between the parties and preventing future violations. Unlike the obligations to make reparation and to cease the wrongful conduct, this obligation will arise only in exceptional situations considering the rank of the obligation breached, the gravity of the breach, and the risk that the responsible State will again incur in the breach of the obligation.[31]

The flagrant or systematic violation of a peremptory norm (*ius cogens*), for instance in case of genocide or torture, in addition will give rise to obligations for the international community as a whole.[32] Article 41 ARSIWA provides for the obligation of all States (1) to cooperate to put an end to the violation, either within the framework of the UN

---

29 *Application of the Convention on the Prevention and Punishment of the Crime of Genocide (The Gambia v. Myanmar* (Request for the Indication of Provisional Measures: Order) [2020] ICJ Rep 3.

30 On the grounds for treaty termination, see Fiskatoris and Svicevic, § 6.1, in this textbook.

31 Ricardo Abello Galvis, 'Introducción al Estudio de las Normas de Ius Cogens en el Seno de la Comisión de Derecho Internacional, CDI' (2011) 60 Vniversitas 75.

32 Ibid.

or through any other lawful means,[33] (2) not to recognise as lawful situations resulting
from the violation, and (3) not to give aid or assistance to the responsible State to
maintain the situation of non-compliance.

II. REPARATION

1. General Principle

Articles 31 and 34 ARSIWA state the obligation to make full reparation for the
damages caused by a wrongful act, including both material and moral damages and
interest. International tribunals, such as the PCIJ, the PCA, the ICJ, or the IACHR,
have reiterated that reparation of the damage is carried out under the principle of
restitutio in integrum, or integral reparation of the damage, enunciated by the ICJ in the
Factory at Chorzów case.[34] According to this principle, the possibility that the reparation
exceeds the damage and may have punitive, sanctioning or preventive functions, as
occurs with the *torts* regime in common law, is excluded.[35]

The forms of reparation may be given in a single or combined form. Some specific
treaties and particular jurisdictions (e.g. regional human rights systems)[36] may require
that the forms of reparation be given concomitantly in the face of serious human rights
violations to achieve true *restitutio in integrum*.[37]

2. The Different Forms of Reparation

a) Restitution

The first measure of reparation, enshrined in article 25 ARSIWA, is restitution,
understood as the return to the situation as it was before the internationally wrongful
act. Usually, it takes the form of a material conduct such as the release of persons
illegally detained, the return of property, the reversal of a judicial decision[38] or a legal
norm that violates an international obligation, the withdrawal of troops, and so forth.
Restitution as a path within reparation is only available in cases where it is materially
possible to return to previous circumstances.

---

33 Andrés Téllez Nuñez, 'Aproximación Multidimensional al Régimen de Responsabilidad Internacional y al
   Principio de No Intervención. El Problema Hermenéutico' (2020) 13 ACDI 79.
34 *Case Concerning the Factory at Chorzów (Germany v Poland)* (Merits) PCIJ Rep Series A No 17.
35 Walter Arévalo Ramírez and Laura Garcia Matamoros, 'Recent Developments in Punitive Damages in Civil
   Law, Common Law, the Interamerican Human Rights System and International Law' (2019) 37 Revista de
   Derecho Privado 183.
36 Eduardo Ferrer Mac-Gregor, 'Conventionality Control the New Doctrine of the Inter-American Court of
   Human Rights' (2015) 109 AJIL Unbound 93.
37 *Case of Velásquez-Rodríguez v. Honduras*, Merits, Inter-American Court of Human Rights Series C No 4
   (29 July 1988) 25.
38 Walter Arévalo Ramírez, 'Resistance to Territorial and Maritime Delimitation Judgments of the International
   Court of Justice and Clashes with 'Territory Clauses' in the Constitutions of Latin American States' (2022)
   35 LJIL 185.

b) Compensation

If restitution is not possible, article 36 provides compensation as another way of redressing an injury caused by an internationally wrongful act. Compensation corresponds to the payment of any damage that is susceptible of financial assessment, including loss of profits insofar as proven.[39] International jurisprudence has repeatedly held that a court that has jurisdiction to declare the international responsibility for a wrongful act has jurisdiction to produce a judgment fixing the amount of compensation, unless otherwise agreed by the parties. The practice of the tribunals has not only recognised compensation to pay for damages caused to the property of a State,[40] but has also for environmental damage,[41] violations of investment regimes, loss of profits, and injuries to individuals. Regularly, the value of compensation corresponds to an average of the market cost of the affected assets. Likewise, loss of profit has generally been predicated on assets whose nature is the production of wealth, such as industries, infrastructure works, merchant ships, investments, and so forth. It has also been recognised that some incidental measures taken by the affected State to mitigate the damage may be subject to compensation.[42]

c) Satisfaction

Exceptionally, when some type of damage with special characteristics has not been repaired through restitution or is not susceptible of financial evaluation, the responsible State must resort to satisfaction to achieve full reparation of the damage caused (article 37 ARSIWA).

Satisfaction responds directly to the moral damages not susceptible of financial evaluation that the affected party may suffer which is of a *symbolic* nature. Examples are affronts to national symbols such as the flag, invasion of territory, or mistreatment of the head of State.

Forms of satisfaction include the express acknowledgment of the act, public apologies, diplomatic notes, reestablishment of diplomatic relations, and expressions of regret by the head of State. In more particular scenarios, more complex forms of satisfaction have been developed to repair wrongful acts relating to serious human rights violations, such as the experience of the IACtHR.[43]

---

39 See *Chorzów Factory Case* (n 33) and *Nicaragua v USA* (n 15).

40 *Corfu Channel Case (UK v Albania)* (Merits) [1949] ICJ Rep 4.

41 Dinah Shelton, 'Righting Wrongs: Reparations in the Articles on State Responsibility' (2002) 96 AJIL 833.

42 Ángela Rey Anaya and Ernesto Rey Cantor, *Medidas Provisionales y Medidas Cautelares en el Sistema Interamericano de Derechos Humanos* (Temis 2005).

43 Juana Inés Acosta López and Álvaro Francisco Amaya Villarreal, 'La Responsabilidad Internacional del Estado Frente al Deber de Custodia: Estándares Internacionales Frente a los Centros Estatales de Detención' (2011) 13 ESJ 301. On reparations in the Inter-American system, see Kahl, Arévalo-Ramírez, and Rousset-Siri, § 21.5, in this textbook.

G. CONCLUSIONS

State responsibility for international wrongful acts, despite the successful attempts of codification by the ILC, is still an evolving subject of international law. Recent discussions mentioned above include the issue of standing in the face of breaches of peremptory norms of international law, the scope of the circumstances precluding wrongfulness and the development of new ways to fulfil the reparations of the damages that can come along with the breach of an international obligation.

BOX 9.3 Further Readings

Further Readings

- M Feit, 'Responsibility of the State Under International Law for the Breach of Contract Committed by a State-Owned Entity' (2010) 28 Berkeley Journal of International Law 142

- D Shelton, 'Righting Wrongs: Reparations in the Articles on State Responsibility' (2002) 96 AJIL 833

---

§ § §

CHAPTER 10
DIPLOMATIC RELATIONS
WALTER ARÉVALO-RAMÍREZ

BOX 10.1 Required Knowledge and Learning Objectives

Required knowledge: Subjects of International Law

Learning objectives: To understand the background, functions, privileges, and
immunities surrounding diplomatic relations.

BOX 10.2 Interactive Exercises

Access *interactive exercises for this chapter*[1] by positioning your smartphone
camera at the dot-filled box, also known as a QR code.

Figure 10.1 QR code referring to interactive exercises.

A. INTRODUCTION

The role of diplomatic relations has fluctuated between periods of history. In the classic
age of diplomacy, from the Renaissance to the Congress of Vienna,[2] it was a tool for
bilateral relations and not part of public international law. It was based on techniques of
negotiation and representation to achieve its main objective: establish political relations
between States, always protecting national interests.

In the contemporary age of diplomacy, the role of diplomats lies in establishing relations
that transcend the realm of politics, including cultural, economic, and scientific
relations. The aim is to foment friendly relations between nations and citizens, often
called 'Public Diplomacy'.

---

1 https://openrewi.org/en-projects-project-public-international-law-diplomatic-relations/
2 Jovan Kurbalija, 'Diplomacy Between Tradition and Innovation' (*DiploFoundation*, 28 January 2021)
   <www.youtube.com/watch?v=_rVKDuABZH0&t=9s> accessed 9 August 2023.

DOI: 10.4324/9781003451327-12

Diplomatic relations have evolved with the emergence of international organisations. They have changed the way States interact, turning international relations from bilateral to multilateral settings, leaving behind the secrecy of diplomacy that was commonplace during the Cold War. Also, the advances in communication means bring new possibilities for multilateral forms of diplomacy.

Diplomatic relations should not be confused with foreign policy. Foreign policy usually refers broadly to the policy and decisions taken by the State in matters of its international relations, while diplomacy is a particular tool by which the State, represented by its government, executes its foreign policy and pursues other goals, such as the protection of its nationals abroad. Moreover, foreign policy includes the decisional processes by which States adopt their position over foreign issues regarding their national interests. It is adjusted to official governmental positions, needs, and global contexts. Meanwhile, diplomacy tends to focus on the study of the permanent relations and the practices of representation and interaction between States.

The aim of this chapter is to give an overview of the functions, privileges, and immunities surrounding diplomatic relations and their legal bases.

B. DIPLOMATIC RELATIONS AND DIPLOMATIC MISSIONS

I. RATIO AND TERMINOLOGY

The concept of *diplomatic relations* refers broadly to the ways in which a State interacts with other subjects of international law, including international organisations. Different levels of diplomatic missions serve to achieve different goals. For instance, embassies are the official representation of one State in the territory of another, usually offering political representation but also services for citizens abroad. Between associations of States, such as the Commonwealth, a permanent representation of a member State in the territory of another member State is fulfilled under a 'High Commission'. A 'Permanent Mission', on the other hand, is usually the name given to the permanent representation of a State before the governing body of an international organisation.

States have the right to entertain diplomatic relations and to end them as a manifestation of their sovereignty. Usually, after a unilateral act of recognition, States begin diplomatic relations under the principle of reciprocity. Each State may, at any moment, terminate its diplomatic relations with another as there is no international obligation to maintain relations. Even if the act of ending diplomatic relations may seem unfriendly, it is not considered a breach of international law. Political crises may lead States to promptly end or suspend diplomatic relations, which can be reinstated quickly by both governments if an agreement is reached.

II. FUNCTIONS OF A DIPLOMATIC MISSION

Diplomatic missions have the following main functions:

1. Representation and protection of citizens abroad;
2. Communication and political representation between the sending State and the receiving State;
3. Encouraging and enhancing relations between citizens of both States.

In addition, some diplomatic missions may include consular services. Although consular missions are not diplomatic missions per se, in practice States tend to merge these functions in the same mission to reduce costs, in accordance with article 3(2) Vienna Convention on Diplomatic Relations (VCDR).[3]

III. MEMBERS AND ADMINISTRATIVE STAFF

Diplomatic missions are composed of civil servants and State representatives. Their status varies. Some members including ambassadors, secretaries, and diplomatic aggregates enjoy diplomatic status, privileges, and immunities. The administrative staff does not usually have diplomatic rank and their status is governed by domestic labour law.

Article 8 VCDR states the general rule, according to which members of a diplomatic mission must have the nationality of the sending State.[4] Furthermore, they ought to have a diplomatic passport, which specifies the rank they hold and the mission they are attending.

Diplomatic immunity which serves as a legal protection is granted to members of the diplomatic mission not for their personal profit, but to allow them to perform their tasks effectively.[5] Diplomatic immunity, as recognised by customary law,[6] exempts diplomats from the application of the laws of a foreign jurisdiction while they perform official duties. Diplomats remain subject to the laws of the State they represent and said State keeps the prerogative to prosecute diplomats for acts committed abroad.

Diplomatic immunity includes protection from the application of criminal, administrative, and civil jurisdiction where the mission is located (jurisdictional immunity[7]), except for private or commercial activity that the diplomat may conduct

---

3 Vienna Convention on Diplomatic Relations (adopted 18 April 1961, entered into force 24 April 1964) 500 UNTS 95.

4 Eileen Denza, *Diplomatic Law: Commentary on the Vienna Convention on Diplomatic Relations* (4th edn, OUP 2016).

5 Ralph Feltham, *Diplomatic Handbook* (8th edn, Martinus Nijhoff 2004) 35.

6 Michael Byers, *Custom, Power and the Power of Rules: International Relations and Customary International Law* (CUP 1999).

7 *Jurisdictional Immunities of the State (Germany v Italy: Greece intervening)* (Judgment) [2012] ICJ Rep 99.

outside the official functions. Additionally, if the jurisdictional immunity were to be breached, decisions or judgments against diplomats that are vested with immunity shall not be enforced by other local administrative authorities (immunity from enforcement).

The members of the service staff are in the domestic service of the mission. Usually, they are not citizens of the State where the mission is located, but they get a permit to stay in the receiving State regularly for a period of no longer than five years. In the case of personnel for technical issues (maintenance, construction or repair work), the usual duration of stay should not exceed 6 months.[8]

The immunities usually granted to representatives of the State can be extended to the service staff, for example to diplomatic agents and dependent family members (articles 31 and 37 VCDR, respectively).

One limit to diplomatic immunity is that those benefitting from it still have to comply with private financial obligations. In case of serious criminal offenses, the receiving State may furthermore ask the sending State permission to remove the diplomatic immunity. Also, the difference between *acta iure imperii* and *acta iure gestionis* implies differences in the regime of immunities applicable to acts related to the mission and private acts.[9]

IV. APPOINTMENT AND 'AGRÉMENT' OF DIPLOMATIC STAFF

The process of appointment of key diplomatic personnel is subject to a specific procedure. Ambassadors are the head of the diplomatic mission in the receiving State. For these persons, the procedure consists of four steps. First, the sending State selects the person to be named. Subsequently, the receiving State must issue a formal acceptance traditionally called 'agrément'. It may reject the proposal without the need of justification. Once there is an approval by the receiving State, the ambassador is accredited. This decision shall be notified to the chancellor or head of State (articles 4 to 7 VCDR).

The majority of the diplomatic mission's staff, however, does not have to undergo a formal appointment procedure. Each State may designate the staff without the need for consent from the hosting State.

V. ENDING AND REVOCATION

All diplomatic staff end their tenure with a formal revocation. Said process is done by the will of each sending State. Yet, in cases in which the receiving State declares someone from the diplomatic staff as *persona non grata*, there is an obligation to retire that person from the mission. It is important to note that the entire staff of the mission may be subject to this procedure, including non-diplomatic members. These types of

---

8   Government of Iceland Ministry for Foreign Affairs, *Diplomatic Handbook* (Protocol Department, Ministry for Foreign Affairs 2022).

9   On this distinction, see Walton, § 11, in this textbook.

declarations are done without the need for justification and at any time. The declaration of a member of the diplomatic mission as *persona non grata* usually happens in reciprocal fashion (articles 9 and 10 VCDR, respectively).

C. CONSULAR RELATIONS

Diplomatic relations usually give way to consular relations but are not the same. The latter can exist without the former. Consular relations are technical and administrative relations aimed to procure the rights of citizens abroad. These are regulated by a mixed regime: public international law and domestic law. Consular relations, similar to diplomatic relations, are born from a mutual agreement between the recipient State and the sending State. At the international level, two conventions are particularly relevant: the aforementioned VCDR and the Vienna Convention for Consular Relations (VCCR).[10]

The objectives and roles of consular relations are extensive. Examples include the protection and promotion of the already existing commercial relations between the two States and connecting industries; procuring ships, aircraft, and crews with legal and administrative assistance; provision of services to citizens; and providing notarial and administrative duties both for the citizens of the State they represent in the receiving State and the services solicited by citizens of the State on which is located the consular relation (e.g. travelling permits, visas, electoral support abroad; article 5 VCCR).

There are two types of consuls: career and honorary consuls (article 1(2) VCCR). Career consuls usually perform all the available consular tasks and are nationals of the sending State. Honorary consuls do not perform all these tasks and are usually nationals of the recipient country. A consul can only be appointed after an agreement with the sending country in the form of an authorisation of the sending State and with the expedition of an acceptance.

D. VIENNA CONVENTION ON DIPLOMATIC RELATIONS

I. INTRODUCTION AND BACKGROUND

The Vienna Convention of 1961 regarding diplomatic relations (VCDR) is the main instrument that regulates diplomatic law. The Convention, which today reflects and develops customary law, includes the functions of diplomatic missions, their rights, privileges, and obligations of both sending and hosting States.[11]

---

10 Vienna Convention on Consular Relations (adopted 22 April 1963, entered into force 19 March 1967) 596 UNTS 261.

11 Richard Langhorne, 'The Regulation of Diplomatic Practice: The Beginnings to the Vienna Convention on Diplomatic Relations, 1961' (1992) 18 Review of International Studies 3.

Diplomatic relations have a history way back in time. However, as for many other issues in international law, Westphalia marks a milestone. As sovereignty was being discussed, delegations from all countries started to gain protection against civil jurisdiction. Since that moment it became a standard practice and later developed into customary international law as recorded, among others, by Hugo Grotius.[12]

One of the main concerns during the negations of the VCDR was communication. Until then, the idea of freedom of communication prevailed. However, new technologies such as wireless communication brought about new questions. Only certain States had access to these technologies, while less developed countries struggled to catch up. In addition, there were fears of broadcasting from an embassy. However, after agreeing to make a respectful use of the electromagnetic spaces, the controversy was resolved. Other big discussions related to the inviolability of the diplomatic pouch and the extent of functional immunity of administrative and technical staff, depending on their nationality.[13]

II. KEY PROVISIONS

1. Inviolability of Missions

The VCDR establishes the inviolability of the diplomatic mission (article 22). Such obligation implies that inspections, registers, or other types of intrusions are strictly prohibited. Not only does this oblige the hosting State to abstain from irrupting into the diplomatic mission, but also to guarantee the safety and well-being of the mission. This includes the duty to prevent public demonstrations in the vicinity of the mission that may escalate to endanger the security of the diplomatic seat. A historical example of this situation is the 1984 storming of the Libyan Embassy in the United Kingdom. Armed subjects from within the Libyan embassy fired against civilians on the street.[14]

2. Protection of Documents

The inviolability of the embassy not only refers to the physical infrastructure of the mission, but also the documents inside it (article 24 VCDR). Such protection includes all the necessary documents that assure the operation of the mission.

3. Freedom of Action

A diplomatic mission must have all the freedoms necessary to fulfil its mission (article 25 VCDR). Accordingly, the hosting State should not impose obstacles that may affect the functions of the diplomatic mission. This includes freedom of circulation and free access to

---

12 Max Sorensen, *Manual de Derecho Internacional Público* (Fondo de Cultura Economica 1973) 389–393.

13 Alan James, 'Diplomacy' (1993) 19 Review of International Studies 91.

14 Veronica Maginnis, 'Limiting Diplomatic Immunity: Lessons Learned from the 1946 Convention on the Privileges and Immunities of the United Nations' (2002) 28 Brooklyn Journal of International Law 989.

citizens of the sending State, as part of its main functions. Not the same applies to the citizens of the hosting State, in the sense that it is not an obligation to grant that access.

4. Diplomatic Pouch

All the diplomatic mail and communication between the mission and the sending State is protected by article 27 of the Convention. Once the State identifies the mail as diplomatic, it is completely prohibited to open it. Yet, the mail must contain material to fulfil the diplomatic objective. If there is a situation which requires the violation of this protection, it could only be done with the agreement of the receiving State.

Questions that arise are whether certain situations may grant the hosting State the exercise of an inspection and whether methods like X-rays and scans are permissible under article 27.

5. Families

Members of a diplomatic household may be granted immunity when they are not nationals of the receiving State. Articles 29 and 31 include the regime of protection for the diplomats. According to article 32, the sending States may revoke and waive immunities and privileges. Other privileges include exemptions from taxes (article 35) and from customs duties (article 36).

6. Other Privileges and Immunities

Article 31 VCLD grants diplomats civil and administrative immunity. It also prohibits the obligation for diplomats to testify. However, this does not grant diplomats absolute immunity – diplomats remain responsible under the jurisdiction of the sending State. Article 31 also foresees certain exceptions.

A sending State may waive the immunity of its staff whenever necessary. For that effect, the waiver must be an express, formal act. In the same way, it must explain the scope of the waiver as it is not understood as a complete relinquishment of the immunity (article 32 VCDR).

The temporal scope of immunities is covered under article 39 VCDR, referring to the beginning and termination of diplomatic immunity. The benefits shall begin from the arrival of the diplomat in the receiving country or when the designation is given. Immunity ceases when the personal mission ends, or upon decision by both countries. In the case of diplomatic death, the family still enjoys immunity until the expiration of a reasonable term.

Immunities are also relevant in transit, a situation regulated by article 40 of the VCDR. If diplomats travel from the receiving State to another State based on the objectives of the mission, the third State has to guarantee that the diplomat still enjoys the immunities enjoyed in the receiving State.

E. DIPLOMATIC IMMUNITIES AND IMMUNITIES OF INTERNATIONAL ORGANISATIONS

While diplomatic relations originate from customary law, the immunities of international organisations are closely tied to its constituent treaty.[15] Accordingly, a tailor-made approach for each scenario will determine what is the regime applicable between the hosting State and each international organisation.

The lack of territory implies that international organisations are based on the territory of a hosting State and therefore exposed to local authorities. In that context, the need for immunity and protection is evident to guarantee their independence.

A key difference relates to the sources of immunity. While in diplomatic relations immunity derives from nationality, in international organisations the link will depend on the functional relation. Since international organisations do not have a population, they usually constitute their staff with nationals of their member States and the host State. These individuals can be covered by privileges and immunities, depending on what is agreed upon in the constitutive treaty or seat agreement as functional immunities needed for the object and purpose of the organisation.

Regarding the jurisdictional process, let us recall that in diplomatic immunity, the individuals shall be processed in their home State as immunity is not a synonym for impunity. In the case of international organisations, since there is no link of national origin, the organisation itself oversees the case.

Another key difference concerns accreditation. While diplomatic missions need to have an exchange of instruments that name a head of mission and a protocol, the immunity of the staff of an international organisation depends exclusively on the agreement inside the headquarters agreement.

F. CONCLUSION

Diplomatic relations are a fundamental element of a globalised world. From the political realm, diplomatic relations have evolved into a cornerstone of international law represented in the functions and immunities of diplomatic missions that nowadays not only represent their State but are essential for the rights and needs of nationals and citizens.

---

15 On international organisations, see Baranowska, Engström and Paige, § 7.3, in this textbook.

BOX 10.3 Further Readings

Further Readings

W Arévalo Ramírez and R Abello-Galvis, 'The Immunity of International
    Organizations in Labour Disputes. Developments Before International
    Tribunals, National Courts and the Colombian Jurisdiction' (2021)
    18 BJIL 137

§ § §

CHAPTER 11
IMMUNITIES

BEATRICE A. WALTON

BOX 11.1 Required Knowledge and Learning Objectives

Required knowledge: Jurisdiction; International Organisations; Sources of
International Law; Diplomatic Relations

Learning objectives: To understand the different types of immunities owed
under international law; the legal sources of immunities; the nature and scope
of immunities; and ongoing debates about the extent to which immunities
are compatible with other features of the international legal system, including
human rights law and international criminal law.

BOX 11.2 Interactive Exercises

Access *interactive exercises for this chapter*[1] by positioning your smartphone
camera at the dot-filled box, also known as a QR code.

Figure 11.1 QR code referring to interactive exercises.

A. INTRODUCTION

International law imposes limits on States with respect to their exercise of domestic
jurisdiction over foreign sovereigns, certain categories of foreign sovereign entities and
persons, and international organisations. These limits, or 'immunities' from jurisdiction,
constitute exceptions to the general power of States to exercise legal authority in their
territory in relation to civil, criminal, and other legal matters.[2] Immunities may apply
both in relation to the adjudication of claims, meaning, the power of a court to hear

---

1 https://openrewi.org/en-projects-project-public-international-law-immunities/
2 On jurisdiction, see González Hauck and Milas, § 8, in this textbook.

DOI: 10.4324/9781003451327-13

a suit, as well as in relation to the enforcement of judgments, such as through the attachment of assets.

This chapter focuses on three main types of immunities: foreign sovereign or 'State-derived' immunities, including immunities owed to the State itself as well as foreign heads of State and other officials; diplomatic and consular immunities; and the privileges and immunities owed to international organisations and individuals involved in the work of those organisations.

B. STATE-DERIVED IMMUNITIES

I. FOREIGN SOVEREIGN IMMUNITY

The immunities owed under international law to States and their officials derive from a combination of principles in international law, including the sovereign equality of States and non-interference. Immunity is ultimately owed to the foreign State and on that basis, to certain classes of persons and entities embodying or representing the State, or carrying out State functions.[3]

1. Sources

Historically, foreign sovereign immunity emerged from the notion that no sovereign, or its courts, could sit in judgment of another sovereign.[4] This notion is reflected in the expression *par in parem non habet imperium*, meaning that one sovereign should not have jurisdiction over another given that the two are equals.[5] While foreign sovereign immunity developed strong roots in domestic legal systems, it has come to be recognised as a rule of customary international law.[6] Today, sovereign immunity may be said to draw roots in the principles of sovereign equality of States,[7] non-intervention, and the peaceful settlement of disputes, as reflected in the UN Charter and other contemporary sources.

Customary international law, as opposed to treaty law, remains the key source of the law on foreign sovereign immunity. However, a few key efforts have been made towards codification. Most important is the work of the ILC, which began in 1978 and culminated in the 2004 United Nations Convention on Jurisdictional Immunity of States and their Property (UN Convention), which has not yet entered into force on account of its limited ratification.[8] Other examples include the 1972 European

---

3   On States, see Green, § 7.1, in this textbook.

4   Malcolm Shaw, *International Law* (6th edn, CUP 2008) 697–698.

5   Brownlie's, *Principles of Public International Law* (James Crawford ed, 9th edn, OUP 2019) 471.

6   *Jurisdictional Immunities of the State (Germany v Italy, Greece Intervening) (Merits)* [2012] ICJ Rep 99 [54]–[58].

7   Charter of the United Nations (adopted 26 June 1945, entered into force 24 October 1945) 1 UNTS XVI, article 2(1).

8   See Gerhard Hafner, 'Historical Background to the Convention' in Roger O'Keefe and others (eds), *The United Nations Convention on Jurisdictional Immunities of States and Their Property: A Commentary* (OUP 2013) 5–12; UN

Convention on State Immunity, which also has not received wide ratification, and the
1982 UN Convention on the Law of the Sea, which provides certain immunities for
State-owned ships.[9]

The extent to which the UN Convention reflects customary international law
continues to generate debate. On the one hand, some provisions likely reflected a
progressive approach to the law of State immunity at their drafting.[10] Nonetheless, a
degree of crystallisation may have taken place since then, and indeed several domestic
and international courts, including the ICJ, have looked to the Convention when
deciding immunity issues under customary international law.[11]

At the domestic level, a few States have adopted legislation codifying rules on foreign
sovereign immunity. In the US and UK, the 1976 Foreign Sovereign Immunity Act
(FSIA) and the 1978 State Immunity Act (SIA) set out the immunities owed to foreign
States and their agencies or instrumentalities in the absence of an applicable exception.
Other States, including Sweden, Egypt, and South Korea, give effect to foreign
sovereign immunity by applying customary international law directly.[12]

The ICJ's opinion in the *Jurisdictional Immunities* case provides an example of how
in practice a variety of different sources may factor into a determination of the
customary rules of State immunity. When determining whether Italy's courts were
prohibited from entertaining suits against Germany for severe violations of human
rights carried out in World War II, the Court looked to 'the judgments of national
courts . . . the legislation of those States which have enacted statutes dealing with
immunity', as well as 'the claims to immunity advanced by States before foreign
courts and the statements made by States' during the drafting of the UN Convention,
among other sources.[13]

As this example shows, foreign sovereign immunity inhabits a unique place within
the international legal system. As a binding rule of international law, sovereign
immunity is more than merely the practice by which municipal courts decline to

---

General Assembly Res. 59/38 (2 December 2004) UN Doc A/59/38, Annex, 'United Nations Convention on
Jurisdictional Immunities of States and Their Property' ('UN Convention on Jurisdictional Immunities').

9 See Peter-Tobias Still, 'State Immunity' (*Max Planck Encyclopedia of International Law*, April 2011) paras 9, 43; see
also COE 'European Convention on State Immunity' (opened for signature 16 May 1972, entered into force
11 June 1976) ETS No 74; United Nations Convention on the Law of the Sea (adopted 10 December 1982,
entered into force 16 November 1994) 1833 UNTS 397 articles 95–96.

10 See Anne Peters, 'Immune Against Constitutionalism?' in Anne Peters and others (eds), *Immunities in the Age of
Global Constitutionalism* (Brill 2015) 10.

11 See Ingrid (Wuerth) Brunk, 'A Primer on Foreign Sovereign Immunity' (*Transnational Litigation Blog*, 13
April 2023) <https://tlblog.org/a-primer-on-foreign-sovereign-immunity/> accessed 9 December 2023;
Roger O'Keefe and Christian J Tams, 'General Introduction' in Roger O'Keefe and others (eds), *The United
Nations Convention on Jurisdictional Immunities of States and Their Property: A Commentary* (OUP 2013) xli.

12 See Brunk (n 11).

13 Hazel Fox and Philippa Webb, *The Law of State Immunity* (revised and updated 3rd edn, OUP 2015) 104–105;
Jurisdictional Immunities, para 55.

hear certain disputes, such as through application of comity or other prudential doctrines.[14] Indeed, States are obligated to respect immunities and their failure to respect immunities amounts to an internationally wrongful act. At the same time, because immunities are predominantly implemented at the municipal level, domestic courts, legislatures, and other ministries continue to impact how immunities operate.[15]

2. Nature and Scope

The most important development over the last century in relation to foreign sovereign immunity is the evolution away from the 'absolute' doctrine of foreign sovereign immunity towards the 'restrictive doctrine'. Under the restrictive approach, immunity is limited to public acts (*jure imperii*) and does not apply to private or commercial acts (*jure gestionis*). This approach typically applies to both immunity from suit and immunity from execution.[16]

Several different factors are said to have driven the evolution away from the absolute approach, including the expanding commercial activities of States in the 20th century and the perception that absolute immunity enabled an unfair commercial advantage for State-owned industries and entities competing internationally.[17] While most States today adhere to the restrictive approach, some, including the Soviet Union, were historically more reluctant to adopt it.[18]

Determining the nature of State acts as either 'sovereign' or 'commercial' is critical when implementing the restrictive approach. As set out in the UN Convention, the 'State' includes all organs as well as constituent units, agencies, and representatives 'exercis[ing] sovereign authority'.[19] Accordingly, the activities of such persons or entities will generally constitute sovereign acts for purposes of immunity.[20] By contrast, more parsing is required under the restrictive approach to determine whether a State is immune in relation to certain contracts or transactions.

When assessing whether certain acts constitute commercial acts, courts primarily look at the 'nature' of these acts, as opposed to the State's 'purpose' in carrying them out, though jurisdictions vary on this issue.[21] For example, under the restrictive approach, a State may not be immune in relation to a commercial contract to buy military

---

14 See Peters (n 10) 1.

15 Fox and Webb (n 13) 1.

16 See UN Convention on Jurisdictional Immunities, articles 10, 19(c).

17 Shaw (n 4) 701.

18 Ibid, 707–708; Maryam Jamshidi, 'The Political Economy of Foreign Sovereign Immunity' (2022) 73 Hastings Law Journal 585, 615–616.

19 UN Convention on Jurisdictional Immunities, article 2(1).

20 Fox and Webb (n 13) 403.

21 Shaw (n 4) 709–711; Fox and Webb (n 13) 403, 411, 415; UN Convention on Jurisdictional Immunities, article 2(2).

equipment, even where the State's ultimate 'purpose' is to outfit its military, a traditional sovereign function. Focusing on the 'nature' of a transaction thus has the effect of limiting immunity.[22]

Another area where jurisdictions may differ with respect to foreign sovereign immunity issues concerns the procedures giving effect to immunities in domestic courts. With respect to timing, the ICJ suggested in *Jurisdictional Immunities* that foreign sovereign immunity is a threshold issue, meaning that courts are 'required to determine whether or not a foreign State is entitled to immunity as a matter of international law before it can hear the merits of the case brought before it and before the facts have been established'.[23] Other procedural issues remain less clear, including which party bears the burden of proving immunity or the application of an exception; the circumstances required to show a waiver of immunity; and whether the government of the forum State bears a duty to intervene to ensure that its courts respect immunity. Some States have also purported to condition immunity on a reciprocal basis, though the permissibility of such an approach remains uncertain.[24]

3. Application and Debates

While foreign sovereign immunity is established as a matter of customary international law, its contours, including the availability of exceptions to it, remain subject to debate.[25] The most important debate has concerned whether foreign sovereign immunity applies in relation to violations of *jus cogens*, or whether a limit or exception to immunity exists in such cases. In the *Jurisdictional Immunities* case, the ICJ rejected Italy's argument in favour of a customary exception to immunity for claims relating to *jus cogens* violations (including large-scale killing of civilians and deportation of civilians to slave labour), reasoning that there was no conflict between the application of immunity and underlying *jus cogens* rules because the 'two sets of rules address different matters'.[26] In reaching this conclusion, the Court held that foreign sovereign immunity was essentially 'procedural' in nature,[27] in contrast to human rights and humanitarian law rules, which are 'substantive'. The ICJ further rejected Italy's argument that customary international law recognises a 'territorial tort' exception for claims in relation to violations carried out in the forum State.[28]

---

22 See generally William S Dodge, 'China's Draft Law on Foreign State Immunity Would Adopt Restrictive Theory' (*Transnational Litigation Blog*, 12 April 2023) <https://tlblog.org/chinas-draft-law-on-foreign-state-immunity-would-adopt-restrictive-theory/> accessed 16 August 2023.

23 *Jurisdictional Immunities* (n 5) [82].

24 See Brunk (n 11); Lori Fisler Damrosch, 'The Sources of Immunity Law – Between International and Domestic Law' in Tom Ruys and others (eds), *The Cambridge Handbook of Immunities and International Law* (CUP 2019) 45–46.

25 See generally Peters (n 10) 2.

26 *Jurisdictional Immunities* (n 5) [93].

27 Ibid.

28 Ibid [79]; see UN Convention on Jurisdictional Immunities, article 12.

The ICJ's approach to the relationship between *jus cogens* and immunity followed a similar holding in *Al Adsani v United Kingdom*, where the European Court of Human Rights (ECtHR) found that there was no violation of the right of access to court in relation to the application of immunity to a complaint alleging violations of torture.[29] Other courts have reached comparable conclusions, including the Supreme Court of Canada in *Kazemi Estate v Islamic Republic of Iran*, which found immunity applicable in relation to civil suits for torture and other serious violations.[30]

The ICJ's decision in *Jurisdictional Immunities* has nonetheless attracted considerable criticism. As Fox and Webb explain, by recognising foreign sovereign immunity as a 'procedural plea', the ICJ effectively held that the alleged illegality of certain sovereign acts does not affect the application of immunity.[31] While this approach has gained prominence, the extent to which such a procedural/substantive distinction can or should persist despite the development of the international human rights system remains open to debate, and a theme returned to throughout this chapter. Indeed, in analysing this case, commentators have questioned the underlying logic of such a dichotomy[32] as well as the Court's deployment of this dichotomy in a way that enabled it to avoid addressing the evolution of international law away from State-centric approaches[33] or balancing competing values.[34]

Not all courts have accepted the ICJ's approach. A few recent examples finding no immunity in relation to serious violations committed in the territory of the forum State include the Seoul Central District Court,[35] the Brazilian Supreme Court,[36] and the Ukrainian Supreme Court.[37]

---

29 *Case of Al-Adsani v The United Kingdom* (ECtHR) Reports 2001–XI 79; see also Stefan Talmon, '*Jus Cogens* after *Germany v Italy*: Substantive and Procedural Rules Distinguished' (2012) 25 LJIL 979, 980.

30 *Kazemi (Estate) v Islamic Republic of Iran* (10 October 2014) (Supreme Court of Canada) 2014 SCC 62, [2014] 3 SCR 176.

31 Fox and Webb (n 13) 4–5.

32 See Claire EM Jervis, 'Jurisdictional Immunities Revisited: An Analysis of the Procedure Substance Distinction in International Law' (2019) 30 EJIL 123–124.

33 See Peters (n 10) 8–9.

34 See Andrea Bianchi, 'Gazing at the Crystal Ball (Again): State Immunity and *Jus Cogens* beyond *Germany v Italy*' (2013) 4 JIDS 462.

35 Seoul Central District Court, Joint Case No. 2016/505092 (8 January 2021); Vessela Terzieva, 'State Immunity and Victims' Rights to Access to Court, Reparation, and the Truth' (2022) 22 International Criminal Law Review 784; Daniel Franchini, 'South Korea's Denial of Japan's Immunity for International Crimes: Restricting or Bypassing the Law of State Immunity? (*Völkerrechtsblog*, 18 January 2021) <doi:10.17176/20210118-144257-0>.

36 Terzieva (n 35) 786; Brazil Federal Supreme Court, ARE 954858/RJ (23 August 2021). See also Lucas Carlos Lima and Aziz Tuffi Saliba, 'The Immunity Saga Reaches Latin America. The Changri-la Case' (*EJIL: Talk!*, 2 December 2021) <www.ejiltalk.org/the-immunity-saga-reaches-latin-america-the-changri-la-case/> accessed 16 August 2023.

37 Ielyzaveta Badanova, 'Jurisdictional Immunities v. Grave Crimes: Reflections on New Developments from Ukraine' (*EJIL: Talk!*, 8 September 2022) <https://www.ejiltalk.org/jurisdictional-immunities-v-grave-crimes-reflections-on-new-developments-from-ukraine/> accessed 9 December 2023.

Another controversial issue pertains to the adoption of a 'State sponsor' of terrorism exception to foreign sovereign immunity by both the US and Canada.[38] Iran raised the issue of the US application of this exception in relation to the attachment of Iranian State-owned assets in the *Certain Iranian Assets* case; however, the ICJ ultimately held that it did not have jurisdiction to decide the issue.[39] In 2023, Iran initiated a new case against Canada at the ICJ arguing that such an exception violates customary international law.[40]

Other exceptions to foreign sovereign immunity which are more commonly recognised pertain to suits over State-owned real estate on the territory of the forum State and suits to enforce awards obtained by arbitration.

BOX 11.3 Advanced: Sanctions and Immunities

In the wake of Russia's war of aggression against Ukraine, questions have surfaced over the relationship between sanctions freezing or seizing State assets and foreign sovereign immunity.[41] One key issue at root of this debate is the extent to which immunities are confined to the judicial branch, or whether they can be invoked in relation to coercive executive or legislative measures, such as sanctions orders. While some commentators have suggested that merely freezing assets is not alone enough to violate immunity,[42] others have suggested that immunity applies regardless of the branch of government involved.[43]

---

38 28 U.S.C. § 1605A; R.S.C., 1985, c. S-18, s. 6.1(1). See Daniel Franchini, 'State Immunity as a Tool of Foreign Policy: The Unanswered Question of *Certain Iranian Assets*' (2020) 60 Virginia Journal of International Law 443.

39 *Certain Iranian Assets (Islamic Republic of Iran v United States of America) (Preliminary Objections)* [2019] ICJ Rep 7, para 80.

40 Islamic Republic of Iran v Canada (Application Instituting Proceedings) (27 June 2023) <www.icj-cij.org/sites/default/files/case-related/189/189-20230628-app-01-00-en.pdf> accessed 27 July 2023.

41 See Daniel Franchini, 'Ukraine Symposium: Seizure of Russian State Assets: State Immunity and Countermeasures' (*Articles of War*, 8 March 2023) <https://lieber.westpoint.edu/seizure-russian-state-assets-state-immunity-countermeasures/> accessed 16 August 2023.

42 Ibid; see Tom Ruys, 'Non-UN Financial Sanctions Against Central Banks and Heads of State: In Breach of International Immunity Law' (EJIL: *Talk!*, 2 March 2017) <www.ejiltalk.org/non-un-financial-sanctions-against-central-banks-and-heads-of-state-in-breach-of-international-immunity-law/> accessed 16 August 2023; Ingrid (Wuerth) Brunk, 'Does Foreign Sovereign Immunity Apply to Sanctions on Central Banks?' (*Lawfare*, 7 March 2022) <www.lawfaremedia.org/article/does-foreign-sovereign-immunity-apply-sanctions-central-banks> accessed 16 August 2023.

43 See Jean-Marc Thouvenin and Victor Grandaubert, 'The Material Scope of State Immunity from Execution' in Tom Ruys and others (eds), *The Cambridge Handbook of Immunities and International Law* (CUP 2019); Christian J Tams and Roger O'Keefe, 'Part I Introduction, Article 1' in Roger O'Keefe and others (eds), *The United Nations Convention on Jurisdictional Immunities of States and Their Property: A Commentary* (OUP 2013) 37–38.

II. FOREIGN STATE OFFICIAL IMMUNITY

International law also extends immunity to foreign State officials in certain circumstances. While in some jurisdictions foreign sovereign immunity may apply in civil suits where a head of State is sued in his public capacity, and thus as a stand-in for the foreign State,[44] different international rules apply to heads of State and other high-ranking officials when sued personally. The rationales offered for foreign State official immunity overlap with those for foreign sovereign immunity (i.e. sovereign equality of States, non-interference). However, foreign official immunity has the added rationale of facilitating orderly international relations, particularly as some high-ranking State officials are routinely required to travel to participate in diplomatic meetings.[45]

1. Sources

Like foreign sovereign immunity, customary international law remains the primary source of the international rules on foreign State official immunity. The ICJ affirmed the customary status of foreign official immunity in the *Arrest Warrant* case.[46] Nonetheless, as with foreign sovereign immunity, the exact scope and contours of the customary international law on foreign State official immunity continue to generate debate. These debates can be seen in response to recent work undertaken by the ILC on the topic of foreign official immunity in the context of criminal proceedings, as discussed further in this section.

Domestic law also plays a considerable role in implementing foreign official immunity, as it does with other immunities discussed in this chapter. In the UK, the SIA affords heads of State acting in a personal capacity privileges and immunities similar to diplomats,[47] whereas in the US, the immunities owed to foreign State officials are instead governed by the common law.[48]

To supplement immunities owed under customary international law, States also frequently enter into bilateral agreements, such as 'status-of-forces' agreements, to afford a broader scope of immunities to personnel stationed abroad.

2. Nature and Application

There are two types of immunities owed to foreign State officials under customary international law. The first, *ratione personae*, or 'status-based' immunity, is owed only to very high-ranking officials, such as the head of State, minister of foreign

---

44 See Fox and Webb (n 13) 550; State Immunity Act (1978), s14(1).

45 Joanne Foakes, *The Position of Heads of State and Senior Officials in International Law* (OUP 2014), 1–2, 10–11; see also Fox and Webb (n 13) 566.

46 *Arrest Warrant of 11 April 2000 (Democratic Republic of the Congo v. Belgium) (Jurisdiction and Admissibility)* [2002] ICJ Rep 3 [51].

47 State Immunity Act (1978), s20(1); Fox and Webb (n 13) 550.

48 See *Samantar v Yousef* (US Supreme Court) 560 U.S. 305 (2010).

affairs, and the head of government, who are often referred to as the 'troika'.[49] These persons are considered inviolable for the duration of their office, meaning that they enjoy full immunity from the exercise of foreign civil and criminal jurisdiction,[50] including both official and private acts.[51] In the words of the ICJ, 'immunity and . . . inviolability protect the individual concerned against any act of authority of another State which would hinder him or her in the performance of his or her duties'.[52]

The second type of immunity, *ratione materiae*, or 'functional' immunity, attaches to acts which are carried out on behalf of the foreign sovereign. Unlike *ratione personae* immunity, which expires at the end of the official's term in office, *ratione materiae* immunity can be raised even after an official leaves office as this form of immunity attaches to conduct which can be considered 'sovereign'.[53] In contrast to *ratione personae* immunity, whose application to high-ranking officials beyond the troika remains uncertain, *ratione materiae* immunity can in principle apply to a much broader range of actors given that immunity is based on the nature of particular acts.[54]

In terms of practicalities, foreign official immunities apply regardless of whether the official is travelling as part of his duties and thus are not contingent on a receiving State's grant of credentials for the official to enter the State.[55] The home State of the official may also waive these immunities as they are ultimately owed to the State and not granted for personal benefit.[56]

Some less settled issues include which party bears the burden of proof in relation to these immunities and the appropriate role of the host government in recognising foreign governments and their officials, as well as in assessing whether officials acted in an 'official' capacity.[57] Along similar lines, question remains as to what role the home State of the official is required to play in raising the official's immunity before a national court. For example, in denying the application of immunity to

---

49 *Arrest Warrant* (n 49) [51].

50 Ibid [54].

51 However, there is some debate over the limited possibility of suits in relation to civil acts not carried out in the individual's official capacity. See Fox and Webb (n 13) 553–554; Sir Arthur Watts and Joanne Foakes, 'Heads of Governments and Other Senior Officials' (*Max Planck Encyclopedia of Public International Law* (October 2010) para 16.

52 *Arrest Warrant* (n 49) [54].

53 Ibid [61].

54 Foakes (n 45) 7. In *Djibouti v France*, the ICJ found that the *procureur de la Republique* and the head of national security were not entitled to immunity *ratione personae*. See *Certain Questions of Mutual Assistance in Criminal Matters (Djibouti v France) (Judgment)* [2008] ICJ Rep 177 [194].

55 See Fox and Webb (n 13) 551.

56 *Arrest Warrant* (n 49) [53]; [61]; see ILC, 'Immunity of State officials from foreign criminal jurisdiction: Texts and titles of the draft articles adopted by the Drafting Committee on first reading' (73rd session) UN Doc A/CN.4/L.969 (31 May 2022), Draft Article 12.

57 William S Dodge and Chimène I Keitner, 'A Roadmap for Foreign Official Immunity Cases in U.S. Courts' (2021) 90 Fordham Law Review 680.

certain high-ranking officials in *Djibouti v France*, the ICJ noted that '[a]t no stage' had Djibouti informed France's courts that the acts in question were State acts or that the individuals in question were carrying out those acts,[58] an approach which the ILC appears to follow in its recent draft articles on *Immunity of State Officials from Foreign Criminal Jurisdiction*, where it requires invocation by the official's home State.[59] By contrast, some courts, including, for example, Germany's Federal Court of Justice in a recent case concerning an Afghan soldier, have considered it their own responsibility to address immunity issues,[60] particularly in response to a plea by the official. How this rule ultimately develops may have broader implications as commentators suggest that requiring foreign States to actively argue immunity may encourage greater waiver of immunity in cases involving abuse or underlying violations.[61]

3. Key Issues

As with foreign sovereign immunity, important debate surrounds the question of whether foreign official immunity is available in cases involving alleged *jus cogens* violations. This question has taken on increased importance as mechanisms for international criminal accountability have solidified, and as States have ratified various human rights treaties requiring the prosecution of violations. Recognition of the principle of *aut dedere aut iudicare* (Latin: 'to extradite or prosecute') and the requirement to prosecute grave breaches of international humanitarian law similarly exist in some tension with foreign official immunity.[62]

In the *Arrest Warrant* case, the ICJ rejected the possibility of an exception to *ratione personae* immunity on the basis of alleged violations, finding that Belgium's issuance of a warrant for the arrest of an incumbent foreign minister violated his immunity despite allegations that he had committed crimes against humanity.[63] While States have largely accepted this relatively absolute approach to *ratione personae* immunity, perspectives are more varied as to whether *ratione materiae* immunity can apply to *jus cogens* violations.

In the UK, the *Pinochet (No 3)* case serves as a prominent example denying *ratione materiae* immunity in relation to prior acts of torture.[64] While the Lords upheld the request made by Spain to arrest Augusto Pinochet, the former president of Chile,

---

58 *Djibouti v. France* (n 57) [196].

59 See ILC Draft Articles (n 59), article 11.

60 See Claus Kress, 'On Functional Immunity of Foreign Officials and Crimes Under International Law' (*Just Security*, 31 March 2021) <www.justsecurity.org/75596/on-functional-immunity-of-foreign-officials-and-crimes-under-international-law/> accessed 16 August 2023.

61 Peters (n 10) 19.

62 Philippa Webb, 'Human Rights and the Immunities of State Officials' in Erika De Wet and Jure Vidmar (eds), *Hierarchy in International Law: The Place of Human Rights* (OUP 2012) 128.

63 *Arrest Warrant* (n 49) [56]–[60].

64 *Regina v Bow Street Metropolitan Stipendiary Magistrate ex parte Pinochet Ugarte (No. 3)* (U.K. House of Lords) [2000] 1 A.C. 147.

while he was present in England on the basis that he was not entitled to immunity in relation to those acts, they were divided as to their reasoning. The majority held that the UN Convention on Torture established an international crime rendering immunity in relation to such acts inapplicable. Some Lords took the perspective that an exception to immunity applied for torture, and others held that torture is not an official function of the head of State.[65] In the *Samantar* case, involving immunity from civil jurisdiction, the US Court of Appeals shared this latter approach in finding that torture and other violations cannot constitute 'official' acts for purposes of immunity.[66]

Debate over these issues has recently followed the ILC's adoption of a draft article recognising an exception for certain international crimes, including genocide, crimes against humanity, and torture as part of its work on the topic of foreign official immunity.[67] As commentators have explained, State practice in support of the exception appears to be limited at present. While only a handful of States have so far provided a clear international crimes exception to immunity *ratione materiae*,[68] a few domestic courts have denied immunity on this basis,[69] including Germany's Federal Court of Justice in 2021.[70] Nonetheless, as with other areas of international law, this area may well be evolving.

BOX 11.4 Advanced: International Criminal Courts and Foreign State Official Immunity

The question of how foreign State official immunity interacts with the jurisdiction of international criminal courts and tribunals has become a key issue in recent years. The charters and statutes of various international criminal tribunals make clear that a defendant's official capacity does not serve as a defence or bar to their international criminal responsibility.[71] The ICJ also recognised this in *Arrest Warrant*, where it noted that foreign State official immunities 'do not represent a bar to criminal prosecution in certain circumstances' as such persons 'may be subject to criminal proceedings before certain international criminal courts, where they have jurisdiction'.[72] Article 27 of the Rome Statute accordingly waives before the International Criminal Court any immunity otherwise entitled to

---

65 Ibid; Fox and Webb (n 13) 557–558.

66 *Yousuf v Samantar* (US Court of Appeals for the Fourth Circuit) 699 F.3d 763 (4th Cir. 2012).

67 See ILC Draft Articles (n 59), article 7.

68 Sean D Murphy, 'Immunity *Ratione Materiae* of State Officials from Foreign Criminal Jurisdiction: Where Is the State Practice in Support of Exceptions?' (2018) 112 AJIL Unbound 5.

69 See Dodge and Keitner (n 57) 705–706.

70 See Kress (n 60).

71 See Webb (n 62) 126–127; see also Aghem Hanson Ekori, 'The ICC or the ACC: Defining the Future of the Immunities of African State Officials' (2020) 6 AJICJ 50.

72 *Arrest Warrant* (n 49) [61].

officials of States parties to the Rome Statute.[73] What is less clear is how, at the domestic level, foreign State official immunity relates to obligations to carry out arrest warrants issued by international courts and tribunals, particularly where the official is from a State which is not party to the Rome Statute.[74]

C. DIPLOMATIC, CONSULAR, AND RELATED IMMUNITIES

States are also obligated to comply with various rules governing diplomatic and consular immunities. These immunities, like foreign sovereign and foreign State official immunity, derive from the concepts of State sovereignty and the sovereign equality of States. However, in comparison with foreign sovereign immunity, the emphasis of diplomatic and consular immunities is less on the dignity of the sovereign and more on the need to ensure the effective functioning of diplomatic missions when operating in foreign territories.[75]

I. SOURCES

Diplomatic and consular immunities are primarily grounded in treaties, though in some cases customary rules exist in parallel. The Vienna Convention on Diplomatic Relations (1961) (VCDR) and the Vienna Convention on Consular Relations (1963) (VCCR), both of which are widely ratified, largely codified pre-existing customary international legal rules with respect to diplomatic and consular immunity.[76] Less widely ratified is the Convention on Special Missions (1985), which provides immunities to special missions sent by one State to another with the consent of the receiving State. At least some privileges and immunities with respect to special missions also exist under customary international law, though the scope and extent of such immunities remain uncertain.[77]

---

73 Rome Statute of the International Criminal Court (adopted 17 July 1998, entered into force 1 July 2002), 2187 UNTS 3 article 27.

74 Cf Ibid, article 98; see also Dapo Akande, 'The Immunity of Heads of States of Nonparties in the Early Years of the ICC' (2019) 112 AJIL Unbound 172; *Judgment in the Jordan Referral re Al-Bashir Appeal* ICC-02/05–01/09 (6 May 2019).

75 See Philippa Webb, 'How Far Does the Systemic Approach to Immunities Take Us?' (2018) 112 AJIL Unbound 17.

76 Eileen Denza, 'Diplomatic and Consular Immunities – Trends and Challenges' in Tom Ruys and others (eds), *The Cambridge Handbook of Immunities and International Law* (CUP 2019) 433.

77 Michael Wood, 'Convention on Special Missions' (*United Nations Audiovisual Library of International Law*) <https://legal.un.org/avl/ha/csm/csm.html> accessed 27 July 2023.

II. NATURE AND SCOPE

The first key aspect of diplomatic and consular immunity is 'inviolability', which was mentioned previously in relation to foreign State official immunity.[78] According to Denza, this means the 'duty to abstain from exercising any sovereign rights, in particular law enforcement rights, in respect of inviolable premises, persons, or property'.[79] VCDR article 22 enshrines this obligation in relation to diplomatic premises and provides that they are 'immune from search, requisition, attachment or execution'.[80] This rule is stated without exception, in comparison with VCCR article 31, which provides that consent may be assumed in case of a disaster requiring prompt protective action on the consular premises.[81] In *Tehran Hostages*, the ICJ described inviolability as a 'fundamental prerequisite for the conduct of relations between States'.[82]

Absent a waiver by the sending State, diplomats are also personally inviolable and absolutely immune from any form of arrest or detention or other exercise of criminal jurisdiction for the duration of their posts.[83] They also enjoy immunity in relation to most civil and administrative proceedings apart from three types of proceedings: real actions involving immovable property; actions relating to succession; and suits relating to commercial or professional activities undertaken outside of official functions.[84]

By comparison, consular officials may be arrested or detained pending trial in the case of a 'grave crime' and pursuant to the decision of a 'competent judicial authority'.[85] Consular officials also only possess immunity for 'acts performed in exercise of consular functions' (article 43(1) VCCR).[86] These provisions reflect a more functional approach to immunity for consular as opposed to diplomatic agents, as well as balance in favour of the interests of the receiving State in ensuring compliance with local laws.[87] At the

---

78 On diplomatic relations, see Arévalo-Ramírez, § 10, in this textbook.

79 Eileen Denza, *Diplomatic Law: Commentary on the Vienna Convention on Diplomatic Relations* (4th edn, OUP 2016) 110.

80 Vienna Convention on Diplomatic Relations (adopted 18 April 1961, entered into force 24 April 1964) 500 UNTS 95 (VCDR), article 22(1).

81 Vienna Convention on Consular Relations (adopted 24 April 1963, entered into force 19 March 1967) 596 UNTS 261 (VCCR), article 31(2).

82 United States Diplomatic and Consular Staff in Tehran (United States v Iran) ('*Tehran Hostages*') (Jurisdiction and Admissibility) [1980] ICJ Rep 3 [91]; see also Ibid (Request for the Indication of Provisional Measures: Order), General List No 64 [1979] [38].

83 VCDR, articles 29, 31.

84 Ibid, article 31.

85 VCCR, article 41(1).

86 An exception exists for contracts concluded while the consular official was not acting as an agent of the sending State and in relation to damage caused to third parties by vehicles or aircraft. See VCCR article 43(2).

87 See Fox and Webb (n 13) 600.

same time, differences exist across jurisdictions in light of the absence of guidance in the VCCR as to the scope of 'grave crimes'.[88]

At the end of a diplomatic or consular term, the virtually absolute immunity afforded to diplomats is replaced by residual functional immunity. As VCDR article 39(2) provides, when a diplomat's term ends, 'such privileges and immunities . . . normally cease at the moment when [the diplomat] leaves the country, or on expiry of a reasonable period in which to do so'.[89] At that point, immunity only remains with respect to acts performed by the diplomat in the exercise of their functions.[90] A similar provision is contained in the VCCR.[91]

As with the restrictive approach to foreign sovereign immunity, the scope of the 'commercial activities' exception to diplomatic immunity has given rise to considerable debate. The issue has arisen prominently in relation to claims by persons employed as domestic workers. In 2022, the UK Supreme Court in *Basfar v Wong*[92] concluded that a serving diplomat was not entitled to immunity from civil jurisdiction in relation to a suit brought by a migrant domestic worker employed in the diplomat's residence under conditions amounting to modern slavery.[93] In explaining its reasoning, the Court observed that while the 'commercial activities' exception did not encompass 'ordinary contracts incidental to daily life in the receiving state', the abusive working conditions complained of were not 'incidental' to the ordinary functioning of the diplomatic post.[94] In comparison with this outcome, US courts have disagreed over whether the commercial activities exception applies in similar circumstances,[95] with most holding that abusive employment only falls outside the scope of a diplomat or consular official's residual immunity.[96]

---

88 See Luke T Lee and John B Quigley, *Consular Law and Practice* (3d edn, OUP 2008) 34–35; SR Subramanian, 'Abuse of Diplomatic Privileges and the Balance between Immunities and the Duty to Respect the Local Laws and Regulations under the Vienna Conventions: The Recent Indian Experience' (2017) 3 CJGG 182, 207–10.

89 VCDR, article 39(2).

90 Ibid.

91 VCCR, article 53(4). For further reading on the scope of functional immunity in the context of diplomatic relations, see Xinxiang Shi, 'Official Acts and Beyond: Towards and Accurate Interpretation of Diplomatic Immunity *Ratione Materiae* under the Vienna Convention on Diplomatic Relations' (2019) 18 Chinese JIL 669.

92 *Basfar v. Wong* [2022] UKSC 20.

93 See Chris Stephen, 'Diplomatic Immunity, Modern Slavery and the "Commercial Activity" Exception: The UK Supreme Court in *Basfar v Wong*' (*EJIL: Talk!*, 11 July 2022) <www.ejiltalk.org/diplomatic-immunity-modern-slavery-and-the-commercial-activity-exception-the-uk-supreme-court-in-basfar-v-wong/> accessed 16 August 2023.

94 *Basfar v Wong* [2022] UKSC 20 [37].

95 Compare *Tabion v Mufti* (US Court of Appeals for the Fourth Circuit) 73 F.3d 535 (4th Cir. 1996) (finding a serving diplomatic official immune from suit by domestic servant because the services provided were incidental to the daily life of the diplomat and therefore not a commercial activity); with *Park v Shin* (US Court of Appeals for the Ninth Circuit) 313 F.3d 1138 (9th Cir. 2002) (finding a consular official not entitled to immunity under the VCCR in relation to employment claims brought by a consular official's personal domestic servant because these activities were not undertaken as part of the consular official's functions).

96 See William S Dodge, 'SDNY Rejects Immunity for Former Diplomat in Trafficking Case' (*Transnational Litigation Blog*, 27 October 2022) <https://tlblog.org/sdny-rejects-immunity-for-former-diplomat-in-trafficking-case/> accessed 16 August 2023; see also *Swarna v Al-Awadi* (US Court of Appeals for the Second Circuit) 622 F.3d 123 (2d Cir. 2010).

Diplomatic and consular immunity differs from the immunity owed to high-ranking State officials in several ways, some more minor than others. One key difference is the relevance of the consent of the State receiving the mission. In comparison with foreign official immunity, which does not depend on whether the individual is traveling in their professional capacity and which applies in all States, diplomatic and consular immunity only applies in the receiving State where the individual enters to take up their post, as well as in States transited by the official en route to or from a post.[97] A sending State must also take into account the views of a receiving State. In *Equatorial Guinea v France*, for example, the ICJ explained that VCDR article 22 did not allow a sending State to unilaterally impose its choice of mission premises upon the receiving State.[98]

As in the case of foreign official immunity, diplomatic and consular immunities may be waived by a sending State. The VCDR and VCCR also provide protections for the receiving State, such as the ability to declare individuals *persona non grata*.[99] These provisions potentially suggest that the VCDR and VCCR constitute 'self-contained regimes' such that receiving States cannot resort to general secondary rules of international law, such as countermeasures, in cases of alleged abuse. The ICJ appears to have taken this position in *Tehran Hostages*, where it categorically rejected Iran's attempted defence that the US had committed abuse in its territory.[100]

D. PRIVILEGES AND IMMUNITIES OF INTERNATIONAL ORGANISATIONS

A separate category of immunities under international law pertains to international organisations and the individuals carrying out the work of such organisations.[101] A variety of legal instruments set out these immunities with the aim of ensuring the protection of an international organisation's headquarters, property, and personnel.[102]

I. SOURCES

The privileges and immunities owed to international organisations are principally rooted in treaties, including both multilateral and bilateral instruments.[103] Article 105(1) of the UN Charter provides that the UN 'shall enjoy in the territory of each

---

97 See Foakes (n 45) 9; see also VCDR, article 40.

98 Immunities and Criminal Proceedings (Equatorial Guinea v France) (Merits) [2020] ICJ Rep 300 [67].

99 Rosanne van Alebeek, 'Immunity, Diplomatic' (*Max Planck Encyclopedia of Public International Law*, May 2009) para 34.

100 *Tehran Hostages*, para 83.

101 On international organisations, see Baranowska, Engström, and Paige, § 7.3, in this textbook.

102 See generally August Reinisch, 'Privileges and Immunities' in Jacob Katz Cogan and others (eds), *The Oxford Handbook of International Organizations* (OUP 2016).

103 The extent to which international organisations enjoy immunity under customary international law is debated. See Brownlie's, Principles (n 5) 173.

of its Members such privileges and immunities as are necessary for the exercise of its functions and the fulfillment of its purposes'.[104] Article 105(2) of the Charter in turn grants to representatives of UN member States and UN officials 'such privileges and immunities as are necessary for the independent exercise of their functions in connection with the Organization'.[105] Two subsequent conventions, the General Convention on the Privileges and Immunities of the United Nations (1946)[106] and the Convention on the Privileges and Immunities of the Specialized Agencies (1947),[107] further specify the content of these immunities.

Other international organisation immunities are found in the constitutive instruments of international organisations, including of UN specialised agencies. For example, the Constitution of the World Health Organization provides that the organisation shall enjoy 'such privileges and immunities as may be necessary for the fulfilment of its objective and for the exercise of its functions', and that representatives of member States and persons serving on various technical boards shall enjoy 'such privileges and immunities as are necessary for the independent exercise of their functions in connection with the Organization'.[108]

Several multilateral agreements also provide international organisations with immunity. One example is the Agreement on Privileges and Immunities of the International Atomic Energy Agency (IAEA),[109] which builds on more general immunity provisions found in the Statute of the IAEA. Because the IAEA is neither a UN organ nor a UN specialised agency, this convention serves the analogous purpose of the Specialized Agencies Convention. Other examples of multilateral instruments setting out privileges and immunities include the UN Convention on the Law of the Sea, which provides privileges and immunities for the International Tribunal for the Law of the Sea,[110] and the statutes of various international tribunals, which afford privileges and immunities to certain classes of employees.[111]

International organisations may also work out host and headquarters agreements with the States in which they are situated to supplement the other sources of immunities

---

104 Charter of the United Nations (adopted 26 June 1945, entered into force 24 October 1945) 1 UNTS XVI, article 105(1).

105 Ibid, article 105(2).

106 Convention on the Privileges and Immunities of the United Nations (adopted 13 February 1946, entered into force 17 September 1946) 1 UNTS 15.

107 Convention on the Privileges and Immunities of the Specialized Agencies (approved 21 November 1947, entered into force 2 December 1948) 33 UNTS 261.

108 Constitution of the World Health Organization (adopted 22 July 1946, entered into force 7 April 1948) 14 UNTS 185, article 67.

109 Agreement on the Privileges and Immunities of the International Atomic Energy Agency (adopted 1 July 1959, entered into force 29 July 1960) 374 UNTS 148 (1959).

110 UNCLOS, Annex VI.

111 See e.g. Rome Statute, article 48; Convention on the Settlement of Investment Disputes between States and Nationals of Other States (concluded 18 March 1965, entered into force 14 October 1966) 757 UNTS 159, section 6.

to which they may be entitled. Key examples include the US-UN headquarters agreement[112] and the Switzerland-UN headquarters agreement.[113] In some countries, domestic statutes, such as the US International Organizations Immunities Act (1945)[114] and the UK International Organisations Act (1968),[115] also give effect to various international organisation immunities.

II. NATURE AND SCOPE

The privileges and immunities granted to international organisations are in many cases quite broad. For example, article II(2) of the General Convention provides that the 'United Nations, its property and assets wherever located and by whomsoever held, shall enjoy immunity from every form of legal process' except where it has been expressly waived.[116] Article II(3)–(4) further provides that the premises of the United Nations and UN documents are 'inviolable' and that the property and the assets of the UN are 'immune from search, requisition, confiscation and any other form of interference, whether by executive, administrative, judicial or legislative action'.[117]

However, not all international organisations possess such extensive immunity. The International Bank for Reconstruction and Development and the International Finance Corporation are two examples of organisations with instruments indicating that they are not immune from judicial process in certain circumstances.[118] One explanation for this is that these organisations more routinely enter into contracts with private parties as part of their functions.

Where international organisation immunities are broadly worded, debate has surrounded the question of whether such immunities are 'absolute' in nature, or 'functional', meaning that they are granted only to the extent necessary for the 'fulfilment' of the organisation's 'purposes'.[119] For its part, the ICJ has referred to international organisation immunities as functional and ultimately owed for the benefit of the international organisation and not, for instance, to the personnel claiming UN

---

112 Agreement regarding the Headquarters of the United Nations (adopted 26 June 1947, entered into force 31 October 1947) 11 UNTS 11.

113 Agreement on the Privileges and Immunities of the United Nations concluded between the Swiss Federal Council and the Secretary General of the United Nations on 19 April 1946 (1946) 1 UNTS 163.

114 22 U.S.C. § 288 et seq.

115 International Organisations Act 1968 (c. 48).

116 General Convention, article II(2).

117 Ibid, article II(3)–(4).

118 See International Bank for Reconstruction and Development, Articles of Agreement (amended effective 27 June 2012), article VII, § 3; International Finance Corporation, Articles of Agreement (amended through 16 April 2020), article VI, § 3; see also Chanaka Wickremasinghe, 'International Organizations or Institutions, Immunities before National Courts' (*Max Planck Encyclopedia of Public International Law*, July 2009) para 13.

119 August Reinisch, 'Convention on the Privileges and Immunities of the United Nations; Convention on the Privileges and Immunities of the Specialized Agencies' <https://legal.un.org/avl/ha/cpiun-cpisa/cpiun-cpisa. html> accessed 16 August 2023.

immunity.[120] At the same time, the ICJ appears to have adopted a rather broad view of international organisation immunities bordering on the absolute approach, particularly in relation to individuals entitled to international organisation immunity.[121]

The key purpose of international organisation immunity is ultimately to enable each organisation to effectively carry out its work unimpeded by the unilateral influence of member States. The UN has previously been proactive in protecting immunities when carrying out projects away from its headquarters, as well as where the immunities of persons carrying out UN work in their home State are implicated. Notably, the UN has on two occasions (namely, in both the *Mazilu* and *Cumaraswamy* cases)[122] requested an advisory opinion from the ICJ on the issue of the immunity of experts on mission from legal process in their home States.

A key issue which has arisen in recent years concerns whether the restrictive approach to immunity can be applied to international organisations. In 2019, the US Supreme Court held in *Jam v International Finance Corporation*[123] that international organisations are only afforded the 'same' immunity as foreign States under US law, meaning that any exceptions available under the restrictive approach also apply to international organisations.[124] This approach has been criticised by academics who have questioned the logic of transferring the restrictive approach to international organisations which by design do not typically act with a commercial purpose.[125]

III. APPLICATION AND DEBATES

The ICJ has emphasised that matters concerning international organisation immunities must be addressed 'expeditiously' and *in limine litis* (Latin: 'at the start of the procedure').[126] In the *Obligation to Arbitrate* case, this resulted in the ICJ finding a dispute between the US and the UN concerning privileges and immunities owed under the US-UN headquarters agreement even where certain coercive measures aimed at Palestine's delegation to the United Nations had only been adopted by the US Congress but not yet enforced.[127] Similarly, in the *Cumaraswamy* case, the ICJ rejected Malaysia's

---

120 See *Difference Relating to Immunity from Legal Process of a Special Rapporteur of the Commission of Human Rights* (*'Cumaraswamy'*) *(Advisory Opinion)* [1999] ICJ Rep 62 [51].

121 See Beatrice Walton, 'Difference Relating to Immunity from Legal Process of a Special Rapporteur of the Commission on Human Rights (Advisory Opinion)' (OXIO 572) in Jean d'Aspremont and others (eds), *Oxford International Organisations*; see also Beatrice Walton, 'Applicability of the Obligation to Arbitrate under Section 21 of the United Nations Headquarters Agreement of 26 June 1947 (Advisory Opinion)' OXIO 590) in Jean d'Aspremont and others (eds), *Oxford International Organisations*.

122 *Cumaraswamy*; Applicability of Article VI, Section 22, of the Convention on the Privileges and Immunities of the United Nations (Advisory Opinion) ('*Mazilu*'), [1989] ICJ Rep 177.

123 *Jam v International Finance Corporation*, 139 S. Ct. 759 (2019).

124 22 U.S.C. § 288a(b).

125 Wickremasinghe (n 118) paras 15–16.

126 *Cumaraswamy* (n 122) [63].

127 Walton (n 121); see *Applicability of the Obligation to Arbitrate under Section 21 of the United Nations Headquarters Agreement of 26 June 1947* (Advisory Opinion) [1988] ICJ Rep 12.

argument that the General Convention imposed only obligations of 'result', such that Malaysia would not be in breach until its courts reached a final decision as to whether the individual in question was entitled to immunity.[128] The Court instead held that Malaysia had an obligation to intervene in its national courts to assert international organisation immunities as soon as was feasible.[129]

Related to the issue of timing is the degree of deference owed to the views taken by an international organisation as to whether the organisation, or a member of its personnel, is entitled to immunity. In *Cumaraswamy*, the ICJ explained that a finding by the UN Secretary-General that one of its officials is entitled to immunity 'creates a presumption which can only be set aside for the most compelling reasons'.[130] Accordingly, States are required to communicate to their domestic authorities and courts the view of the UN Secretary-General as to whether an individual acted in his or her official capacity.[131] Whether this approach makes sense, or whether more room is in fact permitted for national courts to scrutinise whether certain conduct falls within the scope of organisation functions, is a question which remains unsettled, with some jurisdictions, such as the Netherlands, appearing to adopt such an approach.[132]

Another important issue concerns the potential for abuse in relation to the application of immunity, which has prompted considerable debate. Both the General Convention and the Specialized Agencies Convention impose a duty on the UN and specialised agencies to waive immunity in cases where the application of immunity 'would impede the course of justice' and where waiver can be achieved without prejudicing UN interests.[133] Some agreements, such as the UN model status-of-forces agreement for peacekeeping operations, also anticipate potential remedies for abuse by allowing military or national authorities to apprehend, investigate, and prosecute persons involved in the operation in certain circumstances.[134]

A final and related issue concerns the interaction between international organisation immunities and human rights. The ECtHR has considered this issue in relation to article 6(1) of the European Convention on Human Rights, which provides a right of access to a court. In the context of employment disputes, the ECtHR in the *Waite and Kennedy v Germany* case found that the privileges and immunities of international organisations were compatible with article 6(1) where they pursued the legitimate aim

---

128 *Cumaraswamy*, paras 61–63.

129 Ibid; Wickremasinghe (n 118) para 8.

130 *Cumaraswamy* (n 122) [61].

131 Walton (n 121).

132 See Clemens Treichl, 'The Denial of Oral Hearings by International Administrative Tribunals as a Factor for Lifting Organizational Immunity before European Courts' (2019) 16 IOLR 409.

133 General Convention, articles V(20), VI(23); Specialized Agencies Convention, article VI(22).

134 See Report of the Secretary-General, 'Comprehensive Review of the Whole Question of Peace-Keeping Operations in All Their Aspects: Model Status-of-Forces Agreement for Peace-keeping Operations' (9 October 1990) UN Doc A/45/594.

of guarding against interference by States.[135] The ECtHR has nonetheless considered the possibility that international organisations may be required to afford alternative internal proceedings, the exact requirements of which continue to generate debate.[136]

E. CONCLUSION

This chapter has provided an overview of three main types of immunities: foreign sovereign immunity, including foreign State official immunity; diplomatic and consular immunity; and international organisation immunity. Across these immunities, an important and delicate balance is required to respect the purposes served by each type of immunity as well as other key values. While the first exceptions to immunity emerged to protect commercial interests,[137] more recent trends suggest that a shift may be gradually underway towards an expansion of exceptions to address other issues, including human rights and serious violations of international law.

Another key takeaway from the chapter is the breadth of actors involved in immunities issues, and the range of topics impacted by them. While there has been an evolution over the last century towards a greater role for courts (as opposed to governments) in immunities issues, at the practical level, nearly all facets of government, as well as key international actors, such as the UN Secretary General, have the potential to affect immunities issues. Likewise, immunities issues have the potential to implicate an extremely wide range of substantive areas of international law, including commercial law, arbitration, international criminal law, and human rights, to name a few examples touched on in this chapter.

BOX 11.5 Further Readings

Further Readings

- Peace Palace Library, 'Immunities' <https://peacepalacelibrary.nl/research-guide/immunities> accessed 16 August 2023

---

§ § §

---

135 *Waite and Kennedy v Germany* (ECtHR) Reports 1999-I 393.
136 See Treichl (n 137) 425–429.
137 See generally Jamshidi (n 18) 585; see also Peters (n 10) 15.

CHAPTER 12
PEACEFUL SETTLEMENT OF INTERNATIONAL DISPUTES

VISHAKHA CHOUDHARY

BOX 12.1 Required Knowledge and Learning Objectives

Required knowledge: Use of Force; States; International Organisations; History

Learning objectives: Understanding the obligation to pursue peaceful settlement of disputes, its different methods, and the relationship to the maintenance of international peace as a fundamental objective of international law.

BOX 12.2 Interactive Exercises

Access *interactive exercises for this chapter*[1] by positioning your smartphone camera at the dot-filled box, also known as a QR code.

Figure 12.1 QR code referring to interactive exercises.

A. INTRODUCTION

The maintenance and, as necessary, restoration of international peace is a fundamental objective of international law.[2] While traditionally conceived as the 'absence of war', global perceptions of peace have matured significantly today,[3] as captured in this

---

1 https://openrewi.org/en-projects-project-public-international-law-peaceful-settlement-of-disputes/

2 See also Lloydd, § 2.1, in this textbook.

3 See generally, Cecilia M Bailliet and Kjetil Mujezinovic Larsen, 'Introduction' in Cecilia Marcela Bailliet and Kjetil Mujezinovic Larsen (eds), *Promoting Peace Through International Law* (OUP 2015); Paul F Diehl, 'Exploring Peace: Looking Beyond War and Negative Peace' (2016) 60 ISQ 1; Höglund Kristine and Kovacs Mimmisöderberg, 'Beyond the Absence of War: The Diversity of Peace in Post-Settlement Societies' (2010) 36 RIS 367.

DOI: 10.4324/9781003451327-14

statement by the United Nations Security Council (UNSC) in the aftermath of the adversarial decades of the Cold War:

> The absence of war and military conflicts among States does not in itself ensure international peace and security. The non-military sources of instability in the economic, social, humanitarian and ecological fields have become threats to peace and security. The United Nations membership as a whole, working through the appropriate bodies, needs to give the highest priority to the solution of these matters.[4]

Central to this contemporary understanding is that, with the changing world order, the sources of international conflicts are diversifying. The evolution in the meaning of 'peace' and 'conflict' has been accompanied by the mainstreaming of different avenues for resolving disputes on the international plane. From the use of military force, States and non-State actors have gradually shifted towards more peaceful methods of dispute settlement. This chapter discusses such methods, their underlying principles, and how these principles evolved, primarily through the lens of the Charter of the United Nations (UN Charter).

B. HISTORICAL BACKGROUND

Until recently, the international legal order permitted the use of force for the settlement of disputes. Early Western scholars like Hugo Grotius considered warfare to be concerned with the same subject matter as judicial trials and recognised the legality of use of force for the 'execution of a right'.[5] Sovereigns regularly deployed declarations setting out their reasons for waging war, which ranged from obtaining compensation for tortious injuries to the protection of trade or religious interests, and regarded war's outcome as a means of dispute settlement.[6] Indicative examples include the threats and use of force by Western powers against Mexico in 1846–1848 and Venezuela in 1902 over unpaid debts.[7]

Efforts to promote peaceful dispute settlement began with modest goals, that is not to outlaw war as an option, but to procedurally regulate and limit it.[8] For instance,

---

4   UNSC Presidential Statement 47 (1992) UN Doc S/23500. See also Declaration on the Right to Peace, UNGA Res 71/189 (2 February 2017) UN Doc A/RES/71/189, Annex, recital para 17.

5   Hugo Grotius, *Commentary on the Law of Prize and Booty* (first published 1603, Liberty Fund 2006) 102–105; similarly Emer de Vattel, *The Law of Nations, or, Principles of the Law of Nature, Applied to the Conduct and Affairs of Nations and Sovereigns* (first published 1797, Liberty Fund 2008) 279, 289.

6   Oona A Hathaway and Scott Shapiro, *The Internationalists* (Simon and Schuster 2017) 105–107; see generally, Oona A Hathaway and others, 'War Manifestos' (2018) 85 UCLR 1139.

7   Clayton Charles Kohl, *Claims as a Cause of the Mexican War* (1914) 72; Andrew Clapham, *Brierly's Law of Nations: An Introduction to the Role of International Law in International Relations* (OUP 2012) 451.

8   The 1856 Peace of Paris provided that disputing parties, before having recourse to force, should afford each other the possibility of mediation. At the 1874 Brussels Conference, generally considered to have formed the basis for the Hague peace conferences, delegates declared that '[w]ar being thus regulated . . . would tend more surely to that which should be its final object, viz., the re-establishment of good relations, and a more solid and lasting peace between the belligerent States'. *See* Final Protocol of the Brussels Conference of 1874, recital para 5.

at the Hague peace conferences of 1899 and 1907, States undertook to make 'best efforts' towards non-violent dispute settlement, with the view of obviating war 'as far as possible'.[9] The Hague Conventions' rules on mediation exemplify the political will at the time: States agreed to pursue good offices or mediation 'before an appeal to arms' for the resolution of a dispute, but caveated that acceptance of mediation would not hinder measures of preparation for war.[10] If mediation was pursued after the commencement of hostilities, States remained free to continue military operations in progress, absent an agreement to the contrary.[11]

The devastations of the First World War prompted further emphasis on peaceful dispute settlement, as evidenced by the 1920 Covenant of the League of Nations establishing the Permanent Court of International Justice (PCIJ).[12] Articles 12 and 13 mandated recourse to arbitration and judicial settlement in 'suitable' cases,[13] restraining States from resorting to war 'until three months after the award by the arbitrators or the judicial decision'. Simultaneously, article 13 noted the commitment of League members to carry out any award or decision 'in full good faith', and prohibited resort to war against members that so complied.[14] A definitive repudiation of war as an instrument of dispute settlement emerged shortly thereafter, in 1928, when the parties to the Kellogg-Briand Pact 'condemn[ed] recourse to war for the solution of international controversies' and 'agree[d] that the settlement or solution of all disputes . . . shall never be sought except by pacific means'.[15]

The Covenant continued to tolerate war and its parties lacked political will to make use of the sanctioning mechanisms provided therein; the Kellogg-Briand Pact was devoid of an enforcement mechanism altogether. Unsurprisingly, dispute settlement rules in these instruments withered in the face of the Second World War.[16] In the era of the UN, a stronger commitment to pacific dispute settlement has developed in parallel with the prohibition on the use of force.[17] Together, they circumscribe the avenues of international dispute resolution *exclusively* to peaceful methods.

---

9 1899 Convention for the Pacific Settlement of International Disputes (1899 Hague Convention I), article 1; 1907 Convention for the Pacific Settlement of International Disputes (1907 Hague Convention I), article 1.

10 1899 Hague Convention I, articles 2 and 7; 1907 Hague Convention I, articles 2 and 7.

11 1907 Hague Convention I, article 7.

12 Covenant of the League of Nations (adopted 28 June 1919, entered into force 10 January 1920) 108 LNTS 188. For an overview of the role of the PCIJ in the effecting post-war peace, see Christian J Tams, 'Peace Through International Adjudication: The Permanent Court of International Justice and the Post-War Order' in Michel Erpelding, Burkhard Hess, and Hélène Ruiz Fabri (eds), *Peace Through Law: The Versailles Peace Treaty and Dispute Settlement After World War I* (Nomos 2019) 215–238.

13 'Suitable' cases were broadly defined as '[d]isputes as to the interpretation of a treaty, as to any question of international law, as to the existence of any fact which if established would constitute a breach of any international obligation, or as to the extent and nature of the reparation to be made for any such breach'.

14 See also Covenant of the League of Nations (n 12) article 15 providing similar rules for disputes considered by the League's Council or Assembly.

15 General Treaty Providing for the Renunciation of War as an Instrument of National Policy (adopted 27 August 1928, entered into force 24 July 1929) 94 LNTS 57, articles I and II.

16 See Andrew Clapham, *War* (Clarendon Law Series 2021) 86–106 for a detailed discussion.

17 On the use of force, see Svicevic, § 13, in this textbook.

C. THE OBLIGATION TO PURSUE PEACEFUL SETTLEMENT OF INTERNATIONAL DISPUTES

The principle of peaceful dispute settlement is widely regarded as customary international law,[18] and its binding character has been affirmed in numerous international instruments,[19] most prominently article 2(3) of the UN Charter, which sets out in mandatory terms:

> All Members *shall* settle their international disputes by peaceful means in such a manner that international peace and security, and justice, are not endangered.

The precise content of this obligation remains contentious: does the mandatory language in article 2(3) indicate an obligation to settle disputes *per se*? Consider article 33(1) of the UN Charter, which provides that the parties to any dispute, 'the continuance of which is likely to endanger the maintenance of international peace and security, *shall . . . seek*' a solution by peaceful means. Read with the purposes and principles of the UN Charter to maintain international peace and security,[20] article 33(1) may be understood as compelling States to actively seek to resolve, at minimum, those disputes that threaten the same.

The selective focus of article 33(1) could simultaneously be interpreted as suggesting that any obligation to settle international disputes is not universally applicable.[21] Under that view, States are not required to pursue the settlement of disputes *per se* but only to pursue any settlement exclusively through peaceful methods.[22] A common critique

---

18 *Case Concerning Military and Paramilitary Activities in and against Nicaragua (Nicaragua v. United States of America)* (Merits) [1986] ICJ Rep 14, 145; *Aerial Incident of 10 August 1999 (Pakistan v India)* (Jurisdiction) [2000] ICJ Rep 12, 33. On customary international law generally, see Stoica, § 6.2, in this textbook.

19 UNGA Res 2625 (24 October 1970), Annex (or the 'Friendly Relations Declaration'); UNGA Res 37/10 (15 November 1982) UN Doc A/RES/37/10, Annex (or the 'Manila Declaration'), paras 1 and 2; UNGA Res 43/51 (5 December 1988), UN Doc A/RES/43/51; UNGA Res 57/26 (3 February 2003), UN Doc A/RES/57/26, para 2; Millennium Declaration, UNGA Res 55/2 (8 September 2000), UN Doc A/RES/55/2, para 4; Declaration on Rule of Law, UNGA Res 67/1 (19 September 2012), UN Doc A/67/L.1, para 4; Charter of the League of Arab States (signed 22 March 1945, entered into force 10 May 1945) 70 UNTS 237, article 5; Charter of the Organization of American States (signed 30 April 1948, entered into force 13 December 1951) 119 UNTS 3, articles 24–27; Constitutive Act of the African Union (signed 11 July 2000, entered into force 26 May 2001) 2158 UNTS 3, article 4(e).

20 Cf. article 1(1) UN Charter.

21 Alain Pellet, 'Peaceful Settlement of International Disputes' (*Max Planck Encyclopaedia of International Law*, August 2013), para 5; *Tallinn Manual 2.0 on the International Law Applicable to Cyber Operations* (CUP 2016) 306. See also Antonio Cassese, *International Law* (OUP 2005) 283 (arguing that to the extent any dispute can threaten international peace and security, a narrow reading of articles 2(3) and 33 may nevertheless be expansive enough to encapsulate *all* disputes).

22 Tanaka thus argues that disputes may remain frozen in time and illustratively refers to the 1959 Antarctic Treaty freezing claims for territorial sovereignty over Antarctica. *See* Yoshifumi Tanaka, *The Peaceful Settlement of International Disputes* (CUP 2018), 6.

of this view is that it reduces article 2(3) to a restatement of the prohibition on the use of force, essentially comprising an identical negative obligation to refrain from forceful conduct. Many international legal scholars thus posit that, to give effectiveness and meaning to the principle in article 2(3), it must be viewed as requiring the deployment of active efforts for the settlement of all disputes.[23] Debates on the scope of the obligation remain ongoing, and the open-ended objectives and negotiating history of the UN Charter have fostered multiple perspectives.[24]

What is unanimously accepted, as well as explicitly recognised in article 33(1), is that parties are free to choose the specific method of dispute settlement employed,[25] otherwise known as the notion of 'free choice of means'. Barring exceptional situations where States have accepted compulsory dispute settlement through prescribed methods,[26] the notion of free choice or consent remains pervasive in international dispute settlement, as evidenced by numerous treaties that permit States to make reservations or withdraw from dispute settlement provisions.[27] Concurrently, given the natural tension between consent and the obligation of peaceful dispute settlement, some scholars have called for greater weight to be accorded to the latter, especially in matters concerning international peace and security.[28]

The expression 'seek a solution' in article 33(1) indicates that while States may be required to *attempt* to peacefully resolve certain disputes, they are not bound to achieve a settlement. Put differently, any obligation in this regard is an obligation of *conduct* and not of *result*.[29] As recognised in the 1982 Manila Declaration,[30] the central thrust here is on the duty of parties to act in good faith. This duty may manifest in various ways, depending upon the method chosen for dispute resolution. For example,

---

23 Duncan B Hollis and Eneken Tikk, 'Peaceful Settlement in International Law' (2022) 57 TILJ 29; Christian Tomuschat, 'Purposes and Principles, Article 2(3)' in Bruno Simma and others (eds), *The Charter of the United Nations: A Commentary* (OUP 2012) 190; John Merrills, 'The Means of Dispute Settlement' in Malcolm D Evans (ed), *International Law* (OUP 2018) 549.

24 For an extensive discussion, DN Hutchinson, 'The Material Scope of the Obligation under the United Nations Charter to Take Action to Settle International Disputes' (1992) 14 AYIL 1–128.

25 Manila Declaration (n 19), para 3; Friendly Relations Declaration (n 19), 123; Fisheries Jurisdiction (*Spain v Canada*) (Jurisdiction) [1998] ICJ Rep 432, 456; *Aerial Incident of 10 August 1999* (n 18) [53].

26 E.g. Understanding on the Rules and Procedures Governing the Settlement of Disputes (signed 15 April 1994, entered into force 1 January 1995) 1869 UNTS 401, article 23.1; Convention on the Law of the Sea (signed 10 December 1982, entered into force 16 November 1994) 1833 UNTS 397, article 297.

27 E.g. United Nations Convention Against Corruption (signed 31 October 2003, entered into force 14 December 2005) 2349 UNTS 41, article 66(3); Convention against Torture and Other Cruel, Inhuman, or Degrading Treatment or Punishment (signed 10 December 1984) 1465 UNTS 85, articles 21 and 22.

28 Christian Tomuschat, 'Pacific Settlement of Disputes, Article 33' in Bruno Simma and others (eds), *The Charter of the United Nations: A Commentary* (OUP 2012) 1081; Antônio Augusto Cançado Trindade, 'Peaceful Settlement of International Disputes: Current State and Perspectives' <www.oas.org/es/sla/ddi/docs/publicaciones_digital_xxxi_curso_derecho_internacional_2004_antonio_augusto_cancado_trindade.pdf> accessed 2 July 2023.

29 This is expressed clearly in the Spanish text of article 33(1), which uses the expression '*tratarán de buscarle solución*' (in English, 'to try to find a solution').

30 Manila Declaration (n 19), paras 1, 5, 10, 11.

parties engaging in negotiations would fail to act in good faith if they do not conduct themselves in a manner that allows meaningful and fruitful discussions.[31] Parties pursuing adjudication or arbitration should abstain from taking any measure that would entail a prejudicial effect on the execution of a future decision.[32]

I. PERSONAL SCOPE

The peaceful settlement principle in article 2(3) of the UN Charter belongs to a period where the subjects of international law were rigidly understood as States alone.[33] As such, that this provision principally addresses UN members is not surprising.[34] However, as a rule of customary international law, the obligation to settle disputes peacefully binds every State, and not just UN members. The UN Charter itself, in article 35(2), allows non-members to accept 'the obligations of pacific settlement provided in the [Charter]' and bring relevant disputes to the notice of the UNSC or General Assembly (UNGA).

Article 2 of the UN Charter applies to both member States and '[t]he Organization'. Hence, the requirement of peaceful settlement in article 2(3) also binds the UN itself.[35] It is difficult to envisage that non-UN international organisations would be exempted from the corresponding obligation under customary international law, creating a two-tiered system of law that accords greater privileges to some organisations.[36]

Whether the obligation applies or should apply to non-State actors is heavily contested. States increasingly litigate disputes with private persons (such as investor-State disputes and human rights litigation).[37] It is also not uncommon for States to be called upon to resolve disputes with non-State actors peacefully.[38]

---

31 *North Sea Continental Shelf (Germany v Netherlands)* (Judgement) [1969] ICJ Rep 3, 47; *Gabčíkovo-Nagymaros Project (Hungary v Slovakia)* (Judgment) [1997] ICJ Rep 7, 78; *Pulp Mills on the River Uruguay (Argentina v Uruguay)* (Judgment) [2010] ICJ Rep 14 [68].

32 Manila Declaration (n 19), para 8; Friendly Relations Declaration (n 19), 123; *Frontier Dispute (Burkina Faso v Mali)* (Order) [1986] ICJ Rep 3, 9; *Allegations of Genocide under the Convention on the Prevention and Punishment of the Crime of Genocide (Ukraine v Russian Federation)* (Order) [2022] ICJ Rep 211 [213].

33 Cf Engström, § 7, in this textbook.

34 This can also be viewed as a natural consequence of article 2(3) being a complement to the prohibition on the use of force in article 2(4) of the UN Charter, which is also addressed to States.

35 See e.g. articles 34 and 36 of the UN Charter regarding consideration of a dispute by the UN Security Council. Hollis and Tikk (n 23), 24 argue that international organisations have a dual obligation to settle disputes to which they become parties and to facilitate inter-State dispute settlement.

36 See *Interpretation of the Agreement of 25 March 1951 between the WHO and Egypt (Advisory Opinion)* [1980] ICJ Rep 73 [89].

37 On international investment law, see Hankings-Evans, § 23.1, in this textbook; on human rights law, see Ciampi, § 21, in this textbook. See also *Abyei Arbitration (Government of Sudan v Sudan People's Liberation Movement/Army)* (Award) PCA 2008–07.

38 Manila Declaration (n 19), para 12; UNSC Res 322 (22 November 1972), UN Doc S/RES/322(1972), para 3; UNSC Res 389 (22 April 1976), UN Doc S/RES/389(1976), para 5; UNSC Res 1250 (29 June 1999), UN Doc S/RES/1250(1999), para 7; UNSC Res 1339 (31 January 2001), UN Doc S/RES/1339(2001), para 5; UNSC Res 1529 (29 February 2004), UN Doc, S/RES/1529(2004), para 7; UNSC Res 1781 (15 October 2007), UN Doc S/RES/1781 (2007), para 3.

Christian Tomuschat makes the case that, as a logical corollary of the prohibition on the use of force, the obligation of peaceful dispute settlement should extend to all entities enjoying the protection of that prohibition, including *de facto* regimes and national liberation movements that can invoke the right of self-determination.[39] At the same time, he considers that as most private persons are placed under the jurisdiction of one or more States, which internally proscribe resort to forceful or coercive self-help, imposing a reciprocal international obligation on such non-State actors to settle disputes peacefully may have little added value.[40] Implicit in this argument is a narrow reading of article 2(3) of the UN Charter as a mere reformulation of article 2(4) on the prohibition on the use of force.

II. MATERIAL SCOPE

The use of the term 'disputes' in article 2(3) should be distinguished from references to 'situations' in other provisions of the UN Charter.[41] Broadly speaking, a dispute entails a claim by one party, pertaining to a point of law or fact, which another party rejects.[42] While such claims may be subjected to dispute settlement as envisaged in the Charter, to compel States to resolve – either under treaty or under custom – 'situations' involving a general state of discord may be too far-reaching a requirement, given the variety of tensions that characterise international relations, even among friendly nations.[43]

The qualifier 'international' before 'disputes' in article 2(3) should also be given due consideration. Article 2(7) of the UN Charter recognises the *domaine réservé* (French: 'reserved domain') of States over matters that are essentially within their domestic jurisdiction and, accordingly, exempts members from any requirement of pursuing peaceful settlement of such matters.[44] Nevertheless, 'domestic' disputes could implicate international peace and security and consequently be subjected to the requirements of dispute settlement as prescribed in article 33(1) of the Charter.[45] The practice of the UNSC suggests that disputes that threaten international peace and security would not qualify as matters 'essentially' within the domestic jurisdiction of States.[46]

---

39 Christian Tomuschat, 'Purposes and Principles, Article 2(3)' in Bruno Simma and others (eds), *The Charter of the United Nations: A Commentary* (OUP 2012) 193–195.

40 UN Security Council resolutions, nevertheless, often address non-State actors directly in calling upon disputing parties to seek peaceful settlement. See for example UNSC Res 1339 (n 38) para 5; UNSC Res 1781 (n 38) para 3,10.

41 See articles 1(1), 24, 35 and 36 UN Charter.

42 *Mavrommatis Palestine Concessions (Greece v Great Britain)* (Jurisdiction) [1924] PCIJ Ser A No 2, 7, 11; *Right of Passage over Indian Territory (Portugal v India)* (Preliminary Objections) [1957] ICJ Rep 125, 148-149; *South West Africa (Liberia v South Africa)* (Preliminary Objections) [1962] ICJ Rep 319, 328; *Armed Activities on the Territory of the Congo (Democratic Republic of the Congo v Rwanda)* [2006] ICJ Rep 6,40.

43 On the other hand, see UNGA Res 43/51 (n 19) para 25 referring to both 'disputes' and 'situations' in relation to the obligation of peaceful resolution.

44 In similar vein, see Charter of the Organization of American States (n 19), article 24; Constitutive Act of the African Union (n 19), articles 4(e) and (g).

45 Note here that article 33(1) of the UN Charter does not refer to 'international disputes' but 'any dispute'.

46 UNSC Res 7 (26 June 1946), UN Doc S/RES/7(1946) (regarding 'the situation in Spain'); UNSC Res 794 (3 December 1992), UN Doc S/Res/794(1992) (on the conflict in Somalia); UNSC Res 1902 (17

III. TEMPORAL SCOPE

Articles 2(3) and 33 of the UN Charter indicate the existence of a dispute as the trigger with which the obligation under those provisions comes into effect. Alain Pellet describes the obligation as 'continuous': 'the parties to a dispute cannot take shelter from the failure of a particular means of settlement to stop their best efforts to peacefully settle their dispute'.[47] It would also be disingenuous to consider that the obligation ceases to exist once hostilities commence. The nature of the obligation would suggest that it is precisely in those situations that efforts to peacefully resolve disputes should continue.[48]

In recent times, there has been increasing attention on the prevention of international disputes.[49] International organisations place a gamut of institutional mechanisms at States' disposal to facilitate prevention of disputes.[50] However, there is scant practice, in treaties or otherwise, to suggest any binding legal obligation in this regard. Given the various potential sources of conflicts between international legal actors, it is also difficult to see how comprehensive rules of conduct for the prevention of disputes could be developed.

D. PEACEFUL METHODS

In article 33(1), the UN Charter refers to primarily two types of dispute settlement methods:

- *Political-diplomatic* methods (negotiation, inquiry, mediation, conciliation, regional arrangements) characterised by flexible procedures and typically non-binding outcomes
- *Judicial-legal* methods (arbitration and judicial settlement), which are generally formal and binding in terms of both procedure and outcome.[51]

December 2009), UN Doc S/RES/1902(2009) (on the Burundian peace process); UNSC Res 1973 (17 March 2011) UN Doc S/RES/1973(2011) (authorising intervention in the Libyan civil war); See also *Tallinn Manual 2.0* (n 21) 304–305.

47 Alain Pellet (n 21) para 24.

48 See e.g. UNGA Res 41/33 (5 November 1986) UN Doc A/RES/41/33 para 7 (calling for continued efforts to find a political solution during the ongoing foreign armed intervention in Afghanistan); UNGA Res ES-11 (18 March 2022) UN Doc A/RES/ES-11/1, para 14 (urging the immediate peaceful resolution of the conflict between the Russian Federation and Ukraine through political dialogue, negotiations, mediation and other peaceful means).

49 UNGA Res 43/51 (n 19); Report of the Secretary General, Prevention of Armed Conflict (7 June 2001), UN Doc A/55/985; Daniel Shapiro and Adam Kinon, 'The Prevention Principle: A Pragmatic Framework to Prevent Destructive Conflict' (2010) 1 JIDS 301–312.

50 See e.g. Secretariat, Mechanisms established by the General Assembly in the context of dispute prevention and settlement (14 April 2000) UN Doc A/AC.182/2000/INF/2; Report of the Secretary-General, Preventive Diplomacy: Delivering Results (26 August 2011), UN Doc S/2011/552.

51 While there may be practical reasons for referring 'legal' and 'political' disputes to the respective types of dispute settlement, there is no strict demarcation of the methods by which these categories of disputes may be considered. Disputes may involve legal considerations despite their political background, and *vice versa*.

It additionally provides for resort to any 'other peaceful means of [the parties'] own choice'. What 'other peaceful means' may parties have recourse to? Naturally, any act that runs afoul of the prohibition on the use of force cannot be characterised as such. Similarly, acts of intervention that breach the principle of sovereign equality of States may also not be deemed peaceful. One 'peaceful' method notably absent from article 33(1) is recourse to 'good offices',[52] which will be discussed below. While drawing up an exhaustive list of peaceful dispute settlement methods is beyond the scope of this chapter, it is noteworthy that the focus of article 33(1) appears to be on bilateral or multilateral means of dispute settlement, and not any form of self-help.[53]

In line with the notion of free choice of means discussed above, article 33(1) does not stipulate a hierarchical order between the various methods discussed therein.[54] Moreover, parties to a dispute are not confined to choosing only one among several methods of dispute resolution and, in practice, tend to rely on a blended approach.[55]

I. NEGOTIATION

Negotiation involves consultation and exchange of views between disputing parties, generally through diplomatic channels, with a view to arriving at a satisfactory resolution of their conflict.[56] Parties are free to design the process and criteria for such negotiations, including whether any settlement should be guided by legal, political, or a combination of considerations.[57] As confirmed by the UNGA in 1999, the good faith

---

On 'political' questions in judicial-legal dispute settlement, see *Case Concerning United States Diplomatic and Consular Staff in Tehran (United States v Iran)* (Judgement) [1980] ICJ Rep 3 [19]; *Prosecutor v Tadić* (Decision on the Defence Motion for Interlocutory Appeal on Jurisdiction) IT-94-1-A (2 October 1995), [23–25]; WTO, *Russia: Measures Concerning Tariff in Transit – Report of the Panel* (5 April 2019) WT/DS512/R, 7.103 and footnote 183.

52 Good offices do find mention in instruments such as UNGA Res 3283(XXIX) (12 December 1974), UN Doc A/RES/3283(XXIX) on the peaceful settlement of international disputes; Manila Declaration (n 19) para 5; and the Declaration on the Rule of Law (n 18) para 5.

53 On countermeasures as a form of self-help, see Arévalo-Ramírez, § 9, in this textbook.

54 See John Collier and Vaughan Lowe, *The Settlement of Disputes in International Law* (OUP 1999) 7 noting the progressive formality of the methods listed in article 33(1).

55 For instance, the diplomatic crisis between Qatar and its GCC partners was considered by judicial-legal methods at the ICJ, WTO, and before the ICAO Council, while also being mediated by Kuwait, Oman and the United States, subject to *ad hoc* conciliation at the UN Committee on the Elimination of Racial Discrimination, and ultimately resolved through the negotiation of a 'solidarity and stability' agreement between the parties.

56 For a general overview, Kari Hakapää, 'Negotiation' (*Max Planck Encyclopaedia of International Procedural Law*, May 2013) <https://opil.ouplaw.com/display/10.1093/law:epil/9780199231690/law-9780199231690-e67?prd=EPIL>; Valerie Rosoux, 'Theories of Negotiation and International Adjudication' (*Max Planck Encyclopaedia of International Procedural Law*, October 2019) <https://opil.ouplaw.com/display/10.1093/law-mpeipro/e3779.013.3779/law-mpeipro-e3779>.

57 Ian Brownlie, 'The Wang Tieya Lecture in Public International Law: The Peaceful Settlement of International Disputes' (2009) 8 CJIL 267, 270.

conduct of disputants remains the predominant guiding principle for negotiations.[58] In the opinion of the International Court of Justice (ICJ), this means that parties should 'conduct themselves [such] that the negotiations are meaningful, which will not be the case when either of them insists upon its own position without contemplating any modification of it'.[59]

Negotiations are typically associated with dispute mitigation. For example, parties to the World Trade Organization (WTO) Dispute Settlement Understanding[60] and the Convention on Biological Diversity[61] have agreed to first attempt to settle their differences through negotiations before pursuing alternative channels. This does not mean that negotiations must precede recourse to formal methods of dispute resolution.[62] Parties may also negotiate simultaneously with other modes of dispute settlement in order to manage their conflict.[63] Negotiations may further be useful in developing effective solutions for the enforcement of a decision resulting from a judicial-legal process.[64] Given their flexibility and the role they can play in preserving amicable relations between disputants, negotiations are often regarded as the preferred mode of international dispute resolution.[65]

II. MEDIATION AND GOOD OFFICES

Mediation is a negotiation facilitated by an independent third party. If this third party's role is limited to establishing or restoring open channels of communication between disputants without participating in the negotiations themselves, they are considered to be providing good offices.[66] A mediator, strictly speaking, is an active

---

58 UNGA Res 53/101 (8 December 1998) UN Doc S/RES/53/101.

59 *North Sea Continental Shelf* (n 31) 47. This duty of conduct, however, cannot be considered absolute. For instance, if one party advances a view that has no basis in international law, the other(s) may not be reasonably expected to contemplate any 'modification' of their positions taken in response.

60 WTO Dispute Settlement understanding (n 25) article 4.3.

61 Convention on Biological Diversity (signed 5 June 1992, entered into force 29 December 1993) 1760 UNTS 79, article 27(1).

62 *Land and Maritime Boundary between Cameroon and Nigeria (Cameroon v Nigeria)* (Preliminary Objection) [1998] ICJ Rep 275 [303].

63 See for instance, *Trial of Pakistani Prisoners of War (Pakistan v India)* (Order) [1973] ICJ Rep 347 (discontinuing adversarial proceedings to facilitate negotiations between the parties); WTO, *United States: Certain Measures on Steel and Aluminium Products – Recourse to Article 25 of the DSU* (21 January 2022) WT/DS548/19 (commencing arbitration proceedings and suspending them immediately as parties continue to pursue negotiations).

64 For example, WTO Dispute Settlement Understanding (n 25) article 22.2 recognises that parties may negotiate to arrive at a 'mutually acceptable compensation' following formal proceedings. See also *Gabčikovo-Nagymaros Project* (n 31) 76 directing the parties to seek a negotiated agreement on the modalities for execution of the Court's judgment.

65 *Free Zones of Upper Savoy and the District of Gex (France v Switzerland)* (Judgment) PCIJ Rep Series A No 22 [6], [13]; *Passage through the Great Belt Case (Finland v Denmark)* (Order) [1991] ICJ Rep 4 [12]; WTO Dispute Settlement Understanding, (n 25) article 3.7.

66 Merrills (n 23) 551; UN Office of Legal Affairs, *Handbook on the Peaceful Settlement of Disputes between States* (1992) 33; American Treaty on Pacific Settlement (signed 30 April 1948, entered into force 6 May 1949) 30 UNTS 55, article IX.

participant in the negotiations, tasked with facilitating the parties' understanding of each other's perspectives to catalyse a negotiated outcome as well as making proposals aimed at advancing a mutually acceptable solution, based on information shared by parties and their own findings.[67] The distinction between mediation and good offices may be blurred in practice as the role of the third party providing good offices may evolve over time to involve direct participation.[68] A common imperative in the involvement of a third party in either capacity is the requirement to maintain their neutrality.[69]

Early in their conception, mediation and good offices were primarily associated with brokering by third States.[70] Today the UN, and in particular the Office of the Secretary-General,[71] regional and international organisations,[72] peacekeeping missions,[73] State officials, and private actors,[74] are among the other key actors facilitating these processes. While mediation and good offices in inter-State conflicts have a long history, their use is increasingly advocated for disputes between States and private actors, such as investor-State disputes, due to time and cost-effectiveness.[75]

---

67 American Treaty on Pacific Settlement (n 66) article XII; Merrills, (n 23) 551. See generally, Jacob Bercovitch (ed), *Resolving International Conflicts: The Theory and Practice of Mediation* (Lynne Rienner 1996); Sven MG Koopmans, *Negotiating Peace: A Guide to the Practice, Politics, and Law of International Mediation* (OUP 2018).

68 *Handbook on the Peaceful Settlement of Disputes between States* (n 66) 33–34. An example of 'pure good offices' is the role played by Norwegian officials in facilitating meetings between representatives from Israel and the Palestine Liberation Organisation, held secretly in Norway, which catalysed the Oslo Process.

69 See e.g. Andre Härtel, Anton Pisarenko and Andreas Umland, 'The OSCE's Special Monitoring Mission to Ukraine: The SSM's Work in the Donbas and Its Ukrainian Critique in 2014–2019' (2021) Security and Human Rights 121–154 (on criticisms against the OSCE mediation in the Minsk Process).

70 1907 Hague Convention I, article 3 ('*one or more Powers, strangers to the dispute*, should . . . offer their good offices or mediation to the States at variance'). More recent examples include Switzerland's good offices in relation to Iran's nuclear programme ('Switzerland's Good Offices' (*Federal Department of Foreign Affairs*, December 2021) <www.eda.admin.ch/aboutswitzerland/en/home/politik-geschichte/die-schweiz-und-die-welt/die-guten-dienste-der-schweiz.html> accessed 9 July 2023) and mediation by the United Arab Emirates in the conflict between Eritrea and Ethiopia ('UAE Turns Its Attention to Mediating International Disputes' (*Economist Intelligence*, 13 April 2021) <http://country.eiu.com/article.aspx?articleid=330915616> accessed 9 July 2023).

71 Report of the United Nations Mediator on Cyprus to the Secretary-General (26 March 1965) UN Doc S/6253; UNGA Res 65/241 (24 December 2010) UN Doc A/RES/65/241, para 30(a). See also 'Mediation Support Unit' (*United Nations Peacemaker*) <https://peacemaker.un.org/mediation-support> accessed 9 July 2023.

72 Organization of American States, 'Role of the OAS in Mediating the Belize-Guatemala Territorial Disputes' <www.oas.org/es/sap/dsdme/pubs/role_of_the_oas_belize_guatemala.pdf> accessed 9 July 2023; Yoshifumi Tanaka (n 22) 49 referring to mediation by the ICRC and World Bank in armed conflicts and international water disputes respectively.

73 James A Wall, 'Mediation in Peacekeeping Missions' (2022) SSRN 1–35.

74 For instance, good offices offered by the President of Venezuela in the internal armed conflict in Colombia (Vinceç Fisas (ed), *2014 Yearbook on Peace Processes* (Icaria Editorial 2014) 64); mediation by Alexander Haig, US Secretary of State, in the Falkland/Malvinas crisis (Jorge O Laucirica, 'Lessons from Failure: The Falkland/Malvinas Conflict' (2000) 1 JIDR 79); and the activities of the Community of Saint Egidio (Mario Giro, 'The Community of Saint Egidio and Its Peace-Making Activities' (*The International Spectator*, September 1998) <https://ciaotest.cc.columbia.edu/olj/iai/iai_98gim01.html> accessed 9 July 2023.

75 *See generally* International Centre for Settlement of Investment Disputes, 'Background Paper on Investment Mediation' (*World Bank*, July 2021) <https://icsid.worldbank.org/sites/default/files/publications/

III. FACT-FINDING OR INQUIRY

Fact-finding or inquiry consists of independent investigation to establish factual issues surrounding a dispute. While this may *prima facie* appear to resemble judicial-legal dispute settlement, fact-finding or inquiry does not typically involve the application of law to facts.[76] The conclusions resulting from these processes are reported to disputants for them to consider as they deem fit. The underlying rationale is that making objective facts available to the parties can have a preventive effect on disputes or their escalation. The success of these processes, however, can be highly contingent on cooperation by parties.[77]

'Commissions' of inquiry were already envisaged in the 1899 and 1907 Hague conventions.[78] The first commission under these conventions was established to consider the *Dogger Bank* incident of 1904, in which a Russian Baltic fleet fired upon a flotilla of British fishing vessels, having mistaken them for Japanese warships. A five-member commission presented a report attributing responsibility for the casualties to the admiral commanding the Russian Baltic fleet, having determined that there were no Japanese torpedo boats among or near the British vessels.[79] A more recent and striking example is the *Mavi Marmara* incident involving raid by the Israeli Defense Forces (IDF) of the 'Gaza Freedom Flotilla' carrying humanitarian aid, where two different panels of inquiry rendered diverging conclusions on the legality of the IDF's actions.[80] Both cases illustrate that the same body tasked with fact-finding may also be called upon by parties to evaluate such facts and ascertain legal responsibility and consequences. Results from

---

Background_Paper_on_Investment_Mediation.pdf> accessed 9 July 2023; United Nations Commission on International Trade Law, 'Draft UNCITRAL Guidelines on Investment Mediation' (*UNCITRAL*, 21 April 2023) <https://documents-dds-ny.un.org/doc/UNDOC/GEN/V23/027/58/PDF/V2302758.pdf?OpenElement> accessed 9 July 2023.

76 See Brownlie (n 57) 272 also referring to exceptions to this norm.

77 Report of the United Nations High Commissioner for Human Rights on the Situation of Human Rights in the Syrian Arab Republic (15 September 2011) UN Doc A/HRC/18/53 (noting the non-cooperation of Syria and its impact). Similarly, see 'Human Rights Council Discusses Report of UN Fact Finding Mission on Gaza Conflict' (29 September 2009) <www.un.org/unispal/document/auto-insert-201505/> accessed 9 July 2023 (discussing non-cooperation by Israel with the UN Fact-Finding Mission on the Gaza conflict).

78 1899 Hague Convention I, article 9; 1907 Hague Convention I, article 9. The Permanent Court of Arbitration has since developed the 1997 Optional Rules for Fact-Finding Commissions of Inquiry, intended to provide a self-contained procedural framework. See also 1977 Additional Protocol (I) to the Geneva Conventions (signed 9 June 1977, entered into force 7 December 1978) 1125 UNTS 3, article 90; 1997 Convention on Non-Navigational Uses of International Watercourses, 36 ILM 700, article 33; the 2022 ICSID Fact-Finding Rules <https://icsid.worldbank.org/sites/default/files/ICSID_Fact-Finding_Rules.pdf> accessed 9 July 2023; Declaration on Fact-finding by the United Nations in the Field of the Maintenance of International Peace and Security, UNGA Res 46/59 (9 December 1991), UN Doc A/RES/46/59.

79 RDN Lebow, 'Accidents and Crises: The Dogger Bank Affair' (1978) 31 NCWR 66–75.

80 Human Rights Council, Report of the International fact-Finding Mission to Investigate Violations of International Law, Including International Humanitarian and Human Rights Law, Resulting from the Israeli Attacks on the Flotilla of Ships Carrying Humanitarian Assistance (27 September 2010) A/MC/15/21; Report of the Secretary-General's Panel of Inquiry on the 31 May 2010 Flotilla Incident (September 2011).

fact-finding may also be relied upon in the course of judicial-legal dispute settlement proceedings.[81]

IV. CONCILIATION

Conciliation is a more structured form of dispute settlement, involving a person or commission tasked with receiving submissions from disputants and issuing recommendations for a possible solution.[82] Thus it combines characteristics of mediation and fact-finding, relying similarly on the independence and impartiality of the third party involved. While recommendations rendered through conciliation should be considered in good faith,[83] they are not binding on the disputants.

Conciliation features prominently in modern multilateral treaties,[84] usually in one of two forms: optional conciliation, which is contingent on the mutual consent of disputants for the submission of a particular dispute to conciliation procedures,[85] and compulsory conciliation, which has been agreed upon by parties to a treaty in advance and can thus be initiated at the request of any of the disputants.[86] By one author's estimate, as of 2018, there were more than 200 bilateral treaties in force addressing conciliation procedures.[87] Despite this, conciliation has seen relatively low popularity, especially with the proliferation of arbitration.[88] To explain their lack of appeal, Yoshifumi Tanaka traces the origin of conciliation in the Covenant of the League of Nations and the UN Charter to conclude that the mechanism was developed to settle those non-legal disputes which were neither submitted to

---

81 E.g. *Armed Activities on the Territory of the Congo (Democratic Republic of the Congo v. Uganda)* (Judgment) [2005] ICJ Rep 168 (relying on the findings of the Porter Commission, an independent inquiry panel established by Uganda in 2001). See contra, *Application of the Convention on the Prevention and Punishment of the Crime of Genocide (The Gambia v. Myanmar)* (Preliminary Objections) (disputing reliance on findings of a UN Independent International Fact-Finding Mission).

82 *Handbook on the Peaceful Settlement of Disputes between States* (n 66) 46–47. See 1949 Revised Geneva General Act for the Pacific Settlement of International Disputes (signed 28 April 1949, entered into force 20 September 1950) 71 UNTS 101, article 15; 1957 European Convention for the Peaceful Settlement of Disputes (signed 29 April 1957, entered into force 30 April 1958) 320 UNTS 241, article 15.

83 See section C.

84 Vienna Convention on the Law of Treaties (signed 23 May 1969, entered into force 27 January 1980) 1155 UNTS 331, article 66; Convention on the Law of the Sea (n 26) article 284 and annex V; 1992 Convention on Biological Diversity (n 61) article 27(4) and annex II, part 2; UN Framework Convention on Climate Change (signed 9 May 1992, entered into force 21 March 1994) 1771 UNTS 107, article 14; 'ICSID Conciliation Rules' <https://icsid.worldbank.org/sites/default/files/Conciliation_Rules.pdf> accessed 9 July 2023. See also UN General Assembly, United Nations Model Rules for the Conciliation of Disputes between States, UNGA Res 50/50 (29 January 1996), UN Doc A/RES/50/50.

85 E.g. PCA Optional Conciliation Rules <https://docs.pca-cpa.org/2016/01/Permanent-Court-of-Arbitration-Optional-Conciliation-Rules.pdf> accessed 9 July 2023.

86 E.g. Vienna Convention on the Law of Treaties (n 84), article 66.

87 Yoshifumi Tanaka (n 22) 69.

88 Christian Tomuschat (n 28) 1078; Ian Brownlie (n 57) 272; Sean Murphy, 'Non-Binding International Dispute Settlement' (2022) GWLFP 11.

arbitration nor judicial settlement.[89] Tanaka questions the suitability of conciliation for the resolution of such disputes, noting that these disputes often involve sensitive matters that States are unlikely to willingly entrust to third parties with no political authority.[90]

V. REGIONAL AGENCIES OR ARRANGEMENTS

In recognition of their potentially valuable role in resolving localised disputes, the UN Charter prefers the settlement of such disputes through regional agencies or arrangements.[91] The Report of the UN Secretary-General on 'Agenda for Peace' recalls the rich variety of complementary efforts that the UN has benefitted from in cooperating with regional arrangements and organisations.[92] Prominent examples include the Organization of American States,[93] the African Union,[94] the League of Arab States,[95] the Organization for Security and Co-operation in Europe,[96] the Association of Southeast Asian Nations,[97] and the Pacific Islands Forum.[98]

VI. ARBITRATION AND JUDICIAL SETTLEMENT

Like conciliation, judicial-legal methods involve consideration of a dispute by an independent third party chosen by the disputants. The key difference is that decisions resulting from these methods are largely guided by legal considerations and are binding on parties. The two main types of judicial-legal methods are (1) arbitration by temporarily appointed (*ad hoc*) tribunals, whose composition and procedures

---

89 Yoshifumi Tanaka (n 22) 70.

90 Yoshifumi Tanaka (n 22) 71.

91 Article 52(2) UN Charter, calling for 'every effort to achieve pacific settlement of local disputes through such regional arrangements or by such regional agencies before referring them to the Security Council'. Note that there is no such priority in respect of enforcement action (article 53(1)). See also UNGA Res 43/51 (n 19) paras 4, 13, and 17.

92 UN Secretary-General, 'An Agenda for Peace: Preventive Diplomacy, Peacemaking and Peace-keeping' (31 January 1992) UN Doc A/47/277-S-/2411, 35 ff.

93 UNSC Res 841 (16 June 1993) UN Doc S/RES/841 on the cooperation between the UN and the OAS to find a political solution for the crisis in Haiti.

94 UNSC Res 1744 (20 February 2007) UN Doc S/RES/1744 and UNSC Res 1769 (31 July 2007) UN Doc S/RES/1769(2007) on the UN-AU hybrid missions in Somalia and Sudan, respectively.

95 The League was granted observer status in the General Assembly in 1950. See UNGA Res 477(V) (1 November 1950) UN Doc A/RES/477(V).

96 Conference on Security and Co-operation in Europe: Final Act (concluded 1 August 1975) 14 ILM 1292. See also The Helsinki Document 1992 <www.osce.org/files/f/documents/7/c/39530.pdf> accessed 9 July 2023, setting out envisaged cooperation between the OSCE and the UN, including in preventing and settling conflicts.

97 'The Declaration on the Establishment of the Association of South-East Asian Nations' (8 August 1967) 6 ILM 1233.

98 See UNGA Res 65/316 (11 October 2011) UN Doc A/RES/65/316 on promoting and expanding cooperation and coordination with Pacific Islands Forum.

can be flexibly determined by the disputants;[99] and (2) standing international courts or tribunals consisting of elected adjudicators following established rules and procedures.[100]

Modern international law has witnessed a steady growth in the use of judicial-legal methods. In addition to numerous *ad hoc* arbitration mechanisms,[101] the international legal landscape is dotted with multilateral courts and tribunals that operate in different – and sometimes overlapping – domains.[102] Together with a 'general' court in the form of the ICJ, specialised bodies have been set up to examine disputes pertaining to the law of the sea,[103] international economic law,[104] international human rights law,[105] and more. This proliferation is an ongoing phenomenon, as evidenced by growing calls for an international court for the environment and a multilateral investment court.[106]

Judicial-legal methods play a crucial role not only in the resolution of disputes but also in framing our understanding of international legal rules and contributing to their development.[107] As the results of these processes are binding, they also impact the conduct of international legal actors.

1. Jurisdiction and Admissibility

The jurisdiction of an international court or tribunal refers to its competence to entertain a dispute. Yuval Shany offers a useful typology of jurisdiction based on the source of a court or tribunal's authority, advancing two broad categories:[108]

- 'Foundational jurisdiction' is the competence that a court or tribunal derives from its constitutive treaty. This reflects the extent to which treaty parties have delegated

---

99 See generally, Charles Brower, 'Arbitration', and Nisuke Ando, 'Permanent Court of Arbitration' (*Max Planck Encyclopaedia of Public International Law*, 2007).

100 See generally William A Schabas (ed), *International Courts and Tribunals* (Edward Elgar Publishing 2014); Ruth Mackenzie and others (eds), *The Manual on International Courts and Tribunals* (OUP 2010).

101 PCA, 'Cases' <https://pca-cpa.org/cases/>; ICSID, 'Cases Database' <https://icsid.worldbank.org/cases/case-database> accessed 9 July 2023.

102 E.g. Craig D Gaver, 'Lingering Gulf Dispute Gives Rise to Multi-Forum Legal Proceedings' (*American Society of International Law*, 28 January 2020) <www.asil.org/insights/volume/24/issue/1/lingering-gulf-dispute-gives-rise-multi-forum-legal-proceedings> accessed 9 July 2023.

103 On the law of the sea, see Dela Cruz and Paige, § 15, in this textbook.

104 On international economic law, see Hankings-Evans, § 23, in this textbook.

105 On human rights law, see Ciampi, § 21, in this textbook.

106 Stuart Bruce, 'The Project for an International Environmental Court' in Christian Tomuschat and others (eds), *Conciliation in International Law* (Brill 2016); Marc Bungenberg and August Reinisch, *From Bilateral Arbitral Tribunals and Investment Courts to a Multilateral Investment Court* (Springer 2019).

107 Thomas Buergenthal, 'Lawmaking by the ICJ and Other International Courts' (2009) 103 ASIL Proceedings of Annual Meeting 403; Armin Von Bogdandy and Ingo Venzke, 'On the Functions of International Courts: An Appraisal in Light of Their Burgeoning Public Authority' (2013) 26 LJIL 49.

108 Yuval Shany, 'Jurisdiction and Admissibility' in Cesare Romano, Karen Alter, and Yuval Shany (eds), *The Oxford Handbook of International Adjudication* (OUP 2013) 782–786.

decision-making authority to a court or tribunal, and operates from the moment of its establishment.[109] For instance, in concluding the WTO Agreement, States accepted the competence of panels and the Appellate Body over all disputes arising under those agreements,[110] and thus may be made parties to disputes thereunder without requiring any further consent (or, in fact, against their objections). This type of jurisdiction can thus be characterised as 'compulsory'.

- 'Specific jurisdiction' is derived from consent given to a court or tribunal for the adjudication of particular dispute(s). As Shany notes, the main contours of ICJ's powers to adjudicate are in the realm of specific jurisdiction.[111] This is because the jurisdiction of the ICJ is largely established either through (1) a special agreement, *ex post facto* (Latin: 'after the fact') referring a dispute to the Court; or (2) 'compromissory clauses' in treaties, stipulating that the particular matters regulated thereunder be referred to the Court in the event of a dispute.[112] Specific jurisdiction is 'optional' in that it does not accrue automatically to any court or tribunal but requires States to choose to submit to a court or tribunal a particular case or category of cases.

  Note that under the Statute of the ICJ, any State party may also recognise the Court's jurisdiction as compulsory through a declaration to that effect.[113] On the date of writing, 74 States have deposited such declarations,[114] but these generally contain numerous carve-outs and broad reservations, thereby giving the ICJ a selective and diluted form of compulsory jurisdiction at best.

Together, the foundational and specific jurisdiction of a court or tribunal determine its (1) *ratione personae* jurisdiction, that is the persons or actors over which it may exercise decision-making authority;[115] (2) *ratione materiae* jurisdiction, that is the subject matter or the issues of fact and law which it has competence to adjudicate;[116] (3) *ratione temporis* jurisdiction, that is the effect of time on the authority to entertain

---

109 Foundational jurisdiction may be amended over time. For instance, the accession of new members to the constitutive instrument of a court or tribunal would extend the scope of its foundational jurisdiction to more parties (e.g. Agreement Establishing the World Trade Organization (signed 15 April 1994, entered into force 1 January 1995) 1867 UNTS 154, article XII).

110 Agreement Establishing the World Trade Organization, article III.3; WTO Dispute Settlement Understanding, article 23.1.

111 Shany (n 110) 783.

112 Statute of the ICJ (adopted 26 June 1945, entered into force 24 October 1945) 33 UNTS 933, article 36(1).

113 Statute of the ICJ, article 36(2).

114 'Declarations recognizing the jurisdiction of the Court as compulsory' <www.icj-cij.org/declarations> accessed 9 July 2023.

115 E.g. Convention on the Settlement of Investment Disputes Between States and Nationals of other States, 575 UNTS 159 (ICSID Convention), article 25 (jurisdiction extending to disputes between 'a Contracting State . . . and a national of another Contracting State') and 'Energy Charter Treaty' (1994) 10 ICSID Rev 258, articles 17 and 25 (accepting ICSID jurisdiction but limiting it to certain types of investors).

116 E.g. ICSID Convention, article 25 (jurisdiction limited to 'legal dispute arising directly out of an investment'); Hungary-Norway Bilateral Investment Treaty <https://investmentpolicy.unctad.org/international-investment-agreements/treaty-files/5327/download>, article XI (narrowing ICSID jurisdiction for the purposes of that treaty to disputes concerning compensation or expropriation).

a dispute;[117] and (4) *ratione loci* jurisdiction, that is the territorial extent of its competence.[118]

A distinction should be drawn here between jurisdiction and admissibility. While the former concerns whether a court or tribunal has the authority to examine a case, the latter pertains to conditions under which they should exercise or decline to exercise that authority.[119] Conditions that may render a dispute inadmissible include the issue in dispute having been rendered moot or incapable of effective adjudication,[120] failure to exhaust local remedies,[121] non-inclusion of necessary third parties in the proceedings,[122] and pendency or resolution of the same dispute before another forum.[123] In each of these situations, despite the requisite competence, a defect in the manner, the time, or the stage at which a dispute has been advanced may nevertheless preclude its consideration by the relevant court or tribunal.

2. Applicable Law

The international legal rules that an adjudicator should apply in examining disputes falling within their competence and rendering decisions are referred to as the laws applicable to a dispute.[124] Applicable laws may be broadly divided into *primary* rules, which directly govern the conduct of actors, and *secondary* rules, which allow for the identification, creation, alteration, or extinction of primary rules.[125] Exceptionally, courts or tribunals may also be authorised to apply considerations of fairness and equity in deciding a dispute.[126]

---

117 E.g. Comprehensive and Progressive Agreement for Trans-Pacific Partnership (signed 8 March 2018, entered into force 30 December 2018) article 9.21.1; Statute of the International Criminal Tribunal for Rwanda (ICTR), 33 ILM 1598, article 7.

118 E.g. Statute of the ICTR, article 7; Statute of the International Criminal Tribunal for the Former Yugoslavia, 32 ILM 1192, article 8.

119 See also Robert Kolb, *International Court of Justice* (Hart 2014) 202 (referring to admissibility as concerning the formal or material defects of the claim); *Case concerning Oil Platforms (Iran v United States of America)* (Judgement) [2003] ICJ Rep 161, 177; *Waste Management Inc. v Mexico*, ICSID Case No ARB(AF)/98/2, Highet Dissenting Opinion (8 May 2000) [58].

120 *Northern Cameroons (Cameroon v United Kingdom)* (Judgment) [1963] ICJ Rep 15, 33–34; *Nuclear Tests Case (Australia v France)* (Judgment) [1974] ICJ Rep 253, 270–271.

121 *Interhandel (Switzerland v United States)* (Judgment) [1959] ICJ Rep 6, 27–28.

122 *Case concerning East Timor (Portugal v Australia)* (Judgment) [1995] ICJ Rep 90, 105; *Monetary Gold Removed from Rome (Italy v. France, United Kingdom of Great Britain and Northern Ireland and United States)* (Judgment) [1954] ICJ Rep 19, 32–33.

123 *MOX Plant Case (Ireland v United Kingdom)* (Order) [2003] 126 ILR 310.

124 On the relationship between applicable law and jurisdiction, see *Pulp Mills on the River Uruguay (Argentina v Uruguay)* (Judgment) [2010] ICJ Rep 14, 46; Matina Papadaki, 'Compromissory Clauses as the Gatekeepers of the Law to Be "Used" in the ICJ and the PCIJ' (2014) JIDS 560.

125 Sean Murphy, 'The Concept of International Law' (2009) 103 ASIL Proceedings Minutes 165–169 referring to HLA Hart, *The Concept of Law* (OUP 1994) ch 5.

126 Statute of the ICJ (n 115), article 38(2); ICSID Convention (n 117), article 42(3).

For standing courts or tribunals, the law applicable to a dispute is usually specified in the constitutive instruments.[127] Applicable law provisions can also be found in instruments conferring specific jurisdiction, such as choice of law provisions in international investment treaties.[128] Provisions on applicable law are an expression of parties' consent.[129] Their non-application or improper application constitutes an exercise in excess of the jurisdictional authority of a court or tribunal, and can be the grounds for appeal, revision, or annulment of a decision, depending on available procedural rights.[130]

3. Provisional and Final Remedies

Constituent instruments or instruments of special jurisdiction may not explicitly recognise the authority of a court or tribunal to prescribe a remedy for a disputant. In the absence of such authority, though, courts and tribunals would have no means of safeguarding the interests of disputants or ensuring the effectiveness of their own decisions. Hence, the ability to grant remedies is widely regarded as an inherent power of an international court or tribunal.[131] Such remedies may be either provisional or final.

Provisional measures (also known as interim measures of protection) are temporary remedies aimed at preserving the rights of disputing parties,[132] both substantive and procedural,[133] pending the final resolution of the dispute. Examples include preservation of evidence,[134] preventing disclosure of confidential information,[135] measures implemented to protect the life and safety of parties,[136] and measures to secure the non-aggravation of a dispute.[137] Provisional measures are generally indicated by way of

---

127 E.g. Statute of the ICJ (n 115), article 38 (on sources, see Eggett, § 6, in this textbook); WTO Dispute Settlement understanding (n 25) article 3.2.

128 Energy Charter Treaty (n 116), article 25(6); Hungary-Norway BIT (n 117), article X(5).

129 *CME Czech Republic B.V. v The Czech Republic*, UNCITRAL, Legal Opinion by Christoph Schreuer and August Reinisch (20 June 2002) [141–147].

130 E.g. ICSID Convention (n 117), article 52; WTO Dispute Settlement understanding (n 25) article 17.

131 James Crawford, *The International Law Commission's Articles on State Responsibility* (CUP 2002) 201, 218; Chester Brown, *A Common Law of International Adjudication* (OUP 2007) 55; *Factory at Chorzów (Germany v Poland)* (Jurisdiction) PCIJ Ser A No 9 [20–1], [25]; European Court of Human Rights, *Mamatkulov and Askarov v. Turkey*, Application Nos 46827/99 and 46951/99, Judgement (4 February 2005) [124]; *E-Systems, Inc. v. Islamic Republic of Iran*, No. ITM 13–388-FT, Interim Award (4 February 1983) [51–57].

132 Statute of the ICJ (n 115), article 41(1); ICSID Convention (n 117), article 47.

133 *Burlington Resources Inc. and others v. Republic of Ecuador and Empresa Estatal Petróleos del Ecuador (PetroEcuador)*, ICSID Case No ARB/08/5, Procedural Order No 1 (29 June 2009) [60].

134 *Land and Maritime Boundary between Cameroon and Nigeria* (n 61), 23; *Application of the Convention on the Prevention and Punishment of the Crime of Genocide (The Gambia v Myanmar)* (Order) [2020] ICJ Rep 6.

135 *Biwater Gauff (Tanzania) Ltd v. Tanzania*, ICSID Case No ARB/05/22, Procedural Order No 3 (29 September 2006) [163]; *The Loewen Group, Inc. and Raymond L. Loewen v. United States of America*, ICSID Case No ARB (AF)/98/3, Decision on Jurisdiction (5 January 2001) [26].

136 *United States Diplomatic and Consular Staff in Tehran (United States v Iran)* (Order) [1979] ICJ Rep 8, 14; Yoshiyuki Iwamoto, 'The Protection of Human Life Through Provisional Measures Indicated by the International Court of Justice' (2002) 15 LJIL 345.

137 *Frontier Dispute* (n 32), 9; *Land and Maritime Boundary between Cameroon and Nigeria* (n 62), 24.

an 'order' of the relevant court or tribunal that is understood to have binding effect.[138] These measures may be requested at any stage of the proceedings by either party, or alternatively ordered by a court or tribunal on its own initiative.[139]

The type(s) of the final remedy available to parties at the conclusion of proceedings may be dictated by the applicable constitutive treaties.[140] The remedy granted may also depend on the primary rule under consideration in a dispute: for instance, the 1961 Vienna Convention on Diplomatic Relations in article 9 provides remedies for abuses of diplomatic functions in the form of declarations of *persona non grata*.[141] In the absence of any specific rules, courts such as the ICJ award remedies in accordance with customary international law, primarily those set out in ILC Articles on State Responsibility.[142]

4. Advisory Opinions

As the term suggests, an advisory opinion is legal advice given by an international court or tribunal at the request of authorised organs or institutions.[143] Such advice need not pertain to a dispute; opinions can generally be sought on 'legal questions',[144] such as interpretation of or consistency with treaty provisions,[145] rights and obligations under general international law,[146] and issues of legal procedure.[147] In providing these opinions, adjudicators may also be required to make determinations of relevant facts

---

138 *LaGrand (Germany v United States)* (Judgement) [2001] ICJ Rep 466, 502–503; *Mamatkulov and Askarov v. Turkey* (n 133) [128–129]. Interim measures, however, do not have a *res judicata* character due to the lack of finality.

139 E.g. article 75(1) ICJ Rules of Court.

140 WTO Dispute Settlement understanding (n 25), articles 19, 22, and 23; see generally UNGA Res 56/83 (3 August 2001), Articles on Responsibility of States for Internationally Wrongful Acts, UN Doc A/RES/56/83(2001) (recognising that *lex specialis* provisions take precedence over customary rules on the implementation of international responsibility such as compensation).

141 See *United States Diplomatic and Consular Staff in Tehran (United States v Iran)* (Judgment) [1980] ICJ Rep 3, 38–39. Similar provisions can also be found in article 23 of the Vienna Convention on Consular Relations.

142 On State responsibility and remedies, see Arévalo-Ramírez, § 9, in this textbook.

143 Statute of the ICJ (n 115), article 65(1) providing that requests may be made by 'whatever body may be authorized by or in accordance with the Charter of the United Nations to make such a request'. More generally, see Hugh Thirlway, 'Advisory Opinion' (*Max Planck Encyclopaedia of Public International Law*, April 2006); Georges Abi-Saab, 'Reflections on the Nature of the Consultative Function of the International Court of Justice' in Laurence Boisson de Chazournes and Philippe Sands (eds), *International Law, the International Court of Justice and Nuclear Weapons* (CUP 1999) 36.

144 Statute of the ICJ (n 115), article 65; Convention on the Law of the Sea (n 26), article 191; Protocol 2 to the European Convention for the Protection of Human Rights and Fundamental Freedoms (signed 6 May 1963, entered into force 21 September 1970) ETS 44, article 1.

145 Convention on the Law of the Sea (n 26), article 159(10); American Convention on Human Rights (adopted 22 November 1969, entered into force 18 July 1978) 1144 UNTS 123, article 64.

146 *Legality of the Threat or Use of Nuclear Weapons* (Advisory Opinion) [1996] ICJ Rep 226; *Accordance with International Law of the Unilateral Declaration of Independence in Respect of Kosovo* (Advisory Opinion) [2010] ICJ Rep 403; Obligations of States in respect of Climate Change (Request for Advisory Opinion) <www.icj-cij.org/sites/default/files/case-related/187/187-20230412-app-01-00-en.pdf> accessed 9 July 2023.

147 *South West Africa – Voting Procedure* (Advisory Opinion) [1955] ICJ Rep 67.

as necessary.[148] While advisory opinions may not strictly seem to be concerned with the settlement of *disputes*, they have been used for this purpose. For example, advisory opinions have been requested at the ICJ in the context of disputes between a State and an international organisation, the latter of which has no standing to participate in contentious proceedings before the ICJ.[149]

Pertinently, in keeping with the solemnity of consent, international courts and tribunals do not have any inherent advisory jurisdiction. Their competence arises from express provisions in their constitutive legal instruments conferring requisite consent.[150] Typically, advisory opinions do not bind the requesting parties or any other entity affected by the subject matter of the opinion,[151] although exceptions exist.[152]

E. CONCLUSION

This chapter aimed to provide a basic understanding of the principle and methods of peaceful dispute settlement. A key development in international law in the last century, dispute settlement mechanisms are increasingly looked upon as integral for responding to the urgencies of our times, a recent example being the request to the ICJ for an advisory opinion on the obligations of States with respect to climate change. Concurrently, protracted conflicts and outbreaks of new wars suggest that the mechanisms in place are far from perfect. State practice also indicates waning confidence in this regard, as seen in the frequent criticisms of the International Criminal Court for judicial overreach, backlash against investor-State dispute settlement, or the ongoing non-functioning of the WTO's Appellate Body since

---

148 *Western Sahara* (Advisory Opinion) [1975] ICJ Rep 12; *Legal Consequences arising from the Policies and Practices of Israel in the Occupied Palestinian Territory, including East Jerusalem* (Request for Advisory Opinion) <www.icj-cij. org/sites/default/files/case-related/186/186-20230117-REQ-01-00-EN.pdf> accessed 9 July 2023.

149 *Applicability of the Obligation to Arbitrate under Section 21 of the United Nations Headquarters Agreement of 26 June 1947* (Advisory Opinion) [1988] ICJ Rep 12. See also *Legal Consequences of the Construction of a Wall in the Occupied Palestinian Territory* (Advisory Opinion) [2004] ICJ Rep 136.

150 See nn 145–146; Protocol to the African Charter on Human and Peoples' Rights on the Establishment of an African Court on Human and People's Rights <www.refworld.org/docid/3f4b139d4.html>, article 4; By contrast, the WTO Dispute Settlement Understanding confers contentious but no advisory jurisdiction upon panels and the Appellate Body.

151 Advisory opinions are thus distinct from declaratory judgments, which may not contain any executory direction to the parties but are nevertheless binding upon on them. See Victor Stoica, *Remedies before the International Court of Justice: A Systemic Analysis* (CUP 2021) 21–45 on declaratory judgements.

152 Convention on the Privileges and Immunities of the Specialised Agencies (signed 21 November 1947, entered into force 16 August 1949) 33 UNTS 261, article IX, section 32; Convention on the Privileges and Immunities of the United Nations (signed 13 February 1946, entered into force 17 September 1946) 1 UNTS 15, article VIII, section 30; Agreement between the United Nations High Commissioner for Refugees and the Government of Nicaragua (signed 1 November 1990, entered into force 1 November 1990) 1582 UNTS 76, article 16; *Difference Relating to Immunity from Legal Process of a Special Rapporteur of the Commission on Human Rights* (Advisory Opinion) [1999] ICJ Rep 62, 76.

2020. Increasing disregard for and resistance to peaceful dispute settlement may call for repurposing what has been discussed above to render effective and lasting solutions that are fit for purpose.

BOX 12.3 Further Readings and Further Resources

Further Readings

- A Von Bogdandy and I Venzke, *In Whose Name? A Public Law Theory of International Adjudication* (OUP 2014)

- E Bjorge and C Miles, *Landmark Cases in Public International Law* (Hart 2017)

- F Orrego Vicuña, *International Dispute Settlement in an Evolving Global Society: Constitutionalization, Accessibility, Privatization* (CUP 2004)

- I De la Rasilla and JE Viñuales (eds), *Experiments in International Adjudication: Historical Accounts* (CUP 2019)

Further Resources

- L Reed, 'Ninth Annual Charles N. Brower Lecture: Crisis Cases – Not Reconceiving International Dispute Resolution' (*ASIL*, 26 March 2021) <www.youtube.com/watch?v=FjYLEOYrItA> accessed 31 August 2023

- MN Shaw, 'Shabtai Rosenne Memorial Lecture: Peaceful Settlement of Disputes – Paradigms, Plurality and Policy' <https://legal.un.org/avl/ls/Rosenne.html> accessed 31 August 2023

- ICJ, 'Public Hearing on the Request for the Indication of Provisional Measures Submitted by Ukraine in the Case Concerning Allegations of Genocide under the Convention on the Prevention and Punishment of the Crime of Genocide (Ukraine v. Russian Federation)' (7 March 2022) <www.youtube.com/watch?v=4erFL0FSXWs> accessed 31 August 2023

---

§ § §

CHAPTER 13
USE OF FORCE

MARKO SVICEVIC

BOX 13.1 Required Knowledge and Learning Objectives

Required knowledge: History of International Law; Sources of International Law; International Organisations

Learning objectives: Understanding the historical development, scope, and extent of the prohibition of the use of force and being able to identify exceptions to the prohibition both within and outside of the UN Charter.

BOX 13.2 Interactive Exercises

Access *interactive exercises for this chapter*[1] by positioning your smartphone camera at the dot-filled box, also known as a QR code.

Figure 13.1 QR code referring to interactive exercises.

A. INTRODUCTION

One of the most important, and consequently, most controversial subjects in public international law, is the use of force.[2] The use of force predominantly refers to military force, that is, where one or more States use military force against another State. Colloquially, the law on the use of force refers to a State's permissibility to go to war (also known as 'armed conflict' or 'armed force'), and the laws governing the use of force are those which regulate when and under what conditions a State may (legally) go to war.[3]

---

1 https://openrewi.org/en-projects-project-public-international-law-use-of-force/

2 On international law and violence, see Lloydd, § 2.1, in this textbook.

3 ICRC, *What are jus ad bellum and jus in bello?* (22 January 2015) <https://shop.icrc.org/international-humanitarian-law-answers-to-your-questions-pdf-en> accessed 16 August 2023, 8.

DOI: 10.4324/9781003451327-15

The Latin term *jus ad bellum* is also frequently used to refer to the use of force, its literal interpretation being 'right to war'.

It is first and foremost important to note that the rules governing the use of force (*jus ad bellum*) predominantly regulate States' behaviour prior to their engagement in war as well as the decision of going to war. In contrast, the laws of war (*jus in bello*) regulate the permissibility of a State's conduct *during* wartime.[4]

Crucial to the rules on the use of force are the scope and extent to which it is prohibited. The fact that a State has, under certain circumstances, a right to resort to the use of force presupposes that the use of force itself is, in one way or another, prohibited. Although this has not always been the case, the adoption of the United Nations (UN) Charter in 1945 saw the prohibition codified in article 2(4).[5] At the same time, the UN Charter also established and re-affirmed certain exceptions to the prohibition. These include the inherent right of self-defence in article 51, and in cases where the UN Security Council (UNSC) authorises the use of force, as discussed below. The system of collective security put in place with the creation of the UN therefore not only prohibits the use of force, but also regulates it. The aim of this chapter is to give an overview of this system and the scope and exceptions to the prohibition.

B. HISTORICAL ASSESSMENT OF THE USE OF FORCE IN INTERNATIONAL LAW

I. THE JUST WAR DOCTRINE

It may be surprising to many new scholars of international law that war has not always been prohibited. Moreover, prior to the comprehensive prohibition of the use of armed force in the 20th century, States, empires, and kingdoms regularly claimed a right to wage war. Such claims were usually based on religious or moral grounds. As wars progressed and Christianity expanded across Europe, a fundamental issue arose when two Christian States went to war with each other. On this basis, in the 15th century Thomas Aquinas formulated the most comprehensive work on what is considered the 'just war theory'. Aquinas advocated for a moral basis to wage war. War fought for imperial reasons, self-interest, or for the acquisition of territory could not reasonably fit into the just war theory. Of course, the very idea of a 'just' war was never as clear as imagined since it often involved a matter of perspective and discretion.[6] Because of its very construction, just war theory has been perceived as an

---

4   On the laws of war, see Dienelt and Ullah, § 14, in this textbook.

5   Charter of the United Nations (adopted 26 June 1945, entered into force 24 October 1945) 1 UNTS XVI, article 2(4).

6   Alina Kaczorowska, *Public International Law* (4th edn, Routledge 2010) 695.

enabler of wars in support of colonialism and the subjugation of non-Western peoples, drawing (arbitrary, Western-based) distinctions between civilised and uncivilised, and just and unjust.[7]

II. FROM *JUS AD BELLUM* TO *JUS CONTRA BELLO*

Although the just war theory held for some 400 years, the Peace Treaties of Westphalia of 1648 heralded a new right to wage war.[8] Absolute notions of State sovereignty considered the right to wage war as an extension of such sovereignty. Often enough, therefore, the right to wage war not only materialised, but was enshrined in States' national policies.[9]

Despite attempts in particular during the end of the 19th and beginning of the 20th centuries to curtail means and methods of war, the most serious attempt at regulating the resort to war only materialised after the end of World War I. The Treaty of Versailles declared the end to World War I and set in place the Covenant of the League of Nations. The League was meant to serve as an intergovernmental organisation of States which would seek to prevent war, increase international cooperation, place limits on waging war, submit disputes to judicial means, and establish a Permanent Court of International Justice.[10] Despite several commitments under the Covenant, it was only with the adoption of the Kellogg-Briand Pact on 27 August 1928 when the first multilateral international commitment to renounce war was made. Surprisingly, the Pact consists only of three provisions. Article I expresses the parties' condemnation of recourse to war to international issues and renouncement of war as an instrument of national policy.[11] Article II declares the parties' intention to resolve their disputes by pacific means, and article III concerns the treaty's ratification and entering into force.

Despite the Kellogg-Briand Pact's revolutionary renunciation of war in international relations, its success was limited. A decade later, the Pact's provisions were little more than empty promises, and the commencement of World War II laid bare its inability to suppress armed conflict. The comprehensive prohibition on the use or threat of force therefore only came into being following the end of World War II and the adoption of the UN Charter, together with its pivotal article 2(4).

---

7 See Kimberley Hutchings, 'Cosmopolitan Just War and Coloniality' in Duncan Bell (ed), *Empire, Race and Global Justice* (CUP 2019) 211.

8 On Westphalia and international law's founding myths, see González Hauck, § 1, in this textbook.

9 Kaczorowska (n 5) 696.

10 League of Nations, The Covenant of the League of Nations, Including Amendments in Force (1 February 1938), articles 8–16.

11 General Treaty for Renunciation of War as an Instrument of National Policy (Kellogg-Briandt Pact) (adopted 27 August 1928, entered into force 24 July 1929), article I.

C. THE PROHIBITION OF THE THREAT OR USE OF FORCE

I. SCOPE OF PROHIBITION UNDER ARTICLE 2(4) OF THE UN CHARTER

One of the cornerstones of the system of collective security put in place by the UN Charter, and indeed of today's international legal order, involves the encompassing prohibition of the use of force. Article 2(4) of the UN Charter effectively prohibits States from going to war with one another.

From the wording of article 2(4), it is clear that both threats of force and the actual use of force are prohibited. In addition, it is worth noting that the prohibition in article 2(4) is framed within the context of States 'international relations'. The threat or use of force may therefore not be employed between States in their engagements with one another. Internal use of force by a State, such as police action, or the suppression of secessionist or rebel movements, falls outside the scope of the provision. While some argue that the provision's reference to threat or use of force directed against the political independence, territorial integrity, or the purposes of the United Nations narrows down the prohibition, the predominant view is that it is a blanket ban against any use of force in the inter-State context.[12]

One question which arises with the interpretation of the prohibition is what exactly is meant by 'force'. The predominant view is that it refers to military or armed force. Forms of political or economic coercion do not fall under the law on the use of force.[13] This debate continues until today: Is only the use of conventional weapons forbidden? Does one focus on the effects of the act rather than the instruments involved? Do cyberattacks qualify as uses of force?[14] Although difficult to determine precisely, there is sufficient State practice as well as ICJ jurisprudence, to at the least point out instances which clearly are uses of force:

- The use of one State's military to target another State (the use of conventional armed forces for purposes of invasion, occupation, or annexation)
- Acts of aggression (see further below), which may include bombardment, targeting of military forces, and annexation
- Certain forms of support provided to rebel movements
- Targeted killings (frequently undertaken with the use of drones in another State without that State's consent)[15]

---

12 See also Ian Brownlie, *Principles of Public International Law* (7th edn, OUP 2008) 732.

13 On this, see the discussions in United Nations, *Documents of the United Nations Conference on International Organization* (Vol VI, 1945) 334.

14 On weapons, see *Legality of the Threat or Use of Nuclear Weapons* [1996] (Advisory Opinion) ICJ Rep 226 [39]. On cyberspace, see Hüsch, § 19, in this textbook.

15 See Erin Pobjie, 'The Meaning of Prohibited "Use of Force" in International Law' (18 November 2022) Max Planck Institute for Comparative Public Law and International Law (MPIL) Research Paper No. 2022–27,

- Cyberattacks with a scale and effect comparable to kinetic uses of force (physical damage of kinetic effect).[16]

Despite certain situations that clearly represent 'force', the question remains relevant, as recent examples illustrate. Do 'minimal' uses of force qualify as a use of force, and is there a gravity threshold: Would the firing of one bullet across State borders qualify?[17] Does an accidental missile strike from one State into another qualify?[18] Does the poisoning of an individual with a prohibited substance in another State by an 'aggressor' State qualify as a use of force?

II. THREATS OF FORCE

In comparison to actual uses of force, even though they are equally forbidden by the UN Charter, *threats* of force are far less discussed.[19] Generally, threats of force are those actions which fall short of actual use of force. One of the clearest manifestations includes an ultimatum, whereby a State is given a choice to comply with certain requests or demands, failing which, it will face the use of force against it.[20] Other forms in which a threat of force manifests include open verbal communication by one State against another threatening force, as well as demonstrations of force, such as military build-ups or exercises. It is generally understood that threats of force are only unlawful if the envisaged actual use of force which would follow would also be unlawful.[21]

III. REGIONAL AND SUB-REGIONAL ORGANISATIONS INCORPORATING THE PROHIBITION

The prohibition of the use of force in article 2(4) of the UN Charter is similarly found in numerous regional and sub-regional instruments. To name but a few of these:

- Articles 19, 21, and 22 of the *Charter of the Organization of American States* (OAS) curtail the resort to force and prescribe the peaceful settlement of disputes;
- Article 4(f) of the *Constitutive Act of the African Union* (AU), successor to the Organisation of African Unity (OAU), contains a similar provision to article 2(4) of the UN Charter;

---

11. See also Patryk I Labuda, 'The Killing of Soleimani, the Use of Force Against Iraq and Overlooked Ius Ad Bellum Questions' (*EJIL: Talk*, 13 January 2020) <www.ejiltalk.org/the-killing-of-soleimani-the-use-of-force-against-iraq-and-overlooked-ius-ad-bellum-questions/> accessed 16 August 2023.

16 See, Michael N Schmitt (ed), *Tallinn Manual on the International Law Applicable to Cyber Warfare* (CUP 2013), Rule 11; and Michael N Schmitt, *Tallinn Manual 2.0 on the International Law Applicable to Cyber Warfare* (CUP 2017), Rule 69.

17 On this topic, see Tom Ruys, 'The Meaning of "Force" and the Boundaries of the jus ad Bellum: Are "Minimal" Uses of Force Excluded from UN Charter Article 2(4)?' (2014) 108(2) AJIL 159.

18 For an example, see Marko Milanovic, 'As Far as We Know, There Has Been No Armed Attack Against Poland' (*EJIL: Talk!*, 16 November 2022) <www.ejiltalk.org/as-far-as-we-know-there-has-been-no-armed-attack-against-poland/> accessed 16 August 2023.

19 Nikolas Stürchler, *The Threat of Force in International Law* (CUP 2007) 1–4.

20 Ibid 258.

21 *Legality of the Threat or Use of Nuclear Weapons* (n 14) [47].

- Article 1 of the Economic Community of West African States (ECOWAS) *Protocol on Non-Aggression* sets out that member States in their international relations refrain from the threat or use of force or aggression;[22] and
- Articles 3 and 4 of the International Conference on the Great Lakes Region (ICGLR) *Protocol on Non-Aggression and Mutual Defence* similarly include a comprehensive prohibition on the threat or use of force.[23]

Although the prohibition does not appear explicitly in several other regional organisations' instruments, other related principles feature prominently, such as the prevention and resolution of inter-State conflict, good neighbourliness, the resolution of disputes by peaceful means, and the use of force only as a last resort.

D. LEGAL CONSEQUENCES OF A VIOLATION

The main legal consequence of a violation of article 2(4) is that the UNSC is allowed to step in and take measures under Chapter VII of the Charter. In a first step, the Council determines under article 39 whether a 'Chapter VII situation' has arisen; if this is the case, it has a broad range of options to maintain or restore international peace and security, including both non-coercive (non-military) and coercive (military) measures. The UN Security Council can, by way of non-coercive measures, call on the parties to a dispute to comply with provisional measures such as a ceasefire agreement (article 40 UN Charter). It may then go a step further and impose additional measures, such as individual or collective sanctions (article 41 UN Charter), with travel bans and freezing of assets being widespread examples. When non-coercive measures prove insufficient, the UNSC may decide on military measures (see E.I.1.).

In addition to the UN Charter, the use and threat of force bears consequences under other areas of international law. Article 52 of the VCLT states that a treaty is void if its conclusion has been procured by the threat or use of force in violation of the principles of international law embodied in the UN Charter.[24] Any unlawful threat or use of force, considered an internationally wrongful act, also gives rise to State responsibility and may result in reparations.[25] Further, there are obligations on States not to recognise the lawfulness of a situation, such as territorial acquisition caused by the breach of

---

22 Economic Community of West African States Protocol on Non-Aggression (adopted 22 April 1978, entered into force 13 May 1982) 1690 UNTS, article 1. See also article 6(2) of the ECOWAS Convention on Small Arms and Light Weapons, their Ammunition and Other Related Matters (adopted 14 June 2006, entered into force 5 August 2009).

23 Protocol on Non-Aggression and Mutual Defence in the Great Lakes Region (adopted 30 November 2006, entered into force 21 June 2008), articles 3 and 4.

24 Vienna Convention on the Law of Treaties (adopted 23 May 1969, entered into force 27 January 1980) 1155 UNTS 331. On the law of treaties, see Fiskatoris and Svicevic, § 6.1, in this textbook.

25 On State responsibility, see Arévalo-Ramírez, § 9, in this textbook.

peremptory norms, such as the annexation of Crimea by the Russian Federation.[26] Finally, persons involved in the commission of acts during a violation of article 2(4) might be responsible individually under international criminal law.[27] Acts and conduct which therefore breach article 2(4) are in no way isolated and have numerous consequences in other areas of international law. In other words, a violation of article 2(4) never stands alone, always being simultaneously a violation of other principles and rules of international law.

E. EXCEPTIONS TO THE PROHIBITION

I. EXCEPTIONS WITHIN THE SYSTEM OF COLLECTIVE SECURITY

1. UNSC Authorisations Under 'Chapter VII'

The UN Charter puts in place an encompassing system of collective security in that it not only prohibits the use of force, but also regulates its exceptions. The Charter foresees two principal exceptions. The first concerns situations in which the Security Council authorises the use of force (for self-defence, however, see E.I.3.). The basis for the Council's competence can be found in article 24(1) of the Charter, which highlights the Council's 'primary responsibility for the maintenance of international peace and security'. Upon ratifying the UN Charter, member States thus agreed that the UNSC could act on their behalf.

The UNSC has authorised the use of force on a number of occasions. The most notable of these include authorisation to member States during the Korean War (1950) – the first time the Security Council had explicitly authorised force, and the Iraqi invasion of Kuwait (1990) – the first authorisation given following years of stalemate during the Cold War.[28] Since its first employment, the Council has made use of its powers on over a dozen occasions.[29]

Before authorising the use of force, the UNSC must first determine the existence of a threat to international peace and security under article 39 of the Charter. The Council's wording of this determination varies, but it has consistently determined situations as

---

26 ILC, 'Responsibility of States for Internationally Wrongful Acts (53rd Session 23 April–1 June and 2 July–10 August 2001) UN Doc A/RES/56/83 Annex, article 40.

27 On individual responsibility, see Arévalo-Ramírez, § 9, in this textbook.

28 On the Korean War, see S/RES/82 (1950) and S/RES/83 (1950) which determined that the armed attack by North Korean forces constituted a breach of the peace and recommended member States furnish the necessary assistance to the Republic of Korea in order repel the armed attack and restore international peace and security.
   On the Iraqi invasion of Kuwait, see S/RES/678 (1990), which gave Iraq one final opportunity to withdraw its forces from Kuwait, failing which, authorised the use of all necessary means by member States to ensure withdrawal of Iraqi forces.

29 These situations include the Gulf War (1990), the situation in Somalia (1992), the situation in Haiti (1993–1994), the situation in Rwanda (1994), the situation in the Great Lakes Region (1996), and the post-US invasion situation in Iraq (2003).

(1) a threat to international peace and security, (2) a threat to peace and security in the region, or (3) a breach of the peace.[30]

Article 42 of the Charter builds the legal basis for the authorisation of force. In practice, however, the Council has never explicitly invoked this provision. Instead, it has consistently used the terms 'all necessary means' to signal authorisation for the use of force. Moreover, despite the provision's wording, the UNSC authorises member States to use force. The Charter initially envisaged the establishment of UN troops; however, this never materialised. This system of authorisation has therefore come to be known as *delegated* enforcement action.[31]

Resolutions which invoke Chapter VII have consistently been interpreted with a greater gravity and sense of bindingness. To this end, most resolutions authorising the use of force contain, often in the final preambular paragraph, the UNSC's expression that it is 'acting under Chapter VII of the Charter of the United Nations'.[32]

BOX 13.3 Advanced: The United Nations General Assembly (UNGA) and the Uniting for Peace Resolution

Following the Korean War in the 1950s and the paralysis of the permanent members of the UNSC at the time, the UNGA adopted Resolution 377A on 3 November 1950. The resolution came to be known as the 'Uniting for Peace' resolution – aimed principally at allowing the UNGA to consider and take actions on matters of peace and security when the UNSC itself failed to discharge its responsibilities under the UN Charter. One of the most important provisions of the resolution is found in the first operative paragraph. It states that should the Security Council, because of a lack of unanimity among its permanent members, fail to exercise its primary responsibility over matters of international peace and security, the UNGA may consider the matter with a view to make appropriate recommendations to maintain or restore international peace and security.

Despite the resolution's strong wording, there remains debate today as to whether the UNGA has the competence to consider and take actions with respect to breaches of peace, acts of aggression, and threats to peace and security.

---

30 On the nuanced nature of this determination, in particular by the five permanent Members of the UNSC, see Tamsin Phillipa Paige, *Petulant and Contrary: Approaches by the Permanent Five Members of the UN Security Council to the Concept of 'Threat to the Peace' under Article 39 of the UN Charter* (Brill Nijhoff 2019) 277.

31 Erika de Wet, *The Chapter VII Powers of the United Nations Security Council* (Hart Publishing 2004) 257; see also broadly, Niels Blokker, 'Is the Authorization Authorized? Powers and Practice of the UN Security Council to Authorize the Use of Force by "Coalitions of the Able and Willing"' (2000) 11(3) EJIL 541.

32 See for example, fourth preambular paragraph, S/RES/678 (1990).

The resolution has been invoked 13 times (eight times by the Security Council and five times by the UNGA). The most recent instance concerns the Russian invasion of Ukraine on 24 February 2022 under UNSC Resolution 2623 (2022).

2. Collective Action Under Chapter VIII

As much as the UNSC may authorise the use of force by States, it may also, and regularly does, authorise the use of force by regional organisations. This system of authorisation is sometimes known as decentralised collective security insofar as it is regional organisations which act on behalf of the UNSC.

Article 52 of the UN Charter recognises the important role of regional organisations in matters of peace and security. As such, it expressly provides that nothing in the UN Charter precludes 'the existence of [regional organisations] for dealing with such matters relating to the maintenance of international peace and security'.[33] Regional organisations are of course obliged to make use of pacific settlement of disputes prior to their referral to the UNSC.[34]

It is worth noting that the UN Charter consistently refers to 'regional arrangements or agencies'. Nonetheless, this reference clearly speaks of regional organisations to the extent that such organisations are involved in matters of peace and security within a specific geographical region.[35] Examples include the African Union and its Regional Economic Communities, the European Union, and the Organization of American States.[36] One organisation which has evaded being considered as a 'regional arrangement or regional agency' is NATO, which resembles more of a collective defence alliance. Despite this, scholars have convincingly argued that it is not necessarily the nature of the organisation which would determine whether UNSC authorisation of the use of force is required, but rather the nature of the action in question.[37] In other words, an organisation which acts in collective self-defence, that is coming to the aid of another State which has been attacked, need not obtain UNSC authorisation. An organisation which resorts to force for other purposes, however, such as maintaining peace and security, will require UNSC authorisation.

---

33 Article 52(1) UN Charter.

34 Article 52(2) and (3) UN Charter.

35 Erika de Wet, 'Regional Organizations and Arrangements: Authorization, Ratification, or Independent Action' in Marc Weller (ed), *The Oxford Handbook of the Use of Force in International Law* (OUP 2015) 315–316.

36 The African Union has eight Regional Economic Communities. On a brief description of each, see Marko Svicevic, *Compendium of Documents Relating to Regional and Sub-Regional Peace and Security in Africa* (2nd edn, Pretoria University Law Press 2021).

37 Ian Johnstone, 'When the Security Council Is Divided: Imprecise Authorizations, Implied Mandates, and the "Unreasonable Veto"' in Weller (n 35) 229.

When peaceful means of resolving a dispute fail, the UNSC may authorise a regional organisation to use force under article 53(1) of the UN Charter.

The wording of article 53(1) has not been spared of debate surrounding its interpretation. Although the UNSC has authorised the use of force by regional organisations on numerous occasions,[38] some have argued that regional organisations may use force without the approval of the UNSC.[39] This debate becomes particularly relevant considering that some regional organisations and defence alliances have either developed their own treaty law seemingly allowing them to use force unilaterally, or have resorted to the actual use of force without UNSC approval. Examples include the ECOWAS interventions in Sierra Leone and Liberia in the 1990s and the NATO operation against Yugoslavia in 1999.[40] An example of such a provision is article 4(h) of the Constitutive Act of the African Union which allows the AU to intervene in its member States when grave circumstances occur, which include war crimes, genocide, and crimes against humanity. The fact that the Constitutive Act makes no reference to UNSC approval has caused controversy, mostly because it suggests the AU does not require UNSC authorisation when intervening in AU member States.[41]

3. Individual and Collective Self-Defence

a) General Remarks

Arguably the most relied upon exceptions to the prohibition of the use of force involve the right of individual and collective self-defence. Although this right has been codified in article 51 of the UN Charter, it is well established that the right has been at the disposal of States even before the UN Charter was adopted. The ICJ confirmed this position in its *Nicaragua* judgment when it stated that the right of self-defence is a 'natural' or 'inherent' right and its inclusion in the UN Charter 'does not go on to regulate directly all aspects of its content'.[42] The right of self-defence is also considered a

---

38 See for example the authorisation given to the African Union operations in Somalia (AMISOM) under Resolution 1725 (2006); Sudan (UNAMID) under Resolution 1769 (2008); by ECOWAS in the Ivory Coast (ECOMICI) under Resolution 1464 (2003); and Mali (AFISMA) under Resolution 2085 (2012).

39 On this debate, see Erika de Wet, 'The Evolving Role of ECOWAS and SADC in Peace Operations: A Challenge to the Primacy of the United Nations Security Council in Matters of Peace and Security?' (2014) 27 LJIL 353; Suyasha Paliwal, 'The Primacy of Regional Organisations in International Peacekeeping: The African Example' (2010) 51(1) Virginia Journal of International Law 185; Marko Svicevic, 'Re-assessing the (Continued) Need for UN Security Council Authorisation of Regional Enforcement Action: The African Union 20 Years On' (2020) 45(1) SAYIL 1.

40 Johnstone (n 37) 231. UNSC resolutions often cited include on the ECOWAS intervention in Sierra Leone, S/RES/1132 (1997) and S/RES/1181 (1998); on the ECOWAS intervention in Liberia, S/RES/788 (1992) and S/RES/866 (1993); on the NATO intervention in Yugoslavia, S/RES 1244 (1999); and also S/RES/1160 (1998), S/RES/1199 (1998), and S/RES/1203(1998).

41 See for example, arguments raised by Erika de Wet, 'Regional Organizations and Arrangements: Authorization, Ratification, or Independent Action' in Weller (n 35) 314; Paliwal (n 39) 196; and Svicevic (n 39).

42 *Military and Paramilitary Activities in and Against Nicaragua (Nicaragua v. United States of America)* (Merits) [1986] ICJ Rep 14 [176].

rule of customary international law. The right of self-defence means that all States may use military force when they are attacked by other States, or where such an attack is imminent.

While States have resorted to this right historically on many occasions, the contemporary understanding of the right is subject to a number of well-established requirements and limitations that will be discussed in the following sections.

b) The Gravity Threshold of an 'Armed Attack'

In order for a State to lawfully invoke self-defence, there must be an armed attack. That is, before a State may use armed force in self-defence, it must have been attacked. The ICJ in its *Nicaragua* judgment has clarified that an 'armed attack' needs to be of a certain gravity, and that it may include action not only by the regular armed forces of a State. A mere 'frontier incident' does not qualify as such an armed attack; on the other hand, 'the sending by a State of armed bands to the territory of another State' may be of a 'scale and effect' to be considered an armed attack.[43] It is worth noting that the Court's position on outlining more grave and less grave incidents has come under considerable scrutiny over the years.[44] Despite some uncertainties, what is clear is that the threshold for the invocation of article 51 is higher than for the UNSC to become active under 'Chapter VII', or, in other words, that not all unlawful threats or uses of force give rise to lawful self-defence.

c) Limitations to the (Lawful) Exercise of Self-Defence

As can be expected, the right to use force in self-defence is not unlimited. These limitations are not spelled out in article 51 of the UN Charter but are derived from customary international law (as reaffirmed by the ICJ in the *Nicaragua* and the *Oil Platforms* cases[45]).

The reaction to an attack must be necessary and proportionate. This refers to the fact that only those acts are allowed that were strictly necessary to halt or repel an attack that has already begun or is ongoing.[46] By implication, necessity of forceful measures means that other dispute resolution options were not available to the victim State. Reprisals and punitive measures are not allowed. Such measures would not only violate the proportionality requirement under self-defence but may also be a violation of the prohibition of the use of force.

---

43 Ibid [195].

44 Tom Ruys, *'Armed Attack' and Article 51 of the UN Charter: Evolutions in Customary Law and Practice* (CUP 2010) 143.

45 *Oil Platforms (Islamic Republic of Iran v. United States of America)* (Merits) [2003] ICJ Rep 16 [76]; *Nicaragua* (n 42) [194].

46 *Nicaragua* (n 42) [176]. See also *Legality of the Threat or Use of Nuclear Weapons* (Advisory Opinion) [1996] ICJ Rep 226 [41].

d) The Duration of the Right of Self-Defence and the Reporting Requirement

Article 51 of the UN Charter imposes two additional criteria. The first of these criteria impacts the duration of lawful self-defence. States may only resort to self-defence 'until the Security Council has taken measures necessary to maintain international peace and security'. The UNSC may take any number of measures, and it may well be that it authorises the use of force, in order to restore international peace and security.[47] However, of course, that does not mean that the UNSC needs to authorise self-defence; this option remains at the disposal of States without UNSC approval.[48]

The second criteria is a procedural requirement; when States resort to the use of armed force in self-defence, they are obliged to immediately inform the UNSC. In this way, the UNSC is kept informed of latest developments and is able to assess situations as the primary organ responsible for international peace and security.[49]

e) Anticipatory/Pre-emptive Self-Defence and the 'Caroline Test'

One aspect of the right to self-defence which has received its fair share of debate concerns situations where an armed attack has not yet taken place but is imminent. This debate is certainly not new and goes back to the *Caroline* incident, resulting from a dispute between America and Britain in the context of a rebellion in Canada.[50] The *Caroline* was a steamboat which was transporting supplies to Canada, aiding the uprising there. The British set out to halt this, captured the boat, set it alight and sent it over Niagara Falls. The British put forward that these actions amounted to self-defence. The Americans countered this explanation by putting forward the test now famously known as the *Caroline* test. According to this, a State claiming self-defence needs to show that the 'necessity of self-defense was instant, overwhelming, leaving no choice of means, and no moment of deliberation'.[51]

This precedent has arguably enabled anticipatory or pre-emptive self-defence, in which a State may use armed force against another State even before an armed attack has taken place; such armed attack must be imminent, however.[52]

---

47 de Wet (n 31) 262–263.

48 On the distinction between self-defence and collective security (UNSC authorisation of the use of force), see Michael Wood, 'Self-defence and Collective Security: Key Distinctions' in Weller (n 35) 649–660.

49 See also Nick van der Steenhoven, 'Conduct and Subsequent Practice by States in the Application of the Requirement to Report under UN Charter Article 51' (2019) 6(2) JUFIL 247.

50 See Michael Wood, 'The Caroline Incident – 1837' in Tom Ruys, Olivier Corten and Alexandra Hofer (eds), *The Use of Force in International Law: A Case-based Approach* (OUP 2018) 5.

51 See the letter by Secretary of State Daniel Webster dated 24 April 1841 in 'British American Diplomacy: The Caroline Case' in William C Fray and Lisa A Spar, *The Avalon Project at the Yale Law School: Documents in Law, History and Diplomacy* (Avalon Project 1996) <https://avalon.law.yale.edu/19th_century/br-1842d.asp>.

52 Rajeesh Kumar, 'Iraq War 2003 and the Issue of Pre-emptive and Preventive Self-defence: Implications for the United Nations' (2014) 70(2) *India Quarterly* 124–125.

Pre-emptive self-defence was used as one justification for the US invasion of Iraq in 2003. It was then argued by the US, together with Australia and the UK, that Iraq was attempting to acquire weapons of mass destruction and that this threat was too grave to avoid counteraction. No armed attack took place against either of the States involved. Since then, pre-emptive self-defence has been widely criticised for violating article 51 of the UN Charter and arguments in favour of such a notion have significantly decreased.[53]

f) Self-Defence Against Non-State Actors

Traditionally, the main actors in international law have been States.[54] This has been true both for general international law and for the use of force. In contemporary times, however, this position finds some challenge. Nowhere is this clearer than regarding the question of self-defence against non-State actors. Whereas only States were previously able to declare and wage war, there exist today (as has been the case for some time now) non-State actors which are sufficiently sophisticated and organised to wage both terrorist attacks and large-scale conflicts against States. This is especially true of terrorist organisations such as Al Qaeda, Al Shabab, Boko Haram, and the Islamic State. The terrorist attacks of 11 September 2001 against the United States and its corresponding 'War on Terror' marked a turning point in the way international law, and more specifically, the use of force, was viewed.[55]

The question discussed ever since is whether States could rely on self-defence when using force against non-State actors. This in turn preconditions that non-State actors can mount an 'armed attack'. Both literature and State practice on this matter remain moot. Recently, the UNSC held a meeting convened by Mexico to provide States with an opportunity to make submissions on this matter.[56] Submissions by States during this meeting broadly confirmed a divergent approach. While some States took the view that the use of force against non-State actors was acceptable even in the territory of third States, other States submitted that the consent of the host State is required before using force.[57]

II. EXCEPTIONS BEYOND THE UN CHARTER

1. Military Assistance on Request

The sending of military forces by one State to the territory of another remains a surprisingly frequent occurrence. These actions are ordinarily justified in that the

---

53 E.g. Kofi Annan, 'Lessons of Iraq War Underscore Importance of UN Charter – Annan' (16 September 2004) <https://news.un.org/en/story/2004/09/115352-lessons-iraq-war-underscore-importance-un-charter-annan> accessed 16 August 2023.

54 See Green, § 7.1, in this textbook.

55 However, in the *Wall Advisory Opinion*, the ICJ rejected Israel's argument that constructing a wall in occupied Palestinian Territory was consistent with article 51 UN Charter. See *Legal Consequences of the Construction of a Wall in the Occupied Palestinian Territory* (Advisory Opinion) [2004] ICJ Rep 136.

56 UNSC, 'Arria Formula Meeting "Upholding the Collective Security System of the UN Charter: The Use of Force in International Law, Non-state Actors and Legitimate Self-defence"' UNSC Doc. S/2021/247.

57 See the discussions by Adil Ahmad Haque, 'The Use of Force Against Non-state Actors: All over the Map' (2021) 8(2) JUFIL 278.

State sending the armed forces does so on the basis of a request by the inviting State. International law in this regard recognises the principle of 'military assistance on request', often also termed as 'intervention by invitation'.

In other words, State A may request, for one or another reason, that State B send its armed forces to State A's territory. Such a course of action would not violate the article 2(4) prohibition of the use of force since the armed deployment is undertaken with the consent of the 'host State'.[58] Despite its lawful nature, there are, however, a number of conditions which need to be met for such a course of action to be legal under international law.[59]

First, the consent expressed by the host State must be given validly. The State requesting military assistance must therefore have given its consent freely, without coercion.[60]

Second, the authority of the host State giving the consent must be appropriate; that the entity consenting to or requesting military assistance in fact has the power to give such consent or make such request. Ordinarily, the authority entitled to request military assistance is the de jure government of a particular State (the internationally recognised government). In turn, entities which are entitled to make such a request are those acting on behalf of the State (an organ of State), such as the head of State or head of government.[61]

Finally, a State requesting military assistance may not receive it when it is under a state of civil war (the rule of non-intervention in civil wars).[62] The general nature of this prohibition serves as a limitation to military assistance on request and regards that all peoples have a right to self-determination and the right to choose the political, economic, and social characteristics of the State, without external interference from, for example, military forces of another State.[63] Insofar as withdrawal of military forces concerns, it is worth noting that the ICJ in its *DRC v Uganda* case underlined that no particular formalities are required when a State wishes to withdraw its consent.[64]

2. The Use of Force for Humanitarian Purposes: Humanitarian Intervention and the Responsibility to Protect

One of the more controversial uses of force in international law concerns coercive measures taken for humanitarian purposes, with neither the consent of the State

---

58 See further on this, Gregory Fox, 'Intervention by Invitation' in Weller (n 35) 816.

59 See also Martin Faix, *Law of Armed Conflict and Use of Force: Part One: Securing International Peace and Security: International Law on the Use of Force* (Univerzita Palackeho v Olomouci 2013) 92.

60 Erika de Wet, *Military Assistance on Request and the Use of Force* (OUP 2020) 154.

61 Ibid.

62 Fox (n 58) 819.

63 See the principle of equal rights and self-determination of peoples in UNGA, *Declaration of Principles of International Law concerning Friendly Relations and Co-operation among States in Accordance with the Charter of the United Nations* (24 October 1970), UN Doc A/RES/2625 (XXV).

64 *Armed Activities on the Territory of the Congo (Democratic Republic of the Congo v. Uganda)* (Merits) [2005] ICJ Rep 168 [47].

concerned nor the authorisation of the UNSC. One such example includes humanitarian intervention. Such intervention is usually argued for the purpose of 'preventing or putting to a halt gross and massive violations of human rights or international humanitarian law'.[65]

When humanitarian intervention is undertaken with the authorisation of the UNSC, it is followed by far less controversy. This is because the UNSC indeed has the competence to authorise the use of force against a State and for such purposes. With the end of the Cold War and particularly from the 1990s onward, the UNSC has on several occasions authorised the use of force by States for humanitarian purposes. Resolution 794 (1992) addressing the situation in Somalia, Resolution 929 (1994) on Rwanda, and Resolution 1080 (1996) on the Great Lakes Region, all represent to a greater or lesser extent examples where the UNSC has authorised military intervention for humanitarian reasons.[66]

Unilateral humanitarian intervention, on the other hand, is far more controversial. The most notable example of unilateral humanitarian intervention involves the controversial NATO decision to the use of force against the Federal Republic of Yugoslavia in 1999 to halt widespread crimes against humanity, war crimes and ethnic cleansing of Kosovar Albanians by Serbian military forces.[67] Kosovo is not a solitary example, however. The ECOWAS interventions in Liberia and Sierra Leone in the 1990s and the US-led no-fly zone in Northern Iraq in 1991 are equally noteworthy in what have been argued as examples of humanitarian intervention.[68]

On this basis, arguments both in favour of and against humanitarian intervention may be summarised as follows:

Arguments in favour of humanitarian intervention:

- It provides a legal basis for the protection of civilians in situations where the UNSC is inactive or fails to discharge its responsibilities; and
- It may ensure that desperately needed humanitarian aid reaches those affected.

Arguments disfavouring humanitarian intervention:

- There is no firm legal basis in international law for humanitarian intervention;
- Its application remains highly selective by States justifying their actions on this basis; (some States are perceived as insignificant resulting in perceived indifference to specific situations); and

---

65 Danish Institute of International Affairs, *Humanitarian Intervention: Legal and Political Aspects* (Gullanders Bogtrykkeri 2000) 11.
66 See S/RES/794 (1992); S/RES/929 (1994); S/RES/1080 (1996). On authorisation of humanitarian intervention, see Cristina G Badescu, 'Authorizing Humanitarian Intervention: Hard Choices in Saving Strangers' (2007) 40(1) Canadian Journal of Political Science 51.
67 See broadly, Louis Henkin, 'Kosovo and the Law of "Humanitarian Intervention"' (1999) 93(4) AJIL 824.
68 See for example, Sir Nigel Rodley, 'Humanitarian Intervention' in Weller (n 35) 780.

- Politically, humanitarian intervention is opposed by a large majority of the Third World (African States have expressed a preference for UNSC authorised actions, failing which, such action should be undertaken by regional organisations rather than Western States).[69]

Related, but distinct, is the concept of the responsibility to protect (R2P). At its core is the idea that although State sovereignty entails the right of each State to regulate domestic affairs, such a right is accompanied by the responsibility of each State to protect populations living within its borders.[70] Where the State fails to protect its population, the responsibility to protect then rests with the international community. This idea was formally endorsed by the UNGA under its 2005 World Summit Outcome Document.[71] In principle, R2P is based on three pillars:

Pillar I: Each State carries with it the responsibility to protect its populations from genocide, war crimes, ethnic cleansing, and crimes against humanity;
Pillar II: States support each other in their responsibility to protect; and
Pillar III: Where a State fails to protect its population, that responsibility turns to the international community to ensure effective collective action.

Although both the idea of humanitarian intervention and its extension under R2P have been around for some time, its exception to the prohibition of the use of force in article 2(4) remains controversial. Much of the controversy surrounding the concepts concerns the authority of States to intervene in each other's affairs and whether existing institutions such as the UNSC should in fact always authorise military force even in cases of humanitarian intervention. It therefore suffices to say that despite some practice and the ironing out of certain principles on the international level, the broader concept of humanitarian intervention can neither be considered a well-established exception to the prohibition nor accepted by the international community of States as such.

F. CONCLUSION

The use of force, its prohibition, and exceptions to this prohibition have a long-standing history in international law. While resort to armed force was not always regulated, nor was it always prohibited, the developments of the last century represent the greatest attempt to curtail the use of armed force. Article 2(4) of the UN Charter and its prohibition of the threat or use of force remains a cornerstone not only of the

---

69 See broadly, Mohammed Ayoob, 'Third World Perspectives on Humanitarian Intervention and International Administration' (2004) 10 Global Governance 99.

70 International Commission on Intervention and State Sovereignty, 'Report of the International Commission on Intervention and State Sovereignty: The Responsibility to Protect' (December 2001).

71 UNGA, 'World Summit Outcome' (24 October 2005) UN Doc S/RES/60/1.

UN Charter system of collective security but of the entire international legal order. Likewise, well-established exceptions to the prohibition, most notably, self-defence under article 51, and UNSC authorisation, are firmly established and widely accepted in practice. At the same time, the prohibition and corresponding exceptions are not without controversy. Emerging challenges, least of which include terrorism and force used by non-State actors, the continued proliferation of weapons of mass destruction, cybersecurity and cyberthreats, and abusive interpretations of self-defence, pose significant challenges to the regulation of armed force. While the *jus ad bellum* has been resilient, the development of international law and of the use of force cannot be viewed in isolation. Its continued evolution will rest with its ability to meet the challenges of the 21st century, ever present and expanding as they may be.

BOX 13.4 Further Readings and Further Resources

Further Readings

- A Abass, *Regional Organisations and the Development of Collective Security: Beyond Chapter VIII of the UN Charter* (Hart Publishing 2004)

- C Gray, *International Law and the Use of Force* (4th edn, OUP 2018)

- O Corten, *The Law Against War: The Prohibition on the Use of Force in Contemporary International Law* (2nd edn, Hart Publishing 2021)

- M Weller (ed), *The Oxford Handbook of the Use of Force in International Law* (OUP 2015)

- T Ruys, O Corten and A Hofer (eds), *The Use of Force in International Law: A Case-Based Approach* (OUP 2020)

Further Resources

- EJIL: Talk, 'Use of Force' <www.ejiltalk.org/category/use-of-force/> accessed 16 August 2023

- Opinio Juris, 'Use of Force' <http://opiniojuris.org/category/topics/use-of-force/> accessed 16 August 2023

- UN Web TV, 'Security Council' <https://media.un.org/en/search/categories/meetings-events/security-council> accessed 16 August 2023

§ § §

PART III
SPECIALISED FIELDS

14

CHAPTER 14
LAW OF ARMED CONFLICT
ANNE DIENELT AND IMDAD ULLAH

BOX 14.1 Required Knowledge and Learning Objectives

Required knowledge: Sources of International Law; International Human Rights Law; Use of Force; Subjects of International Law.

Learning objectives: Understanding the law of armed conflict considering its historical roots, evolution over the period of various centuries, core principles and norms of the law of armed conflict, and some current challenges.

BOX 14.2 Interactive Exercises

Access *interactive exercises for this chapter*[1] by positioning your smartphone camera at the dot-filled box, also known as a QR code.

Figure 14.1 QR code referring to interactive exercises.

A. INTRODUCTION

The persistence of violence and conflicts over time gave way to efforts to regulate it, first in terms of regulating weapons as in the (Eurocentric) 1868 St. Petersburg Declaration, and later on by specifically protecting civilians from the conduct of hostilities in the four universal Geneva Conventions and their additional protocols (often described as 'international humanitarian law' or 'IHL'). Rules and principles to limit harm to civilian objects and the civilian population were present as early as recorded human history. The content of these rules and principles was (and is) not purely humanitarian but also serves the necessities of war. There is a constant struggle to balance military necessities with humanitarian aims. This also explains why not all

---

1 https://openrewi.org/en-projects-project-public-international-law-law-of-armed-conflict/.

DOI: 10.4324/9781003451327-17

rules and principles in warfare follow humanitarian motives; as warfare has always been cruel and brutal.[2] The *jus in bello* (Latin: 'right in war'), another synonym for the law of armed conflict) should not be mixed with the *jus ad bellum* (Latin: 'right to war')[3] (or *jus contra bellum* [Latin: 'right against war']), which refers to the law prohibiting the use of force (see article 2(4) UN Charter[4]) and its exceptions (e.g., article 51 UN Charter). Even though aggression is prohibited, the law of armed conflict includes rules and principles regulating how an armed conflict can be conducted lawfully.

BOX 14.3 Advanced: Separation of *jus ad bellum* and *jus in bello*

In the *jus ad bellum*, the current situation in Ukraine is phrased as an unlawful aggression by Russia against Ukraine. In the *jus in bello*, Russia and Ukraine are bound by the same legal standards, namely the law of armed conflict, even though Russia started the war with an unlawful invasion.

This chapter explores how civilians and the civilian population are protected in war. How is the tension between military necessity and humanitarian aims resolved? What is lawful conduct in war? It begins with a historical overview to better understand the origins of the law of armed conflict. It then turns to the classification of a conflict (non-international or international), which determines the specific legal framework in the law of armed conflict that regulates the specific conduct of hostilities. Afterward, the relevance of customary international law is highlighted by reference to the core principles of the law of armed conflict, such as distinction or proportionality. The various actors in the law of armed conflict are briefly described, leading to current challenges within the law of armed conflict, including the protection of specific groups and objects particularly vulnerable in war as well as new technologies of warfare. The chapter concludes with a brief description of how the law of armed conflict can interact with other fields of public international law.

B. HISTORICAL OVERVIEW

The modern law of armed conflict emerged as a result of historical norms and traditions. The terrible harm witnessed by Henry Dunant[5] after the Battle of Solferino in 1859 served as a catalyst for this development.[6] Parallel to States coming together to regulate a further warfare escalation with new weapons being developed in the 19th century,

---

2   Marco Sassòli, Antoine Bouvier, and Anne Quintin, *How Does Law Protect in War? Cases, Documents and Teaching Materials on Contemporary Practice in International Humanitarian Law* (Vol I, 3rd edn, ICRC Publications 2011) 1.

3   On *jus ad bellum*, see Svicevic, § 13, in this textbook.

4   Charter of the United Nations (1945), XV UNCIO 335.

5   Henry Dunant, 'A Memory of Solferino' <www.icrc.org/en/doc/resources/documents/misc/57jnvr.htm> accessed 23 June 2022.

6   'The Battle of Solferino' (1859) <www.icrc.org/en/doc/resources/documents/misc/57jnvr.htm> accessed 23 June 2022.

influential pacifists and peace movement figures, such as Bertha von Suttner or Dunant,[7] campaigned to adopt regulations to limit the suffering of the wounded. The creation of the International Committee of the Red Cross (ICRC) in 1863, the first Geneva Convention for the Amelioration of the Condition of the Wounded in Armies in the Field of 1864, and eventually also the 1899/1907 Hague Regulations aim at protecting the wounded in wars. In the beginning, 16 States mainly from Europe and Latin America participated in the first Geneva Conference, which resulted in an agreement on principles that emphasises the care for wounded individuals on the battlefield, regardless of their nationality. Later on, the Hague Peace Conferences further expanded the regulations and also included rules governing naval warfare, which were subsequently confirmed and amended in the four 1949 Geneva Conventions and the two 1977 Additional Protocols (AP I and II).

The 19th-century regulations and the 1899/1907 Hague Regulations could not stop two world wars (and did not intend to do so), nor were they able to prevent all human suffering. However, the two world wars and their devastating consequences for the civilian population underscored the need for universally applicable rules and regulations to curtail the horrendous character of modern warfare. Consequently, diplomatic conferences were held to agree on rules to care for the sick, wounded, and prisoners of war. These conferences also intended to expand the scope of earlier conventions. The 1949 Geneva Conventions enshrine rules on protecting civilian populations during war and under foreign occupation and generally regulate international armed conflicts. Their common article 3 addresses non-international armed conflicts.[8] In the meantime, the Vietnam War, among others, highlighted the need for further warfare regulation. The two Additional Protocols (APs) from 1977 were also adopted in light of colonial wars. While AP II focuses on non-international armed conflicts and includes a set of rules applying to conflicts between States and non-State actors, AP I contains rules that extend the protection of the four Geneva Conventions.

C. CLASSIFICATION OF AN ARMED CONFLICT

When analysing a specific armed conflict, first, one must determine the kind of armed conflict. This so-called classification[9] refers to two categories of conflict: an international armed conflict (IAC) and a non-international armed conflict (NIAC).

---

7   Janne Elisabeth Nijman, 'Bertha von Suttner: Locating International Law in Novel and Salon' in Immi Tallgren (ed), *Portraits of Women in International Law – New Names and Forgotten Faces?* (OUP 2022). Dienelt, 'When Humanitarians go to War: A European Road to "Civilized" Warfare?' in Anne van Aaken et. al (eds.), Oxford Handbook on International Law in Europe (OUP 2024).

8   Frits Kalshoven and Liesbeth Zegveld, *Constraints on the Waging of War: An Introduction to International Humanitarian Law* (ICRC Publications 2001) 27–29.

9   Tristan Ferraro and Lindsey Cameron, 'Article 2 – Application of the Convention' in Philip Spoerri and others (eds), *Commentary on the First Geneva Convention* (ICRC Publications 2016) paras 193 + 210 ff. + 214 <https://ihl-databases.icrc.org/en/ihl-treaties/gci-1949/article-2/commentary/2016?activeTab=1949GCs-APs-and-commentaries#index> accessed 26 June 2022; Dapo Akande, 'Classification of Armed Conflicts: Relevant Legal Concepts' in Elizabeth Wilmshurst (ed), *International Law and the Classification of Conflicts* (OUP 2012) 32–79; Jann K Kleffner, 'Scope of Application of International Humanitarian Law' in Dieter Fleck (ed), *Handbook of International Humanitarian Law* (4th edn, OUP 2021) 52, para 3.

IACs between two or more States are regulated by the four Geneva Conventions, AP I and custom,[10] while NIACs between a State and a non-State actor or between several non-State actors on the territory of a State[11] are governed by common article 3, AP II (for its State parties), and custom. Consequently, a State who is involved in a NIAC but is not a party to AP II is only bound by common article 3 together with customary rules and principles.

BOX 14.4 Example: NIACs

Two examples of NAICs are the conflict in Colombia with the FARC guerrilla group fighting the government, and in the aftermath of 9/11, the US war with Al-Qaeda across several States.[12]

D. CORE PRINCIPLES OF THE LAW OF ARMED CONFLICT

In many instances, parties to a conflict have treated prisoners humanely and exchanged prisoners of war in the aftermath of conflicts. Due to belligerent States' consistent practice and *opinio juris*, these practices gradually emerged as customary rules.[13] These customs[14] were also codified in treaties,[15] such as the 1899/1907 Hague Regulations, the 1949 Geneva Conventions, or the 1977 Additional Protocols.

All fundamental principles of the law of armed conflict, such as humanity, distinction, military necessity, proportionality, and the obligation to take all feasible precautions, enjoy the status of customary law,[16] and apply in IACs and NIACs. Their objective is to 'humanise' warfare without challenging the justifications for the initial aggression (important separation of the right to war from the right in war). They assist in maintaining the balance between military necessity and humanitarian protection. To determine the legality of an attack, all principles as well as specific regulations have to be observed.

---

10 On customary law, see Stoica, § 6, Section 2, in this textbook.

11 On the variety of actors, see Engström, § 7, in this textbook.

12 Geneva Academy, 'Rule of Law in Armed Conflicts (RULAC)' <https://geneva-academy.ch/research/rule-of-law-in-armed-conflicts-rulac> accessed 26 June 2022.

13 Kalshoven and Zegveld (n 8) 15.

14 The ICRC has conducted a study on customary IHL in 2005, Jean-Marie Henckaerts and Louise Doswald-Beck (eds), *Customary International Humanitarian Law* (Vols I and II, CUP 2005), and since then regularly updates the analysis of State practice and *opinio juris*. It is available online at <https://ihl-databases.icrc.org/en/customary-ihl> accessed 26 June 2022.

15 On international treaties, see Fiskatoris and Svicevic, § 6, Section 1, in this textbook.

16 'Fundamental Principles of IHL' <https://casebook.icrc.org/a_to_z/glossary/fundamental-principles-ihl > accessed 26 June 2022.

I. HUMANITY

Following the principle of humanity, States have adopted norms prohibiting cruel and inhumane treatment of opponents, especially regarding prisoners of war.[17] Today, the wounded, sick, shipwrecked, and non-combatants also enjoy protection. Regarding NIACs, the principle can be found in common article 3, which prohibits the inhumane treatment of all those persons not participating in hostilities.[18] In IACs, article 75(1) AP I emphasises the humane treatment of individuals without discrimination.[19] The principle of humanity enjoys customary status,[20] applicable to States and non-States alike.

II. DISTINCTION

The principle of distinction determines *who* and *what* can be targeted in the conduct of hostilities (see e.g. article 48 AP I). It has emerged as a cardinal principle in treaty as well as in customary law.[21] It underscores that civilians and civilian objects are not lawful targets, while military objects and combatants can generally be attacked lawfully. Until and unless civilians participate in hostilities directly, they are legally protected from belligerent attacks.[22] Nevertheless, under very limited conditions, and only if proportionate, collateral damage to civilians and civilian objects can be lawful. The 1899/1907 Hague Regulations (article 25) do not specifically use the word 'civilians', but they outlaw 'the attack or bombardment, by whatever means, of towns, villages, dwellings, or buildings which are undefended'.[23] Regarding IACs, article 57(2)(b) AP I stresses that only direct armed attacks against combatants and military objects are lawful. In NIACs, article 13(2) AP II prohibits attacks on the civilian population and treating civilians and civilian objects as an object of attack. Parallel in IACs, article 57(1) AP I stipulates that 'in the conduct of military operations, constant care shall be taken to spare the civilian population, civilians and civilian objects'.

---

17 'Lieber Code: Instructions for the Government of Armies of the United States in the Field' (24 April 1863) <https://ihl-databases.icrc.org/applic/ihl/ihl.nsf/Article.xsp?action=openDocument&documentId=0E91FD21E67035CCC12563CD00514E42> accessed 24 June 2022.

18 'Convention (I) for the Amelioration of the Condition of the Wounded and Sick in Armed Forces in the Field' (12 August 1949) <https://ihl-databases.icrc.org/applic/ihl/ihl.nsf/WebART/365-570006?OpenDocument> accessed 25 June 2022.

19 'Protocol Additional to the Geneva Conventions of 12 August 1949, and Relating to the Protection of Victims of International Armed Conflicts (Protocol I)' (8 June 1977) <https://ihl-databases.icrc.org/ihl/WebART/470-750096?OpenDocument> accessed 26 June 2022.

20 Jean-Marie Henckaerts and Louise Doswald-Beck, *Customary International Humanitarian Law* (Vol I, CUP 2005) 306–343.

21 Legality of the Threat or Use of Nuclear Weapons (Advisory Opinion) [1996] ICJ Rep 226, paras 78 + 92.

22 Henckaerts and Doswald-Beck (n 20) 3.

23 'Convention (IV) Respecting the Laws and Customs of War on Land and Its Annex: Regulations Concerning the Laws and Customs of War on Land' (18 October 1907) <https://ihl-databases.icrc.org/applic/ihl/ihl.nsf/Article.xsp?action=openDocument&documentId=D1C251B17210CE8DC12563CD0051678F> accessed 26 June 2022.

III. MILITARY NECESSITY

Furthermore, actions that are necessary to accomplish a legitimate military purpose and are not otherwise prohibited by IHL can be lawful. In treaty law and custom, the only lawful military purpose is to weaken the military capacity of the other belligerent parties.[24] Article 23(g) 1899/1907 Hague Regulations prohibits 'to destroy or seize the enemy's property, unless such destruction or seizure be imperatively demanded by the necessities of war'.[25]

IV. PROPORTIONALITY

Proportionality is inter alia enshrined in article 51(5)(b) AP I which states that 'an attack which may be expected to cause incidental loss of civilian life, injury to civilians, damage to civilian objects, or a combination thereof, which would be excessive in relation to the concrete and direct military advantage anticipated'. It puts the damage caused by military activities into relation with the military advantage and requires that the effects of the means and methods of warfare cannot be disproportionate to the military advantage.[26] Hence this principle balances military necessity with humanitarian considerations. It is common understanding that 'direct military advantage' refers to the advantages of the operation as a whole and not separate parts of the attack.[27] While military necessity speaks of the criteria to choose a military target, proportionality lays down the limits of specific military action to neutralise a target.

V. TO TAKE ALL FEASIBLE PRECAUTIONS

The principle of precaution was initially set out in article 2 of the 1907 Hague Convention (IX). It provides that given the presence of a military target inside an undefended town or port, the military commander must 'take all due measures in order that the town may suffer as little harm as possible'.[28] Additionally, article 57 AP I states that it is incumbent upon the warring parties to 'do everything feasible to verify that the objectives to be attacked are neither civilians nor civilian objects and are not subject to special protection'.

---

24 'Military Necessity' <https://casebook.icrc.org/a_to_z/glossary/military-necessity> accessed 26 June 2022.

25 'Convention (IV) Respecting the Laws and Customs of War on Land and Its Annex: Regulations Concerning the Laws and Customs of War on Land' (18 October 1907) <https://ihl-databases.icrc.org/ihl/WebART/195-200033?OpenDocument> accessed 27 June 2022.

26 'Proportionality' <https://casebook.icrc.org/a_to_z/glossary/proportionality> accessed 26 June 2022.

27 Henckaerts and Doswald-Beck (n 20) 49–51.

28 'Convention (IX) Concerning Bombardment by Naval Forces in Time of War' (18 October 1907) <https://ihl-databases.icrc.org/applic/ihl/ihl.nsf/Article.xsp?action=openDocument&documentId=C27C2D1A0E0C2C35C12563CD00516DB5> accessed 28 June 2022.

E. ACTORS IN THE LAW OF ARMED CONFLICT

I. STATES

States as traditional subjects of international law[29] play an important role in the law of armed conflict: States start armed conflicts, they participate in hostilities, they occupy territory, and they negotiate armistices. In collective efforts, States assemble at international peace conferences, like the ones leading to the conclusion of the 1863 Geneva Convention, the 1899/1907 Hague Regulations, and the 1949 Geneva Conventions.

II. NON-STATE ACTORS

Over the past decades, many NIACs took place, with one State fighting an organised armed group or several ones within its territory, and vice versa. These situations are regulated by common article 3 to the Geneva Conventions and AP II. In NIACs, rebel and terrorist groups can be belligerent parties and lawfully participate in the hostilities as armed non–State actors under the law of armed conflict. They are directly addressed in common article 3 and in AP II.

BOX 14.5 Advanced: Non-State Actors

The treatment of non-State actors under non-international armed conflicts does not grant them any legitimacy. This regulation only aims to safeguard innocent civilians in armed conflicts. Despite their active role in conflicts, non-State actors do not participate in the law-making procedure in the law of armed conflict. They are not a party to any treaty, since treaties are concluded between States exclusively. In peace negotiations, in contrast, non-State actors participate together with States. Their actions are also indirectly considered when interpreting the law of armed conflict,[30] and when identifying rules and principles of customary law.[31] Compliance of non-State actors with the law of armed conflict still represents a challenge.[32]

---

29 On States, see Green, § 7, Section 1, in this textbook.

30 Cf. conclusion 7 and its commentary of the ILC's draft conclusions on subsequent agreements and subsequent practice in relation to the interpretation of treaties with commentaries <https://legal.un.org/ilc/texts/1_11.shtml> accessed 23 June 2022.

31 Cf. conclusion 4, para 4 of the ILC's draft conclusions on the identification of customary international law with commentaries <https://legal.un.org/ilc/texts/1_13.shtml> accessed 23 June 2022.

32 Annyssa Bellal and Stuart Casey-Maslen, 'Enhancing Compliance with International Law by Armed Non-State Actors' (2011) 3(1) GoJIL 175–197.

III. THE INTERNATIONAL COMMITTEE OF THE RED CROSS

The International Committee of the Red Cross (ICRC) is the 'guardian'[33] of the law of armed conflict. It is mandated to protect people affected by armed conflicts. It is a subject of international law and has international legal personality. But the ICRC enjoys a special status that is different from the one of NGOs, which are not subjects of international law, or international organisations, which mostly enjoy a derivative subjectivity in international law.[34] The ICRC is guided by seven principles: humanity, impartiality, neutrality, independence, voluntary service, unity, and universality.[35]

F. CURRENT CHALLENGES IN THE LAW OF ARMED CONFLICT

I. PROTECTED GROUPS AND OBJECTS

States originally created the law of armed conflict to spare civilians and the civilian population from the consequences of war. While the principle of distinction generally prohibits direct attacks against civilians, some provisions of the Geneva Conventions and their additional protocols address other specific protected groups or objects, such as medical personnel and infrastructure cultural property, or the natural environment. Their protection is often linked to the protection of civilians and civilian objects, but the provisions install special protection for specific groups and objects that differs from the general protection of civilians and civilian objects.

1. Medical Personnel

The 1864 Geneva Convention was concluded to take care of the wounded and sick combatants of all belligerent States who were *hors de combat* (French: 'out of the battle'). Without medical personnel and medical care, their protection would have remained meaningless. Hence civilians and militaries officially assigned to medical purposes temporarily or permanently are of high value in war due to their essential role in medical care. Medical personnel, medical units, and medical establishments enjoy protection and cannot be targeted lawfully.[36] They are protected when fulfilling their medical duties in conformity with medical ethics.[37] But once they participate in hostilities, they lose their protection.[38] If they fall into the enemy's hands, they are not

---

33 ICRC Blog, 'What Is the ICRC's Role in Developing and Ensuring Respect for IHL?' <https://blogs.icrc.org/ilot/2017/08/14/what-is-the-icrc-s-role-in-developing-and-ensuring-respect-for-ihl/>.

34 On the variety of actors, see Engström, § 7, in this textbook.

35 See ICRC, Research Guide 'The Fundamental Principles of the International Red Cross and Red Crescent Movement' <https://blogs.icrc.org/cross-files/the-fundamental-principles-of-the-international-red-cross-and-red-crescent-movement/> accessed 23 June 2022.

36 For IACs, see articles 24–25 GC I, articles 36–37 GC II, and article 15 AP I; for NIACs, see article 9 AP II.

37 See articles 24–25 GC I, articles 36–37 GC II, and articles 15–16 AP I.

38 See, e.g., The Practical Guide to Humanitarian Law 'Medical Personnel' (*Médecins Sans Frontières*) <https://guide-humanitarian-law.org/content/article/3/medical-personnel/> accessed 22 June 2023.

considered prisoners of war and must be set free.[39] Since they can use the distinctive sign of the red cross, red crescent, red lion, or red crystal to guarantee their special protection, they are visible to the enemy's forces. Attacking them is a war crime under article 8(2) lit. b(xxiv) and 8(2) lit. e(ii) Rome Statute.[40]

2. Cultural Property

Cultural property enjoys special protection in armed conflicts.[41] The two additional protocols contain provisions specifically protecting for cultural property in IAC and NIAC. Additionally, the Hague Convention for the protection of cultural property in the event of armed conflict from 1954 and its two protocols complement the Geneva law.[42] Cultural property is protected in armed conflicts because of its relevance for humanity and because everyone contributes to the world's culture.[43] Destruction of cultural heritage can amount to a war crime under the Rome Statute.[44]

3. Natural Environment

The environment has been called a 'silent victim' of war.[45] Only since the aftermath of the Vietnam War and with the adoption of AP I,[46] the 'natural environment' enjoys direct protection from 'widespread, long-term *and* severe damage' in IACs.[47] However, it is unclear whether 'long-term' is measured in years or decades; based on the *travaux préparatoires* (French: 'preparatory work') the latter seems to be the case.[48] Most scholars assume that this was not even reached in the cases of the Vietnam War and the deployment of Agent Orange, or when burning oil wells in Kuwait in 1991. Additionally, elements of the environment are protected as civilian objects.[49] They rarely serve military purposes and hence only rarely represent a military objective that can be attacked lawfully. Moreover, other provisions indirectly protect the environment, such

---

39 See, e.g., articles 28–32 GC I.

40 On international crimes, see Fiskatoris, § 22, Section 1, in this textbook.

41 See generally, Roger O'Keefe, *The Protection of Cultural Property in Armed Conflict* (CUP 2006).

42 See article 53 AP I and article 16 AP II. Cultural property also enjoys protection under customary law, see ICRC, 'Study on Customary IHL,' Chapter 12, Rules 38–41 <https://ihl-databases.icrc.org/en/customary-ihl/v1/rule38> accessed 22 June 2023.

43 Preamble of the 1954 Hague Convention.

44 See, e.g., the *Al Mahdi* case by the ICC, *The Prosecutor v. Ahmad Al Faqi Al Mahdi* ICC-01/12–01/15; more information <www.icc-cpi.int/mali/al-mahdi> accessed 23 June 2022.

45 UN Environment Programme, 'Rooting for the Environment in Times of Conflict and War' (*UNEP Press Release*, 6 November 2019) <www.unep.org/news-and-stories/story/rooting-environment-times-conflict-and-war> accessed 15 March 2022.

46 See also the Convention on the Prohibition of Military or Any Other Hostile Use of Environmental Modification Techniques (ENMOD Convention), which contains a similar threshold with almost identical wording ('widespread, long-lasting, *or* severe').

47 See articles 35(3) and 55(1) AP I; for custom, see rules 43–45 in ICRC, 'Study on Customary IHL,' Chapter 14 <https://ihl-databases.icrc.org/en/customary-ihl/v1/rule43> accessed 15 March 2022.

48 See Anne Dienelt, *Armed Conflicts and the Environment: Complementing the Laws of Armed Conflict with Human Rights Law and International Environmental Law* (Springer 2022) 57 ff.

49 See Cordula Droege and Marie-Louise Tougas, 'The Protection of the Natural Environment in Armed Conflict – Existing Rules and Need for Further Legal Protection' (2013) 82(1) Nordic Journal of International Law 21, 23.

as article 56 AP I on installations containing dangerous forces like nuclear power plants or dams.

II. NEW TECHNOLOGIES

1. Semi-autonomous Weapons

Warfare technologies have made unprecedented strides in the last few decades. Such a development provides a strategic and operational edge, while it also raises legal questions concerning the principles of distinction, military necessity, proportionality, and so forth. In theory, semi-autonomous weapons like combat drones are more precise and proportionate. This is why combat drones were presented as the 'weapon of choice' at the start of the 'War on Terror'.[50] Where the results on saving the lives of drone operators are certainly positive, the loss of lives when targeting the alleged terrorists is in many cases not proportionate though to the actual security threats they pose. For instance, in case of the US drone attacks against terrorists in Pakistan, Yemen, and Somalia, various governmental and non-governmental studies point to the fact that in contrast to their technological reputation for precision, combat drones are not that more precise, operationally.[51] Nonetheless, the US remains adamant that combat drones avoid losses to the innocent lives, despite the discrepancies surrounding the loss of innocent civilian lives. Undoubtedly, in some instances, combat drones pinpointed and eliminated terrorists with more precision than conventional weapons,[52] complying with 'all feasible precautions' before striking down the intended target, and adequately fulfilling the principles of military necessity and proportionality. Notwithstanding the technological sophistication of combat drones and their ability to be precise and proportionate, their past deployment, specifically against belligerent non-State actors, raises some serious questions about the fulfilment of humanitarian principles. The *actual* practices of the usage of combat drones seriously question their precision and proportionality, as often described in theory.[53]

---

50 Remarks of Director of Central Intelligence Agency, Leon E Panetta, at the Pacific Council on International Policy (18 May 2009) <www.cia.gov/newsinformation/speeches-testimony/directors-remarks-at-pacific-council.html> accessed 23 July 2022.

51 James Cavallaro, Stephan Sonnenberg, and Sarah Knuckey, *Living under Drones: Death, Injury and Trauma to Civilians from US Drone Practice in Pakistan* (International Human Rights and Conflict Resolution Clinic, Stanford Law School and Global Justice Clinic, New York University School of Law 2012); Letta Tayler, 'Between a Drone and Al-Qaeda: The Civilian Cost of US Targeted Killing in Yemen' (Human Rights Watch 2013); Jane Mayer, 'The Predator War: What Are the Risks of the C.I.A.'s Covert Drone Program?' *The New Yorker* (26 October 2009); Ben Emmerson, 'Report of the Special Rapporteur on the Promotion and Protection of Human Rights and Fundamental Freedoms While Countering Terrorism' UN Document A/68/389 (18 September 2013); Philip Alston, 'Report of the Special Rapporteur on Extrajudicial, Summary or Arbitrary Executions' (Presented to the Human Rights Council, 14th Session, 28 May 2010).

52 Imdad Ullah, *Terrorism and the US Drone Attacks in Pakistan: Killing First* (Routledge 2021) 131.

53 See more generally Hugh Gusterson, *Drone: Remote Control Warfare* (MIT Press 2016); Letta Tayler, 'Between a Drone and Al-Qaeda: The Civilian Cost of US Targeted Killing in Yemen' (Human Rights Watch 2013) <www.hrw.org/node/256485/printable/print> accessed 23 July 2022; 'A Wedding That Became a Funeral' (Human Rights Watch 2014); 'France's Shadow War in Mali: Airstrikes at the Bounti Wedding' (Stoke White

2. Autonomous Weapons

Within the context of warfare weapons, autonomy is a relative term. It may range and encompass launching a weapon to the point of successfully selecting, engaging, and neutralising the target.[54] According to the US Department of Defense, a weapons system is autonomous when 'once activated, (it) can select and engage targets without further intervention by a human operator'.[55] In contrast, humans remain in the loop with semi-autonomous weapons when deciding on and targeting enemy combatants. In general, artificial intelligence and autonomous weapons challenges the cardinal principles, such as humanity and proportionality. For instance, articles 51 and 57 AP I stress the importance of avoiding excessive physical and material damages in warfare.[56] Avoidance of excessive damage thus depends upon efficient decision-making. However, autonomous weapons based on data feeds reach decisions within seconds, and thus might undermine the role of human judgment.[57] Moreover, since the algorithm is based on image classifications such as soldier uniforms, insignias, and types of rifles and ammunition, it can be hacked and fed with different image classifications. In other cases, images can be misinterpreted by autonomous weapons.[58] Despite ethical, legal, and political questions[59] about the nature of and about certain characteristics of autonomous weapons challenging the cardinal principles, they may better protect a State's military personnel.[60]

Investigations 2021) <www.swiunit.com/post/france-s-shadow-war-in-mali-airstrikes-at-the-bounti-wedding> accessed 24 July 2022.

54 For a detailed treatment of autonomy in autonomous weapons systems and how may it operate in warfare, see Kenneth Payne, 'Artificial Intelligence: A Revolution in Strategic Affairs?' (2018) 60(5) Survival 7–32; Giovanni Sartor and Andrea Omicini, 'The Autonomy of Technological Systems and Responsibilities for Their Use' in Nehal Bhutta and others (eds), *Autonomous Weapons Systems: Law, Ethics, Policy* (CUP 2016) 40–65.

55 'Autonomy in Weapons Systems' *U.S. Department of Defense*, Directive no. 3000.09 (21 November 2012).

56 See also the St. Petersburg Declaration and the Hague Declarations and Regulations.

57 Dan Saxon, 'A Human Touch: Autonomous Weapons, Directive 3000.09, and the "Appropriate Levels of Human Judgment over the Use of Force"' (Summer/Fall 2014) 15(2) Georgetown Journal of International Affairs 100, 103. For further details, see Bill Boothby, 'How Far Will the Law Allow Unmanned Targeting to Go?' in Dan Saxon (ed), *International Humanitarian Law and the Changing Technology of War* (Martinus Nijhoff/Brill 2013) 62–63; and David Akerson, 'The Illegality of Offensive Lethal Autonomy' in Dan Saxon (ed), *International Humanitarian Law and the Changing Technology of War* (Martinus Nijhoff/Brill 2013) 71.

58 Ibid.

59 Mary E O'Connell, 'Banning Autonomous Killing – The Legal and Ethical Requirement That Humans Make Near- Time Lethal Decisions' in Matthew Evangelista and Henry Shue (eds), *The American Way of Bombing: Changing Ethical and Legal Norms From Flying Fortresses to Drones* (Cornell University Press 2014) 224–235; Rebecca Crootof, 'A Meaningful Floor for "Meaningful Human Control"' (2016) 30 Temple International and Comparative Law Journal 53–62; Peter Asaro, 'Jus nascendi, Robotic Weapons and the Martens Clause' in Ryan Calo and others (eds), *Robot Law* (Edward Elgar 2016) 367–386.

60 Duncan Macintosh, 'Fire and Forget: A Moral Defense of the Use of Autonomous Weapons Systems in War and Peace' in Duncan Macintosh and Jens D Ohlin (eds), *Lethal Autonomous Weapons: Re- Examining the Law and Ethics of Robotic Warfare* (OUP 2021) 9–23.

3. Cyber Weapons

Cyber[61] weapons, such as spyware and malicious software codes, have already brought down governmental digital platforms in Estonia and destroyed certain nuclear reactors in Iran, raising questions of armed attacks in the *jus ad bellum*, possibly triggering the right to self-defence under article 51 UN Charter, and State responsibility. With regard to the *jus in bello*, the cardinal principles of the law of armed conflict are challenged.[62] Due to the easiness and less costly prospects, a military commander might decide to shut down an electricity grid by a cyberattack to disrupt the command and communication structures of a nearby military installation while simultaneously turning off electricity in a nearby hospital, possibly violating the principles of distinction and proportionality. In cyber warfare, like in conventional warfare, there are high chances of indirectly targeting civilian cyber infrastructure.[63]

G. INTERPLAY WITH OTHER FIELDS OF PUBLIC INTERNATIONAL LAW

Decades ago, the law of war represented the *lex specialis* (Latin: 'special law') in war-related matters.[64] With the adoption of the 1949 Geneva Conventions and the 'humanisation' of the law of war, there is agreement today among States and scholars that human rights[65] can complement the law of war under certain conditions, particularly based on non-derogable human rights such as the right to life. In turn, regional and universal human rights systems as well as the ICJ have clarified questions at the intersection of human rights law and the law of war.[66] In 1996, the ICJ in its advisory opinion on the *Legality of the Threat or Use of Nuclear Weapons* stated that

> the protection of the International Covenant of Civil and Political Rights does not cease in times of war, except by operation of Article 4 of the Covenant whereby certain provisions may be derogated from in a time of national emergency. Respect for the right to life is not, however, such a provision. In principle, the right not arbitrarily to be deprived of one's life applies also in hostilities. The test of what is an arbitrary deprivation of life, however, then falls to be determined by the applicable lex specialis, namely, the law *applicable* in armed conflict which is designed to regulate the conduct of hostilities.[67]

---

61 On international law in cyberspace, see Hüsch, § 19, in this textbook.

62 Michael N Schmitt and Liis Vihuk (eds), *Tallinn Manual 2.0 on the International Law Applicable to Cyber Operations* (CUP 2017) 348–350.

63 Ibid 26.

64 See Fleck (n 9) Chapter 14.

65 On international human rights law, see Ciampi, § 21, in this textbook.

66 See, e.g., IACommHR, *Coard et al. v. United States*; IACommHR, *Victor Saldaño v. Argentina*; Walter Kälin/ UNCHR, 'Report of the Special Rapporteur on the Situation of Human Rights in Occupied Kuwait' (16 January 1992) UN Doc. E/CN.4/1992/26, paras 50–63.

67 *Nuclear Weapons* (n 19), para 25.

In 2005, it specified the interplay in the *Wall* Advisory Opinion by stating that

> [a]s regards the relationship between IHL and human rights law, there are thus three possible situations: some rights may be exclusively matters of IHL; others may be exclusively matters of human rights law; yet others may be matters of both these branches of international law.[68]

Other fields also coexist or apply simultaneously to the law of war. The UN International Law Commission in its work on 'The Effects of Armed Conflicts on Treaties' in 2011 confirmed that certain treaties continue to be 'in operation' during an armed conflict.[69] In an annex, the Commission included a list of treaties[70] that presumably continue to apply during armed conflict, among them treaties in human rights law and international environmental law,[71] and are not suspended in case of an armed conflict.[72]

International criminal law is another field of public international law that complements the laws of war.[73] In the Rome Statute, States have codified and criminalised war crimes that are conducted during hostilities, thus relating to the law of war. However, the Office of the Prosecutor of the International Criminal Court can only investigate crimes as agreed upon in the Rome Statute, thus separating the law of war from international criminal law and resulting in differing legal standards.

H. CONCLUSION

The law of armed conflict is built around the tensions between military force on the one hand, and humanitarian considerations on the other. It regulates (and facilitates) the conduct of hostilities, while it also intends to spare civilians and the civilian population from the consequences of warfare, despite a prohibition of aggression under the *jus ad bellum*. The 1899/1907 Hague Regulations, the 1949 Geneva Conventions and their additional protocols, together with customary rules and the cardinal principles of the law of armed conflict determine the legality of today's warfare. Only when the cardinal principles together with the specific regulations are complied with, then a belligerent party can launch a lawful attack against a target. These rules and principles apply to conventional warfare as well as to new technologies; they protect the civilian population, civilian objects, and protected groups and objects alike.

---

68 *Legal Consequences of the Construction of a Wall* (Advisory Opinion) [2004] ICJ Rep 136, para 106.

69 See draft article 7, ILC, 'Draft Articles on the Effects of Armed Conflicts on Treaties' (2011) UN Doc. A/66/10, paras 100–101.

70 On international treaties, see Fiskatoris and Svicevic, § 6, Section 1, in this textbook.

71 See, e.g., Dienelt (n 48) 234 ff. On international environmental law, see Poorhashemi, § 16, in this textbook.

72 On multilateral environmental treaties and armed conflict, see. e.g. Britta Sjöstedt, 'The Role of Multilateral Environmental Agreements in Armed Conflict: "Green-keeping" in Virunga Park. Applying the UNESCO World Heritage Convention in the Armed Conflict of the Democratic Republic of the Congo' (2013) 82 Nordic Journal of International Law 129–153.

73 On international criminal law, see Ciampi, § 22, in this textbook.

BOX 14.6 Further Readings and Further Resources

Further Readings

- Commentaries to the Geneva Conventions, <www.icrc.org/en/war-and-law/treaties-customary-law/geneva-conventions> accessed 20 August 2023.

- D Fleck (ed), *The Handbook of International Humanitarian Law* (OUP 2021).

- ICRC, 'Customary IHL Database', <https://ihl-databases.icrc.org/en/customary-ihl> accessed 20 August 2023.

- ICRC, 'IHL Database', <https://ihl-databases.icrc.org/en> accessed 20 August 2023.

Further Resources

- ICRC, 'Casebook on "How Does Law Protect in War?"', <https://casebook.icrc.org/> accessed 20 August 2023.

- 'Humanity in War Podcast', <https://blogs.icrc.org/law-and-policy/humanity-in-war-podcast/> accessed 20 August 2023.

- 'ICRC Report on IHL and the Challenges of Contemporary Armed Conflicts', <www.icrc.org/en/document/icrc-report-ihl-and-challenges-contemporary-armed-conflicts> accessed 20 August 2023.

- 'In and Around War(s) Podcast by the Geneva Academy of IHL and Human Rights', <https://soundcloud.com/user-230423719> accessed 20 August 2023.

- 'The Laws of War Podcast', <https://jibjabpodcast.com/tag/jus-in-bello/> accessed 20 August 2023.

§ § §

CHAPTER 15
LAW OF THE SEA

ALEX P. DELA CRUZ AND
TAMSIN PHILLIPA PAIGE

BOX 15.1 Required Knowledge and Learning Objectives

Required knowledge: History of International Law, Sources of International Law

Learning objectives: Understanding the law of the sea as a specialised discipline of international law with a specific history; the notion of maritime zones in UNCLOS as a way of allocating rights and obligations among States in respect of the ocean and its resources; and the contemporary issues confronting the law of the sea.

BOX 15.2 Interactive Exercises

Access *interactive exercises for this chapter*[1] by positioning your smartphone camera at the dot-filled box, also known as a QR code.

Figure 15.1 QR code referring to interactive exercises.

A. INTRODUCTION

The significance of the law of the sea lies in the fact that it is an important legal argumentative resource for States and corporations seeking to undertake cooperative endeavours, as well as in asserting their own interests and authority in relation to the ocean. This chapter will offer a brief history of the law of the sea until its codification into the United Nations Convention on the Law of the Sea (UNCLOS).[2] It also

---

1 https://openrewi.org/en-projects-project-public-international-law-law-of-the-sea/.

2 United Nations Convention on the Law of the Sea (opened for signature 10 December 1982, entered into force 16 November 1994) 1833 UNTS 397.

DOI: 10.4324/9781003451327-18

outlines the maritime zones as defined in the UNCLOS, its system of dispute settlement, and presents contemporary challenges confronting the law of the sea.

B. HISTORY OF THE LAW OF THE SEA

The law of the sea has been described as 'a persistently important theme' of international law 'from the very beginning',[3] but remained uncodified as a treaty for many centuries. Prior to the Hague Conference for the Codification of International Law in 1930, the law of the sea referred to a collection of various customs that different nations observed in relation to the ocean. These customs became topics for debate at the 1930 Hague Conference. However, the Conference concluded without producing a law of the sea treaty due to disagreement on the question of the breadth of the territorial sea.

After World War II, the United Nations convened the first Conference on the Law of the Sea (CLOS I) in Geneva in 1958. Four separate Geneva law of the sea conventions were adopted at the end of UNCLOS I, namely the Convention on the Territorial Sea and the Contiguous Zone (CTS); the Convention on the High Seas (CHS); the Convention on Fishing and Conservation of the Living Resources of the High Seas (CFCLR); and the Convention on the Continental Shelf (CCS). UNCLOS I also concluded with the adoption of an Optional Protocol of Signature Concerning the Compulsory Settlement of Disputes (OPSD), but many States refused to ratify it. However, the Geneva Conventions did not achieve high numbers of ratification. A second UN Conference on the Law of the Sea (CLOS II) was soon convened in 1960 in order to address the questions of the breadth of the territorial sea and the settlement of disputes, which remained unresolved under the Geneva law of the sea conventions. Again, sharp disagreements among States over those questions meant that CLOS II did not produce any treaties.

By the late 1960s, a large number of States had gained independence from imperial rule.[4] These States were previously unable to send delegations to CLOS I and II and felt that many of the provisions of the Geneva Conventions did not reflect their needs and issues. Many newly independent States sought greater control over fishery resources, mineral resources in areas beyond national jurisdiction, preservation of the marine environment, national security from threats coming from the ocean, and marine technology.[5] Another source of dissatisfaction with the Geneva Conventions was the fact that the breadth of the territorial sea remained unsettled. On this point, many newly independent States sought a wider territorial sea, while former imperial powers

---

3 RY Jennings, 'A Changing International Law of the Sea' [1972] 31 Cambridge LJ 32.

4 On decolonisation, see González Hauck, § 1, in this textbook.

5 Christopher W Pinto, 'Problems of Developing States and Their Effects on Decisions on Law of the Sea' in Lewis M Alexander (ed), *The Law of the Sea: Needs and Interests of Developing Countries* (University of Rhode Island 1973) 3–13.

wanted to keep the territorial sea as narrow as possible in order to preserve the vast geographical scope of international waters or the high seas.[6]

Both the newly independent States and the former imperial powers agreed the third UN Conference on the Law of the Sea (CLOS III) from 1973 to 1982 should aim to produce a single and universally ratified ocean treaty from which States would not be allowed to make reservations[7] or exceptions. Ratification would mean that States are signing up to the ocean treaty as a single package. Both groups of States recognised that the topics of the law of the sea formed an interrelated field in which compromises between competing interests were essential for the success of the then future ocean treaty.[8] CLOS III adopted provisions through a combination of consensus and majority voting, with a view to preventing a few recalcitrant States from blocking an emerging consensus on a point of law.[9] On 30 April 1982, UNCLOS was adopted by 130 votes in favour, 4 against, and 17 abstentions. It finally entered into force on 16 November 1994. UNCLOS adopted a zonal approach to the ocean, dividing waters into maritime zones with specific dimensions. UNCLOS also codified rules on innocent, transit, and archipelagic types of sea lane passage, the latter two types being UNCLOS's distinctive contribution to the language of international law.[10]

BOX 15.3 Advanced: Reciprocating States Regime

Between the Convention's adoption in 1982 and its entry into force in 1994, the US, Britain, France, Italy, the Netherlands, Belgium, West Germany, and Japan were in an arrangement called the Reciprocating States Regime (RSR). The RSR refuted the universal application of UNCLOS, particularly Part XI of the Convention that established the seabed beyond national jurisdiction as the common heritage of humankind.[11] It was the adoption of the 1994 Agreement relating to the Implementation of Part XI of the United Nations Convention on the Law of the Sea (1994 Implementing Agreement) which removed the objections of the RSR States. The salient feature of the 1994 Implementing Agreement is that it now allows multinational consortia controlled by the RSR States to apply for seabed exploration permits on the same terms applicable to UNCLOS pioneer investors from developing nations.

---

6 Tullio Treves, 'Law of the Sea' *Max Planck Encyclopedias of International Law* (April 2011) [c].

7 On reservations to treaties, see Fiskatoris and Svicevic, § 6.1, in this textbook.

8 James Harrison, *Making the Law of the Sea: A Study in the Development of International Law* (CUP 2011) 44.

9 Daniel Vignes, 'Will the Third Conference on the Law of the Sea Work According to Consensus Rule?' (1975) 69 AJIL 119, 120.

10 Arthur Ralph Carnegie, 'Environmental Law Challenges to the Law of the Sea Convention: Progressive Development of Progressive Development' in Hans Corell and others (eds), *International Law as a Language for International Relations* (United Nations 1996) 551.

11 Surabhi Ranganathan, *Strategically Created Treaty Conflicts and the Politics of International Law* (CUP 2014) 151.

C. MARITIME ZONES

The UNCLOS is the omnibus treaty governing international law regulating ocean spaces. It has been ratified by 168 States (including Palestine in 2015, with Azerbaijan being the most recent in 2016),[12] and is considered to be a codification of customary international law.[13] Even world powers who have not ratified the UNCLOS, such as the US, consider it to be customary in nature with the exception of Part XI of the Convention (concerning the Area).[14] For the most part, UNCLOS sets out how States are entitled to use various parts of the ocean and jurisdictional regimes relating to different ocean regions. UNCLOS was also responsible for a significant reduction in the scope of the high seas (also known as international waters) due to the expansion of the territorial sea and the creation of the exclusive economic zone and of archipelagic waters for certain island-and-water formations.

The different zones of jurisdiction that make up the core of the UNCLOS all start from the definition and premise of maritime baselines. Maritime baselines as a concept are simply the demarcation point between what is considered the landed territory of a State, and what is considered to be part of the ocean and thus governed by the UNCLOS. The starting point for determining baselines (and the rule that applies in most circumstances) is set out in article 5, which states that 'the normal baseline for measuring the breadth of the territorial sea is the low-water line along the coast as marked on large-scale charts officially recognised by the Coastal State'. This rule was relatively uncontroversial as a standard of geographical demarcation for most States. However, additional rules were developed in articles 6, 7, and 10 to account for non-standard coastlines, such as fringing reefs, coastlines with deep indentations or fringing islands, or small entirely enclosed bays. Article 6 sets out that the baseline can be drawn from the low water line of the reef; article 7 sets out the rules for drawing straight baselines to allow for ease of maritime zone measurement in situations where the coastline has deep indentations or fringing islands; and article 10 sets out the rules for baselines enclosing bays. Once the baselines of the State have been established in accordance with articles 7, 9, and 10, and the delimitation drawn in accordance with articles 12 and 15 the coastal State is required to publish these charts and deposit a copy of them with the Secretary-General of the United Nations.[15] It is worth noting that it is generally accepted that baselines move as the coastline changes; however, with climate change causing significant sea level rise and reduction of coast, particularly for small island States, there is a strong argument on ground of equity for fixing baselines.[16] From

---

12　United Nations Treaty Collection, 21(6) *Status of Multilateral Treaties Deposited with the Secretary-General: United Nations Convention on the Law of the Sea* 27 <https://treaties.un.org/doc/Publication/MTDSG/Volume%20II/Chapter%20XXI/XXI-6.en.pdf> accessed 9 August 2023.

13　On customary law, see Stoica, § 6.2, in this textbook.

14　See for example: Joint Statement by the United States of America and the Union of Soviet Socialist Republics 1989.

15　Article 16 UNCLOS.

16　Tim Stephen, 'Warming Waters and Souring Seas: Climate Change and Ocean Acidification' in Donald Rothwell and others (eds), *The Oxford Handbook of the Law of the Sea* (OUP 2015) 790–793.

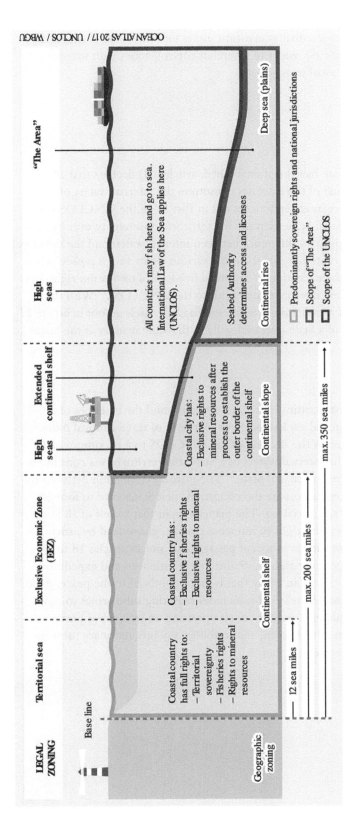

Figure 15.2 UNCLOS maritime and airspace zones.[17]

17 Heinrich Böll Foundation/University of Kiel's Future Ocean Cluster of Excellence – Ocean Atlas, CC BY 4.0 <https://creativecommons.org/licenses/by/4.0> via Wikimedia Commons.

these baselines the law of the sea divides maritime zones into three broad categories (each with specific subcategories): zones of sovereign control, zones with sovereign rights, and areas beyond national jurisdictions.

I. SOVEREIGN ZONES

1. Internal Waters

After the baselines of the State have been established, article 8(1) declares that all territory on the landward side of the baselines constitutes the internal waters of the coastal State (with particular exceptions set out in Part IV of the UNCLOS for archipelagic States). The coastal State exercises full territorial sovereignty over its internal waters,[18] with the primary difference between internal waters and the territorial sea being that internal waters are not subject to the various rights vessels possess when in the territorial sea (with the exception of historical freedom of navigation rights over areas that were not considered internal waters prior to the UNCLOS).[19] With the exception of some limits of jurisdiction over foreign flagged vessels set out in article 27 and 28, the internal waters of a State operate legally in the same manner as the State's landed territory.

2. Territorial Sea

The territorial sea is the first maritime zone that exists beyond the baselines of a State. Historically, the territorial sea had been set to a limit of three nautical miles, with this limit being updated in the drafting of the UNCLOS to a maximum of 12 nautical miles. Much like the internal waters of a State, the territorial sea constitutes the full sovereign territory of the coastal State.[20] The primary distinction between the territorial sea and the internal waters are the obligations that States owe to foreign flagged vessels within their territorial sea. The primary right that vessels of all States possess in the territorial sea is the right of innocent passage, guaranteed by article 17.[21] The details of what constitutes innocent passage is set out in articles 18 to 26 UNCLOS. Innocent passage is the right to transit in a 'continuous and expeditious'[22] manner through the territorial sea in a way that is 'not prejudicial to the peace, good order or security of the coastal State'.[23] This includes requiring submarines to travel surfaced with their flag displayed[24] and for vessels operating under nuclear power to carry documentation making this known, and to follow any precautionary measures set out in international agreements.[25]

---

18 Article 2(1).
19 Article 8(2).
20 Article 2.
21 Article 17.
22 Article 18(2).
23 Article 19(2).
24 Article 20.
25 Article 23.

BOX 15.4 Advanced: Controversy Over the Meaning of 'Innocent Passage'

This last requirement has been a source of long-running contention between New Zealand and the United States. New Zealand prohibits any nuclear vessels from entering its territorial sea, and the US for reasons of military secrecy refuses to disclose which vessels in its navy operate under nuclear power.[26] As such, New Zealand has taken the position since 1984 that no US warships (or any other vessel operating under a nuclear power plant) are exercising innocent passage when entering the New Zealand territorial sea as any of them theoretically may be operating under nuclear power.

The other restrictions on coastal State sovereignty within the territorial sea (with these also applying to the internal waters of the State) are limitations on criminal and civil jurisdictions[27] being exercised over foreign flagged vessels.[28] This is linked with article 92 UNCLOS, which grants exclusive jurisdiction to the flag State over vessels on the high seas. Because the UNCLOS treats vessels as an extension of the territorial jurisdiction of the flag State, limitations on coastal State jurisdiction regarding both criminal and civil law exist. These limitations are set out in articles 27 and 28, respectively.

3. Straits

Part III of the UNCLOS does not specifically define a strait, but the term usually refers to a waterway bordered by one or more coastal States that ships use for international navigation. States bordering straits used for international navigation (strait States) retain sovereignty or jurisdiction over such waters and their airspace, seabed, and subsoil, subject to the regime of transit passage and other rules of international law.[29]

Transit passage is a regime of passage that is less restrictive than the traditional right of innocent passage in the territorial sea. This means that ships navigating through international straits are subject to lesser restrictions that they would normally be when passing through the territorial sea of a coastal State. Article 38(2) UNCLOS defines transit passage as the exercise of the freedom of navigation and overflight 'solely for the purpose of continuous and expeditious transit of the strait between one part of the high seas or an exclusive economic zone and another part of the high seas or an exclusive economic zone'. 'Continuous and expeditious transit', however, does not prevent ships

---

26 Henry Cronic, 'New Zealand's Anti-Nuclear Legislation and the United States in 1985' (*Sources and Methods*, 26 August 2020) <www.wilsoncenter.org/blog-post/new-zealands-anti-nuclear-legislation-and-united-states-1985> accessed 11 April 2022.

27 On jurisdiction, see González Hauck and Milas, § 8, in this textbook.

28 Articles 27 and 28.

29 Article 34.

from using the strait in order to enter, leave, or return from one of the States bordering the strait. A foreign ship using a strait for transit passage may not carry out marine scientific research, hydrographic surveys, or other research activities without prior authorisation from the States bordering the strait.[30]

Strait States are allowed to designate sea lanes and traffic separation schemes for navigation in order to promote safe passage of ships.[31] But before such designation, strait States are required to refer proposed sea lane designations and traffic separation schemes to the International Maritime Organisation (IMO).[32]

4. Archipelagic Waters

The term 'archipelagic waters' refers to a category of waters which form an element of the definition of an archipelago in article 46(b) UNCLOS:

> a group of islands, including parts of islands, interconnecting waters and other natural features which are so closely interrelated that such islands, waters and other natural features form an intrinsic geographical, economic and political entity, or which historically have been regarded as such.

Article 47 UNCLOS outlines the steps through which an archipelagic State might draw its archipelagic baselines joining the outermost points of the outermost islands and drying reefs of the archipelago. The waters encompassed within these baselines are archipelagic waters, except those waters that the archipelagic State might delimit as internal waters in accordance with articles 9, 10, and 11.[33] Archipelagic waters are subject to the sovereignty of an archipelagic State, regardless of those waters' depth or distance from the coast.[34]

Sovereignty over archipelagic waters, however, is subject to a few limitations. For example, an archipelagic State is under an obligation to respect existing agreements with other States and to recognise traditional fishing rights and other legitimate activities of immediately adjacent neighbouring States in archipelagic waters.[35] Archipelagic States are also required to respect existing submarine cables laid by other States and passing through archipelagic waters without making a landfall and permit the maintenance and replacement of those cables.[36]

Two regimes of passage apply to archipelagic waters. These are (1) innocent passage and (2) archipelagic sea lanes passage. Ships of all States enjoy the right of innocent passage in archipelagic waters as they would in the territorial sea of a coastal State, subject to the

---

30 Article 40.
31 Article 41(1).
32 Harrison (n 8) 181.
33 Article 50.
34 Article 49(1).
35 Article 51(1).
36 Article 51(2).

right of archipelagic sea lanes passage and without prejudice to the right of the archipelagic State to delimit internal waters within its archipelagic waters.[37] An archipelagic State may temporarily suspend innocent passage in archipelagic waters without discrimination among foreign ships when essential for the protection of its security.[38]

The right of archipelagic sea lanes passage evolved from the right of transit passage through international straits. Like strait States, archipelagic States may designate sea lanes and air routes for the 'continuous and expeditious passage of foreign ships and aircraft through or over its archipelagic waters and the adjacent territorial sea'.[39] But while article 52(1) UNCLOS guarantees the right of innocent passage through archipelagic waters to 'ships of all States', article 53(2) simply states that 'all ships and aircraft enjoy the right of archipelagic sea lanes passage' in such sea lanes and air routes as the archipelagic State may designate. Similar to the designation of sea lanes and traffic separation in international straits, an archipelagic State's designation and substitution of sea lanes and traffic separation schemes in archipelagic waters also require approval from the IMO.[40] An archipelagic State that chooses not to designate sea lanes and air routes is deemed to have consented to the enjoyment by all ships and aircraft of the right of archipelagic sea lanes passage in all routes within archipelagic waters that are normally used for international navigation.[41]

II. SOVEREIGN RIGHTS

1. Contiguous Zone

The contiguous zone is the first of three zones that constitute areas beyond national jurisdiction where coastal States retain some sovereign rights over the territory. Article 33 sets out the limits of those rights for the contiguous zone. It specifies that the contiguous zone can extend no more than 24 nautical miles from the State's baselines (so 12 nautical miles from the edge of the territorial sea). Within the contiguous zone the State possesses the right to prevent infringement of 'customs, for school, immigration or sanitary laws' within its territory. This right does not allow for an exercise of domestic law over these issues, rather, the State possesses the right to prevent entry to the territorial sea (by declaring passage by the vessel to not be innocent) where the vessel in question would be violating the law should it enter. Within the contiguous zone the coastal State may also exercise a domestic criminal jurisdiction where violations of the law have already been committed within its territory.

2. Exclusive Economic Zone

The exclusive economic Zone (EEZ) is created in Part V of UNCLOS a zone within the oceans of exclusive economic rights for the coastal State. The EEZ regime allows

---

37 Article 52(1).
38 Article 52(2).
39 Article 53(1).
40 Article 53(9).
41 Article 53(12).

coastal States to establish an area of no greater than 200 nautical miles from the baseline where they gain:

> sovereign rights for the purpose of exploring and exploiting, conserving and managing the natural resources, whether living or nonliving, of the waters super adjacent to the seabed and of the seabed and its subsoil, and with regard to other activities for the economic exploitation and exploration of the zone, such as the production of energy from water currents and winds.[42]

In addition to this, the coastal State also gains the jurisdiction regarding marine scientific research, the establishment and use of artificial islands and other structures within the zone, and the protection and preservation of the marine environment. Article 73 also grants the coastal State with rights of law enforcement related to these sovereign rights within the EEZ.[43] Where the resourcing of the EEZ is situated in two or more EEZs and/or the high seas, UNCLOS requires that these resources be managed through regional or subregional mechanisms (e.g. see the Straddling Fish Stocks and Highly Migratory Fish Stocks Agreement and varied regional fisheries management organisations).[44] Where the EEZ of coastal States would overlap, or neighbouring coastal States cannot agree on the delimitation line, article 74 requires an equitable solution, with options for dispute settlement procedures provided in Part XV of UNCLOS if an agreement cannot be reached.[45] Outside of these specific economic rights the EEZ functions in the same manner as the high seas.[46]

3. Continental Shelf

Part VI of the UNCLOS sets out the rights of States over the continental shelf. The continental shelf is the area of the ocean floor seabed and subsoil. Under ordinary circumstances, the continental shelf of the State, much like the EEZ, is limited to a maximum of 200 nautical miles from the baselines of the State; however, article 76 provides grounds under which States can claim an extended continental shelf.[47] Annex II of UNCLOS establishes the Commission on the Limits of the Continental Shelf (CLCS) to assist with the application of the dense rules contained within article 76.[48] The continental shelf grants similar sovereign rights to the coastal State that the EEZ does, except over the resources contained within the seabed rather than within the ocean.[49] Furthermore, while the EEZ needs to be claimed, the continental shelf is considered an inherent right of the coastal State as an extension of the landed territorial.[50]

---

42 Article 56(1)(a).

43 Article 73.

44 Articles 63 and 64.

45 Article 74(2).

46 Article 58.

47 Article 76.

48 Annex II.

49 Article 77.

50 *North Sea Continental Shelf (Federal Republic of Germany v Denmark; Federal Republic of Germany v Netherlands)* [1969] ICJ Reports 3 (International Court of Justice) [43].

III. BEYOND NATIONAL JURISDICTION

1. *The High Seas*

The high seas cover all of the areas of the oceans beyond the zones detailed above (and the EEZ for noneconomic purposes), with it being clear that any claims of sovereignty will be considered invalid over this zone. Article 87 sets out the freedoms that are enjoyed by all States and vessels when on the high seas. These include freedom of navigation and overflight;[51] freedom to lay submarine cables and pipelines (subject to continental shelf restrictions);[52] freedom to construct artificial islands and other installations (subject to international law in particular continental shelf restrictions);[53] freedom of fishing (subject to due regard for the interests of other States, and regulations set out in the Straddling Fish Stocks and Highly Migratory Fish Stocks Agreement or by regional fisheries management agencies);[54] and freedom of scientific research (subject to continental shelf restrictions and Part XIII of UNCLOS).[55]

Article 92 of the UNCLOS sets out that the jurisdiction[56] over a vessel shall belong exclusively to the State whose flag is being flown.[57] Flag States have duties including, but not limited to, maintaining a register of ships flying its flag, ensuring the seaworthiness of vessels, ensuring that vessels have all the appropriate equipment for safety of navigation, assuming jurisdiction of its domestic law over the vessel, and ensuring adequate crewing and labour standards on the vessel and that all crew have appropriate qualifications.[58] This also includes the assumption of criminal jurisdiction over incidences of navigation caused by vessels flying their flag.[59] The high seas section of UNCLOS also sets out the various grounds of jurisdiction in which government or warships may engage in various activities such as the prevention of piracy, suppression of slave trafficking, and unauthorised radio broadcasting.[60] It also contains the obligation of all vessels to render assistance to those in distress within their vicinity.[61] Part VII of UNCLOS also sets out that warships and government vessels on non-commercial service have immunity from the jurisdiction of any State other than the flag State.[62]

---

51 UNCLOS (n 2) article 87(1)(a), (b).

52 Article 87(1)(c).

53 Ibid.

54 Article 87(1)(e).

55 Article 87(1)(f).

56 On jurisdiction, see González Hauck and Milas, § 8, in this textbook.

57 Article 92.

58 Article 94.

59 Article 97.

60 Articles 100–107, 99, 109.

61 Article 98.

62 Articles 95, 96.

2. The Area

The 'Area' is to the high seas as the continental shelf is to the EEZ. It is the subsoil and seabed in the areas beyond national jurisdiction,[63] and is addressed in Part XI and a separate implementing agreement related to Part XI. Part XI sets up the area as part of the common heritage of all humankind,[64] requiring that any exploitation of resources contained within the area to be used for the betterment and benefit of all peoples.[65] With this in mind, UNCLOS also set up the International Seabed Authority (ISA) to govern the activities being undertaken within this zone.[66] To date no commercial exploitation of resources contained within the Area has been deemed viable.

IV. DISPUTE SETTLEMENT

UNCLOS gives States an opportunity to settle their disputes by any peaceful means of their choice.[67] This system has been described to be 'unusual in public international law', since dispute settlement in most other instances depends on whether States agree to submit their dispute to an international court or tribunal.[68] If States do not agree on a mode of dispute settlement, the procedures outlined in Part XV become applicable to such disputes, provided that recourse to further procedures is not excluded.[69] Among these procedures are those that entail binding decisions under Part XV, section 2, namely (1) the International Tribunal for the Law of the Sea, established in accordance with Annex VI of UNCLOS; (2) the International Court of Justice, whose Statute is annexed to the Charter of the United Nations; (3) an arbitral tribunal constituted in accordance with Annex VII of UNCLOS (also known as a compulsory arbitration); and (4) a special tribunal constituted in accordance with Annex VIII of UNCLOS (also known as a special arbitration) for disputes over fisheries, the protection and preservation of the marine environment, marine scientific research, navigation, and marine vessel pollution and dumping.[70]

D. CONTEMPORARY CHALLENGES

I. ENVIRONMENT AND BIODIVERSITY

Part XII of UNCLOS deals with the protection of the marine environment. Specifically, article 237 maintains the ability of States to enter into further agreements relating to the protection and preservation of the marine environment, provided that

---

63 Article 1(1).
64 Article 136.
65 Article 140.
66 Article 156.
67 Article 280.
68 Donald R Rothwell and Tim Stephens, *The International Law of the Sea* (Hart 2010) 439.
69 Article 281(1).
70 Article 287(1).

these agreements are 'concluded in furtherance of the general principles and objectives of this Convention'. This provision enables States to address marine environmental concerns at a regional level. Regional agreements under article 237 have been described as a 'significant source of further development of the law of the sea'.[71]

The proliferation of regional agreements may undermine the near-universal consensus achieved in UNCLOS. Boyle argues that 'fragmentation is an inherent risk in any system of law built on the consent of States'.[72] Yet he also writes that there has been no real basis to suggest that regional cooperation has critically weakened UNCLOS; the opposite is actually true. In the context of the South China Sea, for example, the lack of a specific regional seas convention has meant that the implementation of Part XII of UNCLOS relies heavily on the benevolence or goodwill of South China Sea littoral States. This non-committal and evasive arrangement among the littoral States exposes the South China Sea to the risk of serious and long-term marine environmental damage.[73]

In 2017, the UN General Assembly passed Resolution 72/249 in order to elaborate the text of another international legally binding instrument under UNCLOS on the conservation and sustainable use of marine biological diversity of areas beyond national jurisdiction (BBNJ).[74] The BBNJ agenda includes marine genetic resources, marine protected areas, environmental impact assessment, and capacity building and transfer of technology. Work towards this agenda is currently being done through an Intergovernmental Conference, whose proceedings have been stalled by the COVID-19 pandemic.

II. STATE SPONSORSHIP OF ACTIVITIES IN THE DEEP SEABED

Article 153 of UNCLOS provides that one of the ways in which activities for the exploration and exploitation of the deep seabed beyond national jurisdiction (which the UNCLOS refers to as the Area) may be carried out is when such activities are 'sponsored' by States Parties to the UNCLOS in accordance with the rules, regulations, and procedures of the ISA. 'Sponsorship' refers to the framework created by UNCLOS through which a State Party exercises 'control' over contractors with respect to activities in the Area 'by requiring [contractors] to comply with the provisions of [the Convention]'.[75]

---

71 Alan Boyle, 'Further Development of the Law of the Sea Convention: Mechanisms for Change' (2005) 54 ICLQ 563, 575.

72 Ibid.

73 Alexis Ian P Dela Cruz, 'A South China Sea Regional Seas Convention: Transcending Soft Law and State Goodwill in Marine Environmental Governance?' (2019) 6 Journal of Territorial and Maritime Studies 5, 23.

74 International legally binding instrument under the United Nations Convention on the Law of the Sea on the conservation and sustainable use of marine biological diversity of areas beyond national jurisdiction, UN Doc A/RES/72/249 (24 December 2017).

75 Ximena Hinrichs Oyarce, 'Sponsoring States in the Area: Obligations, Liability and the Role of Developing States' (2018) 95 Marine Policy 317.

> **BOX 15.5** Example: State Sponsorship
>
> Nauru is currently one of four Pacific Island States which use the power of sponsorship in order to generate revenue. In 2015, Nauru passed legislation requiring contractors to pay a sponsorship application fee of US\$ 15,000, an annual administration fee of US\$ 20,000, and 'Seabed Mineral recovery payments' based on a percentage of the still undetermined 'market value of the metal content contained in the Seabed Minerals to be extracted by the Sponsored Party through the Seabed Mineral Activities'. But as the ISA is expected to collect royalties under a forthcoming Mining Code and prospective sponsoring States scramble to attract seabed mining contractors, it is unlikely that Nauru would be able to collect substantive payments from sponsorship under the Convention.[76]

III. ISLANDS AND SEA LEVEL RISE

Article 121(1) UNCLOS defines an island as 'a naturally formed area of land, surrounded by water, which is above water at high tide'. Under article 121(2), islands generate an entitlement to the full suite of maritime zones in UNCLOS (territorial sea, contiguous zone, EEZ, and continental shelf). As the worsening effects of the ongoing climate crisis melt polar ice caps,[77] islands are expected to bear significant impacts from rising sea levels. While large areas of continental landmasses and islands could potentially submerge underwater as a result of sea level rise, small islands and their populations are particularly vulnerable. One possible legal scenario is that the submergence of land areas could lead to an interpretation that an island would also lose entitlement to maritime zones. Article 121(3) seems to lend support to such an interpretation in favour of loss of maritime entitlement.[78] That provision states that islands which are 'rocks' that 'cannot sustain human habitation or economic life of their own shall have no exclusive economic zone or continental shelf'.

In August 2021, the member States of the Pacific Islands Forum (PIF) published the Declaration on Preserving Maritime Zones in the Face of Climate Change-Related Sea Level Rise (Declaration on Sea Level Rise).[79] In it, the PIF declared that UNCLOS 'imposes no affirmative obligation to keep baselines and outer limits of maritime zones under review nor to update charts or lists of geographical coordinates once deposited with the Secretary-General of the United Nations'. The Declaration

---

76 Isabel Feichtner, 'Sharing the Riches of the Sea: The Redistributive and Fiscal Dimension of Deep Seabed Exploitation' (2019) 30 EJIL 601, 631.

77 On international climate change law, see Viveros-Uehara, § 17, in this textbook.

78 Kate Purcell, *Geographical Change and the Law of the Sea* (OUP 2019) 260–61.

79 Pacific Islands Forum, 'Declaration on Preserving Maritime Zones in the Face of Climate Change-related Sea-Level Rise' <www.forumsec.org/2021/08/11/declaration-on-preserving-maritime-zones-in-the-face-of-climate-change-related-sea-level-rise/> accessed 18 June 2023.

also records the official PIF position that 'maintaining maritime zones established in accordance with the Convention, and rights and entitlements that flow from them, notwithstanding climate change-related sea level rise, is supported by both the Convention and the legal principles underpinning it'. But whether maritime entitlements should be preserved or contract as a consequence of sea level rise remains 'very much an open issue'.[80]

E. CONCLUSION

In this chapter, we have provided an outline of some of the most salient features of the law of the sea as a specialised discipline of public international law. It offered an overview of the significant provisions of the Law of the Sea Convention, which since its adoption in 1982 has been regarded as a 'Constitution for the Oceans'.[81] While UNCLOS bears the features of a constitution (such as dispute settlement), the disaggregated character of authority at the international level means that tensions will continue to arise between those constitutional features and the sovereignty that States often invoke as a doctrine that protects often questionable acts from external scrutiny and accountability.

BOX 15.6 Further Readings and Further Resources

Further Readings

- N Klein, *Judging the Law of the Sea* (OUP 2022)

- S Ranganathan, 'Decolonization and International Law: Putting the Ocean on the Map' (2021) 23 JHIL 161–83

Further Resources

- I Papanicolopulu (ed), *Gender and the Law of the Sea* (Brill 2019)

- I Braverman and ER Johnson (eds), *Blue Legalities: The Life and Laws of the Sea* (Duke UP 2020)

---

§ § §

---

80 David Freestone and Duygu Çiçek, *Legal Dimensions of Sea Level Rise: Pacific Perspectives* (World Bank Group 2021) 35 <http://elibrary.worldbank.org/doi/book/10.1596/35881> accessed 29 June 2021.

81 Tommy TB Koh, 'A Constitution for the Oceans' (*Speech*, 6 December 1982) <www.un.org/depts/los/convention_agreements/texts/koh_english.pdf> accessed 13 August 2023.

CHAPTER 16
INTERNATIONAL ENVIRONMENTAL LAW
ABBAS POORHASHEMI

BOX 16.1 Required Knowledge and Learning Objectives

Required knowledge: Sources of International Law, International Human Rights Law

Learning objectives: Understanding the essential elements of the foundation and emergence of IEL as a new branch of public international law; the sources of IEL; ecological challenges facing the international community; the relationship between environment, sustainable development and preservation of the global climate; the importance of international cooperation and collaboration to address environmental challenges.

BOX 16.2 Interactive Exercises

Access *interactive exercises for this chapter*[1] by positioning your smartphone camera at the dot-filled box, also known as a QR code.

Figure 16.1 QR code referring to interactive exercises.

A. INTRODUCTION

The relationship between humans and the environment has been discussed and investigated from different points of view. Many jurists disagree about whether this relationship can be examined from a legal point of view, and some even go so far as to refer to international environmental law (IEL) as global ethics. But looking at the formation and development

---

1   https://openrewi.org/en-projects-project-public-international-law-international-environmental-law/.

DOI: 10.4324/9781003451327-19

of IEL in the last decades, it becomes clear that this field, as one of the branches of public international law, has been able to include principles and rules. Since the environment has no boundaries and all humanity is on a single ship called the Earth, any damage to this ship will cause the destruction and decay of the entire human society. In the shadow of the development and expansion of this legal field, the right to a healthy environment, the common heritage of humanity, the rights of future generations, and the right to development were crystallised as examples of environmental rights.

B. EMERGENCE OF INTERNATIONAL ENVIRONMENTAL LAW

The 'environment' comprises the air, water, and land in or around which people, animals, and plants live.[2] The environment is a balanced set of biotic and abiotic elements that surround a body and can interact with it. The concept of 'environment' includes (but is not limited to) spaces, resources, natural land, and marine environments, sites, day and night landscapes, air quality, living beings and biodiversity, biological processes, soils, and geodiversity. IEL is a body of international law concerned with protecting the global environment by applying legal norms and regulations that address transboundary, regional, or global environmental issues.[3]

IEL as a branch of public international law emerged in the 1970s. Although the conservation of some species of animals and plants dates back to the pre-1970s, the basis for the formation of international environmental law, in its modern concept, is the Stockholm Declaration of the United Nations Conference on the Human Environment in 1972 (Stockholm Declaration).[4] In general, IEL is historically divided into three periods.

I. FIRST GENERATION

The first generation began in the 18th century with the signing of bilateral agreements in the field of fisheries and marine life resources. The most important feature of this historical period is regionalism and the creation of contractual obligations between governments to protect a specific region or species. Examples of these treaties are the Treaty concerning the Regulation of Salmon Fishery in the Rhine River Basin on 30 June 1885,[5] the Paris

---

2 'Environment', *Cambridge Advanced Learner's Dictionary & Thesaurus* (CUP) <https://dictionary.cambridge.org/dictionary/english/environment> accessed 20 August 2023.

3 Alexandre Kiss and Dinah Shelton, *International Environmental Law* (Transnational Publishers 1991) 45–48; Laurence Boisson de Chazournes, 'La Protection de l'Environnement dans le Système des Nations Unies' in Jean-Pierre Cot, Alan Pellet, and Mathias Forteau (eds), *La Charte des Nations Unies: Commentaire Article par Article* (3rd edn, Economica 2005) 27; Abbas Poorhashemi, 'Emergence of "International Environmental Law": As a New Branch of International Public Law' (2020) 1(2) CIFILE Journal of International Law 33, 34.

4 'Declaration of the United Nations Conference on the Human Environment' UN Conference on the Human Environment (Stockholm 5–16 June 1972) (16 June 1972) UN Doc A/CONF.48/14/Rev. 1 3–5.

5 Treaty concerning the Regulation of Salmon Fishery in the Rhine River Basin (adopted 30 June 1885, entered into force 6 June 1886) SR 0.923.414.

Convention for the Protection of Birds Useful to Agriculture on 19 March 1902,[6] and the Treaty relating to the Boundary Waters and Questions arising along the Boundary between Canada and the United States done at Washington on 11 January 1909.[7]

II. SECOND GENERATION

Its expansion to other fields, including wildlife, rare and endangered plants and animal species, continued into the early 20th century. The 1960s, generally known as the decade of student movements, marked a turning point in the destructive process of modernity and addressed many fundamental issues, including environmental matters. Subsequently, environmental activists and scientists declared that if industrial progress continued the same way, the world would be destroyed. As a result, by the end of the decade and the beginning of the 1970s, States were forced to hold the Stockholm Conference.[8] The purpose of this conference was to pay attention to the world's environmental issues and their relationship with human rights, as well as to warn of the harmful effects of human activities on the environment. The Stockholm Conference recognises the right of development to be closely linked to the environment by identifying the right to a healthy environment as a fundamental human right.[9] Furthermore, by considering the establishment of international institutions, it integrated the process of global cooperation in the field of the environment. It provided the direction for the further development and evolution of the relevant international rules to protect the global environment.

BOX 16.3 Advanced: Outcome of the Stockholm Conference

As the main outcome of the conference, the Stockholm Declaration of 1972 recognised 26 principles of IEL. According to the declaration, environmental issues should be at the forefront of international concerns and marked the start of a dialogue between developed and developing countries on the link between economic growth, the pollution of the air, water, and oceans, and the well-being of people around the world.[10] Thereby, the Stockholm Declaration has strongly influenced the further development of international environmental law. Another important outcome of the conference was the establishment of an international

---

6 Convention for the Protection of Birds Useful to Agriculture (adopted 19 March 1902, entered into force 6 December 1905) SR 0.922.71.

7 Treaty Between the United States and Great Britain Relating to Boundary Waters between the United States and Canada (US and Great Britain) (11 January 1909) 36 Stat. 2448.

8 Ben Purvis, Yong Mao, and Darren Robinson, 'Three Pillars of Sustainability: In Search of Conceptual Origins' (2019) 14 Sustainability Science 681, 684.

9 Stockholm Declaration (n 4) principle 1: 'Man has the fundamental right to freedom, equality and adequate conditions of life, in an environment of a quality that permits a life of dignity and well-being'.

10 Stockholm Declaration (n 4).

body called the United Nations Environment Program (UNEP). UNEP is a UN-affiliated[11] environmental protection program that has been one of the most important pillars of environmental protection. One of the important tasks of UNEP is the Global Environmental Assessment, which publishes a collection annually that describes the state of the world's environment. UNEP is also coordinating and managing the world's environmental protection in cooperation with States worldwide.

After the Stockholm Conference, environmental protection became the subject of several treaties and declarations, which illustrate the willingness of the international community to protect the environment, encourage sustainable development, and attenuate the imbalance between the North and the South. These conventions accepted and ratified by States could be considered global responses to contemporary environmental problems. Moreover, international environmental treaties unite developed and developing countries by ensuring that developed countries 'assume their historical responsibility' for global environmental degradation.

III. THIRD GENERATION

The third generation of IEL began with the 1992 United Nations Conference on Environment and Development (Rio Conference) in Rio de Janeiro, Brazil.[12] In discussing the issue of the environment as a global problem, the Rio Conference stressed the need to coordinate the development process of countries with the protection of the environment and introduced environmental protection as an essential international issue for the next century. The 1992 Rio Declaration affirms that States should always be concerned with environmental preoccupations in economic development and industrial growth.[13] States should consider the 'principle of sustainable development' in the formulation of programmatic and ordinary laws, as well as in the drafting of bilateral or multilateral binding instruments. They should recognise the role of social groups and non-governmental organisations in protecting the national, regional, and global environment.[14]

Another development of IEL in this period is the organisation of the 2002 World Summit on Sustainable Development in Johannesburg.[15] The Conference announced the eight Millennium Development Goals for development, among them the promotion

---

11 On the United Nations, see Baranowska, Engström, and Paige, § 7.3, in this textbook.
12 'Rio Declaration on Environment and Development' UN Conference on Environment and Development (Rio de Janeiro 3–14 June 1992) (14 June 1992) UN Doc A/CONF.151/26/Rev.1 (Vol I) Annex I.
13 Ibid.
14 Ibid.
15 'Report of the World Summit on Sustainable Development' World Summit on Sustainable Development (Johannesburg 26 August–4 September 2002) UN Doc A/CONF.199/20*.

of environmental sustainability. In 2012, the international community met again in Rio de Janeiro to review the 20-year achievements of the Rio Conference. This Rio + 20 Conference, while emphasising the commitments made at the Rio Conference of 1992, sought to introduce a new type of engagement in which businesses, governments, and civil society are vital leaders for protecting the global environment. One of the most significant steps toward achieving sustainable development in this decade (from Johannesburg 2002 to Rio 2012) was identifying the causes of recession and economic crisis in the previous decade and combining economic issues with environmental criteria.

Another remarkable event in this period is the 2030 Agenda for Sustainable Development.[16] The purpose of this agenda is a plan of action for sustainable development strengthening universal peace, and eradicating poverty. The 17 Sustainable Development Goals and 169 targets demonstrate the scale and ambition of this new universal Agenda. It seeks to build on the Millennium Development Goals and complete what these did not achieve. It aims to realise the human rights of all and achieve gender equality and the empowerment of all women and girls. The agenda creates a balance between the three dimensions of sustainable development: economy, society, and environment.

The 2015 Paris Agreement on climate change[17] is another significant collective initiative by the international community to address climate change.[18] The agreement aims to limit global warming to less than 2°C above pre-industrial levels and strives to limit temperature increase to 1.5°C. The United Nations Human Rights Council, on 8 October 2021,[19] adopted a resolution recognising the human right to a clean, healthy, and sustainable environment as an essential human right. While this right is already recognised in more than 150 national jurisdictions, its international recognition paves the way for its effective incorporation into international law and strengthened implementation at the national and international levels.

C. SOURCES OF INTERNATIONAL ENVIRONMENTAL LAW

IEL borrows traditional sources from public international law. Some of the leading environmental conventions are:

- *Climate change*: Vienna Convention for the Protection of the Ozone Layer (1985); Montreal Protocol (1987); United Nations Framework Convention on Climate Change (UNFCCC) (1992); Kyoto Protocol (1997); 2015 Paris Agreement on climate change.

---

16 UNGA Res 70/1 (25 September 2015) UN Doc A/RES/70/1.
17 Paris Agreement (adopted 12 December 2015, entered into force 4 November 2016) 3156 UNTS 79.
18 On international climate change law, see Viveros-Uehara, § 17, in this textbook.
19 UNHRC Res 48/14 'Mandate of the Special Rapporteur on the Promotion and Protection of Human Rights in the Context of Climate Change' (8 October 2021) UN Doc A/HRC/RES/48/14.

- *Environmental accidents and civil protection*: Helsinki Convention on Industrial Accidents (1992); Barcelona Convention (1976); Helsinki Convention on the Baltic Sea (1992); OSPAR Convention (1992); Bonn Agreement (1983); Lisbon Agreement (1990); Convention on the Protection of the Black Sea Against Pollution, Bucharest, (1992); Helsinki Convention on Industrial Accidents (1992).
- *Biotechnology and chemicals*: Cartagena Biosafety Protocol (2000); Stockholm Convention on Persistent Organic Pollutants (2001); Rio Convention on Biological Diversity (1992) and its Supplementary Protocol on Liability and Redress (2010); Rotterdam Convention on Prior Informed Consent (1998); Minamata Convention on Mercury (2013).
- *Human rights and environment*: Aarhus Convention on access to information, public participation in decision making, and access to justice in environmental matters (1998); Protocol on Pollutant Release and Transfer Registers (2009); the Espoo Convention on Environmental Impact Assessment (1991); Regional Agreement on Access to Information, Public Participation and Justice in Environmental Matters in Latin America and the Caribbean (Escazú, Costa Rica, 2018).
- *Biodiversity*: Convention on Wetlands of International Importance, Ramsar (1971); Convention on International Trade in Endangered Species of Wild Fauna and Flora (CITES Convention) (1973); Bonn Convention on the Conservation of Migratory Species (CMS) (1979); Convention for the Protection of Vertebrate Animals Used for Experimental and Other Scientific Purposes (1986); Bern Convention on European Wildlife and Habitats (1979); Convention on Biological Diversity CBD (1992); International Tropical Timber Agreement (ITTA) (1994); Agreement on the conservation of African-Eurasian Migratory Waterbirds (AEWA-CMS) (1995); Alpine Convention (1991); Cartagena Protocol on Biosafety (2003); Convention for the Conservation of Antarctic Marine Living Resources (1980); Protocol on Access to Genetic Resources and the Fair and Equitable Sharing of the Benefits arising from Their Utilization, Nagoya (2010); and Agreement on the Protection and Sustainable Development of the Prespa Park Area (2010).
- *Water protection*: Barcelona Convention (1976) and its protocols; Bonn Agreement (1983); Danube River Basin Convention (1987); Helsinki Convention on Watercourses and International Lakes (1992); OSPAR Convention (1992); Convention on the Protection of the Black Sea Against Pollution, Bucharest (1992); Helsinki Convention on the Baltic Sea (1992); Convention on the Protection of the Rhine (1999).[20]
- *Non-binding international instruments*: United Nations Conference on the Human Environment, 5–16 June 1972, Stockholm; the World Charter for Nature of 1982; Rio Declaration on Environment and Development (1992); Agenda 21 UNCED, 1992; United Nations Millennium Development Goals (2000); Johannesburg Declaration (2002); Rio+20 Declaration (2012); Agenda 2030 for Sustainable Development (2015) and the 17 Sustainable Development Goals (SDGs).

Although these conventions have been signed, accepted, and ratified by the majority of the States, the commitments made by the States seem minimalist and insufficient concerning the gravity of problems and challenges facing the development of

---

20 Convention on the Protection of the Rhine [2000] OJ L289/31.

international environmental law. Even though soft law[21] is not binding, it has a crucial impact on the development of IEL. The most significant examples of these sources are the 1972 Stockholm Declaration, the 1982 Universal Charter of Nature, the 1992 Rio Declaration, and Agenda 2030 for Sustainable Development.

D. PRINCIPLES OF INTERNATIONAL ENVIRONMENTAL LAW

Principles of IEL are the basic ideas for the development of this field of law. Some of them are enshrined in the multilateral environmental agreements, and in this case, they obtain clear meaning for the specific international environmental regime. However, even if a treaty does not explicitly recognise a principle in its text, the principle still can play a role in the interpretation and development of the treaty. General environmental principles also can supplement specific rules and express gap-filling functions.[22]

I. PRINCIPLE OF SOVEREIGNTY OVER NATURAL RESOURCES AND RESPONSIBILITY NOT TO CAUSE TRANSBOUNDARY ENVIRONMENTAL DAMAGE

The sovereignty of States in IEL has two bases: one is to recognise the sovereignty of States in the use of their natural resources, and the other is not to cause harm to other territories under the control of other States or areas that are not under the control of States, such as the high seas. The turning point in the principle of sovereignty is in article 21 of the 1972 Stockholm Declaration,[23] which, with a slight modification, was contained in the second principle of the Rio 1992 Declaration, which states:

> States have, in accordance with the Charter of the United Nations and the principles of international law, the sovereign right to exploit their own resources pursuant to their own environmental and developmental policies, and the responsibility to ensure that activities within their jurisdiction or control do not cause damage to the environment of other States or of areas beyond the limits of national jurisdiction.[24]

In the *Trail Smelter* case (*United States v Canada*) of 16 April 1938 and 11 March 1941, the Tribunal found that

> under the principles of international law, as well as of the law of the United States, no State has the right to use or permit the use of its territory in such a manner as to

---

21 On soft law, see Lima, Kunz, and Castelar Campos, § 6.4, in this textbook.

22 Maksim Lavrik 'Customary Norms, General Principles of International Environmental Law, and Assisted Migration as a Tool for Biodiversity Adaptation to Climate Change' (2022) 4 Jus Cogens 99.

23 Stockholm Declaration (n 4).

24 Rio Declaration (n 12).

cause injury by fumes in or to the territory of another or the properties or persons therein, when the case is of serious consequence, and the injury is established by clear and convincing evidence.[25]

II. PRINCIPLE OF COOPERATION

The principle of cooperation is a customary obligation[26] and one of the inseparable principles of the Charter of the United Nations.[27] It is one of the features of contemporary international law. The principle of cooperation is binding in accordance with the Charter of the United Nations. Protection of the global environment is beyond the capacity of one or more States. It requires the international community's cooperation to prevent, reduce, and eliminate the harmful effects of environmental degradation and pollution. According to the principle of cooperation, States have a duty to work together in all circumstances and in good faith to protect the environment.[28] International cooperation could be considered in various fields, such as information exchange, technology transfer, financial resources, participation in international conferences, and even emergency assistance through bilateral or multilateral agreements.

III. PRINCIPLE OF SUSTAINABLE DEVELOPMENT

The principle of sustainable development is confirmed in many international legal instruments, including the Rio Declaration of 1992. According to the principle, States should review national policies and plans for environment and development to enact effective laws and regulations that use economic instruments where appropriate and establish and strengthen institutional structures and procedures to integrate environmental and development issues into all decision-making spheres fully. In addition, the integration of environmental, social, and economic policies also requires transparency and broad public participation in decision-making by the authorities.[29] The concept of sustainable development is an evolutionary process that meets the current generation's needs without diminishing the ability of the next generation to meet their needs – in other words, to provide an opportunity for everyone to live forever on the planet. Today sustainable development is one of the most fundamental issues of IEL.[30] However, implementing sustainable development confronted some challenges in its forms and contents. Its content lacks a comprehensive approach for including

---

25 *Trail Smelter Case (US v Canada)* (1938; 1941) 3 RIAA 1905.

26 On customary law, see Stoica, § 6.2, in this textbook.

27 Charter of the United Nations (signed 26 June 1945, entered into force 24 October 1945) 1 UNTS XVI articles 1, 11, and 13.

28 Neil Craik, 'The Duty to Cooperate in the Customary Law of Environmental Impact Assessment' (2020) 69 ICLQ 239, 243.

29 Abbas Poorhashemi, 'Opportunities and Challenges Facing the Future Development of International Environmental Law' in Hüseyin Gökçekuş and Youssef Kassem (eds), *Climate Change, Natural Resources and Sustainable Environmental Management* (Springer International 2022) 44.

30 Virginie Barral, *Le Développement Durable en Droit International: Essai sur les Incidences Juridiques d'une Norme Évolutive* (Bruylant 2016) 37.

indigenous people, local cultures, good governance, consuming resources, producing goods and services, freedom of expression, employment, and identifying the roots of poverty and gender discrimination.

IV. PRINCIPLE OF PREVENTION

Environmental degradation and pollution prevention are regarded as the 'golden rule' in IEL based on economic and ecological reasons.[31] For instance, extinction of plant or animal species, soil erosion, loss of human life, and leakage of pollutants into the sea create irreparable damage in a way that, even when the damage can be compensated, restoring them to their previous state is not possible. The prevention principle in IEL exists to prevent national and transboundary harm due to the activities of States. This principle forms the basis of many international environmental agreements and conventions, such as the Basel Convention on the Control of Transboundary Movements of Hazardous Wastes and Their Disposal (1989).[32] The principle aims to minimise hazardous waste generation and combat illegal dumping.

V. PRECAUTIONARY PRINCIPLE

The precautionary principle imposes a duty on States to prevent environmental damage. Under this rule, a State may be obligated to take precautionary measures to prevent damage within its jurisdiction. The number of international environmental treaties confirms this duty of stats. In this perspective, article 3 of the United Nations Framework Convention on Climate Change (UNFCC) states that:

> The Parties should take precautionary measures to anticipate, prevent or minimize the causes of climate change and mitigate its adverse effects. Where there are threats of serious or irreversible damage, lack of full scientific certainty should not be used as a reason for postponing such measures, taking into account that policies and measures to deal with climate change should be cost-effective so as to ensure global benefits at the lowest possible cost.[33]

VI. PRINCIPLE OF NOTIFICATION

The principle of notification is one of the basic principles that can be traced back to the International Court of Justice from the 1949 *Corfu Strait* case[34] and other international sources such as environmental treaties and agreements. According to this principle, States must timely notify and share relevant information with every State that may be

---

31 Nicolas de Sadeleer, *Environmental Principles: From Political Slogans to Legal Rules* (2nd edn, OUP 2020) 85–132.

32 Basel Convention on the control of transboundary movements of hazardous wastes and their disposal (adopted 22 March 1989, entered into force 5 May 1992) 1673 UNTS 57.

33 United Nations Framework Convention on Climate Change (adopted 9 May 1992, entered into force 21 March 1994) 1771 UNTS 107 article 3.

34 *Corfu Channel Case* (*UK v Albania*) (Merits) [1949] ICJ Rep 4.

adversely affected by its environmental activities. States shall immediately notify other States of any natural disasters or other emergencies likely to produce transboundary effects. In addition, notification is fundamental when there is a nuclear accident and transboundary pollution.[35] This obligation is primarily related to international cooperation based on a system of information and prior consultation and notification to achieve optimum use of natural resources without causing damage to the legitimate interests of other States.

VII. POLLUTER-PAYS PRINCIPLE

The polluter-pays principle is set out in many national and international regulations.[36] According to this principle, polluters must bear the costs resulting from measures to prevent, reduce, and fight pollution. This principle was adopted by the Organisation for Economic Co-operation and Development (OECD) in 1972[37] as an economic principle for allocating the costs associated with pollution control. The Declaration of the United Nations Conference on Environment and Development in 1992 recognised this principle as one of the 27 guiding principles for future sustainable development. According to Principle 16 of the declaration:

> National authorities should endeavor to promote the internalization of environmental costs and the use of economic instruments, taking into account the approach that the polluter should, in principle, bear the cost of pollution, with due regard to the public interest and without distorting international trade and investment.[38]

VIII. PRINCIPLE OF COMMON BUT DIFFERENTIATED RESPONSIBILITIES (CBDR)

According to the principle of common but differentiated responsibilities (CBDR), all States are responsible for protecting the environment but with different types of responsibilities. Developed countries have a more significant burden due to their historical contributions to environmental degradation. As a result, they should assist developing countries with transferring new technologies and supporting them financially. According to Principle 7 of the 1992 Rio Declaration,[39] States should cooperate in a spirit of partnership to conserve, protect, and restore the health and integrity of the Earth's ecosystem. Given the diversity of roles played in global environmental degradation, States have common but differentiated responsibilities.

---

35 Max Valverde Soto, 'General Principles of International Environmental Law' (1996) 3 ILSA Journal of International & Comparative Law 193.

36 Alexandra Aragão, 'Polluter-Pays Principle' in Javier Cremades and Cristina Hermida (eds), *Encyclopedia of Contemporary Constitutionalism* (Springer 2022).

37 OECD, 'Recommendation of the Council on Guiding Principles Concerning International Economic Aspects of Environmental Policies' (26 May 1972) OECD/LEGAL/0102.

38 Ibid, principle 16.

39 Rio Declaration (n 12).

Developed countries recognise their responsibility in the international effort to promote sustainable development, given their societies' pressures on the global environment and the technologies and financial resources at their disposal.[40] The principle recognises that developed countries have benefited from exploiting natural resources and using fossil fuels, resulting in a disproportionate share of greenhouse gas emissions in the atmosphere.[41] In this perspective, the principle was later included in the 1997 Kyoto Protocol,[42] which sets binding emission reduction targets for developed countries. Based on the Kyoto Protocol, developed countries are responsible for reducing their greenhouse gas emissions by an average of 5% below 1990 levels over the period 2008–2012. In contrast, developing countries were not subject to binding emissions reduction targets but were expected to take voluntary actions to address climate change.

E. GLOBAL ENVIRONMENTAL PROBLEMS AND CHALLENGES

I. STATE SOVEREIGNTY

Regardless of the concept of the sovereignty of States in international law, one of the main obstacles to the development of IEL is the non-acceptance of governments to delegate or limit their sovereignty in favour of environmental organisations. Another conflict also exists between developed and developing countries in enforcing regulations. For instance, according to the principle of CBDR, developed countries should take additional actions such as transferring technologies or contributing finance to developing countries, but this principle is not respected properly.[43]

II. DIVERSITY OF SOURCES

Another substantive challenge to developing international law is the diversity of binding and non-binding sources, which is caused confusion and vagueness in the implementation of international law. The variety of binding and non-binding sources creates a significant challenge for developing and implementing IEL. The absence of a globally applicable environmental treaty, the limited decisions of international courts, and the unclear customary law status of environmental regulations exacerbate these challenges. IEL has fallen between the development of general environmental principles, mainly enunciated in non-binding international instruments (such as the 1992 Rio Declaration on Environmental and Development) and binding international

---

40 Common but differentiated responsibilities.

41 Thomas Deleuil, 'The Common but Differentiated Responsibilities Principle: Changes in Continuity after the Durban Conference of the Parties' (2012) 21 RECIEL 271.

42 Kyoto Protocol to the United Nations Framework Convention on Climate Change (adopted 11 December 1997, entered into force 16 February 2005) 2303 UNTS 162.

43 Poorhashemi (n 29).

environmental treaties, which are nevertheless sector-specific in their orientation, or even when comprehensive in their approach to (several) environmental threats, are regional in their geographical scope of application.

III. INSUFFICIENT GUARANTEE OF IMPLEMENTATION

Many international rules and regulations, including multilateral treaties, are confronted with a deficiency of compliance mechanisms to protect the environment. The failure to provide financial mechanisms in international environmental treaties is one of the principal points of concern of the international community to implement environmental obligations, especially in developing countries.

IV. INSTITUTIONAL CHALLENGE

Global environmental protection has prompted international governmental organisations to participate in environmental conservation efforts since the 1970s. As subjects of international law, these organisations have an important responsibility in this field. The Stockholm Conference reflected the growing recognition of the need for global environmental governance. It led to the establishment of United Nations Environment Programme (UNEP)[44] as the principal body and executive for international environmental protection. However, despite its establishment, UNEP has faced limitations and challenges in effectively protecting the global environment. As environmental challenges continue to intensify and evolve, there is a growing need to assess the feasibility of creating a new organisation specifically dedicated to environmental protection, such as the World Environment Organization (WEO). Creating a WEO could fill the gaps in the existing framework by providing a dedicated institution solely focused on global environmental issues. This organisation can be given resources, authority, and a clear mission to address serious environmental challenges in different sectors and regions. It can also foster stronger coordination and cooperation between States, international organisations, and public participation.[45]

V. EMERGENCE OF ENVIRONMENTAL CHALLENGES IN THE WORLD

From the early 1990s, environmental threats became alarming: the destruction of the stratospheric ozone layer, climate change, sea level rise, ecosystem acidification, sheer loss of biological diversity, overexploitation of marine resources, increased technological risks, and so forth. The emergence of increasingly unpredictable risks enticed the authorities to base their policy on an anticipatory model. This model can be linked to understanding the limitations of scientific expertise. While prevention is based on

---

44 UNGA Res 2997 (XXVII) (15 December 1972) UN Doc A/RES/27/2997.

45 For more about reforming UNEP, see Steffen Bauer, 'Strengthening the United Nations' in Robert Falkner (ed), *The Handbook of Global Climate and Environment Policy* (John Wiley & Sons 2013).

a particular risk, the new model is distinguished by the intrusion of uncertainty.[46] The world is confronted with several environmental problems and challenges, such as climate change;[47] global warming; air, water, soil, and light pollution; resource depletion; massive disappearance of plant and animal species; the depletion of biodiversity; and other environmental degradations. These challenges could have significant implications for human health, social stability, and economic development.

F. CONCLUSION

Global challenges need global solutions; in this perspective, international cooperation between States plays a vital role. Economic growth and increasing technological advances in the contemporary period have caused real damage to the environment. States should be willing to participate actively in drafting, signing, ratifying, and implementing new treaties on environmental issues such as water pollution and climate change in a sustainable way. It is also crucial to recognise the right of public participation in the environmental decision–making process and implementation. The right to 'environment' and right to 'economic development' as a 'human right' should be considered in the concept of sustainable development as a common concern of humanity. Now is the time for the international community to impose absolute responsibility or strict liability on States for any damage and harm to the environment at the national and international levels.

BOX 16.4 Further Readings and Further Resources

Further Readings

- L Duvic-Paoli, *The Prevention Principle in International Environmental Law* (CUP 2018)

- A Kiss and D Shelton, *Guide to International Environmental Law* (Martinus Nijhoff 2007)

- A Poorhashemi, 'Emergence of "International Environmental Law": As a New Branch of International Public Law' (2020) 1 (2) CIFILE Journal of International Law 33.

- P Sands and others, *Principles of International Environmental Law* (3rd edn, CUP 2018)

---

46 Nicolas de Sadeleer, 'The Principles of Prevention and Precaution in International Law: Two Heads of the Same Coin?' in Malgosia Fitzmaurice, David M Ong, and Panos Merkouris (eds), *Research Handbook on International Environmental Law* (Edward Elgar 2010).

47 On international climate change law, see Viveros-Uehara, § 17, in this textbook.

Further Resources

- UN Environment Programme, 'UNEP Training Manual on International Environmental Law' (2006) <https://wedocs.unep.org/20.500.11822/20599> accessed 11 December 2023

§ § §

17

CHAPTER 17
INTERNATIONAL CLIMATE CHANGE LAW

THALIA VIVEROS-UEHARA

BOX 17.1 Required Knowledge and Learning Objectives

Required knowledge: International Environmental Law; International Human Rights Law

Learning objectives: Understanding the multifaceted implications of climate change from a variety of perspectives; the core principles of international climate change law; the role of different stakeholders; and major implementation and oversight mechanisms.

BOX 17.2 Interactive Exercises

Access *interactive exercises for this chapter*[1] by positioning your smartphone camera at the dot-filled box, also known as a QR code.

Figure 17.1 QR code referring to interactive exercises.

A. INTRODUCTION

Today, compelling scientific evidence conclusively shows that the emission of greenhouse gases (GHG) into the atmosphere, a consequence of human activities, has warmed the climate at an unprecedented rate.[2] By altering the composition of the global atmosphere, such anthropogenic release of gases has induced a change in the state of the climate over

---

1   https://openrewi.org/en-projects-project-public-international-law-international-climate-change-law/.

2   IPCC, 'Summary for Policymakers' in Valérie Masson-Delmotte and others (eds), *Climate Change 2021: The Physical Science Basis. Contribution of Working Group I to the Sixth Assessment Report of the Intergovernmental Panel on Climate Change* (CUP 2021) 6.

DOI: 10.4324/9781003451327-20

extended periods, a phenomenon known as 'climate change'.[3] In its most recent Sixth
Assessment Report (AR6), the Intergovernmental Panel on Climate Change (IPCC) –
the lead scientific body on climate change – attests that climate change is already affecting
every region across the globe by altering the frequency and intensity of heatwaves, heavy
precipitations, droughts, and tropical cyclones.[4] Concerningly, the report's projection
about a continuous increase in the global surface temperature until mid-century has
become increasingly evident.[5] This claim has been further corroborated by a recent
update from the World Meteorological Organization (WMO) issued in May 2023.[6] The
WMO states that there is a 66% likelihood that the annual average global temperature,
measured near the Earth's surface, will exceed 1.5°C above pre-industrial levels for at least
one year between 2023 and 2027. In the face of such compelling evidence, it becomes
crucial to drastically reduce GHG emissions in the forthcoming decades.

The complexities of climate change extend beyond the simple correlation between
human-induced emissions and an amplified greenhouse effect – on which the IPCC
concentrated in its earliest reports.[7] This issue is intertwined with how current
socioeconomic and political systems function and distribute resources.[8] For instance,
while the richest 10% of the global population is responsible for half of all CO_2
emissions, the bottom 57% – those living below the World Bank poverty line –
generate only 16%.[9] These latter groups, often experiencing intersecting forms of social
exclusion due to their gender, race, or ethnicity, bear a disproportionate burden of
climate change impacts given their limited coping mechanisms and resources.[10] Indeed,
between 2010 and 2020, such populations suffered 15 times higher mortality from
climate-induced disasters than those in less vulnerable socioeconomic circumstances.[11]
Consequently, climate change – a 'wicked problem', as some have famously labelled it[12] –
demands deep and fast transformations not only in the environmental sphere but also in
how the current social, economic, and even political systems work.

---

3 Article 1.2 of the United Nations Framework Convention on Climate Change (adopted 9 May 1992, entered
  into force 21 March 1994) 1771 UNTS 107 (UNFCCC).
4 IPCC (n 2) 8.
5 Ibid 14.
6 WMO, 'Global Temperatures Set to Reach New Records in Next Five Years' (*World Meteorological Organization*,
  17 May 2023) <https://public.wmo.int/en/media/press-release/global-temperatures-set-reach-new-records-
  next-five-years> accessed 13 June 2023.
7 John T Houghton, Geoff J Jenkins, and Jim J Ephraums (eds), *Climate Change: The IPCC Scientific Assessment*
  (WMO and UNEP 1990) <www.ipcc.ch/site/assets/uploads/2018/03/ipcc_far_wg_I_full_report.pdf>
  accessed 1 August 2022.
8 Susana Borràs, 'Movimientos para la justicia climática global: replanteando el escenario internacional del cambio
  climático' (2016) 33 Relaciones Internacionales 97, 98.
9 Benedikt Bruckner and others, 'Impacts of Poverty Alleviation on National and Global Carbon Emissions'
  (2022) Nature Sustainability 1 <www.nature.com/articles/s41893-021-00842-z> accessed 2 March 2022.
10 Caroline Moser and others, *Pro-Poor Adaptation to Climate Change in Urban Centers: Case Studies of Vulnerability
   and Resilience in Kenya and Nicaragua* (World Bank 2010) <https://openknowledge.worldbank.org/
   handle/10986/3001> accessed 1 August 2022.
11 IPCC (n 2) 12.
12 Richard Lazarus, 'Super Wicked Problems and Climate Change: Restraining the Present to Liberate the Future'
   (2009) 94(5) Cornell Law Review 1153.

To confront this global problem, the international community responded by establishing a multilateral climate change regime.[13] Initiated by the 1990 United Nations General Assembly (UNGA) Resolution 45/212,[14] the United Nations Framework Convention on Climate Change (UNFCCC)[15] became the bedrock for contemporary international climate change law (ICCL). The UNFCCC serves as the foundational framework through which climate change has been comprehended and incorporated into the legal arena. It articulates the core concepts and principles related to climate change and provides a platform for other core instruments like the Kyoto Protocol[16] and the Paris Agreement. Together, these treaties form what is commonly referred to as the UN climate change regime. However, with the global temperature trajectory currently projected to surpass the catastrophic 2°C mark during this century, the efficacy of such regime is under scrutiny. This concern has been increasingly highlighted by young activists,[17] who have recently emerged as vocal advocates for a carbon-free world.

B. OVERVIEW OF THE LEGAL RESPONSE TO CLIMATE CHANGE

I. CONCEPTS

The core objective of ICCL, as established by article 2 of the UNFCCC, is 'to achieve . . . stabilisation of greenhouse gas concentrations in the atmosphere at a level that would prevent dangerous anthropogenic interference with the climate system'.[18] To accomplish this, much of ICCL spans two different sets of actions: mitigation and adaptation. On the one hand, human interventions aimed at mitigating climate change seek to reduce GHG emissions, including preserving carbon sinks such as wetlands and forests.[19] On the other hand, adaptation involves actions geared at adjusting to the actual or expected climate and its effects.[20]

---

13 Rosemary Gail Rayfuse and Shirley V Scott, 'Mapping the Impact of Climate Change on International Law' in Rosemary Gail Rayfuse and Shirley V Scott (eds), *International Law in the Era of Climate Change* (Edward Elgar 2012) 4.

14 United Nations Framework Convention on Climate Change (adopted 9 May 1992, entered into force 21 March 1994) 1771 UNTS 107 (UNFCCC).

15 UN General Assembly, 'Resolution 45/212 – Protection of Global Climate for Present and Future Generations of Mankind' (21 December 1990) <https://documents-dds-ny.un.org/doc/RESOLUTION/GEN/NR0/566/01/IMG/NR056601.pdf?OpenElement> accessed 1 August 2022.

16 Kyoto Protocol to the United Nations Framework Convention on Climate Change (adopted 11 December 1997, entered into force 16 February 2005) 2303 UNTS 162 (Kyoto Protocol).

17 Olivia Lai, '10 Young Climate Activists Leading the Way on Global Climate Action' (*Earth*, 12 August 2022) <https://earth.org/young-climate-activists-leading-the-way-on-global-climate-action/> accessed 19 December 2022.

18 Article 2 UNFCCC.

19 IPCC, 'Annex I: Glossary' in Valérie Masson-Delmotte and others (eds), *Global Warming of 1.5°C. An IPCC Special Report on the Impacts of Global Warming of 1.5°C above Pre-Industrial Levels and Related Global Greenhouse Gas Emission Pathways, in the Context of Strengthening the Global Response to the Threat of Climate Change, Sustainable Development, and Efforts to Eradicate Poverty* (CUP 2018) 554.

20 Ibid 542.

> ## BOX 17.3 Example: Climate Mitigation
>
> Oil-based road transportation is India's third-highest GHG-emitting sector, contributing about 13% of the country's total CO_2. To avoid 9.5 million tons of GHG from this sector, in 2022, the Green Climate Fund approved a project that will promote the use of electric vehicles, thereby supporting India's e-mobility transition.[21] Electric cars emit fewer GHG and air pollutants than petrol and diesel cars.[22]

> ## BOX 17.4 Example: Climate Adaptation
>
> Extreme floods and droughts are expected to intensify in Burundi, making the country's agricultural yield decline by 5%–25% in the coming decades.[23] To increase agricultural productivity and food security amidst such detrimental climatic projections, in 2020 the Green Climate Fund approved a project aimed at building farmers' resilience to climate change by promoting the adoption of agroecosystem management practices to conserve soil and water resources.[24]

However, while both mitigation and adaptation are central tenets of the UN climate regime, it was not until the Convention's second legally binding instrument, the 2015 Paris Agreement,[25] that the operationalisation of adaptation was enhanced, with the agreement establishing a global goal on adaptation.[26]

II. IMPLEMENTATION AND OVERSIGHT MECHANISMS

To fulfil its ultimate objective, the UNFCCC established a Conference of the Parties (COP) and a permanent Secretariat to facilitate State party negotiations.[27] Article 7 of the UNFCCC confers on the COP the status of the supreme body of the UNFCCC and the duty to keep its implementation under regular review.[28] The COP meets every year. The latest meeting (COP28) took place in Dubai, United Arab Emirates, from 30 November until 12 December 2023.[29]

---

21 'FP 186 – India E-Mobility Financing Program' (*Green Climate Fund*, n.d.) <www.greenclimate.fund/project/fp186> accessed 30 August 2022.

22 Paul Wolfram and others, 'Pricing Indirect Emissions Accelerates Low-Carbon Transition of US Light Vehicle Sector' (2021) 12(1) Nature Communications 7121.

23 'SAP017 – Climate Proofing Food Production Investments in Imbo and Moso Basins in the Republic of Burundi' (*Green Climate Fund*, n.d.) <www.greenclimate.fund/project/sap017> accessed 30 August 2022.

24 Ibid.

25 Paris Agreement (adopted 12 December 2015, entered into force 4 November 2016) 3156 UNTS.

26 Ibid article 7.

27 Benoit Mayer, *The International Law on Climate Change* (CUP 2018) 12.

28 Article 7 UNFCCC.

29 UN Climate Change, 'Conference of the Parties (COP)' (UNFCCC, n.d.) <https://unfccc.int/process/bodies/supreme-bodies/conference-of-the-parties-cop> accessed 13 January 2024.

The UNFCCC sets out the commitment for developed countries to provide financial resources to developing countries as an instrumental measure to advance climate action.[30] Because meeting the costs of mitigation and adaptation is instrumental for accomplishing the Convention's objectives, its parties agreed on establishing a financial mechanism and special funds to facilitate the flow of resources.[31] Special funds complement these primary mechanisms and support specific countries and projects.[32]

The UNFCCC also laid the foundation for oversight mechanisms to ensure implementation and compliance. Specifically, the Convention mandated States to periodically report on the progress of their mitigation and adaptation measures, serving as a general means for promoting accountability.[33] The Kyoto Protocol and the Paris Agreement incorporated this oversight model in their respective implementation frameworks.

III. PRINCIPLES

Principles form the bedrock of ICCL, with roots in general[34] and international environmental law.[35] These principles encompass the no-harm rule and the principle of common but differentiated responsibility (CBDR).[36] The no-harm rule, a fundamental tenet of international law, obliges States to ensure activities within their jurisdiction do not inflict harm on the environment of other States or areas beyond national jurisdiction.[37] The UNFCCC broadens the preventive essence of the no-harm rule, based on scientific certainty, to include *potential* harms.[38] The CBDR, initially codified in the Rio Declaration[39] and subsequently adopted by the UNFCCC,[40] acknowledges shared yet differing responsibilities among States for preventing harmful interference with the climate system. This principle considers both historical contributions to the

---

30 Article 4.3 UNFCCC.

31 UN Climate Change, 'Climate Finance' (*UNFCCC*, n.d.) <https://unfccc.int/topics/climate-finance/the-big-picture/climate-finance-in-the-negotiations/climate-finance#:~:text=The%20Financial%20Mechanism%20is%20accountable,and%20eligibility%20criteria%20for%20funding.&text=The%20Kyoto%20Protocol%-20also%20recognizes,activities%20by%20developing%20country%20Parties> accessed 1 August 2022.

32 Ibid.

33 Article 12 UNFCCC.

34 On the principles of public international law, see Eggett, § 6.3, in this textbook.

35 On the principles of international environmental law, see Poorhashemi, § 16, in this textbook.

36 Lavanya Rajamani and Jacob D Werksman, 'Climate Change' in Lavanya Rajamani and Jacqueline Peel (eds), *The Oxford Handbook of International Environmental Law* (2nd edn, OUP 2021) 493.

37 Erkki J Hollo, Kati Kulovesi, and Michael Mehling (eds), *Climate Change and the Law* (Springer Netherlands 2013) 16; *Case concerning Pulp Mills on the River Uruguay (Argentina v Uruguay)* (Judgment) [2010] ICJ Rep 14, 55 [197].

38 Article 3.3 UNFCCC.

39 Rio Declaration on Environment and Development 1992, Principle 7.

40 Cinnamon Carlarne, Kevin R Gray, and Richard Tarasofsky, 'International Climate Change Law: Mapping the Field' in Kevin R Gray, Richard Tarasofsky, and Cinnamon Carlarne (eds), *The Oxford Handbook of International Climate Change Law* (OUP 2016) 14.

problem and current capacities to respond, thus accounting for national and regional development priorities, objectives, and circumstances.[41]

IV. STAKEHOLDERS AND POLITICS

While States have traditionally led ICCL development, both intergovernmental organisations and non-State actors[42] have gained influence within the UNFCCC, participating actively in COPs.[43] Their rise in prominence has, directly or indirectly, impacted the trajectory of the UN climate change regime.[44] Currently, they are grouped into nine constituencies, including business and industry, indigenous peoples' organisations, municipal authorities, trade unions, and youth NGOs.[45]

The IPCC, established in 1988, is another key player of the UN climate change regime. This body of 195 governments provides scientific data on climate change, informing international climate negotiations.[46] To date, six assessment reports highlighting critical areas for climate action have been issued.[47] The work of the IPCC thereby constitutes an essential input for international climate change negotiations.

The varying interests and concerns colliding in the UNFCCC process, due to the diverse participants, expose the political complexities challenging ICCL. Three distinct perspectives on climate change have emerged amongst these actors.[48] Some, mainly European States and organisations, regard climate change primarily as an environmental issue, advocating for a reduction in GHG emissions.[49] Conversely, other entities, including non-European high-income countries like the US, approach climate change as an economic issue.[50] They support emissions reduction only when benefits exceed costs, prioritising economic growth and job creation. Global South countries and organisations, however, frame climate change as a matter of 'climate justice'.[51] Despite contributing minimally to the problem, these nations bear the brunt of its effects.[52]

---

41 Article 4.1 UNFCCC.

42 On the variety of actors of international law, see Engström, § 7, in this textbook.

43 Ronnie D Lipschutz and Corina McKendry, 'Social Movements and Global Civil Society' in John S Dryzek, Richard B Norgaard, and David Schlosberg (eds), *The Oxford Handbook of Climate Change and Society* (OUP 2018) 370.

44 Ibid.

45 UN Climate Change, 'Statistics on Admission' (*UNFCCC*, 2022) <https://unfccc.int/process-and-meetings/parties-non-party-stakeholders/non-party-stakeholders/statistics-on-non-party-stakeholders/statistics-on-admission> accessed 1 August 2022.

46 IPCC, 'About the IPCC' (*IPCC*, 2022) <www.ipcc.ch/about/> accessed 19 December 2022.

47 IPCC, 'Reports' (*IPCC*, 2022) <www.ipcc.ch/reports/> accessed 19 December 2022.

48 Daniel Bodansky, Jutta Brunnée, and Lavanya Rajamani, *International Climate Change Law* (OUP 2017) 4.

49 Council of the EU, 'EU Position for the UN Climate Change Conference in Paris: Council Conclusions' (*Council of the European Union*, 18 September 2015) <www.consilium.europa.eu/en/press-releases/2015/09/18/conclusions-un-climate-change-conference-paris-2015/> accessed 19 December 2022.

50 Bodansky and others (n 48) 5.

51 Brian Tokar, 'On the Evolution and Continuing Development of the Climate Justice Movement' in Tahseen Jafry (ed), *Routledge Handbook of Climate Justice* (Routledge 2019) 13; Paul Routledge, 'Translocal Climate Justice Solidarities' in John S Dryzek, Richard B Norgaard, and David Schlosberg (eds), *The Oxford Handbook of Climate Change and Society* (OUP 2018) 385.

52 Tokar (n 51) 20.

Therefore, they call on high-income countries, which have historically emitted the most GHGs, to acknowledge and assume their responsibilities for contributing significantly to climate change, including making reparations for its adverse effects.[53]

BOX 17.5 Advanced: For Small Island Developing States (SIDS), Climate Change is a Matter of Life and Death

SIDS are extremely vulnerable to climate change–induced hurricanes and sea level rise. They are low-lying territories (one-third of them lay on land less than 5 m above sea level)[54] highly dependent on food imports, and some are considered least developed countries.[55] Yet, SIDS contribute less than 1% of global GHG emissions. Given their distinctive vulnerability to climate change, SIDS have formed a coalition of States through which they have advanced several advocacy efforts to accelerate climate ambition and action. These efforts include the Malé Declaration on the Human Dimension of Global Climate Change signed in 2007; the Agreement for the Establishment of the Commission of Small Island States on Climate Change and International Law in 2021; and the drafting of a resolution adopted by the UNGA in 2023, which requested an Advisory Opinion on climate change from the International Court of Justice.[56]

C. EMERGENCE AND EVOLUTION OF THE INTERNATIONAL CLIMATE CHANGE TREATY REGIME

I. EMERGENCE OF THE UNFCCC

Early scientific research into climate change revealed rising atmospheric CO_2 levels during the 1960s.[57] Enhanced understanding of the issue in the subsequent decades led to the First World Climate Conference convened in Geneva under the WMO in 1979, resulting in an urgent appeal for nations to anticipate and mitigate potential climate changes harmful to humanity.[58] During the 1980s and 1990s, escalating environmental activism and political developments like the adoption of the 1987 Montreal Protocol

---

53 See, for example, 'LDC Chair's Reflections at the Thimphu Ambition Summit 2020' (*LDC Climate Change*, n.d.) <www.ldc-climate.org/thimphuambition-eventdetails/ldc-chairs-reflections/> accessed 19 December 2022.

54 Leila Mead, 'Small Islands, Large Oceans: Voices on the Frontlines of Climate Change' (*IISD*, 29 March 2021) <www.iisd.org/articles/deep-dive/small-islands-large-oceans-voices-frontlines-climate-change>accessed 30 August 2022.

55 Ibid.

56 'Vanuatu ICJ Initiative' <www.vanuatuicj.com/>accessed 18 July 2023.

57 Bodansky and others (n 48) 98.

58 John W Zillman, 'A History of Climate Activities' (*WMO*, 2009) <https://public-old.wmo.int/en/bulletin/history-climate-activities> accessed 8 December 2023.

and the 1992 Rio Conference helped raise public awareness on climate issues.[59] In 1988, the WMO and the UN Environment Programme founded the IPCC and the UNGA recognised climate change as a 'common concern of mankind'.[60]

In 1989, the Netherlands hosted the Hague Summit and the Noordwijk meeting, the first high-level intergovernmental forum devoted exclusively to climate change.[61] That same year, the climate issue was on the agenda of various international summits, including the Small Island States meeting, the Francophone Summit in Dakar, the G7 Meeting, the Non-Aligned Meeting, and the Commonwealth Summit.[62] The Second World Climate Conference in 1990 issued a widely endorsed call for global action on climate change, setting the stage for the negotiation of the UNFCCC.[63] The IPCC also published its inaugural report on climate change's scientific, environmental, and policy implications.[64]

II. EVOLUTION OF THE UNFCCC

In 1990, the UNGA adopted Resolution 45/212, setting in motion the creation of the UNFCCC.[65] Entrusted by the UNGA, the Intergovernmental Negotiating Committee finalised the Convention in 1992, and it came into effect two years later when it achieved ratification by 50 countries.[66] The Convention aims to stabilise GHG concentrations to prevent dangerous interference with the climate system.[67] It sets out five guiding principles: (1) the CBDR principle, urging developed nations to lead in combating climate change and its adverse effects; (2) special attention to the needs of developing countries; (3) the precautionary principle; (4) the right to sustainable development; and (5) the importance of cooperation in an open international economic system.[68] While it did not outline specific emission targets, it established general obligations which provided a base for international climate change regulation.

Tensions between developed and developing countries concerning equity influenced the Convention's commitments.[69] The CBDR principle, in particular, underscored the Convention's distinction between 'Annex I' (developed) and 'non-Annex I' (developing) countries.[70] Annex I countries, including members of the Organisation for Economic Co-operation and Development (OECD) and

---

59 Bodansky and others (n 48) 98.
60 UN General Assembly (n 15).
61 Bodansky and others (n 48) 99.
62 Ibid.
63 Zillman (n 58).
64 Houghton and others (n 7).
65 UN General Assembly (n 15).
66 Article 23.1 UNFCCC.
67 Article 2 UNFCCC.
68 Article 3 UNFCCC.
69 Bodansky and others (n 48) 104.
70 Jacqueline Peel, 'Climate Change Law: The Emergence of a New Legal Discipline' (2008) 32(3) Melbourne University Law Review 922, 928.

nations with economies in transition, were encouraged to limit greenhouse gas emissions to 1990 levels by 2000.[71] Annex II countries, a subgroup of Annex I, were expected to provide financial resources to assist developing countries in adapting to climate change.[72] Non-Annex I parties, mostly developing nations,[73] include the United Nations' 49 classified least developed countries (LDCs), which receive special consideration due to their limited capacity to adapt to climate change.[74]

III. THE KYOTO PROTOCOL

The Kyoto Protocol, adopted in 1997, emerged due to the UNFCCC's lack of specific emission reduction targets.[75] However, its strict provisions led to challenges in securing participation,[76] only entering into force in 2005 when 'enough' Annex I parties (accounting for at least 55% of the total CO_2 emissions for 1990) deposited their instruments of ratification, acceptance, approval, or accession.[77]

The Kyoto Protocol's goal was to enforce emission reduction targets for Annex I countries, introducing a commitment period (2008–2012) during which parties aimed to reduce their GHG emissions by at least 5% below 1990 levels.[78] The protocol also mandated national systems for estimating GHG emissions by 2007[79] and periodic reporting on progress.[80] Perhaps among the most salient features of the Kyoto Protocol are the implementation mechanisms it established. These are three: the Clean Development Mechanism (CDM) set up under article 12, the Joint Implementation (JI) defined by article 6, and the Emissions Trading (ET) set out in article 16bis. The CDM allows countries with emission reduction commitments (Annex I parties) to undertake emission reduction projects in non-Annex I countries. In so doing, the former countries earn saleable certified emission reduction (CER) credits (each equivalent to 1 tonne of CO_2) that count towards their Kyoto targets. Similarly, the JI provided the opportunity for Annex I countries to transfer to, or acquire from, any other such party emission reduction units (ERUs) resulting from emission reduction projects implemented in another Annex I country. Each ERU is equivalent to 1 tonne of CO_2, which counts toward meeting these countries' Kyoto targets.

---

71 Article 4.2(a) UNFCCC.
72 Articles 4.3, 4.4 UNFCCC.
73 UN Climate Change, 'Parties & Observers' (*UNFCCC*, n.d.) <https://unfccc.int/parties-observers> accessed 30 August 2022.
74 Ibid.
75 Peel (n 70) 929.
76 Bodansky and others (n 48) 23.
77 Article 24.1 Kyoto Protocol.
78 Article 3.1 Kyoto Protocol.
79 Article 5 Kyoto Protocol.
80 Article 7 Kyoto Protocol.

> **BOX 17.6** Advanced: Concerns on 'Climate Grabbing' in CDM Projects
>
> The UNFCCC database indicates that 7844 CDM projects have been registered to date.[81] These projects span several sectors, including 67 activities on afforestation and reforestation.[82] While protecting the world's forests is instrumental for reducing GHG emissions, several scholars have raised concerns about how such afforestation and reforestation projects promote 'climate grabbing' in Global South territories.[83] That is because as governments and international NGOs are increasingly incentivised to preserve large areas of forests, they end up appropriating the land and resources of Indigenous peoples and other vulnerable communities for such climate mitigation purposes, thereby reinforcing existing socioeconomic inequalities.[84]

The ET scheme allows countries whose actual emissions did not surpass their emission reduction commitments – and thus had emission units to spare – to sell this excess capacity to countries that were over their targets. In this way, a new commodity was created through emission reductions or removals, whereby carbon is tracked and traded like any other commodity.[85] Since CO_2 is the main GHG, emissions trading is often known as the 'carbon market'. CER and ERU units from the CDM and JI, respectively, can also be transferred under this market.

However, the Kyoto Protocol's architecture, a top-down approach with clear delineations between developed and developing countries,[86] posed some significant challenges. Its prescriptive nature and favour towards developing countries led to the withdrawal of the United States in 2001,[87] one of the largest GHG emitters.[88] Given such a significant withdrawal and the fact that China (a non-Annex I country yet also a major GHG emitter)[89] was not given emission reduction commitments under the

---

81 UN Climate Change, 'Project Search' (*UNFCCC*, n.d.) <https://cdm.unfccc.int/Projects/projsearch. html>accessed 30 August 2022.

82 Ibid.

83 Giulia Parola and Lodovica Toffoletto, 'El "acaparamiento de tierras y el cambio climático": una oportunidad perdida del Acuerdo de París' in Henry Jiménez Guanipa and Marisol Luna Leal (eds), *Crisis climática, derechos humanos y los Acuerdos de París y Escazú* (Fundación Heinrich Böll 2020) 203, 219 <https://co.boell.org/es/2020/03/30/crisis-climatica-transicion-energetica-y-derechos-humanos> accessed 10 August 2022.

84 Ibid.

85 UN Climate Change, 'Emissions Trading' (*UNFCCC*, n.d.) <https://unfccc.int/process/the-kyoto-protocol/mechanisms/emissions-trading> accessed 10 August 2022.

86 Kyoto Protocol (n 16) article 10.

87 Rajamani and Werksman (n 36) 496.

88 Hannah Ritchie and Max Roser, 'CO2 Emissions' (*Our World in Data*, 2020) <https://ourworldindata.org/co2-emissions> accessed 10 August 2022.

89 Ibid.

Protocol, this treaty's emissions targets encompassed less than 24% of global GHG emissions.[90]

IV. THE PARIS AGREEMENT

Replacing the Kyoto Protocol, the Paris Agreement acts as the foundation for specific climate commitments.[91] Adopted by the COP during its 21st session in 2015, it marks the first time human rights have been explicitly mentioned in a climate treaty (yet only in its preamble).[92]

The Paris Agreement's article 2 outlines two central goals: mitigation and adaptation to climate change. The mitigation aim strives to limit the global temperature increase to well below 2°C and urges efforts to restrict the rise to 1.5°C above pre-industrial levels.[93] It also advocates for adaptation to the adverse impacts of climate change and the fostering climate resilience.[94] Furthermore, unlike the Kyoto Protocol, the Paris Agreement refrains from mandating differentiated emission reduction targets based on the countries' development trajectories. Instead, it calls for mitigation actions from all parties, while still infusing the principle of CBDR into some general commitments.[95] For example, it expresses the 'aim' of Parties to 'reach global peaking of greenhouse gas emissions as soon as possible, recognizing that peaking will take longer for developing country Parties, and to undertake rapid reductions thereafter'.[96] It also mandates developed parties to continue 'taking the lead' in emission reduction targets and support developing countries in implementing the Agreement.[97]

New principles introduced in the Paris Agreement include the maximum ambition and progression principles.[98] These principles establish a foundation for increasing ambition, requiring each party to periodically enhance its level of commitment over a 5-year review cycle known as the 'global stocktake'. The Agreement employs tools like the nationally determined contributions (NDCs), long-term strategies (LT-LEDS), adaptation plans (NAPs), and the global stocktake for achieving its objectives. NDCs are action plans that both developed and developing countries must communicate every five years, showing a progressive increase in ambition.[99] The first-ever stocktake is scheduled to conclude at the 2023 COP28 in the United Arab Emirates.

---

90 Bodansky and others (n 48) 108.

91 Rajamani and Werksman (n 36) 502.

92 Paris Agreement (n 25) preamble, para 11.

93 Ibid article 2.1(a).

94 Ibid article 2.1(b).

95 Ibid article 2.2.

96 Ibid article 4.1.

97 Ibid article 4 paras 4, 5.

98 Daniel Klein, 'El Acuerdo de París sobre Cambio Climático: del dicho al hecho' in Henry Jiménez Guanipa and Marisol Luna Leal (eds), *Crisis climática, derechos humanos y los Acuerdos de París y Escazú* (Fundación Heinrich Böll 2020) 227, 235 <https://co.boell.org/es/2020/03/30/crisis-climatica-transicion-energetica-y-derechos-humanos> accessed 10 August 2022.

99 Paris Agreement (n 25) articles 4.3, 4.9.

Unlike the Kyoto Protocol, the Paris Agreement employs a hybrid architecture that blends top-down and bottom-up approaches. The Agreement's objectives and principles, established by multilateral negotiations, reflect a top-down approach, while the NDCs and adaptation arrangements follow a bottom-up template.[100] This structure grants each State the flexibility to set its mitigation ambition level and incorporates these commitments into an international climate accountability system through the global stocktake.[101] The hybrid architecture of the Paris Agreement has enhanced participation levels compared to its predecessor: a record 175 parties signed the Agreement on its opening day, 22 April 2016, and it came into force less than a year after its adoption.[102]

However, there are concerns about the Agreement's potential to meet the urgent need for global decarbonisation, as countries are given the discretion to determine the levels of ambition in their GHG reduction commitments. Despite the Paris Agreement's maximum ambition principle, these concerns are not unfounded, given that governments often express lofty aspirations but shy away from difficult decisions that may conflict with the interests of powerful economic actors, like the oil industry. The current ambition levels of submitted NDCs are insufficient to prevent global warming beyond 1.5°C.[103]

D. INTERNATIONAL CLIMATE CHANGE LAW BEYOND THE UNFCCC

The UNFCCC apparatus serves as a cornerstone of ICCL. Nonetheless, legal provisions pertaining to climate change extend beyond this treaty regime. The relevance and substance of ICCL have expanded considerably, reaching out of its initial confines in environmental law.

I. MULTILATERAL ENVIRONMENTAL AGREEMENTS (MEAs)

1. The Ramsar Convention

Effective since 1975, the Ramsar Convention[104] promotes the conservation of wetlands (areas of marsh, fen, peatland or water, with water that is static or flowing, fresh, brackish or salt)[105] that hold international significance in terms of their environmental characteristics.[106]

100 Klein (n 98) 233.
101 Robert Falkner, 'The Paris Agreement and the New Logic of International Climate Politics' (2016) 92 International Affairs 5.
102 Bodansky and others (n 48) 25.
103 Climate Action Tracker, 'CAT Emissions Gap' (CAT, November 2021) <https://climateactiontracker.org/global/cat-emissions-gaps/> accessed 30 August 2022.
104 Convention on wetlands of international importance especially as waterfowl habitat (adopted 2 February 1971, entered into force 21 December 1975) 996 UNTS 245 (Ramsar Convention).
105 Ibid article 1.1.
106 Ibid article 2.2.

Despite not directly addressing climate change, its implementation has led to a growing awareness of the significant roles that peatlands and mangroves, which are key components of wetlands, play in carbon storage and disaster risk reduction.[107] Recognising the climate mitigation and adaptation capabilities of wetlands, the Conference of the Parties to the Ramsar Convention has incorporated climate change considerations into the management and protection of these vital ecosystems.[108]

2. The Convention on Biological Diversity

Effective since 1993, the Convention on Biological Diversity[109] (CBD) has three primary objectives: conservation of biological diversity, sustainable use of ecosystem components, and equitable sharing of benefits arising from their genetic resources.[110] Recognising the inseparable connection between biodiversity conservation and climate change, the CBD integrates climate change concerns into its core operations. The post-2020 Kunming-Montreal Global Biodiversity Framework includes 23 action-oriented global targets,[111] of which three seek to respond directly to the impacts of climate change. First, target 8 calls for minimising the effects of climate change and ocean acidification on biodiversity and increasing its resilience through mitigation, adaptation, and disaster risk reduction actions. Second, target 11 pursues the restoration, maintenance, and enhancement of nature's contributions to people, including the climate. And third, target 19 commends the increase of financial resources by optimising co-benefits and synergies targeting the biodiversity and climate crises.

3. Environmental Governance Agreements

The Espoo Convention,[112] a European MEA adopted in 1991, guides countries to implement environmental impact assessment (EIA) procedures to manage adverse transboundary environmental impacts.[113] While not fully encompassing climate change in its provisions, its Kyiv Protocol, in force since 2010, requires strategic EIA to consider the effects of proposed activities on the global environment, including the climate.[114] Furthermore, the EU Commission has urged the mainstreaming of climate

---

107 The Ramsar Convention Secretariat, 'Global Wetland Outlook: 2021 Special Edition' (*Ramsar*, 2021)

108 10th Meeting of the Conference of the Parties to the Convention on Wetlands 2008, 'Resolution X.24' (2008) paras 31, 32 <www.ramsar.org/sites/default/files/documents/pdf/res/key_res_x_24_e.pdf> accessed 20 August 2022.

109 Convention on Biological Diversity (adopted 5 June 1992, entered into force 29 December 1993) 1760 UNTS 79 (CBD).

110 Ibid articles 1, 2.

111 Conference of the Parties to the Convention on Biological Diversity, 'Kunming-Montreal Global Biodiversity Framework' (18 December 2022) para 4 <www.cbd.int/doc/c/e6d3/cd1d/daf663719a03902a9b116c34/cop-15-l-25-en.pdf> accessed 18 July 2023.

112 Convention on Environmental Impact Assessment in a Transboundary Context (adopted 25 February 1991, entered into force 10 September 1997) 1989 UNTS 309 (Espoo Convention).

113 Ibid article 2.

114 Benoit Mayer, 'Environmental Assessments in the Context of Climate Change: The Role of the UN Economic Commission for Europe' (2019) 28(1) Review of European, Comparative and International Environmental Law 82.

mitigation measures into member States' legislation on EIA. To this end, it issued guidance documents in 2013[115] and a directive in 2014[116] that impact the implementation of the Espoo Convention and its Protocol.

The Escazú Agreement,[117] focusing on Latin America and the Caribbean, assures access to environmental information, public participation, and justice in environmental matters.[118] Adopted in 2018, it commands countries to provide updated information on climate change sources and encourages public involvement, including in the development of their NDCs.[119] Through these provisions, the agreement emphasises a more inclusive and transparent approach to climate change mitigation and adaptation.[120]

II. HUMAN RIGHTS LAW

Despite climate change impacting nearly every aspect of human well-being, the formal convergence of international climate change and human rights law[121] is a recent development. These two legal domains arose from different historical and political contexts, leading to distinct normative paths. The treaty-based international human rights regime can be traced back to the Universal Declaration of Human Rights in 1948, facilitated by the post–World War II momentum.[122] Conversely, the UNFCCC emerged four decades later in 1992. However, the formal interaction between human rights and climate change only took place in 2008, when the Human Rights Council adopted Resolution 7/23.

---

115 EU Commission, 'Guidance on Integrating Climate Change and Biodiversity into Environmental Impact Assessment' (2013) <https://ec.europa.eu/environment/eia/pdf/EIA%20Guidance.pdf> accessed 20 August 2022; EU Commission, 'Guidance on Integrating Climate Change and Biodiversity into Strategic Environmental Assessment' (2013) <https://ec.europa.eu/environment/eia/pdf/SEA%20Guidance.pdf> accessed 20 August 2022.

116 Directive 2014/52/EU of the European Parliament and of the Council of 16 April 2014 amending Directive 2011/92/EU on the assessment of the effects of certain public and private projects on the environment [2014] OJ L124/1.

117 Regional Agreement on Access to Information, Public Participation and Justice in Environmental Matters in Latin America and the Caribbean (adopted 4 March 2018, entered into force 22 April 2021) 3397 UNTS (Escazú Agreement).

118 Ibid article 1.

119 Ibid article 7.1.

120 Lina Muñoz Ávila and Camilo Quintero-Giraldo, 'El Acuerdo de Escazú sobre democracia ambiental y su relación con el Acuerdo de París sobre cambio climático en Colombia' in Henry Jiménez Guanipa and Marisol Luna Leal (eds), *Crisis climática, derechos humanos y los Acuerdos de París y Escazú* (Fundación Heinrich Böll 2020) 267, 279 <https://co.boell.org/es/2020/03/30/crisis-climatica-transicion-energetica-y-derechos-humanos> accessed 20 August 2022.

121 On international human rights law, see Ciampi, § 21 (and the following sub-chapters), in this textbook.

122 Frans Viljoen, 'International Human Rights Law: A Short History' (*UN Chronicle*, n.d.) <www.un.org/en/chronicle/article/international-human-rights-law-short-history> accessed 20 August 2022.

Resolution 7/23 marked the first time a UN human rights body acknowledged climate change's impact on human rights. This resolution led to a comprehensive analysis by the Office of the UN High Commissioner for Human Rights (OHCHR) on the relationship between the two.[123] The OHCHR report, submitted in 2009, highlighted the effects of rising global temperatures on specific human rights and groups.[124] It also underscored the importance of procedural rights in addressing climate change,[125] providing an early clarification on human rights obligations concerning climate change.[126] Since then, numerous resolutions, studies, and discussions on the relationship between climate change and human rights have been adopted by the UN human rights system.[127]

BOX 17.7 Climate Change and the African Commission on Human and People's Rights

Recognising the intricate link between climate change and human rights, the African Commission has issued several pivotal resolutions. In 2009, Resolution 153 marked the first significant stride, emphasising the need to infuse human rights standards into climate change negotiations. Subsequently, the Commission expanded its focus through Resolution 271 in 2014, engaging an exploratory study on the direct influence of climate change on human rights in Africa. Moving a step further in 2016, it passed Resolution 342 to promote regional cooperation for climate action, which pursued a vision of safeguarding the human rights of Africans now and for future generations. This trajectory culminated in the adoption of Resolution 417 in 2019, which implored State parties to cohesively integrate climate change concerns into broader developmental strategies, thereby reinforcing their commitment to preserving human rights.

---

123 UN Human Rights Council, 'Resolution 7/23 – Human Rights and Climate Change' (28 March 2008) para 1 <https://ap.ohchr.org/documents/E/HRC/resolutions/A_HRC_RES_7_23.pdf> accessed 20 August 2022.

124 Office of the UN High Commissioner for Human Rights, 'Report of the Office of the United Nations High Commissioner for Human Rights on the Relationship between Climate Change and Human Rights' (15 January 2009) para 20 <https://documents-dds-ny.un.org/doc/UNDOC/GEN/G09/103/44/PDF/G0910344.pdf?OpenElement> accessed 20 August 2022.

125 Ibid para 78.

126 Ibid para 69.

127 UN Economic Commission for Latin America and the Caribbean and UN High Commissioner for Human Rights, *Climate Change and Human Rights: Contributions by and for Latin America and The Caribbean* (ECLAC/OHCHR 2019) 17 <www.ohchr.org/sites/default/files/S1900999_en.pdf> accessed 20 August 2022.

BOX 17.8 Advanced: The Inter-American Commission on Human Rights Resolution on the Climate Emergency

In December 2021, the Inter-American Commission on Human Rights adopted Resolution 3/21, Climate Emergency: Scope of Inter-American Human Rights Obligations, the first document of this regional human rights body specifically dedicated to the issue of climate change.[128] Recognising that climate change poses a major threat to the enjoyment of a wide range of rights – including the rights to life, food, health, and a healthy environment – this resolution draws inter alia on the normative and jurisprudential developments of the Inter-American Human Rights System, including the Advisory Opinion 23 of the Inter-American Court of Human Rights,[129] to guide States to make public policy decisions under a rights-based approach in the context of climate change.[130]

This expanding focus on climate change within the universal human rights system has led to recent significant institutional and normative developments[131]. For instance, in 2021, the Human Rights Council appointed a special rapporteurship to make recommendations on addressing and preventing climate change's adverse effects on human rights.[132] Moreover, in July 2022, the UNGA recognised the right to a clean, healthy, and sustainable environment as a human right, which it asserted has been compromised by climate change.[133]

In parallel to international human rights law, the link between human rights and climate change has also evolved within the UN climate change regime, albeit at a slower pace. The COP to the UNFCCC first acknowledged this link at its 10th session in Cancún in 2010.[134] However, a stronger emphasis came with the Paris Agreement, the first legally binding instrument to explicitly refer to human rights, despite the political tension that relegated human rights to a preambular reference.[135]

---

128 Inter-American Commission on Human Rights, 'Resolution 3/2021 Climate Emergency: Scope of Inter-American Human Rights Obligations' (31 December 2021) <www.oas.org/en/iachr/decisions/pdf/2021/resolucion_3-21_ENG.pdf>accessed 30 August 2022.

129 Inter-American Court of Human Rights, 'Advisory Opinion OC-23/17' (15 November 2017) <www.corteidh.or.cr/docs/opiniones/seriea_23_ing.pdf>accessed 18 July 2023.

130 Inter-American Commission on Human Rights (n 128) 7.

131 Verena Kahl, 'A Human Right to Climate Protection – Necessary Protection or Human Rights Proliferation?' (2022) 40 NQHR 2.

132 UN Human Rights Council 2021, 'Resolution 48/14 – Mandate of the Special Rapporteur on the Promotion and Protection of Human Rights in the Context of Climate Change' (8 October 2021) para 2(a) <https://documents-dds-ny.un.org/doc/UNDOC/GEN/G21/285/48/PDF/G2128548.pdf?OpenElement> accessed 18 July 2023.

133 UN General Assembly, 'The Human Right to a Clean, Healthy and Sustainable Environment' (26 July 2022) <https://digitallibrary.un.org/record/3982508?ln=en> accessed 20 August 2022.

134 Conference of the Parties to the UNFCCC 2010, 'Decision 1/CP.16 – The Cancún Agreements: Outcome of the Work of the Ad Hoc Working Group on Long-Term Cooperative Action under the Convention' (10 December 2010) preamble <https://unfccc.int/resource/docs/2010/cop16/eng/07a01.pdf>accessed 18 July 2023.

135 Paris Agreement (n 25) preamble.

E. CONCLUSION

Climate change, one of the most complex challenges of our era, demands robust legal responses. This chapter has endeavoured to provide an overview of the ICCL primarily anchored on the UNFCCC regime. It has traced the historical background, legal architecture, and normative propositions of the UNFCCC, the Kyoto Protocol, and the Paris Agreement aiming to delineate the mechanisms by which they seek to mitigate to and withstand such 'wicked problems'. However, the effectiveness and timeliness of these legal instruments, along with those emerging from their intersection with other legal domains, remain critical questions in preventing and adapting to the effects of the ever-escalating global temperature. The inescapable interlinkages between climate change and global inequality patterns underscore political and socioeconomic conflicts. Untangling these tensions is a prerequisite for achieving climate justice. As the law is a perfectible instrument, its adequacy in addressing climate change largely depends on our ability to prioritise a healthy planet over accumulation and dispossession.

BOX 17.9 Further Readings and Further Resources

Further Readings

- B Mayer, *The International Law on Climate Change* (CUP 2018)

- C Carlarne, KR Gray, and R Tarasofsky, 'International Climate Change Law: Mapping the Field' in Tarasofsky Gray and Carlarne (eds), *The Oxford Handbook of International Climate Change Law* (OUP 2016)

- D Bodansky, J Brunnée, and L Rajamani, *International Climate Change Law* (OUP 2017)

- J Peel, 'Climate Change Law: The Emergence of a New Legal Discipline' (2008) 32 Melbourne University Law Review 922

- L Rajamani and JD Werksman, 'Climate Change' in Rajamani and Peel (eds), *The Oxford Handbook of International Environmental Law* (2nd edn, OUP 2021) 492

Further Resources

- 'CAT Emissions Gap' (*Climate Action Tracker*, 10 November 2022) <https://climateactiontracker.org/global/cat-emissions-gaps/> accessed 18 July 2023

- 'Climate Change Litigation Databases' (*Sabin Center for Climate Change Law*, 2023) <http://climatecasechart.com/> accessed 18 July 2023.

- 'Lancet Countdown: Tracking Progress on Health and Climate Change' (*The Lancet and Wellcome*, 2019) <www.lancetcountdown.org/> accessed 18 July 2023

§ § §

18

CHAPTER 18
INTERNATIONAL MIGRATION LAW

PATRICK LUKUSA KADIMA

BOX 18.1 Required Knowledge and Learning Objectives

Required knowledge: International Human Rights Law; Sources of International Law; International Law and Domestic Law

Learning objectives: Understanding the field of international migration law, which oversees and reviews human rights violations against forcibly displaced people and refugees; the international standards that govern migration policy.

BOX 18.2 Interactive Exercises

Access *interactive exercises for this chapter*[1] by positioning your smartphone camera at the dot-filled box, also known as a QR code.

Figure 18.1 QR code referring to interactive exercises.

A. INTRODUCTION

The rise in conflicts, climate change,[2] poverty and human rights abuses[3] have driven millions of individuals[4] from their countries of birth in order to seek a better life. The often tedious and perilous journeys forcibly displaced people undertake to reach destinations like Europe are often marked, sadly, by death. At least two major

---

1 https://openrewi.org/en-projects-project-public-international-law-international-migration-law/.

2 On international climate change law, see Viveros-Uehara, § 17, in this textbook.

3 On international human rights law, see Ciampi, § 21 (and the following sub-chapters), in this textbook.

4 On individuals, see Theilen, § 7.4, in this textbook.

DOI: 10.4324/9781003451327-21

consequences flow from the steadfast rise in migration numbers globally. The first consequence is how media has narrated stories of migrants. Media reports often depict story of migrants as being 'a story of abuse, violence, and racism'.[5] These media reports often shape an individuals' opinion of how they perceive migrants and migration. The second consequence is the rise in anti-immigrant sentiment as a result of high numbers of migrants, sometimes aided by how media reports migration and the rise of populist politicians. Elsewhere, I have emphasised that

> political leaders around the world are using anti-immigration rhetoric as a pedestal to access public office; this behaviour has not been without consequences such as a high rise in the negative perspective of migrants whether documented or undocumented. The ultimate result is Xenophobia/Afro-phobia.[6]

Tough economic times, a rise in crime, and competition for depleting public goods such as healthcare have led populist leaders in various countries to scapegoat foreigners for the social ills their nations face.

BOX 18.3 Example: The UK-Rwanda Migration Deal

In Britain, the Conservative-led government drew up the controversial UK-Rwanda deal which sought to deport migrants who arrived illegally in the UK to Rwanda to seek asylum there.[7] The UK-Rwanda deal has since faced several legal challenges, the latest being a judgment by the Court of Appeal which overruled an earlier High Court decision by stating that it was unlawful to deport individuals to Rwanda since it was an unsafe Third World country and that the Rwandan asylum system had certain deficiencies in it.[8] Furthermore, the Conservative-led British government has sought to introduce the seemingly controversial and unconstitutional illegal immigration bill, which violates certain clauses of the 1951 Convention relating to the Status of Refugees (Refugee Convention),[9] and the European Convention on Human Rights[10] (ECHR),[11] which Britain are party to.[12]

---

5 Vincent Chetail, 'The Human Rights of Migrants in General International Law: From Minimum Standards to Fundamental Rights' in Mary Crock (ed), *Migrants and Rights* (Routledge 2015).

6 Patrick Lukusa Kadima, 'Afro-phobia and the Law: How Has the South African Judiciary Responded to Cases of Afro-phobia' (LLB Dissertation, University of the Witwatersrand 2019).

7 James Gregory and Sean Seddon, 'Rwanda Policy: Government Committed to Deportation Plan – Braverman' (*BBC News*, 30 June 2023) <www.bbc.com/news/uk-66051292> accessed 30 June 2023.

8 *AA v Secretary of State for the Home Department* [2023] EWCA Civ 745, [2023] CA 282–284.

9 Convention relating to the Status of Refugees (adopted 28 July 1951, entered into force 22 April 1954) 189 UNTS 137.

10 Convention for the Protection of Human Rights and Fundamental Freedoms (adopted 04 November 1950, entered into force 3 September 1953) 213 UNTS 221 (ECHR).

11 On the European human rights system, see Theilen, § 21.4, in this textbook.

12 Tim Baker, 'Illegal Migration Bill: Government Accused of Ignoring International Law During House of Lords Defeats' (*Sky News*, 28 June 2023) <https://news.sky.com/story/illegal-migration-bill-government-accused-of-ignoring-international-law-during-house-of-lords-defeats-12911388> accessed 29 June 2023.

In other parts of Europe, such as Greece,[13] Italy,[14] Hungary,[15] and Poland,[16] hostility towards migrants has developed to a certain extent that it has become State sponsored. In the Global South, countries such as South Africa and Kenya have experienced a surge in migrants arriving on their respective shores. This, too, has not been without backlash.

BOX 18.4 Example: State-Sponsored Hostility Towards Migrants

The South African Operation Fiela (Sotho: 'to sweep clean') was an operation that the government undertook with the goal of reducing the crime rate.[17] However, human rights organisations[18] argue that the operation found itself to be targeting undocumented immigrants and seemingly rushing their deportation of which some termed institutional xenophobia.[19] In East Africa, the Kenyan government in 2018 cracked down on undocumented migrants to a point where they even set up a hotline for citizens to call the immigration department if they suspected any undocumented migrants in their neighbourhood.[20] These actions by government have undoubtedly flared up anti-immigrant sentiments and homed in on the question of migration management.

Against this backdrop, the chapter sets out to discuss international migration law. To this end, the chapter first introduces the concept of migration and the issues that arise from it, before proceeding to discuss global migration governance. The chapter then delves into international refugee law where concepts such as asylum, refugee status determination, *non-refoulement* (French: 'no return'), and standard of treatment are

---

13 Helena Smith, 'Greek Government under Fire after Video Shows Pushback of Asylum Seekers' (*The Guardian*, 19 May 2023) <www.theguardian.com/world/2023/may/19/greek-government-under-fire-after-video-shows-pushback-of-asylum-seekers> accessed 15 June 2023.

14 Marta Silvia Vigano, 'Italy: New Law Curtails Migrants' Rights' (*Deutsche Welle*, 9 May 2023) <www.dw.com/en/italy-new-law-curtails-migrants-rights/a-65552219> accessed 15 June 2023.

15 Reuters, 'Hungary to Defy EU Court Ruling over Migration Policy, Orban Says' (*Reuters*, 21 December 2021) <www.reuters.com/world/europe/hungary-defy-eu-court-ruling-over-migration-policy-orban-says-2021-12-21/> accessed 15 June 2023.

16 Jorge Liboreiro, 'Poland and Hungary Hijack EU Summit with Anti-migration Demands' (*euronews*, 30 June 2023) <www.euronews.com/my-europe/2023/06/30/poland-and-hungary-hijack-eu-summit-with-anti-migration-demands> accessed 30 June 2023.

17 South African Government, 'Police on Operation Fiela/Reclaim 2015' (*South African Government*, 30 April 2015) <www.gov.za/speeches/police-operation-fielareclaim-2015-30-apr-2015-0000> accessed 20 June 2023.

18 On non-governmental organisations, see Chi, § 7.6, in this textbook.

19 Lara Wallis, 'Disturbing Court Judgment Ignores Our Rights' (*Groundup*, 1 July 2015) <https://groundup.org.za/article/disturbing-court-judgment-ignores-our-rights_3082/> accessed 20 June 23.

20 Amnesty International, 'Kenya: Crackdown on Irregular Migrants Risks Sparking Xenophobia' (*Amnesty International*, 1 September 2018) <www.amnesty.org/en/latest/press-release/2018/09/kenya-crackdown-on-irregular-migrants-risks-sparking-xenophobia/> accessed 22 June 2023.

discussed. International migration law without doubt envelopes the whole world and affects every State. However, how international law comes into operation both at a domestic and international level is the focus of this chapter.

B. INTERNATIONAL MIGRATION LAW

Often there is a misconception that the terms 'refugee' and 'migrant' are the same. These terms cannot be used interchangeably because they have different legal meanings. Refugees are specifically defined in international law as individuals who are often fleeing persecution and violence. On the other hand, migrants are not fleeing from persecution but have voluntarily left their country. Article 13(2) of the 1948 Universal Declaration of Human Rights (UDHR)[21] notes, 'Everyone has the right to leave any country, including his own, and to return to his country'.

As contended in the introductory section of this chapter, over the last decade human mobility has been on the rise in view of the increasing interconnectedness of the world. The 2005 Global Commission on International Migration notes that between 1970 and 2005 the number of international migrants has increased from 82 million to 200 million.[22] Similarly, the Interactive World Migration Report of the International Organization for Migration (IOM) states that in 2022 there were approximately 281 million international migrants.[23] In terms of refugee statistics, it is recorded that there were 26.4 million refugees around the world in 2020. In 2020, asylum seekers were said to be 4.1 million. In total, 89.4 million people were said to be displaced in 2020.[24]

The numbers of displaced persons globally is increasing, and this has necessitated the calls for solutions to migration. Often migrants undertake perilous journeys to reach their destinations. These clandestine journeys via unsafe boats or as airplane stowaways usually result in death. The Interactive World Migration Report notes that despite attempts in collecting data on migrants who have gone missing or perished on their routes, there remain severe hiccups in collecting data.[25] Few official sources collect and make data on migrant deaths publicly available. Relying on testimonies of migrants and media sources can be problematic due to inaccuracies and incomplete coverage.[26]

---

21 Universal Declaration of Human Rights (adopted 10 December 1948 UNGA Res 217 A(III) (UDHR).
22 Report of the Global Commission on International Migration, 'Migration in an Interconnected World: New Directions for Action' (2005) <www.iom.int/sites/g/files/tmzbdl486/files/jahia/webdav/site/myjahiasite/shared/shared/mainsite/policy_and_research/gcim/GCIM_Report_Complete.pdf> accessed 20 June 2023.
23 Marie McAuliffe and Anna Triandafyllidou (eds), *World Migration Report 2022* (International Organization for Migration 2021).
24 Ibid 3.
25 Ibid 30–31.
26 Ibid.

I. GLOBAL MIGRATION GOVERNANCE

It is without doubt that international migration has become top of the agenda globally, especially for receiving States[27] (i.e. the States of immigration) and intergovernmental organisations.[28] As noted above, countries such as Britain have gone to an extent of even creating bills to 'stop the boats'.[29] Given the complexity that migration poses both domestically and internationally, it has become essential to understand what the governance of migration entails at a global level.

BOX 18.5 Advanced: Issues of Global Governance

Migration is a trans-boundary issue, and as such the question of global governance is thrust into the limelight. Alexander Betts argues that global governance has been created as a response to dealing with issues that have become trans-boundary.[30] Betts further argues that issues become trans-boundary when the nature of that issue is such that it transcends borders and cannot be solved by a single State in isolation.[31] International trade, transitional crime, and communicable diseases are examples of trans-boundary issues, and as a result of such issues States have developed institutions that seek to address them.[32] The issue of migration affects more than one country, and thus there is a need for a global governance structure that will be responsible for dealing with migration.

II. INTERNATIONAL MIGRATION INSTITUTIONS

Unlike the World Trade Organization (WTO), which deals with issues of international trade,[33] or the World Health Organization, which deals with issues of health, it is notable that migration does not have one single centralised international organisation dedicated to it.[34] Betts emphasises that 'what exists is fragmented and incoherent in comparison to most trans-boundary issue-areas'.[35] This lack of a centralised organisation on migration does indeed contribute to the lack of efficient management of migration at a global level.

---

27 On States, see Green, § 7.1, in this textbook.

28 On international organisations, see Baranowska, Engström, and Paige, § 7.3, in this textbook.

29 The phrase 'stop the boat' is a commonly used phrase used by the Conservative party politicians to indicate their fightback against asylum seekers crossing the channel.

30 Alexander Betts, 'Introduction: Global Migration Governance' in Alexander Betts (ed), *Global Migration Governance* (OUP 2011).

31 Ibid.

32 Ibid.

33 On international trade law, see Agarwalla, § 23.2, in this textbook.

34 Vincent Chetail, *International Migration Law* (OUP 2019).

35 Betts (n 30) 8.

1. A Future World Migration Organisation

Over the years, there has been calls by various scholars and practitioners for the need of a comprehensive organisation at a global stage that should deal with the growing complexities of migration. In 1992, economist Jagdish Bhagwati called for the establishment of a world migration organisation.[36] He argued that

> [t]he world migration organization should seek to develop codes for the rights and obligations of different types of immigrants. Among the issues that need to be addressed by a global organisation on migration are access by illegal migrants to welfare safety nets; the rights of their children to free public education alongside native children; and the voting rights of legal immigrants.[37]

Bhagwati based the idea of a world migration organisation on it being able to carry out three major objectives: the ability of the organisation to codify the rights of migrants, burden sharing indices, and developing periodic country reviews.[38] Bimal Ghosh has also pointed out to the establishment of a central organisation dealing with migration. In supporting the calls for a centralised body that deals with migration, international lawyer Arthur Helton requested 'to make and arbitrate global migration policy, which should be more effective, generous and humane than is currently the case'.[39]

BOX 18.6 Advanced: Institutional Design of a Future World Migration Organisation

International trade lawyer Joel Trachtman has made calls for a centralised body of migration to be created which will resemble the WTO and will comprise a strong secretariat.[40] Christopher Rudolph, in support of a world migration body that will be designed the same way the WTO has been set up, notes that

> given the expansiveness of its scope, the breadth of its membership, the degree of delegation afforded to it by member countries, the precision of its rules and procedures, and the sophistication of its dispute resolution mechanisms, the [WTO] clearly represents a model form for a migration regime to emulate.[41]

---

36 Jagdish Bhagwati, 'A Champion for Migrating Peoples' (*The Christian Science Monitor*, 28 February 1992) <www.csmonitor.com/1992/0228/28181.html> accessed 20 June 2023.

37 Ibid.

38 Ibid.

39 A Helton, 'People Movement: The Need for a World Migration Organization' (*Open Democracy*, 1 May 2003) <www.opendemocracy.net/people-migrationeurope/article_1192. jsp> accessed 19 June 2023.

40 JP Trachtman, *The International Law of Economic Migration: Toward a Fourth Freedom* (WE Upjohn Institute Press 2009) 324–329; see also TJ Hatton, 'Should We Have a WTO for International Migration?' (2007) 22(50) Economic Policy 339–383.

41 Christopher Rudolph, 'Prospects and Prescriptions for a Global Mobility Regime: Five Lessons from the WTO' in B Koslowski (ed), *Global Mobility Regimes* (Palgrave Macmillan 2011) 184.

However, Rudolph points out that creating an institutional design akin to the WTO for addressing migration is a challenging prospect.[42] Vincent Chetail argues that although to certain scholars having a centralised body of migration designed in the same way as the WTO may be attractive, it does not seem to be feasible.[43] Chetail further argues that the model of the WTO cannot be taken as it is and used to create a centralised migration organisation for the mere fact that people are not like goods and services that can be negotiated and exchanged at will.[44]

2. Existing Migration Organisations

Certain aspects of migration have been managed by different agencies or organisations. Two of the leading institutions that deal with different aspects of migration are the United Nations High Commissioner for Refugees (UNHCR) and the International Organization for Migration (IOM). Notably, migration has also been managed on regional levels as well as bilateral levels. Regional organisations have become important role players in the management of migration.[45]

BOX 18.7 Example: Regional Governance on Migration

Examples of regional governance on migration can be found within the European Union (EU) and the African Union (AU). In Europe, member States of the EU, despite maintaining their domestic immigration policies, have sought to cooperate at a regional level where they seek to achieve common goals such as developing a common European asylum system. In Africa, the AU has developed the Revised Migration Policy Framework for Africa and Plan of Action (2018–2030).[46] This framework offers guidelines to member States as well as sub-regional organisations to take into consideration when crafting their migration policies.

a) United Nations High Commissioner for Refugees

The UNHCR is a UN specialised agency that is primarily responsible for the protection of refugees. It was established in 1950 as result of the number of refugees

---

42 Ibid 184.

43 Chetail (n 34) 666.

44 Ibid.

45 Sandra Lavenex and Nicola Piper, 'Regions and Global Migration Governance: Perspectives "From Above", "From Below" and "From Beyond"' (2022) 48(12) Journal of Ethnic and Migration Studies 2837.

46 African Union, *Revised Migration Policy Framework for Africa and Plan of Action* (International Labour Organization 2018) <www.ilo.org/africa/areas-of-work/labour-migration/policy-frameworks/WCMS_671952/lang–en/index.htm#:~:text=The%20AU%20revised%20Migration%20Policy,in%20the%20management%20of%20migration> accessed 28 August 2023.

created by the Second World War. On its website, the UNHCR characterises itself as an organisation that is 'dedicated to saving lives, protecting rights and building a better future for people forced to flee their homes because of conflict and persecution'.[47] The UNHCR does not operate in isolation but maintains constant cooperation with other UN agencies, civil society, and States.[48] The UNHCR also relies heavily on funding, and at times this leads to the interest of its donor States to influence its work one way or another.[49] The UNHCR cannot be individually tasked with achieving its own objectives, but needs assistance from other parties such as the UN General Assembly.[50] However, the UNHCR has come under immense pressure over the years. For example, the institution's responsibilities have been stretched while it experiences a funding shortfall. This shortfall means that the UNHCR will find it difficult to meet its mandate. Although the UNHCR's mandate is to protect refugees, donors increasingly expect the organisation to protect their borders instead.[51]

b) International Organization for Migration

The IOM was established in 1951 as a body responsible for resettling refugees in Europe after the Second World War. The IOM became part of the UN as a related organisation.[52] The IOM is currently the leading intergovernmental organisation on migration. In 2007, Megan Bradley highlights that the member States of the IOM adopted a new vision for the organisation, encompassing 12 priorities, which include:

> the humane and orderly management of migration and the effective respect for the human rights of migrants in accordance with international law; increasing efforts to tackle human smuggling, trafficking, and other forms of irregular migration; participating in coordinated inter-agency humanitarian operations by providing migration services and other support in emergency and post-crisis contexts; and facilitating the voluntary return and reintegration of refugees, IDPs, and other migrants.[53]

---

47 United Nations High Commissioner for Refugees, 'Safeguarding the Rights and Well-Being of People Forced to Flee for over 70 Years' <www.unhcr.org/about-unhcr> accessed 20 June 2023.

48 Alexander Betts, Gil Loescher, and James Milner, *The United Nations High Commissioner for Refugees (UNHCR) The Politics and Practice of Refugee Protection* (Routledge 2012).

49 Ibid.

50 'Statute of the Office of the United Nations High Commissioner for Refugees', UNGA Res 428(V) (14 December 1950) (UNHCR Statute).

51 William Maley, 'A New Tower of Babel? Reappraising the Architecture of Refugee Protection' in E Newman and J van Selm (eds), *Refugees and Forced Displacement: International Security, Human Vulnerability, and the State* (United Nations University Press 2003).

52 IOM, 'IOM Becomes a Related Organization to the UN' (*IOM*, 25 July 2016) <www.iom.int/news/iom-becomes-related-organization-un> accessed 28 August 2023.

53 Megan Bradley, 'The International Organization for Migration (IOM): Gaining Power in the Forced Migration Regime' (2017) 33(1) Refuge: Canada's Journal on Refugees.

BOX 18.8 Advanced: Cooperation Between the UNHCR and the IOM

Despite the UNHCR and IOM having different mandates, this does not mean they have not and cannot cooperate together to achieve common goals, such as ensuring sustainable migration. One such example where the two institutions have worked together is reflected in the memorandum of agreement between the two, which was signed in 1997.[54] More recently, the two bodies released a joint statement on the adoption of the Global Compact for Safe, Orderly and Regular Migration and of the Global Compact on Refugees.[55]

C. INTERNATIONAL REFUGEE LAW

I. BACKGROUND

The occurrence of war, climate change, persecution, and violence has led to the displacement of millions of people. Over the years, international refugee law has responded to increasingly complex humanitarian crises and an ever-increasing number of people who are forced to leave their homes for military, political, social, economic, or climatic reasons. International law responds to these crises by creating institutions and rules. The protection of refugees is primarily dictated by two instruments: the 1951 UN Convention Relating to the Status of Refugees (Refugee Convention or Geneva Convention) and its 1967 Protocol Relating to the Status of Refugees (Protocol).[56] The Protocol broadened the temporal and geographical scope of the Refugee Convention's application, which is no longer restricted geographically to European refugees and temporarily to events occurring before 1 January 1951.

II. DEFINITION OF REFUGEES

Article 1 (A)(2) Refugee Convention sets out the following definition of a refugee:

owing to well founded fear of being persecuted for reasons of race, religion, nationality, membership of a particular social group or political opinion, is outside the country of his nationality and is unable or, owing to such fear, is unwilling to avail himself of the protection of that country; or who, not having a nationality and being outside the country of his former habitual residence as a result of such events, is unable or, owing to such fear, is unwilling to return to it.

---

54 UNHCR and IOM, 'Memorandum of Understanding' (UNHCR, 15 May 1997) <https://emergency.unhcr. org/sites/default/files/IOM-UNHCR%2C%20MoU%2C%201997.pdf> accessed 28 August 2023.

55 UNGA, 'Global Compact for Safe, Orderly and Regular Migration' (19 December 2018) UN Doc A/ RES/73/195.

56 Protocol relating to the Status of Refugees (adopted 31 January 1967, entered into force 4 October 1967) 606 UNTS 267.

However, according to article 1(C) Refugee Convention, individuals are excluded from the refugee status if they enjoy the protection of a country of their new nationality or if they voluntarily resettle in their country of origin. Furthermore, the status of refugee is temporary. For example, one loses their refugee status out of certain voluntary acts or fundamental changes in the country they are fleeing.

At the time the Refugee Convention was adopted, it did not envision protecting all people who have been forcibly displaced.[57] However, the development of international law has shaped the meaning of who a refugee is. Chetail argues that 'following other conventional rules, the Geneva Convention must be construed and applied within the normative context prevailing at the time of its interpretation, including, therefore, in light of the human rights treaties adopted since its entry into force'.[58] The evolutive method of interpretation[59] is therefore the most appropriate interpretation when dealing with the Refugee Convention due to the ever-changing context of forced displacement.[60] Human rights law has 'been instrumental in instilling a common and dynamic understanding of the refugee definition more consonant with, and loyal to, the evolution of international law and the changing realities of forced migration'.[61] Despite this human rights–based approach, individuals forcibly displaced internally are still excluded from refugee status as it presupposes being outside the country of origin.

III. PRINCIPLES OF INTERNATIONAL REFUGEE LAW

1. Asylum

Asylum is defined as 'the protection that a State grants on its territory or in some other place under the control of certain of its organs to a person who comes to seek it'.[62] Notably, asylum is not the same as refugee status. Asylum refers to the institution of protection, while refugee status refers to the content of protection offered to those individuals who benefit from asylum.[63] The right to asylum is not covered in any universal treaty. However, article 14 UDHR expressly notes 'everyone has the right to seek and to enjoy asylum from persecution',[64] Notably, the Refugee Convention and its Protocol make no mention of the right to seek asylum. María-Teresa Gil-Bazo and Elspeth Guild note that despite the right to seek asylum not being mentioned in the Refugee Convention and its protocol, its procedural mechanisms can be found in the principle of *non-refoulement*.[65]

57 Vincent Chetail (n 34) 353.

58 Ibid 353.

59 On treaty interpretation, see Fiskatoris and Svicevic, § 6.1, in this textbook.

60 Vincent Chetail (n 34) 353.

61 Ibid 354.

62 Institute of International Law (5th Commission), 'Asylum in Public International Law', Resolutions Adopted at its Bath Session (September 1950) art 1.

63 María-Teresa Gil-Bazo, 'Asylum as a General Principle of International Law' (2015) 27 IJRL 3, 7–10.

64 UDHR, art 14(1).

65 María-Teresa Gil-Bazo and Elspeth Guild, 'The Right to Asylum' in Cathryn Costello, Michelle Foster, and Jane McAdam (eds), *The Oxford Handbook of International Refugee Law* (OUP 2021).

2. Refugee Status Determination

The refugee status determination (RSD) is an important process which the UNHCR or States that are signatory to the Refugee Convention undertake to ascertain whether an individual can be considered a refugee under international law. This process allows for refugees to realise their rights under international law. The primary responsibility to conduct the RSD rests on the State. However, if a State is not party to the Refugee Convention, the UNHCR can take charge of the process. The UNHCR has been very explicit that this process needs to be transparent, adaptable, and efficient.

BOX 18.9 Example: RSD in South Africa

In South Africa, the RSD is undertaken by the Department of Home Affairs which employs the Refugee Status Determination Officer. This officer holds a vital role in South Africa's RSD as they have the power to accept or reject asylum.

---

3. The Principle of Non-refoulement

The principle of *non-refoulement* offers protection under international human rights law, refugee law, and customary international law.[66] In essence, the principle stipulates that a State is prohibited from removing or transferring an individual out of its territory if there are substantial grounds for believing that the person concerned would face persecution or irreparable harm if returned to their country of origin. It has been noted by several scholars that the aim of the principle of *non-refoulement* is twofold. On one hand, the principle affords asylum seekers protection while awaiting the receiving State to determine whether they meet the criteria of refugee. On the other hand, the principle affords recognised refugees the protection they need and temporary stability.

Article 33(1) Refugee Convention notes that

> no Contracting State shall expel or return ('refouler') a refugee in any manner whatsoever to the frontiers of territories where his life or freedom would be threatened on account of his race, religion, nationality, membership of a particular social group or political opinion.

Article 33(1) applies to both asylum seekers and recognised refugees on the condition they are in the territory of a signatory to the convention. In international human rights law, general human rights treaties,[67] as well as the Convention against Torture and Other Cruel, Inhuman or Degrading Treatment or Punishment[68] and the International

---

66 On customary international law, see Stoica, § 6.2, in this textbook.

67 María-Teresa Gil-Bazo, 'Refugee Protection under International Human Rights Law: From Non-Refoulement to Residence and Citizenship' (2015) 34 Refugee Survey Quarterly 11.

68 Convention against Torture and Other Cruel, Inhuman or Degrading Treatment or Punishment (adopted 10 December 1984, entered into force 26 June 1987) 1465 UNTS 85, article 3(2).

Convention for the Protection of All Persons from Enforced Disappearance,[69] contain
the prohibition of *refoulement*.

BOX 18.10 Advanced: Circumventing the
Non-refoulment Prohibition

One of the challenges that arises from this principle is that of interpreting
article 33(1) Refugee Convention. Several States have interpreted the article
in various ways to circumvent article 33 obligations and accommodate their
domestic immigration policies.[70] According to a sovereignty-based interpretation,
States must only consider the prohibition of *refoulement* if an asylum seeker
enters its borders. It has also been noted that States using this interpretation do
not feel obligated to facilitate the arrival of refugees on their shores. States that
use this interpretation also have designed laws and policies to prevent asylum
seekers from reaching their borders.[71] According to the collective interpretation,
there is no affirmative obligation whatsoever imposed on States to admit
refugees and asylum seekers in their territory. States that support this approach
understand that there is no obligation to grant asylum, and therefore these
States send refugees to a third State as long as the third State does not engage
in *refoulement* of the refugees to a fourth State that would put the individuals at
risk.[72] States supporting a transit zone–based interpretation create transit areas
within their borders (usually at travel hubs
such as airports) to circumvent their article 33 obligations. By creating these
non-sovereign areas, these States employ a procedural method to avoid
determining whether asylum seekers can be granted refugee status.[73]

---

4. Standard of Treatment

The Refugee Convention creates obligations on States to accord refugees the same
treatment as nationals of that State or at a minimum 'the most favourable treatment
accorded to nationals of a foreign country in the same circumstances'.[74] In South Africa,
for example, the courts have emphasised that asylum seekers and refugees enjoy the right
to work as do citizens. In the Supreme Court of Appeal case of *Somali Association of South
Africa and Others v Limpopo Department of Economic Development Environment and Tourism*

---

69 Convention for the Protection of All Persons from Enforced Disappearance (adopted 20 December 2006,
    entered into force 23 December 2010) 2716 UNTS 3, article 16(1),

70 Ellen F D'Angelo, 'Non-Refoulement: The Search for a Consistent Interpretation of Article 33' (2009) 42
    Vanderbilt Law Review 279, 290–310.

71 Ibid.

72 Ibid.

73 Ibid.

74 Articles 4, 7, 13, 15–25 Refugee Convention.

and Others,[75] the Court held that the Constitution does not place a blanket approach on asylum seekers and refugees from seeking employment. The Court went on to further state that section 27(f) of the Refugee Act entitles refugees and asylum seekers to 'seek employment' and does not restrict that expression to wage–earning employment.[76]

D. CONCLUSION

The 2015 European migration crisis and the rise in hatred against migrants in Europe and Africa are just two examples that show that migration has become top of the agenda for any State. As we have noted above, despite the UNHCR and IOM being present, the lack of a centralised migration governance structure will continue to hamper proper coordination of refugees. Regional organisations should play an important role in creating forums and enacting policies and frameworks that will seek to solve the migration issues they face.

BOX 18.11 Further Readings and Further Resources

Further Readings

- A Betts, G Loescher, and J Milner, *The United Nations High Commissioner for Refugees (UNHCR): The Politics and Practice of Refugee Protection* (Routledge 2012)

- K Kamanga, 'International Refugee Law in East Africa: An Evolving Regime' (2002) 3 Georgetown Journal of International Affairs 25

- T Gammeltoft-Hansen, *Access to Asylum: International Refugee Law and the Globalization of Migration Control* (CUP 2011)

- K Vanyoro, *Migration, Crisis and Temporality at the Zimbabwe-South Africa Border: Governing Immobilities* (Bristol University Press 2024)

Further Resources

- Netflix, 'Stateless' (2020) <www.netflix.com/de-en/title/81206211> accessed 28 August 2023

- UNHCR, 'Forced to Flee' <www.unhcr.org/forced-to-flee-podcast/> accessed 28 August 2023

---

§ § §

---

75 *Limpopo Department of Economic Development Environment and Tourism and Others* [2014] 4 All SA 600 (SCA).
76 Ibid.

CHAPTER 19
INTERNATIONAL LAW IN CYBERSPACE

PIA HÜSCH

BOX 19.1 Required Knowledge and Learning Objectives

Required knowledge: General Principles; Jurisdiction; Use of Force; Law of Armed Conflict

Learning objectives: Understanding how existing international law applies in cyberspace and what challenges remain when trying to apply different areas of international law to cyber operations.

BOX 19.2 Interactive Exercises

Access *interactive exercises for this chapter*[1] by positioning your smartphone camera at the dot-filled box, also known as a QR code.

Figure 19.1 QR code referring to interactive exercises.

A. INTRODUCTION

The application of international law to cyberspace is one of the great challenges international law faces in the 21st century. By the third decade of the 21st century, cyber operations have become increasingly common in inter-State relations.[2] Although the applicability of international law to cyberspace was originally contested,[3] today it is

---

1   https://openrewi.org/en-projects-project-public-international-law-international-law-in-cyberspace/

2   Sean Watts, 'Low Intensity Cyber Operations and the Principle of Non-Intervention' (2014) <https://papers.ssrn.com/sol3/papers.cfm?abstract_id=2479609> accessed 5 December 2022, 1.

3   François Delerue, *Cyber Operations and International Law* (CUP 2021) 1.

DOI: 10.4324/9781003451327-22

widely agreed upon. It has been confirmed by individual States,[4] UN working groups,[5] and scholarship.[6] While such consensus is a laudable first step, it is at the same time an agreement that is minimal at best. Since then, the conversation has moved on to the decisive question of *how exactly* international law applies to cyberspace.

Cyberspace, in this context, is broader than the internet and also includes other computer and telecommunications networks.[7] While the term 'space' has often raised questions in how far cyberspace is territorial – a question outside the scope of this chapter – this chapter considers that in line with Betz and Stevens, 'Cyberspace is not a space in any traditional sense . . . but we experience it as though it possesses physical attributes, if only by association and analogy'.[8]

B. INTERNATIONAL LAW-MAKING AND ACTORS IN CYBERSPACE

To understand how international law applies to cyberspace, it makes sense to take a step back and to briefly consider relevant parties involved in determining such application and contributing to the discussion respectively. First, States remain the primary lawmakers of international law.[9] This also holds up in a cyber context where States primarily contribute to the discourse via State statements, setting out their specific interpretation of how the application of international law can be understood in cyberspace.[10]

Furthermore, a number of other actors and initiatives[11] advance norm-making in cyberspace, including non-binding norms.[12] Not all of these actors can be addressed here. Most prominently, however, there are two UN working groups: the US-led UN Group of Governmental Experts (GGE), which came to an end in 2021,[13] and the

---

4 See e.g. New Zealand Ministry of Foreign Affairs and Trade, *The Application of International Law to State Activity in Cyberspace* (2020) §§ 3–4; Federal Government of Germany, *On the Application of International Law in Cyberspace* (2021) 1.

5 UN GGE Report 2013, § 19; UN GGE Report 2015, § 24.

6 See e.g. Delerue (n 3) 1–2.

7 Delerue (n 3) 29.

8 David J Betz and Tim Stevens, 'Analogical Reasoning and Cyber Security' (2013) 44 Security Dialogue 147, 150.

9 On States, see Green, § 7.1, in this textbook.

10 See e.g. Federal Government of Germany (n 3); Finnish Ministry of Foreign Affairs, *International Law and Cyberspace – Finland's National Positions* (2020); French Ministère des Armées, *International Law Applied to Operations in Cyberspace* (2019).

11 On the variety of actors in international law, see Engström, § 7 (and the following sub-chapters), in this textbook.

12 On sources of international law, see Eggett, § 6, in this textbook.

13 E.g. Cyber Peace Institute, 'The UN GGE Final Report: A Milestone in Cyber Diplomacy; but see Where Is the Accountability?', 9 June 2021 <https://cyberpeaceinstitute.org/news/the-un-gge-final-report-a-milestone-in-cyber-diplomacy-but-where-is-the-accountability/> accessed 25 February 2023.

Russian-led UN Open-Ended Working Group (OEWG),[14] which continues to meet at the time of writing. Both groups work on similar issues and publish consensus reports, but their composition differs.[15] Other multilateral fora that have previously positioned themselves on the application of international law to cyberspace are organisations such as NATO[16] and collective groups of States like the G20.[17]

However, States are not the only relevant actors pursuing norm development in cyberspace. They are joined by several multi-stakeholder fora advancing cyber norms, such as the Paris Call,[18] the Internet Governance Forum,[19] the International Telecommunications Union,[20] and the Internet Cooperation for Assigned Names and Numbers (ICANN), which maintains the technical infrastructure of the internet.[21] The number of relevant actors is further complemented by private sector companies such as Microsoft that play an active role in norm development.[22] The most prominent collection of academic interpretations of international law in cyberspace is advanced in the non-binding Tallinn Manuals,[23] referenced frequently throughout this chapter. Whereas all of these organisations and initiatives contribute to the discussion on how international law applies to cyberspace in one way or another, the primary focus of this chapter rests on States' individual and collective interpretations.

C. KEY PRINCIPLES OF INTERNATIONAL LAW

In the absence of a comprehensive cyber treaty that explicitly regulates inter-state cyber operations, the debate on the application of international law to cyberspace primarily revolves around the application of existing principles of international law to cyberspace.

---

14 E.g. Cyber Peace Institute, 'Open-Ended Working Group on Security of and Use of Information and Communications Technologies 2021–2025 (OEWG II)' (25 March 2022) <https://cyberpeaceinstitute. org/news/oewg-security-use-of-information-communications-technologies-2021–2025/> accessed 25 February 2023.

15 Dan Efrony, 'The UN Cyber Groups, GGE and OEWG – A Consensus Is Optimal, But Time Is of the Essence' (*Just Security*, 16 July 2021) <https://www.justsecurity.org/77480/the-un-cyber-groups-gge-and-oewg-a-consensus-is-optimal-but-time-is-of-the-essence/> accessed 11 December 2023.

16 NATO, *AJP-3.20: Allied Joint Doctrine for Cyberspace Operations* (NATO Standardization Office 2020).

17 G20 Leaders' Communiqué, Antalya, Turkey (16 November 2015) <www.consilium.europa.eu/media/23729/ g20-antalya-leaders-summit-communique.pdf> accessed 25 February 2023, § 26.

18 See Paris Call, For Trust and Security in Cyberspace <https://pariscall.international/en/>.

19 Zhixiong Huang and Kubo Mačák, 'Towards the International Rule of Law in Cyberspace: Contrasting Chinese and Western Approaches' (2017) 16 Chinese Journal of International Law 271, 286.

20 Andrew N Liaropoulos, 'Cyberspace Governance and State Sovereignty' in Goerge Bitros and Nicholas Kyriazis (eds), *Democracy and an Open-Economy World Order* (Springer 2017) 30 f.

21 Ibid 31.

22 Brad Smith, 'The Need for a Digital Geneva Convention' (2017) <https://blogs.microsoft.com/on-the-issues/2017/02/14/need-digital-geneva-convention/#sm.001vmxlx4fckfcd11ci132tpwpta8> accessed 17 June 2022.

23 Michael N Schmitt (ed), *Tallinn Manual on the International Law Applicable to Cyber Warfare* (Cambridge University Press 2013); Michael N Schmitt (ed), *Tallinn Manual 2.0 on the International Law Applicable to Cyber Operations* (Cambridge University Press 2017).

These principles include the prohibition of the use of force and, when a cyber operation amounts to an armed attack, the right to self-defence.[24] This section also addresses the application of sovereignty to cyberspace before turning to the principle of non-intervention.[25]

I. USE OF FORCE AND SELF-DEFENCE IN CYBERSPACE

The prohibition of the use or threat of force is also applicable in cyberspace. This has been confirmed by States such as Finland and New Zealand,[26] as well as the UN working groups,[27] and is also reflected in the Tallinn Manual[28] and wider scholarship.[29] Thus, there is no longer any debate on the applicability of the prohibition of the use of force in cyberspace, but as is the case for so many principles of international law, the question remains how its application can be understood exactly, including the question of what amounts to a use of force in cyberspace.

As the term 'force' is not defined in the UN Charter, its exact scope and meaning have been subject to much scholarly debate. In light of the development of modern technologies and weapons, including biological and chemical weapons, 'the debate . . . comes across as relatively outdated' and it seems no longer 'accurate to limit the prohibition of the use or threat of force to armed force'.[30]

Yet even where such first hurdle is taken, still not every use of a cyber operation amounts to a use of force. Delerue identifies three different approaches that determine whether a use of force has occurred: the target-based approach, the instrument-based approach, and the consequence-based approach.[31] The target-based approach considers that a cyber operation amounts to a use of force where it penetrates critical national infrastructure. However, as there is no minimum threshold that has to be met here, the approach is generally considered as too inclusive.[32] The second, instrument-based approach emphasises the 'similarity between cyber operations and traditional weapons', which, however, is often far-fetched. As such, this approach seems outdated and mismatched to the realities of low-intensity cyber operations.[33] Finally, it is the consequence-based or effects-based approach that finds most support. It stresses the importance of the effects caused by cyber operations and foresees that

---

24 On the use of force, see Svicevic, § 13, in this textbook.

25 On sovereignty, see Green, § 7.1, in this textbook.

26 Finnish Ministry of Foreign Affairs (n 9) 6–7; The Federal Government of Germany (n 3) 6; New Zealand Ministry of Foreign Affairs and Trade (n 3) §§ 6–8.

27 UN GGE Report 2015, § 26.

28 Schmitt (ed), *Tallinn Manual 2.0 on the International Law Applicable to Cyber Operations* (n 22), Rule 68.

29 Confirming that 'The Absence of Specific References to Cyber Operations Does Not Render the UN Charter Law Inapplicable to Cyber Operations', Delerue (n 3) 277.

30 Ibid 287.

31 Ibid 288.

32 Ibid 289.

33 Ibid.

any cyber operation resulting in physical destruction or loss of life amounts to a use of force.[34] Several criteria have been established to determine whether the effects caused by a cyber operation amount to a use of force, including severity, immediacy, and invasiveness.[35]

Even where this nowadays most popular interpretation is followed, what is less clear is whether non-physical effects can also amount to a use of force and whether there is a *de minimis* (Latin: 'the smallest') threshold that has to be met to constitute force.[36] Currently, there is no scholarly agreement on these matters. And although many States support an effects-based interpretation, these categories remain largely based on an existing legal framework tailored around kinetic uses of force. Consequently, the question remains whether a cyber-specific approach may still add value to the discourse.[37]

Closely related to the prohibition of the use of force is the question when such force amounts to an armed attack, triggering another State's customary right to self-defence.[38] In a cyber context, such assessment considers the scale, that is 'the magnitude and intensity of the cyber operation (amount of force used, its location and its duration)'; and its effects, that is 'the consequences of the cyber operation (damage and casualties)'.[39] Taking into account non-physical effects for this assessment is still controversial, but not every cyber operation with physical effects amounts to a most grave form of the use of force, either. Instead, a case-by-case assessment needs to be made. The Tallinn Manual 2.0, for example, speaks of 'all reasonably foreseeable consequences of the cyber operation' that must be taken into account.[40] Equally controversial is the question whether the accumulation of events can mean that several cyber operations not meeting the threshold individually can collectively meet the threshold of an armed attack.

BOX 19.3 Example: Stuxnet Cyber Operation in Iran

A prominent example of a cyber operation that is often referred to when discussing the use of force and armed attack thresholds in cyberspace is Stuxnet. From late 2009 to 2010, malware (i.e. malicious software) was used to infiltrate and subsequently attack the control system at Natanz, 'Iran's largest

---

34 Russell Buchan and Nicholas Tsagourias, *Regulating the Use of Force in International Law: Stability and Change* (Edward Elgar 2021) 118.

35 Michael Schmitt, 'Computer Network Attack and the Use of Force in International Law: Thoughts on a Normative Framework' (1998–1999) 37 *Columbia Journal of Transnational Law* 885, 914–915.

36 Buchan and Tsagourias (n 33) 119 ff.

37 Delerue (n 3) 290.

38 *Nicaragua* case, § 195.

39 Delerue (n 3) 330–331, referencing Ruys, 139.

40 Schmitt (n 23), commentary to rule 71, § 13.

nuclear fuel enrichment facility'.[41] Moore has previously referred to Stuxnet as a magnum opus, crediting its outstanding effectiveness in causing harm.[42] Indeed, it stopped a considerable percentage of the facility's centrifuges from working properly. The intention was to make them spin faster and slower until they break, thus having physical effects. Given its complexity and sophistication, Stuxnet is widely considered to be of a State-sponsored nature, presumably a joint US-Israeli operation, but no public attribution has been made, nor has Iran declared that it constituted a use of force.[43] Despite the fact that there is widespread (scholarly) agreement that Stuxnet amounted to a use of force,[44] Iran never publicly qualified it as such. Ultimately, the legal question as to what amounts to a use of force remains distinct from the strategic and political decisions that a State has to make when it publicly qualifies it as such.[45] Next to the question whether Stuxnet amounted to a use of force, it must further be considered whether Stuxnet also met the threshold of an armed attack. Generally speaking, both interpretations here are possible, also depending on whether or not all uses of force are understood to amount to an armed attack. Delerue finds that to this date Stuxnet is 'the only publicly known cyber operation that caused grave effects; it therefore demonstrates that a qualification as an armed attack is unlikely in the vast majority of cyber operations'.[46]

II. SOVEREIGNTY

Already outside a cyber context, the principle of sovereignty is a highly complex principle of international law. While no authoritative definition of the principle exists and scholarly debates on the role of sovereignty in a globalised world remain divided, there is no doubt that States still consider it highly relevant, including in a cyber context. States have repeatedly stressed that State sovereignty applies to cyberspace.[47]

The question that often receives the most attention when discussing the application of sovereignty to cyberspace is whether sovereignty constitutes a principle or a rule of international law. Many States and scholars have since positioned themselves in this so-called principle versus rule debate. On the one hand, there is the United Kingdom, which has repeatedly confirmed its interpretation

---

41 Andrew (I) Moore, 'Stuxnet and Article 2(4)'s Prohibition against the Use of Force: Customary Law and Potential Models' (2015) 64 Naval Law Review 1, 1–2.

42 Ibid.

43 Buchan and Tsagourias (n 33) 118–119.

44 Russell Buchan, 'Cyber Attacks: Unlawful Uses of Force or Prohibited Interventions?' (2012) 17 Journal of Conflict and Security Law 212, 219–221.

45 Delerue (n 3) 297.

46 Ibid 333.

47 For example in UN GGE, Report 2013, para 20; UN GGE, Report 2021, para 71(b).

that sovereignty merely constitutes a principle of international law.[48] This means that although many specific rights are closely related to this principle, where a cyber operation does not violate any of these specific rights, it does not constitute a violation of international law and, thus, no international wrongful act. The targeted State therefore cannot resort to lawful countermeasures. Some scholars have supported this view,[49] but overall, support for this interpretation remains limited. In contrast, many States have positioned themselves in the 'sovereignty as a rule' camp, confirming that they understand sovereignty as a primary rule of international law and that where such rule is violated, the activity in question amounts to an international wrongful act. Finland, for example, explicitly confirms this view by stating that it 'sees sovereignty as a primary rule of international law, a breach of which amounts to an internationally wrongful act and triggers State responsibility'.[50] So do New Zealand,[51] Germany,[52] and France.[53] The interpretation that sovereignty constitutes a rule of international law has also been supported by the experts of the Tallinn Manuals[54] and many other international legal scholars.[55] Under this interpretation, sovereignty almost serves as a catch-all function for those cyber operations that otherwise do not meet the threshold of other primary rules of international law.

Whereas the majority view thus sides with the sovereignty as a rule interpretation, this does not mean that States in this camp agree on one definition of sovereignty. To the contrary, considerable differences amongst these States remain, especially when determining the relevant threshold that has to be met for a violation of sovereignty. Some States, like France, consider any penetration of their networks a violation of sovereignty;[56] others require a certain *de minimis* threshold to be met.[57] Thus it remains unclear how the principle of sovereignty applies to cyberspace exactly.

---

48 Jeremy Wright, 'Cyber and International Law in the 21st Century' (*Gov.uk*, 2018) <https://www.gov.uk/government/speeches/cyber-and-international-law-in-the-21st-century> accessed 11 December 2023; Suella Braverman, 'International Law in Future Frontiers' (*Gov.uk*, 2022) <https://www.gov.uk/government/speeches/international-law-in-future-frontiers> accessed 11 December 2023.

49 Most prominently, see Gary P Corn and Robert Taylor, 'Sovereignty in the Age of Cyber' (2017) 111 AJIL Unbound 207.

50 Finnish Ministry of Foreign Affairs (n 9) 3.

51 New Zealand Ministry of Foreign Affairs and Trade (n 3) § 12.

52 The Federal Government of Germany (n 3) 3–4.

53 French Ministère des Armées (n 9) 6–7.

54 Schmitt (n 22), see commentary for rule 4.

55 E.g. Przemyslaw Roguski, 'Layered Sovereignty: Adjusting Traditional Notions of Sovereignty to a Digital Environment' (11th International Conference on Cyber Conflict: Silent Battle); Kevin Jon Heller, 'In Defense of Pure Sovereignty in Cyberspace' (2021) 97 International Law Studies 1432; Michael N Schmitt and Liis Vihul, 'Respect for Sovereignty in Cyberspace' (2017) 95 Texas Law Review 1639.

56 French Ministère des Armées (n 9) 6–7; Przemyslaw Roguski, 'Violations of Territorial Sovereignty in Cyberspace – an Intrusion-Based Approach' in Dennis Broeders and Bibi van den Berg (eds), *Governing Cyberspace – Behavior, Power, and Diplomacy* (Rowman & Littlefield 2020) 72.

57 E.g. The Federal Government of Germany (n 3) 4.

BOX 19.4 Advanced: Cyber Espionage

Espionage constitutes a legal grey zone in international law. As it is not explicitly prohibited by any treaty or customary law, some have argued that espionage is not per se unlawful but may violate other norms of international law. The same reasoning applies to cyber espionage, which therefore also is not explicitly prohibited.[58] However, it has been argued that the threshold debate with respect to the principle of sovereignty actually revolves around the question whether cyber espionage is considered a violation of sovereignty.[59] So far, even States that have advanced a strict sovereignty in cyberspace interpretation have not explicitly clarified whether they consider cyber espionage as unlawful. Taking past State practice as an indication, it seems unlikely that there will be a more explicit discussion of the lawfulness of espionage by States who benefit from the ambiguity and the existing legal grey zone.

III. NON-INTERVENTION IN CYBERSPACE

A further principle of international law that applies to cyberspace is that of non-intervention. The principle of non-intervention is based on the idea of sovereign equality and that as all States are equal, one State may not intervene in the affairs of another State.[60] The application of the principle to cyberspace has been widely agreed upon, including in the UN working groups,[61] State statements,[62] the Tallinn Manuals,[63] and academia[64] more widely. But although there is general agreement that the principle of non-intervention also constitutes a primary rule of international law,[65] its application remains subject to many uncertainties.[66] Whereas a military intervention is the most

---

58 Delerue (n 3) 198.

59 Heller (n 55) 1454 ff.

60 For a more detailed analysis preceding the cyber debate see, e.g. Christian Tomuschat, *International Law: Ensuring the Survival of Mankind on the Eve of a New Century General Course on Public International Law (Volume 281)* (Collected Courses of the Hague Academy of International Law, Brill 1999) 231 ff.

61 UN GGE Report 2021, § 71; UN GGE Report 2015, § 28(b).

62 The Federal Government of Germany (n 3) 4–6; New Zealand Ministry of Foreign Affairs and Trade (n 3) § 9–10; Finnish Ministry of Foreign Affairs (n 8) 3–4.

63 Schmitt (n 22), Rule 66.

64 Thibault Moulin, 'Reviving the Principle of Non-Intervention in Cyberspace: The Path Forward' (2020) 25 Journal of Conflict and Security Law 423; Nicholas Tsagourias, 'Electoral Cyber Interference, Self-Determination and the Principle of Non-Intervention in Cyberspace' in Dennis Broeders and Bibi van den Berg (eds), *Governing Cyberspace – Behavior, Power, and Diplomacy* (Rowman & Littlefield 2020); Ido Kilovaty, 'Doxfare: Politically Motivated Leaks and the Future of the Norm on Non-Intervention in the Era of Weaponized Information' (2018) 9 Harvard National Security Journal 146.

65 Oppenheim, for example, made clear 'That Intervention Is, as a Rule, Forbidden by International Law There Is No Doubt' in Robert Jennings and Arthur Watts (eds), *Oppenheim's International Law* (Vol 1, 9 edn, Addison Wesley Longman 1996); Moulin (n 64) 428.

66 Kunig, for example, says that 'the exact meaning of the principle remains unclear', Philip Kunig, *Prohibition of Intervention* (OUP 2008) Max Planck Encyclopedia of International Law, § 1.

obvious form of intervention, the discussion on the application of non-intervention to cyberspace primarily revolves around those cyber operations that remain below the use of force threshold.

A first look at the principle raises the impression that the principle of non-intervention is – as far as principles of international law go – not just well established but also well defined. The ICJ's *Nicaragua* case is the key reference in this context when stating that the activity in question must target another State's *domaine réservé* (French: 'reserved area') and must be coercive.[67] The *domaine réservé* is typically defined as an area in which a State can decide freely.[68] Coercion distinguishes mere influence, which may be unwanted but not unlawful, from unlawful intervention. Much like is the case for the term *domaine réservé*, the exact definition of coercion remains unclear, particularly so in the cyber context. Some scholars consider whether the acting State needs to aim for a specific goal, whether advantages need to be secured, or whether it needs to fulfil an intention requirement.[69] These uncertainties are a problem that is further augmented in the cyber context, where interaction between States is constant and often disruptive, but not always easily defined as coercive. Most low-intensity cyber operations do not reach the high thresholds set out by the non-intervention principle. While some academic suggestions to redefine these thresholds exist,[70] they remain purely academic at this point. As the law stands, this means that most cyber operations fall short of these thresholds.

BOX 19.5 Example: Russian Election Interference

Legal analysis around the lawfulness of Russian election interference in the 2016 US presidential elections is a prominent example of how challenging it is to apply non-intervention to cyber operations. More precisely, the question arises whether Russian activities, which included 'hacking into the Democratic National Committee e-mails and the release of confidential information as well as disinformation operations',[71] amounted to an unlawful intervention. The US has attributed these activities to Russia but has not referred to them as an unlawful intervention.

Scholarship is divided over the question whether these activities met the high thresholds of the principle of non-intervention. While it is uncontroversial that targeting another State's elections falls within the targeted State's *domaine réservé*, it is unclear whether the coercion requirement was fulfilled. As Russia

---

67 *Military and Paramilitary Activities in and against Nicaragua (Nicaragua v. United States of America)* [1986] ICJ Rep 14 [202].

68 Kunig (n 66) § 3.

69 Maziar Jamnejad and Michael Wood, 'The Principle of Non-Intervention' (2009) 22 Leiden Journal of International Law 2, 347–348, 368.

70 Kilovaty (n 64) 169 f.

71 Tsagourias (n 64) 48–49.

did not meddle with the vote count or directly change the outcome, which would have amounted to an unlawful intervention, some argue that it was not fulfilled given that the US was not forced into a specific outcome.[72] Others consider that the activities assessed collectively[73] or the fact that the election interference meddled with the people's ability to choose their own government by influencing their choices[74] amounted to an unlawful intervention.

D. JURISDICTION IN CYBERSPACE

Exercising jurisdiction[75] is 'the legal competence of a State . . . to make, apply, and enforce legal rules'.[76] As with many of the principles discussed here, there is little doubt that jurisdiction generally applies to cyberspace. States have repeatedly confirmed that they enjoy jurisdiction over information and communications technology (ICT) infrastructure in their territory.[77] Similarly, academia has also argued in favour of its applicability,[78] and so do the Tallinn Manuals.[79] This includes prescriptive/legislative jurisdiction, enforcement jurisdiction, and adjudicative jurisdiction alike.

Different approaches illustrate the difficulty of establishing jurisdiction in cyberspace. Let us take the example of a French website globally selling items online. Some argue that in this instance, the *destination approach* should be followed (i.e. granting a State jurisdiction if the website in question has been locally accessed).[80] Whereas this reasoning has been applied in the past,[81] it is ultimately not considered practical: given that customers from all over the world might be able to order from this website, it allows for too many competing claims for jurisdiction. This is because there is hardly any threshold that has to be met for a State to argue it has jurisdiction. As a consequence, it comes close to a universal jurisdiction which, traditionally, is only reserved for the most severe crimes, such as piracy,[82] but not to regular activities in cyberspace, such as online shopping.

---

72 Michael N Schmitt, 'Virtual' Disenfranchisement: Cyber Election Meddling in the Grey Zones of International Law' (2018) 19 Chicago Journal of International Law 30, 49–50.

73 Steven J Barela, 'Cross-Border Cyber Ops to Erode Legitimacy: An Act of Coercion' (*Just Security*, 12 January 2017) <https://www.justsecurity.org/36212/cross-border-cyber-ops-erode-legitimacy-act-coercion/> accessed 11 December 2023.

74 Tsagourias (n 64) 54.

75 On jurisdiction, see González Hauck and Milas, § 8, in this textbook.

76 Gleider I Hernández, *International Law* (Oxford University Press 2019) 194.

77 UN GGE, Report 2015, § 28(a).

78 See e.g. Uta Kohl, 'Jurisdiction in Cyberspace' in Nicholas Tsagourias and Russell Buchan (eds), *Research Handbook on International Law and Cyberspace* (Edward Elgar 2015).

79 Schmitt (ed), *Tallinn Manual on the International Law Applicable to Cyber Warfare* (n 22), Rule 2; Schmitt (ed), *Tallinn Manual 2.0 on the International Law Applicable to Cyber Operations* (n 22), Rule 8.

80 Kohl (n 78) 38.

81 See e.g. *LICRA v. Yahoo! Inc & Yahoo France* (Tribunal de Grande Instance de Paris, 22 May 2000); *Arzneimittelwerbung im Internet* BGH (30 March 2006) I ZR 24/03, § 27–30.

82 Bernard Oxman, *Jurisdiction of States* (2007) Max Planck Encyclopedia of International Law § 37 ff.

Therefore, a variation of the destination approach, the *targeted destination approach*, has been advanced that foresees that jurisdiction can no longer be established by any State that can access the website but only by those that have been targeted by a website.[83] The targeted destination approach has been applied by the European Court of Justice but has been criticised for advancing fragmentation of otherwise global cyberspace and has been considered unsuitable for intangible services (e.g. streaming films).[84]

Finally, there is the *origin approach*, the idea that jurisdiction is granted to the State where a website is either registered or hosted. Coming back to our example, this means that the French-registered website would only have to comply with French law even when it sells items to customers in other States. While such an approach is appreciated by businesses who under this approach merely have to comply with the law of one State, it also bears the risk of a 'race to the bottom' as businesses are thus tempted to register in the State with the most lenient regulation in place.[85] As is the case for many other principles addressed here, there is little doubt that jurisdiction applies in cyberspace. The realities of the cyber context, however, often mean that it is challenging or unsatisfying to apply established principles of determining jurisdiction to the interconnected world.

E. INTERNATIONAL HUMANITARIAN LAW IN CYBERSPACE

Unlike some of the other areas of international law examined here, the applicability of international humanitarian law[86] (IHL) in cyberspace is a controversial topic amongst States. For example, the failure to reach agreement over the 2017 UN GGE report arguably at least partially stems from disagreement regarding the applicability of IHL in cyberspace.[87] The experts of the Tallinn Manual 1.0, published in 2013, had already clearly supported the applicability of IHL to cyber operations conducted in the context of an armed conflict.[88] Since then, individual States have confirmed this interpretation.[89]

---

83 Kohl (n 78) 45.

84 Edouard Treppoz, 'Jurisdiction in the Cyberspace' (2016) 26 Swiss Review of International and European Law 273, 281–284.

85 Kohl (n 78) 49–50.

86 On international humanitarian law, see Dienelt and Ullah, § 14, in this textbook.

87 Samuele De Tomas Colatin, 'A Surprising Turn of Events: UN Creates Two Working Groups on Cyberspace' (*CCDCOE*) <https://ccdcoe.org/incyder-articles/a-surprising-turn-of-events-un-creates-two-working-groups-on-cyberspace/> accessed 6 August 2023.

88 Schmitt (ed), *Tallinn Manual on the International Law Applicable to Cyber Warfare* (n 22), Rule 80.

89 See e.g. The Federal Government of Germany (n 3) 1; New Zealand Ministry of Foreign Affairs and Trade (n 3) § 3; Finnish Ministry of Foreign Affairs (n 8) 6.

Generally speaking, the application of IHL is triggered where an international or non-international armed conflict exists.[90] However, to this day, no individual cyberattack has reached this threshold and it remains unlikely that this threshold will be reached.[91] As such, IHL will most likely apply to cyber operations where these form part of a conventional armed conflict. Where a cyber operation does form part of an international or non-international armed conflict and constitutes an attack, it has to comply with the same principles of IHL that also apply to kinetic attacks, including but not limited to the principles of distinction, proportionality, and precaution. Details of their application, however, remain challenging.

The principle of distinction, for example, may at times be difficult to apply to cyber operations, where the interconnectivity of ICT infrastructure means that it is not always clear how to distinguish between civilian and military structures. To enable greater distinction, the ICRC has suggested a digital emblem marking hospitals and other digital infrastructure that may not be directly targeted.[92] The involvement of cyber 'hacktivists' and volunteers in the cyber domain also poses further challenges to the distinction between combatants and civilians directly participating in hostilities through cyber means.[93]

Similarly, the principle of proportionality can also be challenging to apply, especially in light of the controversial question whether attacks that do not cause or are not intended to cause physical effects are also subject to the proportionality assessment. The Tallinn Manual, for example, argues that this is not the case. Accordingly, information operations or electronic warfare against communications systems would not be subject to the proportionality assessment.[94]

Finally, the principle of precaution must be applied when planning cyberattacks. The Tallinn Manual provides insights on how precautions can be taken for cyberattacks (e.g. by including technical experts in the planning of attacks).[95]

---

90 For definitions thereof, see ICRC Opinion Paper, 'How Is the Term "Armed Conflict" Defined in International Humanitarian Law?' (March 2008) <www.icrc.org/en/doc/assets/files/other/opinion-paper-armed-conflict.pdf> accessed 25 February 2023.

91 Terry D Gill, 'International Humanitarian Law Applied to Cyber-Warfare: Precautions, Proportionality and the Notion of "attack" Under the Humanitarian Law of Armed Conflict' in N Tsagourias and R Buchan (eds), *Research Handbook on International Law and Cyberspace* (Edward Elgar 2021) 458.

92 Tilman Rodenhäuser and Mauro Vignati, 'How Can a "Digital Emblem" Help Protect Medical Facilities Against Cyber Operations?' (27 January 2023) <www.lawfareblog.com/how-can-digital-emblem-help-protect-medical-facilities-against-cyber-operations> accessed 25 February 2023.

93 Kubo Macak and Mauro Vignati, 'Civilianization of Digital Operations: A Risky Trend', 5 April 2023, *Lawfare* <www.lawfareblog.com/civilianization-digital-operations-risky-trend> accessed 20 August 2023; Russell Buchan and Nicholas Tsagourias, 'Ukranian "IT Army": A cyber levée en masse or civilians directly participating in hostilities?' (*EJIL Talk!*, 9 March 2022) <www.ejiltalk.org/ukranian-it-army-a-cyber-levee-en-masse-or-civilians-directly-participating-in-hostilities/> accessed 19 June 2023.

94 Gill (n 91) 465.

95 Schmitt (ed), *Tallinn Manual 2.0 on the International Law Applicable to Cyber Operations* (n 22), rule 114.

F. HUMAN RIGHTS IN CYBERSPACE

Early versions of cyberspace and the development of the internet were seen as revolutionary opportunities to advance human rights standards globally, the development of one fertilising the development of the other.[96] Such development, however, was not appreciated by authoritarian States which, by relying on notions of sovereignty and non-intervention, restricted access to the internet as a form of opposing US soft power.[97] Nowadays, the intersection of cyberspace and human rights often raises associations of internet restrictions, internet shutdowns, and human rights infringements. Examples that come to mind are the Great Firewall in China,[98] the heavy free speech restrictions in Russia,[99] and repeated internet shutdowns in Iran in response to protests.[100]

There is widespread agreement that human rights also apply online.[101] But that does not mean that the application of human rights online is straightforward. The freedom of expression and its application to cyberspace is a particularly contentious topic.[102] Varying restrictions of the freedom of expression are particularly evident when comparing restrictive practices of authoritarian and liberal States, highlighting the need for procedural protections of the right to free speech.[103] This is also true for global social media platforms like X (formerly Twitter) and Facebook (part of Meta), where content moderation or the lack thereof is a reoccurring topic of controversy.[104]

The right to privacy is another key human right that is central to the debate on how human rights law applies online. While acts such as the EU's General Data Protection Regulation (GDPR) have been highly influential in setting standards of data protection

---

96 David P Fidler, 'Cyberspace and Human Rights' in Nicholas Tsagourias and Russel Buchan (eds), *Research Handbook on International Law and Cyberspace* (Edward Elgar 2021) 132.

97 Fidler (n 96) 132–133.

98 Elizabeth C Economy, 'The Great Firewall of China: Xi Jinping's Internet Shutdown' (*The Guardian*, 29 June 2018) <www.theguardian.com/news/2018/jun/29/the-great-firewall-of-china-xi-jinpings-internet-shutdown> accessed 6 August 2023.

99 Sarah Rainsford, 'Russia Internet: Law Introducing New Controls Comes into Force' (*BBC*, 20 February 2021) <www.bbc.co.uk/news/world-europe-50259597> accessed 6 August 2023.

100 Weronika Strzyznska, 'Iran Blocks Capital's Internet Access as Amini Protests Grow' (*The Guardian*, 22 September 2022) <www.theguardian.com/world/2022/sep/22/iran-blocks-capitals-internet-access-as-amini-protests-grow> accessed 25 February 2023.

101 See e.g. Human Rights Council, Promotion and Protection of All Human Rights, Civil, Political, Economic, Social and Cultural Rights, Including the Right to Development, 7 July 2021, UN Doc A/HRC/47/L.22.

102 See e.g. Barrie Sander, 'Freedom of Expression in the Age of Online Platforms: The Promise and Pitfalls of a Human Rights-Based Approach to Content Moderation' (2019–2020) 43 Fordham International Law Journal 939.

103 Fidler (n 96) 136.

104 Kate Klonick, 'The Facebook Oversight Board: Creating an Independent Institution to Adjudicate Online Free Expression' (2020) 129 Yale Law Journal 2418; Natalie Alkiviadou, 'Hate Speech on Social Media Networks: Towards a Regulatory Framework?' (2019) 28 Information & Communications Technology Law 1, 19–35.

in and beyond Europe,[105] significant discrepancies between the standards set out in human rights treaties such as the ICCPR and 'the reality of government practices on privacy' remain, such as expansive surveillance practices.[106]

Finally, human rights law online also addresses the realisation of economic, social, and cultural rights that also apply online but typically require digital access and a stable and secure internet connection to be fulfilled in the first place. Therefore, some scholars find that internet access is key to realising the right to development, while others have gone even further and advocated for a self-standing human right to internet access.[107] However, such argument is highly controversial and points out that many details of the question of how human rights law plays out online are in fact still unclear and under development.

G. CONCLUSION

In a highly digitalised world, almost all aspects of life are interconnected with online activities. This is also true for subject matter that typically falls under the scope of international law, such as key principles of international law, humanitarian law, or the law of human rights law. This chapter has demonstrated that existing norms of international law find application in cyberspace, whether it is to inter-State cyber operations targeting foreign elections or those conducted in connection with armed conflicts, or whether it affects human rights law and the freedom of speech online. However, this chapter has also pointed out that although the application of international law to cyberspace is widely agreed upon, the discussions on how it applies exactly are just beginning. Both technology and State practice are developing further, feeding into the discourse on how international law exactly applies to cyberspace. Furthermore, numerous initiatives on norm development in cyberspace add to the discourse. Against this backdrop, many of the details on the interpretation and application of international law remain unclear at this stage, requiring further research and clarification by both academia and State practice.

BOX 19.6 Further Readings and Further Resources

Further Readings

- H Moynihan, 'The Application of International Law to State Cyberattacks' (Chatham House) <www.chathamhouse.org/sites/default/files/publications/research/2019-11-29-Intl-Law-Cyberattacks.pdf> accessed 20 August 2023

---

105 Giovanni Buttarelli, 'The EU GDPR as a Clarion Call for a New Global Digital Gold Standard' (2016) 6 International Data Privacy Law 77.

106 Fidler (n 96) 138–139.

107 Stephen Tully, 'A Human Right to Access the Internet? Problems and Prospects' (2014) 14 Human Rights Law Review 2, 175–195.

- ICRC, 'International Humanitarian Law and Cyber Operations During Armed Conflicts' (ICRC Short Papers, Paper Series) <www.icrc.org/en/document/short-papers-on-international-humanitarian-law-and-cyber-operations-during-armed-conflicts> accessed 20 August 2023

Further Resources

- Jack Rhysider (*Darknet Diaries*) <https://darknetdiaries.com> accessed 20 August 2023
- 'NATO CCDCOE Cyber Toolkit, Examining How International Law Applies to Example Scenarios and Providing an Overview of States' National Positions', <https://cyberlaw.ccdcoe.org/wiki/Main_Page> accessed 20 August 2023

§ § §

CHAPTER 20
SPACE LAW

DEEPA KANSRA

BOX 20.1 Required Knowledge and Learning Objectives

Required knowledge: Sources of International Law

Learning objectives: Understanding the international norms which govern the activities of States and other actors in outer space; the core principles and concepts that shape decision-making and developments in international and national space law; the challenges faced by countries and international organisations in the implementation of space laws; and the interface of space law with other domains namely human rights law, environmental law, and so forth.

BOX 20.2 Interactive Exercises

Access *interactive exercises for this chapter*[1] by positioning your smartphone camera at the dot-filled box, also known as a QR code.

Figure 20.1 QR code referring to interactive exercises.

A. INTRODUCTION

International space law (ISL) can be described as the body of law which governs space activities.[2] It is a specialised branch of general international law[3] with its objectives and principles adopted in treaty law and resolutions. ISL, in terms of nature, is multidimensional, with its formation and development shaped by concerns from the

---

1 https://openrewi.org/en-projects-project-public-international-law-space-law/.

2 Frans von der Dunk and Fabio Tronchetti (eds), *Handbook of Space Law* (EEPL 2015) xxvi.

3 Carl Q Christol, 'International Outer Space Law' (1987) 3 Space Policy 65.

DOI: 10.4324/9781003451327-23

public, private, and technological, economic, security, and political domains.[4] The present chapter discusses some of the core concepts and principles of space law along with the challenges posed to their implementation and reform.

B. HISTORY

Historically, the United Nations constituted an international forum to codify rules for the regulation of activities in outer space to establish an effective, fair, and transparent international legal regime and to respond to geopolitical considerations, particularly the competition between the superpowers, the United States and the Soviet Union.[5] The first step, under the aegis of the UN, was the constitution of the Committee on the Peaceful Uses of Outer Space (COPUOS). The mandate of the COPUOS included the formulation and codification of ISL and guiding its development based on principles of cooperation and equality amongst States. The COPUOS, along with its two sub-committees, the Scientific and Technical Sub-Committee and the Legal Sub-Committee, were created to play a central role in the regulation of activities in outer space. Since its inception, the contributions of the COPUOS can be viewed in three phases.[6] The first is the pre-treaty phase, wherein the COPUOS drafted a handful of UN declarations and resolutions with considerable political and moral force, but no binding legal character. The second phase is the golden age of ISL treaty-making, in which the five core treaties on outer ISL were created. In the third phase, COPUOS adopted non-binding resolutions to address the new conditions concerning outer space.[7]

C. SOURCES

The regulatory framework for space activities comprises standards of binding and non-binding nature[8] incorporated in the space treaties, international resolutions, and rules of international organisations.

I. SPACE TREATIES

In 1963, the UN General Assembly (UNGA) adopted the Declaration of Legal Principles Governing the Activities of States in the Exploration and Use of Outer

---

4   Ram S Jakhu and Paul Stephen Dempsey (eds), *Routledge Handbook of Space Law* (Routledge 2017) 26.

5   Frans von der Dunk, 'International Space Law' in Frans von der Dunk and Fabio Tronchetti (eds), *Handbook of Space Law* (EEPL 2015) 35. For events prior to the adoption of rules and principles of international space law, see Glenn H Reynolds and Robert Merges, *Outer Space Problems of Law and Policy* (Routledge 1997) Chapter: Some History and Background.

6   von der Dunk (n 5) 38.

7   Oleg Danilyan and Alexander Dzeban, 'Space Law at 21st Century: The Security Issues, Philosophy and Cosmology' (2019) 22 Filosofiâ I Kosmologiâ 8.

8   On the variety of sources in international law, see Eggett, § 6 (and the following sub-chapters), in this textbook.

Space, 1963 (Principles Declaration).[9] The Principles Declaration was followed by five treaties, referred to as the 'heart of international space law'.[10] These include the Outer Space Treaty (OST);[11] the Agreement Governing the Activities of States on the Moon and Other Celestial Bodies (Moon Agreement);[12] the Rescue Agreement;[13] the Liability Convention;[14] and the Registration Convention.[15]

1. The Outer Space Treaty

The OST is the 'main legal framework'[16] containing the key principles concerning the use and exploration of outer space.[17] Under the OST, State parties are required to carry out activities in the exploration and use of outer space, including the moon and other celestial bodies, in accordance with international law, including the UN Charter.[18] By referring to the UN Charter, the fundamental principles of international law are included in the scope of ISL (e.g. sovereign equality, the maintenance of international peace and security).[19]

The importance of the OST as an authoritative guide for space actors has been widely discussed. First, its provisions were shaped by the geopolitical considerations, competition, and possible confrontation of the two superpowers, the United States and Soviet Union.[20] Second, the OST covers principles that have been 'recognised as customary law', including non-appropriation and equality of States.[21] Some view the obligations as provided under the OST (and other treaties) as obligations *erga omnes* (Latin: 'towards all').[22] Third, the OST is an important guide for States and other actors

---

9 UNGA, 'Declaration of Legal Principles Governing the Activities of States in the Exploration and Use of Outer Space' <www.unoosa.org/oosa/en/ourwork/spacelaw/principles/legal-principles.html> accessed 2 August 2023.

10 von der Dunk (n 5) 43.

11 Treaty on principles governing the activities of States in the exploration and use of outer space, including the moon and other celestial bodies (adopted 27 January 1967, entered into force 10 October 1967) 610 UNTS 205 (OST).

12 Agreement governing the Activities of States on the Moon and Other Celestial Bodies (adopted 5 December 1979, entered into force 11 July 1984) 1363 UNTS 3 (Moon Agreement).

13 Agreement on the rescue of astronauts, the return of astronauts and the return of objects launched into outer space (adopted 22 April 1968, entered into force 3 December 1968) 672 UNTS 119 (Rescue Agreement).

14 Convention on the international liability for damage caused by space objects (adopted 29 March 1972, entered into force 1 September 1972) 961 UNTS 187 (Liability Convention).

15 Convention on registration of objects launched into outer space (adopted 12 November 1974, entered into force 15 September 1976) 1023 UNTS 15 (Registration Convention).

16 Bin Cheng, *Studies in International Space Law* (OUP 1997) 6.

17 David Lindgren, *An Assessment Framework for Compliance with International Space Law and Norms: Promoting Equitable Access and Use of Space for Emerging Actors* (Springer 2020) 25.

18 Charter of the United Nations (adopted 26 June 1945, entered into force 24 October 1945) 1 UNTS XVI (UN Charter).

19 Article 1 UN Charter.

20 Peter Jankowitsch, 'The Background and history of Space Law' in Frans von der Dunk and Fabio Tronchetti (eds), *Handbook of Space Law* (EEPL 2015) 2.

21 Ram S Jakhu and Paul Stephen Dempsey (eds), *Routledge Handbook of Space Law* (Routledge 2017) 8.

22 Ibid 7.

in the field. The principles enshrined in the treaty have assisted in the development of international and domestic rules.

2. The Moon Agreement

The Moon Agreement substantially reaffirms many of the provisions of the OST.[23] In terms of participation and compliance, the Moon Agreement is often viewed as a failure for its low number of ratifications in comparison to other treaties. To some, this is because many of its provisions are in contrast to a more market-friendly world.[24] To others, the Moon Agreement is the least popular due to its restrictive terms and provisions. For example, article 11 declares the Moon and its natural resources to be the 'Common Heritage of Mankind' and calls for the establishment of an international regulatory regime to govern the exploitation of the natural resources of the Moon.[25] States advanced opposite views about the interpretation and application of the Common Heritage of Mankind concept to the management and exploitation of lunar resources.[26] Further, the Moon Agreement fails to meet the necessary geopolitical and economic realities of the current space environment and the priorities of those engaging in activities in the domain.[27]

Despite low participation, the principles incorporated under the Moon Agreement have been cited time and again. To a few, the Moon Agreement contains several articles that tighten restrictions on State activities and powers.[28] To others,

> the treaty aims to establish a number of best practices and guiding principles for the cooperative use and exploitation of the Moon and celestial bodies, which particularly from a Global South perspective emphasise on the distribution of benefits to developing countries who may otherwise lack access to such resources and the ability to benefit from them.[29]

The principles and objectives of the Moon Agreement have also been endorsed under several instruments adopted by COPUOS, member States, and other agencies.[30]

---

23 Courtney Trombly, 'The Space Race: Futile Fighting for Finite Findings' (2021) 31 Albany Law Journal of Science & Technology 127–128.

24 Jankowitsch (n 20) 13.

25 Fabio Tronchetti, 'The Exploitation of Natural Resources of the Moon and Other Celestial Bodies: A Proposal for a Legal Regime' (Brill 2009) 41.

26 Ibid 56–57.

27 David Lindgren (ed), *An Assessment Framework for Compliance with International Space Law and Norms: Promoting Equitable Access and Use of Space for Emerging Actors* (Springer 2020) 28.

28 Katherine Latimer Martinezt, 'Lost in Space: An Exploration of the Current Gaps in Space Law' (2021) 11: 2 Seattle Journal for Technology, Environmental & Innovation Law 328.

29 Lindgren (n 17) 28.

30 European Space Agency Earth-Moon System Agendas <http://lunarexploration.esa.int/explore/science/218> accessed 2 August 2023.

3. *The Liability Convention*

Under the OST, articles VI, VII, and VIII relate to State liability. The Liability Convention elaborates upon the provisions of the OST by establishing a framework for claiming compensation for damage caused by space objects. In 1971, the UNGA underlined that the 'Convention fulfils the need of the international community for a separate international instrument on the rights and obligations pertaining to liability for damage'.[31] In 2005, the UNGA Resolution on the Application of the Concept of the Launching State reaffirmed that 'the Liability Convention identifies those States which may be liable for damage caused by a space object and which would have to pay compensation in such a case'.[32]

The notable features of the Convention include article I, which defines damage as loss of life, personal injury, or other impairments of health; or loss of or damage to property of States or of persons, natural or juridical, or property of intergovernmental organisations. Article XII of the Convention specifies that the compensation which the launching State shall be liable to pay for damage under this Convention shall be determined in accordance with international law and the principles of justice and equity.[33]

II. NON-BINDING RULES

Non-binding rules, although voluntary, have been found to have considerable influence on the development of outer ISL. In the case of the space resolutions of the UNGA, for instance, they carry 'notable political weight especially when adopted with the full support of the Assembly's members'.[34] To Jankowitsch, the resolutions form a code of conduct and reflect a wide legal conviction of the present international space community on special categories of space activities. If followed, as is the case, by constant practice of States and international organisations, the resolutions 'may play a significant role either in establishing customary rules of international law[35] or serve as a basis for future international negotiations on treaties to regulate the same subjects but this time in a legally binding manner'.[36] In this way, the documents adopted by COPUOS 'have been a constant driver for the development of space law and international cooperation of Member States in their space activities'.[37]

---

31 UNGA (1971) Resolutions adopted on the reports of the First Committee, 26th Session, 25.

32 UNGA, 'Application of the Concept of the "Launching State"' (25 January 2005) 59th Session (2004) UN Doc A/RES/59/115.

33 Christol (n 3) 67.

34 Hao Liu and Fabio Tronchetti, 'United Nations Resolution 69/32 on the "No First Placement of Weapons in Space": A Step Forward in the Prevention of an Arms Race in Outer Space?' (2016) 28 Space Policy 1.

35 On customary international law, see Stoica, § 6.2, in this textbook.

36 Jankowitsch (n 20) 8.

37 UN Office for Outer Space Affairs, 'Space Law: Resolutions' <www.unoosa.org/oosa/en/ourwork/spacelaw/resolutions.html> accessed 2 August 2023.

> **BOX 20.3** Example: Non-binding Rules of ILS
>
> One can look at the UNGA Principles Declaration,[38] which incorporates the fundamental principles of outer ISL. The Principles Declaration informs the development of ISL in treaties, declarations, national policies, and other agreements. Other notable instruments include the Declaration on International Cooperation in the Exploration and Use of Outer Space for the Benefit and in the Interest of All States, Taking into Particular Account the Needs of Developing Countries (the Benefits Declaration, 1997); Resolution on No First Placement of Weapons in Outer Space (2014);[39] and the Voluntary Guidelines on Long-Term Sustainability (LST Guidelines, 2019).[40]

III. NATIONAL LAWS

The legislative and policy instruments of States are an important source for regulating outer space activities. Much ISL develops within the varied municipal legal systems of the world, particularly those of space-active States.[41] As per the Working Group on National Legislation Relevant to the Peaceful Exploration and Use of Outer Space, national laws of States are backed by

> the need to fulfil obligations under treaties to which a State had become a party, the need to achieve consistency and predictability in the conduct of space activities under the jurisdiction of the State, and the need to provide a practical regulatory system for private sector involvement.[42]

The enactment of national laws fulfils the responsibility of States to adopt and comply with rules of international ISL.[43] Although individual States enact legislative frameworks per their constitutional processes and security considerations, the structure and content of these rules are modelled primarily on the international space treaties and other instruments of voluntary and non-binding nature.

The COPUOS has encouraged the formulation of model national frameworks to guide the adoption of uniform national laws. A few notable frameworks are

---

38 UNGA, 'Declaration of Legal Principles Governing the Activities of States in the Exploration and Use of Outer Space' (13 December 1963) 1280th Plenary Meeting (1962) UN Doc A/RES/1962/XVIII.

39 UNGA, 'No First Placement of Weapons in Outer Space' (14 October 2016) 71st Session First Committee, UN Doc A/Res/71/32.

40 UN Report, 'Guidelines for the Long-Term Sustainability of Outer Space Activities' (2019) <www.unoosa. org/oosa/en/informationfor/media/2019-unis-os-518.html> accessed 2 August 2023.

41 Francis Lyall and Paul B Larsen, *Space Law: A Treatise* (Ashgate 2009) 35.

42 COPUOS National Legislation Relevant to the Peaceful Exploration and Use of Outer Space, 'Draft Report of the Working Group' (2012) <www.unoosa.org/pdf/limited/c2/AC105_C2_2012_CRP09Rev2.pdf> accessed 2 August 2023.

43 Lyall and Larsen (n 41) 35.

the Draft Model Law on the National Space Legislation of the International Law Association,[44] the Project 2001 Plus 'Building Blocks' for National Space Laws (2004),[45] the UNGA Recommendations on National Legislation Relevant to the Peaceful Exploration and Use of Outer Space (2013),[46] and Building Blocks for the Development of an International Framework on Space Resource Activities (2019).[47]

D. CORE PRINCIPLES AND CONCEPTS

I. SPACE SECURITY

Outer space constitutes a major concern in terms of security and long-term sustainability.[48] Security in the context of outer space is a matter of concern for States and the international community.[49] According to Sheehan, space security is an international security concept and relates to effective international governance of the space environment. Traditionally, the term 'space security' was associated with the military security of States (still the predominant understanding of the term). Today, the scope of 'space security' is wider, bringing other crucial issues to the front.[50] To Gandhi, the safety and security of space assets assume paramount importance today, considering the exercise of unlimited freedom by States.[51] This broader framework is represented in the recent Space Security Index Report, according to which space security encompasses the sustainability of the unique outer space environment, the physical and operational integrity of human-made objects in space and their ground

---

44 UNGA, 'Information on the Activities of International Intergovernmental and Non-Governmental Organizations Relating to Space Law' (19 April 2013) 52nd Session Committee on the Peaceful Uses of Outer Space, UN Doc A/AC.105/C.2/2013/CRP.6.

45 The five building blocks proposed under the Project 2001 Plus include Authorization of space activities, Supervision of space activities, Registration of space objects, Compensation, regulation, and Additional regulation. See UNCOPUOS, 'Information on the Activities of International Intergovernmental and Non-governmental Organizations Relating to Space Law' (2013) <www.unoosa.org/pdf/limited/c2/AC105_C2_2013_CRP06E.pdf> accessed 2 August 2023.

46 UNGA, 'Recommendations on National Legislation Relevant to the Peaceful Exploration and Use of Outer Space' (16 December 2013) 68th Session (2013) UN Doc A/RES/68/74.

47 The Hague International Space Resources Governance Working Group, 'Building Blocks for the Development of an International Framework on Space Resource Activities' (2019) <www.universiteitleiden.nl/binaries/content/assets/rechtsgeleerdheid/instituut-voor-publiekrecht/lucht-en-ruimterecht/space-resources/final-bb.pdf> accessed 20 August 2023.

48 Oleg Danilyan and Alexander Dzeban, 'Space Law at 21st Century: The Security Issues' (2019) 22 Philosophy and Cosmology 9.

49 See Detlev Wolter, Common Security in Outer Space and International Law (United Nations Institute for Disarmament Research 2006).

50 Michael Sheehan, 'Defining Space Security' in Kai-Uwe Schrogl, Peter L Hays Jana Robinson, Denis Moura Christina Giannopapa (eds), Handbook of Space Security (Springer 2015) 8.

51 Manimuthu Gandhi, 'Towards a Legal Regime for the Protection of Space Assets' in R Venkata Rao, V Gopalkrishnan, and Kumar Abhijeet (eds), Recent Developments in Space Law Opportunities & Challenges (Springer 2017) 120–122.

stations, and security on Earth from threats and natural hazards originating in space.[52]

II. PEACEFUL PURPOSES

Maintenance of space for peaceful purposes is the leading challenge of ISL.[53] The principle of peaceful purposes is fundamental in addressing the growing risk of an arms race in outer space, including the advancement in anti-satellite technology and the growing dependence on satellites from a civil and military perspective.[54] References to the principle have been made in the Principles Declaration,[55] article IV of the OST, which expressly outlaws 'the establishment of military bases, installations, and fortifications, the testing of any weapons and the conduct of military manoeuvres on celestial bodies'.[56] The Moon Agreement, under article 3 provides,

> the Moon shall be used by all States Parties exclusively for peaceful purposes . . . Any threat or use of force or any other hostile act or threat of hostile act on the Moon is prohibited. It is likewise prohibited to use the Moon to commit any such act or engage in any such threat about the earth, the Moon, spacecraft, the personnel of spacecraft or man-made space objects.[57]

The more recent Resolution on Practical Measures for the Prevention of an Arms Race in Outer Space (2019) reaffirms that an arms race in outer space would be a grave threat to international peace and security. The resolution urges member States, particularly those with major space capabilities, to contribute actively to the prevention of an arms race in outer space to promote and strengthen international cooperation in the exploration and use of outer space for peaceful purposes. The resolution further supports the agenda for a binding legal regime to prevent the weaponisation of outer space.[58]

III. PROVINCE OF MANKIND AND BENEFITS

The OST explicitly confirms the equality of all States under international law, regardless of their degree of economic or scientific development. According to Trombly, the

---

52 Project Ploughshares & The University of Adelaide, 'Space Security Index' (2019) <https://spacesecurityindex.org> accessed 20 August 2023.

53 Ram S Jakhu, Kuan-Wei Chen, and Bayar Goswami, 'Threats to Peaceful Purposes of Outer Space: Politics and Law' (2020) 18 1 Astropolitics 22–50, 22.

54 Liu and Tronchetti (n 34) 1.

55 UNGA, 'International Cooperation in the Peaceful Uses of Outer Space' (15 December 2021) 76th Session, UN Doc A/Res/76/76.

56 Jankowitsch (n 20) 15.

57 Ibid.

58 UNGA Resolution, 'Practical Measures for the Prevention of an Arms Race in Outer Space' (December 2019) A/RES/74/34 <https://digitallibrary.un.org/record/3846403>.

notion of outer space as a resource for all has been recognised in several international agreements.[59] Article IX of the OST provides:

> [I]n the exploration and use of outer space, including the Moon and other celestial bodies, State Parties to the treaty shall be guided by the principle of co-operation and mutual assistance and shall conduct all their activities in outer space, including the Moon and other celestial bodies, with due regard to the corresponding interests of all other State Parties to the treaty.[60]

IV. NON-APPROPRIATION

The principle of non-appropriation has been emphasised in several binding and non-binding rules on outer space. Article II of the OST provides: 'outer space, including the Moon and other celestial bodies, is not subject to national appropriation by claim of sovereignty, by means of use of occupation, or any other means'. The scope of article II of the OST has been subject to two divergent opinions. According to one view, it prohibits any exclusive rights over space and celestial bodies. This view designates outer space as the province of all mankind or international commons. The other view suggests that the provision is ambiguous and consequently, it could not be considered an explicit prohibition.[61] According to the Moon Agreement, the principle of non-appropriation applies to celestial bodies. Article 11 of the Agreement provides: 'the Moon and its natural resources are the common heritage of mankind . . . The Moon is not subject to national appropriation by any claim of sovereignty, by means of use or occupation, or by any other means'. In essence, the principle 'prohibits claims to ownership in outer space'.[62] The principle is also emphasised in the Benefits Declaration,[63] and the Guidelines on National Systems.[64]

V. LONG-TERM SUSTAINABILITY

Long-term sustainability means

> the ability to maintain the conduct of space activities indefinitely into the future in a manner that realises the objectives of equitable access to the benefits of the

---

59 Trombly (n 23).

60 Jakhu and Dempsey (n 4) 9.

61 Stephan Hobe and Philip de Man, 'National Appropriation of Outer Space and State Jurisdiction to Regulate the Exploitation, Exploration and Utilization of Space Resources' (2017) 66 ZLW 460, 462.

62 Stephan Hobe and Kuan-Wei Chen, 'Legal Status of Outer Space and Celestial Bodies' in Ram S Jakhu and Paul Stephen Dempsey (eds), *Routledge Handbook of Space Law* (Routledge 2017) 30.

63 UNGA, 'Declaration on International Cooperation in the Exploration and Use of Outer Space for the Benefit and in the Interest of All States, Taking into Particular Account the Needs of Developing Countries' (4 February 1997) 51st Session UN Doc A/RES/51/122.

64 UNGA (n 46).

exploration and use of outer space for peaceful purposes, in order to meet the needs of the present generations while preserving the outer space environment for future generations.[65]

The responsibility for the sustainable use of outer space rests on all space actors, including States and non-State actors. It is the responsibility of national governments, regional and international organisations, and commercial operators to find a common approach to the sustainable use of outer space.[66]

The COPUOS Space 2030 Agenda invests in a comprehensive understanding of space sustainability. The agenda includes the commitment of States and other actors around four pillars: space economy, space society, space accessibility, and space diplomacy. The core objectives are (1) enhancing space-derived economic benefits and strengthening the role of the space sector as a major driver of sustainable development; (2) harnessing the potential of space to solve everyday challenges and leverage space-related innovation to improve the quality of life; and (3) improving access to space for all and ensuring that all countries can benefit socioeconomically from space science and technology applications and space-based data, information, and products, thereby supporting the achievement of the Sustainable Development Goals.[67] In 2019, the COPUOS Working Group on the Long-Term Sustainability of Outer Space Activities adopted 21 Voluntary Guidelines on the sustainable use of outer space. These guidelines cover sub-agendas including sustainable space utilisation and sustainable development on Earth, space situational awareness, weather, and regulatory regime and guidance for actors in space.[68]

VI. INTERNATIONAL RESPONSIBILITY AND COOPERATION

International responsibility[69] vis-à-vis outer space brings the focus on the rule-making authority of States (including the making and content of national space law frameworks and strategies), the responsibility of States for the activities conducted in outer space (including regulation of activities of non-States, the responsibility to cooperate towards the formation of rules concerning outer space (including collaboration with other space actors), and the responsibility to comply and coordinate.

---

65 UN Office for Outer Space Affairs, 'Guidelines for the Long-Term Sustainability of Outer Space Activities of the Committee on Peaceful Uses of Outer Space Adopted' (2019) <www.unoosa.org/oosa/en/informationfor/media/2019-unis-os-518.html> accessed 20 August 2023.

66 Gerard Brachet, 'The Origins of the Long-term Sustainability of Outer Space Activities Initiative at UN COPUOS' (2012) 28 Space Policy 165.

67 UN Committee on the Peaceful Uses of Outer Space, 'Consolidated draft "Space2030" Agenda and Implementation Plan, Working Paper Submitted by the Bureau of the Working Group on the "Space2030" Agenda' (June 2021/A/AC.105/L.321) <https://undocs.org/A/AC.105/L.321> accessed 2 August 2023.

68 Annette Froehlich and Vincent Seffinga (eds), *The United Nations and Space Security Conflicting Mandates Between UNCOPUOS and the CD* (Springer 2020) 114.

69 On State responsibility in international law, see Arévalo Ramírez, § 9, in this textbook.

On the rule-making powers of States, Hobe and de Man write:

> no single state has at all jurisdiction on this question as outer space, celestial bodies and thereby also space resources are not subject to national jurisdiction'. Further, the role of municipal legislation in this context should be limited to ensuring that State nationals adhere to the international framework.[70]

On international responsibility for activities in outer space, article VI of the OST provides:

> States Parties to the treaty shall bear international responsibility for national activities in outer space, including the Moon and other celestial bodies, whether such activities are carried on by governmental agencies or by non-governmental entities, and for assuring that national activities are carried out in conformity with the provisions as outlined in the present Treaty.

The responsibility to comply, coordinate, and cooperate includes the general responsibility to abide by rules of international law. The OST provides, under article III:

> State Parties to the Treaty shall carry on activities in the exploration and use of outer space, including the Moon and other celestial bodies, in accordance with international law, including the Charter of the United Nations, in the interest of maintaining international peace and security and promoting international co-operation and understanding.

E. RELATION TO OTHER FIELDS OF INTERNATIONAL LAW

A fascinating area of study is the intersection of space rules with other legal rules including those under environmental law,[71] human rights law, disaster management law, and climate change law.[72] These intersections are leading to the creation of new concepts, strategies, and institutional mechanisms. At the same time, they uncover the gaps in international rules.

In the case of sustainable development, for instance, efforts have been made to extend the use of space technology and resources towards attainment of various development

---

70 Hobe and de Man (n 61) 475.

71 UNCOUPUS, 'Report on Space Technologies for Monitoring and Protecting Biodiversity and Ecosystems: A Proposed New Thematic Priority for the United Nations Programme on Space Applications (2015) <www.unoosa.org/res/oosadoc/data/documents/2016/stspace/stspace69_0_html/st_space_69E.pdf> accessed 20 August 2023.

72 UNGA, 'Special Report of the Inter-Agency Meeting on Outer Space Activities on the Use of Space Technology within the United Nations System to Address Climate Change Issues' (31 March 2011) Committee on the Peaceful Uses of Outer Space, UN Doc A/AC.105/991.

goals.[73] In the Resolution on International Cooperation in the Peaceful Uses of Outer Space (2021),[74] the UNGA emphasised on the need

> to contribute to an orderly growth of space activities favourable to sustained economic growth and sustainable development in all countries, including strengthening sustainable spatial data infrastructure at the regional and national levels and building resilience to reduce the consequences of disasters, in particular in developing countries.

In the case of human rights and ISL, a strong case has been advanced for the application of existing international human rights standards to outer space and the utilisation of space technology and other benefits for the fulfilment of human rights objectives. Many have spoken of the need to extend international human rights instruments including the Universal Declaration of Human Rights (UDHR) to outer space. According to Bonilla, in the advent of private-funded settlements on Mars, human rights under the UDHR will have to be protected. These include the right against arbitrary detention (article 9), the right to privacy (article 12), the right to nationality (article 15), the right to marriage and family (article 16), and the right to freedom of assembly and association (article 20).[75] Other proposals emphasise the need for a resolution to recognise outer space as 'conflict-free for the enjoyment of fundamental rights and freedoms as enumerated in the Universal Declaration of Human Rights'.[76]

F. CONCLUSION

Outer ISL is a unique framework of international law. Its strength is its reliance on a set of higher principles and consensus-based development of rules. However, in its bid to regulate the challenges concerning outer space, it requires innovative reforms. Regarding ISL and associated reforms, commonly proposed ideas include the need for changes in existing treaty frameworks. This can be achieved either through amending current treaties or adopting new ones. Additionally, there is a call for greater clarity regarding the responsibilities of States towards treaties they have not ratified. Questions also arise about the influence of soft law on State behaviour and the necessity for consistency in national space laws.

---

73 UNGA, 'International Cooperation in the Peaceful Uses of Outer Space' (27 February 2001) 55th Session, UN Doc A/Res/55/122.

74 UNGA, 'International Cooperation in the Peaceful Uses of Outer Space' (15 December 2021) 76th Session, UN Doc A/Res/76/76.

75 Juan García Bonilla, 'How Five Fundamental Human Rights Could Be Violated in Privately-Funded Space Settlements and the Role of the Mars Agreement in Their Protection' in Annette Froehlich (ed), *Assessing a Mars Agreement Including Human Settlements* (Springer 2021).

76 Jakhu, Chen, and Goswami (n 53) 37.

BOX 20.4 Further Readings and Further Resources

Further Readings

- T Gangale, *How High the Sky? The Definition and Delimitation of Outer Space and Territorial Airspace in International Law* (Brill Nijhoff 2017)

- DH Kim, *Global Issues Surrounding Outer Space Law and Policy* (IGI Global 2021)

- I Kostenko, 'Current Problems and Challenges in International Space Law: Legal Aspects' (2020) Advanced Space Law 48–57

- KL Martinez, 'Lost in Space: An Exploration of the Current Gaps in Space Law' (2021) 11 Seattle Journal of Technology, Environmental and Innovation Law 4

- V Rao, V Gopalkrishnan, and K Abhijeet (eds), *Recent Developments in Space Law: Opportunities & Challenges* (Springer 2017)

Further Resources

- 'The International Law Academy, International Space Law' <www.youtube.com/playlist?list=PLT6MLtynHn4S1688ErDyEzMUVIiBcAqIS> accessed 2 August 2023

- 'Outer Space Law-An Interview with Leading Space Law Professor, TALKSONLAW' <www.youtube.com/watch?v=8VTT4IESHEg> accessed 2 August 2023

- Georgetown Law, 'Space Law: The Law of Outer Space' <https://guides.ll.georgetown.edu/spacelaw> accessed 2 August 2023

§ § §

CHAPTER 21
INTERNATIONAL HUMAN RIGHTS LAW

ANNALISA CIAMPI, MAX MILAS, THAMIL VENTHAN ANANTHAVINAYAGAN, GRAŻYNA BARANOWSKA, ADAMANTIA RACHOVITSA, JENS T. THEILEN, VERENA KAHL, WALTER ARÉVALO-RAMÍREZ, AND ANDRÉS ROUSSET-SIRI

INTRODUCTION

ANNALISA CIAMPI

BOX 21.1 Required Knowledge and Learning Objectives

Required knowledge: History of International Law

Learning objectives: Understanding the evolution of international human rights law as a separate branch of international law and a separate domain of global government.

BOX 21.2 Interactive Exercises

Access *interactive exercises for this chapter*[1] by positioning your smartphone camera at the dot-filled box, also known as a QR code.

Figure 21.1 QR code referring to interactive exercises.

---

1 https://openrewi.org/en-projects-project-public-international-law-international-human-rights-law/.

DOI: 10.4324/9781003451327-24

A. INTRODUCTION

This chapter traces back the evolution of human rights from its inception leading to structural changes within international law, away from State-centrism towards a stronger focus on the individual, to its recent crisis and current developments. It shows how the divide between human rights and other branches of international law (e.g. trade, investment, development) is the result of numerous failures, which date back to the aftermath of the Second World War, proceeded during and beyond the Cold War, and continued up into the 21st century.[2]

B. THE HISTORY OF INTERNATIONAL HUMAN RIGHTS LAW

I. THE FAILURE OF THE UNITARY DESIGN OF THE UNIVERSAL DECLARATION OF HUMAN RIGHTS AND THE SPLIT INTO 'GENERATIONS' OF RIGHTS

The Universal Declaration of Human Rights (UDHR)[3] is generally agreed to be a milestone document in the foundation of international human rights law. Drafted by representatives with different legal and cultural backgrounds from all regions of the world, the Declaration was proclaimed by the United Nations General Assembly in Paris on 10 December 1948 as a common standard of achievements for all peoples and all nations. As a single document, it encapsulated the progressive realisation of democracy and development through the universal and effective recognition and observance of rights. And it made no distinction between mostly 'negative' (freedoms from), classical civil and political rights, and (essentially 'positive': freedom of) social, economic, and cultural rights, or collective rights. It was, however, proclaimed as a not binding document:[4] several authoritarian States abstained, while even liberal democracies were not ready to commit themselves to binding legal obligations. Then came the Cold War and human rights became yoked to the ideological conflict between the United States and the former Soviet Union.

Deep political disagreement and profoundly different conceptions of rights between the Western and non-Western world – which included the former socialist States but also the newly independent, developing States – led to the sub-division of human rights into three categories: the 'first-generation' rights, known as civil and political rights; economic, social, and cultural rights as 'second generation' rights; and 'group rights' as 'third generation' rights.

---

2   On the history of international law, see González Hauck, § 1, in this textbook.
3   UNGA Res. 217 A (III) (1948) GAOR 3rd session, UN Doc. A/810 (1948).
4   On non-binding rules in international law, see Lima, Kunz, and Castelar Campos, § 6.4, in this textbook.

It took 18 years for the signature of the International Covenant on Civil and Political Rights (ICCPR)[5] and the International Covenant on Economic, Social and Cultural Rights (ICESCR)[6] in 1966, and then another decade for their entry into force. The adoption of these first international human rights treaties marked the setting aside of collective rights and the formal split between the first generation of rights in the ICCPR and the second generation of rights in the ICESCR. The vision of rights into 'generations' has remained also at the regional level, particularly within the Council of Europe, long considered the most advanced system for human rights protection. Yet, the UDHR is widely recognised as having inspired, and paved the way for, the adoption of more than 70 human rights treaties, all containing references to it in their preambles, both at the global level (see the United Nations human rights system[7]) and regionally (the African human rights system;[8] the European human rights system;[9] the Inter-American human rights system;[10] the Arab and Islamic human rights system;[11] and the Asian human rights system[12]).

II. THE 'INFLUENCE' OF HUMAN RIGHTS DURING THE DECOLONISATION PERIOD AND THE END OF THE COLD WAR

It is generally acknowledged that during decolonisation[13] beginning in the 1960s and more prominently in the 1970s and 1980s, human rights became to exercise their influence and became a major force in international relations.

The Soviet Union ratified the ICCPR in 1973 and 1975 set the beginning of the Helsinki process. Despite their lack of formal status as international treaties setting out binding commitments, the Helsinki Accords provided a framework for the scrutiny of human rights practice in the former Soviet Union and its satellite States. In 1977, the US Congress passed a law conditioning certain types of aids to compliance with human rights. The Convention on the Elimination of All Forms of Discrimination against Women was adopted in 1979,[14] based on a General Assembly resolution sponsored by 22 developing countries and some East European States.

---

5 International Covenant on Civil and Political Rights (adopted 16 December 1966, entered into force 23 March 1976) 999 UNTS 171.

6 International Covenant on Economic, Social and Cultural Rights (adopted 16 December 1966, entered into force 3 January 1976) 993 UNTS 3.

7 On the universal human rights system, see Ananthavinayagan and Baranowska, § 21.2, in this textbook.

8 On the African human rights system, see Rachovitsa, § 21.3, in this textbook.

9 On the European human rights system, see Theilen, § 21.4, in this textbook.

10 On the Inter-American human rights system, see Kahl, Arévalo-Ramírez, and Rousset-Siri, § 21.5, in this textbook.

11 On the Arab and Islamic human rights system, see Rachovitsa, § 21.6, in this textbook.

12 On the Asian human rights system, see Rachovitsa, § 21.7, in this textbook.

13 On decolonisation, see González Hauck, § 1, in this textbook.

14 Convention on the Elimination of All Forms of Discrimination against Women (adopted 18 December 1979, entered into force 3 September 1981) 1249 UNTS 13.

The Convention against Torture[15] – a milestone in the protection of the most fundamental human rights – was signed in 1984. Following a proposal by Poland and other countries of the Soviet bloc, the Convention on the Rights of the Child[16] was opened to signature in 1989.

III. THE DIVIDE BETWEEN THE THEORY AND PRACTICE OF HUMAN RIGHTS IN THE LAST DECADE OF THE 20TH CENTURY

In the post–Cold War, post-decolonisation era, the existence of an international human rights regime was well established. While not all countries had ratified all human rights treaties,[17] most countries ratified most of them. Nowadays, some treaties have been ratified nearly by all States (most notably, the ICCPR with 173 State parties and the Convention on the Rights of the Child with 196) and each of the six major human rights treaties has more than 150 parties.

In 1993 the United Nations Office of the High Commissioner for Human Rights was established. Its task includes preventing human rights violations and securing respect for all human rights, promoting international cooperation and coordinating related activities throughout the United Nations, and leading efforts to integrate a human rights approach within all activities carried out within the United Nations system.

Taking on human rights–related causes became one of the most important functions of non-governmental organisations (NGOs)[18] around the world. NGOs with a focus on human rights issues increased in number and activities, working with or against governments in developing agendas for action, participating in treaty negotiations, investigating, and reporting human rights abuses and offering direct assistance to victims of those abuses, lobbying political officials, corporations, international financial institutions, intergovernmental organisations, and the media. NGOs became also increasingly involved in providing services, such as training programmes on the rule of law and humanitarian assistance in disaster areas.

This was also the era when the legal theory of *jus cogens*[19] (Latin: 'peremptory norms') emerged and started to permeate diplomatic intercourses, judicial arguments in national and international fora, and the academic debate to include the prohibition of torture, genocide, and other serious breaches of human rights. More broadly, the '90s were characterised by the general blossoming of multilateralism and have become known as the 'golden age' of international law and international institutions.

---

15 Convention against Torture and Other Cruel, Inhuman or Degrading Treatment or Punishment (adopted 10 December 1984, entered into force 26 June 1987) 1465 UNTS 85.

16 Convention on the Rights of the Child (adopted 20 November 1989, entered into force 2 September 1990) 1577 UNTS 3.

17 On international treaties, see Fiskatoris and Svicevic, § 6.1, in this textbook.

18 On non-governmental organisations, see Chi § 7.6, in this textbook.

19 On legal sources in general, see Eggett, § 6, in this textbook.

Notwithstanding these developments at the normative, institutional, operational, and theoretical level, however, the decade between the end of the Cold War and the end of the 20th century sets the beginning of a divide between the legal aspirations and the actual implementation of human rights. While the 1970s had seen the human rights movement acquiring prominence in international law, in the 1990s there was consensus that all countries must respect human rights; yet some of the worst atrocities of our modern era are committed in many parts of the world, including within the European borders.

Countless international crimes were committed by all sides to the conflict in the former Yugoslavia in 1991. In 1994, the Rwandan genocide, during the Rwandan Civil War, which had started in 1990, killed between 500,000 and 1,000,000 Rwandans constituting an estimated 70% of the Tutsi population. Following the dissolution of the Soviet Union on 26 December 1991, the establishment of the Russian Federation was marked by the First Chechen War (1994–1996), which set the prelude to the ten-year-long Second Chechen War (1999–2009), with estimates of military and civilian casualties varying in the number of tens of thousands.

Another manifestation of the rising divide between human rights theory and practice is in the response to the Chinese government's armed repression of the political unrest in Tibet in 1987–1989 and violent suppression of the pro-democracy movement at Tiananmen Square in June 1989. Western countries imposed severe economic sanctions and arms embargoes on Chinese entities and officials, which led in turn to a spiral of harsher measures of suppression of other protests around China and heavier condemnation by the West. Initially, the US adopted strong measures against the Chinese government, including the suspension of military sales, the cancellation of high-level visits and regular meetings between the two countries, a request to stop all new loans from the International Monetary Fund and the World Bank, the revocation of China's most favoured nation status and the connection of the issue of human rights with trade. In 1994, however, the Clinton administration decided not to link these two issues and the 'American bilateral monitoring' of Chinese human rights conditions officially ended. It was not well into the 21st century that Western countries were again to impose significant sanctions related to human rights violations in China.

IV. AUTONOMY OR ISOLATION FROM OTHER DOMAINS OF GLOBAL GOVERNANCE? THE 'EFFECTIVENESS' CRISIS OF HUMAN RIGHTS AT THE DAWN OF THE 21ST CENTURY

By the turn of the century, most States had ratified the majority of the most important human rights treaties. Institutionally, the Human Rights Council was established in 2006 to replace the Commission on Human Rights – long criticised for including some of the most prominent human rights violators and the uneven selection of situations subject to its scrutiny. While special procedures continue to monitor, examine, advise, and publicly report on specific rights or country-specific situations under the Universal Periodic Review, set up by the Human Rights Council, all State

members of the United Nations are subject to a periodic assessment in relation to all
human rights issues – not just those enshrined in treaties to which they are parties.
Human rights institutions also flourish and expand at the regional level. Thanks to the
automatic right of individual application introduced in 1998, the European Court of
Human Rights can hold the then 47 member States accountable for violations of the
rights and freedoms guaranteed under the European Convention of Human Rights to
over 800 million persons. The Inter-American Court of Human Rights, the African
Court on Human and Peoples' Rights, and the Arab Human Rights Commission are
all functioning institutions overseeing compliance with their respective human rights
charter. Law schools – where future generations of judges, lawyers, and lawmakers
are formed – include international human rights courses in their curricula – which
in turn prompts private litigation, in the US and elsewhere, based upon human rights
violations. Human rights language is used everywhere and is routinely invoked to
criticise governments in political and diplomatic discourse, while human rights NGOs
continue to grow in number and in the outreach of their reporting, lobbying, and
advocacy activities.

Yet, the beginning of the 21st century was indelibly marked by two events: the
September 11 attacks of 2001 by the Islamic extremist group al-Qaeda against US
targets – which exposed the fragility of the most powerful democracy, triggering
the most geographically and temporally undefined war in history, the war against
international terrorism – and the global financial shock of 2008 with the ensuing
economic crisis.

And human rights practices worsened in many parts of the world. Following a period
of deteriorating relations between Russia and Georgia, a war erupted between Georgia,
Russia, and the Russian-backed self-proclaimed Republics of South Ossetia and
Abkhazia in August 2008. Another war erupted in 2014, when Russia seized Crimea
from Ukraine violating the territorial integrity of the former Soviet Republic. Africa
is afflicted in the East by a major armed conflict in the Darfur region of Sudan that
began in February 2003 between rebel groups and the government of Sudan, which
they accused of oppressing Darfur's non-Arab population. The government responded
to attacks by carrying out a campaign of ethnic cleansing against Darfur's non-Arabs.
The North is marked by the Arab Spring, a series of anti-government protests,
demonstrations and armed rebellions that commenced in Tunisia in 2010 and spread,
in early 2011, across North Africa and the Middle East, as a response to oppressive
regimes and low living standards. One of the consequences was the multi-State military
intervention in Libya in March 2011, led by the North Atlantic Treaty Organization,
and the ensuing chaos that still dominates the country. As part of the Arab Spring in the
Middle East, the Syrian civil war grew out of a popular uprising against the regime of
President Bashar al-Assad in March 2011 and the brutal response of the security forces,
which dragged the country into an ongoing full-scale civil war. At the same time, the
pillars of European integration are challenged by the ensuing influx of migrants and
refugees, terrorist attacks and its own war against terrorism, and ultimately, Brexit and
the rise of anti-establishment populist parties.

The distance between the theory and practice of human rights became more profound, posing dramatically the question of the 'effectiveness' of the international human rights regime. Human rights themselves are increasingly the object of criticism,[20] with some States even backlashing against the European Court of Human Rights or the Inter-American Court of Human Rights.

1. The 'Effectiveness' of International Human Rights Law

Human rights rules and principles differ from those governing international trade, investment, development, or the protection of the environment in their normative structure, institutional settings, and dispute settlement mechanisms. International human rights law is relatively weak compared, for example, to the regime of international trade or direct investment abroad. No competitive market forces push countries towards compliance, nor are States generally consistent in their application of human rights standards to their foreign policy, and only exceptionally employ political, economic, military, or other sanctions to coerce other countries to improve their human rights records. This is because, contrary to trade openness or the protection of foreign investments, a State and its citizens are hardly affected if the human rights of citizens of other countries are violated in the territory of their home State. This is the conundrum and the eternal dilemma of human rights, which impose obligations *erga omnes* (Latin: 'towards all') – respect for which should be imposed in the name of the international society as a whole – but which in fact are generally enforced only when specific national interests are at stake. And without powerful States taking a strong interest in the effectiveness of human rights, there is little cost for countries with a poor human rights reputation to ratify human rights treaties as a symbolic gesture of goodwill, while maintaining their actual practices in reality.

Human rights did bring about significant positive changes in State behaviours *visa-à-vis* (French: 'face-to-face') individuals in the second half of the 20th century. Accounts, however, differ as to the precise contribution of international law to the improvement of human rights conditions worldwide in the second half of the 20th century. Unlike growth in gross domestic product, import and export data and foreign direct investment stocks and flows, the effectiveness of human rights is hardly measurable because numerical values are not entirely attributable to human rights practices. The development of human rights indicators by international organisations[21] does not fundamentally alter this picture. It is also difficult to deny that human rights improvements on the ground in various areas of the world in the last decade of the 20th century were not the product of the human rights movement, but are rather attributable to economic growth, the collapse of communism, and other offsetting factors. And, at the beginning of the 21st century, international human rights law is undergoing a profound crisis.[22]

---

20 On critique of human rights, see Ananthavinayagan and Theilen, § 21.8, in this textbook.
21 See e.g. the OHCHR, Human Rights Indicators. A Guide to Measurement and Implementation (2012).
22 Beth A Simmons, *Mobilizing for Human Rights. International Law in Domestic Politics* (CUP 2012).

2. COVID-19 and New Technologies

All international law fields are affected by the pervasiveness of the new technologies, as discussed in depth elsewhere in this textbook.[23] The internet and social networks can both significantly facilitate and impede the exercise of human rights. They offer a powerful means for society and individuals to express their rights, but also a new, online environment in which such rights can be curtailed by powerful States, public and private institutions, and individuals. As a consequence, international human rights rules need to be interpreted and adapted and new rules need to be enacted in order to ensure cybersecurity and to protect against hate speech, misinformation, disinformation, incitement of violence, and other digital content that can also cause real-world harm. New technologies have also contributed to make both small- and large-scale human rights breaches well detected and documented, with no corresponding decline, however, in human rights breaches. Also, the human rights implications of artificial intelligence and big data, due to their enormous scope and global reach, could not be overestimated. This phenomenon had been going on for several decades, but modern technologies increased incrementally over the second decade of the 21st century, and the outbreak of COVID-19, even before it unleashed its catastrophic economic and social consequences, precipitated it.

BOX 21.3 Advanced: COVID-19 and Human Rights

While human rights are more important than ever in times of crisis, the COVID-19 pandemic exposed gaps in respecting the fundamental rights to health, education, employment, and social protection across society. Measures taken to curb its spread to safeguard public health and provide medical care to defend the human rights of health and of life itself limited fundamental freedoms to an extent rarely experienced in peacetime.

C. EFFORTS AT REUNITING HUMAN RIGHTS WITH OTHER DOMAINS OF GLOBAL GOVERNANCE

As highlighted above, the history of international human rights law is primarily a story of separation of human rights from other realms of international law. One of the causes of their ineffectiveness is precisely in its relative isolation from other domains of global governance. Hence, it is desirable to overcome such a separation.

---

23 On international law in cyberspace, see Hüsch, § 19, in this textbook.

I. BRIDGING EXISTING DIVIDES FROM WITHIN THE HUMAN RIGHTS REGIME

With a view to filling the considerable gap between the recognition of human rights and their implementation on the ground, the UN has put great emphasis, in the first quarter of the 21st century, on the universality, indivisibility, and interdependence of human rights. The principle of universality means that human rights shall enjoy universal protection across all boundaries and civilisations, regardless of political, economic, or cultural systems. Indivisibility implies that all civil, cultural, economic, political, and social rights are equally important and that the improvement in the enjoyment of any right cannot be at the expense of the realisation of any other. Human rights are seen as interdependent because the level of enjoyment of any one right is considered as dependent on the level of realisation of the other rights.

While very few would not wish theoretically for a world where all rights are equally protected, respected, and fulfilled for everyone, the debate is intense at the level of implementation and enforcement. There is no evidence that the adoption and promotion of these principles by the United Nations was ever informed by empirical facts. Indeed, it is possible to fully implement or secure certain human rights (e.g. the right not to be enslaved or tortured) without fully implementing or securing other human rights (e.g. the right to education or food), and vice versa. The realisation of rights requires choices as to ways in which to implement them and to what extent, and by employing which resources.

BOX 21.4 China's New International Human Rights Diplomacy

A more radical attempt at bridging the divide between human rights and international economic and development law and a fundamental challenge to the universality of human rights is China's 'cultural relativism' and collectivist conception of human rights, including its emphasis on 'development first'. Along with the former Soviet Union, China contributed to the rise of the second generation of rights and played an important role in the three-generation debate. After Tiananmen Square, however, human rights had become a structural weakness that China had to overcome through active diplomacy. In the 21st century, China still promotes the concept that human rights must be 'based on national conditions, with the right to development as the primary basic human right', a point emphasised in the Beijing Declaration in 2017. As part of its broader effort to redefine its role on the world scene since the turn of the millennium, China aims to establish itself as an international human rights world champion, with the Human Rights Council as the natural arena for the display of such a move – a dimension that has received little attention so far.

II. REUNITING HUMAN RIGHTS WITH TRADE, INVESTMENT, AND DEVELOPMENT THROUGH FREE TRADE AGREEMENTS, SUSTAINABLE DEVELOPMENT GOALS, AND OTHER TOOLS

For 70 years, the development of international legal rules was the main strategy to promote respect for and observance of human rights. International human rights law continues to grow, enriching itself with new treaties, declarations, and resolutions, because States, international organisations, and NGOs continue to feel a need for such international instruments covering certain areas of human rights.

Many countries, however, also began to negotiate bilateral and regional trade agreements, which primarily aim to establish or further deepen preferential economic relations between the parties, but also include chapters on core human rights, the environment and development. It is too early to assess this new generation of free trade agreements with respect to their stated aim of fostering trade and investment while at same time promoting human rights, particularly labour rights, the protection of the environment, and other third generation rights (such as the right to clean water and other essential goods, usually provided by State public services). Whether they will be successful or not, they represent a clear sign that there exists a need to 'reunite' within a single normative framework these multiple areas of the law.

A number of Western States have also introduced a series of new unilateral measures in order to ensure respect for human rights around the world, such as bans on the import of goods suspected to have been produced with forced labour or as a result of other human rights violations, and corporate due diligence requirements, which aim to anchor human rights in companies' operations and governance. These are also tools which aim to link human rights to international trade and the economic realm, more broadly.

In the same perspective, following the Millennium Development Goals adopted in 2000, the 2030 Agenda for Sustainable Development set, in 2016, the Sustainable Development Goals (SDGs): 17 global goals covering social and economic development issues including poverty, hunger, health, education, global warming, gender equality, water, sanitation, energy, urbanisation, environment, and social justice. The right to development has thus been linked to economic growth and poverty reduction, rather than political rights and personal freedoms. It is also linked to the right to security. This is another important recognition that the furtherance of development away from international cooperation in economic matters is an unattainable goal and that international trade and investment are human rights' most natural allies.

D. CONCLUSION

At the dawn of the 21st century, international human rights law seemed to have lost much of its influence and ability to bring about changes in the human rights situation around the world. Yet recent developments, particularly in the last decade (most prominently, the advent of new technologies and their applications, the SDGs, and Western countries' new set of unilateral measures) have set the ground for a general return of human rights to the centre of international politics and the public debate. This is in principle a welcome development and one that can contribute to reunite human rights to other domains of global governance and hence to make international human rights law more effective.

BOX 21.5 Further Readings and Further Resources

Further Readings

- A Ciampi, 'The Divide Between Human Rights, International Trade, Investment and Development Law' (2018) 61 German Yearbook of International Law 251

- BA Simmons, *Mobilizing for Human Rights. International Law in Domestic Politics* (CUP 2012)

- DL Shelton, *Advanced Introduction to International Human Rights Law* (Edward Elgar 2014)

Further Resources

- 'Message to Mark the 75th Anniversary of the Universal Declaration of Human Rights, UN High Commissioner for Human Rights Volker Türk' <www.ohchr.org/en/human-rights-75> accessed 20 August 2023

---

§ § §

§ 21.1 RECURRING THEMES IN HUMAN RIGHTS DOCTRINE

MAX MILAS

BOX 21.1.1 Required Knowledge and Learning Objectives

Required knowledge: International Human Rights Law; Sources of International Law; Treaties; Interaction

Learning objectives: Understanding what the legal sources of international human rights law are; how international human rights operate; who reviews human rights violations and how.

BOX 21.1.2 Interactive Exercises

Access *interactive exercises for this chapter*[24] by positioning your smartphone camera at the dot-filled box, also known as a QR code.

Figure 21.1 QR code referring to interactive exercises.

A. INTRODUCTION

International human rights law (IHRL) now affects almost every corner, every living being, and every political entity on this planet. However, how IHRL *doctrinally* governs almost every phenomenon on this planet is the subject of this chapter. To this end, the chapter first introduces the positive legal sources of international human rights law before proceeding to present actors, obligations, dispute resolution mechanisms, and the structure of judicial review of IHRL.

---

24 https://openrewi.org/en-projects-project-public-international-law-international-human-rights-law/.

B. SOURCES

I. TREATIES

Most contemporary international human rights are codified in treaties.[25] States have labelled human rights treaties with different names, ranging from charter and covenant to convention and protocol. However, this confusing labelling should not obscure the fact that international agreements for the protection of human rights, regardless of their name, constitute treaties under international law according to article 2(1)(a) VCLT[26] if they are concluded between at least two States and contain binding obligations.[27] The most emblematic human rights treaties due to their wide scope are the 1966 International Covenant on Civil and Political Rights[28] (ICCPR) and the International Covenant on Economic, Social and Cultural Rights[29] (ICESCR) at the universal level[30] and the 1950 European Convention for the Protection of Human Rights and Fundamental Freedoms[31] (ECHR),[32] the 1969 American Convention on Human Rights[33] (ACHR),[34] and the 1981 African Charter on Human and Peoples' Rights[35] (AfCHPR)[36] at the regional level. These general human rights treaties are supplemented by many specialised treaties for the protection of specific population groups, for example, women's rights[37] in the Inter-American Convention on the Prevention, Punishment, and Eradication of Violence against Women[38] and prohibitions on discrimination in the International Convention on the Elimination of All Forms of Racial Discrimination.[39]

---

25 Sarah Chinkin, 'Sources' in Daniel Moeckli and others (eds), *International Human Rights Law* (3rd edn, OUP 2018) 67; Walter Kälin and Jörg Künzli, *The Law of International Human Rights Protection* (2nd edn, OUP 2019) 33–34. On international treaties, see Fiskatoris and Svicevic, § 6.1, in this textbook.

26 Vienna Convention on the Law of Treaties (adopted 23 May 1969, entered into force 27 January 1980) 1155 UNTS 331.

27 Rhona KM Smith, *International Human Rights Law* (10th edn, OUP 2022) 1.

28 International Covenant on Civil and Political Rights (adopted 16 December 1966, entered into force 23 March 1976) 999 UNTS 171 (ICCPR).

29 International Covenant on Economic, Social and Cultural Rights (adopted 16 December 1966, entered into force 3 January 1976) 999 UNTS 3 (ICESCR).

30 On the UN human rights system, see Ananthavinayagan and Baranowska, § 21.2, in this textbook.

31 Convention for the Protection of Human Rights and Fundamental Freedoms (adopted 04 November 1950, entered into force 3 September 1953) 213 UNTS 221 (ECHR).

32 On the European human rights system, see Theilen, § 21.4, in this textbook.

33 American Convention on Human Rights 'Pact of San José, Costa Rica' (adopted 22 November 1969, entered into force 18 July 1978) 1144 UNTS 123 (ACHR).

34 On the Inter-American human rights system, see Kahl, Arévalo-Ramírez, and Rousset-Siri, § 21.5, in this textbook.

35 African Charter on Human and Peoples' Rights (adopted 27 June 1981, entered into force 21 October 1986) 1520 UNTS 217 (AfCHPR).

36 On the African human rights system, see Rachovitsa, § 21.3, in this textbook.

37 On the role of women in international law, see Santos de Carvalho and Kahl, § 7.5, in this textbook.

38 Inter-American Convention on the Prevention, Punishment and Eradication of Violence against Women (adopted 9 June 1994, entered into force 5 March 1995) (Convention of Belem do Para).

39 International Convention on the Elimination of All Forms of Racial Discrimination (adopted 7 March 1966, entered into force 4 January 1969) 660 UNTS 195.

BOX 21.1.3 Advanced: Interpreting International Human
Rights Treaties

In principle, the 'general rules on the interpretation of international treaty law'
in articles 31–33 VCLT are also applicable to human rights treaties.[40] Human
rights adjudicative bodies add a 'dynamic approach' to these general rules for
interpreting international law. According to this, human rights treaties are 'living
instruments' that have to be interpreted 'in light of present-day conditions'.[41]
This progressive mode of interpretation is used to interpret human rights
as 'proactively' and 'favourably' as possible for individuals.[42] However, this
generally positive account of interpretive techniques should not obscure the
fact that human rights treaties are also defined and applied deferentially. For
example, in its case law on migration law, the ECtHR refers to the 'principle of
state control' to leave States leeway in curtailing rights of refugees.[43] Similarly,
the ECtHR uses the 'culpable conduct doctrine' to deprive migrants of human
rights protections for failing to comply with procedures that exist only in law,
not in fact.[44]

II. CUSTOM

Some human rights are also customary international law[45] and are therefore binding
even for States that have not ratified a human rights treaty, provided sufficiently stable
State practice and *opinio juris* (Latin: 'legal opinion') exist. Two developments indicate
the required State practice and *opinio juris* for some customary human rights. First,
many States recognise the legal principles of the Universal Declaration of Human
Rights (UDHR)[46] as binding. Second, almost all States have now signed at least one
human rights treaty.[47] To identify State practice and *opinio juris* for specific human
rights, reference can be made in particular to the Universal Periodic Review of the
Human Rights Council or judgments of the International Court of Justice (ICJ).[48]

---

40 Kälin and Künzli (n 25) 34.

41 Kälin and Künzli (n 25) 34 referring to: *Tyrer v The United Kingdom* [1978] [31]; *Atala Riffo and Daughters v
Chile* [2012] 83.

42 Matthias Herdegen, 'Interpretation in International Law' in *Max Planck Encyclopedia of Public International Law*
(OUP 2009) [45–46].

43 Cabales Abdulaziz and Balkandali v. United Kingdom [1985] ECtHR Applications 9214/80, 9473/81 and
9474/81 [67–68]; Alan Desmond, 'The Private Life of Family Matters: Curtailing Human Rights Protection
for Migrants under Article 8 of the ECHR?' (2018) 29 European Journal of International Law 261, 264.

44 *N.D. and N.T. v. Spain* [2020] ECtHR Applications 8675/15 and 8697/15 [200–231].

45 On customary law, see Stoica, § 6.2, in this textbook.

46 Universal Declaration of Human Rights (adopted 10 December 1948 UNGA Res 217 A(III) (UDHR).

47 William A Schabas, *The Customary International Law of Human Rights* (OUP 2021) 342–343.

48 *Reservations to the Convention on the Prevention and Punishment of the Crime of Genocide (Advisory Opinion)* [1951]
ICJ I.C.J. Reports 1951, p. 15 23; *Questions relating to the Obligation to Prosecute or Extradite (Belgium v Senegal)*
[2012] ICJ Rep 422 [99]; Schabas (n 48) 342–343.

Nowadays, at least the prohibition of torture, racial discrimination, and slavery are considered to be customary international law.[49]

III. GENERAL PRINCIPLES

General principles of international law[50] sometimes clarify the content of international human rights. For example, in the *Golder Case*, the European Court of Human Rights (ECtHR) held that the right to a fair trial incorporates the general principle that 'a civil claim must be capable of being submitted to a judge'.[51] Similarly, the Inter-American Court of Human Rights (IACtHR) applies general principles of international law in its case law.[52]

IV. *JUS COGENS* AND *ERGA OMNES*

The prohibition of torture, racial discrimination, and slavery are recognised not only as customary international law, but also as *jus cogens*[53] norms (Latin: 'peremptory norms').[54] Hence, all rules (whether in treaties, custom or principles) that contradict these *jus cogens* human rights are invalid.[55]

BOX 21.1.4 Advanced: International Human Rights and *Jus Cogens*

The status of *jus cogens* is reserved only for the most important human rights. A majority of human rights can be limited or suspended. However, in addition to the three recognised *jus cogens* human rights, there are other *jus cogens* human rights. For example, the IACtHR recognises protection against enforced disappearance[56] and the Inter-American Commission on Human Rights (IACmHR), the African Court on Human and Peoples' Rights (AfCmHPR), and the Human Rights Committee (CCPR) recognise the right to life[57] as *jus cogens* rights.[58]

---

49 Chinkin (n 26) 71–72; James Crawford, *Brownlie's Principles of Public International Law* (9th edn, OUP 2019) 618; Kälin and Künzli (n 25) 59–60.

50 On customary law, see Eggett, § 6.3, in this textbook.

51 *Golder v United Kingdom* [1975] ECtHR Application 4451/70 [35–36].

52 *Denunciation of the American Convention on Human Rights and the Charter of the Organization of American States and the Consequences for State Human Rights Obligations* [2020] IACtHR Advisory Opinion OC-26/20 [96, 100, 110].

53 On legal sources in general, see Eggett, § 6, in this textbook.

54 International Law Commission, 'Peremptory Norms of General International Law (jus cogens)' (2022) UN General Assembly, A/CN.4/L.967, Annex.

55 Chinkin (n 26) 73–74; Kälin and Künzli (n 25) 61–62.

56 IACtHR, 'García and Family Members v. Guatemala, Judgment' (2012) Series C No. 258 [96].

57 IACmHR, 'Victims of the Tugboat '13 de Marzo' v. Cuba' (1996) Case 11.436, Report 47/96 (Merits) [79]; AfCmHPR, 'General Comment 3 on the African Charter on Human and Peoples' Rights: The Right to Life (Article 4)' (2015) [5]; CCPR, 'General Comment 29, Article 4: Derogations during a State of Emergency' (2001), CCPR/C/21/Rev.1/Add.11 [11].

58 Schabas (n 48) 62–67.

> Ultimately, the list of human rights included among *jus cogens* norms remains ill-defined and is continuously evolving.[59]

Because all *jus cogens* norms are also *erga omnes*[60] (Latin: 'towards all') rules, violations of these three human rights can be invoked by all States before international tribunals.

BOX 21.1.5 Advanced: International Human Rights and *Erga Omnes*

Non–*jus cogens* norms can also be *erga omnes* rules. However, at least in 1970, the ICJ stated that 'on the universal level, the instruments which embody human rights do not confer on States the capacity to protect the victims of infringements of such rights irrespective of their nationality'.[61] Only if certain human rights can be considered 'rules concerning the basic rights of the human person'[62] can they give rise to obligations *erga omnes*.[63] This restrictive approach only applies to universal human rights treaties. In contrast, regional human rights treaties are based on the collective enforcement of human rights by all parties to the treaty.[64] States can, for example, bring cases against other States to human rights adjudicative bodies based on so-called State complaints.[65]

C. OBLIGATIONS

I. OBLIGATED ACTORS

According to the traditional understanding, human rights first and foremost bind the State[66] as the primary duty bearer.[67] In exercising its legislative, administrative, or judicial power, the State must comply with human rights obligations arising from treaties and customary law.[68] This also applies to acts of individual security officers,[69]

---

59 Olivier de Schutter, *International Human Rights Law: Cases, Materials, Commentary* (3rd edn, CUP 2019) 85.

60 On legal sources in general, see Eggett, § 6, in this textbook.

61 *Barcelona Traction, Light and Power Company, Limited (Belgium v Spain) (Second Phase)* [1970] ICJ Rep 3 [91].

62 CCPR, 'General Comment No 31 the Nature of the General Legal Obligation Imposed on State Parties to the Covenant' (2004) [2].

63 International Law Commission, 'Report of the International Law Commission' (2006) General Assembly, Official Records 61st session, Supplement No. 10 (A/61/10) 421–423.

64 *Barcelona Traction, Light and Power Company, Limited (Belgium v. Spain) (Second Phase)* (n 22) [91].

65 Article 46 AfCHPR, article 45 ACHR, article 33 ECHR.

66 On States, see Green, § 7.1, in this textbook.

67 Article 1 ECHR, article 2(1) ICCPR, article 2(1) ICESCR, article 1(1) ACHR, article 1 AfCHPR.

68 Sarah Joseph and Sam Dipnall, 'Scope of Application' in Daniel Moeckli and others (eds), *International Human Rights Law* (3rd edn, OUP 2018) 111; Kälin and Künzli (n 25) 69.

69 *Velásquez-Rodríguez v Honduras* [1988] [170].

private persons performing State functions,[70] or subsequent explicit acceptance of acts[71]. While States have wide discretion in implementing obligations under international law in general, human rights obligations are more specific: States must respect, protect, and fulfil human rights.[72]

Certainly, almost all human rights treaties oblige (only) States to respect human rights. However, non-State actors[73] may also have human rights obligations.[74] Some human rights treaties even contain clauses under which individuals have obligations. In this case, human rights obligations of private actors can be derived directly from the treaty text.[75]

BOX 21.1.6 Example: Obligations of Non-State Actors

Article 27(1) AfCHPR provides that 'Every individual shall have duties towards his family and society, the State and other legally recognised communities and the international community'.[76]

In addition, direct human rights obligations of non-State actors are discussed for a variety of cases if they threaten the human rights of individuals in a State-equivalent manner. This is discussed for terrorists,[77] insurgencies (when they exercise de facto State power in armed conflicts), and large corporations.[78]

II. PROTECTED ACTORS

Human rights bind the State vis-à-vis all individuals[79] within its territory and under its jurisdiction.[80] Unless human rights are not explicitly limited to nationals, they apply

---

70 Kälin and Künzli (n 25) 70–71.

71 *Case concerning United States Diplomatic and Consular Staff in Tehran (United States of America v Iran)* [1980] 3 [63 ff.].

72 Frédéric Mégret, 'Nature of Obligations' in Daniel Moeckli and others (eds), *International Human Rights Law* (3rd edn, OUP 2018) 97; Schutter (n 61) 292.

73 On the variety of actors, see Engström, § 7, in this textbook.

74 While it is disputed whether these obligations of non-State actors can also be called 'obligations' or 'duties' or 'responsibilities', for the sake of consistency, the term 'obligations' is used in this chapter.

75 Kälin and Künzli (n 25) 73.

76 See also article 29(1) UDHR: 'Everyone has *duties* to the community in which alone the free and full development of his personality is possible'.

77 IACmHR, 'Report on Terrorism and Human Rights' (2002) OEA/Ser.L/V/II.116, Doc. 5 rev. 1 corr. [48].

78 David Bilchitz, 'The Ruggie Framework: An Adequate Rubric for Corporate Human Rights Obligations?' (2010) 7 SUR – International Journal On Human Rights 198. Sir Nigel Rodley, 'Non-State Actors and Human Rights' in *Routledge Handbook of International Human Rights Law* (Routledge 2012); Kälin and Künzli (n 25) 72. On business and human rights, see González Hauck, § 7.7, in this textbook.

79 On individuals, see Theilen, § 7.4, in this textbook.

80 Joseph and Dipnall (n 68) 111; see also article 2(1) ICCPR.

equally to nationals and non-nationals.[81] Human rights protect vulnerable groups[82] in particular, such as undocumented migrants, disabled people, elderly people, and indigenous peoples as well as women, transgender people, and children.[83]

BOX 21.1.7 Example: Human Rights and Nationality

Article 25 ICCPR limits the right to political participation to citizens, while the prohibition of torture or inhuman and degrading treatment (article 7 ICCPR) applies equally to nationals and non-nationals (e.g. asylum seekers).

The unborn have no international human rights.[84] According to article 4(1) ACHR, life does not begin with birth, but already with conception. However, this clause has never been successfully invoked on behalf of an unborn and other regional and universal human rights treaties do not contain such a clause. On the contrary, both the ECtHR and the CCPR reject rights of the foetus independent of the pregnant person.[85] This approach is consistent with the wording of article 1 UDHR ('all human beings are *born* free'). Nowadays, many human rights systems provide a (sometimes limited) right to abortion.[86]

A uniform approach to human rights of corporations[87] does not exist. While in the European human rights system corporations have standing before the ECtHR, in the UN and Inter-American systems only individuals have human rights. However, insofar as rights of individuals are protected by a company, individuals can also invoke rights of companies.[88] For the rights of indigenous peoples,[89] on the other hand, most human rights systems provide for distinctive rights.[90]

---

81 Ibid 111–112.

82 For a critical reflection on vulnerability in the human rights discourse, see Pamela Scully, 'Vulnerable Women: A Critical Reflection On Human Rights Discourse and Sexual Violence' (2009) 23 Emory International Law Review 113.

83 Article 2(2), (3) ICESCR; see also CESCR, 'General Comment No. 14: The Right to the Highest Attainable Standard of Health (Article 12 of the Covenant)' (2000) E/C.12/2000/4; Roberto Andorno, 'Is Vulnerability the Foundation of Human Rights?' in Aniceto Masferrer and Emilio García-Sánchez (eds), *Human Dignity of the Vulnerable in the Age of Rights* (Vol 55, Springer International 2016).

84 Kälin and Künzli (n 25) 112.

85 *Vo v France* [2004] ECtHR Application 53924/00; *Peter Michael Queenan v Canada* [2005] CCPR CCPR/C/84/D/1379/2005.

86 Rebecca Smyth, 'Abortion in International Human Rights Law at a Crossroads: Some Thoughts on Beatriz v El Salvador' [2023] Völkerrechtsblog <https://voelkerrechtsblog.org/abortion-in-international-human-rights-law-at-a-crossroads/> accessed 21 June 2023; Spyridoula Katsoni, 'The Right to Abortion and the European Convention on Human Rights: In Search of Consensus among Member-States' [2021] Völkerrechtsblog <https://voelkerrechtsblog.org/the-right-to-abortion-and-the-european-convention-on-human-rights/> accessed 21 June 2023.

87 On corporations, see González Hauck, § 7.7, in this textbook.

88 Joseph and Dipnall (n 68) 112–114.

89 On indigenous peoples, see Viswanath, § 7.2, in this textbook.

90 Article 1, 47 ICCPR; article 20(1) AfCHPR; *Indigenous Communities of the Lhaka Honhat (Our Land) Association v Argentina* [2020] IACtHR Series C 400; *Maya Kaqchikel Indigenous Peoples of Sumpango et al. v Guatemala* [2021] IACtHR Series C 440.

BOX 21.1.8 Example: Rights of Indigenous Peoples

Article 20(1) AfCHPR provides that 'All peoples shall have the right to existence. They shall have the unquestionable and inalienable right to self-determination. They shall freely determine their political status and shall pursue their economic and social development according to the policy they have freely chosen'.

III. TYPES OF OBLIGATIONS

Obligated actors must respect human rights by refraining from interference with rights (so-called negative obligations) and by protecting rights through action (so-called positive obligations).[91] Negative obligations require duty-bearers to refrain from unlawfully interfering with human rights. States may therefore only restrict human rights if they can provide a justification for the interference. This requires a restriction that is prescribed by law, serves a legitimate aim, and is necessary in a democratic society. Thereby, negative obligations correspond to the duty to respect human rights.[92]

BOX 21.1.9 Example: Negative Obligations

A State that uses judicial birching as a form of corporal punishment violates the prohibition of degrading punishment in article 7(1) ICCPR. Since this is a *jus cogens* obligation, the State cannot justify such an intrusion by referring to societal interests. In contrast, a COVID-19 related ban on public indoor assemblies interferes with the freedom of assembly under article 21 ICCPR but can be justified (at least during the initial spread of COVID-19) by reference to public health.

Duty-bearers cannot, however, fulfil their human rights obligations by mere omission. Instead, they must also respect their positive obligations. Positive obligations oblige duty-bearers to actively protect human rights. States must protect individuals from State, human, and natural threats (so-called duty to protect), provide effective access to justice (so-called procedural rights), share information, and enable participation in political and social processes.[93] These duties apply to all State organs and to economic, social, and cultural rights as well as civil and political rights.[94] Thereby, positive obligations correspond to the duties to protect and to fulfil human rights.

---

91 Kälin and Künzli (n 25) 87.
92 This is discussed in more detail in: Mégret (n 70) 97; Schutter (n 61) 292.
93 Eckart Klein (ed), *The Duty to Protect and to Ensure Human Rights* (Berlin-Verl, Spitz 2000); Alastair Mowbray, 'Duties of Investigation Under the European Convention on Human Rights' (2002) 51 International and Comparative Law Quarterly 437; Kälin and Künzli (n 25) 87–89.
94 Ibid 106.

BOX 21.1.10 Example: Positive Obligations

If a State is aware, or should have been aware, that a landslide is imminent as a result of private coal mining and nevertheless fails to take legislative or executive measures to protect the population, the State violates the right to life in article 6(1) ICCPR of the victims. Similarly, impoverished persons are entitled to legal aid to enforce their legal claims.[95]

D. INTERNATIONAL REVIEW OF HUMAN RIGHTS OBLIGATIONS

In IHRL there is no global forum that monitors human rights as the final authority. Instead, State compliance with human rights is supervised simultaneously by universal and regional courts, committees, and commissions in judicial, quasi-judicial, and non-judicial forums.[96] Courts are authorised to exercise judicial review of human rights. In a similar way, quasi-judicial bodies can also rule on individual complaints. Non-judicial bodies operate alongside this (quasi-)judicial supervision by documenting and evaluating the general, not complaint-specific, human rights situation.[97]

I. JUDICIAL REVIEW

The most famous supervisors of human rights are certainly the three regional human rights courts in Europe, America, and Africa. The ECtHR, the IACtHR, and the AfCHPR have been influential in shaping human rights development not only in their regional human rights systems, but worldwide. In these forums, individuals can file cases against actions taken by the State (individual complaints) or States against other States (inter-State complaints). The ICJ also interprets human rights in its case law.[98]

BOX 21.1.11 Advanced: Standards of Review

Standards of review generally describe whether and to what extent a court adheres to the view of an institution or entity that was previously engaged in examining the facts and the law regarding a specific case.[99] In international law,

---

95 These examples are based on decisions mentioned in Kälin and Künzli (n 25) 97–98, 105.

96 Chinkin (n 26) 64.

97 'Courts & Monitoring Bodies' (*International Justice Resource Center*, 4 March 2014) <https://ijrcenter.org/courts-monitoring-bodies/> accessed 26 July 2022.

98 *Ahmadou Sadio Diallo (Republic of Guinea v Democratic Republic of the Congo)* [2010] 639 [64–98].

99 Martha S Davis, 'A Basic Guide to Standards of Judicial Review' (1988) 33 South Dakota Law Review 469, 469–470; Amanda Peters, 'The Meaning, Measure, and Misuse of Standards of Review' (2009) 13 Lewis & Clark Law Review 233, 235.

standard of review is understood as the intensity with which an international adjudicative body[100] scrutinises the respondent State's own assessment of a factual situation and legal assessment of alleged violations of international law.[101]

International human rights adjudicative bodies do not take a uniform approach to standards of review. The ECtHR recognises a certain 'margin of appreciation' of States in the interpretation and implementation of human rights (legal margin) and in the assessment of the facts (factual margin).[102] However, the notion of standards of review should not be confused with the term 'margin of appreciation' mentioned in the case law of the European Court. The margin of appreciation presupposes a degree of deference and can therefore be better described as one deferential standard of review.[103] Although the IACmHR and the IACtHR referred to the margin of appreciation and thus to deferential review in some decision,[104] their settled case law rather suggests a review with less deference to States.[105] Similarly, the CCPR has mentioned the margin of appreciation in communications concerning questions of public morals[106] and national security,[107] but for the most part has rejected it,[108] even though the drafting history of the ICCPR contained an explicit endorsement of the margin of appreciation.[109] The CCPR justifies its strict standard of review considering State's voluntary accession to human rights treaties, the universalism of IHRL, and its own function and competence.[110] In the African human rights system, the AfCmHPR seems to assume a margin of appreciation on the part of member States,[111] whereas the AfCtHR is less deferential.[112]

---

100 On dispute settlement in international law, see Choudhary, § 12, in this textbook.

101 Lukasz Gruszczynski and Wouter Werner (eds), 'Introduction' in *Deference in International Courts and Tribunals* (OUP 2014) 1–2; Caroline Henckels, *Proportionality and Deference in Investor-State Arbitration: Balancing Investment Protection and Regulatory Autonomy* (1st paperback edn, CUP 2018) 29–30.

102 Kälin and Künzli (n 25) 93–95; Mégret (n 74) 102–103.

103 L Gruszczynski and W Werner, 'Introduction' in L Gruszczynski and W Werner (eds), *Deference in International Courts and Tribunals: Standard of Review and Margin of Appreciation* (OUP 2014) 1 at 4.

104 *Advisory Opinion on Proposed Amendments to the Naturalization Provision of the Constitution of Costa Rica* [1984] IACtHR OC-4/84 [58, 62, 63]; *Ricardo Canese v Paraguay* [2004] IACtHR Series C 111 [97].

105 Antônio Augusto Cançado Trindade, *El Derecho Internacional de Los Derechos Humanos En El Siglo XXI* (2nd edn, actualizada, Editorial Jurídica de Chile 2006) 386–387; Gary Born, Danielle Morris and Stephanie Forrest, '"A Margin of Appreciation": Appreciating Its Irrelevance in International Law' (2020) 61 Harvard International Law Journal 70, 53; *Walter Humberto Vásquez Vejarano v Peru* [2000] IACmHR Case 11.166 [24, 34].

106 *Leo Hertzberg et al v Finland* [1982] CCPR CCPR/C/OP/1 [10.3].

107 *Vjatseslav Borzov v Estonia* [2004] CCPR CCPR/C/81/D/1136/2002 [7.3].

108 *Länsman et al v Finland* [1992] CCPR CCPR/C/52D/511/1992 [9.4]; *General Comment No 29: Article 4: Derogations during a State of Emergency* [2001] CCPR Adopted at the Seventy-second Session of the Human Rights Committee [6]; CCPR, 'General Comment No 34 Article 19 Freedoms of Opinion and Expression' (2011) [36].

109 Report of the Third Committee, 'Draft International Covenants on Human Rights' (1963) UN Doc. A/5655 [49].

110 CCPR, 'General Comment No 34 Article 19 Freedoms of Opinion and Expression' (2011) [36].

111 *Garreth Anver Prince v South Africa* [2004] AfCmHPR Communication 255/02 [50–53].

112 *The Tanganyika Law Society and Legal and Human Rights Centre v United Republic of Tanzania* [2013] AfCtHPR Application 009/2011 [107–111, 112]; Adem Kassie Abebe, 'Right to Stand for Elections as an Independent Candidate in the African Human Rights System: The Death of the Margin of Appreciation

II. QUASI-JUDICIAL REVIEW

The quasi-judicial human rights commissions and committees complement the judicial supervision of human rights. On the one hand, these institutions are court-like when they decide on human rights violations in individual cases, as the IACmHR, the CCPR, and the Committee against Torture do. Thereby, they also contribute to the progressive development of their respective human rights treaties. On the other hand, unlike court decisions, the decisions of these adjudicative bodies are not binding. Moreover, the work of quasi-judicial institutions is not limited to individual or inter-State complaints. Instead, the commissions and committees also assess the general human rights situation in States in so-called State reports.[113]

III. NON-JUDICIAL REVIEW

In addition to the (quasi-)judicial review of human rights violations, politicised proceedings based on IHRL are also taking place. The most notorious forum is certainly the UN Human Rights Council (UNHRC). The non-judicial bodies are not concerned with developing a coherent interpretation of human rights, but with balancing political interests.[114] These mechanisms are often criticised for their politicisation and infectivity.[115] However, the key advantage of political review of human rights violations is its applicability to all States. Political review is neither spatially nor temporally limited, and can therefore also be applied to States that do not accept the jurisdiction of judicial and quasi-judicial adjudicative bodies.[116] Moreover, it is precisely the process of political negotiation that brings the human rights discourse into previously unattainable areas.[117] In addition to these institutionalised forms of human rights monitoring, there is also a vast field of non-governmental organisations, grassroots movements, and activist litigators that also participate in the interpretation and monitoring of human rights.[118]

E. (QUASI-)JUDICIAL REVIEW OF HUMAN RIGHTS VIOLATIONS

Human rights adjudicative bodies review human rights violations in individual and (more and more frequently lately[119]) inter-State complaints using a two-tiered structure.

Doctrine?' (*AfricLaw*, 19 August 2013) <https://africlaw.com/2013/08/19/right-to-stand-for-elections-as-an-independent-candidate-in-the-african-human-rights-system-the-death-of-the-margin-of-appreciation-doctrine-2/> accessed 29 June 2022.

113 Kälin and Künzli (n 25) 192–193.

114 Ibid 192.

115 Jane Connors, 'United Nations' in Daniel Moeckli and others (eds), *International Human Rights Law* (3rd edn, OUP 2018) 385–386; Kälin and Künzli (n 25) 242–243.

116 Kälin and Künzli (n 25) 193.

117 Connors (n 119) 386–387; Kälin and Künzli (n 25) 243.

118 Chinkin (n 26) 78.

119 Isabella Risini, *The Inter-State Application under the European Convention on Human Rights: Between Collective Enforcement of Human Rights and International Dispute Settlement* (Brill Nijhoff 2018); Justine Batura and Isabella

In a first step, adjudicative bodies examine whether they have jurisdiction to hear the case, answer procedural preliminary questions, and usually review whether the complaint is manifestly ill-funded. In a second step, the adjudicative bodies examine the actual human rights violation using a two-step structure consisting of scope and interference as well as justification. This second step is the focal point of human rights complaints.

I. JURISDICTION AND ADMISSIBILITY

1. Jurisdiction

Adjudicative bodies can decide on a complaint only if they have jurisdiction.[120] Human rights treaties contain precise requirements for jurisdiction. In general, the person whose human rights have been violated must file a complaint (*ratione personae*; Latin: 'on the basis of the person') concerning the interpretation of human rights provided in the treaty under discussion (*ratione materiae*; Latin: 'on the basis of the matter'), provided that the facts of the case relate to the jurisdiction of the respondent State (*ratione loci*; Latin: 'on the basis of the place') and the human rights violation occurred after the respondent State became a party to the human rights treaty (*ratione temporis*; Latin: 'on the basis of the place').[121]

BOX 21.1.12 Advanced: Extraterritorial Application of International Human Rights

Human rights are applicable whenever the State has jurisdiction. The State has jurisdiction over its own territory.[122] However, States do not only act within their own territory, but also foreign territory to the detriment of human rights. For this case, the various human rights adjudicative bodies have found different approaches, which are discussed under the umbrella term of extraterritorial application. In the European system, the State has jurisdiction when it exercises effective control over a foreign territory or over the rights of an individual.[123] The African human rights system follows this approach.[124] The UN human rights system also echoes the effective control test but only requires that the individual be under the effective control of the State. The decisive factor is therefore the

---

Risini, 'Symposium: Inter-State Cases under the European Convention on Human Rights' (*Völkerrechtsblog*, 26 April 2021) <https://voelkerrechtsblog.org/on-current-developments-and-reform/>.

120 On jurisdiction of international courts, see Choudhary, § 12, in this textbook.

121 Article 32–34 ECHR, article 44–47 ACHR, and article 3–4 Protocol on the Establishment of an African Court on Human and Peoples' Rights.

122 Article 2(1) ICCPR.

123 *Al-Skeini and Others v the United Kingdom* [2011] ECtHR Application 56721/07 [131–150]; Joseph and Dipnall (n 68) 122.

124 AfCmHPR, 'General Comment No. 3 on the African Charter on Human and Peoples' Rights: The Right to Life (Article 4)' (2015) [14].

relationship of the State to the person affected, not the relationship of the rights violation to the territory.[125]

BOX 21.1.13 Advanced: IHRL and International Humanitarian Law

Another common issue is whether the dispute concerns the interpretation of human rights or international humanitarian law (IHL).[126] While IHL regulates armed conflict, IHRL protect almost all human behaviour. However, human rights adjudicative bodies usually only have jurisdiction over international human rights violations and not on violations of IHL. Nevertheless, overlaps may occur between IHRL and IHL due to the substantive and territorial expansion of IHRL.[127] There are situations that are exclusively subject to IHL (e.g. requisitioning of property in occupied territory) or IHRL (e.g. violations of non-derogable rights) and situations in which both fields are applied concurrently.[128] In the case of parallel application of IHRL and IHL, the overlap between the fields must be resolved based on article 31(3)(c) VCLT. Thus, the provisions of both areas of law influence each other.[129] The concurrent application of IHR L and IHL is important due to the insufficient individual protection in armed conflict, as well as uncertainties in the applicability and lack of enforcement mechanisms of IHL.[130]

2. Admissibility

However, jurisdiction is not sufficient for the adjudicative bodies to decide the substance of the claim. Instead, complainants must have exhausted domestic remedies,[131] must observe certain time limits between the violation and the filing of the complaint,[132] and must not abuse their right to appeal.[133] In addition, anonymous complaints are not permitted.[134]

---

125 CCPR, 'General Comment No 31 The Nature of the General Legal Obligation Imposed on State Parties to the Covenant' (2004) [10]; Joseph and Dipnall (n 68) 125.

126 On the international humanitarian law, see Dienelt and Ullah, § 14, in this textbook.

127 Marko Milanovic, *Extraterritorial Application of Human Rights Treaties: Law, Principles, and Policy* (OUP 2011).

128 Sandesh Sivakumaran, 'International Humanitarian Law' in Daniel Moeckli and others (eds), *International Human Rights Law* (3rd edn, OUP 2018) 512–513.

129 *Hassan v the United Kingdom* [2014] ECtHR Application 29750/09 [104–105]; Sivakumaran (n 128) 515–516.

130 Sivakumaran (n 128) 507–511.

131 Article 35(1) ECHR, article 46(1)(a) ACHR, article 2 Optional Protocol to the ICCPR, and article 50 AfCHPR.

132 Article 35(1) ECHR, article 46(1)(b) ACHR, article 56(6) AfCHPR.

133 Article 35(3) ECHR, article 3 Optional Protocol to the ICCPR, article 56(3) AfCHPR.

134 Article 35(2) ECHR, article 3 Optional Protocol to the ICCPR. Nevertheless, the identity of the complainant may be kept secret in the proceedings if necessary.

3. Cursory Examination of Merits

Furthermore, the adjudicative body may dismiss a case as inadmissible if the complaint is manifestly ill-founded,[135] gives no indication of a significant violation,[136] or has already been addressed before the body or another international body.

II. MERITS

1. Scope and Interference

Human rights adjudicative bodies examine whether the State's conduct falls within the scope of a human right. Only when the State intrudes into a sphere protected by a human right does the question of justification arise. However, this question cannot be answered in the abstract, but only depending on the concrete human right. Each human right defines its own scope.[137]

2. Justifications

Human rights are not absolute but depend on other human rights and conflict with public interests. The conflict between two human rights or human rights and public interest can be resolved through limitations and derogations of human rights. However, certain rights cannot be restricted under any circumstances. This applies to all *jus cogens* human rights.[138]

BOX 21.1.14 Example: Conflicts of Human Rights

The freedom of the press of a tabloid allows reporting on the lives of celebrities (negative obligation). This reporting usually interferes with the personal rights of the celebrities (positive obligation). This overlap can be resolved by balancing both rights. On the other hand, a conflict between the (*jus cogens*) prohibition of torture on the one hand and the interest in uncovering a criminal act must always be decided in favour of the prohibition of torture.

---

a) Limitations

Human rights limitations must satisfy a three-step test. Although the specific requirements of the test depend on the human right in question, the basic structure of the test is similar among all human rights. First, the restriction must be prescribed by law. The law must be formulated in an accessible and sufficiently precise manner.[139] Second, the limitation must serve a legitimate aim.

---

135 Article 35(3) ECHR.
136 Article 12 Protocol 14 to the ECHR.
137 Kälin and Künzli (n 25) 118.
138 Mégret (n 74) 99.
139 Ibid 100–101.

BOX 21.1.15 Example: Legitimate Aims

Article 10 ECHR stipulates that limitations of the right to freedom of expression must serve 'the interests of national security'.

States usually meet the first two requirements. Therefore, the third requirement is decisive. The limitation must serve the purpose from the second step, there must be no less intrusive means, and the means must be proportionate, that is the interest in human rights protection must not outweigh the interest in the limitation.[140] An interference is proportionate if the interest of the individual in exercising their human right does not outweigh the interest of the State in protecting the public interest.[141]

b) Derogations

In emergencies, States in the European, American, Arabic, and universal human rights systems can not only restrict human rights, but also derogate from them. Derogations are permitted if a state of emergency is declared and exists, the emergency measure is necessary and non-discriminatory, and provided that no non-derogable rights are violated.[142] The AfCHPR does not contain a derogation clause. Therefore, even in states of emergency, the parties to the AfCHPR can justify infringements on human rights only by relying on the general limitation clause.[143]

c) Economic, Social, and Cultural Rights

Economic, social, and cultural rights (ESC rights) do not oblige the State to refrain from doing something (non-interference with human rights), but to do something (providing resources). Therefore, the test for justifying interferences with these rights differs from other rights. Article 2 ICESCR contains the two decisive State obligations for ESC rights: progressive realisation and the prohibition of discrimination.[144] According to the requirement of progressive realisation, States are obliged to implement incrementally those rights for which they have sufficient resources.[145] The prohibition of discrimination furthermore requires States to guarantee all rights without discrimination.[146] The regional human rights systems further stipulate these State obligations.

---

140 Kälin and Künzli (n 25) 92–93; Mégret (n 74) 101.

141 Ibid 93; for an introductory discussion of the problems during this balancing, see Schutter (n 61) 388–390.

142 Article 4 ICCPR, article 15 ECHR, and article 27 ACHR.

143 *Commission Nationale des Droits de l'Homme et des Libertes v Chad* [1992] AfCmHPR Communication 74/92 [21].

144 Ben Saul, David Kinley, and Jacqueline Mowbray, *The International Covenant on Economic, Social and Cultural Rights: Commentary, Cases, and Materials* (OUP 2014) 133–134.

145 Ibid 143, 151–152.

146 Ibid 174–175.

F. CONCLUSION

This chapter has shown that IHRL derives from multiple sources of law, binds and obligates different actors in international law, various mechanisms exist to review human rights, and international courts around the world apply a similar scheme to review human rights violations. However, the information presented in this chapter can only serve as an introduction to a thorough discussion of IHRL. The following chapters show how different universal and regional systems regulate human rights standards by adapting them to global or local specificities.

BOX 21.1.16 Further Readings and Further Resources

Further Readings

- S Chinkin, 'Sources' in Daniel Moeckli and others (eds), *International Human Rights Law* (3rd edn, OUP 2018)

- S Joseph and S Dipnall, 'Scope of Application' in Daniel Moeckli and others (eds), *International Human Rights Law* (3rd edn, OUP 2018)

- F Mégret, 'Nature of Obligations' in Daniel Moeckli and others (eds), *International Human Rights Law* (3rd edn, OUP 2018)

- O de Schutter, *International Human Rights Law: Cases, Materials, Commentary* (3rd edn, CUP 2019)

Further Resources

- University of Pretoria Centre for Human Rights, 'Africa Rights Talk' <www.chr.up.ac.za/africa-rights-talk> accessed 17 July 2023

- D Kennedy, *The Dark Sides of Virtue: Reassessing International Humanitarianism* (Princeton University Press 2005)

- R Perkins, 'Mabo' (*ABC iView*, 2012) <https://www.youtube.com/watch?v=MwChtmA1Qr4> accessed 7 December 2023

---

§ § §

§ 21.2 UNITED NATIONS HUMAN RIGHTS SYSTEM

THAMIL VENTHAN ANATHAVINAYAGAN AND GRAŻYNA BARANOWSKA

BOX 21.2.1 Required Knowledge and Learning Objectives

Required knowledge: History of International Law; Sources of International Law; International Organisations

Learning objectives: Understanding the relevance of the United Nations human rights system and meaning of the Universal Declaration of Human Rights; the United Nations treaty- and charter-based system; and the United Nations treaty bodies and their functions.

BOX 21.2.2 Interactive Exercises

Access *interactive exercises for this chapter*[147] by positioning your smartphone camera at the dot-filled box, also known as a QR code.

Figure 21.1 QR code referring to interactive exercises.

A. INTRODUCTION

The UN human rights system differs from the regional human rights systems in its universality. The Universal Declaration of Human Rights (UDHR)[148] adopted in 1948 was crucial in triggering the codification of human rights, which on the UN level led to the creation of the core international human rights treaties and their monitoring bodies.

---

147 https://openrewi.org/en-projects-project-public-international-law-international-human-rights-law/.
148 Universal Declaration of Human Rights (adopted 10 December 1948 UNGA Res 217 A(III) (UDHR).

B. UNIVERSAL DECLARATION OF HUMAN RIGHTS

The UDHR is hailed as the first document of global reach that encompassed a wide range of human rights, touching upon civil and political rights on the one hand and, on the other hand, also economic and social rights. It also set the stage for various other human rights documents to follow, such as the twin human rights covenants, the International Covenant on Civil and Political Rights (ICCPR)[149] and the International Covenant on Economic and Social Rights (ICESCR).[150] While the UDHR is a non-binding document, some of its provisions have passed into customary international law.[151]

In face of the destruction caused by the Second World War – and to this end with the failure of the League of Nations – the world leaders of the post-war world assembled in New York to create the United Nations,[152] an assembly of States to prevent the outbreak of the Third World War. At the same time, the UDHR was drafted by persons from different cultural backgrounds, such as Charles Malik, Carlos P. Romulo, Peng-chun Chang, and Eleanor Roosevelt. It cannot be denied, however, that the UDHR has European origins.[153] Despite its rather elitist and hegemonic origins, the UDHR triggered a larger discussion and codification of human rights in different parts of the world, especially in the Global South amid its decolonisation period.[154]

The United Nations General Assembly has given the Office of the High Commissioner for Human Rights (OHCHR) the responsibility of promoting and defending the enjoyment and complete realisation of all human rights by all people. To that end, the OHCHR is mandated by the United Nations General Assembly with its resolution 48/141 to promote human rights internationally and domestically.

C. TREATY BODIES AND CORE INTERNATIONAL HUMAN RIGHTS TREATIES

The aforementioned UDHR triggered the creation of the prime human rights treaties, namely the ICESCR and the ICCPR. While the work initially was supposed to lead to

---

149 International Covenant on Civil and Political Rights (adopted 16 December 1966, entered into force 23 March 1976) 999 UNTS 171 (ICCPR).

150 International Covenant on Economic, Social and Cultural Rights (adopted 16 December 1966, entered into force 3 January 1976) 999 UNTS 3 (ICESCR). Magdalena Sepulveda, and others (eds), *Human Rights Reference Handbook* (3rd edn, University for Peace 2004) 77–113.

151 On customary law, see Stoica, § 6.2, in this textbook.

152 On the United Nations, see Baranowska, Engström, and Paige, § 7.3, in this textbook.

153 Susan Waltz, 'Reclaiming and Rebuilding the History of the Universal Declaration of Human Rights' (2002) 23 Third World Quarterly 437.

154 Johannes von Aggelen, 'The Preamble of the United Nations Declaration of Human Rights' (2000) 129 Denver Journal of International Law and Policy 129. On decolonisation, see González Hauck, § 1, in this textbook.

one general treaty on human rights, the different perspective on political and economic rights led to the adoption of two treaties, each called a 'Covenant': one on civil and political rights and the other on economic, social and cultural rights. The remaining core human rights treaties are called 'Conventions'. While the negotiations to adopt the two covenants were ongoing, States within the UN decided to work on a specialised treaty on racial discrimination, which was adopted in 1965, a year before the two covenants.[155] Since then, specialised conventions on discrimination against women, torture, rights of the child, migrant workers, persons with disabilities, and enforced disappearances have been adopted.

The UN treaty-based human rights system is based on nine core international human rights treaties (and associated optional protocols). Each of those treaties is monitored by a committee, called a treaty body. Besides the nine committees set up to monitor the core treaties, an additional treaty body was created with a preventive mandate: the Subcommittee on Prevention of Torture and other Cruel, Inhuman or Degrading Treatment or Punishment. The Subcommittee differs slightly from the other treaty bodies, as it created a two-pillar system of monitoring places of detention. Consequently, there are currently ten UN treaty bodies:

- International Convention on the Elimination of All Forms of Racial Discrimination[156] (1969): Committee on the Elimination of Racial Discrimination (CERD)
- International Covenant on Economic, Social and Cultural Rights (1976): Committee on Economic, Social and Cultural Rights
- International Covenant on Civil and Political Rights (1976): Human Rights Committee (CCPR)
- Convention on the Elimination of All Forms of Discrimination against Women[157] (1981): Committee on the Elimination of Discrimination against Women (CEDAW)
- Convention against Torture and Other Cruel, Inhuman or Degrading Treatment or Punishment[158] (1987) Committee against Torture
- Convention on the Rights of the Child[159] (1990) Committee on the Rights of the Child International
- Convention on the Protection of the Rights of All Migrant Workers and Members of Their Families[160] (2003) Committee on the Protection of the Rights of All Migrant Workers and Members of their Families

---

155 David Keane, 'Mapping the International Convention on the Elimination of All Forms of Racial Discrimination as a Living Instrument' (2020) 20 Human Rights Law Review 236.

156 International Convention on the Elimination of All Forms of Racial Discrimination (adopted 7 March 1966, entered into force 4 January 1969) 660 UNTS 195 (ICERD).

157 Convention on the Elimination of All Forms of Discrimination against Women (adopted 18 December 1979, entered into force 3 September 1982) 1249 UNTS 13 (CEDAW).

158 Convention against Torture and Other Cruel, Inhuman or Degrading Treatment or Punishment (adopted 10 December 1984, entered into force 26 June 1987) 1465 UNTS 85.

159 Convention on the Rights of the Child (adopted 20 November 1989, entered into force 2 September 1990) 1577 UNTS 3 (CRC).

160 Convention on the Protection of the Rights of All Migrant Workers and Members of Their Families (adopted 18 December 1990, entered into force 1 July 2003), 2220 UNTS 3.

- Optional Protocol to the Convention against Torture and other Cruel, Inhuman or Degrading Treatment or Punishment[161] (2006): Subcommittee on Prevention of Torture and other Cruel, Inhuman or Degrading Treatment or Punishment (SPT)
- Convention on the Rights of Persons with Disabilities[162] (2008): Committee on the Rights of Persons with Disabilities International
- Convention for the Protection of All Persons from Enforced Disappearance[163] (2010): Committee on Enforced Disappearances (CED).

I. MEMBERS

The members of treaty bodies are independent human rights experts, who are nominated and elected by the respective State parties to the covenants. The exception is the Committee on Economic, Social and Cultural Rights, whose members are elected by the Economic and Social Council (ECOSOC). While treaty body members should be elected with the aim to ensure diversity, this has not been achieved yet, with regard to neither gender nor geographic representation.[164] They serve in their personal capacity and are expected to carry out their duties impartially (see also Addis Ababa Guidelines[165]). The UN does not pay the treaty bodies members; they do receive an allowance for the sessions, which usually take place twice a year in Geneva.

II. COMPETENCES

1. Periodic Reports

States that have ratified a treaty are obliged to submit regularly reports to the relevant committee. Those reports are usually submitted every four years. The treaty bodies analyse the State report, considering also information submitted by non-governmental organisations and national human rights institutions. Afterwards, they discuss with State representatives each State report and adopt a non-binding document called 'concluding observations', which contains recommendations to the relevant State party.

2. Individual Communications

Treaty bodies also have the competence to review individual and inter-State communications. This competence requires an additional approval of a State – either

---

161 Optional Protocol to the Convention against Torture and other Cruel, Inhuman or Degrading Treatment or Punishment (adopted 18 December 2002, entered into force 22 June 2006) 2375 UNTS 237 (OPCAT).

162 Convention on the Rights of Persons with Disabilities (adopted 13 December 2006, entered into force 3 May 2008) 2525 UNTS 3.

163 Convention for the Protection of All Persons from Enforced Disappearance (adopted 20 December 2006, entered into force 23 December 2010) 2716 UNTS 3 (ICPPED).

164 'Diversity in Membership of the UN Human Rights Treaty Bodies' (*Geneva Academy*, February 2018) <Diversity in Treaty Bodies Membership.pdf (geneva-academy.ch)> accessed 18 July 2023.

165 OHCHR, 'Guidelines on the Independence and Impartiality of Members of the Human Rights Treaty Bodies' <https://www.ohchr.org/Documents/HRBodies/TB/AnnualMeeting/AddisAbebaGuidelines_en.doc> accessed 11 December 2023.

through the ratification of an Additional Protocol (for example the CCPR) or through a declaration by the State to the relevant treaty body (see for example the declarations to the CEDAW). Communications can concern only those States that have accepted the communication procedure. Currently, eight of the treaty bodies have the competence to review individual communications. Communications are reviewed by the treaty bodies, both regarding their admissibility and substance. After reviewing the case, the committees issue non-binding 'views', in which they state whether the provisions of the relevant treaty have been violated. Finally, the treaty bodies monitor whether and how States implement the views.

3. Inter-State Communications

Seven of the treaty bodies allow State parties to raise alleged violations of the treaty by another treaty body. Inter-State procedures at treaty bodies are extremely rare. So far, the CERD reviewed has *Qatar v the Kingdom of Saudi Arabia*[166] and *Qatar v the United Arab Emirates*,[167] which were suspended, as well as *State of Palestine v Israel*.[168]

4. Adopting General Comments

All treaty bodies adopt general comments, which explain how the respective treaty bodies interpret a treaty provision, thematic issues, or methods of work. Some treaties provide for this competence within the treaty (e.g. article 21 of the Convention on the Elimination of All Forms of Discrimination against Women).

5. Other Competences

Treaty bodies also have other competences that are specific to their mandate. For example, the CED's urgent action procedure is a request from the committee to the State to immediately take all necessary measures to search for, locate, and protect a disappeared person and investigate the disappearance. Another example is the SPT establishes a system of regular visits by independent national and international bodies to places where people are deprived their liberty.

---

166 Decision on the jurisdiction of the Committee in respect of the inter-State communication submitted by Qatar against Saudi Arabia, CERD-C-99–5, 19 October 2020; Decision of the ad hoc Conciliation Commission on the termination of the proceedings concerning the interstate communication Qatar v. the Kingdom of Saudi Arabia, <www.ohchr.org/sites/default/files/documents/hrbodies/cerd/decisions/2022-12-02/AHCC-CERD-Qatar-v-KSA-DECISION-TERMINATION.pdf> accessed 18 July 2023.

167 Decision on the jurisdiction of the Committee in respect of the inter-State communication submitted by Qatar against the United Arab Emirates, CERD/C/99/3, 18 June 2020; Decision of the ad hoc Conciliation Commission on the termination of the proceedings concerning the interstate communication Qatar v. the United Arab Emirates, <www.ohchr.org/sites/default/files/documents/hrbodies/cerd/decisions/ahcc-cerd-qatar-v-uae-decision-termination-adopted-26-01-2023.doc> accessed 18 July 2023.

168 Inter-State communication submitted by the State of Palestine against Israel: decision on admissibility, 17 June 2021, CERD/C/103/4; Complete list of Documents concerning the case State of Palestine v. Israel: <tbinternet.ohchr.org/_layouts/15/treatybodyexternal/TBSearch.aspx?Lang=en&TreatyID=6&DocTypeID=187> accessed 18 July 2023.

D. CHARTER-BASED SYSTEM

The UN human rights machinery, in addition to the treaty-based strand of human rights protection and promotion, has a charter-based strand. At the beginning of the UN, this consisted of the United Nations Human Rights Commission, replaced by its successor, the United Nations Human Rights Council (UNHRC). The reason for this development and replacement was the perception of the United Nations Human Rights Commission as being increasingly politicised. Throughout the 1990s and the 2000s, debate arose about the human rights records of a few commission members who were widely viewed as persistent human rights violators. The credibility of the commission was seriously impacted by these incidents.[169]

The UNHRC was created on 15 March 2006 by the UN General Assembly 'to establish the Human Rights Council, based in Geneva, in replacement of the Commission on Human Rights' according to United Nations General Assembly Resolution 60/251.[170] The UNHRC has different mechanisms to ensure the promotion and protection of human rights: the Universal Periodic Review, the Special Procedures, the Advisory Committee and the Complaint Procedure. Up to now, the UNHRC proved to be a body of universal relevance.

E. UN SYSTEM AND REGIONAL SYSTEMS

In 1993, the Commission on Human Rights adopted several resolutions that encouraged the United Nations Secretary General to strengthen cooperation and knowledge exchange with international and regional human rights bodies, while inviting the treaty bodies to explore ways to increase the exchange of information and cooperation with regional human rights mechanisms. To this end, the Resolution 1993/51 states that the Secretary-General is requested to continue fostering exchanges between the UN and regional intergovernmental organisations that deal with human rights.

F. CONCLUSION

The emergence of an international human rights infrastructure was crucial to address human rights violations at a global scale. Human rights became a dominant force for the liberation of Third World peoples. As Antony Anghie writes:

> The international human rights law that emerged as a central and revolutionary part of the United Nations period offered one mechanism by which Third

---

169 Congressional Research Service, 'The United Nations Human Rights Council: Background and Policy Issues' (26 January 2022) <https://sgp.fas.org/crs/row/RL33608.pdf> accessed 1 August 2023.

170 UNGA Res 60/251. Human Rights Council (3 April 2006), 60th session (A/RES/60/251).

World peoples could seek protection, through international law, from the depredations of the sometimes pathological Third World state. It was for this reason that international human rights law held a special appeal for Third World scholars.[171]

The ability of State parties to fulfil their responsibilities, the effectiveness of the treaty and charter bodies, and eventually the access to the system by rights holders – the system's true beneficiaries – are in a constant flux of development. More than ever, it is obvious that strengthening depends on choices being made by States parties, treaty bodies, and the Office of the High Commissioner within the bounds of their respective powers and in cooperation with one another. All must contribute in order for the system to work correctly. This specifically implies that individuals must make highly critical judgments. The United Nations has established a worldwide framework for the promotion and protection of human rights, generally in accordance with its Charter, legally enforceable treaties, and other initiatives aimed at promoting democracy and human rights globally. However, the human rights system still has a long way to go in a rapidly changing world.

BOX 21.2.3 Further Readings and Further Resources

Further Readings

- P Alston and J Crawford (eds), *The Future of UN Human Rights Treaty Monitoring* (CUP 2000)

- TV Ananthavinayagan, 'Uniting the Nations or Dividing and Conquering? The United Nations' Multilateralism Questioned – A Third World Scholar's Perspective' (2018) 29 Irish Studies in International Affairs 35

- AS Bradley, 'Human Rights Racism' (2019) 32 Harvard Human Rights Journal 1

- MW Mutua, 'The Ideology of Human Rights' (1996) 36 Virginia Journal of International Law 589.

- S Waltz, 'Reclaiming and Rebuilding the History of the Universal Declaration of Human Rights' (2002) 23 Third World Quarterly 437

Further Resources

- Congressional Research Service, 'The United Nations Human Rights Council: Background and Policy Issues' <https://sgp.fas.org/crs/row/RL33608.pdf> accessed 26 April 2022

---

171 Antony Anghie, 'The Evolution of International Law: Colonial and Postcolonial Realities' (2006) 27 Third World Quarterly 739.

- UN Treaty Body Database <https://tbinternet.ohchr.org/_layouts/15/TreatyBodyExternal/TBSearch.aspx> accessed 26 July 2023

- OHCHR Jurisprudence Database <https://juris.ohchr.org> accessed 26 July 2023

- UN Human Rights Bodies Database <https://ap.ohchr.org/Documents/gmainec.aspx> accessed 26 July 2023

§ § §

§ 21.3 AFRICAN HUMAN RIGHTS SYSTEM

ADAMANTIA RACHOVITSA

BOX 21.3.1 Required Knowledge and Learning Objectives

Required knowledge: Sources of International Law; Individuals; Recurring Themes in Human Rights Doctrine

Learning objectives: Understanding the basic substantive and institutional features of the African human rights system.

BOX 21.3.2 Interactive Exercises

Access *interactive exercises for this chapter*[172] by positioning your smartphone camera at the dot-filled box, also known as a QR code.

Figure 21.1 QR code referring to interactive exercises.

A. INTRODUCTION

Although human rights were part of the agenda of the Pan-African Congress in the anti-colonial struggle prior to the independence of the African States, the Organisation of African Unity (OAU), established in 1963, made no reference to human rights. Instead, it emphasised decolonisation, State sovereignty, and development. The language of human rights was (re)introduced with the negotiations for the African Charter on Human and Peoples' Rights (ACHPR or Banjul Charter),[173] adopted in 1981.[174] Subsequently, the Constitutive Act of the African Union (AU), which succeeded

---

172 https://openrewi.org/en-projects-project-public-international-law-international-human-rights-law/

173 African Charter on Human and Peoples' Rights (adopted 27 June 1981, entered into force 21 October 1986) 1520 UNTS 217.

174 For discussion on the Third World approaches in international law, see Hauck, § 3.2, in this textbook. For critique on human rights and discussion of human rights as a colonial construction, see Ananthavinayagan and Theilen, § 21.8, in this textbook.

the OAU in 2002, placed human rights values among the AU's own objectives and principles (see article 3(h) and article 4(m), respectively).[175]

This section first explains the substantive guarantees of human and peoples' rights in Africa by way of selectively highlighting certain aspects of the African Charter on Human and Peoples' Rights and other treaties adopted under the auspices of the OAU/AU. Second, the discussion focuses on the protective mechanisms available in the African human rights system, including the African Commission on Human and Peoples' Rights, the African Court on Human and Peoples' Rights as well as the human rights–protective mandate of certain sub-regional African courts.

B. THE SUBSTANTIVE GUARANTEES OF HUMAN AND PEOPLES' RIGHTS

I. THE AFRICAN CHARTER ON HUMAN AND PEOPLES' RIGHTS

The ACHPR is not only the lighthouse of the African system of human and peoples' rights protection (with 54 State parties), but also a human rights treaty with many features that distinguish it from other regional human rights systems. The ACHPR is the only regional human rights treaty that accords equal weight to the different generations of human rights. The text provides for most civil and political rights and a few economic, social, and cultural rights, such as the right to work, the right to health, and the right to education, as well as peoples' rights (also known as solidarity rights). Peoples' rights hold a prominent place and include the right to self-determination,[176] the right to dispose freely of natural resources, the right to development, and the right to a healthy environment (articles 20–24).[177] Another unique characteristic of the ACHPR is its emphasis on the duties of the individual towards the community and the State (articles 27–29).[178] An example of such a duty is the duty of the individual to preserve and strengthen positive African values (article 29(7)). Finally, in contrast to other human rights instruments, the ACHPR does not contain a derogation clause, which means that limitation on ACHPR rights cannot be justified by emergencies.[179]

---

175 Ilias Bantekas and Lutz Oette, *International Human Rights Law and Practice* (OUP 2020) 280–281.

176 On self-determination, see Bak McKenna, § 2.4, in this textbook.

177 For the groundbreaking reparations' judgment of the ACtHPR on the recognition of the Ogiek community as a holder of rights collectively and the legal implications of the notion of collective harm when deciding moral prejudice and non-pecuniary reparations, see The African Commission on Human and Peoples' Rights vs Republic of Kenya Application No 006/2012 (ACtHPR, 23 June 2022) paras 44, 92–93, 113–114, 116, 160(iv).

178 For the presence of duties of individuals in Islamic and Arab documents on human rights, see Rachovitsa, § 21.6, in this textbook.

179 Abdi J Ali, 'Derogation from Constitutional Rights and Its Implication under the African Charter on Human and Peoples' Rights' (2013) 17 Law, Democracy & Development 78; Mohamed N Bhuian, 'African (Banjul) Charter: A Unique Step to Protect Human Rights in Africa' (2001) 5 Bangladesh Journal of Law 35.

At the same time, the ACHPR features certain notable shortcomings most of which have been addressed by the African Commission on Human and Peoples' Rights (ACmHPR) and the African Court on Human and Peoples' Rights (ACtHPR). First, the text omits certain rights (e.g. the right to privacy).[180] Second, the ACHPR is less detailed (compared to other human rights treaties) in setting out essential safeguards with regard to, for instance, the right to a fair trial. The ACtHPR's case law has incorporated the guarantees of the right to a fair trial under international human rights law into the protective scope of article 7.[181] Third, the ACHPR is silent on the requirements for a restriction on a human right to be lawful. Article 27(2) ACHPR provides only that 'the rights and principles of each individual shall be exercised with due regard to the rights of others, collective security, morality and common interest' without referring to the principles of legality and proportionality. In response to this, the ACtHPR pronounced, in its very first judgment on the merits in 2013, that the restrictions imposed on human rights must conform to the three-part test under international human rights law: restrictions must be prescribed by law, serve a legitimate aim, and be proportionate to the aim pursued.[182] Fourth, the ACtHPR, by affirming the ACmHPR's practice,[183] 'neutralised' the so-called claw-back clauses contained in the ACHPR. A claw-back clause subjects the exercise of a right provided under an international treaty on human rights to domestic law. The ACHPR subjects the exercise of many rights, such as the right to freedom of expression or the right to political participation, to domestic law. For example, article 9(2) ACHPR reads: 'every individual shall have the right to express and disseminate opinions *within the law*' (emphasis added). In contrast, most human rights treaties do not contain such clauses.[184] The ACtHPR ruled that domestic law ought to be in correspondence with international standards and should not nullify the scope and essence of the rights it regulates.[185] This ruling has also been confirmed by the ICJ in the *Diallo* case.[186]

---

180 Certain rights omitted from the text of the ACHPR, including the right to privacy, could be read into the right to human dignity, as provided under article 5 ACHPR.

181 For example, Alex Thomas v United Republic of Tanzania Application No 005/2013 (ACtHPR, 20 November 2015) para 124.

182 Tanganyika Law Society and Legal and Human Rights Centre and Reverend Christopher R Mtikila v Tanzania Application No 009/2011 (ACtHPR, 14 June 2013) para 106.

183 Media Rights Agenda and Constitutional Rights Project v Nigeria Application No 224/1998 (ACmHPR, 2000) paras 65–70.

184 Adamantia Rachovitsa, 'The African Court on Human and Peoples' Rights: A Uniquely Equipped Testbed for (the Limits of) Human Rights Integration?' in Emmanuelle Bribosia, Isabelle Rorive, and Ana Maria Correa (eds), *Human Rights Tectonics: Global Dynamics of Integration and Fragmentation* (Intersentia 2018) 69.

185 Tanganyika Law Society and Legal and Human Rights Centre and Reverend Christopher R Mtikila v Tanzania Application No 009/2011 (ACtHPR, 14 June 2013) paras 108–109.

186 The International Court of Justice in *Case concerning Ahmadou Sadio Diallo (Republic of Guinea v Democratic Republic of the Congo)* [2010] ICJ Rep 639, para 65 while discussing article 12(4) of the ACHPR and article 13 of the ICCPR, clarified that when a human rights provision requires national authorities to make a decision in accordance with the law, acting in accordance with domestic law is a necessary but not sufficient condition for complying with international law. The applicable domestic law must be compatible with the other requirements of a given human rights treaty.

II. OTHER HUMAN RIGHTS AND PEOPLES' TREATIES

In addition to the ACHPR, the African system of human and peoples' rights includes other treaties adopted under the auspices of the OAU/AU, such as

- The 1969 Convention regarding the Specific Aspects of Refugee Problems in Africa
- 1990 African Charter on the Rights and Welfare of the Child
- The 2007 African Charter on Democracy, Elections and Governance
- The 2009 Convention for the Protection and Assistance of Internally Displaced Persons in Africa
- The 2003 Protocol to the African Charter on Human and Peoples' Rights on the Rights of Women in Africa
- The 2018 Protocol to the African Charter on Human and Peoples' Rights on the Rights of Older People in Africa.

C. PROTECTIVE MECHANISMS

I. THE AFRICAN COMMISSION ON HUMAN AND PEOPLES' RIGHTS

The ACmHPR is an autonomous treaty body entrusted with the mandate of promoting and protecting human and peoples' rights in Africa. Its views and findings are non-binding but carry strong persuasive authority and have contributed to the progressive development of States' obligations under the ACHPR.

1. State Reporting

Parties to the ACHPR have the obligation to report on progress and challenges concerning its implementation every two years. Non-governmental organisations[187] (NGOs) are allowed to submit non-expert reports. The ACmHPR, in its early practice, did not publish the reports submitted by States and did not adopt concluding observations. Subsequently, it changed its approach in the interest of transparency. From 2001, the ACmHPR began adopting concluding observations and publishing State reports and its own observations on its website.[188] However, many States have never submitted a report or tend to be very late in doing so.

2. Inter-State Communications

A State party may bring a complaint concerning an alleged violation of the ACHPR against another party before the ACmHPR. This procedure has been used only once. In 2003, in *Democratic Republic of the Congo v Burundi, Rwanda and Uganda,*[189]

---

187 On NGOs, see Chi, § 7.6, in this textbook.

188 ACmHPR <https://achpr.au.int/statereportsandconcludingobservations> accessed 20 August 2021.

189 Democratic Republic of Congo v. Burundi, Rwanda and Uganda Application No 227/99 (ACmHPR, May 2003).

the ACmHPR held that the armed forces of the respondent States committed multiple violations of the ACHPR during their occupation of the eastern province of the Congo.

3. Communications Submitted by Individuals and NGOs

The ACHPR provides that communications other than those of State parties may be submitted to the ACmHPR. Although the text does not clarify who may bring these communications, the ACmHPR accepts that individuals and NGOs may do so. According to article 56 ACHPR, a communication needs to meet certain requirements to be admissible. The author of the communication does not have to be the victim of the alleged violation. This is significant since victims may lack access to resources or awareness of their rights and available remedies, or they may be hesitant, perhaps even afraid, to submit complaints themselves. NGOs regularly make use of this broad standing, bringing many communications before the ACmHPR, which testifies to their prominent role in the ACmHPR's activities. The ACmHPR has adopted many foundational views.[190]

4. Other Functions of the ACmHPR

In fulfilling its mandate, the ACmHPR also exercises a number of other functions, including:

- Creating special mechanisms, such as special rapporteurs, committees, and working groups[191]
- Publishing general comments, guidelines, or declarations with a view to progressively developing the African human rights law
- Carrying out on-site visits, promotional or protective missions, and investigative measures on the territory of States, where appropriate.

II. THE AFRICAN COURT OF HUMAN AND PEOPLES' RIGHTS

The Arusha-based ACtHPR may be the youngest court among its regional counterparts, but its jurisdiction and case law not only present unique features but also offer valuable lessons to be studied. The ACtHPR's mandate is provided for in the 1998 Protocol to the African Charter on Human and Peoples' Rights on the Establishment of the African Court on Human and Peoples' Rights (Protocol),[192] which entered into force in 2003, and in its Rules of Procedure. As far the relationship between the ACtHPR and the ACmHPR is concerned, they are independent and the former

---

190 For example, Social and Economic Rights Action Center (SERAC) and Center for Economic and Social Rights (CESR) v Nigeria Application No 155/96 (ACmHPR, 2001).

191 For discussion, see, Christopher Heyns and Magnus Killander, 'Africa' in D Moeckli, Sangheeta Shah, and Sandesh Sivakumaran (eds), *International Human Rights Law* (OUP 2018) 474–475.

192 Protocol to the African Charter on Human and Peoples' Rights on the Establishment of the African Court on Human and Peoples' Rights (adopted 10 June 1998; entered into force 25 January 2004).

complements the protective mandate of the latter.[193] In addition, the ACmHPR may submit cases to the ACtHPR.[194]

In 2004, the AU Assembly of Heads of State and Government decided that the African Court on Human and Peoples' Rights should be integrated into one court with the Court of Justice of the AU, referencing financial and logistical constraints. In 2008 and 2014, the Protocol on the Statute of the African Court of Justice and Human Rights and the Protocol on Amendments to the Protocol on the Statute of the African Court of Justice and Human Rights were adopted respectively, merging the two courts into a single new court, named the African Court of Justice and Human Rights. Neither protocol is yet in force and, consequently, the African Court on Human and Peoples' Rights is still in operation.

1. The Jurisdiction of the ACtHPR

The ACtHPR's jurisdiction may be divided into advisory and contentious. As far as its advisory jurisdiction is concerned, the ACtHPR may, at the request of an AU member State, any AU organ or any African organisation recognised by the AU, provide an opinion on any legal matter relating to the ACHPR or any other relevant human rights instrument. The ACtHPR has rendered 15 Advisory Opinions thus far. Turning to its contentious jurisdiction, under article 3(1) of the Protocol, the ACtHPR has jurisdiction to deal with all cases and disputes submitted to it regarding the interpretation and application of the ACHPR, the Protocol and any other relevant human rights instrument ratified by the States concerned. Thirty-four State parties to the ACHPR have currently ratified the Protocol.[195]

The Court may receive applications from the ACmHPR, State parties to the Protocol, or African intergovernmental organisations (article 5(1) of the Protocol). Individuals and NGOs do not have direct access to the ACtHPR unless the State against which the application is submitted has deposited the declaration described in article 34(6) of the Protocol, accepting the ACtHPR's competence to decide such complaints. In the absence of such a declaration, a complaint can be only submitted to the ACmHPR, which may decide to refer the communication to the ACtHPR. As of June 2023, only eight States have accepted the competence of the ACtHPR to decide complaints brought by individuals and NGOs (Burkina Faso, The Gambia, Ghana, Guinea Bissau, Mali, Malawi, Niger, and Tunisia). Since 2016, Benin, Rwanda, Côte d'Ivoire and even Tanzania – the ACtHPR's host State – withdrew their declarations, marking an unfortunate landmark in the ACtHPR's history.[196] However, in November 2021, the

---

193 Ibid, article 2.

194 Ibid, article 5.

195 AfCtHPR, 'List of Ratifications' <www.african-court.org/wpafc/wp-content/uploads/2023/03/36393-sl-PROTOCOL_TO_THE_AFRICAN_CHARTER_ON_HUMAN_AND_PEOPLESRIGHTS_ON_THE_ESTABLISHMENT_OF_AN_AFRICAN_COURT_ON_HUMAN_AND_PEOPLES_RIGHTS_0.pdf> accessed 20 August 2023.

196 Nicole de Silva and Misha Plagis, 'A Court in Crisis: African States' Increasing Resistance to Africa's Human Rights Court' (*Opinio Juris*, 19 May 2020) <http://opiniojuris.org/2020/05/19/a-court-in-crisis-african-

Republic of Guinea Bissau and the Republic of Niger deposited respective declarations under article 34(6) of the Protocol allowing direct access to the ACtHPR.[197]

Pursuant to articles 3(1) and 7 of the Protocol to the African Charter on Human and Peoples' Rights on the Establishment of the African Court on Human and Peoples' Rights, the ACtHPR enjoys a unique material jurisdiction. Its mandate extends to the interpretation and application of not only the ACHPR but also any other relevant human rights instrument ratified by the States concerned. In contrast, the material jurisdiction of UN human rights bodies and of other regional human rights courts is limited to matters concerning only their respective constitutive instruments.[198]

The future African Court of Justice and Human Rights is expected to have a different structure and a considerably broader material jurisdiction. More specifically, it will have three separate sections: a general affairs section, a human and peoples' rights section and an international criminal law section. The AU decided to add individual and corporate criminal responsibility to the jurisdiction of the merged court. This comes as a response to the strong dissatisfaction among many African States about the International Criminal Court's (perceived) biased focus on Africa.[199]

2. The ACtHPR's Case Law

Overall, the ACtHPR has an unfolding case law ordering provisional measures and ruling on matters pertaining to jurisdiction, admissibility, merits, and reparations. The subject matter of the cases spans, for instance:

- The right to political participation in connection to the prohibition of independent candidature[200] or the arbitrary revocation of one's passport[201]
- The right to freedom of expression and whether criminal defamation statutes are proportionate and necessary restrictions[202]
- Several aspects of the right to a fair trial[203]
- Indigenous peoples and collective rights.[204]

---

states-increasing-resistance-to-africas-human-rights-court/#:~:text=To%20date%2C%20no%20state%20 has,African%2C%20continental%20human%20rights%20court.> accessed 20 August 2023.

197 Press Release (*ACtHPR*, 3 November 2021) <www.african-court.org/wpafc/the-republic-of-guinea-bissau-becomes-the-eighth-country-to-deposit-a-declaration-under-article-346-of-the-protocol-establishing-the-court/> accessed 20 August 2023.

198 Adamantia Rachovitsa, 'On New "Judicial Animals": The Curious Case of an African Court with Material Jurisdiction of a Global Scope' (2020) 19 Human Rights Law Review 255.

199 Geoff Dancy and others, 'What Determines Perceptions of Bias toward the International Criminal Court? Evidence from Kenya' (2020) 64 Journal of Conflict Resolution 1443.

200 Tanganyika Law Society and Legal and Human Rights Centre and Reverend Christopher R Mtikila v Tanzania Application No 009/2011 (ACtHPR, 14 June 2013).

201 Kennedy Gihana and Others v Rwanda Application No 017/2015 (ACtHPR, 28 November 2019).

202 Lohe Issa Konate v Burkina Faso Application No 004/2013 (ACtHPR, 5 December 2014).

203 Mohamed Abubakari v United Republic of Tanzania Application No 007/2013 (ACtHPR, 3 June 2016).

204 African Commission on Human and Peoples' Rights v Republic of Kenya Application No 006/2012 (ACtHPR, 23 June 2018).

State parties are under the obligation to comply with the ACtHPR's judgments. The AU Executive Council monitors the execution of judgments on behalf of the Assembly. The reality on the ground is that the level of compliance with the decisions is poor: of the over 200 decisions and judgments rendered by the ACtHPR, less than 10% have been fully complied with, 18% partially implemented, and 75% not implemented at all.[205] Certain alternative measures to ensure better implementation of the judgments are under discussion, including the introduction of a monitoring role for the ACtHPR, under a newly established Monitoring Unit, or the possibility for the ACtHPR to issue compliance judgments.

III. SUB-REGIONAL COURTS PROTECTING HUMAN AND PEOPLES' RIGHTS

Individuals and NGOs regularly resort to sub-regional African courts, established in the context of regional economic communities, to raise and litigate human rights claims.

The most active in the field of human rights is the Economic Community of West African States (ECOWAS). The ECOWAS Community Court of Justice can hear complaints on human rights violations and applies the ACHPR as its standard of assessment.[206] The fact that it grants direct access to individuals, without requiring them to have exhausted domestic remedies, offers a notable litigation advantage for applicants.

The East African Court of Justice does not have explicit jurisdiction to address human rights complaints but nonetheless deals with such complaints as long as they are considered to be violations falling within the scope of the East African Community treaty.[207]

The Tribunal of the Southern African Development Community (SADC) followed the approach of the East African Court of Justice, namely, to address human rights claims without a clear mandate to do so.[208] However, this choice was more politically controversial than expected and it seriously backfired. After several judgment rulings against Zimbabwe and its refusal to comply, the Tribunal was de facto suspended in 2010.[209] In 2014, the SADC adopted a new protocol that will confine the Tribunal's mandate to the interpretation and application of the SADC treaty and protocols in inter-State disputes. The protocol is not yet in force, and the Tribunal remains effectively suspended.

---

205 Activity Report of the African Court on Human and Peoples' Rights, Executive Council, Forty Second Ordinary Session, 16 January–16 February 2023, EX.CL/1409(XLII), para 85.

206 *Omar Jallow v The Gambia* Application No 33/16 (ECOWAS Court, 10 October 2017) para 10.

207 *Katabazi and 21 Others v Secretary General of the East African Community* and Application No 1/2007 (East African Court of Justice, 29 August 2007).

208 *Mike Campbell (PTV) and Others v Zimbabwe* Application No 2/2007 (Southern African Development Community (SADC) Tribunal, 11 October 2007).

209 Michelo Hansungule, 'The Suspension of the SADC Tribunal' (2013) 35 Strategic Review for Southern Africa 135.

D. CONCLUSION

There is still room for the ACtHPR to develop the ACHPR's unique characteristics as well as for other human rights courts and bodies to draw inspiration from the ACHPR's features and the ACtHPR's case law. The ACmHPR and the ACtHPR continuously elaborate upon their functions and jurisdiction, respectively. They also develop the scope of rights and guarantees under the ACHPR. Although the practice of progressively elevating the level of protection for peoples' and individuals' rights may be arguably linked to the backlash consisting of the four States having withdrawn their declarations under article 34(6) of the Protocol, new States have recently deposited such declarations. Consequently, States' political choices about accepting/withdrawing their declarations allowing direct access to the ACtHPR need to be assessed in light of many factors. The ACtHPR's function is undermined by the low number of States accepting its jurisdiction for complaints brought by individuals and NGOs and the poor compliance record with its judgments. Despite these challenges, the ACtHPR is a resilient court addressing its increasing workload and evolving its case law.

BOX 21.3.3 Further Readings and Further Resources

Further Readings

- JT Gathii (ed), *The Performance of Africa's International Courts: Using Litigation for Political, Legal, and Social Change* (OUP 2020)

- C Heyns, 'The African Regional Human Rights System: In Need of Reform?' (2001) 2 African Human Rights Law Journal 155

- R Murray, *The African Charter on Human and Peoples' Rights* (OUP 2010)

- F Ouguergouz, *La Charte Africaine des Droits de l'Homme et des Peuples* (Graduate Institute Publication 1993)

Further Resources

- 'Documentary on the African Court on Human and Peoples' Rights' <www.youtube.com/watch?v=OfUNQIL9Zoc> accessed 20 August 2023

- 'YouTube Channel of the African Court on Human and Peoples' Rights' <www.youtube.com/@AfricanCourtEnglishChannel> accessed 20 August 2023

- Annual Activity Reports (*African Court on Human and Peoples' Rights*) <www.african-court.org/wpafc/activity-report/> accessed 20 August 2023

---

§ § §

§ 21.4 EUROPEAN HUMAN RIGHTS SYSTEM

JENS T. THEILEN

BOX 21.4.1 Required Knowledge and Learning Objectives

Required knowledge: Recurring Themes in Human Rights Doctrine

Learning objectives: Understanding the institutional setup and regional idiosyncrasies of human rights protection in Europe.

BOX 21.4.2 Interactive Exercises

Access *interactive exercises for this chapter*[210] by positioning your smartphone camera at the dot-filled box, also known as a QR code.

Figure 21.1 QR code referring to interactive exercises.

A. INTRODUCTION

The institutionalisation of rights in Europe has developed primarily within two organisations: the Council of Europe (CoE), with a broad range of member States extending to the east of Europe, on the one hand; and the European Union (EU) and its predecessors, the European Communities, on the other.[211] Under EU law, the primary reference point nowadays is the Charter of Fundamental Rights, which was originally proclaimed in 2000 and received formal legal force in 2009 under the Treaty of Lisbon (article 6 (1) TEU). Given the many particularities of the EU as a supranational legal order, the development and scope of its fundamental rights protection are beyond the remit of this chapter, except to note that it largely shares

---

210 https://openrewi.org/en-projects-project-public-international-law-international-human-rights-law/.

211 As of 16 March 2022, Russia is no longer a member State of the CoE following its expulsion in reaction to the invasion of Ukraine; see *Resolution CM/Res(2022)2 (CoM, 16 March 2022)*.

the market-based outlook of EU law as a whole.[212] The focus in what follows will be on the human rights protection developed in the context of the CoE, notably but not exclusively the Convention for the Protection of Human Rights and Fundamental Freedoms – informally known as the European Convention on Human Rights (ECHR)[213] – and the European Court of Human Rights (ECtHR), whose task it is to interpret it. All 46 member States of the CoE are party to the ECHR. The EU is not, nor is it likely to be in the foreseeable future given concerns about the legality of accession to the ECHR under EU law.[214]

B. THE EUROPEAN CONVENTION ON HUMAN RIGHTS

I. HISTORICAL ORIGINS AND DEVELOPMENT

The ECHR was the first treaty to be drafted under the auspices of the CoE and is still widely considered to be its crowning achievement. Originally a product of Western European States in the immediate post-war period, it was conceived of to prevent the backsliding of newly democratic States into totalitarianism and to provide a bulwark against the perceived threat of communism.[215] It is also worth noting that several of the States involved were major colonial powers. With the period of formal decolonisation not yet at its peak, they acted on the assumption that they would maintain their colonial territories for a significant time yet and drafted the ECHR in such a way that it would not run counter to their interests in doing so.[216] The ECHR thus 'embodies in its very text the contradictions between the proclamation of universal aspirations and realpolitik interests of political subjugation'.[217]

BOX 21.4.3 Example: Colonial Elements

A particularly stark example of this is the so-called colonial clause (article 56, previous article 63 ECHR), which puts the applicability of the ECHR and the possibility of individual complaints at the discretion of a State party for

---

212 Alexander Somek, *Engineering Equality. An Essay on European Anti-Discrimination Law* (OUP 2011).

213 Convention for the Protection of Human Rights and Fundamental Freedoms (adopted 04 November 1950, entered into force 3 September 1953) 213 UNTS 221 (ECHR).

214 See *Opinion 2/13 (ECJ, 18 December 2014).*

215 Andrew Moravcsik, 'The Origins of Human Rights Regimes: Democratic Delegation in Postwar Europe' (2000) 54 International Organization 217; Ed Bates, *The Evolution of the European Convention on Human Rights* (OUP 2011); Alexandra Huneeus and Mikael Rask Madsen, 'Between Universalism and Regional Law and Politics: A Comparative History of the American, European, and African Human Rights Systems' (2018) 16 ICON 136.

216 On this period, see González Hauck, § 1, in this textbook.

217 Marie-Bénédicte Dembour, *When Humans Become Migrants* (OUP 2015) 95.

'territories for whose international relations it is responsible'. It thus gives the option of placing (neo-)colonial acts outside the purview of the ECtHR. Far from being 'anachronistic', as the ECtHR has claimed, it is relevant to this day since various States parties continue to hold overseas territories and the ECtHR regards article 56 ECHR as 'a provision of the Convention which is in force and cannot be abrogated at will by the Court'.[218]

The ECHR was opened for signature in 1950 and came into force in 1953. From the very beginning, it has been supplemented by various protocols, which can broadly be divided into two groups. The first group, optional protocols, can enter into force despite not being ratified by all the States parties to the ECHR. According to the general principle of *pacta tertiis non nocent* (Latin: 'agreements do not harm third parties'),[219] they are binding only on those States which do ratify them,[220] and provide additional substantive guarantees (e.g. the rights to property, to education, and to free elections in Protocol No. 1) or procedural mechanisms for those States only. The second group, mandatory protocols, enter into force only after being ratified by all parties and amend the text of the ECHR itself. Most importantly, Protocol No. 11 to the ECHR fundamentally transformed the system of judicial oversight when it entered into force in 1998. While this system was originally conceived of as optional (and individual complaints were directed to the now-defunct European Commission of Human Rights, with the ECtHR acting only as a second instance), Protocol No. 11 turned the ECtHR into a permanent court with obligatory jurisdiction vis-à-vis all States parties – subject to the limitations of article 56 ECHR mentioned earlier. Another key change around the same time was the significant enlargement of the CoE, which generated a great deal of discussion as to whether and how the accession of many Central and Eastern European States to the ECHR should entail a different role for the ECtHR.[221]

II. THE EUROPEAN COURT OF HUMAN RIGHTS AND ITS PROCEDURES

The ECtHR is composed of 46 full-time judges (still with a clear male majority despite some tepid attempts to increase the number of women[222]), one for each State

---

218 Chagos Islanders v the United Kingdom *App no 35622/04 (ECtHR, 11 December 2012)*.

219 On which, see Fiskatoris and Svicevic, § 6.1.B.II.4, in this textbook.

220 But see as the exception to the rule *Öcalan v Turkey* App no 46221/99 (ECtHR, 12 May 2005) paras 163–165; *Al-Saadoon and Mufdhi v the United Kingdom* App no 61498/08 (ECtHR, 2 March 2010) para 120, where the ECtHR controversially read the prohibition of the death penalty contained in Protocols No. 6 and 13 to the ECHR into article 3 ECHR although they were not (quite) unanimously ratified.

221 Wojciech Sadurski, 'Partnering with Strasbourg: Constitutionalisation of the European Court of Human Rights, the Accession of Central and East European States to the Council of Europe, and the Idea of Pilot Judgments' (2009) 9 HRLR 397.

222 Stéphanie Hennette Vauchez, 'More Women – But Which Women? The Rule and the Politics of Gender Balance at the European Court of Human Rights' (2015) 26 EJIL 195; Helen Keller, Corina Heri, and

party. The majority of applications is dealt with by individual judges, committees of three judges, or Chambers of seven judges (articles 26 to 29 ECHR). Particularly important cases may be decided by the Grand Chamber consisting of 17 judges, either by relinquishment of jurisdiction by the Chamber (article 30 ECHR) or by referral at a party's request after the Chamber's judgment (article 43 ECHR).

The individual complaint procedure (article 34 ECHR) is the basis of the majority of applications to the ECtHR. Admissibility criteria (article 35 ECHR) include, inter alia, the ECHR's temporal and spatial applicability, the victim status of the applicant(s), the exhaustion of domestic remedies, and a four-month time limit (as of February 2022, according to Protocol No. 15 to the ECHR, previously six months). While seemingly of a formal nature, some of these requirements can become quite politically loaded and have generated as much case law and academic commentary as certain substantive provisions. This goes in particular for cases involving extraterritorial jurisdiction, which often relate to politically sensitive topics such as wartime measures, migration management, or – as in several pending cases – climate change.[223]

Compared to individual complaints, inter-State applications (article 33 ECHR) and advisory opinions at the request of the CoE's Committee of Ministers (article 47 ECHR) are significantly less common.[224] When they are used, however, inter-State applications tend to be high-profile cases, as with various cases brought by Georgia and Ukraine in the context of Russian invasions before Russia was expelled from the CoE. As of 2018, Protocol No. 16 to the ECHR, an optional protocol, allows the ECtHR to also give advisory opinions at the request of the highest national courts with regard to cases pending before the latter. Protocol No. 16 is viewed by many as an important step towards strengthening judicial dialogue between national courts and the ECtHR,[225] but it remains to be seen to what extent national courts will make use of the new procedure.[226]

III. CURRENT DISCUSSIONS AND FUTURE CHALLENGES

An idiosyncrasy of the ECtHR compared to other regional human rights courts is the extremely high number of cases it deals with: in 2022, for example, 45,500 new

---

Myriam Christ, 'Fifty Years of Women at the European Court of Human Rights' in Freya Baetens (ed), *Identity and Diversity on the International Bench: Who Is the Judge?* (OUP 2020).

223 E.g. *Banković and others v Belgium and others* App no 52207/99 (ECtHR, 12 December 2001); *Al-Skeini and others v the United Kingdom* App no 55721/07 (ECtHR, 7 July 2011); *Hirsi Jamaa and others v Italy* App no 27765/09 (ECtHR, 23 February 2012).

224 The most recent Advisory Opinion is of 22 January 2010 *on certain legal questions concerning the lists of candidates submitted with a view to the election of judges to the European Court of Human Rights (No. 2)*.

225 See e.g. the speech by *Guido Raimondi, then President of the ECtHR, at the high-level conference 'Continued Reform of the European Court of Human Rights Convention System – Better Balance, Improved Protection' Copenhagen, April 2018.*

226 At the time of writing, the ECtHR has rendered seven advisory opinions under Protocol No. 16.

applications were allocated and overall 74,650 applications were pending. (By way of contrast, the number of pending cases before the IACtHR and the AfCtHR does not exceed three-digit numbers.) While legal analysis often focuses on 'landmark cases' which deal with politically sensitive topics or develop the material standards set by the ECtHR, the overwhelming majority of applications are disposed of by means of an admissibility decision. Protocol No. 14 to the ECHR, a mandatory protocol, introduced various measures to streamline the procedure for such decisions and thereby manage the case load: for example, single judges may now declare cases inadmissible (article 27 ECHR), and applicants must usually have suffered a 'significant disadvantage' for their application to be considered admissible (article (3) lit. b ECHR).[227]

Another area of discussion, particularly in recent years, concerns the legitimacy of the ECtHR and the *backlash* its case law has generated, particularly in cases on prisoners' voting rights[228] and immigration.[229] This has led to increasing fears that the efficiency of the Strasbourg system might be endangered if the States parties were to withdraw their support. In particular, the State parties might no longer regularly abide by the ECtHR's judgments: while these are legally binding and their execution is supervised by the CoE's Council of Ministers (article 46 ECHR), there is no truly effective mechanism to ensure compliance.[230] Some States claim primacy for their national constitutions over the ECHR and use this internal legal hierarchy to prevent the implementation of certain judgments.

Debates on how the ECtHR should respond in such a situation involve questions of judicial strategy and principle, often connected to doctrinal figures such as the margin of appreciation and the notion of subsidiarity.[231] But these discussions also draw attention to the limits of what is considered possible within institutionalised human rights protection: if even incremental change is controversial and may draw the ire

---

227 On the controversies these changes have led to, see e.g. Steven Greer and Luzius Wildhaber, 'Revisiting the Debate about "Constitutionalising" the European Court of Human Rights' (2012) 12 HRLR 655; Dinah Shelton, 'Significantly Disadvantaged? Shrinking Access to the European Court of Human Rights' (2016) 16 HRLR 303; Janneke H Gerards and Lize R Glas, 'Access to Justice in the European Convention on Human rights System' (2017) 35 NQHR 11.

228 Particularly Anchugov and Gladkov v Russia *App nos 11157/04 and 15162/05 (ECtHR, 4 July 2013)*; Hirst v the United Kingdom (No. 2) *App no 74025/01 (ECtHR, 6 October 2005)*.

229 Marie-Bénédicte Dembour, *When Humans Become Migrants* (OUP 2015) 1. See generally on 'backlash' and responses to it Mikael Rask Madsen, Pola Cebulak, and Micha Wiebusch, 'Backlash against International Courts: Explaining the Forms and Patterns of Resistance to International Courts' (2018) 14 International Journal of Law in Context 197; Silvia Steininger, 'With or Without You: Suspension, Expulsion, and the Limits of Membership Sanctions in Regional Human Rights Regimes' (2021) 81 ZaöRV 533; see also Kunz, § 5 C.II, in this textbook.

230 For an overview and evaluation, see Raffaela Kunz, 'Securing the Survival of the System: The Legal and Institutional Architecture to Supervise Compliance with the ECtHR's Judgments' in Rainer Grote, Mariela Morales Antoniazzi, and Davide Paris (eds), *Research Handbook on Compliance in International Human Rights Law* (Edward Elgar 2021) 12.

231 On standards of review in international human rights law, see Milas, § 21.1, in this textbook.

of the States parties to such an extent, then more fundamental forms of injustice are bound to go unchallenged.[232]

C. OTHER COUNCIL OF EUROPE TREATIES AND DOCUMENTS

Human rights protection within the CoE is shaped by the ideological distinction between civil and political rights, on the one hand, and economic, social, and cultural rights, on the other.[233] The ECHR's guarantees focus on the prior, although they cannot be entirely separated from the latter.[234] Some economic and social rights, particularly various labour rights and the right to social security, are guaranteed in the European Social Charter (ESC), which was first adopted in 1961 and is gradually being replaced by a revised version of 1996. Many rights included in the International Covenant on Economic, Social and Cultural Rights are notably absent at the European level: 'private property is a right for Europeans, but food is not'.[235]

These priorities are reflected in the institutional and procedural design of the European Committee of Social Rights, which is responsible for monitoring compliance with the ESC. It does so primarily by reference to reports submitted by the States parties (comparable with the reporting system in place for many human rights treaties at the global level[236]). An additional protocol from 1995 further introduced the possibility of collective complaints, for example by trade unions and certain non-governmental organisations with consultative status within the Council of Europe. As of 2023, however, it has been ratified only by 14 States. In stark contrast to the ECtHR, there is no complaint procedure for individuals.

To round off the picture, it is worth gesturing towards the manifold other treaties developed under the auspices of the CoE, many of which can be considered specialised human rights treaties or at least touch upon human rights issues, such as data protection or the legal status of migrant workers. Some of these treaties, such as the European Convention for the Prevention of Torture and Inhuman or Degrading Treatment and the Council of Europe Convention on preventing and combating violence against women and domestic violence, are equipped with a monitoring body which provides more specific but not legally binding guidance. The ECtHR at times refers to these treaties and other documents as part of its interpretation of the ECHR,[237] thus

---

232 Jens T Theilen, *European Consensus between Strategy and Principle* (Nomos 2021) chs 9–11.
233 See Ciampi, § 21.B.I., in this textbook.
234 Ingrid Leijten, *Core Socio-Economic Rights and the European Court of Human Rights* (CUP 2018).
235 Jose Luis Vivero Pol and Claudio Schuftan, 'No Right to Food and Nutrition in the SDGs: Mistake or Success?' [2016] BMJ Global Health 1, 3.
236 See Ananthavinayagan and Baranowska, § 21.2, in this textbook.
237 Lize R Glas, 'The European Court of Human Rights' Use of Non-Binding and Standard-Setting Council of Europe Documents' (2017) 17 HRLR 97; Theilen (n 232) ch 6.

indirectly giving them binding legal force even when this was not envisaged at the time of their drafting or when they are not widely ratified.

D. CONCLUSION

Overall, what stands out in the European system of human rights protection is the elevated position granted to the ECtHR and, with it, the focus on civil and political rights in a highly institutionalised form. This brings with it in particularly stark form all the advantages and disadvantages of institutionalising human rights.[238] In the European self-perception, the ECtHR is often lauded as a beacon of human rights protection, to be emulated by other regions.[239] The ECtHR has indeed contributed significantly to the development of human rights in Europe over the years, but this assessment should not distract from the cautious and oftentimes timid stance which it tends to take in its judgments: on topics ranging from religious freedom over gay and trans rights to racial violence, other regional courts and quasi-judicial bodies at the global level have challenged injustices by finding human rights violations while the ECtHR demurred.[240] It is important, then, to not overemphasise the achievements of the ECtHR but rather to read its case law with a critical eye[241] and to remain alert to other approaches to human rights, both in Europe and elsewhere.[242]

BOX 21.4.4 Further Readings and Further Resources

Further Readings

- HP Aust and E Demir-Gürsel (eds), *The European Court of Human Rights. Current Challenges in Historical Perspective* (Edward Elgar 2021)

- RR Churchill and U Khaliq, 'The Collective Complaints System of the European Social Charter: An Effective Mechanism for Ensuring Compliance with Economic and Social Rights?' (2004) 15 EJIL 417

- J Gerards, *General Principles of the European Convention on Human Rights* (CUP 2019)

---

238 On the critique of (institutionalised) rights, see further Ananthavinayagan and Theilen, § 21.8, in this textbook.

239 E.g. Michael O'Boyle, 'The Future of the European Court of Human Rights' (2011) 12 GLJ 1862.

240 For criticism, see e.g. Eva Brems and others, 'Head-Covering Bans in Belgian Courtrooms and Beyond: Headscarf Persecution and the Complicity of Supranational Courts' (2017) 39 HRQ 882; Damian A Gonzalez Salzberg, *Sexuality and Transsexuality Under the European Convention on Human Rights* (Hart 2019); Ruth Rubio-Marín and Mathias Möschel, 'Anti-Discrimination Exceptionalism: Racist Violence before the ECtHR and the Holocaust Prism' (2015) 26 EJIL 881.

241 On critique of human rights, see Ananthavinayagan and Theilen, § 21.8, in this textbook.

242 On case analysis, see also Milas, § 4.1, in this textbook.

- C Heri, *Responsive Human Rights. Vulnerability, Ill-Treatment and the ECtHR* (Hart 2021)
- E Demir-Gürsel and JT Theilen, 'Framing Europe in Human Rights, Framing Human Rights in Europe – Authoritarianism, Migration, and Climate Change in the Council of Europe' (2023) 12/4 ESIL Reflections 1

Further Resources

- The website of the ECtHR includes various factsheets on different topics within its case law as well as other helpful summaries <www.echr.coe.int/Pages/home.aspx?p=press/factsheets&c=> accessed 20 August 2023
- There are several excellent blogs covering developments related to the ECtHR; see in particular *Strasbourg Observers* (providing case notes for important judgments of the ECtHR <https://strasbourgobservers.com/> accessed 20 August 2023), *ECHR Blog* (with a wide variety of content including updates on institutional developments and new academic publications <www.echrblog.com/> accessed 20 August 2023) and *ECHR Sexual Orientation Blog* (focusing on case law related to sexual orientation <http://echrso.blogspot.com/> accessed 20 August 2023)

§ § §

§ 21.5 INTER-AMERICAN HUMAN RIGHTS SYSTEM

VERENA KAHL, WALTER ARÉVALO-RAMÍREZ, AND ANDRÉS ROUSSET-SIRI

BOX 21.5.1 Required Knowledge and Learning Objectives

Required knowledge: Sources of International Law; Human Rights Law; Indigenous Peoples; TWAIL; Decolonisation

Learning objectives: Understanding the activity and the scope of the human rights protection bodies and instruments in the Americas.

BOX 21.5.2 Interactive Exercises

Access *interactive exercises for this chapter*[243] by positioning your smartphone camera at the dot-filled box, also known as a QR code.

Figure 21.1 QR code referring to interactive exercises.

A. INTRODUCTION

In April 1948, after the end of a devastating Second World War, delegates from 21 countries met in Bogotá, Colombia, to strengthen cooperation among American States. In their quest for institutionalisation, they created the Organization of American States (OAS), which today comprises 35 member States. During the Ninth International Conference of American States, the first international human rights instrument of a general nature was adopted,[244] which laid the foundation for the Inter-American Human Rights System: the American Declaration of the Rights and Duties of Man (ADRDM).

---

243 https://openrewi.org/en-projects-project-public-international-law-international-human-rights-law/
244 Inter-American Commission of Human Rights, Annual Report 2019, OEA/Ser.L/V/II. Doc. 9, 24 February 2020, para 48.

While the Inter-American human rights system had thereby formally been established even shortly before the Universal Declaration of Human Rights came into being, it took several years before the system actually went into operation. An important driver of this operationalisation was the adoption of the American Convention on Human Rights (ACHR),[245] a legally binding human rights instrument which established the Inter-American Court of Human Rights (IACtHR) as a competent organ alongside the Inter-American Commission on Human Rights (IACmHR), which had already been established by a resolution of the OAS in 1959. With regard to institutional safeguards, the Inter-American human rights system thus follows a twofold structure, which can also be found in the African human rights system and had formerly been applied in the European system of human rights.[246] Besides this institutional setting, it is important to note that the Inter-American human rights system developed in the context of long-lasting dictatorships and civil wars in the region, which also shaped the system's case law.[247]

In comparison to its European[248] and African[249] counterparts, distinguishing features include a unique system of reparations, intensive use of the IACtHR's advisory function and remarkable case law with regard to specific topics, such as indigenous communities, forced disappearance, amnesty laws, or environmental rights.[250] One of the main challenges of the Inter-American system is, besides continuous financial constraints,[251] to find an adequate position in the balancing act between progressive human rights protection on the one hand and member State protest on the other hand, which can go as far as turning away from the system itself.[252]

---

245 American Convention on Human Rights 'Pact of San José, Costa Rica' (adopted 22 November 1969, entered into force 18 July 1978) 1144 UNTS 123 (ACHR).

246 See Philip Leach, 'The European Court of Human Rights: Achievements and Prospects' in Gerd Oberleitner (ed), *International Human Rights Institutions, Tribunals, and Courts* (Springer 2018) 425.

247 See Lea Shaver, 'The Inter-American Human Rights System: An Effective Institution for Regional Rights Protection? for Regional Rights Protection?' (2010) 9(4) Washington University Global Studies Law Review 639, 660, 666 f, 670.

248 On the European human rights system, see Theilen, § 21.4, in this textbook.

249 On the African human rights system, see Rachovitsa, § 21.3, in this textbook.

250 Emblematic decisions on these topics include, inter alia, IACtHR, The Environment and Human Rights (State obligations in relation to the environment in the context of the protection and guarantee of the rights to life and to personal integrity – interpretation and scope of articles 4(1) and 5(1) of the American Convention on Human Rights), Advisory Opinion OC-23/17, 15 November 2017, Series A No. 23; IACtHR, Case of the Indigenous Communities of the Lhaka Honhat Association (Our Land) v. Argentina (Merits, Reparations and Costs) Judgment, 6 February 2020, Series C No. 400; IACtHR, Case of the Yakye Axa Indigenous Community v. Paraguay (Merits, Reparations and Costs) Judgment of 17 June 2005, Series C No. 125; IACtHR, Case of Barrios Altos v. Peru (Merits), Judgment of 14 March 2001, Series C No. 75.

251 See, by mode of example, Raffaela Kunz, 'The Inter-American System Has Always Been in Crisis, and We Always Found a Way Out' An interview with Eduardo Ferrer Mac-Gregor Poisot (*Völkerrechtsblog*, 17 October 2016) <https://voelkerrechtsblog.org/de/the-inter-american-system-has-always-been-in-crisis-and-we-always-found-a-way-out/> accessed 20 August 2023.

252 Note the ACHR's denunciations of Trinidad Tobago (1998) and Venezuela (2012), while the latter re-ratified the Convention in 2019, see <www.oas.org/dil/treaties_B-32_American_Convention_on_Human_Rights_sign.htm> accessed 20 August 2023.

B. LEGAL FRAMEWORK

I. AMERICAN DECLARATION OF THE RIGHTS AND DUTIES OF MAN

The ADRDM was signed on 2 May 1948. Following natural law theory,[253] the American Declaration emphasises that 'the essential rights of [a hu]man are not derived from the fact that he[*she] is a national of a certain state, but are based upon attributes of his[*her] human personality'. Besides traditional civil and political rights, it also includes economic, social and cultural rights which, for the most part, were at that time not yet part of the signatory States' national legal systems.[254] While the ADRDM is not constructed as a treaty and by its nature not legally binding, it has both been considered as a means of interpretation regarding the ACHR and the OAS Charter[255] and even as 'a source of international obligations for the Member States of the OAS'.[256] In this sense, the ADRDM has served as a yardstick in cases before the IACmHR regarding those American countries that have not ratified the ACHR.[257]

II. AMERICAN CONVENTION ON HUMAN RIGHTS

The ACHR was adopted during the Inter-American Specialized Conference on Human Rights, which took place in 1969 in San José, Costa Rica. Pursuant to article 74(2), the ACHR entered into force in 1978. Currently, 24 States have ratified the ACHR. In 1998, Trinidad and Tobago denounced the Convention. Venezuela, which had also presented an instrument of denunciation in 2012, decided to re-ratify the Convention in 2019. Although the ACHR is, according to article 74(1), open to all OAS member States for signature and ratification, the United States, Canada, and several other English-speaking countries have not ratified the Convention.

The ACHR can be considered the legal centrepiece of the Inter-American human rights system. It is divided into three parts, from which the first enshrines fundamental human rights and corresponding State obligations (articles 1–32), the second establishes the means of protection (articles 33–73), and the third consists of general and transitory provisions (articles 74–82). The main focus of the ACHR lies on the protection of traditional civil and political rights, such as the right to life (article 4), the right to humane treatment (article 5), the right to personal liberty (article 7), the right to a fair trial (article 8),

---

253 Robert K Goldman, 'History and Action: The Inter-American Human Rights System and the Role of the Inter-American Commission on Human Rights' (2009) 31(4) Human Rights Quarterly 856, 859.

254 Cf. Ibid 860.

255 See IACtHR, Interpretation of the American Declaration of the Rights and Duties of Man within the Framework of Article 64 of the American Convention on Human Rights, Advisory Opinion OC-10/89 of 14 July 1989, Series A No. 10, para 44.

256 Ibid paras 42, 45.

257 IACmHR, James Terry Roach and Jay Pinkerton v. United States, Case 9647, Resolution No. 3/87, Annual Report 1986–1987, 22 September 1987, paras 47–49; for the case of Canada, see Bernard Duhaime, 'Canada and the Inter-American Human Rights System: Time to Become a Full Player' (2012) 67(3) International Journal 639, particularly 641 f.

freedom of thought and expression (article 13), or the right to judicial protection (article 25). However, article 26 provides for the progressive and full realisation of the rights 'implicit in the economic, social, educational, scientific, and cultural standards set forth in the Charter of the Organization of American States', which has been used to innovatively incoporate second generation rights, such as job security or a healthy environment.[258]

Besides the rights and freedoms expressly codified in the ACHR, other rights have been read into the Convention through progressive interpretation. Particularly worth mentioning is the right to (know) the truth, whose emergence is related to the systematic practice of forced disappearance in situations of civil war or dictatorship that have for long periods dominated large parts of the Inter-American hemisphere.[259]

III. OTHER RELEVANT INSTRUMENTS

The diversification of international human rights law in the decades following the Universal Declaration of Human Rights has equally taken place in the context of the Inter-American human rights system connecting to the historical process of human rights codification in different subsequent agreements. The Additional Protocol to the American Convention on Human Rights in the Area of Economic, Social and Cultural Rights was adopted in November 1988 and entered into force only 11 years later in 1999.

Similarly, human rights expansion in international and regional treaty law was directed towards groups that suffer from structural discrimination or generally require specific protection, such as women, Black, indigenous and people of colour, persons with disabilities, or children. Besides a general agreement on non-discrimination, the Inter-American Convention against all Forms of Discrimination and Intolerance, several other instruments were adopted with regard to specific groups. These include, inter alia, the Inter-American Convention against Racism, Racial Discrimination and Related Forms of Intolerance; the Inter-American Convention on the Prevention, Punishment and Eradication of Violence against Women; the Inter-American Convention on International Traffic in Minors; or the Inter-American Convention on the Elimination of All Forms of Discrimination against Persons with Disabilities. Taking into account the presence of many indigenous communities in the region, the OAS General Assembly has also adopted the American Declaration on the Rights of Indigenous Peoples.

---

258 Oswaldo R Ruiz-Chiriboga, 'The American Convention and the Protocol of San Salvador: Two Intertwined Treaties – Non-Enforceability of Economic, Social and Cultural Rights in the Inter-American System' (2013) 31(2) Netherlands Quarterly of Human Rights 159, 160; IACtHR, Case of Lagos del Campo Vs. Peru (Preliminary Objections, Merits, Reparations and Costs), Judgment of 31 August 2017, Series C No. 340, paras.141-154; IACtHR, Case of Dismissed Employees of Petroperú et al. Vs. Peru (Preliminary Objections, Merits, Reparations and Costs), Judgment of 23 November 2017, Series C No. 344 (in Spanish only), paras. 192, 193; IACtHR, Case of the Indigenous Communities of the Lhaka Honhat Association (Our Land) Vs. Argentina (Merits, Reparations and Costs), Judgment of 6 February 2020, paras. 201, 202–209.

259 IACHR, 'The Right to the Truth in the Americas', 13 August 2014, OEA/Ser.L/V/II.152 Doc. 2, paras 43, 56 et seq.

C. INSTITUTIONAL FRAMEWORK

I. INTER-AMERICAN COURT OF HUMAN RIGHTS

The IACtHR was created as a permanent and autonomous organ of the OAS by the ACHR in 1969. As the Convention did not enter into force until 1978, it took a decade for the Court to make it from paper to an actual operating institution. In 1979, the IACtHR's first judges were elected and the Court was officially installed.

1. Composition

According to article 52(1) ACHR, the IACtHR is composed of seven judges which have to be OAS member State nationals and jurists of the highest moral authority and of recognised competence in the field of human rights. They are elected by the OAS General Assembly for a term of six years with the possibility of a single re-election (article 54(1) ACHR). Since the election in November 2021, for the first time in the history of the IACtHR there have been three women among the sitting judges.[260]

2. Jurisdiction and Functions

According to article 1 of its Statute, the IACtHR is an 'autonomous judicial institution whose purpose is the application and interpretation of the American Convention on Human Rights'. Article 2 of the Statute describes the functions of the Court as twofold. First, in the realm of its judiciary or contentious function, which is governed by articles 61 to 63 of the ACHR, the Court has the competence to hear and rule on cases submitted by the IACHR or a State Party to the Convention (article 61(1) ACHR), provided that the State, which is party to the case, has recognised the Court's jurisdiction according to article 62(3) ACHR and that the procedure before the Commission enshrined in articles 48 to 50 ACHR has been exhausted (article 61(2) ACHR). For cases to reach the IACtHR, States must have recognised the jurisdiction of the Court pursuant to article 62(1) ACHR. In addition, based on article 63(1) ACHR, the Court has ordered a great variety of reparatory measures,[261] which has become a distinguishing feature of its jurisprudence.[262] In contrast to its regional counterparts, the IACtHR has also developed an innovative network of institutions and procedures to supervise compliance with its decisions in accordance with articles 67 and 68(1) ACHR,[263] including monitoring mediums such as requests for information,

---

260 Corte Interamericana sesionará con cuatro hombres y tres mujeres, Servindi, 17 November 2021 <www. servindi.org/actualidad-noticias/17/11/2021/corte-interamericana-sesionara-cuatro-hombres-y-tres-mujeres> accessed 20 August 2023.

261 Jo M Pasqualucci, *The Practice and Procedure of the Inter-American Court of Human Rights* (2nd edn, Cambridge University Press 2013) 188 ff.

262 Dinah Shelton, 'Remedies in the Inter-American System' (1998) 92 Proceedings of the Annual Meeting (American Society of International Law) 202, 203.

263 IACtHR, Annual Report of the Inter-American Court of Human Rights 2010, San José 2011, p. 9 et seq.

monitoring hearings, on-site visits, and issuing orders on monitoring compliance.[264] Second, article 64 ACHR provides for an advisory function. Due to a lack of contentious cases during its first years of operation, the IACtHR built its jurisprudence by relying heavily on its responses to requests for advisory opinions.[265]

II. INTER-AMERICAN COMMISSION OF HUMAN RIGHTS

Like the IACtHR, the IACmHR has seven members, who must have high moral authority and a recognised understanding of human rights law. The Commission has 11 rapporteurs on indigenous peoples, women, freedom of expression, children, human rights defenders and justice operators, persons deprived of liberty, LGBTI persons, migrants, rights of Afro-descendants and against racial discrimination, older persons, economic, social, cultural, and environmental rights that prepare specialised recommendations addressed to OAS member States and advise the Commission in the processing of petitions.

Three types of reports are produced by the IACmHR: country reports; reports where the results of the in loco visit (on-site visit) for OAS States are condensed; and thematic reports on specific topics and annuals report, which includes data on the processing of petitions, the activities carried out in relation to the IACtHR, and other human rights bodies.

The IACmHR decides cases in a quasi-judicial manner after receiving individual petitions (article 44 ACHR) and inter-State communications (article 45). The jurisdictional procedure before the IACHR is divided into four procedural stages: initial processing, admissibility, merits, and referral of the case to the Court. Thereby, the IACmHR acts as a gatekeeper for cases before they are submitted to the IACtHR. In the merits stage, if the Commission determines that there is State responsibility for an international wrongful act, it will issue a preliminary report that will be notified to the State (article 50). If within the time period conferred, the State does not comply with the recommendations made by the IACmHR, it will decide between issuing the report on the merits (article 51) and publishing it or referring the case to the IACtHR.

D. MONITORING COMPLIANCE WITH JUDGMENTS

1. EFFECTIVENESS

Compliance with judgments of the IACtHR is still relatively low, with only 44 of 365 rulings submitted for full implementation to date (July 2023). The progress of

---

264 For a detailed overview, see Rene Urueña, 'Compliance as Transformation: The Inter-American System of Human Rights and Its Impact(s)' in Rainer Grote, Mariela Morales Antoniazzi, and Davide Paris, *Research Handbook on Compliance in International Human Rights Law* (Edward Elgar 2021) 226, 233–237.

265 See Thomas Buergenthal, 'Remembering the Early Years of the Inter-American Court of Human Rights' (2005) 37 New York University Journal of International Law and Politics 259, 265 f.

compliance with the measures ordered by the IACtHR is influenced by the (lack of) domestic implementation of the IACHR and structural (non-)compliance with human rights standards. Problems are caused by the general ignorance of international law, the lack of prior debate on how to comply, or even unwillingness to comply with the rulings of the Inter-American adjudicative bodies. This generates a notable gap between decisions and their execution.

2. JUDGMENTS ON SUPERVISION

The part of a judgment that stipulates compensatory damages may be executed in the country concerned in accordance with domestic procedure governing the execution of judgments against the State (article 68.2). The IACtHR issues specific judgments on supervision where it condenses the information collected and progress in compliance, which is then described and compiled in its annual report. Pursuant to article 65 ACHR, the IACtHR must submit a report each year to the General Assembly of the OAS in which it indicates – among other things – the cases in which a State has not complied with a judgment of the IACtHR.

E. THE DOCTRINE OF 'CONVENTIONALITY CONTROL'

The doctrine of conventionality control is one of the most effective efforts of the IACtHR to increase the level of compliance with the ACHR. The concept of conventionality control was developed in the concurring opinion of Judge Sergio García-Ramírez in the judgment for the *Mack Chang v Guatemala* case.[266] Two years later, in the *Almonacid-Arellano* case,[267] the IACtHR, for the first time, used the notion in the reasoning of one of its decisions.

Conventionality control is a guarantee designed to obtain the harmonious application of international and domestic law. This, according to the jurisprudence of the IACtHR includes all organs of the State, at all levels, within the framework of their competences. It encompasses both the ACHR as well as specialised treaties of the Inter-American human rights system. It also includes the decisions of the IACtHR, both in its contentious and advisory jurisdiction. The doctrine allows the repeal of internal regulations incompatible with the ACHR, but at the same time it functions as a parameter to eradicate practices contrary to the rules of the Inter-American human rights system.

---

266 IACtHR, Case of Myrna Mack Chang v. Guatemala (Merits, Reparations and Costs), Judgment of 25 November 2003, Series C No. 101 Reasoned concurring opinion of Judge Sergio García Ramírez, p. 2.
267 IACtHR, Case of Almonacid-Arellano et al v. Chile (Merits, Reparations and Costs), Judgment of 26 September 2006, Series C No. 154, para 124.

The IACtHR recognises two types of conventionality control. The first type, known as *internationally performed conventionality control*, is carried out by the judges of the IACtHR when the Court, as part of its decisions, orders the suspension, revision, or withdrawal of domestic norms of the State.[268] The second type, known as *national conventionality control*, implies that every organ or agent of the State is capable to perform a control of conventionality to the extent of its competences. Accordingly, all State authorities must interpret and apply all domestic laws in a way that complies with the Convention, its protocols, and the case law of the IACHR and the IACtHR. Thereby, the national conventionality control ensures that no State authority applies a norm contrary to the Convention.

F. CONCLUSION

The present contribution took a closer look at the institutions and legal framework of the Inter-American human rights system with a particular focus on the corresponding case law and specific distinguishing features of its two institutional pillars: the Inter-American Commission of Human Rights and the Inter-American Court of Human Rights. Besides covering core provisions of the American Convention on Human Rights as well as the composition, jurisdiction and functions of Court and Commission, the chapter also casted a spotlight on the monitoring of compliance with the IACtHR's decisions, which distinguishes the Inter-American human rights system from its European and African counterparts. Finally, the contribution dived deeper into the doctrine of 'conventionality control', which is of particular importance for the implementation of Inter-American human rights standards at the domestic level.

BOX 21.5.3 Further Readings and Further Resources

Further Readings

- JL Cavallaro, C Vargas, C Sandoval, B Duhaime, *Doctrine, Practice, and Advocacy in the Inter-American Human Rights System* (OUP 2019)

- Y Haeck, O Ruiz-Chiriboga, and C Burbano-Herrera, *The Inter-American Court of Human Rights: Theory and Practice, Present and Future* (Intersentia 2015)

- L Hennebel and H Tigroudja, *The American Convention on Human Rights: A Commentary* (OUP 2022)

- JM Pasqualucci, *The Practice and Procedure of the Inter-American Court of Human Rights* (2nd edn, CUP 2013)

---

268 IACtHR. *Caso Vargas Areco v. Paraguay* (Merits, Reparations and Costs), Judgments of 26 September 2006. Serie C No. 155, Reasoned concurring opinion of Judge Sergio García Ramírez, p. 6.

- X Soley and S Steininger, 'Parting Ways or Lashing Back? Withdrawals, Backlash and the Inter-American Court of Human Rights' (2018) 14 International Journal of Law in Context 237

Further Resources

- Annual reports with detailed information and statistics on the Court's jurisprudence are published in four different languages <www.corteidh.or.cr/informes_anuales.cfm?lang=en> accessed 20 August 2023

- The IACtHR regularly publishes Journals of Jurisprudence (Cuadernillos de Jurisprudencia) concerning specific topics and member States, available in Spanish only at <www.corteidh.or.cr/publicaciones.cfm?lang=en> accessed 20 August 2023

- Interactive Map of member States with updated information on pending cases, cases with judgment and provisional measures, <www.corteidh.or.cr/mapa_casos_pais.cfm?lang=en> accessed 20 August 2023

- The movie 'Helena from Sarayaku' (2022) directed by Eriberto Gualinga follows Helena and the indigenous community of the Kichwa people of Sarayaku in their struggle to protect their ancestral lands and the 'living forest'

§ § §

§ 21.6 ARAB AND ISLAMIC HUMAN RIGHTS SYSTEM

ADAMANTIA RACHOVITSA

BOX 21.6.1 Required Knowledge and Learning Objectives

Required knowledge: Sources of International Law; Individuals; Recurring Themes in Human Rights Doctrine

Learning objectives: Understanding the basic substantive and institutional features of the Arab/Islamic human rights mosaic.

BOX 21.6.2 Interactive Exercises

Access *interactive exercises for this chapter*[269] by positioning your smartphone camera at the dot-filled box, also known as a QR code.

Figure 21.1 QR code referring to interactive exercises.

A. INTRODUCTION

The geographies of the 'Middle East', 'Arab region', or 'Islamic world' are difficult to capture. Regional arrangements of States involving these geographies do not fall squarely into the orderly and familiar forms of regionalism.[270] Take the example of the League of Arab States: a regional organisation of 22 States across two continents. The Organisation of Islamic Cooperation defies geographical distance, bringing together 57 member States (with a population of over 1.8 billion) across four continents. One should also note that a number of States belonging in these regional arrangements are also members to the African Union[271] and parties to the African Charter on Human

---

269 https://openrewi.org/en-projects-project-public-international-law-international-human-rights-law/.

270 Antony T Anghie, 'Identifying Regions in the History of International Law' in Bardo Fassbender and Anne Peters (eds), *The Oxford Handbook of the History of International Law* (OUP 2012) 1058.

271 For example, Egypt, Libya or Morocco.

and Peoples' Rights.[272] In these instances, groupings of States are not driven solely by physical proximity but mostly by a 'regionalism of ideas'[273] and various markers of common identity, such as Arab heritage and Islamic solidarity. Therefore, it does not come as a surprise that these regional arrangements are reflected in a diversity of treaties and instruments on human rights.[274]

The sub-chapter starts with discussing two early Islamic human rights documents which, although non-binding, seem to have set the tone for the Arab/Islamic human rights system. The discussion then focuses on the institutional and substantive aspects of protecting human rights in the League of Arab States, including the Arab Independent Committee on Human Rights and the Revised Arab Charter on Human Rights. Finally, some insights are highlighted from the more recent Gulf Cooperation Council Declaration on Human Rights.

B. EARLY ISLAMIC HUMAN RIGHTS DOCUMENTS

Two Islamic documents concerning human rights protection, which have taken the form of international declarations and are therefore non-binding, stand out. The first document is the 1981 Universal Islamic Declaration of Human Rights. It was prepared under the auspices of the Islamic Council of Europe, which is a private, London-based organisation affiliated with the Muslim World League, an international non-governmental organisation (NGO)[275] headquartered in Saudi Arabia that tends to support the views of conservative Muslims. The second instrument, influenced by the Universal Islamic Declaration of Human Rights, is the Cairo Declaration on Human Rights in Islam, adopted by the Organisation of Islamic Cooperation in 1990.[276] The Cairo Declaration on Human Rights in Islam was the contribution of the Organisation of Islamic Cooperation to the 1993 World Conference on Human Rights. In line with the Organisation of Islamic Cooperation's religious nature, the Cairo Declaration on Human Rights in Islam contains consistent references to Islamic law (also known as Sharia).[277]

---

272 For example, Egypt, Libya or Morocco. On the African human rights system, see Rachovitsa, § 21.3, in this textbook.

273 Malcolm D Evans, 'The Future(s) of Regional Courts on Human Rights' in Antonio Cassese (ed), *Realizing Utopia: The Future of International Law* (OUP 2012) 261, 271.

274 On how the notions of diversity and coherence play out in the regional development of the Asian system of human rights, see Rachovitsa, § 21.7, in this textbook.

275 On NGOs, see Chi § 7.6, in this textbook.

276 Cairo Declaration on Human Rights in Islam, adopted 5 August 1990 by the Conference of Foreign Ministers of the Organisation of the Islamic Conference, Resolution 49/19-P.

277 For the basic sources of Islamic law also known as Sharia, see Christopher G Weeramantry, *Islamic Jurisprudence – An International Perspective* (Macmillan 1998) 30–58; Mashood A Baderin, *International Human Rights and Islamic Law* (OUP 2005) 33–48.

Many of the rights and freedoms contained in both the Cairo Declaration on Human Rights in Islam and the Universal Islamic Declaration of Human Rights fall short of universal standards, as encapsulated in the international bill of rights,[278] as well as from an Islamic perspective. This is because, in many instances, the language and scope of rights provided in these documents do not measure up to Islamic standards of human rights.[279] Two notable examples of how the rights and freedoms contained in these two documents fall short of universal human rights standards concern the scope of rights of women (e.g. women's right to work, polygamy, right to inheritance, equality of rights in marriage) and freedom of religion.[280]

A defining feature of both the Cairo Declaration on Human Rights in Islam and the Universal Islamic Declaration of Human Rights is that they subject the exercise of human rights to Islamic law. The Cairo Declaration on Human Rights in Islam states that 'all the rights and freedoms stipulated in this Declaration are subject to the Islamic Sharia' (article 24). The Universal Islamic Declaration of Human Rights lacks such an explicit clause but clarifies that any reference to law, to which human rights are subordinated throughout the text, denotes Sharia.[281]

BOX 21.6.3 Advanced: Legal Challenges of Unconditionally Subjecting the Exercise of Human Rights to Islamic Law

Unconditionally subjecting the enjoyment of internationally protected rights to Islamic law is as problematic as subjecting them to domestic law, since this renders the scope of rights and freedoms uncertain. This uncertainty is further amplified by concerns regarding Islamic law and, in particular, its foreseeability, predictability, and accessibility. The content of Islamic law is frequently elusive due to the lack of codification and the different schools of Islamic thought. There is no systematisation of the case law and, in fact, judgments in the Middle East or Arab region are not published. Moreover, since the protective scope of the rights is subjected to Islamic law, there is no clarification of what this means with respect to different interpretations of Islamic law in case of differences in jurisprudential views and across schools of thought.

---

278 The International Bill of Human Rights consists of the Universal Declaration of Human Rights, the International Covenant on Economic, Social and Cultural Rights, and the International Covenant on Civil and Political Rights and its two Optional Protocols.

279 Mashood A Baderin, 'The Human Rights Agenda of the OIC: Between Pessimism and Optimism' in Marie J Petersen and Turan Kayaoglu (eds), *The Organization of Islamic Cooperation and Human Rights* (University of Pennsylvania Press 2019) 40, 51–52.

280 On the rights of women under Islamic law and human rights law, see Baderin (n 277) 133–155.

281 Explanatory note 1(b).

An additional notable characteristic of the Cairo Declaration on Human Rights in Islam and the Universal Islamic Declaration of Human Rights is that they set out a series of individual duties towards society[282] and duties of the community towards the individual. Such duties express Arab and Islamic ideals of social justice and a community-oriented approach to human rights. These ideals and approaches have contributed to the apparatus of positive human rights law and may also advance novel perspectives for conceptualising aspects of human rights law as well as alternative systems for protecting human dignity.[283]

Overall, the rationale for creating the Islamic human rights documents is not clear. Both the Cairo Declaration on Human Rights in Islam and the Universal Islamic Declaration of Human Rights were intended to develop an Islamic response to the Universal Declaration on Human Rights.[284] Many also argue that the underlying rationale of these Islamic human rights documents as well as the specific encapsulation of rights therein are intended more as rhetorical devices serving political interests, ideologies, and (perceived) hegemonic politics and repressive policies of certain autocratic regimes.[285]

C. THE PROTECTION OF HUMAN RIGHTS IN THE LEAGUE OF ARAB STATES

The League of Arab States, based in Cairo, has 22 member States. Non-interference in domestic affairs is a key policy of the League of Arab States, which is historically linked to decolonisation[286] and pan-Arab nationalism forged during and in the aftermath of the independence of many Arab States.[287] In contrast to the Organisation of Islamic Cooperation, the League of Arab States is primarily a non-religious organisation.

I. ARAB INDEPENDENT COMMITTEE ON HUMAN RIGHTS

The Arab Independent Committee on Human Rights (Committee) is a body of the League of Arab States, established in 1998. The Committee meets twice per year in

---

282 For discussion on the notion of the duties of the individual see Rachovitsa, § 21.3, in this textbook.

283 Weeramantry (n 277) 125–127; Patrick Glenn, *Legal Traditions of the World* (OUP 2014) 224.

284 International Law Association, Committee on Islamic Law and International Law, *Islamic Law and the Rule of Law in Light of the Right to Freedom of Expression*, Final Report, 7 November 2018, para 80.

285 Ibid; Salim Farrar, 'The Organisation of Islamic Cooperation: Forever on the Periphery of Public International Law?' (2014) 12 Chinese Journal of International Law 787, 802–805; Ann E Mayer, *Islam and Human Rights* (Westview Press 2007) 192–197.

286 On decolonisation, see González Hauck, § 1, in this textbook.

287 For discussion on the Third World approaches in international law, see González Hauck, § 3.2, in this textbook. For critique on human rights and discussion of human rights as a colonial construction, see Ananthavinayagan and Theilen, § 21.8, in this textbook.

Cairo and consists of one political representative from each member State. According to its mandate,[288] the Committee is responsible for:

- Establishing rules of cooperation among member States in the field of human rights
- Formulating an Arab position on human rights issues at the regional and international levels
- Drafting human rights treaties and assessing the compatibility of agreements with human rights principles
- Promoting the implementation of human rights
- Promoting cooperation in human rights education.

Despite its broad mandate on paper, the Committee is limited to considering issues referred to it by specific bodies of the League of Arab States or member States. It has neither a mechanism to consider the human rights situation in member States nor any special procedures.

II. THE REVISED ARAB CHARTER ON HUMAN RIGHTS

The Revised Arab Charter on Human Rights (Charter)[289] was adopted in 2004 and entered into force in 2008. As of January 2021, 16 out of 22 member States to the League of Arab States have ratified the Charter.[290] The Charter affirms the universality and indivisibility of human rights (article 1) and contains a clause safeguarding the more favourable level of protection for the individual (article 43). The text of the treaty ensures peoples' right to self-determination (article 2) and safeguards key civil and political rights (articles 5–33) and many economic, social, and cultural rights (articles 34–42). There are a few novel provisions, too, such as the right to a decent life for persons with mental or physical disability (article 40).

Nonetheless, the Charter presents certain shortcomings. First, it omits important human rights. For instance, it does not prohibit cruel, inhuman, or degrading punishment but only treatment (see article 8(1)). This is troubling, since many States in the region retain corporal forms of punishment that may be in violation of the Convention Against Torture.[291] Some rights are protected only with regard to State parties' own citizens, such as the right to association and peaceful assembly (article 24(6)) and most economic and social rights. Second, the death penalty may be imposed on

---

288 Internal Regulations of the Arab Permanent Committee on Human Rights, adopted by Resolution 6826, Regular Session 1285 of the Council of Ministers of Foreign Affairs, September 2007.

289 Revised Arab Charter on Human Rights (adopted 22 May 2004, entered into force 15 March 2008) reprinted in 18 Human Rights Law Journal 151.

290 These are Algeria, Bahrain, Egypt, Iraq, Jordan, Kuwait, Lebanon, Libya, Mauritania, Palestine, Qatar, Saudi Arabia, Sudan, Syria, United Arab Emirates, and Yemen. Comoros, Djibouti, Morocco, Oman, Somalia, and Tunisia have not yet ratified the Charter.

291 Convention against Torture and Other Cruel, Inhuman or Degrading Treatment or Punishment (adopted 10 December 1984, entered into force 26 June 1987) 1465 UNTS 85.

minors, if stipulated in a State party's domestic law (article 7(1)). Third, women's rights are not sufficiently protected in accordance with international standards. Fourth, the Charter contains so-called claw-back clauses, as is the case with the African Charter on Human and Peoples' Rights.[292]

III. MONITORING THE REVISED ARAB CHARTER

1. The Arab Human Rights Committee

The Arab Human Rights Committee, created in 2009, is the treaty body entrusted with supervising the implementation of the Revised Arab Charter (articles 45–48). The Committee consists of seven independent human rights experts who serve in a personal capacity.

The Committee is responsible for monitoring States' human rights performance and reviewing State reports. The Committee cannot receive individual complaints. States parties are required to submit a report on their compliance with the Charter within one year of ratification, and thereafter every three years. The Committee reviews these reports and issues conclusions and recommendations. Civil society organisations can submit reports and attend meetings. Although the Committee does not require them to have observer status to take part in the reporting procedure, they must have NGO status in their country of origin. Since many State parties have rigid requirements under their domestic law for registering an NGO, many organisations are prevented from accessing the reporting procedure. In practice, the reporting system suffers from huge delays, since States are often late in submitting their national reports.

2. The Arab Court of Human Rights

In 2014, the League of Arab States concluded the Statute of the Arab Court of Human Rights.[293] The Court's jurisdiction extends over disputes resulting from the interpretation and application of the Charter, or any other Arab convention in the field of human rights involving a member State (article 16). Moreover, upon request of the League of Arab States' Assembly, the Court may also issue an advisory opinion regarding any legal issues related to the Charter or to any other Arab convention on human rights (article 21).

The personal jurisdiction of the Court is severely limited, depriving individuals of the right to access it directly. According to article 19, only State parties may bring applications before the Court. State parties may accept, pursuant to a separate

---

292 On the role of the claw-back clauses in the African Charter on Human and Peoples' Rights, see Rachovitsa, § 21.3, in this textbook. On the relationship between domestic and international law, see Kunz, § 5, in this textbook.

293 Council of the LAS Resolution no 7790 EA (142) C 3. Unofficial translation in English. For discussion, see Ahmed Almutawa, 'The Arab Court of Human Rights and the Enforcement of the Arab Charter on Human Rights' (2021) 21 Human Rights Law Review 506.

declaration, that a civil society organisation has standing to bring cases on behalf of individuals. As of yet, no States have ratified the Statute.

D. THE GCC DECLARATION ON HUMAN RIGHTS

In 2014, the member States of the Cooperation Council for the Arab States of the Gulf (GCC), namely Bahrain, Kuwait, Oman, Qatar, Saudi Arabia, and the United Arab Emirates, adopted the GCC Human Rights Declaration.[294] The Declaration embodies an expression of the subregional level of human rights protection. The text consists of 47 provisions concerning civil and political rights and social, economic, and cultural rights. Some of these rights are novel, including article 39 which sets out a joint responsibility for the State and the community with regard to addressing the consequences of disasters and emergencies; and article 4 which criminalises trade in human organs but also frames it as a violation of human rights. With that being said, the GCC Human Rights Declaration overemphasises the role of domestic law when limiting human rights and subjects the exercise of human rights to Islamic law.

E. CONCLUSION

The development of the Arab/Islamic system on human rights gives rise to a polymorphous regionalism, wherein human rights documents and treaties capture different geographies and reflect various interests and priorities. The potential for certain novel provisions, as provided in the Arab/Islamic human rights instruments to support, in certain instances, different conceptualisations of human rights law remains largely unexplored in human rights law and practice. The restrictive scope of many of the human rights provided in the early Islamic human rights documents and the Revised Arab Charter on Human Rights and the subjection of the exercise of human rights to domestic law and/or Islamic law deviate from universal human rights standards. The ineffective functioning of international bodies casts a long shadow over the progressive development of human rights standards in the Arab/Islamic human rights system.

BOX 21.6.4 Further Readings

Further Readings

- AA An-Na'im, 'Human Rights in the Arab World: A Regional Perspective' (2001) 23 Human Rights Quarterly 701

---

294 Human Rights Declaration for the Member States of the Cooperation Council for the Arab States of the Gulf, adopted by the High Council, Thirty-fifth session, Doha, 9 December 2014.

- S Farrar, 'The Organisation of Islamic Cooperation: Forever on the Periphery of Public International Law?' (2014) 12 Chinese Journal of International Law 787

- MMO Mohamedou, 'Arab Agency and the UN Project: The League of Arab States Between Universality and Regionalism' (2016) 37 Third World Quarterly 1226

§ § §

§ 21.7 ASIAN HUMAN RIGHTS SYSTEM

ADAMANTIA RACHOVITSA

BOX 21.7.1 Required Knowledge and
Learning Objectives

Required knowledge: Sources of International Law; Individuals; Recurring
Themes in Human Rights Doctrine

Learning objectives: Understanding the reasons that the Asian human rights
system takes a different path comparing to other regions; to become
familiarised with the notion of Asian values in human rights law; to highlight
the major human rights developments in the ASEAN.

BOX 21.7.2 Interactive Exercises

Access *interactive exercises for this chapter*[295] by positioning your smartphone
camera at the dot-filled box, also known as a QR code.

Figure 21.1 QR code referring to interactive exercises.

A. INTRODUCTION

Asia is one of the regions in the world which lacks a regional system for the
protection of human rights. A few remarks are warranted so as to understand why
this is so. Any hastiness of the non-Asian observer in expecting of Asia what may
be expected of other regions in the world may be misguided. Conceptualising Asia
as a region, that is, a geographical area with sufficient historical, economic, social,
religious, and cultural cohesion, is a complex matter.[296] Asia consists of a great
number of States: 53 members of the Asia-Pacific Group at the UN, out of a 193

---

295 https://openrewi.org/en-projects-project-public-international-law-international-human-rights-law/.

296 Antony T Anghie, 'Identifying Regions in the History of International Law' in Bardo Fassbender and Anne
      Peters (eds), *The Oxford Handbook of the History of International Law* (OUP 2012) 1058.

United Nations (UN) member States.[297] Asia is by far the most populous region in the world: 4.5 billion people out of 7.6 billion on the planet. Asia's self-identification as a continent is also subject to discussion.[298] Despite commonalities among States and peoples, the diversity within Asia is remarkable, perhaps inhibiting a systematic, coherent approach to regional development, at least in the form that this is witnessed in other regions.

The absence of regional human rights instruments and institutions needs to be also understood within the broader framework of Asian States' engagement with international law. Asian States are the least likely to accept international obligations. They tend to be mistrustful of delegating sovereignty, either on an international or regional basis. This is due to the diversity in the continent and the influences of the great powers (China, India, and Japan). Historical[299] and cultural reasons,[300] as well as the experience(s) of colonialism, should not be understated either (e.g. India and colonialism, China and unequal treaties,[301] the trials that followed the Second World War in Japan).[302] These experiences have cemented the perception that international law is primarily an instrument of political power to be used selectively.[303]

Against this background, regional human rights law in Asia is considerably less developed and amorphous compared to other regions. The deepening of human rights law is more likely to occur at the sub-regional level in smaller and more coherent groupings of States. At the same time, Asian States have existing human rights obligations under customary international law and under the UN human rights framework.[304]

First, this section briefly explains the concept and role of Asian values in human rights law and discourse. The discussion subsequently focuses on the sub-regional level for protecting human rights and, more specifically, the bodies and human rights instruments created by the Association of Southeast Nations (ASEAN).

---

297 On the United Nations, see Baranowska, Engström, and Paige, § 7.3, in this textbook.

298 Teemu Ruskola, 'Where Is Asia? When Is Asia? Theorizing Comparative Law and International Law' (2011) 44 University of California at Davis Law Review 879, 882; Simon Chesterman, 'Asia's Ambivalence about International Law and Institutions: Past, Present and Futures' (2016) 27 EJIL 945, 965.

299 On the history of international law, see González-Hauck, § 1, in this textbook.

300 'Culture' in Susan Marks and Andrew Clapham (eds), *International Human Rights Lexicon* (OUP 2005) 33, 39.

301 For the concept of unequal treaties and their function in the context of colonialism, see, Mathew Craven, 'What Happened to Unequal Treaties? The Continuities of Informal Empire' (2005) 74 Nordic Journal of International Law 335–382; Mitchell Chan, 'Rule of Law and China's Unequal Treaties: Conceptions of the Rule of Law and Its Role in Chinese International Law and Diplomatic Relations in the Early Twentieth Century' (2018) 25 Penn History Review 9.

302 Chesterman (n 298) 962–965. For discussion on the Third World approaches in international law (TWAIL), see González-Hauck, § 3.2, in this textbook.

303 Chesterman (n 298) 962–965.

304 For the ratification record of the main UN human rights treaties by Asian States, see Office of the United Nations High Commissioner for Human Rights, OHCHR Management Plan 2022–2023, Asia-Pacific, 154–155. On the UN human rights system, see Ananthavinayagan and Baranowska, § 21.2, in this textbook.

B. THE 'ASIAN VALUES' DEBATE

An infrequent occasion when Asian States formed and presented a united front on their position on human rights was their contribution to the 1993 World Conference on Human Rights. They drafted and submitted the Bangkok Declaration,[305] which embodies the so-called Asian values. 'Asian values' is a term coined by Asian officials to contest the Western conceptualisation of civil and political freedoms.[306] A major claim raised in this regard is that communitarian values and duties of the individual towards society should be placed on an equal footing to (or even take precedence over) individual freedoms. Paragraph 8 of the Bangkok Declaration reads:

> While human rights are universal in nature, they must be considered in the context of a dynamic and evolving process of international norm-setting, bearing in mind the significance of national and regional particularities and various historical, cultural and religious backgrounds.

The 1998 Asian Charter on Human Rights,[307] which is a peoples' charter drafted by civil society in response to the Bangkok Declaration, holds that the idea of 'Asian values' legitimises the 'deprivation of the rights and freedoms of . . . citizens, which are denounced as foreign ideas inappropriate to the religious and cultural traditions of Asia'.[308] A distinction is also drawn between Asian values as a 'thin disguise for . . . authoritarianism',[309] on the one hand, and the relevance of bearing in mind the social, economic, and cultural contexts in which rights are to be enjoyed, on the other.[310] In other words, it is not debated whether social, economic, and cultural contexts have a bearing on the enjoyment of rights (they do), but rather the specific weight of this bearing on the protective scope of rights as well as this weight's potentially disguised abuse for political purposes.

C. DEVELOPMENTS IN THE ASSOCIATION OF SOUTHEAST ASIAN NATIONS

While the number of human rights developments have taken place (e.g. South Asian Association for Regional Cooperation)[311] or are likely to take place (e.g. Pacific Islands Forum) in specific sub-regional corners of Asia, the Association of Southeast Asian

---

305 Final Declaration of the Regional Meeting for Asia of the World Conference on Human Rights (Bangkok Declaration), Bangkok, 7 April 1993, UN Doc UNGA A/CONF.157/ASRM/8A/CONF.157/PC/59.

306 For critique on human rights and discussion of human rights as a colonial construction, see Ananthavinayagan and Theilen, § 21.8, in this textbook.

307 Asian Charter on Human Rights – A Peoples' Charter, Kwangju – South Korea, 17 May 1998.

308 Article 1(5).

309 Article 1(5).

310 Article 2(3).

311 Human rights treaties adopted under the auspices of the South Asian Association for Regional Cooperation are: the Social Charter, (adopted 4 January 2004); the Convention on Regional Arrangements for the Promotion of

Nations (ASEAN) stands out for its progress. ASEAN is a political and economic union created in 1967 by Indonesia, Malaysia, the Philippines, Singapore, and Thailand, which were subsequently joined by Brunei, Vietnam, Laos, Myanmar, and Cambodia. In 2007, ASEAN member States decided to deepen their political, security-related, economic and socio-cultural cooperation by creating the ASEAN Charter. Respect for sovereignty, non-interference in domestic affairs, and the consensus approach remain the foundational principles of States' engagement.[312] In a surprising move, the protection of human rights and social justice features prominently in the purposes and principles of the ASEAN Charter. It was additionally agreed that a human rights body would be established, which eventually became the ASEAN Intergovernmental Commission on Human Rights (AICHR).

I. THE ASEAN INTERGOVERNMENTAL COMMISSION ON HUMAN RIGHTS

The AICHR, established in 2009, is an intergovernmental, consultative body. Its decision-making is based on consultation and consensus, following a non-confrontational approach. The AICHR's mandate is to promote and protect human rights in the regional context, bearing in mind different cultural and religious backgrounds. Its tasks are promotional of human rights with no remit for receiving individual complaints or conducting investigations. According to its Terms of Reference,[313] the AICHR is tasked with:

* Developing strategies and capacity-building
* Consulting, and engaging in dialogue with other bodies and institutions, including civil society
* Enhancing public awareness of human rights.

The AICHR has been criticised for lack of engagement with civil society organisations and the general public.[314]

II. THE ASEAN HUMAN RIGHTS DECLARATION

Since the 1993 Bangkok Declaration, States in Asian and ASEAN fora have made many unsuccessful attempts to form a consensus on drafting a human rights instrument. These attempts came to fruition in 2012 with the adoption of the ASEAN Human Rights Declaration.[315] The Declaration, a non-binding instrument, provides for both civil and

---

the Child Welfare in South Asia (adopted 5 January 2002); and the Convention on Preventing and Combating Trafficking in Women and Children for Prostitution (adopted 5 January 2022).

312 Vitit Muntarbhorn, 'The South East Asian System for Human Rights Protection' in Scott Sheeran and Nigel Rodley (eds), *Routledge Handbook of International Human Rights Law* (Routledge 2013) 467.

313 See articles 1–4, 2009 Terms of Reference, adopted pursuant to article 14 of the ASEAN Charter.

314 Yuyun Wahyuningrum, 'A Decade of Institutionalizing Human Rights in ASEAN: Progress and Challenges' (2021) 20 Journal of Human Rights 158.

315 Association of Southeast Asian Nations, ASEAN Human Rights Declaration, adopted by the Phnom-Penh Statement, 18 November 2012.

political rights (articles 10–25) and economic, social, and cultural rights (articles 26–34), plus the right to development (articles 35–37) and the right to peace (article 38). Following in the footsteps of the Bangkok Declaration, the ASEAN Human Rights Declaration stresses that 'the realisation of human rights must be considered in the regional and national context bearing in mind different political, economic, legal, social, cultural, historical and religious backgrounds' (article 7). The Declaration also emphasises that the enjoyment of human rights must be balanced with the performance of corresponding duties towards other individuals and the community (article 6). The rights are drafted almost telegraphically as to their protective scope, and the limitations on human rights provided are broad (article 8). This may be understandable since declarations are not commonly drafted in the same detail as treaties.

BOX 21.7.3 Advanced: Potential Normative, Legal, and Political Impact of the ASEAN Human Rights Declaration

Notwithstanding the absence of international obligations stemming from a declaration, the potential impact of non-binding instruments (soft-law) should not be dismissed altogether.[316] Other well-known examples of non-binding instruments (e.g. the Universal Declaration on Human Rights) have developed a significant normative impact. In this way, the ASEAN Human Rights Declaration, first, transforms human rights from a solely domestic concern into an issue to be addressed in inter-State relations; second, may form the basis for a treaty in the future; third, can be referenced and used before/by national bodies and in international practice; and fourth, legitimises human rights language for political debate at the domestic level.

III. OTHER ASEAN HUMAN RIGHTS BODIES AND INSTRUMENTS

A few other developments in the ASEAN should be noted.[317] The ASEAN Commission on the Promotion and Protection of the Rights of Women and Children, formally established in 2010, is a consultative, intergovernmental human rights body. It is tasked with promoting and protecting the human rights of women and children upholding rights contained in the Convention on the Elimination of All Forms of Discrimination against Women[318] and the Convention on the Rights of the Child[319] (all ASEAN member

---

316 Anthony J Langlois, 'Human Rights in Southeast Asia: ASEAN's Rights Regime after Its First Decade' (2021) 20 Journal of Human Rights 151.

317 For discussion on how the ASEAN human rights system informally evolves, see Tan Hsien-Li, 'Adaptive Protection of Human Rights: Stealth Institutionalisation of Scrutiny Functions in ASEAN's Limited Regime' (2022) 22 Human Rights Law Review 1.

318 Convention on the Elimination of All Forms of Discrimination Against Women (adopted 18 December 1979, entered into force 3 September 1981) 1249 UNTS 13.

319 Convention on the Rights of the Child (adopted 20 November 1989, entered into force 2 September 1990) 1577 UNTS 3.

States have ratified both treaties). Its functions are very similar to those of the AICHR and include:

- Promoting the implementation of international and ASEAN instruments on the rights of women and children
- Advocating on behalf of women and children
- Assisting, upon request by ASEAN member States, in fulfilling their international human rights reporting obligations on women and children's rights
- Encouraging ASEAN member States to collect and analyse sex-disaggregated data, and undertake periodic reviews of national legislation, policies, and practices related to the rights of women and children.[320]

Like the AICHR, the ASEAN Commission on the Promotion and Protection of the Rights of Women and Children does not have a specific mandate to receive and investigate (individual) complaints of human rights violations. Decision-making in the ASEAN Commission on the Promotion and Protection of the Rights of Women and Children is based on consultation and consensus (see article 20 of the ASEAN Charter), which means that the Commission cannot act without the full agreement of all representatives.[321]

Finally, in 2007, representatives of the ASEAN member States adopted the ASEAN Declaration on the Protection and Promotion of the Rights of Migrant Workers.[322] The same year, the ASEAN Committee in the Implementation of the Declaration on the Protection and Promotion of the Rights of Migrant Workers was created, mandated to ensure the implementation of commitments made under the previously mentioned Declaration as well as to develop an ASEAN instrument on the protection and promotion of the rights of migrant workers.[323] In 2017, following ten years of negotiations, ASEAN States did adopt the ASEAN Consensus on the Protection and Promotion of the Rights of Migrant Workers, a treaty that sets out standards for the treatment of migrant workers in source and destination countries.

D. CONCLUSION

In the ASEAN the development of human rights both on a substantive level and on an institutional level is notable. It remains to be seen though whether the ASEAN example can and will be extrapolated to other sub-regional corners in Asia. The so-called Asian values, as reflected in the Bangkok Declaration and the ASEAN Human Rights

---

320 ASEAN Commission on the Promotion and Protection of the Rights of Women and Children, article 5, Terms of Reference, ASEAN Secretariat 2010.

321 Ibid, article 3.6.

322 ASEAN Declaration on the Protection and Promotion of the Rights of Migrant Workers, Cebu – Philippines, 13 January 2007.

323 Statement of the Establishment of the ASEAN Committee on the Implementation of the ASEAN Declaration on the Protection and Promotion of the Rights of Migrant Workers, Manila – Philippines, 31 July 2007.

Declaration, do not necessarily contest the universality of human rights law but rather aim at crafting more political and legal space for deference to national and regional particularities. With that being said, communitarian values or the role of duties of the individual hold conceptually certain untapped potential and therefore merit further study in human rights law.

BOX 21.7.4 Further Readings and Further Resources

Further Readings

- AT Anghie, 'Identifying Regions in the History of International Law' in Bardo Fassbender and Anne Peters (eds), *The Oxford Handbook of the History of International Law* (OUP 2012) 1058

- T Hsien-Li, 'Adaptive Protection of Human Rights: Stealth Institutionalisation of Scrutiny Functions in ASEAN's Limited Regime' (2022) 22 Human Rights Law Review 1

- Y Wahyuningrum, 'A Decade of Institutionalizing Human Rights in ASEAN: Progress and Challenges' (2021) 21 Journal of Human Rights 158

Further Resources

- The ASEAN Intergovernmental Commission on Human Rights publishes Annual Reports, Thematic Studies and Annual Activity Reports <https://aichr.org/reports/> accessed 20 August 2023

- YouTube video, Quick Facts About the Protection of Human Rights in ASEAN and by the ASEAN Intergovernmental Commission on Human Rights <www.youtube.com/watch?v=_gBYrWMyGC0&t=105s> accessed 20 August 2023

---

§ § §

§ 21.8 CRITIQUE OF HUMAN RIGHTS

THAMIL VENTHAN ANANTHAVINAYAGAN AND JENS T. THEILEN

BOX 21.8.1 Required Knowledge and Learning Objectives

Required knowledge: International Human Rights Law

Learning objectives: Understanding how to question the progress narrative of human rights as always already pointing towards a better world; different strands of human rights critique.

BOX 21.8.2 Interactive Exercises

Access *interactive exercises for this chapter*[324] by positioning your smartphone camera at the dot-filled box, also known as a QR code.

Figure 21.1 QR code referring to interactive exercises.

A. INTRODUCTION

In the popular imaginary and in large parts of legal scholarship, human rights are thought of as an unquestioned social good: they have persisted as humanity's 'last utopia' and are believed to express our 'highest moral precepts and political ideals'.[325] Many of those who work within human rights institutions assume that human rights are inherently benign. Critique aims to disrupt that assumption. It thus performs a killjoy function[326] – it aims to disenchant human rights, to present them not as part of a progress narrative in which they are always already pointing towards a better world, but rather as one of many discursive spaces in which different visions of a just society may clash and be fought out.[327]

---

324 https://openrewi.org/en-projects-project-public-international-law-international-human-rights-law/.

325 Samuel Moyn, *The Last Utopia. Human Rights in History* (Harvard UP 2012) 1, 4.

326 For the figure of the feminist killjoy, see Sara Ahmed, *Living a Feminist Life* (Duke UP 2017); in the context of human rights, see Jens T Theilen, *European Consensus between Strategy and Principle* (Nomos 2021) 412.

327 Ratna Kapur, 'Human Rights in the 21st Century: Take a Walk on the Dark Side' (2006) 28 Sydney LR 665, 668–673.

Critique in this sense takes a very different perspective from criticism of individual human rights decisions on the basis of legal doctrine.[328] The latter accepts the system of human rights law as given and merely aims to make minor adjustments on its own terms. By contrast, critique works to uncover the structure of human rights and their connection to other social phenomena, notably to relations of marginalisation, oppression, and exploitation.[329] Most critics of human rights share a commitment to radical social transformation in the face of a status quo that is perceived as fundamentally unjust. Beyond this, however, there are myriads of complex and diverse traditions of critique, with plenty of internal contradictions. We cannot do justice to all of these here, but merely aim to sketch some broad lines of thought building in particular on feminist, decolonial, and Marxist critiques.[330]

B. SOME CRITICAL LINES OF THOUGHT

I. HUMAN RIGHTS ARE NOT NEUTRAL OR APOLITICAL

Human rights are commonly understood as innate and inalienable. With this understanding comes a self-image of human rights as apolitical – they are said to be simply inherent in every human being, rather than being politically constructed. Contesting this self-image is a common starting point for critiques of human rights.[331] Understanding human rights as political opens up space to question the notion of the 'human' which is otherwise naturalised as self-evident, and to analyse the ways in which it is entangled with various structures of oppression.

BOX 21.8.3 Advanced: Struggles Around the Notion of the 'Human'

Feminists have pointed to the ways in which the ostensibly gender-neutral notion of the 'human' in fact privileges the male subject of human rights, for example by focusing on 'public' violations, while women's issues are consigned

---

328 On doctrinal perspectives on human rights, see Milas, § 21.1, in this textbook.

329 See for international law in general Robert Knox, 'Strategy and Tactics' (2010) 21 Finnish YBIL 193, 203; see also Susan Marks, *The Riddle of All Constitutions* (OUP 2000) chapter 6.

330 Other critical approaches include Critical Race Theory, critical disability studies, and queer theory. Labels such as these should not be taken as categorical divisions, however; there are overlaps, intersections and subfields as well as tensions and disagreements. For example, see E Tendayi Achiume and Devon W Carbado, 'Critical Race Theory Meets Third World Approaches to International Law' (2021) 67 UCLA L Rev 1462.

331 E.g. Balakrishnan Rajagopal, 'International Law and Social Movements: Challenges of Theorizing Resistance' (2003) 41 Columbia Journal of Transnational Law 397, 420; Wendy Brown, '"The Most We Can Hope For . . .": Human Rights and the Politics of Fatalism' (2004) 103 SAQ 451, 453.

to the 'private' sphere.[332] Colonised peoples were often construed as outside of the notion of humanity altogether, a mindset that continues to resonate in the disregard for the lives of the 'Wretched of the Earth' in the Global South and the treatment of migrants of colour.[333]

In the context of international human rights law, the idea that human rights are apolitical carries particular weight since the legal form, too, is commonly construed as an antithesis to politics. Critiques of human rights in the legal context thus share ground with critical international legal theory more generally, insisting on the indeterminacy of (human rights) law and thus on the decisional, political aspect involved in any specification of its meaning: the content of human rights is not predetermined by law itself, but rather actively constructed by the actors involved in its formulation and interpretation.[334]

II. HUMAN RIGHTS AS COLONIAL

Once politics are admitted onto the scene, it also becomes possible to question the claims to universality commonly invoked in the discourse on human rights. Refusing to take universality as an apolitical given allows us to analyse the particular interests which are embedded within it. An especially stark instance of this is how claims to universality cover up the Eurocentric origins of human rights and their historical and ongoing use to legitimise (neo-)colonial domination by industrialised Western States.[335] The Third World Approaches to International Law (TWAIL)[336] perspective, in particular, 'helps one to be conscious of the oppressive potential of universality' and to 'scrutinise which aspects of human rights may be made universal and which aspects need to be re-examined'.[337]

Makau Mutua, to this end, sketches the savages-victims-saviours metaphor. This three-dimensional metaphor aims to capture a dynamic central to human rights discourse, in which the victim – a 'powerless, helpless innocent' – has her dignity and worth violated by the barbaric savage, necessitating intervention by the saviour or 'the good

---

332 Hilary Charlesworth, Christine Chinkin, and Shelley Wright, 'Feminist Approaches to International Law' (1991) 85 AJIL 613; on different figures of the 'woman' in human rights law, see Dianne Otto, 'Lost in Translation: Re-scripting the Sexed Subjects of International Human Rights Law' in Anne Orford (ed), *International Law and Its Others* (CUP 2006) 318, and below, B.II., on the figure of the female 'victim'.

333 See e.g. P Khalil Saucier and Tryon P Woods, 'Ex Aqua. The Mediterranean Basin, Africans on the Move and the Politics of Policing' (2014) 61 Theoria 55; for the phrase 'Wretched of the Earth' see Frantz Fanon, *The Wretched of the Earth* (Penguin 1967).

334 Martti Koskenniemi, 'The Effect of Rights on Political Culture' in *The Politics of International Law* (Hart 2011); Theilen (n 326).

335 Davinia Gómez Sánchez, 'Transforming Human Rights Through Decolonial Lens' (2020) 15 The Age of Human Rights Journal 276; see generally on critiques of ostensible universality e.g. Makau Mutua, 'What Is TWAIL?' (2000) 94 Proceedings of the ASIL Annual Meeting 31.

336 For discussion on the Third World approaches in international law, see González-Hauck, § 3.2, in this textbook.

337 Opeoluwa Adetoro Badaru, 'Examining the Utility of Third World Approaches to International Law for International Human Rights Law' (2008) 10 ICLR 379, 384.

angel who protects, vindicates, civilizes, restrains, and safeguards' and who finds expression in the human rights corpus and its institutions.[338] The metaphor builds on colonial notions of civilisation and barbarism and in turn further solidifies 'the international hierarchy of race and color'.[339] It is also profoundly gendered: the 'Third World woman' is constructed as the paradigmatic victim subject that human rights law is thought to respond to.[340] Rights-based justifications for military interventions in the Middle East are an unsurprising continuation of these dynamics.[341]

However, the coloniality of human rights is not limited to the context of military interventions – rather, it is built into the manifold everyday contexts in which human rights are invoked, covering a wide range of subject matter and many international institutions. International financial institutions such as the International Monetary Fund and the World Bank,[342] in particular, make use of human rights and the language of 'good governance' to justify interventions in the political, social, and economic structures of Third World States.[343] Human rights thus remain entangled with (neo-) colonial forms of governance, and notably cannot be separated from the neoliberal economic regimes imposed on the Global South by international institutions.[344] At the same time, human rights have been used both by Third World States in attempts to emphasise political and economic self-determination vis-à-vis the Global North, and by academics, activists, and social movements seeking to contest authoritative regimes and abuses of power by Third World States themselves. Despite the coloniality of human rights, then, their liberatory promise – albeit so far unfulfilled and perhaps based, in the end, only on 'illusions of love or at least mutual interest'[345] – remains a recurring theme. We will return to this ambivalence in the concluding section below.

III. HUMAN RIGHTS AS A LEGITIMATION OF THE STATUS QUO

Several interrelated lines of critique focus on how human rights tend to legitimise the status quo and thus preclude social transformation. For one thing, any demarcation of

---

338 Makau Mutua, 'Savages, Victims, and Saviors: The Metaphor of Human Rights' (2001) 42 Harvard International Law Journal 201, 203–204.

339 Ibid, 207.

340 Ratna Kapur, 'The Tragedy of Victimization Rhetoric: Resurrecting the "Native" Subject in International/ Post-Colonial Feminist Legal Politics' (2002) 15 Harvard Human Rights Journal 1; see also Chandra Talpade Mohanty, *Feminism without Borders* (Duke University Press 2003); for an analysis of similar dynamics in the context of LGBT rights, see e.g. Cynthia Weber, *Queer International Relations* (OUP 2016).

341 See e.g. Vasuki Nesiah, 'From Berlin to Bonn to Baghdad: A Space for Infinite Justice' (2004) 17 Harvard Human Rights Journal 75.

342 On international monetary law, see Bagchi, § 23.3, in this textbook.

343 Antony Anghie, 'The Evolution of International Law: Colonial and Postcolonial Realities' (2006) 27 TWQ 739, 749.

344 See also e.g. Upendra Baxi, *The Future of Human Rights* (3rd edn, OUP 2008); Jessica Whyte, *The Morals of the Market. Human Rights and the Rise of Neoliberalism* (Verso 2019); Radha D'Souza, *What's Wrong With Rights? Social Movements, Law and Liberal Imaginations* (Pluto Press 2018).

345 Nikitah Okembe-Ra Imani, 'Critical Impairments to Globalizing the Western Human Rights Discourse' (2008) 3 Societies Without Borders 270, 271.

what human rights are necessitates an assessment of what they are *not* – and given the high moral value generally accorded to human rights, refusal to see claims that involve social transformation as an issue of human rights will often delegitimise those claims.[346] But the status quo can also be reinforced, and perhaps even more potently so, by virtue of what *is* considered a human right. Once elements of the current social order are integrated into the institutionalised human rights framework, they become extremely difficult to challenge.[347]

BOX 21.8.4 Advanced: Human Rights Entrenching Social Relations

The right to property may be considered the paradigmatic example of this, since it can transparently serve to impede claims to economic redistribution as well as hindering various other large-scale policy changes, which run counter to corporations' established interests. Marxist critiques have long argued that the dominant understandings of human rights are constitutive of the social relations of capitalism.[348] Human rights law also cements many other foundations of the current social order. For example, it foregrounds the nuclear family and the institution of marriage as foundational units of society. Queer critique not only takes issue with the way in which marriage is still understood in hetero- and cisnormative terms by prevailing doctrine, but it also questions the prevalence of marriage as such over other forms of kinship and community.[349] Another example is the normalisation of the prison-industrial complex through human rights. While certain prison conditions might be the subject of rights-based scrutiny, human rights courts simultaneously require States to criminalise an ever-increasing range of behaviours.[350] It thus becomes more difficult to mount prison abolitionist claims,[351] since States will point to their human rights obligations to justify a coercive approach.

---

346 Frédéric Mégret, 'The Apology of Utopia' (2013) 27 Temple International and Comparative Law Journal 455, 488.

347 On the double-bind this creates, see Jens T Theilen, 'The Inflation of Human Rights: A Deconstruction' (2021) 34 LJIL 831, 850.

348 Paul O'Connell, 'On the Human Rights Question' (2018) 40 HRQ 962, 966–967.

349 Ratna Kapur, *Gender, Alterity and Human Rights. Freedom in a Fishbowl* (Edward Elgar 2018) chapter 2; Aeyal M Gross, 'Sex, Love, and Marriage: Questioning Gender and Sexuality Rights in International Law' (2008) 21 LJIL 235, 245–249; Dean Spade, 'Under the Cover of Gay Rights' (2013) 37 NYU Review of Law & Social Change 79.

350 Karen Engle, 'Anti-Impunity and the Turn to Criminal Law in Human Rights' (2015) 100 Cornell Law Review 1069; Mattia Pinto, 'Historical Trends of Human Rights Gone Criminal' (2020) 42 HRQ 729; Natasa Mavronicola, *Torture, Inhumanity and Degradation under Article 3 of the ECHR* (Hart 2021) chapter 6.

351 On prison abolition, see Angela Y Davis, Are Prisons Obsolete? (Seven Stories Press 2003); Mariame Kaba, *We Do This 'Til We Free Us. Abolitionist Organizing and Transforming Justice* (Haymarket 2021).

A further way in which human rights law may reinforce the status quo relates to the patterns of analysis it brings with it. In particular, human rights law aims to establish whether a rights violation has taken place with little attention to underlying structures which bring about and perhaps even necessitate such violations. Even when the causes of human rights are investigated, the focus tends to be more on superficial causes, which can be 'translated into remedial proposals, themselves capable of being translated into bullet-point conclusions at the end of reports'.[352] Often, integration into global markets is presented as a way to empower rights holders, with insufficient attention paid to the power dynamics within markets themselves and to the impact of neoliberal globalisation, which has contributed to the deterioration of living conditions across the globe and especially in the Global South. By virtue of the way judgments, reports, and other documents structure human rights law, then, root causes like the socio-economic conditions underlying human rights violations tend to remain unexamined[353] – and thus unchallenged.

IV. WHO SPEAKS IN THE NAME OF HUMAN RIGHTS?

The proliferation of formal documents like judgments and reports within institutionalised human rights brings us to a related point: who speaks in the name of human rights? Postcolonial feminist Gayatri Spivak famously asked whether the subaltern can speak – and answered in the negative, indicating that the impossibility of speaking constitutes the position of the subaltern subject.[354] This provocation raises questions not only about speaking or not-speaking but also about being heard or not-heard. More generally, it draws our attention to the relationships of (knowledge) production which prefigure discursive fields such as human rights.[355]

In this vein, a common critique of human rights – at least in their institutionalised form – is that they have become a language of legal experts.[356] Human rights are thus conceived of as a managerial issue, an aspect of governance: 'normative standards to guide administrative actions and less and less the basis for justice'.[357] This not only

---

352 Susan Marks, 'Human Rights and Root Causes' (2011) 74 MLR 57, 71–72; see also Wendy Brown, '"The Most We Can Hope for . . .": Human Rights and the Politics of Fatalism' (2004) 103 SAQ 451, 460.

353 David Kennedy, 'The International Human Rights Movement: Part of the Problem?' (2002) 15 Harvard Human Rights Journal 101, especially 109–110 and 118–119.

354 Gayatri Chakravorty Spivak, 'Can the Subaltern Speak?' in Patrick Williams and Laura Chrisman (eds), Colonial Discourse and Post-Colonial Theory. A Reader (Columbia UP 1994) 66.

355 See Sara Ahmed, *Strange Encounters. Embodied Others in Post-Coloniality* (Routledge 2000) 60–61.

356 For a detailed exploration of expertise as a governance feature in the context of rights, see Bal Sokhi-Bulley, 'Government(ality) by Experts: Human Rights as Governance' (2011) 22 Law & Critique 251; on expertise and managerialism in international law more broadly, see Martti Koskenniemi, 'The Politics of International Law – 20 Years Later' (2009) 20 EJIL 7.

357 Radha D'Souza, *What's Wrong With Rights? Social Movements, Law and Liberal Imaginations* (Pluto Press 2018) 18.

obscures their political character, it also establishes certain professional standards for how to think and talk about human rights and sidelines those actors who fail to live up to these expectations. While processes of public consultation on human rights issues are common, they tend to focus on 'civil society' in the shape of large, well-funded non-governmental organisations[358], usually based in (or funded by actors based in) the Global North.[359] Differently put: while human rights institutions have much to say about how to improve the plight of those one might deem subaltern, they rarely seek to listen to them.

C. CONCLUSION

The question of what comes after critique is a difficult one. Having delivered often searing critiques of human rights, many writers end on a hopeful note – they end up 'attempting to reimagine (and in doing so, reinforce) the human rights project itself'.[360] But perhaps such a turn to reimagination and hope is misplaced, a form of cruel optimism?[361] After all, reimagining human rights in a more emancipatory vein cannot displace their legal, institutional, and material realities and the various ways in which they help to constitute relations of marginalisation, oppression, and exploitation.[362] But it is also true that human rights are invoked outside of institutions by a broad variety of political and social movements, asserted in resistance to market logics and forming part of a struggle to survive in the face of global capitalism.[363]

It is from within this space of ambivalence that we suggest approaching human rights, which implies a high measure of caution as to their emancipatory potential when institutionalised within international law. For human rights to become truly international, we would need engagement with the Global South, beyond those elites who tend to play a role in the legal context.[364]

---

358 On NGOs, see Chi, § 7.6, in this textbook.

359 Upendra Baxi, *The Future of Human Rights* (3rd edn, OUP 2008) 218–219; Frédéric Mégret, 'Where Does the Critique of International Human Rights Stand? An Exploration in 18 Vignettes' in José María Beneyto and David Kennedy (eds), *New Approaches to International Law: The European and American Experiences* (Asser 2012) 3, 10–11 and 13–14.

360 Ben Golder, 'Beyond Redemption? Problematising the Critique of Human Rights in Contemporary International Legal Thought' (2014) 2 LRIL 77, 79; for different perspectives on this issue, see e.g. Ratna Kapur, *Gender, Alterity and Human Rights. Freedom in a Fishbowl* (Edward Elgar 2018); Kathryn McNeilly, *Human Rights and Radical Social Transformation* (Routledge 2018).

361 Lauren Berlant, *Cruel Optimism* (Duke UP 2011).

362 Radha D'Souza, *What's Wrong with Rights? Social Movements, Law and Liberal Imaginations* (Pluto Press 2018).

363 Paul O'Connell, 'On the Human Rights Question' (2018) 40 HRQ 962; on social movements, see also Balakrishnan Rajagopal, *International Law from Below* (CUP 2003).

364 Thamil Venthan Ananthavinayagan, *Sri Lanka, Human Rights and the United Nations – A Scrutiny into the International Human Rights Engagement with a Third World State* (Springer 2019) 247.

BOX 21.8.5 Further Readings

Further Readings

- U Baxi, *The Future of Human Rights* (3rd edn, OUP 2008)

- R D'Souza, *What's Wrong With Rights? Social Movements, Law and Liberal Imaginations* (Pluto Press 2018)

- R Kapur, *Gender, Alterity and Human Rights. Freedom in a Fishbowl* (Edward Elgar 2018)

- S Marks, 'Human Rights and Root Causes' (2011) 74 MLR 57

- M Mutua, 'Savages, Victims, and Saviors: The Metaphor of Human Rights' (2001) 42 Harvard International Law Journal 201

---

§ § §

CHAPTER 22
INTERNATIONAL CRIMINAL LAW

ANNALISA CIAMPI, TAXIARCHIS FISKATORIS, AND RAGHAVI VISWANATH

INTRODUCTION
ANNALISA CIAMPI

BOX 22.1 Required Knowledge and Learning Objectives

Required knowledge: Subjects and Actors in International Law; Law of Armed Conflict; International Human Rights Law

Learning objectives: Understanding the notion, foundation, purpose, and importance of international criminal law.

BOX 22.2 Interactive Exercises

Access *interactive exercises for this chapter*[1] by positioning your smartphone camera at the dot-filled box, also known as a QR code.

Figure 22.1 QR code referring to interactive exercises.

A. INTRODUCTION

International criminal law (ICL) refers to principles and rules of international law for the prevention and repression of international crimes.[2] It is a relatively new branch of

---

1 https://openrewi.org/en-projects-project-public-international-law-international-criminal-law/.
2 On international crimes, see Fiskatoris, § 22.1, in this textbook.

DOI: 10.4324/9781003451327-25

international law, which owes its very foundation to the emergence of the principle of individual criminal responsibility in international law.

Under classical international law, with States[3] as the main international actors, individuals[4] could not be held accountable, in the same way as they could not claim international rights. The origin of the principle of individual criminal responsibility lies in the idea that in addition to States, individuals may be held responsible for serious violations of international law. This implies that certain international obligations (the prohibition of war crimes, crimes against humanity, genocide, torture, aggression, and others) are not only addressed to States, but also to individuals. ICL emerged rapidly in the aftermath of World War II and underwent tremendous developments during the post-1990 years to become a body of international law which plays an important role in upholding fundamental values shared by the international community.

From a normative point of view, ICL includes both substantive and procedural rules concerning the prosecution of international crimes, which are examined in the subsequent chapters. Substantive rules indicate the prohibited criminal activities and the circumstances (excluding criminal responsibility). They also either authorise States, or impose upon them the obligation, to prosecute and punish persons accused of such criminal acts. Procedural rules govern international proceedings before international courts and tribunals, from the investigative and prosecutorial phases to the various stages of international trials.[5]

B. THE PRINCIPLE OF INDIVIDUAL CRIMINAL RESPONSIBILITY IN INTERNATIONAL LAW

The notion of international crimes refers to those criminal activities, harmful to values that transcend the interests of individual States, in relation to which a need for repression arises in the international community. Therefore, an international crime can be defined as a criminal activity of an individual in relation to which the international community organises some form of international repression.

The first and most important consequence that international law attaches to the commission of an international crime is the criminal responsibility of the individual who commits it. This is the core of the principle of individual criminal responsibility for international crimes. The principle of individual criminal responsibility also operates – where necessary – as an exception to the general rule according to which the activity carried out in the name and on behalf of the State is attributable to the latter and not to the individual concerned (principle of individual criminal responsibility for

---

3   On States, see Green, § 7.1, in this textbook.

4   On individuals as actors in international law, see Theilen, § 7.4, in this textbook.

5   On international and domestic prosecution of international crimes, see Viswanath, § 22.2, in this textbook.

international crimes committed by State-organs). The rationale for this exception could not be explained more effectively than with the words of the Nuremberg Tribunal:

> Crimes against international law are committed by men, not by abstract entities, and only by punishing individuals who commit such crimes can the provisions of international law be enforced.[6]

Hence, when an international crime is committed by an individual acting on behalf of the State or the conduct of an individual is attributable to a State, the principle of individual criminal responsibility constitutes an exception to the general immunities of State organs under international law,[7] including persons in leadership positions (both military and civilian). This was first affirmed after WWI with reference to war crimes and then reiterated in numerous subsequent instruments, and it is now part of customary international law.[8] It applies equally to all persons without any distinction based on official capacity before international criminal courts and tribunals (see e.g. article 27 of the Statute of the International Criminal Court). For serving heads of States, however, customary international law keeps open the possibility of impunity in limited circumstances.

As in national legal systems, also in international law, crimes consist of two elements: a conduct, that is an act or omission contrary to a substantive rule prohibiting or imposing a specific behaviour (*actus reus* [Latin: 'criminal act']), and a mental element, that is a state of mind directed to or linked to the commission of the criminal act (*mens rea* [Latin: 'criminal intent']). International crimes are often committed by a plurality of persons with the same (co-perpetration) or different modalities of participation (joint criminal enterprise). A person may only be held criminally responsible if they are somehow culpable for the commission of the crime. Furthermore, according to the principle of legality of crimes, only the law can define a crime and prescribe a penalty (*nullum crimen* [Latin: 'no crime'], *nulla poena sine lege* [Latin: 'no punishment without law').

I. COEXISTENCE OF INTERNATIONAL CRIMINAL LAW AND STATE RESPONSIBILITY

Individual criminal responsibility arises alongside international State responsibility when the crime is committed by a State-organ and/or is attributable to a State under any of the rules on the attribution to States of internationally wrongful acts.[9] In this respect, a basic distinction can be drawn between crimes committed by private individuals, crimes generally or necessarily committed by State organs, and crimes that are likely to be committed by individuals either in their private or official capacity.

---

6   Nuremberg Tribunal, judgment of 1 October 1946, in *Trial of the Major War Criminals before the International Military Tribunal, Nuremberg, 14 November 1945–1 October 1946.*

7   On State immunity, see Walton, § 11, in this textbook.

8   On customary international law, see Stoica, § 6.2, in this textbook.

9   On State responsibility, see Arévalo-Ramírez, § 9, in this textbook.

The most ancient category of crimes which are always or generally committed by State organs, are war crimes. Genocide and crimes against humanity also originate, as a rule, from State conduct, either in the sense that their authors are State organs or because they are the result of policies or choices indirectly favoured or supported by a State. The commission of one of these international crimes implies the commission of an internationally wrongful act by the State of which the individual is an organ or to which the conduct in question is attributable, according to the general rules of State responsibility.[10] The need remains, however, to keep the two forms of responsibility distinct.

II. ENFORCEMENT MECHANISMS

ICL possesses two main enforcement mechanisms: the so-called direct enforcement system and the indirect enforcement system of ICL. The establishment of an international criminal court or tribunal relates to the direct enforcement system of ICL. The prosecution and punishment of international crimes takes place before international courts or tribunals, directly at the international level. Indirect enforcement mechanisms refer to domestic prosecution and punishment before national courts. In this case, criminal repression is organised by national jurisdictions: States have the power and sometimes the duty to prosecute and, where appropriate, punish perpetrators of international crimes. In relation to core crimes (genocide, crimes against humanity and war crimes), the principle of universal jurisdiction[11] provides for the possibility – if not the obligation – of repression by any State, regardless of the place where the crimes were committed or the nationality of the suspect. Another system is enforcement by the so-called internationalised or hybrid (mixed) tribunals, which combine features of international and national tribunals.[12]

C. THE HISTORICAL EVOLUTION OF INTERNATIONAL CRIMINAL LAW

I. BEFORE WORLD WAR II

One of the first and most notable manifestation of the principle of individual criminal responsibility is the Treaty of Versailles, which set the terms ending World War I. The victorious Allies – Britain, France, and Italy and the United States – ultimately agreed to investigate and prosecute the defeated German Emperor Kaiser Wilhelm II. Article 227 of the Treaty of Versailles stated that Kaiser Wilhelm would be tried by an international court for the 'supreme crime against international morality and the sanctity of treaties'. The provision was unprecedented in at least two important respects. First, the very notion of holding a leader responsible for crimes committed in

---

10 See articles 4–11 of the Draft Articles on State Responsibility for International Wrongful Acts.

11 On jurisdiction, see González Hauck and Milas, § 8, in this textbook.

12 On hybrid tribunals, see Viswanath, § 22.2, in this textbook.

conflict was unprecedented. It was also the first time in history that States imagined the possibility of an international tribunal for the prosecution of an individual.[13]

II. FROM NUREMBERG TO THE HAGUE

The international prosecution of crimes against peace began with the Nuremberg and Tokyo trials of the major war criminals following WWII.

1. The Nuremberg Trials

The Nuremberg trials were a series of 13 trials carried out in Nuremberg, Germany, between 1945 and 1949 by a tribunal established under the London Charter of the International Military Tribunal (IMT) by the Allies France, Great Britain, the former Soviet Union, and the United States. The Tribunal was endowed with the power to try and punish persons who, acting in the interest of the European Axis countries, committed any act falling in the three categories of crimes defined in article 6 of the London Charter: crimes against peace (including planning, preparing, starting, or waging wars of aggression or wars in violation of international agreements); war crimes (including violations of customs or laws of war, improper treatment of civilians, and prisoners of war); and crimes against humanity (including murder, enslavement, or deportation of civilians or persecution on political, religious, or racial grounds). Article 7 stipulated that even heads of State could not claim immunity.

The best known of the Nuremberg trials was the Trial of Major War Criminals, held from 20 November 1945 to 1 October 1946. Although Nazi leader Adolf Hitler (1889–1945) committed suicide and was never brought to trial, 24 individuals, including Nazi Party officials and high-ranking military officers, were indicted along with six Nazi organisations determined to be criminal. The IMT found all but three of the defendants guilty. Twelve of the accused were sentenced to death, one *in absentia* (Latin: 'in absence'), and the rest were given prison sentences ranging from ten years to life imprisonment.

The Nuremberg trials were controversial even among those who wanted punishment for the Nazis' main criminals. The main criticism, and the most common defence strategy, was that the crimes defined in the London Charter criminalised actions committed before the relevant provisions were drafted. Another criticism, and defence, was that the trial was a form of victor's justice – the Allies were applying a harsh standard to crimes committed by Germans and leniency to crimes committed by their own soldiers. On the other hand, the Nuremberg Tribunal itself responded that the defendants knew that what that they were doing was wrong and therefore the principle of legality, as a principle of justice, was respected.

2. Tokyo Trials

The IMT's trials and findings set a step forward for the development of international criminal law. They were paralleled by the trials of the leaders of the Empire of Japan

---

13 William Schabas, *The Trial of the Kaiser* (OUP 2018).

in Tokyo by the International Military Tribunal for the Far East (IMTFE). Besides prosecuting Japanese leaders, the IMT supplied a useful precedent for future prosecution of international crimes by national courts, most notably the 1961 trial of Nazi leader Adolf Eichmann by the Supreme Court of Israel.[14]

3. Developments After Nuremberg and Tokyo

The experience of the IMT and the IMTFE inspired the Convention on the Prevention and Punishment of the Crime of Genocide and the Universal Declaration of Human Rights, adopted by the United Nations General Assembly (UNGA) on 8 and 10 December 1948, respectively, as well as the four Geneva Conventions on the Laws and Customs of War adopted on 12 August 1949 by the Diplomatic Conference for the Establishment of International Conventions for the Protection of Victims of War. The UNGA entrusted the International Law Commission (ILC) with the task of drafting a Statute for the establishment of an international criminal tribunal, together with a code of crimes, the so-called Code of Crimes Against Peace and Security of Mankind. The two projects were interrelated, but the failure of the latter brought about a halt to the works for draft statute as well. The Cold War prevented any progress.

4. International Criminal Courts and Tribunals

It was only in 1989 that the UNGA asked the ILC once again to draft a statute for the institution of an international criminal court. The end of the Cold War also made it possible to establish two *ad hoc* (Latin: 'for this purpose') international criminal tribunals as subsidiary organs of the UN Security Council (UNSC): the International Criminal Tribunal for the former Yugoslavia (ICTY) and the International Criminal Tribunal for Rwanda (ICTR). During its mandate, which lasted from 1993 to 2017, the ICTY prosecuted those responsible for serious violations of international humanitarian law committed in the territory of the former Yugoslavia since 1991, in accordance with UNSC Resolution 827 and the Statute annexed thereto.[15] The ICTR, established by UNSC Resolution 955,[16] prosecuted those considered most responsible for genocide and other serious violations of international humanitarian law committed in the territory of Rwanda and neighbouring States in 1994.

The ILC eventually approved a draft statute for an international criminal court in 1994, which provided the basis for the further works which were entrusted to the Preparatory Committee (Prep Com), an *ad hoc* group of people established by the General Assembly. The draft of the Prep Com was the basis of the further negotiations, which took place in Rome in 1998 and finally resulted in the adoption by 120 States of the Statute of the International Criminal Court (ICC)[17] on 17 July 1998. The Rome Statute entered into force on 1 July 2002, making the ICC the first permanent international criminal court.

---

14 Randolph L Braham, *The Eichmann Case: A Source Book* (World Federation of Hungarian Jews 1969).

15 UNSC Res 827 (25 May 1993) UN Doc S/RES/827.

16 UNSC Res 955 (8 November 1994) UN Doc S/RES/955.

17 Rome Statute of the International Criminal Court (adopted 17 July 1998, entered into force 1 July 2002) 2187 UNTS 90.

The ICTY and the ICTR terminated their mandates on 31 December 2017 and 2015, respectively, following the establishment of the International Residual Mechanism for Criminal Tribunals by the UNSC to ensure that the closure of the two pioneering *ad hoc* tribunals does not open the way for impunity.

D. CONCLUSION

Built heavily on the law of armed of conflict,[18] at its inception, for the identification of the violations which give rise to individual criminal responsibility, ILC continues to draw significantly upon international humanitarian law and international human rights law[19] – the latter also in relation to the fundamental rights of suspects, accused persons, victims and witnesses, and the basic safeguards of a fair trial. Albeit a relatively new branch of international law, ICL has become of prominent importance with the establishment of the ICC in 1998 and in subsequent years. And it remains complementary to other branches of international law, in particular, human rights and international humanitarian law.

BOX 22.3 Further Readings and Further Resources

Further Readings

- A Cassese and P Gaeta, *Cassese's International Criminal Law* (3rd edn, OUP 2013)

- R Cryer, D Robinson, and S Vasiliev, *An Introduction to International Criminal Law and Procedure* (4th edn, CUP 2019)

Further Resources

- Judgment at Nuremberg, Film Directed by S Kramer (1961) <www.youtube.com/watch?v=50fR251R_Ck> accessed 20 August 2023

- Nuremberg, Film Directed by Y. Simoneau (2000) <www.youtube.com/watch?v=f7p7DDihpvQ> accessed 20 August 2023

- RJ Golsan and SM Misemer (eds), *The Trial That Never Ends: Hannah Arendt's Eichmann in Jerusalem in Retrospect* (University of Toronto Press 2017)

- S Minerbi, *The Eichmann Trial Diary. An Eyewitness Account of the Trial that Revealed the Holocaust* (RL Miller, trans., Enigma Books 2011)

---

§ § §

---

18 On the law of armed conflict, see Dienelt and Ullah, § 14, in this textbook.
19 On international human rights law, see Ciampi, § 21 (and the following sub-chapters), in this textbook.

§ 22.1 INTERNATIONAL CRIMES

TAXIARCHIS FISKATORIS

BOX 22.1.1 Required Knowledge and Learning Objectives

Required knowledge: International Criminal Law; Law of Armed Conflict

Learning objectives: Understanding the foundations and purpose of international criminal justice; the most prominent international crimes; the content of international crimes and its dynamic evolution in time; and the elements of international crimes to practical situations.

BOX 22.1.2 Interactive Exercises

Access *interactive exercises for this chapter*[20] by positioning your smartphone camera at the dot-filled box, also known as a QR code.   .

Figure 22.1 QR code referring to interactive exercises.

A. INTRODUCTION

A conceptual definition of international crimes does not exist in international law. The constitutive instruments of international or internationalised courts and tribunals enumerate their subject matter jurisdiction without explicitly labelling the punishable offences as international crimes. The jurisdictional remit of such institutions cannot be considered a substitute for a comprehensive international criminal code, which does not exist. The preamble to the Rome Statute of the International Criminal Court[21] (Rome Statute or ICC Statute) implies that the International Criminal Court's (ICC) jurisdiction does not cover all 'international crimes'.[22] Scholars usually distinguish between 'international crimes *lato sensu*' (Latin: 'in the broad sense') and 'international

---

20 https://openrewi.org/en-projects-project-public-international-law-international-criminal-law/.

21 On the International Criminal Court, see Viswanath, § 22.2, in this textbook.

22 Mark Klamberg (ed), *Commentary on the Law of the International Criminal Court* (TOAEP 2017) 2 fn 7.

crimes *stricto sensu*' (Latin: 'in the narrow sense').[23] International crimes *stricto sensu*, also known as *core crimes*, coincide to a great extent with Rome Statute crimes.

B. ROME STATUTE CRIMES

The ICC Statute qualifies the offences within the jurisdiction of the ICC as 'the most serious crimes of concern to the international community as a whole'.[24] All Rome Statute crimes have a similar structure, which consists of a catalogue of offences, and an introductory sentence about their contextual elements. The offences may overlap, but the contextual elements distinguish the crimes from one another.

BOX 22.1.3 Example: Overlapping Offences

A murder is an ordinary crime, which can take the form of a war crime, a crime against humanity, or genocide, depending on what contextual elements are fulfilled.

Additionally, according to article 30, 'unless otherwise provided', the mental element of 'intent and knowledge' applies to all offences within the ICC's ambit.

I. WAR CRIMES

1. The Nature of War Crimes

War crime is the oldest category among the four Rome Statute crimes. Individual accountability for war crimes has its origins in the process of progressive criminalisation of customary and conventional rules of the law of armed conflict.[25] War crimes generally pertain to the use of prohibited weapons and methods of warfare, and to attacks on protected persons or property.

2. The Underlying Offences

In its 1951 Draft Code of Offences against the Peace and Security of Mankind, the International Law Commission (ILC) commented that war crimes were relevant not only in cases of declared war, but also in 'any other armed conflict which may arise between two or more States, even if the existence of a state of war is recognized by none of them'.[26] The content of war crimes was further elaborated by the ILC in its review

---

23 On this distinction, see Ciampi, § 22, in this textbook.

24 Rome Statute of the International Criminal Court (adopted 17 July 1998, entered into force 1 July 2002) 2187 UNTS 3 preamble.

25 On the law of armed conflict, see Dienelt and Ullah, § 14, in this textbook.

26 Draft Code of Offences against the Peace and Security of Mankind (1957) 2 YILC 1951 134 Comment 11 to article 2.

of the Draft Code, and in the Statutes of the International Criminal Tribunals for the former Yugoslavia (ICTY) and Rwanda (ICTR). All of them confirmed that 'grave breaches' of the Geneva Conventions give rise to individual criminal accountability. Nowadays, war crimes are incorporated into article 8(2) of the ICC Statute.

The enumeration of war crimes in the context of non-international armed conflicts is modest in comparison to that of war crimes in international armed conflicts. For example, the war crime of 'intentionally launching an attack in the knowledge that such attack will cause . . . widespread, long-term and severe damage to the natural environment' can only be prosecuted by the ICC if linked to an international, and not an internal conflict.[27] However, through the amendment procedure of the Rome Statute, the number of punishable war crimes committed in non-international armed conflicts incrementally converges with that of war crimes perpetrated in international conflicts.

3. The Contextual Elements

In its first case, the ICTY clarified that the prerequisite for war crimes, the existence of an armed conflict, was fulfilled whenever 'there is a resort to armed force between States or protracted armed violence between governmental authorities and organized armed groups or between such groups within a State'.[28] That meant, essentially, that war crimes can be committed in both international and internal armed conflicts. A mere resort to force, such as in occasions of riots, does not meet the required level of intensity of 'protracted armed violence', and thus criminal conduct in such contexts does not constitute war crimes.

However, even in the event of an armed conflict, not every offence is necessarily a war crime. The perpetrator's ability or decision to commit the offence, the purpose for which it was committed, or the manner in which it was committed must be substantially linked to the conflict.[29] Furthermore, the perpetrator must fulfil the threshold of the mental element. For instance, the accidental destruction of historic monuments may not qualify as a war crime, but 'intentionally directing attacks' against them, provided they are not used for military purposes, most probably will.[30]

II. GENOCIDE

1. The Material Element

Genocide was explicitly recognised in the 1948 Genocide Convention as a 'crime under international law' whether committed in time of war or peace.[31]

---

27 Article 8(2)(b)(iv) Rome Statute.

28 *ICTY*, Prosecutor v Duško Tadić (AC Decision on the Defence Motion for Interlocutory Appeal on Jurisdiction) IT-94-1-AR72 (2 October 1995) para 70.

29 *ICTY, Prosecutor v Dragoljub Kunarac et al. (AC Judgement) IT-96-23&IT-96-23/1-A (12 June 2002) para 58.*

30 Article 8(2)(b)(ix) and 8(2)(e)(iv) Rome Statute.

31 Convention on the Prevention and Punishment of the Crime of Genocide (adopted 9 December 1948, entered into force 12 January 1951) 78 UNTS 277; see also UNGA 'The Crime of Genocide' (11 December 1946) UN Doc A/Res/96(I).

According to article 2 of the Genocide Convention and article 6 of the Rome Statute:

> Genocide means any of the following acts committed with intent to destroy, in whole or in part, a national, ethnical, racial or religious group, as such:
> (a) killing members of the group;
> (b) causing serious bodily or mental harm to members of the group;
> (c) deliberately inflicting on the group conditions of life calculated to bring about its physical destruction in whole or in part;
> (d) imposing measures intended to prevent births within the group;
> (e) forcibly transferring children of the group to another group.

The material element of genocide may take the form of any one of five alternative prohibited acts, directed against any one of four alternative protected groups. The ICTR has attempted to define the four protected groups based on scientific criteria.[32] However, jurisprudence has progressively accepted that whether one belongs to a protected group does not exclusively depend on objective facts, but also on the subjective perceptions of the victims or the perpetrators.[33] In any case, prohibited acts committed against other groups, such as political, social, or gender groups, do not fall within the definition.

Genocide is not confined to acts of killing. Echoing the judgment of the first international genocide trial in history, the ICC Elements of Crimes accept that, among others, 'torture, rape, sexual violence or inhuman or degrading treatment' may constitute underlying genocidal offences as causing serious bodily or mental harm.[34]

2. The Mental Elements

The legal definition of genocide consists of two mental elements. First, the general intent to execute one of the underlying offences of the material element. However, genocide's distinctive feature is the second and more stringent mental element of a specific intent (Latin: 'dolus specialis') of the perpetrator to destroy 'in whole or in part' a protected group 'as such'.[35] The actual destruction of the group is not required. The wording 'in part' suggests that even the intention to destroy a small but 'substantial part' of the group, not only in the sense of numeric size but also of emblematic prominence, counts as genocide.[36] It is usually 'difficult, even impossible' to unequivocally establish genocidal intent, especially when there are other reasonable explanations.[37]

---

32 *ICTR, The Prosecutor v. Jean-Paul Akayesu (TC Judgement), ICTR-96–4-T (2 September 1998)* paras 512–515.

33 See Carola Lingaas, 'Defining the Protected Groups of Genocide through the Case Law of International Courts' (2015) ICD Brief 18, 12/2015 <www.internationalcrimesdatabase.org/upload/documents/20151217T122733-Lingaas%20Final%20ICD%20Format.pdf> accessed 26 June 2023.

34 ASP, 'Elements of Crimes' in ASP 'Official Records, First Session, New York, 3–10 September 2002' (2002) ICC-ASP/1/3 Part II.B article 6(b), element 1 fn 3; *ICTR, The Prosecutor v. Jean-Paul Akayesu (TC Judgement), ICTR-96–4-T (2 September 1998)* paras 731–733.

35 See *ICTY, The Prosecutor v Goran Jelisić (TC Judgement), IT-95–10-T (14 December 1999)* para 66.

36 *ICTY, The Prosecutor v Radislav Krstić (AC Judgement) IT-98–33-A (19 April 2004)* para 12.

37 *ICTR, The Prosecutor v. Jean-Paul Akayesu (TC Judgement), ICTR-96–4-T (2 September 1998)* para 523.

III. CRIMES AGAINST HUMANITY

1. The Nature of Crimes Against Humanity

The essential characteristic of crimes against humanity (CAH) is that humanity rather than the individual is their ultimate victim.[38] Some CAH overlap with genocide and war crimes. They differ, though, from genocide because they lack the mental element of special intent to destroy a group, and from war crimes because they apply equally in wartime and peacetime.

2. The Underlying Offences

Article 7 of the Rome Statute establishes that persecuting an identifiable group or community on political, racial, national, ethnic, cultural, religious, gender, or other grounds; sexual violence such as sexual slavery, enforced prostitution, forced pregnancy, and enforced sterilisation; enforced disappearance of persons; and the crime of apartheid are considered to be CAH.[39] Furthermore, other inhumane 'acts of similar character intentionally causing great suffering, or serious injury to body or to mental or physical health' are also included in the list of CAH.[40] Forced marriage has been prosecuted by the Special Court for Sierra Leone and the ICC as falling into the latter category.

> ## BOX 22.1.4 Advanced: Apartheid as a Crime Against Humanity
>
> The 1967 UN Convention on the Non-Applicability of Statutory Limitations to War Crimes and Crimes Against Humanity, the 1973 Apartheid Convention, and numerous UN General Assembly (UNGA) Resolutions explicitly declared apartheid a CAH. This categorisation is based on the vigorous efforts of countries in the Global South that felt empowered by the decolonisation movement.[41] Nonetheless, States from the Global South had to fight until the very last moment of the Rome Conference in order to achieve the inclusion of apartheid as an underlying CAH into the Rome Statute.

3. The Contextual Element

According to the contextual element of CAH in the Rome Statute, CAH must be 'committed as part of a widespread or systematic attack directed against any civilian

---

38 *ICTY*, Prosecutor v Erdemović *(TC Sentencing Judgement) IT-96–22-T (29 November 1996)* para 28.
39 Article 7 Rome Statute.
40 Article 7(1)(k) Rome Statute.
41 On decolonisation, see González Hauck, § 1, in this textbook.

population, with knowledge of the attack'.[42] Article 7(2) further specifies that the attack must be 'pursuant to or in furtherance of a state or organizational policy to commit such attack'. According to the ICC's Elements of Crimes, attack is not necessarily military, but understood as 'involving the multiple commission' of an underlying offence.[43]

To this date, apart from the Rome Statute, there is not any international convention on crimes against humanity. The ICTY stated that CAH are part of customary international law, but a number of States reject this. The ILC has concluded Draft Articles on the Prevention and Punishment of Crimes Against Humanity, but the UNGA has not yet adopted these draft articles.[44]

IV. THE CRIME OF AGGRESSION

Article 8bis of the Rome Statute provides that the crime of aggression requires the planning, preparation, initiation, or execution of an act of aggression which, by its character, gravity, and scale, constitutes a manifest violation of the UN Charter. Aggression covers the 'use of armed force by a State against the sovereignty, territorial integrity or political independence of another State, or in any other manner inconsistent with the UN Charter . . . regardless of a declaration of war'. The person committing the crime of aggression must be in a position effectively to exercise control over or to direct the political or military action of a State.

C. OTHER INTERNATIONAL CRIMES

Depending on the definition of international crimes one adopts, the catalogue of international crimes can be much broader than the list presented above. For instance, M. Cherif Bassiouni, one of the pioneers of modern international criminal law (ICL), having studied international conventions with penal characteristics, had compiled a list of no less than 25 international crimes in the broad sense.[45] Most of these crimes are to be found in conventions that establish for States parties a duty to domestically criminalise acts as well as a right or duty to either prosecute or extradite the offenders and to cooperate in prosecution and punishment. A majority of modern scholars prefers to call such offences transnational crimes or treaty crimes.[46]

---

42 Article 7(1) Rome Statute.
43 ASP, 'Elements of Crimes' in ASP 'Official Records, First Session, New York, 3–10 September 2002' (2002) ICC-ASP/1/3 Part II.B article 7, introduction, para 3.
44 2019 Draft Articles on Prevention and Punishment of Crimes Against Humanity 2(2) YILC 2019.
45 M Cherif Bassiouni, *International Criminal Law Conventions and Their Penal Provisions* (Transnational Publishers 1997) 20–21.
46 Neil Boister, *An Introduction to Transnational Criminal Law* (2nd edn, OUP 2018).

Among others, piracy,[47] human trafficking,[48] torture,[49] terrorism,[50] and drug trafficking[51] belong to this category. The Malabo Protocol, which establishes the subject–matter jurisdiction of a future African Criminal Court,[52] lists terrorism, mercenarism, corruption, money laundering, trafficking in persons, drugs and hazardous wastes, illicit exploitation of natural resources, and the crime of unconstitutional change of government as other, non–core international crimes.[53]

BOX 22.1.5 Advanced: Ecocide

The relevance of ICL to the protection of the environment has been debated and occasionally put on the UN agenda at least since the 1970s. However, with the exception of the ICC Statute, where widespread, long-term, and severe environmental damage is mentioned as an underlying war crime in international armed conflicts, ICL remains anthropocentric. In recent years, the recognition of environmental offences as international crimes worthy of prosecution at the international level has gained significant importance. The connotative term 'ecocide' is used in order to raise awareness. Non-governmental organisations and eminent legal scholars have attempted to vest ecocide with a definition that could become the fifth autonomous Rome Statute crime:

> For the purpose of this Statute, 'ecocide' means unlawful or wanton acts committed with knowledge that there is a substantial likelihood of severe

---

47 United Nations Convention on the Law of the Sea (adopted 10 December 1982, entered into force 16 November 1994) *1833 UNTS 3 (UNCLOS)* article 101.

48 Protocol to Prevent, Suppress and Punish Trafficking in Persons, Especially Women and Children, supplementing the United Nations Convention against Transnational Organized Crime (adopted 15 November 2000, entered into force 25 December 2003) *2237 UNTS 319* article 3(a).

49 Convention against Torture and Other Cruel, Inhuman or Degrading Treatment or Punishment (adopted 10 December 1984, entered into force 26 June 1987) 1465 UNTS 85; see Antonio Cassese and others, *Cassese's International Criminal Law* (3rd edn, OUP 2013) 132.

50 *STL, The Prosecutor v. Ayyash et al (AC Interlocutory Decision on the Applicable Law: Terrorism, Conspiracy, Homicide, Perpetration, Cumulative Charging) STL-11–01/I (16 February 2011)* para 85; See also A Cassese, 'The Multifaceted Criminal Notion of Terrorism in International Law' (2006) 4 JICJ 933; cf Kai Ambos, 'Judicial Creativity at the Special Tribunal for Lebanon: Is there a Crime of Terrorism under International Law?' (2011) 24 LJIL 655.

51 Single Convention on Narcotic Drugs (adopted 30 March 1961, entered into force 13 December 1964) 520 UNTS 151; Convention on Psychotropic Substances (adopted 21 February 1971, entered into force 16 August 1976) 1019 UNTS 175; United Nations Convention against Illicit Traffic in Narcotic Drugs and Psychotropic Substances (adopted 20 December 1988, entered into force 11 November 1990) 1582 UNTS 95; 'Final Act of the United Nations Diplomatic Conference of Plenipotentiaries on the Establishment of an International Criminal Court' (17 July 1988) UN Doc A/CONF.183/10 Annex E.

52 On the African Criminal Court, see Rachovitsa, § 21.3, and Viswanath, § 22.2, in this textbook.

53 See Charles C Jalloh, 'A Classification of the Crimes in the Malabo Protocol' in Charles C Jalloh, Kamari M Clarke, and Vincent O Nmehielle (eds), *The African Court of Justice and Human and Peoples' Rights in Context* (CUP 2019) 225–256.

and either widespread or long-term damage to the environment being caused by those acts.[54]

D. CONCLUSION

The concept and extend of international crimes are still open to doctrinal scrutiny. There is little doubt that war crimes, genocide, crimes against humanity, and the crime of aggression, all prosecutable by the ICC, are international crimes. They differ from one another and from other international offences due to their particular contextual elements.

BOX 22.1.6 Further Readings and Further Resources

Further Readings

- MC Bassiouni, *International Criminal Law Conventions and their Penal Provisions* (Transnational 1997)

- A Cassese and others, *Cassese's International Criminal Law* (3rd edn, OUP 2013)

- T Fiskatoris, 'The Global South and the Drafting of the Subject-Matter Jurisdiction of the ICC' in F Jeßberger, L Steinl, and K Mehta (eds), *International Criminal Law: A Counter-Hegemonic Project?* (TMC Asser Press 2023)

- M Klamberg (ed), *Commentary on the Law of the International Criminal Court* (TOAEP 2017)

- C Stahn, *A Critical Introduction to International Criminal Law* (CUP 2018)

Further Resources

- M Gillett, 'A Tale of Two Definitions: Fortifying Four Key Elements of the Proposed Crime of Ecocide' (*Opinio Juris*) <https://opiniojuris. org/2023/06/20/a-tale-of-two-definitions-fortifying-four-key-elements- of-the-proposed-crime-of-ecocide-part-i/> and <https://opiniojuris. org/2023/06/20/a-tale-of-two-definitions-fortifying-four-key-elements-of-the- proposed-crime-of-ecocide-part-ii/> accessed 26 June 2023

- SLU LAW Summations Podcast, 'Episode 41: International Criminal Law and the War in Ukraine' <www.slu.edu/law/podcast/international-criminal-law- ukraine.php> accessed 26 June 2023

---

§ § §

---

54 Stop Ecocide International, 'Legal Definition of Ecocide Drafted by Independent Expert Panel' <www. stopecocide.earth/legal–definition> accessed 20 August 2023.

§ 22.2 INTERNATIONAL CRIMINAL COURTS AND TRIBUNALS

RAGHAVI VISWANATH

BOX 22.2.1 Required Knowledge and Learning Objectives

Required knowledge: Sources of International Law; Jurisdiction; Law of Armed Conflict; International Criminal Law; International Crimes; Interaction

Learning objectives: Understanding the various types of international criminal tribunals; the mandate and legacy of contemporary international criminal tribunals; how domestic courts apply international criminal law; and the application of universal jurisdiction in domestic law.

BOX 22.2.2 Interactive Exercises

Access *interactive exercises for this chapter*[55] by positioning your smartphone camera at the dot-filled box, also known as a QR code.

Figure 22.1 QR code referring to interactive exercises.

A. INTRODUCTION

This chapter introduces readers to a range of contemporary international criminal courts and tribunals, the political contexts in which they were set up, and the workings of such tribunals. It is in international criminal courts and tribunals that the substantive principles of international criminal law (ICL) are applied on a case-by-case basis. The International Criminal Court (ICC), a permanent and universal international criminal tribunal based in The Hague, is arguably the most prominent international tribunal for criminal responsibility. Additionally, so-called hybrid criminal tribunals and domestic courts apply international criminal law and interact with the ICC.

---

55 https://openrewi.org/en-projects-project-public-international-law-international-criminal-law/.

B. THE INTERNATIONAL CRIMINAL COURT

The ICC is distinct for being the first permanent tribunal that applies ICL with jurisdiction in over 123 States. The idea of a permanent international criminal tribunal was mooted much before even the Nuremberg Tribunal was set up. In 1872, Gustav Moynier from the International Committee of the Red Cross articulated the concern that national judges would find it difficult to be impartial when prosecuting humanitarian law violations orchestrated by their own State.[56] This apprehension developed into a request for a standing court. Following a study by the International Law Commission (ILC), the United Nations General Assembly prepared a draft code for such a court.[57] This effort lost steam during the negotiations of the Genocide Convention. The demand was later picked up in 1989. The Prime Minister of Trinidad and Tobago approached the ILC to set up a court that would be able to prosecute drug crimes. The ILC, paying heed to the request, drafted a statute by 1994 and a separate conference was eventually held in Rome to deliberate the draft.[58] The deliberations saw multiple States participating directly and contributions from non-governmental organisations. However, the jurisdiction of the Court (particularly for war crimes) generated great controversy. Yet, the Court received the approval of 120 out of the 148 participating States.[59] The Rome Statute of the International Criminal Court (Rome Statute) was adopted in 1998 and came into force on 1 July 2002.[60]

BOX 22.2.3 Advanced: The Seat of the ICC

The selection of The Hague as the seat of the ICC has faced great censure, given that it places significant distance between the Court and those it admittedly serves. Recently, the counsels for the defence in the Bangladesh/Myanmar situation requested the ICC to move its seat within reasonable proximity of the affected populations.[61] The Court rejected the request, citing reasons of prematurity and immobility during the pandemic.[62] In this context,

---

56 Christopher Keith Hall, 'The First Proposal for a Permanent International Criminal Court' (1998) 322 International Review of the Red Cross 57.

57 UNGA, 'Report of the Committee on International Criminal Jurisdiction', UNGAOR 9th session UN Doc. A/2645 (1953).

58 UNGA, 'Report of the International Law Commission on the Work of Its Forty-sixth Session', UNGAOR 49th session Suppl. No. 10, A/49/10 (1994).

59 Mark Klamberg, *Commentary on the Law of the International Criminal Court* (TOAEP 2016).

60 Rome Statute of the International Criminal Court (adopted 17 July 1998, entered into force 1 July 2002) 2187 UNTS 3.

61 *Situation in the People's Republic of Bangladesh/Republic of the Union of Myanmar* (Request), ICC-01/19–34 (4 August 2020).

62 *Situation in the People's Republic of Bangladesh/Republic of the Union of Myanmar* (Corrected version of 'Decision on Victims' joint request concerning hearings outside the host State'), ICC-01/19 (27 October 2020), para 26.

it is important to acknowledge that the Rome Statute – under article 3 – does allow for the seat to be moved wherever deemed necessary. The new design of the Court has also been called out by critical scholars as not being encouraging for victims with its opaque setting, monochromatic colour scheme, less visible witness boxes – all of which impede the interests of reflexivity.[63]

I. COMPOSITION AND ORGANISATION

The Court is composed of four organs – the Presidency, the Chambers, Office of the Prosecutor, and the Registry (under article 34 Rome Statute).

1. Presidency

The Presidency of the ICC oversees the constitution of the judicial chambers of the ICC. It is also the organ that liaises with States by concluding cooperation agreements and organising outreach activities.

2. Chambers

The three Chambers – Pre-Trial, Trial, and Appeals – are responsible for various stages of the proceedings. The Pre-Trial Chamber is tasked with determining whether the Prosecutor's request for the opening of an investigation under article 15 should be granted, and also for reviewing the Prosecutor's decision not to open an investigation.[64] The Pre-Trial Chamber is also in charge of confirming the charges pinned by the Prosecutor. The Trial Chamber's jurisdiction is triggered after this stage is crossed. The Trial Chamber conducts the trial and, where required, awards the sentence. Appeals against the decisions of both the Pre-Trial Chamber and the Trial Chamber are heard and decided by the Appeals Chamber.[65]

At any point of time, the Chambers are constituted by a total of 18 judges, who are elected for nine-year terms by signatories of the Rome Statute. Article 36(8) (a) calls for equitable geographical representation determined through regional groupings (being the African States, Asia-Pacific States, Eastern European States, Latin American and Caribbean States, and Western Europe and Others Group) with only one judge of the same nationality eligible to sit at one time. The Raising the Bar report identifies that minimum voting requirements in practice reflect 'an alarming concentration of the ICC's judiciary in only a small handful of states,

---

63 Stephanie Maupas, 'The New Clothes of the ICC' (*Justice info.net*, 19 December 2015) <https://theblacksea.eu/stories/secrets-of-the-international-criminal-court-jolie-clooney-and-the-world-fixer-psychosis/> accessed 20 March 2023.

64 Rome Statute of the International Criminal Court (adopted on 17 July 1998, entered into force on 1 July 2002) 2187 U.N.T.S. 90 (hereinafter 'Rome Statute').

65 Article 82 of the Rome Statute.

as well as a decline in the engagement of States Parties in the judicial selection process over time'.[66]

3. Office of the Prosecutor

The Office of the Prosecutor has been envisaged as an independent and impartial investigating authority, drawing on the Yugoslavia and Rwanda models.[67] Under article 15, the Prosecutor is empowered to initiate investigations in situations, based on information received from States, organs of the UN, intergovernmental and nongovernmental organisations, or other reliable sources. Before doing this, the Prosecutor must obtain approval from the Pre-Trial Chamber. Under article 15, when the Prosecutor decides not to open such an investigation, the Pre-Trial Chamber may order the Prosecutor to reconsider their decision.

4. Registry

The Registry helps the Court to conduct fair, impartial, and public trials. The core function of the Registry is to provide administrative and operational support to the Chambers and the Office of the Prosecutor.

II. APPLICABLE LAW

Article 21 Rome Statute prescribes the sources of law that the ICC can apply. Earlier tribunals predominantly relied on custom[68] and general principles[69] as gap filling tools.[70] This invited severe criticism about it impugning the principle of legality and vesting unreasonable law-making authority on the Court. The most important sources are the Statute, the Court's Rules of Procedure and Evidence, and the Elements of Crimes.[71] If this fails to yield an effective solution, then the Court may consult general principles of international law and failing that, rules derived from national legislations and human rights.[72] Article 21 was inserted with the motive of restricting the Court's discretion and ensuring that the principle of legality (*nullum crimen sine lege* [Latin: 'no crime without law']) is respected.[73] The construction of article 21 that the Statute finally retained does not create any room for oral sources, customs, or indigenous legal

---

66 Open Society Justice Initiative, 'Raising the Bar: Improving the Nomination and Election of Judges to the International Criminal Court' <www.justiceinitiative.org/publications/raising-the-bar-improving-the-nomination-and-election-of-judges-to-the-international-criminal-court> accessed 12 July 2023.

67 Article 42 of the Rome Statute and Rule 11 of the Rules of Procedure and Evidence.

68 On customary law, see Stoica, § 6.2, in this textbook.

69 On general principles, see Eggett, § 6.3, in this textbook.

70 Mia Swart, 'Judicial Lawmaking at the ad hoc Tribunals: The Creative Use of the Sources of International Law and "Adventurous Interpretation"' (2010) 70 Heidelberg Journal of International Law 459, 461–462.

71 ASP, 'Elements of Crimes' in ASP Official Records, First Session, New York, 3–10 September 2002' (2002) ICC-ASP/1/3.

72 On international human rights law, see Ciampi, § 21 (and the following sub-chapters) in this textbook.

73 Margaret M deGuzman, 'Article 21, Applicable Law' in Otto Triffterer and Kai Ambos (eds), *The Rome Statute of the International Criminal Court: A Commentary* (3rd edn, C.H. Beck 2016) 933.

orders.[74] It imposes Western epistemologies governing the formation of treaties[75] and 'international legal principles' on Global South peoples who forge relationships with the Court.[76] Substantively, article 21 – as the Court's own jurisprudence has demonstrated – has made it difficult for the Court to recognise the evolving nature of ICL and the victimhood triggered by crimes that the original Statute did not codify.[77]

III. JURISDICTION

There are four bases for the Court's jurisdiction: personal, territorial/nationality, subject matter, and temporal. In terms of *ratione materiae* (Latin: 'on the basis of the matter'), the Court is authorised to exercise jurisdiction over 'the most serious crimes of international concern': genocide, crimes against humanity, war crimes, and aggression (article 5(1)). On *ratione personae* (Latin: 'on the basis of the person') and *tertii* (Latin: 'on the basis of the place'), the first condition is one of age. The Court can only try natural persons above the age of 18.[78] The second is that of territoriality. Article 12 of the Rome Statute confers territorial jurisdiction on the Court in cases where the 'conduct in question' was committed on the territory of a State party to the Statute or by a national of a State party. The third condition, nationality, has not been defined in the Statute. The Court has implicitly imported the domestic understanding of nationality as the legal bond between the natural person and the sovereign State.[79] Importantly, the Court's jurisdiction cannot be activated through passive nationality (when only victims bear a nationality link to State parties). Nationality under article 12(2)(b) is limited to active nationality.[80] The temporal starting point of the Court's jurisdiction has been spelled out in article 11. The provision notes that the Court's jurisdiction is prospective and can be invoked only for crimes committed following the Statute's coming into force on 1 July 2002.

Exceptionally, article 12(3) allows non-State parties to file declarations accepting the Court's jurisdiction on an *ad hoc* (Latin: 'for this purpose') basis for crimes committed within their territories or by their nationals. This option, some argue, also offers the facility of circumventing the temporal limits of the Court's jurisdiction. Palestine, for instance, has lodged an article 12(3) declaration accepting the Court's jurisdiction over crimes committed against its nationals prior to Palestine's own accession of the Statute in 2015.[81]

---

74 On indigenous peoples, see Viswanath, § 7.2, in this textbook.

75 On treaties, see Fiskatoris and Svicevic, § 6.1, in this textbook.

76 Sujith Xavier, John Reynolds, and Asad Kyani, 'Foreword: Third World Approaches to International Criminal Law' (2016) 14(4) Journal of International Criminal Justice 915.

77 Alain Pellet, 'Revisiting the Sources of Applicable Law before the ICC' in Margaret deGuzman and Diane Marie Amann (eds), *Arcs of Global Justice: Essays in Honour of William A. Schabas* (OUP 2018).

78 Article 24 of the Rome Statute.

79 James Crawford, *Brownlie's Principles of Public International Law* (9th edn, CUP 2019) 443.

80 *Situation in the State of Palestine* (Prosecutor of the International Criminal Court, Fatou Bensouda, Re-opens the preliminary examination of the situation in Iraq), OTP Press Release (13 May 2014).

81 *Situation in the State of Palestine* (Palestine declares acceptance of ICC jurisdiction since 13 June 2014), ICC-CPI-20150105-PR1080 (5 January 2015).

IV. THE TRIGGERING MECHANISMS

The ICC can be accessed following a referral by a State party, a referral by the UN Security Council (UNSC) acting under Chapter VII of the UN Charter,[82] and the institution of an investigation by the Prosecutor acting on their own initiative (article 13). The first mode is a *proprio motu* (Latin: 'with his own motion') investigation by the Prosecution. To do this, the Prosecutor must obtain the approval of the Pre-Trial Chamber by showing how and why the selected situation meets the admissibility and jurisdiction requirements prescribed by the Statute. The Prosecutor must also obtain the consent of the States implicated. The second mode is self-referral. The bulk of the cases that the Court has heard have been self-referrals by the States in which the crimes were committed. A recurring concern with self-referrals has been that States have fashioned it into a tool to pursue retributive prosecutions of rebel non-State actors to bolster the 'legitimacy of its own military operations'.[83] Article 13(b) of the Statute allows the Court – a treaty-based creature modelled to exercise jurisdiction purely based on nationality and territoriality – to extend jurisdiction over crimes and accused persons even in non-State parties.

BOX 22.2.4 Advanced: Hegemonial Structure of the ICC

The UNSC referral route raises important questions about the legitimacy of the Court. The ICC originally postured itself as a mechanism to rectify the failures of past international criminal tribunals. The deliberations in Rome reveal that the drafters were clear about avoiding accusations of Eurocentric exercise of judicial discretion. However, the Security Council referral in the Statute suffers from the same vices. The Security Council referral departs from the nationality-based and territoriality-based jurisdictional framework that the ICC otherwise rests on. This route of referral has faced much censure, primarily on account of its vulnerability to political misuse. Scholars argue that it offers a free pass to the permanent members to exercise 'unilateral negative control' and exempt their own nationals from criminal responsibility for the same acts that they refer other individuals to the ICC for. The recent political clashes triggered by the Palestine and Afghanistan situations have shown that the Court still 'reifies White supremacy' and 'works to mask the core-periphery relations' that sustain economic and power inequalities.[84]

V. ADMISSIBILITY

According to article 17 Rome Statute, admissibility at the Court hinges on two aspects. The first is complementarity. Complementarity requires an assessment of whether the referring

---

82 Charter of the United Nations 1945, 1 UNTS XVI (1945).

83 Parvathi Menon, 'Self-Referring to the International Criminal Court: A Continuation of War by Other Means' (2015) 109 AJIL Unbound, 260–265.

84 Kamari Maxine Clarke, 'Affective Justice: The Racialized Imaginaries of International Justice' (2019) 42:2 Political and Legal Anthropology Review 244, at 247.

State/host State is unwilling or unable to prosecute the case. The defence – in order to challenge admissibility – must demonstrate that the national jurisdiction is investigating and taking genuine steps to interrogate witnesses, collecting evidence, and so forth.[85] The second part of the admissibility test relates to the analysis of the 'gravity threshold', in order to determine whether the case is of sufficient gravity to justify further action by the Court.

VI. ENFORCEMENT OF JUDGMENTS AND STATE COOPERATION WITH THE ICC

The primary challenge plaguing the ICC is its enforcement powers. Although decisions of the Court are binding on parties, the ICC does not possess its own enforcement infrastructures. Illustratively, the ICC does not have its own police that could accost those who are charged by the Court and bring them to the Court's premises in The Hague. The only recourse left for the Court is to rely on cooperation of the State parties to the Rome Statute. State parties to the Statute have an obligation to cooperate with the Court in all stages of the investigation and trial: from surrendering suspects/accused and seizing assets to detaining convicts.[86]

BOX 22.2.5 Advanced: Pushback Against the ICC

Of the 36 arrest warrants issued by the Court, only 20 have been enforced. The Court's warrants against Bosco Ntaganda, Simone Gbagbo, and Omar Al-Bashir were flouted for many months.[87] The Court's chiding of African States' failure in Bashir's case triggered a string of withdrawals (from Burundi, South Africa, and The Gambia). In all three cases, the withdrawals were intended to protect and immunise State officials, including sitting heads of State, from the ICC's reach.[88] The Philippines also notified the ICC of its withdrawal, pushing back on the Prosecutor's efforts to investigate the drug war and former President Duterte's complicity in its violence.[89] Withdrawals have becoming increasingly popular tools for States to express their discontent with the Court, and to curb the Court's prosecutorial reach. This pushback is seemingly quite alive to the Court's treaty-based character and the powers that such a design vests in treaty parties.

---

85 *Prosecutor v. Muthaura, Kenyatta and Ali* (Judgment on the appeal of the Republic of Kenya against the decision of Pre-Trial Chamber II of 30 May 2011 entitled 'Decision on the Application by the Government of Kenya Challenging the Admissibility of the Case Pursuant to Article 19(2)(b) of the Statute'), ICC-01/09–02/11–274 (30 August 2011), paras 1 and 40.

86 Articles 86 and 88 of the Rome Statute.

87 Saumya Uma, 'State Cooperation and the Challenge to International Criminal Justice' (*The Wire*, 31 January 2022) <https://thewire.in/law/state-cooperation-and-the-challenge-to-international-criminal-justice> accessed 16 July 2023.

88 Ssenyonjo, Manisuli, 'State Withdrawals from the Rome Statute of the International Criminal Court: South Africa, Burundi, and The Gambia' in Charles Chernor Jalloh and Ilias Bantekas (eds), *The International Criminal Court and Africa* (Online edn, Oxford Academic 2017).

89 ICC, 'Situation in the Republic of the Philippines' <www.icc-cpi.int/philippines> accessed 20 August 2023.

These challenges are compounded by the opposition to the ICC's jurisdiction by powerful States. To impede the Court's reach, the US Congress has passed the American Service-Members' Protection Act in 2002, empowering the government to stop financial aid to the ICC's State parties who surrender American nationals to the ICC.[90] When the Prosecutor expressed her desire to prosecute CIA officials in relation to the opening of an investigation in Afghanistan, the US government also went so far as to issue sanctions against ICC officials.[91] Similar non-cooperation quagmires have plagued the opening of investigations in Palestine against Israeli nationals[92] and in Iraq against British nationals.[93]

C. HYBRID (MIXED) TRIBUNALS

Hybrid tribunals are those tribunals that are governed by and have the authority to apply both international and domestic laws.

I. SPECIAL COURT OF SIERRA LEONE

The Special Court of Sierra Leone (SCSL) was established by treaty between Sierra Leone and the UN to prosecute crimes committed during the 1991 civil war between militia and the governments in Sierra Leone and Liberia.[94] The Court is independent of both the UN and the domestic legal system. The Court is composed of judges – the majority of whom are elected by the UN and the remaining by the government of Sierra Leone.[95] The jurisdiction of the Court is circumscribed to crimes against humanity and war crimes committed in non-international armed conflicts. Like the ICC, the Court's prosecutorial strategy is to prosecute those persons who are most responsible for serious violations of international humanitarian law and Sierra Leonese law.[96] The Court commenced its work in 2002 and wrapped up in 2013, entrusting its pending cases to the Residual Court for Sierra Leone.

---

90 Department of State of the Office of Electronic Information, Bureau of Public Affairs, 'American Service-Members' Protection Act' (July 2003) <https://2001-2009.state.gov/t/pm/rls/othr/misc/23425.htm> accessed 16 July 2023.

91 Federal Register, 'Blocking Property of Certain Persons Associated With the International Criminal Court' <www.federalregister.gov/documents/2020/06/15/2020-12953/blocking-property-of-certain-persons-associated-with-the-international-criminal-court> accessed 14 July 2023.

92 NBC News, 'Netanyahu Calls ICC Investigation "Undiluted Anti-Semitism"' <www.youtube.com/watch?v=fa8m2KkHJuw> accessed 14 July 2023.

93 Ronan Cormacain, 'Overseas Operations Bill: Getting Away When Powerful States Are Implicated (Particularly Those Who Are Members of the Council or Strong Allies of Council Members' (UK Human Rights Blog, 20 January 2021) <https://ukhumanrightsblog.com/2021/01/20/overseas-operations-bill-getting-away-with-murder-dr-ronan-cormacain/> accessed 16 July 2023.

94 UNSC Res 1315 (14 August 2000), UN Doc S/RES/1315.

95 Statute of the Special Court for Sierra Leone (16 January 2002), 2178 U.N.T.S. 145, article 14 ('SCSL Statute').

96 Article 1(1) of the SCSL Statute. The date relates to an earlier peace agreement between the Government of Sierra Leone and RUF, signed in Abidjan on 30 November 1996.

II. KOSOVO SPECIALIST CHAMBERS

The Kosovo Specialist Chambers – and the Specialist Prosecutor's Office – was established in 2011 following a report by the Parliamentary Assembly of the Council of Europe which shed light on the detention, torture, and enforced disappearances of Serbs and Kosovo Albanians during the 1999 conflict in Kosovo.[97] The Specialist Chambers comprises two organs, the Chambers and the Registry. The Specialist Chambers are staffed with international judges, prosecutors and officers and have a seat in The Hague.

III. EXTRAORDINARY CHAMBERS IN THE COURTS OF CAMBODIA

In 1997, the Cambodian government approached the UN to set up a tribunal to prosecute the crimes committed by the Khmer Rouge (English: 'Red Khmer') against political dissidents from 1975 to 1979. The Extraordinary Chambers in the Courts of Cambodia (ECCC) was established through a 2003 agreement between the UN and Cambodia. The ECCC has been absorbed into the Cambodian domestic legal system, albeit supported by the UN. The jurisdiction of the ECCC extends to genocide, crimes against humanity, and war crimes (solely in international armed conflicts). The Cambodian government insisted that the ECCC be predominantly staffed by local judges and prosecutors. This demand was honoured. Although the dominance of local staff has not inspired much confidence in the impartiality of the bench, all the judges and prosecutors are appointed by the Cambodian Supreme Council of Magistracy with the UN Secretary-General nominating international personnel.

D. REGIONAL AND DOMESTIC PROSECUTION OF INTERNATIONAL CRIMES

I. THE PROPOSED AFRICAN CRIMINAL COURT

Right from the mid-2000s when the ICC's docket was almost completely populated by cases seeking prosecution of African rebel groups or heads of State, the African Union has voiced its strong objection to being disproportionately targeted by the ICC. Fair to say that the ICC found it difficult to retain the trust of the 34 African States who signed onto its Statute, with States like Burundi choosing to exit the Statute altogether.[98]

The distrust in the ICC prompted the African Union to call for an African Criminal Court and dissuading African States from cooperating with the ICC. In 2014, the statute of this court – which came to be called the African Court of Justice and Human Rights –

---

97 Council of Europe Committee on Legal Affairs and Human Rights, 'Inhuman Treatment of People and Illicit Trafficking in Human Organs in Kosovo' (12 December 2010), AS/Jur (2010) 46.

98 'Burundi Is Officially Not a Member of the International Criminal Court (ICC)' (*Africanews*, 27 October 2017) <www.africanews.com/2017/10/27/burundi-is-officially-not-a-member-of-the-international-criminal-court-icc/> accessed 16 July 2023.

was passed.[99] The jurisdiction of the African court and the ICC greatly overlap. Article 46Ebis of the African Criminal Court's Statute is different only insofar as it allows the Court to exercise jurisdiction when the victim is a national of a State party or when a State party's vital interests have been threatened. The Court has jurisdiction over 14 unique offences, including the core crime but crimes outside the Rome Statute such as collective punishment.[100] However, the protocol of the Court is not yet in force and, consequently, the African Court of Justice and Human Rights is still to be established.[101]

II. DOMESTIC PROSECUTION OF INTERNATIONAL CRIMES

Domestic courts can exercise universal jurisdiction[102] over certain crimes. Universal jurisdiction allows the prosecution of certain crimes by any State, unconnected to the commission of the crime, the place it occurred, the accused or the victim because the conduct is of universal concern.[103] Universal jurisdiction does not replace domestic or international prosecutions. It elevates certain crimes because of their seriousness and ensures that impunity is eliminated for such crimes. It is also implicit in this rationale that powerful States actively shield their senior officials who commit core crimes; this would hold them back from prosecuting such actors.[104]

Universal jurisdiction was conceived as a way out of such conflicts of interest. Universal jurisdiction was first recognised for the crime of piracy. Ever since, a longer list of crimes can now trigger universal jurisdiction. The 1948 Genocide Convention,[105] for instance, enjoins all State parties to punish and prosecute perpetrators of genocide. The 1984 Convention against Torture[106] codifies universal jurisdiction for the crime of torture. Crimes against humanity,[107] apartheid,[108] and enforced disappearance[109] have also been added to this list.

---

99 Protocol on Amendments to the Protocol on the Statute of the African Court of Justice and Human Rights (Malabo Protocol) (adopted 27 June 2014, entered into force 2 April 2019).

100 Article 28D(b)(v), (xxviii), (xxix)–(xxxiii), and article 28D(e)(xvi)–(xxii), but also (g) of the Statute.

101 On the African Criminal Court, see Rachovitsa, § 21.3, in this textbook.

102 On jurisdiction, see González Hauck and Milas, § 8, in this textbook.

103 Kenneth C Randall, 'Universal Jurisdiction Under International Law' (1988) 66 Texas Law Review 785, 788 as cited in Steven W Becker, 'Universal Jurisdiction: How Universal Is It? A Study of Competing Theories' (2002–3) 12 Palestine Yearbook of International Law 49, 50; Roger O'Keefe, 'Universal Jurisdiction: Clarifying the Basic Concept' (2004) 2(3) Journal of International Criminal Justice 735.

104 Comments From Kenya, 'The Scope and Application of the Principle of Universal Jurisdiction: The Report of the Sixth Committee' A/64/452-Res64/117 (2018).

105 Convention on the Prevention and Punishment of the Crime of Genocide (adopted 9 December 1948, entered into force 12 January 1951) 78 UNTS 277.

106 Convention against Torture and Other Cruel, Inhuman or Degrading Treatment or Punishment (adopted 10 December 1984, entered into force 26 June 1987) 1465 UNTS 85.

107 Charles Jalloh, 'Universal Criminal Jurisdiction' in *Report of the International Law Commission on the Work of Its Seventieth Session* (ILC 2018), A/73/10 (2018).

108 International Convention on the Suppression and Punishment of the Crime against Apartheid (adopted 30 November 1973, entered into force 18 July 1976), 105 UNTS 243.

109 International Convention for the Protection of All Persons from Enforced Disappearance (adopted 20 December 2006, entered into force 23 December 2010), G.A. res. A/61/177 (2006), reprinted in (2007) 14 Int'l. Hum. Rts. Rep. 582.

Many scholars laud universal jurisdiction for creating a globalised jurisprudence, involving transnational networks.[110] This does not mean that universal jurisdiction is not political. This is evident in the statistics compiled by TRIAL International annually. Although universal jurisdiction has acquired much traction in terms of geographical reach (almost 92 States initiated universal jurisdiction cases in 2021–2022), these prosecutions are concentrated on crimes committed mostly in the Global South. The African Union has been vocal in its opposition to such exercise of jurisdiction. It has instead adopted a Model Law calling on African States to legislate on universal jurisdiction and prosecute 'international crimes, trafficking, and terrorism crimes'.[111] This addition of terrorism and trafficking departs from the internationally recognised list of crimes warranting universal jurisdiction.

When seen from a positivist[112] lens, the validity of exercises of universal jurisdiction rest majorly on the source which confers such jurisdiction. This is done by referring to either domestic laws,[113] international treaties,[114] or customary international law.[115]

E. CONCLUSION

This chapter homed in on the workings of contemporary international criminal tribunals, including the ICC. In so doing, the chapter not only looked at the legal framework supporting the mandate of such tribunals, but also the political hegemonies upon which these tribunals rest. In particular, the chapter discussed the political pushback experienced by the ICC. For instance, the control exercised by powerful Western States and the Security Council on the ICC's budget and case selection. The chapter also looked at the political contexts in which other hybrid tribunals are situated. The final parts of the chapter examined the sources of universal jurisdiction, common trends in the invocation of universal jurisdiction, and the transnational mobilisation universal jurisdiction cases entail.

---

110 Anne-Marie Slaughter, *A New World Order* (Princeton University Press 2004) 150.

111 African Union (Draft) Model National Law on Universal Jurisdiction over International Crimes, adopted at 21st Ordinary Session of the Executive Council Addis Ababa (9–13 July 2012).

112 On positivism, see Etkin and Green, § 3.1, in this textbook.

113 See *Federal Prosecutor's Office v. Anwar R* (Higher Regional Court, Koblenz 2022); *R v. Kumar Lama*, Case no. 2013/05698 (Central Criminal Court 2016).

114 See 'Universal Jurisdiction Annual Review 2022' (*TRIAL International*, March 2022) <https://trialinternational.org/wp-content/uploads/2022/03/TRIAL_International_UJAR-2022.pdf> accessed 16 July 2023; chapter 1, section 7 of the Criminal Code of Finland, 39/1889, amendments up to 766/2015 included, translation from Finnish by Ministry of Justice, Finland; Asetus rikoslain 1 luvun 7 §:n soveltamisesta (unofficial translation: Decree on the Application of Chapter 1, Section 7 of the Criminal Code), 16 August 1996/627, 1996; on international treaties, see Fiskatoris/Svicevic, § 6.1, in this textbook.

115 See *Attorney General v. Eichmann* (Supreme Court of Israel 336/31), 36 ILR 28; Arrest Warrant of 11 April 2000 (Democratic Republic of the Congo v. Belgium), Judgment, 14 February 2002, ICJ Reports (2002) 3, Joint Separate Opinion of Judges Higgins, Kooijmans and Buergenthal, at 63; on customary international law, see Stoica, § 6.2, in this textbook.

BOX 22.2.6 Further Readings and Further Resources

Further Readings

- R Cryer and others, *An Introduction to International Criminal Law and Procedure* (2nd edn, CUP 2010)

- C Schwöbel, *Critical Approaches to International Criminal Law: An Introduction* (Routledge 2014)

- G Werle, *Principles of International Criminal Law* (2nd edn, TMC Asser 2009)

Further Resources

- D Guilfoyle, Introduction to International Criminal Law, Introduction to International Criminal Law (*YouTube* 2011) <www.youtube.com/watch?v=BdX3n1dbla4> accessed 16 July 2023

§ § §

23

CHAPTER 23
INTERNATIONAL ECONOMIC LAW

ANNA HANKINGS-EVANS, SHUBHANGI AGARWALLA, AND KANAD BAGCHI

INTRODUCTION
ANNA HANKINGS-EVANS

BOX 23.1 Required Knowledge and Learning Objectives

Required knowledge: History of International Law; Sources of International Law; Subjects and Actors in International Law

Learning objectives: Understanding how the different fields of international economic law operate; and how trade, investment and monetary law interact.

BOX 23.2 Interactive Exercises

Access *interactive exercises for this chapter*[1] by positioning your smartphone camera at the dot-filled box, also known as a QR code.

Figure 23.1 QR code referring to interactive exercises.

A. INTRODUCTION

In October 2020, the World Trade Organization (WTO) in Geneva ruled that the European Union (EU) could impose punitive tariffs of EUR 3.4 billion on the

---

1 https://openrewi.org/en-projects-project-public-international-law-international-economic-law/.

DOI: 10.4324/9781003451327-26

US in a trade dispute over illegal State subsidies to aircraft manufacturer Boeing.[2] On 29 July 2022, WTO members were notified that South Africa had requested WTO dispute settlement consultations with the EU over certain measures imposed by the EU on imports of South African citrus fruit.[3] In 2007 South Africa faced an investment arbitration case[4] brought against its Black Economic Empowerment policies, intended to redress historical, social, and economic inequalities.[5] These examples, among many, illustrate the practical importance of international economic law (IEL) for the international movement of goods, services, and capital, as well as for national policy objectives. IEL can be broadly described as the regulation governing economic globalisation, that is economic affairs between two or more States. At the same time, IEL is seemingly undergoing a legitimacy crisis, not least driven by the increasing State protectionism since the global COVID-19 pandemic.[6] Reasons may be the rise of powerful private actors, which has led IEL to increasingly address relationships between private entities,[7] or growing inequality exacerbated by international economic regulation.[8]

IEL covers a very broad range of topics and,[9] in its modern manifestation, has developed into a distinct and clearly definable area of law. In 1944, the Bretton Woods institutions were established, including the International Bank for Reconstruction and Development (World Bank) and the International Monetary Fund (IMF).[10] The goal of establishing an International Trade Organization as the third Bretton Woods institution, however, failed due to US opposition in ratifying the Havana Charter. It took until 15 April 1994 for the Marrakesh Agreement to be signed, which entered into force on 1 January 1995, establishing the WTO, an organisation whose dispute settlement system now finds itself in crisis 28 years after its inception.[11] The following section will provide an introduction into concepts, developments, and significance of international economic law.

---

2 Boeing Subsidy Case: World Trade Organization Confirms EU Right to Retaliate Against $4 Billion of U.S. Imports, EU Commission (13 October 2020) <https://ec.europa.eu/commission/presscorner/detail/en/ip_20_1895> accessed 23 August 2023.

3 South Africa Initiates WTO Dispute Complaint Challenging EU Citrus Fruit Measures, WTO, (29 July 2022) <www.wto.org/english/news_e/news22_e/ds613rfc_29jul22_e.htm> accessed 23 August 2023.

4 *Piero Foresti, Laura de Carli and others v Republic of South Africa*, ICSID Case No ARB(AF)/07/1.

5 'ICSID Arbitration Filed Over South Africa's Black Empowerment Program' (*Opinio Juris*, 20 February 2007) < https://opiniojuris.org/2007/02/20/icsid-arbitration-filed-over-south-africas-black-empowerment-program/> accessed 23 August 2023.

6 UNCTAD, *World Investment Report* (United Nations Publications 2020) 127.

7 Steve Charnovitz, 'What Is International Economic Law?' (2011) 14(1) Journal of International Economic Law 5.

8 Frank J Garcia, 'Globalization, Inequality & International Economic Law' (2017) 8(5) Religions 78.

9 Surya P Subedi, *International Economic Law, Section A: Evolution and principles of international economic law* (University of London 2006) 21.

10 Kelvin Mbithi, 'Supervising Sovereign Debt Restructuring Through the United Nations' in James Thuo Gathii (ed), *How to Reform the Global and Financial Architecture* (Sheria Publishing House 2023) 197, 198.

11 Simon Lester, *Ending the WTO Dispute Settlement Crisis: Where to from Here?* (IISD 2022).

B. SUBJECTS

International economic relations encompass a wide range of activities, subjects,[12] and disciplines. For example, it may encompass the cross-border exchange of goods and services, the cross-border transfer of capital and means of payment, but also the cross-border movement of people (companies and individuals).[13] While IEL may be described in various ways, no clear definition has been acknowledged in practice or in theory.[14] In its broadest sense, IEL could be said to encompass all areas of law that have both an international and an economic component. However, the core of IEL includes primarily the law of international trade,[15] the law of foreign investment,[16] and the law of international monetary and financial transactions.[17]

C. HISTORY

The topic of IEL has gained scholarly attention in recent years due to a perceived loss in legitimacy.[18] Economic activities (particularly cross-border trade), however, date back to ancient times and were conducted mostly on a reciprocal basis.[19] It was in fact the Industrial Revolution under the pretext of a 'civilising mission' that drove the need expansion of colonial spheres of influence and led to the political subjugation of (resource-rich) colonies and the systematic exploitation of raw materials.[20] The conclusion of international treaties to further the expansion and maintenance of economic power was another significant factor of imperialism from the 15th century onward.[21]

In July 1944, the UN Monetary and Financial Conference, also known as the Bretton Woods Conference, was held in the US in Bretton Woods, New Hampshire. The purpose of this meeting was to restructure the international monetary order and to create an international mechanism for emergency aid and the opening of markets. Following the establishment of the Bretton Woods Institutions, the General Agreement on Tariffs and Trade (GATT) was established in 1947 with the goal of eliminating trade protectionism, abolishing tariffs, promoting international trade, and rebuilding

---

12 On subjects of international law, see Engström, § 7 (and the following sub-chapters), in this textbook.

13 Markus Krajewski, *Wirtschaftsvölkerrecht* (5th edn, CF Müller 2021) 2.

14 Steve Charnovitz, 'What Is International Economic Law?' (2011) 14(1) Journal of International Economic Law 3, 4.

15 On international trade law, see Agarwalla, § 23.2, in this textbook.

16 On international investment law, see Hankings-Evans, § 23.1, in this textbook.

17 Charnovitz (n 7) 3. On international monetary law, see Bagchi, § 23.3, in this textbook.

18 Chris Brummer, *Soft Law and the Global Financial System: Rule Making in the 21st Century* (2nd edn, CUP 2015) 183.

19 Jinyuan Gao, 'China and Africa: The Development of Relations Over Many Centuries' (1984) 83(331) African Affairs 241, 242; David H Shinn and Joshua Eisenman, *China and Africa: A Century of Engagement* (University of Pennsylvania Press 2012) 17.

20 Bharath Gururagavendran, 'The Coloniality of Sovereign Debt in the Global South' in James Thuo Gathii (ed), *How to Reform the Global and Financial Architecture* (Sheria Publishing House 2023) 312.

21 Charnovitz (n 7) 7.

the world economy after the devastation of World War II. The International Centre for Settlement of Investment Disputes (ICSID Centre) was added in 1966 as an independent institution within the World Bank Group.[22]

D. SOURCES

The recognised sources of IEL are those generally found in article 38 of the Statute of the International Court of Justice (ICJ Statute).[23] Nowadays, international agreements can be considered the main source of law in IEL.[24] International economic treaty practice has thereby often evolved from bilateral to multilateral agreements, especially in international trade law, which has created cross-border markets through its free trade agreements and customs unions. Conversely, the prevalence of a network of predominantly bilateral treaties, as seen in international investment law, can hinder a more equitable multilateral solution, as it fragments the bargaining power of developing countries, and makes the system more vulnerable to the replication of (post-colonial) power dynamics.[25]

E. CONCLUSION

The legitimacy and accountability of the global economic system has been the focus of heated debates in IEL.[26] Similar to debates in international investment law,[27] the global debt and financial architecture has been accused of forming part of the colonial legacy.[28] Both regimes are said to have evolved without the participation of the majority of developing countries, enabling post-colonial economic dependencies of less powerful States.[29] This led to a coalition of newly independent States of the Global South challenging existing rules and calling for the establishing a New International Economic Order[30] in the 1970s.[31]

---

22 Meg Kinnear, 'The Role of ICSID in International Economic Law' (2023) 26(1) Journal of International Economic Law 35.

23 On sources of international law, see Eggett, § 6 (and the following sub-chapters), in this textbook.

24 Ohio Omiunu and Titilayo Adebola, 'Sovereign Debt as Investments: Dispute Resolution and Restructuring in Times of Crises' in James Thuo Gathii (ed), *How to Reform the Global and Financial Architecture* (Sheria Publishing House 2023) 131.

25 See Antony Anghie, 'The Evolution of International Law: Colonial and Postcolonial Realities' (2006) 27(5) Third World Quarterly 739, 749.

26 E.g. Hector R Torres, 'Reforming the International Monetary Fund – Why Its Legitimacy Is at Stake' (2007) 10(3) Journal of International Economic Law 443.

27 Asha Kaushal, 'Revisiting History: How the Past Matters for the Present Backlash Against the Foreign Investment Regime' (2009) 50(2) Harvard International Law Journal 491.

28 Gururagavendran (n 20) 311 et seq.

29 Anghie (n 25) 749; Mbithi (n 10) 197; Kate Miles, 'International Investment Law and Universality: Histories of Shape-Shifting' (2014) 3(4) Cambridge Journal of International and Comparative Law 986.

30 Declaration on the Establishment of a New International Economic Order (1 May 1974) UN Doc. A/RES/S-6/3201; Bhupinder S Chimni, 'A Just World Under Law: A View from the South' (2007) 22(2) American University International Law Review 199, 219; Mohammed Bedjaoui, *Towards a New International Economic Order* (UNESCO 1979).

31 Gururagavendran (n 20) 314.

States of the Global South are once again increasingly seeking to redress historical injustice by, for instance, recalibrating existing international investment agreements[32] and articulating demands for inclusion in international agenda and standard-setting organisations such as the G-20.[33] For instance, Africa's 55 States remain underrepresented in the governance structures of the IMF,[34] where they have merely 6.01% in voting rights.[35] Another critical issue highlighted particularly in light of the COVID-19 pandemic was the undersupply of COVID-19 vaccine to developing countries.[36] Finally, a lack of corporate responsibility in cross-border economic activities contributed to impunity for human rights violations in extraterritorial settings.[37] Increasingly, however, international standards for corporate social responsibility are developing.[38] It remains to be seen whether these challenges can be overcome in the coming years. The following s will provide both overview and insight into the specific features and shortcomings of different regimes collectively referred to as IEL, namely the law of international trade, investment, and finance.

BOX 23.3 Further Readings

Further Readings

- A Anghie, 'The Evolution of International Law: Colonial and Postcolonial Realities' (2006) 27(5) Third World Quarterly 739

- S Charnovitz, 'What Is International Economic Law?' (2011) 14(1) Journal of International Economic Law 5

- B Gururagavendran, 'The Coloniality of Sovereign Debt in the Global South' in James Thuo Gathii (ed), *How to Reform the Global and Financial Architecture* (Sheria Publishing House 2023)

---

§ § §

---

32 Uche Ewelukwa Ofodile, 'Africa-China Bilateral Investment Treaties: A Critique' (2013) 35(1) Michigan Journal of International Law 131, 143 et seq.

33 Ovigwe Eguegu, 'Why the G20 Needs African Union as a Member', The Africa Report (29 July 2022) <www.theafricareport.com/226417/why-the-g20-needs-african-union-as-a-member/>.

34 Hector R Torres, 'Reforming the International Monetary Fund – Why Its Legitimacy Is at Stake' (2007) 10(3) Journal of International Economic Law 443.

35 James Thuo Gathii, 'Introduction' in James Thuo Gathii (ed), *How to Reform the Global and Financial Architecture* (Sheria Publishing House 2023) xi; see also Chris Brummer, *Soft Law and the Global Financial System: Rule Making in the 21st Century* (2nd edn, CUP 2015) 201.

36 Vaccine inequity undermining global economic recovery, WHO (22 July 2021) <www.who.int/news/item/22-07-2021-vaccine-inequity-undermining-global-economic-recovery> accessed 23 August 2023.

37 Steven R Ratner, 'Fair and Equitable Treatment and Human Rights: A Moral and Legal Reconciliation' (2022) 25(4) Journal of International Economic Law 568.

38 Lucinda A Low, 'Corporate Power and Accountability in International Economic Law' (2023) 26(1) Journal of International Economic Law 66, 67, 72 et seq.

§ 23.1 INTERNATIONAL INVESTMENT LAW

ANNA HANKINGS-EVANS

BOX 23.1.1 Required Knowledge and Learning Objectives

Required knowledge: History of International Law; Methodology; Interaction; Sources of International Law; Subjects and Actors in International Law; State Responsibility

Learning objectives: Understanding the objective and purpose of international investment law; the power implications in the regime's emergence; the substantive and procedural guarantees provided to foreign investors; the policy issues around balancing foreign investment protection with public interests.

BOX 23.1.2 Interactive Exercises

Access *interactive exercises for this chapter*[39] by positioning your smartphone camera at the dot-filled box, also known as a QR code.

Figure 23.1 QR code referring to interactive exercises.

A. INTRODUCTION

Authors have described international investment law (IIL) as a field subject to controversy and contestation.[40] This is not least because international economic laws and policies have essentially played – and continue to play – a prominent role in the establishment and maintenance of (post-)colonial power structures and the accumulation of wealth in the Global North.[41] This controversy manifests itself in

---

39 https://openrewi.org/en-projects-project-public-international-law-international-economic-law/.

40 Muthucumaraswamy Sornarajah, *The International Law on Foreign Investment* (5th edn, OUP 2021) 46.

41 Antony Anghie, 'The Evolution of International Law: Colonial and Postcolonial Realities' (2006) 27(5) Third World Quarterly 739.

contemporary scrutiny of a system that is believed to lack balance and legitimacy, and which has increasingly drawn criticism and calls for reform in recent years.[42] A primary concern is that IIL grants significant privileges and protections to foreign investors, thereby appearing as an imbalanced regime, favouring corporate interests over the rights of States and their citizens. The Global South and scholarly proponents of Third World Approaches to International Law (TWAIL)[43] attribute international investment law's power imbalances and deficiencies to its colonial origin.[44] This chapter first provides an introduction to the actors and sources of international investment law. It then examines the historical legacy of the regime and the continuity of power structures. What were the shaping factors in its emergence, and to what extent does it affect the reception of legitimacy among States today? The chapter then outlines the substantive and procedural safeguards benefitting foreign investors, and finally addresses current policy issues in the quest for a more balanced regime.

B. STRUCTURE OF INTERNATIONAL INVESTMENT LAW

IIL mainly governs foreign direct investment (FDI) and the resolution of disputes between foreign investors and sovereign host States, meaning the State in which the investment was made. FDI is governed and protected predominantly by international investment agreements (IIAs) entered into between sovereign States, regularly on a bilateral level in the form of bilateral investment treaties (BITs), for the reciprocal benefit of foreign investors and which are therefore amenable to the general rules of interpretation under international law. Other sources of law include double taxation treaties (DTTs) that are also considered IIAs;[45] investment dispute settlement conventions such as the 1965 Convention on the Settlement of Investment Disputes between States and Nationals of Other States (ICSID Convention),[46] which entered into force on 14 October 1966; customary international law; and, secondarily, the decisions of various arbitration tribunals. The creation of the International Centre for Settlement of Investment Disputes (ICSID) further solidified the development of international investment law.[47]

---

42 Kavaljit Singh and Burghard Ilge, 'Introduction' in Kavaljit Singh and Burghard Ilge (eds), *Rethinking International Investment Treaties: Critical Issues and Policy Choices* (Both Ends 2016) 1 et seq.

43 On TWAIL, see González Hauck, § 3.2, in this textbook.

44 Muthucumaraswamy Sornarajah, 'Mutations of Neo-Liberalism in International Investment Law' (2011) 3(1) Trade, Law and Development 203, 205 et seq.

45 Kavaljit Singh and Burghard Ilge, 'Introduction' in Kavaljit Singh and Burghard Ilge (eds), *Rethinking International Investment Treaties: Critical Issues and Policy Choices* (Both Ends 2016) 1.

46 'Convention on the Settlement of Investment Disputes between States and Nationals of Other States' (14 October 1965) <https://icsid.worldbank.org/sites/default/files/ICSID%20Convention%20English.pdf>.

47 Anna Hankings-Evans, 'The Africanization of International Investment Disputes – From Past to Present' (*Verfassungs Blog*, 2020) <https://verfassungsblog.de/the-africanization-of-international-investment-disputes-from-past-to-present/>; Antonio R Parra, *The History of ICSID* (OUP 2012).

I. THE DEFINITION OF 'FOREIGN INVESTMENT'

While IIAs generally aim at promoting and protecting FDI, a natural or legal person can only claim protection under the respective IIA in cases where the person also falls under the treaty's scope of application. Each IIA therefore offers a definition of what constitutes 'foreign investment' under the IIA and who benefits from its protection, meaning who is to be considered a 'foreign investor'. In negotiating IIAs, States usually aim at allocating the maximum possible protection to their own citizens, companies, and corporations,[48] depending on whether they are likely to find themselves as a capital exporter or importer in the specific legal relationship, while making sure that nationals from third States are excluded from benefitting from the IIAs' material guarantees.

Foreign investments can be broadly defined as the transfer, acquisition, establishment, or expansion of business operations by individuals, companies, or governments from one country (the home State) in another country (the host State). These investments may involve various types of assets, including financial resources, technology, expertise, and physical infrastructure. Although many investment agreements have the tendency to include a broad definition of FDI, thereby widening the scope of application of the respective IIA, it is generally agreed that IIL excludes so-called portfolio investments from its subject matter.[49]

The 'Salini test' is a set of factors derived from the *Salini Costruttori S.p.A. v Kingdom of Morocco*[50] proceedings, a dispute concerning the tender for and contractual commitment to the construction of a highway.[51] It provides guidance on determining the existence of an 'investment' under IIL by utilising a so-called triple identity test.[52] The tribunal established that an 'investment' required (1) a contribution of money, assets, or services by the investor, (2) a certain duration, and (3) a participation in the risks of the transaction.[53]

II. PRINCIPAL ACTORS

Traditionally, only States were considered subjects of international law.[54] This led to the customary law doctrine of diplomatic protection being the only remedy available to the foreign investor that wished to challenge host State measures affecting their property rights abroad.[55] Diplomatic protection, however, represents a distinct right of the home State, not the foreign investor, and accordingly depends on the political willingness of the home State to challenge the host State's action against its national by bringing an

---

48 On corporations, see González Hauck, § 7.7, in this textbook.

49 Sornarajah (n 40) 15, 16.

50 *Salini Costruttori S.p.A. and Italstrade S.p.A. v. Kingdom of Morocco [I]*, ICSID Case No. ARB/00/4.

51 Ibid Decision on Jurisdiction.

52 Ibid para 43–58.

53 Ibid para 52.

54 On subjects and actors in international law, see Engström, § 7, in this textbook.

55 Frank J Garcia, Lindita Ciko, Apurv Gaurav and Kirrin Hough, 'Reforming the International Investment Regime: Lessons from International Trade Law' (2015) 18(4) Journal of International Economic Law 861, 865.

international action for compensation.[56] The development of substantive and procedural IIL thus also served to depoliticise investment relations.[57]

IIL typically involves three actors, namely:

1. The capital-exporting home State
2. The capital-importing host State
3. The foreign investor.

In this context, the foreign investor, in particular, can take different forms. Whereas in the past it was a businessperson operating abroad for a limited time, foreign investors today are predominantly multinational enterprises (MNEs).[58]

III. INTERNATIONAL INVESTMENT AGREEMENTS

International agreements are the foundation of foreign investment protection today.[59] In addition to BITs, which are the most common manifestation type of IIAs, there are investment chapters in free trade agreements (FTAs) and regional treaties that contain investment chapters. International agreements, including IIAs, are generally interpreted in accordance with article 31 et seq. of the Vienna Convention on the Law of Treaties (VCLT).[60] Despite the VCLT only entering into force on 27 February 1980, its provisions have been considered customary international law by tribunals in investment disputes and are thus applied in accordance with their customary law content to IIAs that were concluded prior to 1980.[61]

IV. BILATERAL INVESTMENT TREATIES

BITs are considered the primary source of IIL today.[62] Germany became a pioneer in the legalisation process in 1959, following its defeat in World War II, by seeking ways to legally protect its capital exports.[63] Eventually other European countries joined in launching their respective BIT programs. Western States – such as France in 1960 with

---

56 Peter Muchlinski, 'Policy Issues' in Peter Muchlinski, Frederico Ortino, and Christoph Schreuer (eds), *The Oxford Handbook of International Investment Law* (OUP 2008) 6.

57 Ibrahim FI Shihata, 'Towards a Greater Depoliticization of Investment Disputes: The Roles of ICSID and MIGA' (1986) 1(1) ICSID Review 1, 5; Kenneth J Vandevelde, 'A Brief History of International Investment Agreements' (2005) 12 Davis Journal of International Law & Policy 157, 175.

58 Sornarajah (n 40) 79, 80.

59 Rudolf Dolzer, Ursula Kriebaum, and Christoph Schreuer, *Principles of International Law* (3rd edn, OUP 2022) 35 et seq.

60 *Siemens v. Argentina*, Decision on Jurisdiction, 3rd August 2004, ICSID Case No. ARB/02/8, para 80. On the VCLT, see Fiskatoris and Svicevic, § 6.1, in this textbook.

61 Dolzer and others (n 59) 36.

62 Ibid 16.

63 Ingo Venzke and Philipp Günther, 'International Investment Protection Made in Germany? On the Domestic and Foreign Policy Dynamics behind the First BITs' (2022) 33(4) European Journal of International Law 1183.

Chad,[64] Italy in 1964 with Guinea,[65] Great Britain in 1975 with Egypt,[66] and the US in 1977 with Panama[67] – all concluded their first BITs with States of the Global South.[68] Numerous African States supported a liberal approach to their foreign economic policy, which led to the majority of BITs being concluded between European and African States in the early years. In the 1960s, African States were more involved in concluding BITs than any other region in the world.[69]

V. CUSTOMARY INTERNATIONAL LAW

Besides IIAs, customary international law[70] plays a significant role in international investment law. Long before efforts to create bilateral treaty obligations, customary international law existed with respect to aliens and their foreign property,[71] although the precise content of the scope of protection under customary law initially remained controversial.[72] A foreign national who saw their investment threatened by the actions of a host State could only assert their claims through so-called diplomatic protection by their home State, which was regularly associated with risks and major consequences.[73] Under the doctrine of diplomatic protection, an injury to the foreign investor was assumed an injury of their State, the violation of which could even trigger a right to intervene.[74] Diplomatic protection was thereby the only remedy available, since 'foreign nationals' as natural or legal persons had no legal personality under international law and could assert claims only as claims of the home State.[75]

VI. FOREIGN (PRIVATE) INVESTMENT CONTRACTS

Foreign (private) investment contracts are the basis of many large-scale investment projects.[76] They are contractual agreements between a foreign investor (or a local affiliate of a foreign

---

64 UNCTAD, Bilateral Investment Treaties 1959–1999 (2000), UN Doc. UNCTAD/ITE/IIA/2 <https://unctad. org/system/files/official-document/poiteiiad2.en.pdf>.

65 Guinea-Italy BIT (1964), UNCTAD, IIA Navigator <https://investmentpolicy.unctad.org/international-investment-agreements/treaty-files/1497/download>.

66 Egypt-UK BIT (1975), UNCTAD, IIA Navigator <https://investmentpolicy.unctad.org/international-investment-agreements/treaty-files/1122/download>.

67 Panama-USA BIT (1982), UNCTAD, IIA Navigator <https://investmentpolicy.unctad.org/international-investment-agreements/treaty-files/3353/download>.

68 UNCTAD (n 64); Chester Brown, 'The Development by States of Model Bilateral Investment Treaties' in Wenhua Shan and Jinyuan Su (eds), *China and International Investment Law: Twenty Years of ICSID Membership* (Brill Nijhoff 2015) 119.

69 UNECA, Investment agreements landscape in Africa, 2015, UN Doc. E/ECA/CRCI/9/5; Zachary Elkins, Andrew T Guzman, and Beth A Simmons, 'Competing for Capital: The Diffusion of Bilateral Investment Treaties, 1960–2000' (2006) 60(4) International Organization 811, 814–816.

70 On customary law, see Stoica, § 6.2, in this textbook.

71 Dolzer and others (n 59) 22.

72 Sornarajah (n 40) 154.

73 Miles (n 29) 14, 15.

74 Ibid; Sornarajah (n 40) 155.

75 Sornarajah (n 40) 155.

76 Lorenzo Cotula, 'Foreign Investment Contracts' (International Institute for Environment and Development, Briefing 4, 2008) <www.iied.org/sites/default/files/pdfs/migrate/17015IIED.pdf>.

investor) and a government (or a government-owned entity). They do not constitute agreements codifying international obligations within the meaning of article 38(1) lit. a of the ICJ Statute but set out the terms and conditions for a specific investment project in the territory of the relevant host State. Investment contracts are thereby oftentimes drafted as mixed contracts under private and public law. The nature and content of investment contracts may vary, depending on sector, host State, and investment type.[77]

C. THE EVOLUTION OF INTERNATIONAL INVESTMENT LAW

The evolution of the international law relating to foreign investment was accompanied by a long history of dispute over applicable rules and standards.[78] The minimum standard of treatment can be traced as far as to the first half of the 20th century. These developments were thereby largely shaped by major powers and the protection of their nationals' assets in Latin American States.[79] As for the rest of the colonised world, no participation in the law-making was possible and, from a European perspective, hardly needed. Protection was rather achieved through occupation and the subsequent imposition of colonial administrative systems.[80] It was not until the period of decolonisation,[81] particularly of Africa and Asia after World War II, that formerly colonised States were able to contribute to the development of today's IIL regime.

I. UNEQUAL TREATIES

The forerunner of the modern BITs were bilateral so-called Treaties of Friendship, Commerce and Navigation (FCN), of which the Treaty of Amity and Commerce between the United States and France of 1778 or the Treaty of Amity, Commerce and Navigation between United States and Great Britain of 1794 are often cited as the first of its kind.[82] FCN treaties contained far-reaching procedural rights and codified the principle of 'national treatment' and the principle of 'most-favoured-nation treatment'.[83] Conversely, in non-European yet uncolonised countries, trade and investment protection was often safeguarded on the basis of contractually agreed non-reciprocal principles of extraterritoriality that favoured European and American States.[84] Due to the one-sidedness of privileges accorded by these FNC Treaties with non-European entities, they were later referred to as 'unequal'.[85]

---

77 Dolzer and others (n 59) 122 et seq.
78 Sornarajah (n 40) 155 et seq.; Kenneth J Vandevelde, 'A Brief History of International Investment Agreements' (2005) 12 Davis Journal of International Law & Policy 157.
79 Miles (n 29), 17 et seq.
80 Muthucumaraswamy Sornarajah, 'Power and Justice in Foreign Investment Arbitration' (1997) 14 Journal of International Arbitration 103.
81 On decolonisation, see González Hauck, § 1, in this textbook.
82 Dolzer and others (n 59) 8; Miles (n 29) 5, 6.
83 Miles (n 29) 5.
84 Sornarajah (n 40) 28.
85 Miles (n 29) 6, 7.

II. THE STATUS OF FOREIGNERS, DIPLOMATIC PROTECTION, AND THE QUEST FOR A (CUSTOMARY) INTERNATIONAL MINIMUM STANDARD

Latin American States resisted the assertion of a customary 'international minimum standard'. Instead, they argued for 'national treatment' of foreign investors, according to which they should not be treated more favourable than local investors, but should be granted foreign investment protection to the standard accorded by domestic law. The risk of foreign investment protection was thereby shifted to the private investor, who, the argument goes, voluntarily submitted to the national legal system of the host State. The conception became known as the so-called Calvo Doctrine, developed by the Argentinian diplomat and legal scholar Carlos Calvo (1822–1906).[86]

Conversely, capital-exporting States such as the United States maintained the existence of an international (minimum) standard of treatment that, according to them, exists independently of local laws. The 'Hull Formula' was coined in 1938 by former US Secretary of State, Cordell Hull (1871–1955), who argued for 'prompt, adequate and effective' as alleged minimum standard under international law.[87] The Hull formula corresponded with the predominant practice of Western States.[88]

Today, IIAs regularly codify the approach of the United States.[89] The widespread adoption of the Hull formula has been regularly achieved by capital-exporting States of the Global North, but also by reform requirements imposed by institutions such as the World Bank or the International Monetary Fund.[90]

III. THE ERA OF DECOLONISATION AND THE SECOND WAVE OF EXPROPRIATION

The gradual decolonisation of the Global South marks the beginning of the modern history of the development of IIL and arbitration, curbed by a major wave of expropriations[91] and the Western need to protects assets in formerly colonised States.[92] With

---

86 Muthucumaraswamy Sornarajah, 'The Past, Present and Future of the International Law on Foreign Investment' in Wenhua Shan and Jinyuan Su (eds), *China and International Investment Law: Twenty Years of ICSID Membership* (Brill Nijhoff 2015) 26.

87 Sornarajah (n 40) 51.

88 Andreas F Lowenfeld, *International Economic Law* (2nd edn, OUP 2008) 473 et seq.

89 Asha Kaushal, 'Revisiting History: How the Past Matters for the Present Backlash Against the Foreign Investment Regime' (2009) 50(2) Harvard International Law Journal 491, 500.

90 Kaushal (n 27) 505 et. seq. On international monetary law, see Bagchi, § 23.3, in this textbook.

91 Chester Brown, 'The Development by States of Model Bilateral Investment Treaties' in Wenhua Shan and Jinyuan Su (eds), *China and International Investment Law: Twenty Years of ICSID Membership* (Brill Nijhoff 2015) 138.

92 Antony Anghie, *Imperialism, Sovereignty and the Making of International Law* (CUP 2005) 214 et seq.; Jeswald W Salacuse, 'The Emerging Regime for Investment' (2010) 15(2) Harvard International Law Journal 427.

decolonisation of the Global South, newly independent States had increasingly challenged
the customary rules on foreign investments.[93]

BOX 23.1.3 Examples: Expropriation

Among the best-known cases of expropriation are the expropriation of Anglo-
Iranian oil companies in Iran in 1951 or the expropriation of the French Suez
Canal Company in Egypt in 1956.[94]

These expropriations involved compensation payments, which regularly did not
correspond to the amount demanded in terms of a minimum standard under
international law advocated by Western States.[95] Developing States often cited their level
of development and the economic impossibility of paying compensation, especially when
the expropriations occurred as part of an economic reform program. Today, virtually all
BITs entail a substantive provision protecting foreign property against expropriation.

IV. INTERNATIONAL INVESTMENT LAW'S LEGITIMACY CRISIS

Beginning with the Argentine financial crisis in 2001 and due to the many lawsuits
filed by foreign investors against developing countries, individual States in the Global
South have increasingly limited the jurisdiction of investor–State dispute settlement
(ISDS) arbitration tribunals. In the literature, this has been referred to as a 'legitimacy
crisis' of or 'backlash' against IIL in general and ISDS specifically.[96] Some authors have
accordingly attributed the resistance of these States to the regime's colonial legacy and
the resulting asymmetrical contractual relations between the South and the North, that
subordinates public interests such as human rights or environmental concerns, through
the broad and incongruent interpretation of ambiguous investment protection clauses
by ISDS arbitral tribunals, which is seen as another trigger for the perceived loss of
legitimacy.[97] Conversely, the resistance generally referred to as 'of the Global South' is in
reality not limited to States of the Global South, but must be understood, at least today,
as a reaction to systemic challenges of a rather unbalanced system.[98]

---

93 Frank J Garcia and Lindita V Ciko, 'Theories of Justice and International Economic Law' in John Linarelli (ed),
   Research Handbook on Global Justice and International Economic Law (Edward Elgar 2013) 55.

94 Lowenfeld (n 90) 483 et seq.

95 UNCTAD, *Taking of Property. Series on Issues on International Investment Agreements* (United Nations Publication
   2000) 5.

96 UNCTAD, Denunciation of the ICSID Convention and BITs: Impact on Investor–State Claims, IIA Issue
   Note No. 2 (2010); José E Alvarez, 'Contemporary International Law: An 'Empire of Law' or the 'Law of
   Empire?' (2009) 24(5) American University International Law Review 811; Susan D Franck, 'The Legitimacy
   Crisis in Investment Treaty Arbitration: Privatizing Public International Law Through Inconsistent Decisions'
   (2005) 73(4) Fordham Law Review 1521; Kaushal (n 28) 491.

97 Sornarajah (n 40) 101. Suzanne A Spears, 'The Quest for Policy Space in a New Generation of International
   Investment Agreements' (2010) 3(4) Journal of International Economic Law 1037, 1064 ff.

98 Singh and Ilge (n 45) 4, 5.

D. SUBSTANTIAL GUARANTEES OF INTERNATIONAL INVESTMENT AGREEMENTS

I. NATIONAL TREATMENT

The national treatment (NT) standard requires host countries to treat foreign investors and their investments in a non-discriminatory manner, that is no less favourably than domestic investors in comparable circumstances. Once a foreign investor has made an investment in a host State, they should be treated in the same way as domestic investors. The NT standard generally applies to various aspects of investment, such as establishment, operation, expansion, and sale of investments.

II. MOST FAVOURED NATION

Most favoured nation (MFN) is a principle that requires a host State to extend any privileges, advantages, or preferential treatment it grants to one foreign investor to all other foreign investors from other States.[99] It ensures that foreign investors are treated equally and prohibits discriminatory treatment of investors from different countries.[100] The principles of NT and MFN are regularly included in all international economic agreements, that is also in those of international trade law.

III. FAIR AND EQUITABLE TREATMENT

The fair and equitable treatment (FET) principle is a fundamental principle in international investment law guaranteeing that foreign investors are treated fairly and without discrimination by host States.[101] It requires host States to provide foreign investors with a certain level of protection and security for their investments, including, for instance, protecting investors from arbitrary or discriminatory measures, creating a stable and predictable legal framework and/or afford procedural fairness and due process to foreign investors and their investments. One major challenge of the FET principle is that it lacks a precise definition, meaning that its content and scope may vary in different treaties. In general, however, it encompasses the principles of good governance, due process, non-arbitrariness, and protection against targeted or discriminatory treatment.[102]

IV. EXPROPRIATION

The legality of expropriation or expropriation-like measures of the territorial host State and the corresponding obligation to compensate are among the core aspects

---

99 Sornarajah (n 40) 249.
100 Dolzer and others (n 60) 264.
101 Sornarajah (n 40) 248.
102 Sornarajah (n 40) 248, 249.

of investment protection under international law.[103] BITs generally all contain
an expropriation clause, which regularly sets out the conditions under which
expropriation and measures equivalent to expropriation are permissible. As a rule,
expropriation or nationalisation is only permissible if it has been carried out in the
public interest, in a non-discriminatory manner, in accordance with the rule of
law and in return for compensation.[104] Besides direct expropriation, an investor can
experience an expropriation-like measure that amounts to indirect expropriation.[105]
The legality of such regulatory measures largely depends on the preservation of
regulatory space in a host State's IIA regime and will be further addressed below when
discussing the right to regulate.

V. FULL PROTECTION AND SECURITY

The 'full protection and security' standard requires host States to provide foreign
investments with adequate security and protection against any harm, including physical
and political risks.[106] In general, this means that investments must be protected from
unlawful interference and destruction. Some BITs extend this standard explicitly to
legal protection of an investment.[107]

VI. SECURITY INTERESTS

A number of BITs contain provisions that provide for the protection of essential
security interests of the host State as a justification for otherwise prohibited State
action. The provisions appear to be explicitly self-judging in nature, as they grant
a State party the right to take any action it deems necessary to protect its essential
security interests.

E. INVESTOR-STATE DISPUTE SETTLEMENT

Underlying international investment protection law is one of the most powerful
dispute settlement mechanisms of the modern era.[108] Most IIAs and BITs contain
procedural guarantees in the form of the right to resort to ISDS. According to critics,
ISDS not only promotes the shift of power to private actors, but also favours the shift
of jurisdiction away from host-State courts to seemingly 'secretive' ISDS arbitration
proceedings that restrict the regulatory freedom and decision-making power of host-
State legislative bodies.[109]

---

103 Dolzer and others (n 59) 146 et seq.
104 Sornarajah (n 40) 252 et seq.
105 Dolzer and others (n 60) 153 et seq.
106 Sornarajah (n 40) 250.
107 Dolzer and others (n 59) 231.
108 Sornarajah (n 44) 103.
109 Gus van Harten, 'A Critique of Investment Treaties' in Kavaljit Singh and Burghard Ilge (eds), *Rethinking International Investment Treaties: Critical Issues and Policy Choices* (Both Ends 2016) 41.

I. THE INTERNATIONAL CENTRE FOR SETTLEMENT OF INVESTMENT DISPUTES

The ICSID is an international arbitration institution based in Washington, DC, that is part of the World Bank Group. As the principal institution for investment arbitration, ICSID supports dispute resolution primarily in ISDS under BITs and sometimes multilateral investment treaties by providing procedural rules, premises, a secretariat, and administrative support for arbitration and mediation. The ICSID is established by the ICSID Convention in its article 1. The purpose of the Centre is to provide facilities for conciliation and arbitration of investment disputes between member States and nationals of other member States in accordance with the provisions of this Convention.

BOX 23.1.4 Advanced: Participation of African States in ICSID

Often overlooked in legal scholarship is the fact that the participation of African States was crucial to the creation of the ICSID Convention.[110] In 1964, the World Bank had convened the first of four regional conferences in Addis Ababa to discuss the creation of a new international institution for the settlement of investment disputes. Fifteen newly independent African States participated actively in the drafting process and played a critical role in the entry into force of the ICSID Convention in 1966.[111] Recent series of publications dedicated to the investment law engagement of the African continent highlight this crucial role of the 15 African States.[112]

By establishing a secure enforcement framework, African States believed they would increase foreign investors' confidence in the legal security of their respective African States. And in fact, the first ISDS case in 1972 was against an African host State.[113] In 2020, nine ICSID proceedings were registered against an African host State, against Algeria, Cameroon, Zambia, Benin, Tanzania, South Sudan, Nigeria, and Egypt, resulting in the adoption of the Declaration on COVID-Related ISDS Risks at the 14th meeting of the AU Ministers of Trade in November 2020.[114]

---

110 Antonio R Parra, 'The Participation of African States in the Making of the ICSID Convention' (2019) 34(2) ICSID Review 270.

111 Hankings-Evans (n 47).

112 ICSID Review – Foreign Investment Law Journal, Volume 34, Issue 2, Spring 2019, Special Focus Section: Africa and the ICSID Dispute Resolution System.

113 *Holiday Inns S.A. and others v. Morocco*, ICSID Case No. ARB/72/1.

114 UNCTAD, Recent Developments in the IIA Regime: Accelerating IIA Reform, IIA Issue Notes (2021) 7 <https://unctad.org/system/files/official-document/diaepcbinf2021d6_en.pdf>.

II. THE UNITED NATIONS COMMISSION ON INTERNATIONAL TRADE LAW

The United Nations Commission on International Trade Law (UNCITRAL) is a subsidiary body of the UNGA that was established in 1966,[115] with the mandate to promote the harmonisation and modernisation of international trade law. It aims at facilitating the development and adoption of uniform rules and standards in the field of international trade law, particularly in the areas of commercial transactions, arbitration, and dispute resolution. Foreign investors are often provided with a choice in IIAs between initiating ICSID arbitration proceedings under the ICSID Convention or to opt for ad hoc arbitration under the UNCITRAL Arbitration Rules. The UNCITRAL Arbitration Rules were adopted in 1976 and constitute comprehensive procedural rules for the conduct of international commercial arbitrations.

F. PUBLIC POLICY ISSUES: ENVIRONMENTAL PROTECTION, HUMAN RIGHTS, AND SUSTAINABLE DEVELOPMENT

I. THE RIGHT TO REGULATE AND INTERNATIONAL INVESTMENT LAW

The right to regulate refers to a State's authority and sovereign power to regulate its internal affairs and to adopt measures in the public interest, even when those measures may adversely affect foreign investors and their investments. The tension between the need to adopt measures for the benefit of the general public by the domestic legislator and the protection of the foreign investments guaranteed in international investment agreements, is often not adequately resolved in the BITs themselves.[116] The State's right to regulate can be enshrined in a variety of clauses and typically appear as exceptions, carve-outs, or safeguard measures that allow States to adopt and maintain measures that may impact investments in pursuit of legitimate policy objectives.[117]

II. GLOBALISATION AND LEGITIMACY IN INTERNATIONAL INVESTMENT LAW

An important aspect of the question of systemic legitimacy is the increasing shift of State power to the private sector by means of extensive and unilateral international treaty protection mechanisms in favour of private investors.[118] This has been particularly

---

115 Establishment of the United Nations Commission on International Trade Law, Resolution 2205(XXI) 17 December 1966.

116 Sornarajah (n 40) 77, 78.

117 See articles 13(2), 15, 24 of the Morocco-Nigeria BIT (2016).

118 José E Alvarez, 'North American Free Trade Agreement's Chapter Eleven' (1997) 28(2) University of Miami Inter-American Law Review 303.

highlighted in TWAIL scholarship.[119] The globalisation process is the driving force behind the increasing diffusion of State power, which makes State borders in economic matters increasingly blurred.[120] In particular, transnationally operating MNEs have gained economic, social, and political importance through globalisation processes. It has been reported that with increasing activity of MNEs in developing States, especially in extractive sectors, the risk of human rights violations increases at the same time.[121]

In addition, the vagueness and broad interpretation of investment protection clauses favours the increasing shift of power to private actors.[122] For example, the often broad interpretation of the personal scope of protection allows for the possibility of so-called forum shopping, that is investors 'shopping' for the BITs most advantageous to them and initiating proceedings through their subsidiary/branch offices, while the headquarters of the company is located in a third country. In extreme cases, this may even lead to the initiation of ISDS proceedings against one's own nation State.[123]

G. CONCLUSION

International investment law, which in its modern form is based on reciprocal treaties under international law, was historically shaped by power relations between States. Debates about the legitimacy of IIL are indicative of such prevailing power structures. In its classical and modern history, IIL only knew the foreign investor as subject of protection, while corresponding obligations of the foreign investor were largely excluded. The extensive use of IIAs as an instrument to protect and promote FDI is not without consequences, especially since they regularly limit the regulatory sovereignty of host States. This fosters the emergence of legal loopholes with regard to the effective protection of human rights and the environment. Moreover, the far-reaching powers of arbitral tribunals in non-transparent ISDS procedures, the fragmentation caused by different arbitral interpretations of vague principles, and the high costs of ISDS procedures are highlighted by critics. On the other hand, developing States in particular seem to embrace the conclusion of IIAs as a means to attract foreign capital for economic development. While in the 1970s the call for a realignment of the global economic order was articulated by States in the Global South, today States predominantly take the approach of recalibrating their respective IIAs to align them

---

119 Sornarajah (n 40) 46 et seq.

120 Peter Muchlinski, *Multinational Enterprises and The Law* (2nd edn, OUP 2007) 507.

121 Report of the Panel of Experts on the Illegal Exploitation of Natural Resources and Other Forms of Wealth of the Democratic Republic of Congo, 12 April 2001, UN Doc. S/2001/357; Jun Zhao, 'Human Rights Accountability of Transnational Corporations: A Potential Response from Bilateral Investment Treaties' (2015) 8(1) Journal of East Asia & International Law 47, 48.

122 Stephan W Schill, 'Enhancing International Investment Law's Legitimacy: Conceptual and Methodological Foundations of a New Public Law Approach' (2011) 52(1) Virginia Journal of International Law 57, 66 et. seq.; Suzanne A Spears, 'The Quest for Policy Space in a New Generation of International Investment Agreements' (2010) 3(4) Journal of International Economic Law 1037; Singh and Ilge (n 45) 3.

123 Dolzer and others (n 59) 71; Gus van Harten (n 109) 42.

with public interests by balancing 'public' and 'private' power through the formulation of more balanced norms.

BOX 23.1.5 Further Readings and Further Resources

Further Readings

- R Dolzer, U Kriebaum, and K Schreuer, *Principles of International Law* (3rd edn, OUP 2022)

- A Kaushal, 'Revisiting History: How the Past Matters for the Present Backlash Against the Foreign Investment Regime' (2009) 50(2) Harvard International Law Journal 491

- K Miles, 'International Investment Law: Origins, Imperialism and Conceptualizing the Environment' (2010) 21(1) Colorado Journal of International Environmental Law and Policy 1

- M Sornarajah, *The International Law on Foreign Investment* (5th edn, CUP 2021)

- SW Schill, 'Enhancing International Investment Law's Legitimacy: Conceptual and Methodological Foundations of a New Public Law Approach' (2011) 52(1) Virginia Journal of International Law 57

Further Resources

- M Bedjaoui, *Towards a New International Economic Order* (UNESCO 1979)

---

§ § §

§ 23.2 INTERNATIONAL TRADE LAW

SHUBHANGI AGARWALLA

BOX 23.2.1 Required Knowledge and Learning
Objectives

Required knowledge: Sources of International Law; Subjects and Actors in
International Law

Learning objectives: Understanding the evolution, essential principles, and
challenges of international trade law; interdisciplinary insights that stimulate
critical thinking.

BOX 23.2.2 Interactive Exercises

Access *interactive exercises for this chapter*[124] by positioning your smartphone
camera at the dot-filled box, also known as a QR code.

Figure 23.1 QR code referring to interactive exercises.

A. INTRODUCTION

The effects of trade rules are all around us. At this very moment, dozens of violent
cartels in the State of Michoacán, Mexico, are fighting for power over one of its most
secretive markets. Buses are being burnt. Armed civilians are fighting back. Surprisingly,
the market in question is not marijuana or methamphetamines but a fruit that has
seen an astonishing uptick in demand, largely due to the North American Free Trade
Agreement (NAFTA), a trade agreement signed by the United States, Canada, and
Mexico. NAFTA lifted the United States ban on Mexican avocados, making it the
most successful import to the United States year round. However, the disproportionate
demand for avocados has also wreaked havoc on the environment in Mexico.[125] In light

---

124 https://openrewi.org/en-projects-project-public-international-law-international-economic-law/.
125 Mesfin Mekonnen and Arjen Hoekstra, 'The Green, Blue and Grey Water Footprint of Crops and
Derived Crop Products' (UNESCO-IHE 2010) <www.waterfootprint.org/media/downloads/Report47-
WaterFootprintCrops-Vol1.pdf> accessed 17 July 2023.

of this event, it is clear that engaging in international trade comes with its own set of trade-offs.

International trade law (ITL), as important as it is, must thus be put into perspective. This is what this chapter attempts to do. Not only will we identify key principles of ITL but we will also ponder the following questions: What advantages and disadvantages does trade liberalisation offer? What fundamental components make up the structure of ITL? How can we strike a balance between establishing laws to combat unwarranted protectionism and the legitimate regulatory autonomy of individual States? How does ITL relate to other rules of international law? We conclude this chapter by discussing some of the pressing challenges, such as digital trade and climate change, to ITL today.

B. SETTING THE CONTEXT

I. PURPOSE OF INTERNATIONAL TRADE AGREEMENTS

There are several reasons why States choose to enter into trade agreements. First, trade agreements allow States to enlist export-oriented industries, through improved access to foreign markets, as a counterweight to domestic political constituencies in import-impacted industries through the reciprocal exchange of binding trade concessions or commitments with other countries. Second, trade agreements provide security and transparency to investors who might be otherwise deterred by domestic politics. Third, trade agreements resolve terms-of-trade driven prisoners' dilemma problems in international trading relationships, where major trading powers might otherwise engage in mutually destructive high tariff policies.[126]

These rationales and the expansion of trade agreements have not gone uncontested. Scholars have lamented the materialism of ITL and the application of market logic to goods that are unmarketable. According to Rosset, for instance, 'food is not just another commodity, to be bought and sold like a microchip, but something which goes to the heart of human livelihood, culture and society'.[127] Others still have questioned the relevance and gains from trade agreements in developing countries where arguments in favour of open markets need to be modified by other considerations.[128]

II. HISTORY OF INTERNATIONAL TRADE LAW

In 1916, US Democratic Congressman Cordell Hull argued for the establishment of 'a permanent international trade congress' in response to the growing opinion that high US tariffs favoured Northern manufacturers to the detriment of Southern agriculture. The United States ensued negotiations with Britain to present a shared vision for

---

126 Kyle Bagwell and Robert Staiger, *The Economics of the World Trading System* (MIT Press 2002).

127 Peter M Rosset, *Food Is Different: Why We Must Get the WTO Out of Agriculture* (Zed Books 2006).

128 On inequalities in the international economic order, see Hankings-Evans, § 23.1, in this textbook.

the global economic order. The notion that all States could trade freely with each other guided by a common set of laws was understood to be an integral step towards achieving peace.[129] By the end of the Second World War, this Anglo-American idea led to several economic and political conferences. They also agreed on a set of 'proposals for consideration by an international conference on trade and employment' and for an International Trade Organization (ITO).[130] Although the ITO never came into being due to a lack of support from the international community, it formed the foundation for the influential General Agreement on Tariffs and Trade[131] (GATT) and the World Trade Organization (WTO).

While the ITO never came into existence, its objectives continued to be considered in the negotiations to establish the GATT, which came into force in 1948. The GATT served to promote international trade by eliminating or reducing tariffs and quotas. Despite the early success of the GATT, John H. Jackson proposed the creation of a new trade institution. This idea was supported by Canada and the European Community because they feared that the GATT regime was too weak, fragmented, and provisional to adopt and enforce disciplines on the new issues.

In 1995, the WTO entered into force. In particular, the WTO expanded the scope of the GATT regime. Furthermore, economic and political power is more widely distributed in the WTO compared to the GATT. Even though the European Union and the United States remain arguably the most influential members of the WTO, they hold much less influence than they did during the GATT period. The WTO framework includes multiple multilateral trade agreements. All Members are legally bound to oblige with these multilateral trade agreements.

C. WORLD TRADE ORGANIZATION

Established by the Marrakesh Agreement in 1995, the WTO acts as an umbrella organisation that provides multilateral laws on goods, services, and intellectual property, and provides a forum for negotiation, decision-making, and dispute settlement. According to the preamble to the Marrakesh Agreement, the two main ways to achieve the objectives of the WTO are the reduction of trade barriers and the elimination of discrimination in international trade.

The GATT, which started with just 23 contracting parties, had 128 member States when it transitioned to the WTO in 1995. At the time of writing, the WTO has 164

---

129 Jeffry Frieden, *Global Capitalism: Its Fall and Rise in the Twentieth Century* (Norton 2006).

130 'Proposals for consideration by an international conference on trade and employment: As Transmitted by the Secretary of State of the United States to His Majesty's Ambassador at Washington' (1945) International Law Quarterly 3, 4.

131 General Agreement on Tariffs and Trade (adopted 30 October 1947, entered into force 01 January 1948) 814 UNTS 187 (GATT).

members and 25 observer governments. The International Monetary Fund and the World Bank[132] have permanent observer status under their respective agreements with the WTO.

BOX 23.2.3 Advanced: Withdrawals and Expulsion

Any Member may, at any time, unilaterally withdraw from the WTO after providing a 6-month notice of the decision to withdraw. However, no member has withdrawn from the WTO yet. Disappointed with the decision in *EC – Bananas III*, a number of Caribbean countries had threatened withdrawal but had not gone ahead with it. Additionally, there is no procedure to expel a member who breaches their obligations under the WTO agreements. There is, however, a provision providing for expulsion of a member who fails to accept an amendment.

I. INSTITUTIONAL STRUCTURE

The institutional structure of the WTO includes, at the highest level, the Ministerial Conference, the General Council, the Dispute Settlement Body, and the Trade Policy Review Body and, at lower levels, specialised councils, committees, and working parties. It also includes quasi-judicial and other non-political bodies, as well as the WTO Secretariat.

The Ministerial Conference is the highest body of the WTO. It is composed of representatives, often ministers, from all Members and has decision-making powers on all matters under any of the multilateral WTO agreements. These powers include adopting authoritative interpretations of the WTO agreements, granting waivers, appointing the director-general, and adopting staff regulations.

The General Council is composed of ambassador-level diplomats and normally meets once every two months. The General Council is responsible for the day-to-day management of the WTO and its many activities. The General Council also acts as the Dispute Settlement Body and the Trade Policy Review Body, both of which convene at least once a month.

The WTO Secretariat is based in Geneva and is headed by a director-general, who is appointed by the Ministerial Conference. Only citizens of Members can be employed in the WTO Secretariat, but beyond that, there are no national quotas. Article 27.1 of the Dispute Settlement Understanding provides that 'the Secretariat shall have the responsibility of assisting panels, especially on the legal, historical and procedural aspects of the matters dealt with, and of providing secretarial and technical support'.

---

132 On international monetary law, see Bagchi, § 23.3, in this textbook.

II. LEGITIMACY CRISIS

The move to liberalise international trade in services has attracted intense criticisms from many quarters. An ongoing criticism is that it poses serious threats to the domestic political autonomy of States to decide issues concerning essential services such as water, healthcare, and education. For instance, the Alliance for Democracy circulated a pamphlet, 'Don't Let the WTO Get Hold of Our Water', which captures some of the concerns of civil society about the implications of the trade agreements for water distribution services. Crucially, these critiques are not only mounted by non-governmental organisations (NGOs),[133] but also by inter-governmental organisations, such as the World Health Organization (WHO) and the United Nations High Commissioner for Human Rights (UNHCHR).

BOX 23.2.4 Example: The Role of NGOs

An excellent example of the role of NGOs is the campaign for access to affordable medicines against infectious diseases, such as HIV. The patents for most of these essential medicines are held by multinational corporations and thus, this issue is governed by the TRIPS Agreement. In 1999, a number of NGOs launched a massive campaign for the production of affordable generics for patients in developing countries. By the year 2001, the WTO members in the Doha Declaration affirmed that TRIPS should not prevent countries from protecting public health and promoting access to essential medicines. In 2003, they enabled countries that cannot produce such medicines to import pharmaceuticals made under compulsory licence, and in 2005 this decision was turned into a permanent amendment to the TRIPS.

There have also been informal social movements such as the protests during the Seattle ministerial conference in 1999 which saw disenchantment with the WTO from trade unions concerned about immense competition from cheap labour from developing countries, environmentalists concerned about the outsourcing of hazardous activities, consumer unions concerned about unsafe imports, and labour rights and human rights activists concerned about the lack of labour protections in other countries.

D. KEY RULES OF INTERNATIONAL TRADE LAW

I. MOST FAVOURED NATION PRINCIPLE

Once tariff commitments have been agreed to in tariff negotiations and become binding under article II of the GATT, these must be extended to all members of the

---

133 On non-governmental organisations, see Chi, § 7.6, in this textbook.

GATT/WTO system under the most favoured nation (MFN) principle. According to the MFN principle, any benefits or immunities given to one class of product from an exporting country has to be given to all exporters of 'like products' from other countries. Members are forbidden to discriminate among like products by imposing an equal treatment on all members of the GATT.

Determination of the threshold requirements of like products has been the subject of much debate in both case law[134] and in scholarly commentary. Some cases have adopted quite narrow interpretations of like products, essentially requiring products to be almost identical in their physical characteristics. While determining likeness is a controversial exercise, it is usually admitted that when the only differentiating factor between two products is their origin, then the products are like. Factors that are also considered include the physical characteristics of the product, consumer habits and tastes, end uses of the products, and tariff classification of the products. Determination of 'likeness' takes place on a case-by-case basis, taking into account all these factors. Furthermore, article 1 of GATT explicitly states that any trade advantages granted to one member must be 'unconditionally' and 'immediately' offered to all members of the WTO. This means that if a country is accorded any trade advantage, the same trade advantage shall be accorded 'unconditionally and immediately' to all other members of WTO. There are differing interpretations of this requirement. For instance, some cases provide that there can be no conditions that force other countries to make further concessions. Another line of cases is that there can be no conditions altogether. A further interpretation is that some conditions may be applied but these cannot discriminate according to the country of origin. In *Belgium – Family Allowances*, Belgium imposed a charge on foreign goods purchased by public bodies when these goods originated in a country whose system of family allowances did not meet specific requirements that rendered their system comparable to that in place in Belgium. Only few States were given an exemption. A GATT Panel considered that conditioning the imposition of this internal tax on the kind of system of family allowances introduced by foreign countries violated the MFN principle. In *EC – Seal Products*, the Appellate Body further clarified the meaning of 'unconditionality' and said that it did not prevent a State from attaching conditions that might grant it an advantage. Instead, what the provision was meant to capture was the prohibition on condition that might have a detrimental impact on competitive opportunities for imported products.

While the MFN principle has often been called the cornerstone of the multilateral trading system, two major exceptions to the principle increasingly challenge its preeminence: first, the proliferation of preferential trade agreements (PTAs), negotiated on a bilateral, regional, or cross-regional basis among subsets of members of the WTO, that by their nature treat members more favourably than non-members; and second, special and differential treatment of developing countries, including the existence of unilateral, non-reciprocal preferences granted to many such countries by developed countries.

---

134 On case analysis in international law, see Milas, § 4.1, in this textbook.

II. NATIONAL TREATMENT PRINCIPLE

The national treatment principle (NTP) in article III.2 GATT is another core principle of ITL. Broadly, it means that the commerce of any State is treated no less favourably than the domestic product. This prevents countries from taking discriminatory measures on imports and prevents countries from offsetting the effects of tariffs through non-tariff measures.

BOX 23.2.5 Example: Violation of the NTP

In a case where State A reduces the import tariff on product X from 10% to 5%, only to impose a 5% domestic consumption tax only on imported product X, this State is effectively offsetting the 5-percentage-point tariff cut and violates the NTP.

The NTP applies to 'internal taxes'. Common examples of internal taxes are value added taxes, sales taxes, and excise taxes. The consistency of a measure with the first sentence of article III.2 GATT depends on whether the impugned measure is an internal tax that is directly or indirectly applied on the products in question; whether the imported and domestic products are like products; and whether the imported products are taxed in excess of the domestic products. The second sentence of article III.2 expands the scope of the MTP to other measures using a four-part test considering (1) whether the impugned measure is an internal tax that is directly or indirectly applied on the products in question; (2) whether the imported and domestic products are directly competitive or substitutable; (3) whether these products are similarly taxed; and (4) whether the dissimilar taxation is applied to give protection to domestic producers. According to article III.4 GATT, products of the territory of any Contracting Party imported into the territory of any other Contracting Party shall be accorded treatment no less favourable than that accorded to like products of national origin in respect of all laws, regulations, and requirements affecting their internal sale, offering for sale, purchase, transportation, distribution, or use.

III. TRADE IN SERVICES

As developing countries started gaining a comparative advantage in the production of many manufactured goods, developed countries became preoccupied with exploiting their comparative advantage in many service sectors, such as financial services, telecommunications, transportation, and professional services, by broadening the scope of the multilateral trade regime to include the liberalisation of international trade in services. Therefore, negotiating a multilateral agreement on international trade in services became a priority for many developed countries and resulted in the General Agreement on Trade in Services (GATS)[135] that came into force in 1995. Similar to the GATT, the primary objectives of the GATS were to create a credible and reliable

---

135 General Agreement on Trade in Services (adopted 15 April 1994, entered into force 01 January 1995) 1869 UNTS 183 (GATS).

system of ITL, ensure fair and equitable treatment of all States, stimulate economic activity through guaranteed policy bindings, and promote trade and development through progressive liberalisation.

Services in the sense of GATS are intangible and non-durable products of commercial value necessitating simultaneous production and consumption.[136] The GATS applies to 'measures by members affecting trade in services'. It distinguishes between general obligations for all Members and all services sectors, and obligations applying only to sectors for which Members, on an individual basis, decide to be bound. Determination of whether a particular measure is a measure affecting trade in services is integral for the application of the GATS. In *EC – Bananas III*, the Appellate Body opted for a wide understanding of the term 'affecting trade in services':

> The use of the term 'affecting' reflects the intent of the drafters to give a broad reach to the GATS. The ordinary meaning of the word 'affecting' implies a measure that has 'an effect on', which indicates a broad scope of application.

IV. GENERAL EXCEPTIONS

According to article XX of the GATT, measures that contravene rules of ITL are justified if they are necessary to protect public morals, human, animal or plant life or health, to secure compliance with laws or regulations which are not inconsistent with the provisions of the GATT, if they are imposed for the protection of national treasures of artistic, historic, or archaeological value, or relating to the conservation of exhaustible natural resources if such measures are made effective in conjunction with restrictions on domestic production or consumption. Article XIV of the GATS is identical to article XX of the GATT.

Article XX is only invoked after the measure at issue has been found inconsistent with one of the primary obligations in the GATT. Once the complainant has established such an inconsistency, the respondent may invoke the exception clause to justify the measure. To do this, the respondent must show that the measure meets the requirements set out in one of the subparagraphs of article XX (it relates to or is necessary to achieve the objective set out in the relevant subparagraph) and the measure is not inconsistent with the introductory clause of article XX (so-called *chapeau*).

In the case of subparagraphs (a), (b), and (d) of article XX, the measure must be 'necessary' to achieve the objective listed. In *Brazil – Retreaded Tyres*, the Appellate Body explained its test to determine whether a measure is 'necessary':

> In order to determine whether a measure is 'necessary' within the meaning of Article XX(b) of the GATT 1994, a panel must assess all the relevant factors, particularly

---

136 Diana Zacharias, 'Art. I GATS' in Rüdiger Wolfrum, Peter-Tobias Stoll, and Clemens Feinäugle (eds), *Max Planck Commentaries on World Trade Law: WTO – Trade in Services* (Martinus Nijhoff 2008).

the extent of the contribution to the achievement of a measure's objective and its trade restrictiveness, in the light of the importance of the interests or values at stake. If this analysis yields a preliminary conclusion that the measure is necessary, this result must be confirmed by comparing the measure with its possible alternatives, which may be less trade restrictive while providing an equivalent contribution to the achievement of the objective pursued.[137]

Unlike clauses (a), (b), and (d) of article XX which use the word 'necessary', subparagraph (g) only requires that measures 'relate' to the conservation of exhaustible natural resources. In *US – Gasoline*, the Appellate Body held that the word 'relating' does not require 'the same kind or degree of connection or relationship between the measure under appraisal and the State interest or policy sought to be promoted or realised' as the term necessary.

According to the chapeau of article XX, the measure at issue additionally must not be applied in a manner that constitutes 'arbitrary or unjustifiable discrimination' and that the measure must not be a 'disguised restriction on international trade'. Therefore, a balance must be struck between the right of a member to use the exception and the rights of other members under other provisions of the GATT. The exception should not be read so broad that the primary obligation ceases to exist. Similarly, the primary obligation should not be read so widely that the exception is useless.[138]

BOX 23.2.6 Advanced: Application of the General Exception Clause

In *Brazil – Retreaded Tyre*, Brazil had imposed an import ban on retreaded tyres, which had a shorter life span and thus, led to the creation of tyre dumps that increased the incidence of cancer, dengue, reproductive problems, environmental contamination, and other associated risks. Brazil argued that the ban was justified under article XX(b) ('necessary to protect human, animal or plant life or health') which bore particular concern for developing countries and was not inconsistent with the requirements of the chapeau. The European Communities, on the other hand, argued that even though Brazil tried to pretend that the case was about human life and health, this was not the case. As the first prong of its analysis, the Appellate Body noted that the Panel had found the ban prima facie inconsistent with article XI:1 of the GATT because it was a quantitative restriction on imports. As the second prong of its analysis, the Appellate Body noted that the purpose of the ban was to protect human life and health and found that the ban was necessary to achieve that objective.

---

137 Appellate Body Report, *Brazil – Measures Affecting Imports of Retreaded Tyres*, W T/DS332/AB/R (adopted 17 December 2007) para 156.

138 Appellate Body Report, *European Communities – Measures Prohibiting the Importation and Marketing of Seal Products*, WT/DS400/AB/R (adopted 18 June 2014).

Finally, the Appellate Body found that Brazil was applying the ban in a manner constituting arbitrary or unjustifiable discrimination by providing exemptions to some countries but not others for reasons unrelated to the protection of life or health. Thus, the import ban could not be justified under article XX(b) and was inconsistent with article XI:1 of the GATT 1994.[139]

V. RULES ON UNFAIR TRADE

Article VI of the GATT provides for the right of contracting parties to apply anti-dumping measures. These are measures against imports of a product at an export price below its 'normal value'. States are allowed to enact anti-dumping measures if imports cause or threaten to cause injury to a domestic industry in the territory of the importing contracting party. A product is to be considered as being introduced into the commerce of an importing country at less than its normal value if the price at which the product is exported from one country to another is less than the comparable price, in the ordinary course of trade, for the like product when destined for consumption in the exporting country, or in the absence of such domestic price, is less than either (1) the highest comparable price for the like product for export to any third country in the ordinary course of trade, or (2) the cost of production of the product in the country of origin plus a reasonable addition for selling costs and profit.

Under article VI of the GATT, Members can impose countervailing duties on imports into their domestic markets in an amount not in excess of the estimated bounty or subsidy determined to have been granted, directly or indirectly, on the manufacture, production, or export of such product in the country of origin or exportation. Under article VI, as with dumping, no countervailing duties may be imposed unless there has been a determination that the subsidy has caused or has threatened to cause material injury, or cause material retardation to an industry producing like products.[140]

According to article XIX of the GATT, if, as a result of unforeseen developments any product is being imported into the territory of that contracting party in such increased quantities and under such conditions as to cause or threaten serious injury to domestic producers in that territory, the contracting party shall be free to suspend the obligation in whole or in part or to withdraw or modify the concession. The increase in imports must be due to 'unforeseen developments'. An unforeseen development is one that was 'unexpected' by trade negotiators when the concessions were being negotiated.[141]

139 *Brazil – Measures Affecting Imports of Retreaded Tyres* (n 21).
140 Appellate Body Report, *European Communities – Measures Affecting Trade in Large Civil Aircraft*, WT/DS316/R (adopted 1 June 2011); Appellate Body Report, *United States – Final Countervailing Duty Determination with Respect to Certain Softwood Lumber from Canada* (2004) WT/DS257/AB/R.
141 Panel Report, *Argentina – Safeguard Measures on Imports on Footwear* (1999) WTO Docs WT/DS121/R and Appellate Body Report, *Argentina – Safeguard Measures on Imports on Footwear* WT/DS121/AB/R.

Notably, the safeguards regime calls for a 'serious injury' as opposed to the term 'material injury' which is the requirement in anti-dumping and countervailing duty investigations. This implies a higher threshold for injury.[142] The GATS also contains a specific safeguard regime in article 5.

E. DISPUTE SETTLEMENT IN INTERNATIONAL TRADE LAW

The members of the GATT created panels of first five and then three members as dispute settlement bodies in ITL. The initial panel reports used vague, compromise language, constituting over time, in Robert Hudec's words, a 'diplomat's jurisprudence'.[143] Gradually the members grew more comfortable with the idea of greater legalisation in light of their experience with the system. Nevertheless, dissatisfaction with the GATT dispute settlement mechanism remained until the 1980s as States continued to block the establishment of panels and the adoption of reports.

Simultaneously, members of the GATT were also getting dissatisfied with the ability of parties to needlessly delay the appointment of panels, settlement of their terms of reference, and adoption of their findings. Several States argued successfully for a strengthened dispute settlement system that included strict deadlines, the establishment of a negative consensus rule, the creation of a standing Appellate Body, and the prohibition of any unilateral action seeking to redress violation of obligations. The rules governing this revised system of dispute settlement are in large part set out in the Understanding on Rules and Procedures Governing the Settlement of Disputes (DSU).[144]

I. SCOPE OF DISPUTES

Only WTO members can initiate a dispute. Article 3.7 DSU gives Members the responsibility to decide whether it would be fruitful to bring a case before the WTO.[145] The scope of disputes is limited to rights and obligations arising from the provisions of those agreements listed in appendix 1 DSU. These include all multilateral agreements on trade in goods, the TRIPS, the GATS, and plurilateral agreements. Regional trade agreements cannot be used as the basis for a complaint. The Panel and the Appellate

---

142 *United States – Safeguard Measures on Imports of Fresh, Chilled or Frozen Lamb Meat from New Zealand and Australia* (2000) WTO Docs WT/DS/177/R and WT/DS178/R.

143 Robert Hudec, *Enforcing International Trade Law: The Evolution of the Modern GATT Legal System* (Lexis Law 1993).

144 Understanding on Rules and Procedures Governing the Settlement of Disputes, annexed to the Agreement Establishing the World Trade Organization (adopted 15 April 1994) 1867 UNTS 3.

145 Appellate Body Report, Mexico – Anti-Dumping Investigation of High-Fructose Corn Syrup (HFCS) from the United States, WT/DS132/AB/RW (adopted 21 November 2001) para 73.

Body are not legal bodies that have general jurisdiction akin to other international courts[146]. Nonetheless, the Panel in *Korea – Government Procurement* observed that they

> can see no basis . . . for an a contrario implication that rules of international law other than rules of interpretation do not apply. . . . [T]here is no conflict or inconsistency, or an expression in a covered WTO agreement that implies differently, . . . the customary rules of international law apply to the WTO treaties and to the process of treaty formation under the WTO.[147]

II. PROCEDURE

According to article 4 DSU, the proceedings begin with consultations aimed at clearing the factual situation between the parties to the dispute. Parties have broad discretion regarding the manner in which consultations are to be conducted. In case consultations do not resolve the dispute within 60 days after the request for consultations, the complainant may request the DSB to establish a panel. This may also happen earlier if the respondent either did not respect the deadlines for responding to the request for consultations or if the consulting parties jointly consider that consultations have failed to settle the dispute.

Throughout the process of dispute settlement, panels have discretion to seek information and technical advice from experts in order to help them to understand and evaluate the evidence submitted and the arguments made by the parties. Panels submit their draft reports to the parties for a so-called interim review. After this interim review, the panel finalises the report and issues it to the parties. Finally, the report is made public by circulating it to all WTO Members.

Within 60 days of it being circulated to all Members, a panel report is either adopted by the DSB or appealed to the Appellate Body. In contrast to panels, the Appellate Body has detailed standard working procedures set out in the Working Procedures for Appellate Review[148] on the basis of the mandate and pursuant to the procedure stipulated in article 17.9 DSU. Unlike in panel proceedings, third parties have broad rights to participate in appellate review proceedings.

III. ROLE OF DEVELOPING COUNTRIES

About two-thirds of the WTO's members are developing countries. The dispute settlement safeguards the interests of developing States by providing special provisions in favour of developing countries[149] and technical assistance for developing countries

---

146 On international courts, see Choudhary, § 12, in this textbook.
147 Panel Report, *Korea – Measures Affecting Government Procurement*, WT/DS163/R (adopted 19 June 2000) para 7.96.
148 WTO, 'Working Procedures for Appellate Review' (4 January 2005) <www.wto.org/english/tratop_e/dispu_e/ab_e.htm> accessed 20 August 2023.
149 See articles 8.10, 12.10, 24 DSU.

as well as by supporting developing countries through a Committee on Trade and Development.

The WTO Secretariat provides for legal advisers to help developing countries in any WTO dispute. The service is offered by the WTO's Training and Technical Cooperation Institute. Some States also helped set up an Advisory Centre on WTO law in 2001. All least-developed countries are automatically eligible for advice. The WTO also holds regular training sessions on trade policy in Geneva.

Despite this assistance, most developing countries have been unable to meaningfully invoke the dispute settlement mechanisms in ITL.[150] This can be attributed to a lack of bargaining power which becomes particularly relevant during consultations which is aimed at a negotiated solution;[151] fear of extra-legal retaliation by more powerful trading partners; costs and resource constraints which can affect things such as the ability to collect information and evidence on the effects of WTO-inconsistent measures, and hiring quality lawyers and economists; lack of legal capacity and expertise;[152] and asymmetries or unevenness in the effectiveness of remedies as the WTO only provides for prospective remedies.[153]

F. CONCLUSION

This chapter has attempted to provide an account of the fundamental components of ITL. However, many emerging issues related to other areas of international law, such as digital trade and climate change, require further attention. There is no question that digital trade has become ubiquitous over the last decade and will only become more prominent in the years to come. Some of the key contentious areas include the divergence of services and goods disciplines in ITL; classifications of digital services in the services classification schedule; trade secret protection under TRIPS and other recent FTAs; restrictions on forced disclosure of source code and algorithms; and applications of exceptions in trade agreements to protect policy space for domestic regulation. That being said, several WTO Members have strongly expressed the desire to achieve significant progress on electronic commerce so that WTO agreements remain relevant in the age of the digital economy.[154] On the issue of climate change,[155]

---

150 Gregory Shaffer and Ricardo Melendez-Ortiz, *Dispute Settlement at the WTO: The Developing Country Experience* (CUP 2011).

151 Request for Consultations by the United States, *Argentina – Patent Protection for Pharmaceuticals and Test Data Protection for Agricultural Chemicals*, WT/DS171/1 (10 May 1999); Request for Consultations by the United States, *Pakistan – Patent Protection for Pharmaceutical and Agricultural Chemical Products*, WT/DS36/1 (6 May 1996).

152 Andrew Guzman and Beth Simmons, 'Power Plays & Capacity Constraints: The Selection of Defendants in WTO Disputes' (2005) 34 Journal of Legal Studies 557, 557–58.

153 Alan Sykes, 'The Remedy for Breach of Obligations Under the WTO Dispute Settlement Understanding: Damages or Specific Performance?' in Marco Bronckers and Reinhard Quick (eds), *New Directions in International Economic Law* (Kluwer Law International 2000) 347.

154 Junichi Ihara, 'Ambassador & Permanent Representative to WTO, Japan, WTO in the Era of Mega-Regional Trade Agreements' <http://archive.ipu.org/splze/trade16.htm.> accessed 20 August 2023.

155 On international climate change law, see Viveros-Uehara, § 17, in this textbook.

there is a sense that the competition brought about by free trade pressures governments to lower environmental standards. Recently, however, States are keen to factor environmental considerations into their trade policies. A notable example is the effort by six countries (Costa Rica, Fiji, Iceland, New Zealand, Norway, and Switzerland) to negotiate the Agreement on Climate Change Trade and Sustainability.[156] All in all, it is an exciting time to be interested in ITL. While there is no telling how these new issues will transform the discipline in the years to come, it is likely that the same principles will play a prominent role in the debate.

BOX 23.2.7 Further Readings and Further Resources

Further Readings

- EH Leroux, 'Eleven Years of GATS Case Law: What Have We Learned?' (2007) 10 Journal of International Economic Law

- J Pauwelyn and others, *International Trade Law* (3rd edn, Wolters Kluwer 2016)

- M Trebilcock, R Howse, and A Eliason, *The Regulation of International Trade* (4th edn, Routledge 2013)

- P Van den Bossche and W Zdouc, *The Law and Policy of the World Trade Organization, Text, Cases and Materials* (4th edn, CUP 2017)

Further Resources

- The official website of the WTO contains the official documents of the WTO, the official documents issued under the GATT 1947, the WTO Analytical Index, an article-by-article commentary on the agreements <www.wto.org> accessed 20 August 2023

- Summaries of each case excerpted in this chapter can be found at <www. worldtradelaw.net/dsc/dscpage.htm> accessed 20 August 2023

---

§ § §

---

156 New Zealand Foreign Affairs & Trade, 'Agreement on Climate Change, Trade and Sustainability (ACCTS) negotiations' < www.mfat.govt.nz/en/trade/free-trade-agreements/trade-and-climate/agreement-on-climate-change-trade-and-sustainability-accts-negotiations/> accessed 20 August 2023.

§ 23.3 INTERNATIONAL MONETARY LAW

KANAD BAGCHI

BOX 23.3.1 Required Knowledge and Learning Objectives

Required knowledge: International Investment Law; International Trade Law; Subjects and Actors in International Law; TWAIL

Learning objectives: Understanding the rules pertaining to the regulation of money in international law; the institutions which are important in this respect; and the kind of politics that international monetary governance is embedded within.

BOX 23.3.2 Interactive Exercises

Access *interactive exercises for this chapter*[157] by positioning your smartphone camera at the dot-filled box, also known as a QR code.

Figure 23.1 QR code referring to interactive exercises.

A. INTRODUCTION

Even though money has been a crucial instrument of political and social control, the international legal framework around it still remains largely understudied. International monetary law (IML) occupies much less attention within debates on international economic law, as against international trade and investment, for instance.[158] This has meant that questions concerning monetary autonomy, sovereignty, and the way international law deals with monetary conflicts and determines the distribution of rights and obligations remain largely ignored in legal scholarship. What is also missing is a systematic engagement with how money sustains not only the infrastructure of world capitalist expansion, but is also an important instrument of hierarchy, subordination, and imperial expropriation.

---

157 https://openrewi.org/en-projects-project-public-international-law-international-economic-law/.
158 On international economic law, see Hankings-Evans, § 23.1, and Agarwalla, § 23.2, in this textbook.

In this chapter, I attempt to open up a conversation about the manifold transformations that the field has witnessed in the last decades and how the study of monetary law accordingly needs to be reoriented. I focus on the structural changes in IML and the kind of questions which have become relevant today. In addition, I place IML in conversation with the politics of money and hierarchy in the international monetary system (IMS).

B. HISTORIES OF INTERNATIONAL MONETARY LAW

Most accounts of IML trace the origins of the field to the Bretton Woods Conference in 1945 and to the establishment of the International Monetary Fund (IMF, or Fund). To be sure, Bretton Woods was a landmark event. It was the first time that a multilateral instrument for monetary coordination was established. It was also the first time that some semblance of participation of the Third World[159] in monetary affairs was envisioned, albeit in a very limited way.[160] Against the backdrop of the inter-war years that witnessed several episodes of monetary and financial instability accompanied by discriminatory currency practices, the intention at Bretton Woods was to put in place an international organisation with legal powers to enforce a code of conduct for monetary affairs.[161] Thus, the IMF was given a *permanent* mandate for international monetary cooperation and far-reaching powers to impose sanctions.[162]

This highly abstract and sanitised version of the origins of IML erases the role that money and international law played in the long history of capitalism and imperialism. From the powerful Economic and Financial Organization (EFO) of the League of Nations (League) to the erstwhile gold standard adopted among imperial powers in the 19th century, money represented a crucial terrain for the civilising mission[163] as well as resistance to it. Control over money in the colonies was both a means to limit sovereignty and a method to conditionally grant it upon satisfactory transformation.[164] Colonial currency systems were systematically placed subordinate to currency systems in the metropoles enabling the exploitation and extraction of wealth from the former.[165] Moreover, the League was singularly responsible for the unequal economic integration of the mandated territories into the circuits of global capitalist accumulation.[166]

---

159 On Third World Approaches to International Law (TWAIL), see González Hauck, § 3.2, in this textbook.
160 Eric Helleiner, *Forgotten Foundations of Bretton Woods: International Development and the Making of the Postwar Order* (Cornell University Press 2016).
161 Joseph Gold, 'Continuity and Change in the International Monetary Fund' in *Legal and Institutional Aspects of the International Monetary System: Selected Essays* (IMF 1984) 408.
162 IMF Articles of Agreement, art I (1) 'To promote international monetary cooperation through a permanent institution'.
163 On colonialism, see González Hauck, § 3.2, and González Hauck, § 1, in this textbook.
164 Allan ES Lumba, *Monetary Authorities: Capitalism and Decolonization in the American Colonial Philippines* (Duke University Press 2022).
165 Wadan Narsey, *British Imperialism and the Making of Colonial Currency Systems* (Springer 2016).
166 On Marxism, see Bagchi, § 3.4, in this textbook.

Much of what the IMF came to embody at Bretton Woods was an extension of the League's powers of monetary and financial oversight – what we broadly refer to as monetary surveillance in contemporary IMF law.

C. THE SCOPE OF INTERNATIONAL MONETARY LAW

The scope and subject matter of IML continues to be a matter of debate. The term 'international monetary system' was first introduced in the IMF Agreement.[167] Yet, it was left undefined. This meant that much of what this 'system' would include and consequently the legal framework around it would be elaborated through institutional practise and adaptation. This gave international monetary institutions, including the IMF, tremendous leeway in shaping the contours of the discipline and in expanding its own mandate for the regulation of money.[168]

It was only in 2012 that the IMF would make the first attempt at defining the international monetary system, as well as the law governing it.[169] In it, the IMF defined IML as the collection of rules that govern the *balance-of-payments* (BOP) relations among States. These include, as the IMF notes, rules on (1) exchange relations, (2) international payments, (3) cross-border capital flows, and (4) monetary reserve management – all of which determine a particular State's monetary relationship with the rest of the world.

BOX 23.3.3 Advanced: Balance of Payments

In monetary law, the BOP relationship is the governing anchor and the institutional link among States. This is because national economies do not exist in isolation but are intimately tied through a vast network of closely interconnected balance sheets and currency relations. BOP, however, is a zero-sum game in the sense that one country's BOP *deficit* is another country's BOP *surplus*. Much of the politics over money revolves around BOP *adjustment* and who bears the burden of such adjustment.[170]

---

167 See article IV, section 1 IMF Agreement.
168 Joseph Gold, 'Strengthening the Soft International Law of Exchange Arrangements' (1983) 77(3) American Journal of International Law 443–489.
169 See '*Modernizing the Legal Framework for Surveillance – An Integrated Surveillance Decision*' (IMF 2012); Gold, 'Public International Law in the International Monetary System' (1984) 38 SMU Law Review 799–852; Lucía Satragno, 'Chapter 1: The International Monetary System in the Post-Crisis Era' in *Monetary Stability as a Common Concern in International Law: Policy Cooperation and Coordination of Central Banks* (Brill 2022) 11.
170 Benjamin J Cohen, 'The Macro foundations of Monetary Power' in David M Andrews (ed), *International Monetary Power* (Cornell University Press 2006).

D. EXPANDING INSTITUTIONS

I. INTERNATIONAL MONETARY FUND

For the most part, IML has had an outsized focus on the IMF. This is, of course, for good reasons. The Bretton Woods system (BWS) put the IMF at the centre of international monetary relations. It was tasked with enforcing the par-value system of fixed but adjustable exchange rates – a purpose which it lost in 1971 when the US under President Nixon refused convertibility of the dollar in exchange for gold – an event that sent shockwaves across the international monetary system.[171] Indeed, since then, the IMF evolved in multiple ways and its role within the IMS has changed significantly.[172] The Second Amendment to the IMF agreement in 1979 granted it a new mandate for 'firm surveillance' and changed fundamentally the character of the IMS.[173] Currencies that were tied to each other through an interlocking system of par values came to be free-floating in the international market.[174]

II. BANK FOR INTERNATIONAL SETTLEMENTS

The IMF is neither the first nor the only institution tasked with monetary cooperation. We must go further back to the Bank for International Settlements (BIS) established in 1929 with a specific mandate 'to promote the cooperation of central banks'.[175] The uniqueness of the BIS lies in the fact that its membership comprises not States, but 63 central banks across the world. From an institution envisioned with a mandate to determine and settle financial reparations stemming from the First World War,[176] the BIS has evolved into a credible forum for central bank cooperation – hosting a number of influential committees dedicated towards promoting financial and monetary stability. Its role in the international monetary system has been variously described as an anchor and think tank for monetary policy coordination.[177] At least since the demise of the BWS of exchange rates in the 1970s, the BIS has 'emerged as [a] competing source of international monetary authority'.[178]

III. INFORMALISATION OF INTERNATIONAL MONETARY LAW AND COOPERATION

The fall of BWS also resulted in the *informalisation* of IML and cooperation. This shift was transformational in the way it ushered a whole range of new actors in the monetary

---

171 Michael D Bordo, 'The Operation and Demise of the Bretton Woods System; 1958 to 1971' (2017) NBER Working Paper No. 23189.
172 François Gianviti, 'Evolving Role and Challenges for the International Monetary Fund' (2001) 35(4) The International Lawyer 1371–1403.
173 Article IV, section 3 IMF Agreement.
174 Robert Triffin, *Gold and the Dollar Crisis* (Yale University Press 1960).
175 Article 3 Statutes of the Bank for International Settlements, 1930.
176 Beth Simmons, 'Why Innovate? Founding the Bank For international Settlements, 1929–30' (1993) 45 World Politics.
177 Carola Westermeier, 'The Bank of International Settlements as a Think Tank for Financial Policy-Making' (2018) 37 Policy and Society 170–187.
178 Bordo (n 171) 8.

field. Already in the 1960, an influential group of ten (G10) industrial nations agreed to establish the General Agreements to Borrow (GAB) to supplement the resources of the IMF.[179] GAB resulted in a system of a 'double lock'[180] on the resources of the IMF, such that decisions on conditional lending by the IMF would now also require the concurrence of the G10. Thereafter, informality would become a regular feature of international monetary law. The 1970s and the 1980s saw the rise of the G5 and the G7 as the principal forums for international monetary cooperation, much of which was transpiring outside of the IMF.[181] As one commentator put it, '[T]he 1970s was a low point for the IMF as the official hub of international monetary coordination'.[182] The developing world too resorted to informality and minilateralism[183] by establishing the G24, with the mandate to coordinate joint actions, especially on international monetary and financial affairs.[184]

With the Global Financial Crisis (GFC) in 2008, another informal body, the G20, would acquire a lead role in the global governance of financial and monetary matters. The G20 was not simply a political forum comprising heads of States, but also a technical forum, which brought together finance ministers and central bankers. It gathered a greater legitimacy than the G5/G7 given the broader representation of developing countries in the G20. The G20 has engaged with several issues, such as the governance reform of the IMF, augmenting global monetary liquidity through additional SDR allocation, inducing BOP adjustments, and legitimising the use of capital controls to reduce the volatility of international capital flows. Alongside the IMF, the G20 is regarded as an important 'hub of global economic governance'.[185]

IV. DECENTRALISATION IN INTERNATIONAL MONETARY LAW

The GFC also prompted a *decentralisation* in international monetary law, characterised by the creation of a number of regional monetary institutions in the Global South.[186] Especially in Asia, three new institutions – Chiang Mai Initiative Multilateralization

---

179 On GAB, see Michael Ainley, 'The General Agreements to Borrow' (IMF Pamphlet Series No. 41) <www.elibrary.imf.org/downloadpdf/book/9781451981278/9781451981278.pdf> accessed 20 August 2023.

180 As cited in Rakesh Mohan and Muneesh Kapur 'Emerging Powers and Global Governance: Whither the IMF?' (2015) IMF Working Paper WP/15/219, 41.

181 Andrew Baker, *The Group of Seven: Finance Ministers, Central Banks, and Global Financial Governance* (Routledge 2006).

182 Michael D Bordo, 'Monetary Policy Cooperation/Coordination and Global Financial Crises in Historical Perspective' (2021) 32 Open Economics Review 587–611.

183 Orfeo Fioretos, 'Minilateralism and Informality in International Monetary Cooperation' (2019) 26(6) Review of International Political Economy 1136–1159.

184 James M Boughton, 'Southern Accents: The Voice of Developing Countries in International Financial Governance' (2017) CIGI Paper No. 141.

185 Andrew Cooper, 'The G20 as an Improvised Crisis Committee and/or a Contested "Steering Committee" for the World' (2010) 86(3) International Affairs 741–57.

186 William W Grimes, 'East Asian Financial Regionalism in Support of the Global Financial Architecture? The Political Economy of Regional Nesting' (2006) 6(3) Journal of East Asian Studies 353–380; William W Grimes, 'East Asian Financial Regionalism: Why Economic Enhancements Undermine Political Sustainability'

(CMIM),[187] BRICS Contingent Reserve Arrangement (CRA),[188] and Eurasian Fund for Stabilization and Development (EFSD) – were established in quick succession following the GFC. A common theme underlying the establishment of these arrangements was a sense of deep dissatisfaction with the nature and exclusivity of international monetary governance and the need for 'self-insurance' against short-term liquidity shortages.[189] The emergence of regional monetary institutions has been heralded as a new era of 'South-South' monetary coordination.[190] Its distinctiveness lies in the fact that, unlike in the past, these newer mechanisms of coordination are being systematically institutionalised through an elaborate system of rules for monitoring, surveillance, and dissemination of monetary policy standards. Much of legal scholarship has hardly paid any attention to monetary institutions outside the 'West'.[191]

E. EXPANDING INTERACTIONS

The emerging institutional landscape is thus highly segmented, scattered, and multi-layered.[192] In contrast to the top-down centralised system of international monetary coordination, which the BWS put in place, what we have today is a 'decentralized, heterogeneous, pluripolar' global order for monetary coordination.[193] In this setting, multiple institutions interact and compete for authority and also legitimacy.

F. EXPANDING INSTRUMENTS

Conditional lending is an important function of international monetary institutions. Simply put, conditionality is the device by which monetary institutions lend financial resources on the satisfactory fulfilment of certain prescriptions by the receiving State, which is expected to solve its BOP crisis. For the IMF, the legal basis of

(2015) 21(2) Contemporary Politics 145–160; José Antonio Ocampo and Daniel A Titelman, 'Regional Monetary Cooperation in Latin America' (2012) ADBI Working Paper No. 373, 6.

187 Chalongphob Sussangkarn, 'The Chiang Mai Initiative Multilateralization: Origin, Development and Outlook' (2010) ADBI Working Paper No. 230.

188 Aike I Würdemann 'The BRICS Contingent Reserve Arrangement: A Subversive Power Against the IMF's Conditionality?' (2018) 19(3) Journal of World Investment & Trade 570–593.

189 Ocampo and Titelman (n 186) 6.

190 Barbara Fritz and Laurissa Mühlich, 'Regional Monetary Cooperation in Emerging, Transition, and Developing Economies' in J Hölscher and H Tomann (eds), *Palgrave Dictionary of Emerging Markets and Transition Economics* (Palgrave Macmillan 2015).

191 For some exceptions, see Laurissa Mühlich and Barbara Fritz, 'Safety for Whom? The Scattered Global Financial Safety Net and the Role of Regional Financial Arrangements' (2016) KFG Working Paper Series, No. 75; Pradumna B Rana, 'The Evolving Multi-Layered Global Safety Net: The Case of the Association of Southeast Asian Nations+3 Regional Financial Safety Net and the International Monetary Fund' (2017) ADBI Working Paper Series No. 733.

192 Ibid.

193 Ilene Grabel, 'Continuity, Discontinuity and Incoherence in the Bretton Woods Order: A Hirschmanian Reading' (2019) 50(1) Development and Change 46–71, 49.

conditionality is usually traced to article V, section 3(a) of the IMF agreement, which refers to 'conditions governing use of the Fund's general resources' and calls upon the IMF to establish 'adequate safeguard' for the use of its funds. The parameters for conditionality, its content and scope have, however, evolved through practise and internal law-making.[194] Over the years, conditional lending has transformed into a mammoth exercise with several distinct regimes, facilities, and adjustment programmes depending on the development parameters of the member in question and its capacity for repayment.[195] Conditional lending, especially its more structural kind, has faced tremendous criticism, and rightly so, as being 'overly extensive, intrusive and deflationary' – often drawing the ire of governments and civil society organisations.[196] Conditionality has been associated with a 'one-size-fits-all' approach where standard prescriptions for deregulation, greater capital account openness, labour market reforms, deficit reduction, and large-scale austerity programmes are prescribed across the board.

The resistance against IMF conditionality and later World Bank structural adjustment programmes ushered in a change of strategy within these institutions. In the last decades and at least since the fall of the BWS in 1971, a big part of the function of monetary institutions has focused on monetary surveillance. The Second Amendment to the IMF Agreement in 1979 and revised article IV reoriented the objectives of the IMF towards prompting 'a stable system of exchange rates'. For this purpose, the Fund was also granted a new mandate to exercise 'firm surveillance' over exchange rate policies of its members, as well as broad powers to 'oversee' the international monetary system.[197]

Monetary surveillance typically entails both bilateral consultations and multilateral reporting. *Bilateral* surveillance consists of country visits, which are then followed up with the publication of a Consultation Report.[198] These reports contain analysis and recommendations on a range of structural problems associated with a member State's financial and monetary infrastructure, including financial soundness, monetary stability, and exchange rate misalignment. *Multilateral* surveillance, on the other hand, entails information gathering and dissemination, analysis of macroeconomic spillovers, monitoring of cross-country linkages, standard setting, and knowledge production on key monetary policy frameworks.

---

194 See Guidelines on Conditionality (IMF 2002) <www.imf.org/en/Publications/Policy-Papers/ Issues/2016/12/31/Guidelines-on-Conditionality-PP167> accessed 20 August 2023.

195 Rosa M Lastra, *Legal Foundations of International Monetary Stability* (OUP 2006) 406–425; Rosa M Lastra, 'IMF Conditionality' (2002) 4(2) Journal of International Banking Resolution 167–182.

196 William W Grimes and William N Kring, 'Alternatives to the International Monetary Fund in Asia and Latin America: Lessons for Regional Financial Arrangements' in D Barrowclough and others (eds), *South–South Regional Financial Arrangements: Collaboration Towards Resilience* (Palgrave Macmillan 2022) 293–339, 296.

197 Article IV, section 3 IMF Agreement.

198 CMIM published article V Consultation Reports. See <www.imf.org/en/Publications/SPROLLs/Article-iv-staff-reports#sort=%40imfdate%20descending & www.amro-asia.org/category/amro-country-surveillance-reports/annual-consultation-reports/> accessed 20 August 2023.

BOX 23.3.4 Advanced: Monetary Surveillance

The objective of monetary surveillance is twofold. On the one hand, bilateral surveillance provides an opportunity for 'dialogue and persuasion' where international monetary institutions interact closely with domestic central banks and other monetary authorities of member States.[199] On the other hand, multilateral surveillance is geared towards cross-country references, ranking, standardising, and creating coherent cognitive frameworks around contested monetary issues. The recommendations, which are part of the multilateral and bilateral surveillance, are not legally binding. They are offered as advice in the form of best practices.[200] Yet, they carry tremendous weight and have visible impact as they engage processes of peer review, public scrutiny, and induce market pressure.[201] In other words, monetary surveillance operates at the interface of informal and formal law-making. Through surveillance, monetary institutions do not seek to change legal relations directly, but indirectly shape preferences and background assumptions of the actors involved in the process. Surveillance is a typical example of the exercise of cognitive and communicative power, which builds on knowledge, expertise, and information instruments that structure cognitive conditions.[202] The inherently evaluative character of surveillance also makes it a highly political instrument, through which certain forms of knowledge systems, standards, and monetary practices are privileged over others.[203]

G. CONTESTED ISSUES IN INTERNATIONAL MONETARY LAW

I. CURRENCY MANIPULATION

The issue of currency manipulation – the practice of directly or indirectly tinkering with the value of a particular currency to gain a competitive trade advantage – has been

---

199 IMF Legal and Strategy, Policy and Review Departments, *Modernizing the Legal Framework for Surveillance – An Integrated Surveillance Decision* (IMF 2012) 9.

200 Sabine Schlemmer-Schulte, 'International Monetary Fund' in Rüdiger Wolfrum (ed), *Max Planck Encyclopaedia of Public International Law* (OUP 2011) 54.

201 Franz Christian Ebert, 'A Public Law Perspective on Labour Governance by International Financial Institutions: The Case of the IMF's Article IV Consultations' (2020) 17(1) International Organizations Law Review 105–132.

202 Witold J Henisz, Bennet A Zelner, and Mauro F Guillén, 'The Worldwide Diffusion of Market-Oriented Infrastructure Reform, 1977–1999' (2005) 70(6) American Sociological Review 871–897; Leonard Seabrooke, 'Epistemic Arbitrage: Transnational Professional Knowledge in Action' (2014) 1(1) Journal of Professions and Organization 49–64.

203 Michael Breen and Elliott Doak, 'The IMF as a Global Monitor: Surveillance, Information, and Financial Markets' (2021) 30(1) Review of International Political Economy 307–331; Terence C Halliday, 'Legal Yardsticks: International Financial Institutions as Diagnosticians and Designers of the Laws of Nations' In Kevin Davis and others (eds), *Governance by Indicators: Global Power through Quantification and Rankings* (OUP 2012).

a recurring concerning in IML.[204] The central provision that deals with the question of currency manipulation is article IV:1(iii) of the IMF agreement, which reads that member States ought to 'avoid manipulating exchange rates or the international monetary system in order to prevent effective balance of payments adjustment or to gain an unfair competitive advantage over other members'. The IMF has the ultimate authority to find a country in violation of the above provision. Despite the clear nature of the obligation, the process of determining whether a country is, in fact, manipulating its exchange rate has been fraught with economic, legal, and political hurdles. In economic theory, currency manipulation remains a contested concept, with no strict rules capable of determining a particular practice or set of practices as currency manipulation.[205] This allows a great deal of deference to be afforded to a country's interpretation.[206] Moreover, article IV:1(iii) requires the indication of a subjective intent ('in order to') for the purposes of determining whether a particular action, even if considered as manipulation, actually falls foul of the provision. Consequently, the IMF has never found any member in violation, even though accusations of currency manipulation are rife in international monetary relations.

II. CROSS-BORDER MONETARY SPILLOVERS

Monetary spillovers refer to the phenomenon whereby monetary policy actions by one State have negative effects and consequences for monetary policy decisions on others.[207] While monetary spillover is not a new problem, it came back into focus after the GFC when core economy central banks such as the US Federal Reserve and the ECB experimented with a number of unconventional monetary policy measures (UMP).[208] UMP generated large-scale financial and monetary stability implications for the developing world, such as exchange rate volatility, asset price mismatches, and currency appreciations across the developing world.[209] Monetary spillovers also negatively affect the pursuit of monetary autonomy in the periphery. Central banks in the latter are forced to respond to decisions taken elsewhere, steering them away from monetary policy which might be otherwise optimal for domestic circumstances. The regulatory framework for monetary spillovers remains dispersed and is hardly settled. The IMF's multilateral surveillance infrastructure, the G20 MAP as well as the BIS's standardisation

---

204 Lan Cao, 'Currency Wars and the Erosion of Dollar Hegemony' (2016) 38(1) Michigan Journal of International Law 57.

205 See Claus D Zimmermann, 'Chapter 3: Exchange Rate Misalignment and International Law' in *A Contemporary Concept of Monetary Sovereignty* (OUP 2013) 85–142.

206 IMF ISD 2012, Annex para 3.

207 Boris Hofmann and Előd Takáts, 'International Monetary Spillovers' (*BIS Quarterly Review*, 2015) <www.bis.org/publ/qtrpdf/r_qt1509i.htm> accessed 20 August 2023; Jonathan Kearns, Andreas Schrimpf, and Fan Dora Xia, 'Explaining Monetary Spillovers: The Matrix Reloaded' (2020) CEPR Discussion Paper No. DP15006.

208 Kanad Bagchi, 'Revisiting the Taper Tantrum: A Case for International Monetary Policy Coordination' (2017) 3(2) Journal of Financial Regulation 280–289; Liaquat Ahamed, 'Currency Wars, Then and Now: How Policymakers Can Avoid the Perils of the 1930s' (2011) 90(2) Foreign Affairs 92–103.

209 Barry Eichengreen and Poonam Gupta, 'Tapering Talk: The Impact of Expectations of Reduced Federal Reserve Security Purchases on Emerging Markets' (2014) World Bank Policy Research Working Paper No. 6754.

frameworks[210] form the core set of rules regulating monetary spillovers. Yet, they all suffer from a fundamental asymmetry. They fall short of explicitly requiring 'source' countries, that is those largely responsible for monetary spillovers in the first place, to adjust their monetary policy decisions.[211]

III. CROSS-BORDER CAPITAL FLOWS

The movement of international capital has been a defining feature of 21st-century globalisation, far outpacing international trade in recent decades. International capital, however, exhibits a dual quality. Even when it comes with several benefits, capital flows can also be accompanied by financial and monetary instability.[212] Several periods of financial crisis, in the past, attests to the inherently volatile and disruptive nature of capital flows.[213] Despite being allowed under the IMF Agreement, capital controls were shunned for the most part of the 20th century.[214] International institutions like the IMF and Organisation for Economic Co-operation and Development, as well as the regime for international trade and investment, pushed for capital liberalisation, often with devastating consequences for the Global South.[215] The GFC witnessed a change in perspective.[216] A number of States and their central banks resorted to capital controls to protect financial and monetary stability. Today, IMF law, as illustrated in its 2012 Institutional View on the Liberalization and Management of Capital, recognises capital controls as a legitimate monetary policy tool, which can be used under certain circumstances, even pre-emptively.[217]

IV. INTERNATIONAL LIQUIDITY AND MONETARY RESERVES

States typically require access to international liquidity, that is the provision of monetary reserves to finance its BOP and intervene in foreign exchange market to stabilise its exchange rate. How States can access reserves and what indeed counts as reserves have been a source of much of contestation. The IMF sought to provide a solution to the problem of international liquidity by creating Special Drawing Rights (SDR) as a

---

210 IMF Legal and Strategy, Policy and Review Departments (n 199); Ranjit Teja and Rishi Goyal, *Consolidated Spillover Report – Implications from the Analysis of the Systemic-5* (IMF 2011).

211 Laurence Ball, *IMF Advice on Unconventional Monetary Policies* (Independent Evaluations Office of the IMF 2019) 41.

212 Eric Helleiner, 'Controlling Capital Flows' At Both Ends': A Neglected (but Newly Relevant) Keynesian Innovation from Bretton Woods' (2015) 58(5) Challenge 413–427, 414.

213 Barry Eichengreen, *Globalizing Capital: A History of the International Monetary System* (Princeton University Press 2019); Stijn Claessens and Ayhan Kose, 'Financial Crises: Explanations, Types, and Implications' (2013) IMF Working Paper 13/28.

214 Antoine Martin and Bryan Mercurio, 'The IMF and Its Shifting Mandate Towards Capital Movements and Capital Controls: A Legal Perspective' (2017) 44(3) Legal Issues of Economic Integration 211–235.

215 David Howarth and Tal Sadeh, 'In the Vanguard of Globalization: The OECD and International Capital Liberalization' (2011) 18(5) Review of International Political Economy 622–645'.

216 Kevin P Gallagher, 'Regaining Control? Capital Controls and the Global Financial Crisis' in Wyn Grant and Graham K Wilson (eds), *The Consequences of the Global Financial Crisis: The Rhetoric of Reform and Regulation* (OUP 2012) 110–138.

217 Vivek Arora, Karl Habermeier, Jonathan D Ostry and Rhoda Weeks-Brown, *The Liberalization and Management of Capital Flows – An Institutional View* (IMF Policy Paper 2012).

global reserve asset in 1969.[218] SDRs were to be assigned automatically to countries in proportion to their respective quotas and did not come with any strings attached. In fact, the intention was to promote SDR as the 'principal reserve asset in the international monetary system'.[219] Yet, for the most part, the key role of the US dollar as the leading currency for international transactions and payments also made it the de facto reserve asset for the world.[220] This meant that the Federal Reserve, that is the only central bank with unlimited access to dollar liquidity, effectively became the international lender of last resort, sometimes even outpacing the Fund.[221] For the rest of the world, access to dollar liquidity depends on either the largesse of the Federal Reserve or tied to the coerciveness of IMF conditionality.[222] This makes the international monetary system and especially the provision of international liquidity highly asymmetric in that deficit countries are perennially forced to accumulate dollar reserves despite the costs associated with it.

H. CONCLUSION

The illustrated list of issues in IML reveals a number of elements about the international monetary system. First, money is not a neutral instrument of economic policy, but a highly political one through which a range of contestations over key distribution and allocation of resources transpire.[223] The rules pertaining to international monetary cooperation reflect the underlying distribution of international monetary power and how the burdens and benefits of monetary adjustment are ultimately shared.[224] Second, the international monetary system is an inherently hierarchical one.[225] In this, some currencies enjoy what is called 'exorbitant privilege', that is the ability to act as a medium of exchange and store of value both domestically and internationally.[226] In other words, as one moves from the financial core to the periphery, neither monetary sovereignty nor monetary autonomy is necessarily guaranteed.

---

218 Parmeshwar Ramlogan and Fritz-Krockow Bernhard, 'Chapter 4. Special Drawing Rights' in *International Monetary Fund Handbook* (International Monetary Fund 2007).

219 Article VIII, section 7 IMF Agreement.

220 Rohini Hensman and Correggia Marinella, 'US Dollar Hegemony: The Soft Underbelly of Empire' (2005) 40(12) Economic and Political Weekly 1091–1095.

221 Emmanuel Carré and Laurent Le Maux, 'Financial Instability and International-Lender-of-Last-Resort Theory from the Gold Standard to the Dollar System' (2022) 63(2) Jahrbuch für Wirtschaftsgeschichte/ Economic History Yearbook 311–344.

222 Aditi Sahasrabuddhe, 'Drawing the Line: The Politics of Federal Currency Swaps in the Global Financial Crisis' (2019) 26(3) Review of International Political Economy 461–489; Devika Dutt, 'Exorbitant Privilege or Ultimate Responsibility?: Access to the International Lender of Last Resort' (October 2020) <www. researchgate.net/publication/344821791_Exorbitant_Privilege_or_Ultimate_Responsibility_Access_to_the_ International_Lender_of_Last_Resort> accessed 20 August 2023.

223 Gerald Epstein, 'The Contested Terrain Approach to the Political Economy of Central Banking' (2014) Political Economy Research Institute Working paper series No 354.

224 David Andrews (ed), *International Monetary Power* (Cornell University Press 2006); Jonathan Krishner, *Currency and Coercion: The Political Economy of International Monetary Power* (Princeton University Press 1995).

225 Karina Patrício Ferreira Lima, 'Sovereign Solvency as Monetary Power' (2022) 25(3) Journal of International Economic Law 424–446.

226 Barry Eichengreen, *Exorbitant Privilege: The Rise and Fall of the Dollar and the Future of the International Monetary System* (OUP 2011).

Many thus view international monetary and currency relations as a manifestation of imperial power in contemporary society.[227] Much like how colonial currency systems were systematically subordinated to currency systems in the metropole, the present monetary system creates and sustains bonds of subordination and dependency between the core and the periphery. This is the case not only for direct forms of subordination but also indirect forms of control through the provision of international liquidity and reserve accumulation. In this, money operates as a 'neo-colonial' tool which binds the prospects for growth, economic development, and social transformation of the periphery to the economic and political imperatives of the core.[228] Control over money, then, is a crucial element of economic self-determination.

BOX 23.3.5 Further Readings and Further Resources

Further Readings

- R Abdelal, *Capital Rules: The Construction of Global Finance* (Harvard University Press 2009)

- S Eich, *The Currency of Politics: The Political Theory of Money from Aristotle to Keynes* (Princeton University Press 2022)

- AES Lumba, *Monetary Authorities: Capitalism and Decolonization in the American Colonial Philippines* (Duke University Press 2022)

- P Mehrling, *Money and Empire: Charles P. Kindleberger and the Dollar System* (CUP 2022)

- F Pigeaud and N Samba Sylla, *Africa's Last Colonial Currency: The CFA Franc Story* (Pluto Press 2021)

Further Resources

- G Epstein, 'Central Banks as Agents of Economic Development' (2005) Political Economy Research Institute Working Paper Series No. 104

- LR Wray, *Modern Money Theory: A Primer on Macroeconomics for Sovereign Monetary Systems* (2nd edn, Springer 2022)

---

§ § §

---

227 Kanad Bagchi, 'Rosa Luxemburg and the Imperialism of Money' (*Critical Legal Thinking Blog*, 17 November 2022) <https://criticallegalthinking.com/2022/11/17/rosa-luxemburg-and-the-imperialism-of-money/> accessed 20 August 2023.

228 Ndongo Samba Sylla, 'The CFA Franc: French Monetary Imperialism in Africa' (LSE Blog 12 July 2017); Juliet Johnson, *Priests of Prosperity: How Central Bankers Transformed the Postcommunist World* (Cornell University Press 2016).

INDEX

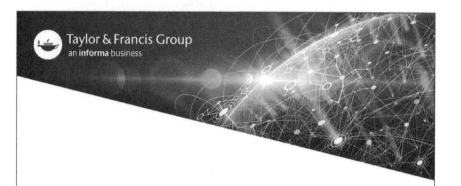